AMERICA'S FAMILIES

GENEALOGICAL TREE.
TO TRACE AND PRESERVE A FAMILY HISTORY FOR FIVE OR MORE GENERATIONS

"First family of Virginia" or "Mayflower descendants" became titles for families only in the nineteenth century when the craze for genealogy was born. Genealogical or family trees such as this were filled in or constructed and census, family and public records scoured to find roots in and connections with the past. The highest ambition was to find an American "aristocrat" to embellish a family's claim to status. Such great branches on the family tree, provided "eligibility" for good marriages, superiority to recent immigrants or commoner folk and even a white family's freedom from race mixture. This blank genealogical tree was an inexpensive printed form that the interested family could purchase and fill in with the findings. Hiring specialists to do the search and to supply such dignities as coats-of-arms, crests and links to European nobility or royalty were other strange preoccupations for ostensible democrats. *Library of Congress*

AMERICA'S FAMILIES
A Documentary History

Donald M. Scott & Bernard Wishy

Editors

1817

HARPER & ROW, PUBLISHERS, New York

Cambridge, Philadelphia, San Francisco
London, Mexico City, São Paulo, Sydney

For Our Children

AMERICA'S FAMILIES. Copyright © 1982 by Donald M. Scott and Bernard Wishy. All rights reserved. Printed in the United States of America. No part of this book may be used or reproduced in any manner whatsoever without written permission except in the case of brief quotations embodied in critical articles and reviews. For information address Harper & Row, Publishers, Inc., 10 East 53rd Street, New York, N.Y. 10022. Published simultaneously in Canada by Fitzhenry & Whiteside Limited, Toronto.

FIRST EDITION

Designer: Ruth Bornschlegel

Library of Congress Cataloging in Publication Data

Main entry under title:
America's families.
   Bibliography: p.
   Includes index.
      1. Family—United States—History—Sources.
I. Scott, Donald M.   II. Wishy,
Bernard, 1925–
HD535.A6 1982   306.8'0973   79–3402
                                        AACR2
ISBN 0–06–014048–8
ISBN 0–06–090903–X (pbk.)

82 83 84 85 10 9 8 7 6 5 4 3 2 1
82 83 84 85 10 9 8 7 6 5 4 3 2 1

Contents*

PREFACE *xv*

ACKNOWLEDGMENTS *xix*

PART ONE A SENSE OF ORDER AND THE CHALLENGE OF DISORDER 1607–1820

Introduction 2

Perspectives 9
PEOPLING THE NEW WORLD *9*
Passengers Bound for Virginia *10*
Passengers Bound for New England *11*
Records from the Nemasket Cemetery, Middleborough, Mass. *13*
LAW AND DEVIANCE *17*
Laws of New Haven Colony, 1656 *18*
The Declaration, Dying Warning, and Advice of Rebekah Chamblit *22*

Courtship 26
COURTSHIP IN CONTRAST *26*
John Lawson, *A New Voyage to Carolina* *27*
LOVE ACROSS CULTURAL BOUNDARIES *29*
John Rolfe to Sir Thomas Dale *29*
CONCERNING SERVANTS, BASTARDS, MULATTOES, AND SLAVES *33*
The Laws of Virginia *33*
A PURITAN PARSON GOES A-COURTING *37*
The Diary of Michael Wigglesworth *37*
Increase Mather to Michael Wigglesworth, March 8, 1679 *40*
Michael Wigglesworth to Mrs. Avery, March 23, 1691 *41*
COURTSHIP AMONG THE HIGH VIRGINIA GENTRY *45*
The Correspondence of William Byrd II *46*
A PHILADELPHIA TRADESMAN MAKES A MATCH *53*
The Autobiography of Benjamin Franklin *53*

* For those interested in a topical rather than a chronological organization of these documents there is a thematic index at the end of the volume.

Benjamin Franklin to a Friend, June 25, 1745 55
A QUAKER WOOING 57
Hannah Logan's Courtship 57
COURTSHIP IN BALLAD AND BROADSIDE 61
The Amorous Sailor's Letter to His Sweetheart 61
The Jolly Orange Woman 63
Young Roger 64
A New Bundling Song 65
A New Song in Favour of Courting 67

Marriage 70
THE TIES THAT BIND: MARRIAGE CONTRACTS 70
Marriage Contract of John French and Eleanor Veazie 70
Marriage Contract of Jacob Mygatt and Sarah Whiting 72
Marriage Gift of Ralph Wormley to Agatha Stubbings 73
THE TIES THAT BIND: MARRIAGE CEREMONIES 75
The Laws of Virginia 76
The Form of Solemnization of Marriage 76
Letters to Quakers on Marriage, 1660 79
"Remonstrance Presented to the Common's House of
    Assembly of South Carolina, Nov. 1767" 82
THE GOOD MARRIAGE EXTOLLED 85
The Duties of Husbands and Wives 85
MARRIAGES IN COURT 91
Salem Quarterly Court, 1676–1682 91
THE SAGA OF A SEVENTEENTH-CENTURY MARRIAGE 97
Rachel Halfield and Lawrence Clenton 98
TO A DEAR AND LOVING HUSBAND 103
Anne Bradstreet, *To My Dear and Loving Husband* 103
Anne Bradstreet, *A Letter to Her Husband, Absent Upon Public
    Employment* 103
MARRIAGE AMONG THE VIRGINIA GENTRY 105
The Secret Diary of William Byrd of Westover 105
William Byrd to John Custis 108
BETWEEN WIFE AND HUSBAND 109
Benjamin Franklin, *A Poem to My Wife* 110
Deborah and Benjamin Franklin, Correspondence, 1756–
    1774 111
Abigail and John Adams Correspondence, 1776 118
THE MARRIAGES OF NEGRO DICK, A SLAVE 122
The Story of Dick the Negro 122
MEMORIALS TO A MARRIAGE 125
Judith and Mann Page 125

Parents and Children: Children and Parents 128
THE BIRTH AND DEATH OF CHILDREN—AND MOTHERS 128
Anne Bradstreet, *Before the Birth of One of Her Children* 128

Anne Bradstreet, *To the Memory of My Dear Daughter-in-Law,
    Mrs. Mercy Bradstreet, Who Deceased Sept. 6, 1669 in the 28
    Year of Her Age* 129
The Diary of Michael Wigglesworth 130
THE WELL-ORDERED FAMILY, OR, RELATIVE DUTIES 132
The School of Good Manners 132
The Duties of Children to Their Parents 133
CHILD NURTURE 137
Anne Bradstreet, *In Reference to Her Children, 23 June,
    1659* 139
Cotton Mather, *Some Special Points Relating to the Education of
    My Children* 141
John Witherspoon, *Letters on Education* 143
Customs of the Indian Natives 149
Parson Weems, *Life of Washington* 152
ORPHANS AND APPRENTICES 158
Laws of Virginia 158
Bonds of Apprenticeship, 1655–1705 160
THE PASSING OF GENERATIONS 164
Court Records, 1682–1715 164
The Will of Martha Emons 166
The Will of Thomas Makepeace 168
Benjamin Franklin's Memorial to His Parents 169

Selected Bibliography for Part One 171

PART TWO   TESTING THE LIMITS OF LIFE   1820–1900

Introduction 174

Westward and Onward the Course of Families 181
    One Family's Moves: *Strong Family Papers* 183
    A Ballad About Moving: *Rolling Stone* 184
    Father Sells the Farm 186
    First Seasons on the Frontier 189
    Frontier Demands on the Family 195
    Homesteading and the Family 196

Democracy and the Family 198
    Influence of Democracy on the Family: Alexis de Tocqueville,
        Democracy in America 199
    Parents *v.* a Son: Wilson Family Letters 201
    A Daughter *v.* Her Parents: Norcom Family Letters 205
    A Daughter's Inequality: Elizabeth Cady Stanton, *Eighty Years
        and More* 208
    Inequality in the Scriptures: Elizabeth Cady Stanton, *The
        Woman's Bible* 210

From Farms to Factories *213*
    Farm Life in Ante-Bellum New England *214*
    Escaping the Mills, *Elias Nason Papers* *216*
    Family Labor Contracts *218*
    The Factory Boarding House *219*

The Family Circle *222*
    Family Reunion: *A Family Gathering* *223*
    My Aunt *227*
    Reveries of a Batchelor *230*
    I Wish I Were Single Again *232*
    The Stepchild: William Tyler, *The Blind Girl* *233*

Courtship *235*
    Courtship of Lucien Boynton: *The Journal of Lucien C. Boynton* *236*
    Love Letters: Nelson-Kemper Letters *239*
    Courting Manners for Ladies: Catharine E. Beecher, *Truth Stranger Than Fiction* *243*
    Courting Manners for Men: Richard Wells, *Manners, Culture and Dress* *243*

Wives and Husbands *246*
    Duties of Young Wives: William A. Alcott, *The Young Wife* *249*
    Marriage Songs and Poems *254*
    On Chastity: Sylvester Graham, *A Lecture to Young Men on Chastity* *255*
    On Birth Control: Robert Dale Owen, *Moral Physiology* *258*
    The General to His Lady *262*
    A Wife's Travail: Willis R. Williams Papers *263*
    Every-day Marriage Life *265*
    Marriage Conduct *267*
    A Planter's Bride *269*

Home and Mother *271*
    George Washington's Mother *276*
    Woman's True Profession: Catharine Beecher and Harriet Beecher Stowe, *The American Woman's Home* *278*
    Songs and Poems of Home and Parents *280*
    Sarah J. Hale *284*
    Eugene Field *285*
    Redeeming the Family: Reverend Leigh Richmond, *The Dairyman's Daughter* *285*
    The Pious Child: John S. C. Abbott, *The Mother at Home* *287*

Child-Rearing: The Mission So Sacred *290*
    Dewees on Pediatrics: Dr. William P. Dewees, *A Treatise on the Physical and Medical Treatment of Children* *292*

Guardianship: *Foster and Wife, Appellants,* v. *Alston   295*
Breaking the Will: Francis Wayland, *A Case of Conviction   297*
A Glimpse at Family Government: Catharine M. Sedgwick,
    Home   300
The Sovereign Parent: Lydia M. Child, *The Mother's Book   304*
Children at Play: Horace Bushnell, *Views of Christian
    Nurture   305*
Science and Nurture: Jacob Abbott, *Gentle Measures in the
    Management and Training of the Young   306*
Children's Rights: Kate Douglas Wiggin, *Children's
    Rights   308*
Childhood Idealized: Henry Wadsworth Longfellow, *The
    Children's Hour   308*

The Black Family Under Slavery and After   310
Slave Children in Court: *Howard* v. *Howard   314*
A Slave Marriage in Court: *Kyler* v. *Dunlap   316*
"Dear Master": Letters from Slaves   *318*
Slave Family Customs: *American Freedman's Inquiry Commission
    Interviews   320*
Slave Narrative: Federal Writers' Project, *Slave Narrative
    Collection   321*
Family Ties, Slave and Free   *323*
Uncle Tom's Cabin   *325*
Defending Slavery: George Fitzhugh, *Sociology for the
    South   330*
Black Women of the Rural South   *333*

Families in Utopia   335
The Shakers: The General Organization of Society   *337*
Brook Farm Observed   *339*
The Family at Brook Farm   *340*
Mormon Polygamy Explained: Orson Pratt, *Celestial Marriage
    Explained   342*
A Mormon Wife: Jennie Frosieth, *The Women of
    Mormonism   344*

Breakdown and Pathology   348
Family and Drink: T. S. Arthur, *Ten Nights in a Bar-Room   352*
Temperance Songs   *356*
Home Protection by Law: Frances E. Willard, *Home Protection
    Manual   360*
Divorce Difficulties: *Hansley* v. *Hansley   363*
Adultery Among the Genteel   *367*
Violent Families, 1835: Henry Ward Beecher, *Journal   373*
Family Violence, 1890s: Edwin H. Porter, *The Fall River
    Tragedy   375*

Family, Society, and State   379
    The Reformatory: *Ex Parte* Crouse   *380*
    Adoption, 1853: Wisconsin Adoption Law, 1853   *381*
    The Ohio Reform Schools: *Commissioners . . . Annual Report,*
       1856   382
    Dangerous Families, 1870s: Charles Loring Brace, *The*
       Dangerous Classes of New York   383
    Foster Homes   *385*

Selected Bibliography for Part Two   388

PART THREE   BEYOND BIOLOGY   1890 TO THE PRESENT

Introduction   392

Nice Homes and Other Halves, 1890–1940   401
    CREATING AND COPING WITH THE "OTHER HALF"   *401*
    The Lower Other Half: Jacob Riis, *How the Other Half*
       Lives   402
    Reforming the Tenements: Robert W. De Forest and
       Lawrence Veiller, *The Tenement House Problem   406*
    U.S. Senate Report on Woman and Child Labor   *412*
    Social Insurance for Old Age: I. M. Rubinow, *Social*
       Insurance   426
    GROWING UP IN SAN FRANCISCO, 1900–1915   *430*
    Old San Franciscans Remember   *430*
    MIDDLE-CLASS MARRIAGE, 1920s   *436*
    Marriage in Middletown   *436*
    DEPRESSION FAMILIES   *441*
    The Donners   *442*
    Family Budget, 1939   *447*
    Migrant Family Life   *451*

Family as Will and Idea   458
    THE NOT-SO-NICE "NICE HOME"   *458*
    Making Nice Homes Better: Charlotte Perkins Gilman, *The*
       Home, Its Work and Influence   459
    THE NEW WOMAN *v.* THE MODERN HOME   *465*
    The Century of the Child   *465*
    THE CONTRACEPTION REVOLUTION   *469*
    Margaret Sanger's Fight for Birth Control   *470*
    Sixth International Neo-Malthusian and Birth Control
       Conference, 1925   *476*
    The Pope on Human Life   *480*
    Christian Tradition and Contraception   *482*
    Catholic Marriages   *483*

OUT OF CORNERS AND CLOSETS *487*
Married Love *490*
Companionate Marriage *492*
California Family Law, 1970 *497*
Homosexual Marriage and the Law *500*
Live Births, Deaths, Marriages, and Divorces: 1910 to
  1978 *504*
ABORTION—UNFINISHED DEBATE *505*
The Abortion Revolution *506*
Death Peddler Abortionists *511*
Abortion and Sexual Caste *512*
Abortion and Privacy *513*
FAMILY LIBERATION *514*
The Politics of Housework *515*
Training for Woman's Place *520*
Parents in Poems: Sylvia Plath, *Daddy 523;* Phyllis McGinley,
  Girl's-Eye View of Relatives 525; Elizabeth Swados, To the
  Dead of Family Wars *526*
THREE CLASSICS ON CHILD-REARING *528*
Infant Care *528*
Conditioned Behavior, 1925 *532*
Dr. Spock, 1976 *535*
FLAMING YOUTH *539*
The Case Against the Younger Generation *540*

Intervening 544
A RATIONALE FOR INTERVENTION *544*
Legislating for Better Families *545*
CRUSADES FOR HOME AND FAMILY *553*
National Congress of Mothers *553*
California Congress of Mothers *557*
Camp Fire Girls *558*
MAKING FAMILIES HEALTHIER *561*
Modern Family Health *562*
ONE CAREER IN PUBLIC HEALTH, **1915–1965** *566*
Dr. R. A. Bolt *566*
THE VOTE AND FAMILY LIFE *569*
Jane Addams, *Why Women Should Vote* *570*
Rhymes for Suffrage Times *578*
THE WORLD OF THERAPY *579*
A Family Interview *580*

Many Nations, Many Races 587
MAKING FAMILIES AMERICAN *587*
Jews and America *593*
Chinese and America *596*
Swedish-Americans and "Ethnics" *600*

The American Catholic Family   *602*
BLACK FAMILIES: DILEMMA AND DEBATE   *605*
Black Families and American Life   *607*

Families as Fiction and Fantasy   613
FAMILIES IN THE MEDIA   *613*
Families in Magazines   *616*
Families in Advertising   *620*
Families in Comics   *625*
Families in Movies   *627*
The Ten Best   *632*
Families on Radio   *633*
Families on Television   *635*
Marriage in Songs   *637*

How Families Live Now   646
VARIATIONS ON THE THEME "FAMILY"   *646*
Family Living: A Radical Solution   *648*
Parents Without Partners   *649*
The Half-Parent   *650*
A Totalitarian Therapeutic Family   *653*

Family Horizons, 1980   657
STRUCTURE AND STRESSES   *657*
The Future of the American Family   *657*
Perspectives on Husbands and Wives   *662*
Saving the Family from Intervention   *666*
Family: An Endangered Species   *670*
Women Workers, 1980   *671*

Selected Bibliography for Part Three   673

General Bibliography   674

Thematic Index   677

Illustrations

Genealogical Tree   *frontispiece*
"Courtship and Marriage"   71
Colonial New England House, exterior   112
Colonial New England House, spinning room   113
Colonial New England House, buttery   113
"A Token for Children"   145
"The Frank Confession"   153
Indian Family, 1890s, tribal dress   192
Indian Family, 1890s, contemporary dress   193
Texas Log House, 1830s   196
"The Family Reunion," 1871   223
"The Grandmother's Gift"   228
"The Grandfather's Advice"   229
Marriage Certificate   247
"The Seven Stages of Matrimony"   253
"Four Seasons of Life"   272–273
"Our Baby," tombstone   288
"Home Education"   306
Five Generations of a Slave Family   311
"Belle Grove," plantation house, exterior   331
"Belle Grove," floor plan   331
Family Funeral   374
"The Dakota," exterior   394
"The Dakota," floor plan   395
Four Tenement Air Shafts   408–409
Tenement Homework   424
California Fruit Tramp Family   450
The Endless Trek   455
Migration of Fruit Tramp Family   457

Mothers' Day Proclamation   466
The Flapper   541
Telegraph Messenger Boys   548
"He Is a Messenger Boy," warning sign   548
First International Congress of Mothers   554–555
Tenement Inspection Report, 1903   567
"Chinatown" Family, 1911   588
Soap Advertisements, 1915–1955   620–624
The Jazz Singer   627
Andy Hardy Meets Debutante   628
The Grapes of Wrath   628
The Magnificent Ambersons   629
Meet Me in St. Louis   629
The Best Years of Our Lives   630
Shane   630
Giant   631
Cat on a Hot Tin Roof   631
The Godfather Part II   632

Preface

It has long been recognized that families have histories. But that *the* family has a history is a recent discovery. The amount, range, and richness of the work in family history over the past twenty years has been impressive indeed. In the attempt to analyze how the family has at once helped make and responded to social and cultural change, historians have delved deeply into such things as fertility, nuptuality, and mortality, sexual ideas and behavior, family and sex roles, the composition of households, childbearing and child-rearing, adolescence and old age, and the role of the family in preparing the young for adulthood and citizenship, organizing work, and facilitating migration. This volume is a logical product of this astonishing efflorescence of family history. It is designed to introduce readers to the richness and diversity of the historical materials that contain the story of families and the family in America. The documents begin in the European world of the early seventeenth century. They end almost four centuries later in the middle of contemporary controversies over the future of the family.

The selections do not reflect any particular notion of *the* American family or any theory of the historical evolution of the family. The wealth and diversity of the materials, as well as the conflicting findings and interpretations of scholars, make those impossible endeavors. And the editors also specifically eschew other interpretive ambitions. It makes little sense to insist upon the dominant role of any American family type which would have to be traced across nearly four centuries to encompass hundreds of millions of lives with extraordinarily different roots, lived across a huge continent and under vastly differing conditions. Better to be content, at least for the time being, with the axiom that the history of the family in America is based on the facts that family has been an essential part of the experience of all who have been Americans and that "family" has thus helped make Americans.

Neither does it seem to us to be very useful or enlightening to try to impose upon our own notes a monistic interpretation of what the story of the American family has been over its four-century course. After all, what appears to be change from one point of view looks suspiciously like continuity from another. Divorce was extremely rare in the seventeenth and eighteenth centuries, while under the current divorce rate over four of every ten marriages contracted in the 1970s will end in divorce. Certainly this suggests an extremely important and far-reaching change. It could also be argued, however, that since the vast majority of these divorces are followed by at least one more marriage with additional offspring, a large number of late-twentieth-century children are experiencing families with stepparents and step-siblings rather similar to those that many seventeenth-century children experienced because of the death of one parent and the remarriage of the surviving one. But is being a stepchild or sibling really the same experience in a Puritan household and in a child-centered Freudian or post-Freudian home? Probably not, although a reading of Anne Bradstreet's poem concerning her children (p. 128) and the report on twentieth-century "family therapy" (p. 580)—and the realization that the psychoanalytic idiom has entered the educated middle class far more readily than it has penetrated Appalachia or the urban ghetto—should lend caution to our conclusions about cultural change.

The point, perhaps, is sufficiently made. This book does not pretend to offer one interpretation of American family history or give readers the documents to adjudicate arcane scholarly disputes. Instead it is designed to provide newcomers with what might well be construed as a basic guide to the materials of American family history. The editors have selected documents that bear on the recurrent experiences, events and activities, functions and relationships that make up family life. The pages that follow also contain documents concerning the family as idea and problem, selections which express values and ideals associated with the institution, which condemn the familial order and practices of others, or which reject dominant patterns and offer alternative or counter arrangements. The book also tries to recognize the differences of circumstance, social class, and cultural tradition that at any one time and across time have made some of America's families different from others.

As important as our quest for range and diversity in substance is our desire to provide as full a sample as possible of the extraordinarily different *kinds* of materials that can be used to ferret out information about what the family has been and meant in America. The editors have been struck repeatedly with how rich and deep the veins run from which family history can be mined. Although the holdings of college and university libraries and archive and manuscript collections are often not organized or catalogued to make items of family history obvious, they contain far richer lodes than is usually assumed. If this volume succeeds in alerting teachers and students to the materials for family history already within reach and suggests some ways to recover and use them, it will have fulfilled one of its goals.

The editorial commentary reflects the book's character as a map to the terrain traversed by America's families. The introductory material is designed more to assist readers in using the documents for whatever line of inquiry they choose than to lead them to particular conclusions; in short, to open up the potential of the selections rather than impose theme or meaning upon them. The introductions to the three broad chronological sections of the book offer context by suggesting some of the things that seem to have impinged most pressingly upon familial forms, ideas, and experiences during that period. Most of our documents have been chosen because they bear on the forms and dilemmas of family life rather than because of the particular author or source of the document. We have, therefore, given only the briefest information about the writers and instead have tried to say something about the kind of document and how it might be used. Our guiding inclination in setting up the particular selections has been to put questions and to suggest modes of analysis rather than state findings or dictate meaning. Finally, so that readers might break out of the confines of our own arrangement and range across time, theme, and genre to weave their own patterns of inquiry and interpretation, we have provided a thematic index.

Inevitably, regretfully, we have had to be ruthlessly selective—the documents that follow represent less than a third of those we had initially chosen as noteworthy and indispensable. Every topic, every group, and every genre simply could not be included for every period. However much we have tried to be sensitive to the complexity and variety in the substance, methods, and materials of family history, some readers are sure to think that we have slighted one or more aspects of the very diversity of American family life that we profess to portray. Could we not have done more, for example, to set off the American Protestant sects from each other or to pay attention to free black families before 1865 or to the lives of each one of America's multitude of national or other minorities? We acknowledge that such charges have merit, while responding that the extraordinary variety of family experiences, the commentary about them through 400 years, and the unavoidable limits of our space meant that for anything added or substituted an existing selection with equal claims for inclusion would have to go. All this is simply another way of expressing what every anthropologist knows: Not everyone will be pleased with someone else's "reading" of a culture. Like those explorers of the past who for decades sought and finally found the headwaters of North America's great rivers, we stand at the beginnings of scholarly explorations of family history and are only certain that the thick and discoverable sources for family history do exist, however hidden they may seem. We hope that finer maps tracing them may be drawn as a result of this early foray.

Acknowledgments

As is common with collaborations, the names of the co-editors of this volume are shown alphabetically and should suggest our equal scholarly and intellectual contributions. Every document and all the introductions and illustrations have been read or considered by both editors. Only what was acceptable to both of us found its way into these pages. We are thus equally responsible for both the pleasure and criticism the book may bring.

Donald Scott prepared the sources, introductions and illustrations for Part I. Bernard Wishy did the same for Part III. The documents and supporting texts for Part II involved a division of work; a majority of the documents themselves came from Scott, the rest from Wishy. The writing of the introductions to sources in Part II was shared equally by Scott and Wishy with Wishy preparing the general introduction. All of the bibliographies for the volume came from Scott.

We want to thank several people for special help in planning and finishing the book. Both editors thank Barbara Welter for working on the general design and for suggesting a number of documents that appear in the final version. Bernard Wishy has a special debt to Willa Baum, Head of the Regional Oral History Office at the Bancroft Library in Berkeley for guidance to sources in and the use of oral histories. David Brody suggested materials about working class families. Tamara Hareven offered important discriminations about the value of different parts of the enormous record of American family life. William Leuchtenburg and Jane D. Mathews suggested themes and materials in recent family history that merited inclusion. The staff of the Photograph Division of the Library of Congress was swift, expert and unpretentious in guiding Bernard Wishy through the immense thickets of their holdings. Thanks for similar reasons go to the Music Division of the Library.

Donald Scott wishes to thank David Allmendinger and Stephen Botein for various specific and general suggestions, Stanley Katz and Jamil Zainaldin for aid in locating legal materials, and Herbert Gutman and Ira Berlin for suggestions concerning slave families. The staff at the American Antiquarian Society was particularly helpful and special thanks are due G. G. Baumgartner, curator of graphics, William Joyce, curator of manuscripts,

and Nancy Burkett, director of reader services. Donald Scott also wishes
to thank Arthur Schrader for directing him to "Rolling Stone" and Hamlin
Garland's use of the song in *Son of the Middle Border.*

Jeff Adams was the model "dogged researcher" as he burrowed successfully for many weeks to locate or copy many sources whose locations were
intially known to us only vaguely. He also gave us much help in the final
assembling of the manuscript. Ingrid Kremer Finnell cheerfully typed many
versions of our prefaces and introductions.

Part One

A SENSE OF ORDER AND
THE CHALLENGE OF DISORDER

1607–1820

Introduction

The diversity that characterizes the family throughout American society today has been there since the beginning. The indigenous peoples who greeted the invaders from across the sea lived under a wide variety of familial arrangements quite alien to the newcomers. The migrants who transplanted themselves to American soil came in many ways and for various reasons—as families and as unmarried individuals; in groups of religious refugees; and as single adventurers seeking fortune or at least an initial stake in life. They came under different conditions of wealth and poverty and in different degrees of freedom and bondage—as lords with vast tracts of land; as gentlemen merchants and planters; as yeoman freeholders with just enough land to build and sustain a family; as renters, as indentured servants, selling four or seven years of their labor for fifty or a hundred acres of uncleared land; and as captive chattel slaves. They set up remarkably different societies, ranging from the compact theocratic communities of New England through quasi-feudal Maryland and the scattered farms and plantations of Virginia to the largely unorganized backcountry of the Carolinas. Still, however they came and whatever conditions they faced and whatever social arrangements they forged, they all in one way or another had to confront the uncertainty of life, the need for property, and the question of authority.

What demographic evidence we now have suggests that death held considerable dominion over life in the seventeenth century. Life expectancy at birth for both males and females was only just above thirty-five years, while those who survived to the age of twenty-five could expect to live on only into their early fifties. Only slightly over half of all children born probably survived into adulthood, and of those who did only about one out of two reached the age of fifty. Like death, birth too has a history. In colonial America a mother who lived through her childbearing years bore eight children, on the average, though it was probably relatively rare for as many as six of the eight to survive to adulthood.

These demographic constraints profoundly influenced the character and duration of married life. Today most women (having on the average three children)

2

complete their childbearing well before they reach the early thirties. With life expectancy over seventy for both men and women, couples can look forward to fifteen to twenty or more years together after all their children have left home and before they themselves become infirm. But for many colonial women, most of marriage was spent (or ended, given the high incidence of deaths in childbirth) bearing and raising children. Childbirth usually occurred within the first year and a half of marriage and continued until menopause. Under these conditions, couples rarely had many years free from the responsibilities of child-rearing. Marrying in their mid-twenties and having eight children, the average couple would see their youngest child reach adulthood only when they were well into their sixties. But with one out of every two men and women dying before fifty, it was not at all certain that either or both partners would survive that long. Though half the adults did live to fifty and beyond and thus enjoyed thirty or more years of married life, not more than a third of them probably had a single marriage which endured much over ten years. Instead, to enjoy thirty or more years of married life, one often had to have two or more spouses. Moreover, the death of a spouse was not something to be expected as one approached "old age" but an event that was more likely to occur sometime during what we now would regard as the prime of life. And it was something many men and women went through more than once in their lifetime.

Neither did childhood escape the ravages of death, a fact that affected attitudes toward children as well as the style and content of parental affection no less than it affected the duration of parent-child ties. One demographer notes that "in one out of every two cases, the death of young children occurred before that of their fathers [or mothers] and half the remaining children saw their fathers [or mothers] die before attaining their majority."* Death, moreover, could give siblings very different kinds of child-parent relationships. Those born first had a far better chance than the last-born of being brought to adulthood by their biological parents. In addition, younger children were as often reared and trained by older siblings as by parents. They were also much more likely to see one or both their parents die before reaching adulthood. If a father died, they might well find themselves transferred to a household governed by their mother's second husband. If the mother died, a second wife usually entered the household, often with children from a previous marriage, and she soon had children by her new mate. If both parents died, or if the mother was too old or poor to care for young children, they might be farmed out to an uncle, brother, or stepbrother or even to the household of a stranger, if no kin were available and willing to take them in.

Parental death thus often disrupted families and shoved them into different channels. Whenever possible, the surviving spouse remarried, often within a

---

* Roland Pressot, *Population* (Baltimore, 1971), p. 51.

year or two. Indeed, it was not at all rare for people who lasted into their sixties to have a succession of two or three spouses. With little restraint on fertility, this often yielded families with an extremely dense and complex mix of natural and stepparents and full and half siblings, not to mention the vast network of kin outside this core. A man who married at age twenty-five, for example, might lose his wife when he was thirty-five, after she had borne him four or five children. He might then marry a young widow with one or two children who would then provide him with several more. He might then die and she herself might remarry and have children in that marriage. One such "chain of marriage and remarriage" in Virginia from about 1655 to 1693, made up of "six marriages among seven people," yielded at least twenty-five children. A visit to this household in 1680 would have found the presence of children (ranging from infancy to the early twenties) from four of the marriages, some of whom did not have any parents in common. *

Birth and death people and depopulate and thereby alter the composition of households, but it is marriage that forms and reconstitutes families. In the seventeenth and eighteenth centuries, death and birth were largely uncontrollable "natural" occurrences: People were largely helpless against disease, and births followed as the inevitable consequence of conjugal life. But a marriage itself was a human contrivance, a matter of deliberate choice and decision. And nuptuality, like fertility and mortality, has a history; when one marries, whom one chooses, and what contraints affect the decision to marry are all subject to social and historical circumstances. Marriage and independence went hand in hand in colonial America. Property—or the lack of it—determined whether one was free to marry; for those in a state of formal, propertyless dependence— servants, slaves, apprentices, and youths still in their minority—marriage was absolutely forbidden. Moreover, unbound young adults usually could not marry until they had the property to attain the economic independence necessary to establish and maintain a separate household. But control over the property they needed ordinarily rested in the hands of the father or some other guardian. This gave elders considerable control over the timing of marriage. A daughter usually could not marry until father or guardian was ready to provide a dowry, and a son usually had to delay marriage until father or guardian provided him with the "portion" he needed to set up his own household. This control over property also carried considerable leverage over the choice of a partner. Consent was needed, and it was conferred only if the intended spouse was approved of, if the parent accepted both the person and the dowry or portion she or he brought to the match. The wishes of the prospective partners clearly played a part in making a marriage. Elders did not usually choose

---

* Darrett B. and Anita H. Rutman, "Now-wives and Sons-in-law: Parental Death in a Seventeenth-Century Virginia County," in Thad Tate and David Ammerman, eds., *The Chesapeake in the Seventeenth Century* (Chapel Hill, 1979), p. 156.

partners for their children or force an unwanted spouse upon them. But they could and often did veto matches they didn't consider suitable.

Behind this control were familial considerations that went well beyond the desires and interests of the individual couple. The entire family, present as well as unborn generations, often had or was alleged to have a clear stake in the "suitability" of a marriage of any of its members, and oftentimes the interests of property, religion, or European origins and survival of the "line" outweighed the romantic interests and attachments of any particular son or daughter. The father (or the mother, in some cases of widowhood) as the head of household was the guardian of the economic resources which family and line needed for its survival and status. Suitability, moreover, often had a clear social dimension. Colonial societies contained firm hierarchies of social rank and order, ranging from the "gentry," set apart by wealth, manner, title, and dress, through the growingly numerous yeomanry down to those in indentured or permanent servitude. Marriages—though not all sexual relationships—across social boundaries were scarcely permissible. Among the wellborn, a suitable marriage was one made or arranged with the right sort of person and was often a kind of economic and social alliance, one that would assure that the son or daughter remained in the station to which he or she was bred or one that would secure if not enhance the status and fortune of the family as a whole. But property was no less important to the making of the marriages of more ordinary folk. Among the less well off, when people married depended upon economic circumstance—such as the well-being of the family, business conditions, the number of sons and daughters who had to be settled, or whether their labor was still needed within the family. The size of the dowry or settlement as well as the timing of the marriage could vary greatly among siblings. In places where either by law or tradition primogeniture— the transfer of the family estate to the eldest surviving male—held sway, the eldest son stood to receive the greatest portion, but he had to wait until his father died or was willing to "retire" and surrender his headship of the household. Younger sons, of course, stood a greater chance of inheriting their "portion" and thereby being able to marry at an earlier age. On the other hand, by the time they reached young adulthood, the settlements on their older siblings might well have depleted the available resources. Then they would have to wait for a perhaps meager inheritance or attain a stake through apprenticeship or formal education. Sometimes they simply departed from the family place and set out for new settlements where they might easily attain the land needed to start a household and where they were free of the control of parents and, often, outside the easy reach of religious or legal authority.

The importance of the family in providing life with some semblance of orderliness went well beyond these regulations and protections provided for its members and their property. In many respects, the social order of seventeenth- and eighteenth-century America was a familial order. Communities depended upon households and families to carry out many of the tasks that the twentieth century simply assumes are the business of government. With the exception of a very small elite at the top of society which might employ tutors and later send its sons to college for education in the liberal arts, the young were trained and taught in the household of father, guardian, or master. Even in New England, where schools early shared the child with the family, the school years were few and the curriculum largely the basic "three R's" with a gloss of religious and moral instruction acceptable to parents. The household rather than the school was where one learned the skills and lore needed for adulthood: Girls learned domestic manufacture—of foodstuffs, clothes and bedding, candles, and the like—from older women in the household, while boys picked up the varied skills needed for farming or a craft from older brothers and their fathers. Skill in specialized crafts like smithing or tanning were usually gained by apprenticing oneself to a craftsman and living within his household. Even more formal training ordinarily took place in a household: Since most of America lacked schools, the parent or master usually taught whatever rudimentary skills in reading, writing, and ciphering were needed. Moreover, the family organized patterns of work. A household provided space for production as well as for domestic affairs. In all but the households of the high gentry, all people above the age of ten participated in the domestic and farm or craft production that maintained the family economy.

Most people thus lived their lives firmly embedded in a household structure, either the one into which they had been born, the one they themselves had established, or the one to which they had been indentured. Moreover, the colonists went to great lengths to keep people from falling outside this ordering and protective structure of the family. Orphans, not surprisingly, posed a particularly acute problem. In southern Maryland from 1658 to 1705, for example, nearly 70 percent of the married or widowed men who died left only minor children behind them. The problem was met by placing the children in other households, if at all possible, under the legal guardianship of a relative, designated by parental will. Frequently, however, suitable kin could not be found, or a widow was too old or poor to care for her children. Then they would be bound out by the mother or the court to the household of a stranger, who in exchange for their labor and service would maintain them until they reached their majority. In addition, others—like the aged, the destitute and abandoned, and the feebleminded—who could not care for themselves were placed not, as was done later, in asylums or other specialized custodial institutions but in households. Thus everyone in a household lived in close proximity to the whole range of life experiences—birth, disease, dementia, death—incorporating the extremes from which modern society seeks to protect its members as part of the normal or ordinary routines of life. Finally, colonial communities went to considerable (but not always entirely successful) lengths to prevent young adults, especially servants and apprentices who were not free to marry, from producing illegitimate children whom they could not support and who would fall outside the legal family. Since conception and birth were hard to control, the colonists tried to control sexuality itself by making fornication a crime, subject to corporal punishment and fines.

The colonial family not only gave some semblance of orderliness to individual lives and to a society so beset by the chances of life, it was also itself an order, with certain rules and ideals of internal governance. Paternal authority was at the center of the notion of the "well-ordered family" that the European settlers brought with them to the New World. By nature and by ordination, the ideal family was a hierarchy, and the good order of the family depended upon the sovereign authority of its head. Religion and custom decreed the basic ideals. Obedience and harmony were the values most persistently attached to family governance and most often invoked by the guardians of social order. Only if all its members yielded unquestioning deference to paternal authority could a family maintain the order and harmony it needed if it was to carry out its responsibilities to its members and to society. So dense and so changing was the composition of the family, and so shifting were the relationships within it, that it seemed that only a clear skein of unabridged authority could give it order. Most colonial families probably did ordinarily operate within a frame of paternal authority. They often probably did manage to balance the interests and wishes of an enormously complex mix of people and get them to subordinate individual preferences to the needs of the whole. Yet the very complexity that demanded such mechanisms of orderliness also contained enormous possibilities for disorder. As documents of all sorts attest, obedience and harmony were often honored in the breach, as defiance and conflict sabotaged many a "well-ordered family." Thus the relationship between rhetoric and reality was, as always, a complex one. The invocation of the ideals of the "well-ordered family" in some ways reflected what people of the seventeenth and eighteenth centuries liked to believe or were taught about their own behavior. But the steady incantation of the need for obedience and harmony could also reflect fears that the opposite traits were, in fact, coming to dominate their society. Indeed, ours is not the first American age to decry the "breakdown of the family."

The threat of death, the dominion of property, the need for obedience and harmony, then, together provided the contours of family life in seventeenth- and eighteenth-century America. Neither these constraints nor the family structures and experiences they molded remained constant. By the last quarter of the eighteenth century, the age-old dominion of death had not been broken. But, as in Western Europe, it had been diminished: Surviving one's early childhood remained problematical, but in most places and among most populations those who reached twenty could expect to live into their mid-sixties or beyond. The ready availability of land and the relative ease with which people could move to new settlements or even beyond the fringes of settlement had profoundly altered how the constraints of property affected individual and family life and had corroded many of the traditional forms of paternal and social authority. And by 1776, when the colonists decided to overthrow kingly control, authority and obedience were not the only values that Americans invoked and by which they applauded or condemned behavior and institutions. Although 1776 had much less meaning at the time for the conduct of family life, it did provide ideals of liberty, equality, and happiness that in the nineteenth century deeply affected family conduct, ideals, and law.

PERSPECTIVES

Peopling the New World

The documents in this section concern the peopling of North America by Europeans and their descendants. The first two record a shipload of passengers bound for Virginia in 1634 and a shipload bound for Massachusetts in the same year. The two lists differ, however, in how they are arranged and in the kinds of information they do or do not contain and, consequently, in what they might suggest about the experience of coming to the New World, the character of the enterprises that brought them, and the kind of society that received them and that they built once they arrived. Taken alone, these lists may not enable us to draw many firm conclusions. They do, however, let us begin to inquire into how different ways of organizing the apparently simple act of coming to the New World affected family ties and institutions. What, for example, do the lists suggest about the effects of migration on family ties? What kind of demographic constraints might these different patterns of migration have imposed upon the setting up of new families and the structure of households in the New World?

The second document alphabetically lists the inscriptions for one surname found in a cemetery established in the eighteenth century. It is not, of course, a complete source, but it nonetheless indicates some of the kinds of information that have been used to recapture family history. When organized into possible chronological or sexual patterns, for example, it can suggest the different or changing ways in which death struck colonial families. The document also permits us to engage in a rudimentary way in one of the analytical techniques, "family reconstitution," by which historians have been able to uncover the demographic and familial spine of social history. A fuller reconstitution of either the Woods or the population of Middleborough, Massachusetts, would, of course, have to draw upon additional sources of information if they were available—wills, death and birth records, tax and census lists, genealogies. But by arranging the data into family groups over time, we can use this document to begin to discern the demographic structure of at least a portion of the Wood family or families which lived—and died—in the environs of Middleborough from 1719 to 1876. Moreover, with its notations of particular ties and monuments, the document points to another way in which cemeteries can yield historical evidence. Burial is a cultural activity: A cemetery not only contains physical remains, its also embeds attitudes and ideals in its arrangments and icons.

PASSENGERS BOUND FOR VIRGINIA

Edward Towers	26	Allin King	19
Henry Woodman	22	Rowland Sadler	19
Richard Seems	26	Jo. Phillips	28
Vyncent Whatter	17	Daniel Endick	16
James Whithedd	14	Jo. Chalk	25
Jonas Watts	21	Jo. Vynall	20
Peter Loe	22	Edward Smith	20
Geo. Brocker	17	Jo. Rowlidge	19
Henry Eeles	26	Wm. Westlie	40
Jo. Dennis	22	Jo. Smith	18
Tho. Swayne	23	Jo. Saunders	22
Charles Rinsden	27	Tho. Bartcherd	16
Jo. Exston	17	Tho. Dodderidge	19
Wm. Luck	14	Richard Williams	18
Jo. Thomas	19	Jo. Ballance	19
Jo. Archer	21	Wm. Baldin	21
Richard Williams	25	Wm. Pen	26
Francis Hutton	20	Jo. Gerie	24
Savill Gascoyne	29	Henry Baylie	18
Rich. Bulfell	29	Rich. Anderson	50
Rich. Jones	26	Robert Kelum	51
Tho. Wynes	30	Richard Fanshaw	22
Humphrey Williams	22	Tho. Bradford	40
Edward Roberts	20	Wm. Spencer	16
Martin Atkinson	32	Marmaduke Ella	22
Edward Atkinson	28		
Wm. Edwards	30	*Women*	
Nathan Braddock	31	Ann Swayne	22
Jeffrey Gurrish	23	Eliz. Cote	22
Henry Carrell	16	Ann Rice	23
Tho. Ryle	24	Kat. Wilson	23
Gamaliel White	24	Maudlin Lloyd	24
Richard Marks	19	Mabell Busher	14
Tho. Clever	16	Annis Hopkins	24
Jo. Kitchin	16	Ann Mason	24
Edmond Edwards	20	Bridget Crompe	18
Lewes Miles	19	Mary Hawkes	19
Jo. Kennedy	20	Ellin Hawkes	18
Sam Jackson	24		

The New England Historical and Genealogical Register, XV (1861), p. 142; XXV (1871), pp. 13–15.

PASSENGERS BOUND FOR NEW ENGLAND

1. Joseph Hull, of Somerset, a minister, aged 40 years
2. Agnes Hull, his wife, aged 25 years
3. Joan Hull, his daughter, aged 15 years
4. Joseph Hull, his son, aged 13 years
5. Tristram, his son, aged 11 years
6. Elizabeth Hull, his daughter, aged 7 years
7. Temperance, his daughter, aged 9 years
8. Grissell Hull, his daughter, aged 5 years
9. Dorothy Hull, his daughter, aged 3 years
10. Judith French, his servant, aged 20 years
11. John Wood, his servant, aged 20 years
12. Robert Dabyn, his servant, aged 28 years
13. Musachiell Bernard, of Batcombe, clothier in the county of Somerset, 24 years
14. Mary Bernard, his wife, aged 28 years
15. John Bernard, his son, aged 3 years
16. Nathaniel, his son, aged 1 year
17. Rich. Persons, salter and his servant, 30 years
18. Francis Baber, chandler, aged 36 years
19. Jesope, joyner, aged 22 years
20. Walter Jesop, weaver, aged 21 years
21. Timothy Tabor, in Somerset of Batcombe, tailor, aged 35 years
22. Jane Tabor, his wife, aged 35 years
23. Jane Tabor, his daughter, aged 10 years
24. Anne Tabor, his daughter, aged 8 years
25. Sarah Tabor, his daughter, aged 5 years
26. William Fever, his servant, aged 20 years
27. John Whitmarke, aged 39 years
28. Alice Whitmarke, his wife, aged 35 years
29. James Whitmarke, his son, aged 11 years
30. Jane, his daughter, aged 7 years
31. Onseph Whitmarke, his son, aged 5 years
32. Rich. Whitmarke, his son, aged 2 years
33. William Read, of Batcombe, taylor in Somerset, aged 28 years
34. [name not entered]
35. Susan Read, his wife, aged 29 years
36. Hannah Read, his daughter, aged 3 years
37. Susan Read, his daughter, aged 1 year
38. Rich. Adams, his servant, 29 years
39. Mary, his wife, aged 26 years
40. Mary Cheame, his daughter, aged 1 year
41. Zachary Bickewell, aged 45 years
42. Agnes Bickewell, his wife, aged 27 years
43. John Bickewell, his son, aged 11 years

44. John Kitchin, his servant, 23 years
46. George Allin, aged 24 years
47. Katherine Allin, his wife, aged 30 years
48. George Allin, his son, aged 16 years
49. William Allin, his son, aged 8 years
50. Matthew Allin, his son, aged 6 years
51. Edward Poole, his servant, aged 26 years
52. Henry Kingman, aged 40 years
53. Joan, his wife, being aged 39
54. Edward Kingman, his son, aged 16 years
55. Joanne, his daughter, aged 11 years
56. Anne, his daughter, aged 9 years
57. Thomas Kingman, his son, aged 7 years
58. John Kingman, his son, aged 2 years
59. John Ford, his servant, aged 30 years
60. William King, aged 40 years
61. Dorothy, his wife, aged 34 years
62. Mary King, his daughter, aged 12 years
63. Katheryn, his daughter, aged 10 years
64. William King, his son, aged 8 years
65. Hannah King, his daughter, aged 6 years
66. Thomas Holbrooke, of Broadway, aged 34 years
67. Jane Holbrooke, his wife, aged 34 years
68. John Holbrooke, his son, aged 11 years
69. Thomas Holbrooke, his son, aged 10 years
70. Anne Holbrooke, his daughter, aged 5 years
71. Elizabeth, his daughter, aged 1 year
72. Thomas Dible, husbandman, aged 22 years
73. Francis Dible, sawyer, aged 24 years
74. Robert Lovell, husbandman, aged 40 years
75. Elizabeth Lovell, his wife, aged 35 years
76. Zacheus Lovell, his son, 15 years
77. Anne Lovell, his daughter, aged 16 years
78. John Lovell, his son, aged 8 years
79. Ellyn, his daughter, aged 1 year
80. James, his son, aged 1 year
81. Joseph Chickin, his servant, 16 years
82. Alice Kinham, aged 22 years
83. Angell Hollard, aged 21 years
84. Katheryn, his wife, 22 years
85. George Land, his servant, 22 years
86. Sarah Land, his kinswoman, 18 years
87. Richard Jones, of Dinder
88. Robert Martin, of Batcombe, husbandman, 44
89. Humphrey Shepard, husbandman, 32
90. John Upham, husbandman, 35

91. Joan Martin, 44
92. Elizabeth Upham, 32
93. John Upham, Junior, 7
94. Sarah Upham, 26
95. William Grane, 12
96. Nathaniel Upham, 5
97. Elizabeth Upham, 3
98. Dorset Richard Wade, of Simstyly, cooper, aged 60
99. Elizabeth Wade, his wife, 6[?]
100. Dinah, his daughter, 22
101. Henry Lush, his servant, aged 17
102. Andrew Hallett, his servant, 28
103. John Hoble, husbandman, 13
104. Robert Huste, husbandman, 40
105. John Woodcooke, 2[?]
106. Rich. Porter, husbandman, 3[?]

RECORDS FROM THE NEMASKET CEMETERY, MIDDLE-BOROUGH, MASS.

Wood

[Ab]iel, died 10 October, 1719, in his 61st year. "A W" is on the foot-stone. [Near the stone of Mrs. Abijah Wood, probably her husband.]

Abiel, son of Silas and Priscilla, died 9 April, 1790, aged 19 years, 2 months, 20 days.

Abigail, wife of Capt. Nelson, died 31 March, 1843, aged 60 years. [On Nelson Wood monument.]

Abigail T., died 1 December, 1856, aged 43 years. [On Nelson Wood monument.]

Abigail T., wife of Thomas, died 19 March, 1880, aged 75 years. [On Thomas Wood monument.]

Abigail W., wife of Horatio G.; daughter of Thomas and Abigail Weston; born 15 March, 1801; died 7 January, 1854.

_____, son of Horatio G. and Abigail W., born and died 10 August, 1831, aged 5 hours.

Abijah, widow of Abial, died 21 May, 1746, in her 83d year.

Alexander, born 5 November, 1796; died 17 December, 1867. [On Alexander Wood monument.]

Alfred, born 5 May, 1777; died 29 June, 1864. [On Alfred Wood monument.]

Alfred, born 21 January, 1802; died 23 August, 1876. [On Alfred Wood monument.]

Benjamin F., born 19 February, 1804; died 12 May, 1879. [On Alfred Wood monument.]

Wood *(cont'd)*

Benjamin P., Colonel, born 18 March, 1793; died 12 September, 1882. [On Benjamin P. Wood monument.]

Betsey, wife of Hon. Wilkes, died 21 September, 1803, in her 25th year.

Betsey T., daughter of Hon. Wilkes and Betsey W., died 16 September, 1829, aged 7 years, 12 days.

Betsey W., wife of Hon. Wilkes, died 12 December, 1822, in her 34th year.

Betty, daughter of Ichabod and Thankful, died 28 December, 1774, in her 20th year.

Caleb T., died 18 February, 1888, aged 80 years. [On Nelson Wood monument.]

Daniel, died 11 January, 1825, aged 46 years. [On Daniel Wood monument.]

Daniel, son of Daniel and Rhoda, aged 6 years. [The date was omitted. On Daniel Wood monument.]

Deliverance, daughter of Henry and Lydia, died 19 August, 1769, in her 15th year.

Ebenezer, died 5 December, 1768, aged 71 years, 3 months, 20 days.

Ebenezer, died 2 September, 1800, aged 26 years. [On Nelson Wood monument.]

Ebenezer, died "by an apoplexy" 13 February, 1803, aged 64 years, 11 months.

Ebenezer G., son of Gorham and Elizabeth, died 7 April, 1809, aged 1 year, 11 months, 18 days.

Edmund, died 29 December, 1805, aged 84 years. . . .

Elnathan, died 20 April, 1752, aged 66 years, 13 days.

Elnathan, died 17 September, 1808, in his 64th year.

Ephraim, died 8 November, 1783, in his 68th year.

Gorham, born 4 May, 1774; died 21 January, 1836. . . .

Hiram Nelson, son of Nelson and Mary B., died 7 June, 1850, aged 5 months, 25 days. [In lot with Nelson Wood monument.]

Ichabod, Lieut., died 8 August, 1787, in his 69th year.

Ichabod, born 6 June, 1751; died 30 December, 1825.

Irena, died 18 April, 1848, aged 62 years.

Isaac, died 16 June, 1727, aged 8 years.

Israel, "M^r".

Israel, Jr., died 9 December, 1802, aged 22 years, 8 months, 25 days.

Israel, died 12 May, 1829, in his 85th year.

Jacob, died 24 January, 1824, in his 69th year.

Jane, wife of Levi, died 24 September, 1797, aged 48 years. [On Nelson Wood monument.]

Jeremiah, born 18 January, 1791; drowned with Sylvanus Wood, Jr., 10 February, 1818. [On Benjamin P. Wood monument.]

Joanna, wife of Sylvanus, born 21 December, 1761; died 1 August, 1853. [On Benjamin P. Wood monument.]

WOOD *(cont'd)*

Joanna T., wife of Caleb T., died 11 February, 1896, aged 81 years. [On Nelson Wood monument.]

Josiah, son of Thomas and Lydia, died 22 July, 17 [*broken*], aged 2 years, 3 months, 2 days.

Levi, died 15 January, 1807, aged 67 years. [On Nelson Wood monument.]

Levina, daughter of Jacob and Lydia, died 27 October, 1803, aged 7 years, 11 months, 26 days. . . .

Lucy, daughter of Jacob and Lydia, died 23 May, 1786, aged 2 months, 1 day.

Lucy C., wife of Hon. Wilkes, died 26 September, 1848, aged 61 years. . . .

Lydia, widow of Ebenezer, died 3 October, 1789, in her 83d year.

Lydia, born 27 August, 1794; died 27 July, 1817. [On Benjamin P. Wood monument.]

Lydia, wife of Thomas, died 24 January, 1822, aged 62 years. [On Thomas Wood monument.]

Lydia, wife of Jacob, died 13 February, 1849, aged 82 years.

Mary, wife of Elnathan, died 30 May, 1733, in her 48th year.

Mary, wife of Horatio G.; daughter of Abner and Huldah Weston, of Randolph, Vt.; born 8 April, 1787, and died 30 September, 1827.

Nelson, Capt., died 7 July, 1854, aged 77 years. [On Nelson Wood monument.] . . .

Patience, wife of Edmund, died 9 April, 1791, in her 74th year.

Polly, daughter of Jacob and Lydia, died 6 November, 1787, aged 4 months, 12 days.

Polly, daughter of Reuben and Jenney, died 13 June, 1790, aged 7 months, 4 days.

Priscilla, wife of Silas, died 19 August, 1788, in her 58th year.

Priscilla, wife of Israel, died 12 April, 1808, in her 59th year.

Priscilla, widow of Ichabod, died 9 August, 1824, aged 88 years. . . .

Rebecca, died 10 February, 1718, aged 67 years.

Reuben, died 31 October, 1790, in his 29th year.

Rhoda, wife of Alfred, born 21 November, 1780; died 4 June, 1860. [On Alfred Wood monument.]

Rhoda, wife of Daniel, died 9 July, 1838, aged 57 years. [On Daniel Wood monument.]

Sally, widow of Ebenezer, died 23 October, 1811, "in the 64 year of her age having survived all her Father's family except one Brother whom with five Children she has left to bewail her death."

Samuel, died 3 February, 1718, aged 70 years.

Samuel, died 19 April, 1798, in his 22d year.

Sarah, wife of Ichabod, died 20 September, 1846, aged 89 years.

Serena, wife of Col. Benjamin P., born 22 May, 1792; died 25 August, 1876. [On Benjamin P. Wood monument.]

WOOD *(cont'd)*

Seth, died 12 May, 1770, in his 26th year.

Sophronia, daughter of Jacob and Lydia, died 25 January, 1800, aged 2 years, 7 days. . . .

Susan, wife of Israel, died 24 June, 1824, in her 73d year.

Susanna, died 1 October, 1720, aged 30 years.

Sylvanus, born 15 September, 1758; died 12 October, 1841. [On Benjamin P. Wood monument.]

Sylvanus, Jr., born 12 October, 1796; drowned with Jeremiah, 10 February, 1818. [On Benjamin P. Wood monument.]

Thankful, wife of Ichabod, died 4 January, 1776, in her 53d year.

Thomas, died 23 November, 1808, aged 56 years. [On Thomas Wood monument.]

Thomas, died 28 February, 1882, aged 85 years. [On Thomas Wood monument.]

Wilkes, Hon., died 1 October, 1843, aged 73 years.

Law and Deviance

Outposts of the mother country, the colonies were under the jurisdiction of the Crown and its agents. But the Crown's authority was remote, and the British government had more important things to do than watch over a few thousand settlers three thousand miles away. Moreover, the grants of power bestowed upon the stock and trading companies which carried out the colonial endeavor were vague. Thus, almost from the beginning, the colonists had to improvise governmental institutions and lay down some formal rules of behavior. The documents below reflect this process. The first, typical of the compendia of laws and liberties by which the Puritan colonies of New England bound themselves into full polities, contains the laws governing family relations and order in the New Haven Colony, founded in 1636. The second, a broadside or poster concerning the execution of a woman for infanticide, is an example of a standard ritual that colonial societies used to deal with their transgressors.

The act of codification, of arranging laws into a comprehensive and fundamental "body," is an act which objectifies the norms that define a community as an order and set the boundaries of what is acceptable civilized behavior. It is no accident that the Pilgrim and Puritan leaders who came to New England should have shown such eagerness to codify their laws. They had come as refugees from a world they considered corrupt and anarchic. From the outset they strove to establish well-ordered communities, communities arranged to contain the corruptions sown in human nature. "In Adam's fall, we sinned all" was how their first schoolbook put it. They began their new social order with the family. They insisted that all people be subject to the family order, that all households in the community be subject to church and civil discipline, and that all communities be subject to Divine ordinance. The New Haven code thus permits us to explore the notions of order and disorder that bound the Puritan communities together and to examine the place of the family within that vision.

A society also reveals a good bit about itself by how it defines and deals with deviance. Acts that one society condemns and punishes may well be tolerated by others. (Ancient Sparta, for example, practiced selective infanticide as a matter of public policy.) How a society treats violators of its

17

laws and norms—when it is willing to wink at certain transgressions and when it employs its most extreme forms of punishment—reveals what it takes most seriously and, perhaps, why it takes it so seriously. This broadside thus not only narrates the life and fate of Rebekah Chamblit, it also indicates how the ritual of confession and punishment was used to hold up a mirror of the culture to itself, to confront it with its own norms and its capacity to trammel them.

LAWS OF NEW HAVEN COLONY, 1656

Capitall Laws

. . . If any man or woman, shall lye with any beast, or bruite creature by carnall copulation, he, or she, shall surely be put to death, and the beast shall be slaine, buried, and not eaten. . . .

If any man lyeth with mankinde, as a man lyeth with a woman, both of them have committed abomination, they both shall surely be put to death. . . . And if any woman change the naturall use, into that which is against nature, . . . she shall be liable to the same sentence, and punishment, or if any person, or persons, shall commit any other kinde of unnaturall and shamefull filthinesse, called in Scripture the going after strange flesh, or other flesh then God alloweth, by carnall knowledge of another vessel then God in nature hath appointed to become one flesh, whether it be by abusing the contrary part of a grown woman, or child of either sex, or unripe vessel of a girle, wherein the naturall use of the woman is left, which God hath ordained for the propagation of posterity, and Sodomiticall filthinesse (tending to the destruction of the race of mankind) is committed by a kind of rape, nature being forced, though the will were inticed, every such person shall be put to death. Or if any man shall act upon himself, and in the sight of others spill his owne seed, by example, or counsel, or both, corrupting or tempting others to doe the like, which tends to the sin of Sodomy, if it be not one kind of it; or shall defile, or corrupt himself and others, by any other kind of sinfull filthinesse, he shall be punished according to the nature of the offence; or if the case considered with the aggravating circumstances, shall according to the mind of God revealed in his word require it, he shall be put to death, as the court of magistrates shall determine. Provided that if in any of the former cases, one of the parties were forced, and so abused against his or her will, the innocent person (crying out, or in due season complaining) shall not be punished, or if any of the offending parties were under fourteen year old, when the sin was committed, such person shall onely be severely corrected, as the court of magistrates considering the age, and other circumstances, shall judge meet.

John Trumbull, *Blue Laws of Connecticut* (Hartford, 1878), pp. 199–201, 211, 216–18, 241–43, 258.

If any man married, or single, commit adultery with a marryed or espoused wife, the adulterer and adulteresse shall surely be put to death. . . .

If any child, or children, above sixteen year old, and of competent understanding, shall curse, or smite, his, her, or their naturall father, or mother, each such child shall be put to death . . . unlesse it be proved, that the parents have been very unchristianly negligent in the education of such child, or children, or so provoked them by extream and cruell correction, or usage, that they have been urged or forced thereunto, to preserve themselves from death or maiming.

If any man have a stubborn rebellious son, of sufficient age and understanding, namely sixteen year old, or upward, which will not obey the voyce of his father, or the voyce of his mother; and that when they have chastned him, will not hearken unto them, then shall his father and his mother (being his naturall parents) lay hold on him, and bring him to the magistrates assembled in court, and testifie unto them, that their son is stubborn and rebellious, and will not obey their voyce and chastisement, but lives in sundry notorious crimes; such a son shall be put to death. . . .

Children's Education

Whereas too many parents and masters, either through an over tender respect to their own occasions, and businesse, or not duly considering the good of their children, and apprentices, have too much neglected duty in their education, while they are young, and capable of learning, it is ordered, That the deputies for the particular court, in each plantation within this jurisdiction for the time being; or where there are no such deputies, the constable, or other officer, or officers in publick trust, shall from time to time, have a vigilant eye over their brethren, and neighbours, within the limits of the said plantation, that all parents and masters, doe duly endeavour, either by their own ability and labour, or by improving such schoolmaster, or other helps and means, as the plantation doth afford, or the family may conveniently provide, that all their children, and apprentices as they grow capable, may through God's blessing, attain at least so much, as to be able duly to read the Scriptures, and other good and profitable printed books in the English tongue, being their native language, and in some competent measure, to understand the main grounds and principles of Christian Religion necessary to salvation. . . .

Divorce, or a Marriage declared a Nullity. Desertion, &c.

If any marryed person proved an adulterer, or an adulteresse, shall by flight, or otherwise, so withdraw or keep out of the jurisdiction, that the course of justice (according to the mind and law of God here established) cannot proceed to due execution, upon complaint, proof, and prosecution, made by the party concerned, and interested, a separation or divorce, shall by sentence of the court of magistrates be granted and published, and the innocent party shall in such case have liberty to marry again. . . .

And if any man marrying a woman fit to bear children, or needing and requiring conjugall duty, and due benevolence from her husband, it be found (after convenient forbearance and due tryall) and satisfyingly proved, that the husband, neither at the time of marriage, nor since, hath been, is, nor by the use of any lawfull means, is like to be able to perform or afford the same, upon the wive's due prosecution, every such marriage shall by the court of magistrates, be declared voyd, and a nullity, the woman freed from all conjugall relation to that man, and shall have liberty in due season, if she see cause, to marry another; but if in any such case, deceipt be charged and proved, that the man before marriage knew himself unfit for that relation, and duty, and yet proceeded, sinfully to abuse an ordinance of God, and in so high a measure to wrong the woman, such satisfaction shall be made to the injuried woman, out of the estate of the offendor, and such fine paid to the jurisdiction, as the court of magistrates shall judge meet. But if any husband after marriage, and marriage duty performed, shall by any providence of God be disabled, he falls not under this law, nor any penalty therein. And it is further declared, that if any husband shall without consent, or just cause shewn, willfully desert his wife, or the wife her husband, actually and peremptorily refusing all matrimoniall society, and shall obstinately persist therein, after due means have been used to convince and reclaim, the husband or wife so deserted, may justly seek and expect help and relief. . . .

Dowryes

Every marryed woman (living with her husband in this jurisdiction, or other where absent from him, with his consent, or through his meer default, or inevitable providence, or in case of divorce where she is the innocent party) that shall not before marriage be estated by way of joynture (according to agreement) in some housing, lands, tenements, hereditaments, or other means for tearm of her life, shall immediately after the death of her husband, have right and interest by way of dower, in and to one third part of all such houses, lands, tenements and hereditaments, as her said husband was seized of to his own use, either in possession, reversion, or remainder, within this jurisdiction, at any time during the marriage, to have and enjoy for tearm of her naturall life, according to the estate of such husband, free, and freely discharged of and from all titles, debts, rents, charges, judgments, executions, and other incumbrauces whatsoever, had, made, or suffered by her said husband, during the said marriage between them, or by any other person claiming by, from, or under him, otherwise then by any act, or consent of such wife, as this court shall ratifie, and allow. And if the heir of the husband, or other person interessed, shall not within one month after lawfull demand made, assign, and set out to such widow, her just third part with conveniency, or to her satisfaction, according to the intent of this law, then upon due complaint, and prosecution either before the court of magistrates, or plantation court, as the case may require, her dower, or third part, shall be assigned and set forth by such persons as the court shall appoint, with due costs and damages.

Marriage

For the preventing of much inconvenience which may grow by clandestine and unlawful marriages: It is ordered, That no persons shal be either contracted, or joyned in marriage before the intention of the parties proceeding therein, hath been three times published, at some time of publick lecture, or town meeting in the town, or towns where the parties, or either of them dwel, or do ordinarily reside; or be set up in writing upon some post of their meeting house door, in publick view, there to stand so as it may be easily read by the space of fovrteen daies; and that no man unless he be a magistrate in this jurisdiction, or expressly allowed by the general court shall marry any persons, and that in a publick place, if they be able to go forth under the penalty of five pounds fine for every such miscarriage.

And the court considering that much sin hath been committed against God, and much inconvenience hath growen to some members of this jurisdiction by the irregular and disorderly carriage of young persons of both sexes, upon purpose or pretence of marriage, did and do order, that whosoever within this jurisdiction shal attempt, or indeavor to inveagle, or draw the affections of any maide, or maide-servant, whether daughter, kinswoman, or in other relation, for himself, or for any other person, without the consent of father, master, guardian, governor, or such other, who hath the present interest, or charge, or (in the absence of such) of the nearest magistrate, whether it be by speech, writing, message, company-keeping, unnecessary familiarity, disorderly night meetings, sinful dalliance, gifts, or any other way, directly or indirectly, every such person (beside all damages which the parent, governor or person intrusted or interested, may sustain by such unlawful proceedings) shall pay to the plantation forty shillings for the first offence; and for the second offence towards the same party four pounds; and for the third offence he shal be further fined, imprisoned, or corporally punished. . . .

And whereas some persons men or women do live, or may come to settle within this colony, whose wives, or husbands are in England or elsewhere, by means whereof they are exposed to great temptations, and some of them live under suspition of uncleanesse, if they do not fal into lewd and sinful courses: It is therefore ordered, That all such persons living within this jurisdiction, shal by the first opportunity, repair to their said relations, (unless such cause be shewen to the satisfaction of the plantation court, that further respite and liberty be given) under the penalty of paying twenty pounds fine, for contempt, or neglect herein. Provided that this order do not extend to such as are, or shal come over to make way for their families, or are in a transient way for traffick, merchandise, or other just occasions for some smal time. . . .

Single Persons

To prevent, or suppress inconvenience, and disorder in the course and carriage of sundry single persons, who live not in service, nor in any family relation, answering the mind of God in the fift commandement: It is ordered, That no single person of either sex, do henceforward board, diet, sojourn, or be permitted so to do, or to have lodging; or house room within any of the plantations of this jurisdiction, but either in some allowed relation, or in some approved family licensed thereunto, by the court, or by a magistrate, or some officer, or officers in that plantation, appointed thereunto, where there is no magistrate; the governor of which family, so licensed, shal as he may conveniently, duly observe the course, carriage, and behaviour, of every such single person, whether he, or she walk diligently in a constant lawful imployment, attending both family duties, and the publick worship of God, and keeping good order day and night, or otherwise.

THE DECLARATION, DYING WARNING, AND ADVICE OF REBEKAH CHAMBLIT

A Young Woman Aged near Twenty-seven Years, Executed at Boston September 27th. 1733. according to the Sentence pass'd upon her at the Superiour Court holden there for the County of Suffolk, in August last, being then found Guilty of Felony, in concealing the Birth of her spurious Male Infant, of which she was Deliver'd when alone the Eighth Day of May last, and was afterwards found Dead, as will more fully appear by the following Declaration, which was carefully taken from her own Mouth.

Being under the awful Apprehensions of my Execution now in a few Hours; and being desirous to do all the Good I can, before I enter the Eternal World, I now in the fear of GOD, give this Declaration and Warning to the Living.

I Was very tenderly brought up, and well Instructed in my Father's House, till I was Twelve Years of Age; but alass, my Childhood wore off in vanity. However, as I grew in Years, my Youth was under very sensible Impressions from the SPIRIT of GOD; and I was awakened to seek and obtain Baptism, when I was about Sixteen Years of Age; and lived for some time with a strictness somewhat answerable to the Obligations I was thereby brought under. But within two or three Years after this, I was led away into the Sin of Uncleanness, from which time I think I may date my Ruin for this World. After this, I became again more watchful, and for several Years kept my self from the like Pollutions, until those for which I am now to suffer.

"The Declaration, Dying Warning, and Advice of Rebekah Chamblit" (Boston, 1733). Used by permission of the American Antiquarian Society.

And as it may be necessary, so doubtless it will be expected of me, that I give the World a particular account of that great Sin, with the aggravations of it, which has brought me to this Shameful Death: And accordingly in the fear of GOD, at whose awful Tribunal I am immediately to appear, I solemnly declare as follows;

That on Saturday the Fifth Day of May last, being then something more than Eight Months gone with Child, I was about my Household Business reaching some Sand from out of a large Cask, I received considerable hurt, which put me into great Pain, and so I continued till the Tuesday following; in all which time I am not sensible I felt any Life or Motion in the Child within me; when, on the said Tuesday the Eighth Day of May, I was Deliver'd when alone of a Male Infant; in whom I did not perceive Life; but still uncertain of Life in it, I threw it into the Vault about two or three Minutes after it was born; uncertain, I say, whether it was a living or dead Child; tho', I confess it's probable there was Life in it, and some Circumstances seem to confirm it. I therefore own the Justice of GOD and Man in my Condemnation, and take Shame to my self, as I have none but my self to Blame; and am sorry for any rash Expressions I have at any time uttered since my Condemnation; and I am verily perswaded there is no Place in the World, where there is a more strict regard to Justice than in this Province.

And now as a Soul going into Eternity, I most earnestly and solemnly Warn all Persons, particularly YOUNG PEOPLE, and more especially those of my own Sex, against the Sins which their Age peculiarly exposes them to; and as the Sin of Uncleanness has brought me into these distressing Circumstances, I would with the greatest Importunity Caution and Warn against it, being perswaded of the abounding of that Sin in this Town and Land. I thought my self as secure, a little more than a Year ago, as many of you now do; but by woful Experience I have found, that Lust when it has conceived bringeth forth Sin, and Sin when it is finished bringeth forth Death; it exposes the Soul not only to Temporal, but to Eternal Death. And therefore as a Dying Person, let me call upon you to forsake the foolish and live: Do not accompany with those you know to be such, and if Sinners entice you do not consent. I am sensible there are many Houses in this Town, that may be called Houses of Uncleanness, and Places of Dreadful Temptations to this and all other Sins. O Shun them, for they lead down to the Chambers of Death and Eternal Misery.

My mispence of precious Sabbaths, lies as a heavy burden upon me; that when I might have gone to the House of GOD, I have been indifferent, and suffer'd a small matter to keep me from it. What would I now give, had I better improv'd the Lord's Day! I tell you, verily, your lost Sabbaths will sit heavy upon you, when you come into the near prospect of Death and Eternity.

The Sin of Lying I have to bewail, and wou'd earnestly caution against; not that I have took so great a pleasure in Lying; but I have often done so to conceal my Sin: Certainly you had better suffer Shame and Disgrace, yea the greatest Punishment, than to hide and conceal your Sin, by Lying. How much better had it been for me, to have confess'd my Sin, than by hiding of it provoke a holy GOD, thus to suffer it to find me out. But I hope I heartily desire to bless GOD, that even in this way, He is thus entring into Judgment with me; for I have often thought, had I been let alone to go on undiscovered in my Sins, I might have provok'd Him to leave me to a course of Rebellion, that would have ripen'd me for a more sudden, and everlasting Destruction; and am fully convinc'd of this, that I should have had no solid ease or quiet in my mind, but the Guilt of this undiscover'd Sin lying upon my Conscience, would have been a tormenting Rack unto me all my Days; whereas now I hope GOD has discover'd to me in some measure the evil of this, and all my other Sins, enabled me to repent of them in Dust and Ashes; and made me earnestly desire and plead with Him for pardon and cleansing in the precious Blood of the REDEEMER of lost and perishing Sinner: And I think I can say, I have had more comfort and satisfaction within the Walls of this Prison, than ever I had in the ways of Sin among my vain Companions, and think I wou'd not for a World, nay for ten Thousand Worlds have my liberty in Sin again, and be in the Same Condition I was in before I came into this Place.

I had the advantage of '' ing in several religious Families; but alass, I disregarded the Instructions and Warnings I there had, which is now a bitterness to me; and so it will be to those of you who are thus favoured, but go on unmindful of GOD, and deaf to all the Reproofs and Admonitions that are given you for the good of your Souls. And I would advise those of my own Sex especially, to chuse to go into religious Families, where the Worship and Fear of GOD is maintained, and submit your selves to the Orders and Government of them.

In my younger Years I maintain'd a constant course of Secret Prayer for some time; but afterwards neglecting the same, I found by experience, that upon my thus leaving GOD, He was provoked to forsake me, and at length suffer'd me to fall into that great and complicated Sin that has brought me to this Death: Mind me, I first left GOD, and then He left me: I therefore solemnly call upon YOUNG PEOPLE to cherish the Convictions of GOD's Holy SPIRIT, and be sure keep up a constant course of fervent Secret prayer.

And now I am just entering into the Eternal World, I do in the fear of GOD, and before Witnesses, call upon our YOUNG PEOPLE in particular, to secure an Interest in the Lord JESUS CHRIST, and in those precious Benefits He has purchased for His People; for surely the favour of GOD, thro' CHRIST, is more worth than a whole World: And O what Comfort will this yield you when you come to that awful Day and Hour I am now arriving unto. I must tell you the World appears to me vain and empty, nothing like what it did in my past Life, my Days of Sin and Vanity, and as doubtless it appears now to you. Will you be perswaded by me to that which will yield you the best Satisfaction and Pleasure here, and which will pre-

pare you for the more abundant Pleasures of GOD's Right Hand for evermore.

Sign'd and Acknowleg'd in the Presence of divers Witnesses, with
a desire that it may be publish'd to the World, and read at the
Place of Execution.

Rebekah Chamblit.

September 26th
1733

COURTSHIP

Courtship in Contrast

It is sheer myth that Europeans "discovered" America and that the English found in North America a "virgin land" largely devoid of peoples and civilization. The New World contained Indian populations that went back thousands of years. Their customs, beliefs, and appearances seemed so alien to the Europeans that some refused to include the native populations within their notions of civilization. The penetration of Europe into the Americas, then, involved the confrontation of European and native cultures just as it did in Africa and Asia. The presence of Indians and their resistance to the incursions of the English and others into the lands they had inhabited, as well as their existence in fact and fantasy at the fringes of settler society, make this cultural confrontation a significant but often neglected aspect of post-Columbian American history.

There is not much direct evidence, especially in writing, about these native Americans, and we often have to rely upon the observations of outsiders—explorers, missionaries, and captives—for information about their families and tribal cultures. As sources, such observations need to be used with some care (the same care that has to be taken with any attempt by an outsider to read a culture alien to her or his own) to assess the operations of white European and Christian bias as well as the circumstances that might have operated to produce accurate observation. Such accounts by outsiders have another historical value. The act of trying to figure out and interpret, for folks back home, the family and other arrangements of a "strange" people often reveals as much about the writer's culture as it does about the people being described. In the implicit and explicit comparisons of such accounts, in what they select to describe and the tone and language with which they portray it, they often operate as simultaneous commentary on two cultures. The account of John Lawson, an English gentleman who explored the Carolinas in the early 1700s, thus contains a description of Indian courtship and marriage which betrays something of the settler societies' own attitudes and concerns about love, courtship, and marriage.

JOHN LAWSON, *A NEW VOYAGE TO CAROLINA*

When any young Indian has a Mind for such a Girl to his Wife, he, or some one for him, goes to the young Woman's Parents, if living; if not, to her nearest Relations, where they make Offers of the Match betwixt the Couple. The Relations reply, they will consider of it; which serves for a sufficient Answer, till there be a second Meeting about the Marriage, which is generally brought into Debate before all the Relations (that are old People) on both Sides, and sometimes the King with all his great Men, give their Opinions therein. If it be agreed on, and the young Woman approve thereof (for these Savages never give their Children in Marriage without their own Consent) the Man pays so much for his Wife; and the handsomer she is the greater Price she bears. Now, it often happens, that the Man has not so much of their Money ready as he is to pay for his Wife; but if they know him to be a good Hunter, and that he can raise the Sum agreed for, in some few Moons, or any little time they agree, she shall go along with him as betrothed, but he is not to have any Knowledge of her till the utmost Payment is discharged; all which is punctually observed. Thus they lie together under one Covering for several Months, and the Woman remains the same as she was when she first came to him. I doubt our Europeans would be apt to break this Custom, but the Indian Men are not so vigorous and impatient in their Love as we are. Yet the Women are quite contrary, and those Indian Girls that have conversed with the English and other Europeans, never care for the Conversation of their own Countrymen afterwards.

They never marry so near as a first Cousin, and although there is nothing more coveted amongst them than to marry a Woman of their own Nation, yet when the Nation consists of a very few People, (as nowadays it often happens) so that they are all of them related to one another, then they look out for Husbands and Wives amongst Strangers. For if an Indian lies with his Sister, or any very near Relation, his Body is burnt, and his Ashes thrown into the River, as unworthy to remain on Earth; yet an Indian is allowed to marry two Sisters, or his Brother's Wife. Although these People are called Savages, yet Sodomy is never heard of amongst them, and they are so far from the Practice of that beastly and loathsome Sin, that they have no Name for it in their Language.

The Marriages of these Indians are no farther binding than the Man and Woman agree Together. Either of them has Liberty to leave the other upon any frivolous Excuse they can make, yet whosoever takes the Woman that was another Man's before, and bought by him, as they all are, must certainly pay to her former Husband whatsoever he gave for her. Nay, if she be a Widow, and her Husband died in Debt, whosoever takes her to Wife pays all her Husband's Obligations, though never so many; yet the Woman is not required to pay anything (unless, she is willing) that was

John Lawson, *A New Voyage to Carolina* (Richmond, 1937), pp. 196–99.

owing from her Husband, so long as she keeps Single. But if a Man courts her for a Night's Lodging and obtains it, the Creditors will make him pay her Husband's Debts, and he may, if he will take her for his Money, or sell her to another for his Wife. I have seen several of these Bargains driven in a day; for you may see Men selling their Wives as Men do Horses in a Fair, a Man being allowed not only to change as often as he pleases, but likewise to have as many Wives as he is able to maintain. I have often seen that very old Indian Men (that have been Grandees in their own Nation) have had three or four very likely young Indian Wives, which I have much wandered at, because, to me they seemed incapacitated to make good Use of one of them.

The Young Men will go in the Night from one House to another to visit the young Women, in which sort of Rambles they will spend the whole Night. In their Addresses they find no Delays, for if she is willing to entertain the Man, she gives him Encouragement and grants him Admittance; otherwise she withdraws her Face from him, and says, I cannot see you, either you or I must leave this Cabin and sleep somewhere else this Night.

They are never to boast of their Intrigues with the Women. If they do, none of the Girls value them ever after, or admit of their Company in their Beds. This proceeds not on the score of Reputation, for there is no such thing (on that account) known amongst them; and although we may reckon them the greatest Libertines and most extravagant in their Embraces, yet they retain and possess a Modesty that requires those Passions never to be divulged.

The Trading Girls, after they have led that Course of Life, for several Years, in which time they scarce ever have a Child; (for they have an Art to destroy the Conception, and she that brings a Child in this Station, is accounted a Fool, and her Reputation is lessened thereby) at last they grow weary of so many, and betake themselves to a married State, or to the Company of one Man; neither does their having been common to so many any wise lessen their Fortunes, but rather augment them.

The Woman is not punished for Adultery, but tis the Man that makes the injured Person Satisfaction, which is the Law of Nations practised amongst them all; and he that strives to evade such Satisfaction as the Husband demands, lives daily in Danger of his Life; yet when discharged, all Animosity is laid aside, and the Cuckold is very well pleased with his Bargain, whilst the Rival is laughed at by the whole Nation, for carrying on his intrigue with no better Conduct, than to be discovered and pay so dear for his Pleasure.

The Indians say, that the Woman is a weak Creature, and easily drawn away by the Man's Persuasion; for which Reason, they lay no Blame upon her, but the Man (that ought to be Master of his Passion) for persuading her to it.

Love Across Cultural Boundaries

One of the most famous of all American matches is that of John Rolfe, an adventurer who came to the Virginia Colony in the earliest years, and Pocahontas, the daughter of Powhatan, chief of the Indians, whose help or anger could save or destroy the colony. According to John Smith, Pocahontas intervened with her father to save his life, and when she married Rolfe in 1610 there followed a period of peace between Englishmen and Indians. In 1613, Rolfe, Pocahontas, and their young son returned to England, where Pocahontas, an object of great curiosity, died in 1615. The selection below is taken from Rolfe's letter defending and justifying his desire to marry the Indian princess.

JOHN ROLFE TO SIR THOMAS DALE

. . . To avoid tedious preambles, and to come neerer the matter: first suffer me with your patence, to sweepe and make cleane the way wherein I walke, from all suspicions and doubts, which may be covered therein, and faithfully to reveale unto you, what should move me hereunto.

Let therefore this my well advised protestation, which here I make betweene God and my own conscience, be a sufficient witnesse, at the dreadfull day of judgement (when the secret of all mens harts shall be opened) to condemne me herein, if my chiefest intent and purpose be not, to strive with all my power of body and minde, in the undertaking of so mightie a matter, no way led (so farre forth as man's weakenesse may permit) with the unbridled desire of carnall affection: but for the good of this plantation, for the honour of our countrie, for the glory of God, for my owne salvation, and for the converting to the true knowledge of God and Jesus Christ, an unbeleeving creature, namely Pokahuntas. To whom my hartie and best thoughts are, and have a long time bin so intangled, and inthralled in so intricate a laborinth, that I was even awearied to unwinde my selfe thereout. But almighty God, who never faileth his, that truely

Lyon Gardiner Tyler, ed., *Narratives of Early Virginia, 1606–1625* (New York, 1907), pp. 240–43.

invocate his holy name hath opened the gate, and led me by the hand that I might plainely see and discerne the safe paths wherein to treade.

To you therefore (most noble Sir) the patron and Father of us in this countrey doe I utter the effects of this my setled and long continued affection (which hath made a mightie warre in my meditations) and here I doe truely relate, to what issue this dangerous combate is come unto, wherein I have not onely examined, but throughly tried and pared my thoughts even to the quicke, before I could finde any fit wholesome and apt applications to cure so daungerous an ulcer. I never failed to offer my daily and faithfull praiers to God, for his sacred and holy assistance. I forgot not to set before mine eies the frailty of mankinde, his prones[s] to evill, his indulgencie of wicked thoughts, with many other imperfections wherein man is daily insnared, and oftentimes overthrowne, and them compared to my present estate. Nor was I ignorant of the heavie displeasure which almightie God conceived against the sonnes of Levie and Israel for marrying strange wives, nor of the inconveniences which may thereby arise, with other the like good motions which made me looke about warily and with good circumspection, into the grounds and principall agitations, which thus should provoke me to be in love with one whose education hath bin rude, her manners barbarous, her generation accursed, and so discrepant in all nurtriture from my selfe, that oftentimes with feare and trembling, I have ended my private controversie with this: surely these are wicked instigations, hatched by him who seeketh and delighteth in mans destruction; and so with fervent praiers to be ever preserved from such diabolical assaults (as I tooke those to be) I have taken some rest.

Thus when I had thought I had obtained my peace and quietnesse, beholde another, but more gracious tentation hath made breaches into my holiest and strongest meditations; with which I have bin put to a new triall, in a straighter manner then the former: for besides the many passions and sufferings which I have daily, hourely, yea and in my sleepe indured, even awaking mee to astonishment, taxing mee with remisnesse, and carelesnesse, refusing and neglecting to performe the duetie of a good Christian, pulling me by the eare, and crying: why dost not thou indevour to make her a Christian? And these have happened to my greater wonder, even when she hath bin furthest seperated from me, which in common reason (were it not an undoubted worke of God) might breede forgetfulnesse of a farre more worthie creature. Besides, I say the holy spirit of God hath often demaunded of me, why I was created? If not for transitory pleasures and worldly vanities, but to labour in the Lords vineyard, there to sow and plant, to nourish and increase the fruites thereof, daily adding with the good husband in the Gospell, somewhat to the tallent, that in the end the fruites may be reaped, to the comfort of the laborer in this life, and his salvation in the world to come? And if this be, as undoubtedly this is, the service Jesus Christ requireth of his best servant: wo unto him that hath these instruments of pietie put into his hands, and wilfully despiseth to worke with them. Likewise, adding hereunto her great apparance of love to me, her desire to be taught and instructed in the knowledge of God, her capablenesse of understanding, her aptnesse and willingnesse to receive anie good impression, and also the spirituall, besides her owne incitements stirring me up hereunto.

What should I doe? shall I be of so untoward a disposition, as to refuse to leade the blind into the right way? Shall I be so unnaturall, as not to give bread to the hungrie? or uncharitable, as not to cover the naked? Shall I despise to actuate these pious dueties of a Christian? Shall the base feare of displeasing the world, overpower and with holde mee from revealing unto man these spirituall workes of the Lord, which in my meditations and praiers, I have daily made knowne unto him? God forbid. I assuredly trust hee hath thus delt with me for my eternall felicitie, and for his glorie: and I hope so to be guided by his heavenly graice, that in the end by my faithfull paines, and christianlike labour, I shall attaine to that blessed promise, Pronounced by that holy Prophet Daniell unto the righteous that bring many unto the knowledge of God. Namely, that they shall shine like the starres forever and ever. A sweeter comfort cannot be to a true Christian, nor a greater incouragement for him to labour all the daies of his life, in the performance thereof, nor a greater gaine of consolation, to be desired at the hower of death, and in the day of judgement.

Againe by my reading, and conference with honest and religious persons, have I received no small encouragement, besides *serena mea conscientia,* the cleerenesse of my conscience, clean from the filth of impurity, *quoe est instar muri ahenei,* which is unto me, as a brasen wall. If I should set down at large, the perturbations and godly motions, which have striven within mee, I should but make a tedious and unnecessary volume. But I doubt not these shall be sufficient both to certifie you of my tru intents, in discharging of my dutie to God, and to your selfe, to whose gracious providence I humbly submit my selfe, for his glory, your honour, our Countreys good, the benefit of this Plantation, and for the converting of one unregenerate, to regeneration; which I beseech God to graunt, for his deere Sonne Christ Jesus his sake.

Now if the vulgar sort, who square all mens actions by the base rule of their own filthinesse, shall taxe or taunt me in this my godly labour: let them know, it is not any hungry appetite, to gorge my selfe with incontinency; sure (if I would, and were so sensually inclined) I might satisfie such desire, though not without a seared conscience, yet with Christians more pleasing to the eie, and lesse fearefull in the offence unlawfully committed. Nor am I in so desperate an estate, that I regard not what becommeth of mee; nor am I out of hope but one day to see my Country, nor so void of friends, nor mean in birth, but there to obtain a mach to my great content: nor have I ignorantly passed over my hopes there, or regardlesly seek to loose the love of my friends, by taking this course: I know them all, and have not rashly overslipped any.

But shal it please God thus to dispose of me (which I earnestly desire to fulfill my ends before sette down) I will heartely accept of it as a godly taxe appointed me, and I will never cease, (God assisting me) untill I have accomplished, and brought to perfection so holy a worke, in which I will daily pray God to blesse me, to mine, and her eternall happines. And thus desiring no longer to live, to enjoy the blessings of God, then [than] this my resolution doth tend to such godly ends, as are by me before declared: not doubting of your favourable acceptance, I take my leave, beseeching Almighty God to raine downe upon you, such plenitude of his heavenly graces, as your heart can wish and desire, and so I rest,

At your commaund most willing to be disposed off
JOHN ROLFE.

Concerning Servants, Bastards, Mulattoes, and Slaves

Authorities in colonial society were much concerned about the mingling of the lower orders. This document, consisting of the acts of the Virginia Burgesses from 1642 to 1732, dealing with the marriage of servants, bastardy, and interracial coupling, permits us to chart the unfolding of this concern, to inquire into the nature and dimensions of the problem, and to consider why there was such anxiety about the sexual and marital behavior of certain classes of people.

THE LAWS OF VIRGINIA

March 1661–62

AGAINST SECRETT MARRIAGE

WHEREAS much losse and detriment doth arise to diverse masters of ffamilyes by the secrett marriage of servants, the said servants through that occasion neglecting their works and often perloyning their masters goods and provisions, *Bee it therefore enacted* that noe minister either publish the banns or celebrate the contract of marriage betweene any servants unless he have from both their masters a certificate that it is done with their consent, and the minister doing otherwise shalbe fined ten thousand pounds of tobacco, and the said servants both man and woman that shall by any indirect meanes procure themselves to be marryed without consent of his and her master, shall for such their offence each of them serve their respective masters one whole yeare after their tyme of service by indenture is expired, and if any person being free shall clandestinely marry with a servant as aforesaid, hee or shee soe marrying shall pay to the master of the servant ffifteen hundred pounds of tobacco or a yeares service, and the servant soe being marryed shall abide with his or her master, the time by indenture or custome and a yeare after as aforesaid.

W. W. Hening, ed., *The Statutes at Large, Being a Collection of all the Laws of Virginia,* 1619–1792 (Richmond, 1809–1823), III, pp. 166–70; VII, pp. 86–87; IX, pp. 443–44.

AGAINST FFORNICATION

FOR restraint of the ffilthy sin of ffornication, *Be it enacted* that what man or woman soever shall commit ffornication, he and she soe offending, upon proofe thereof by confession or evidence shall pay each of them five hundred pounds of tobacco fine, *(a)* to the use of the parish or parishes they dwell in, and be bound to their good behavior, and be imprisoned untill they find security to be bound with them, and if they or either of them committing ffornication as aforesaid be servants then the master of such servant soe offending shall pay the said ffive hundred pounds of tobacco as aforesaid to the use of the parish aforesaid, for which the said servant shall serve half a yeare after the time by indenture or custome is expired; and if the master shall refuse to pay the ffine then the servant to be whipped; and if it happen a bastard child to be gotten in such ffornication then the woman if a servant in regard of the losse and trouble her master doth sustaine by her haveing a bastard shall serve two yeares after her time by indenture is expired or pay two thousand pounds of tobacco to her master besides the ffine or punishment for committing the offence and the reputed father to put in security to keep the child and save the parish harmelesse.

December 1662

WOMEN SERVANTS GOT WITH CHILD BY THEIR MASTERS . . .

WHEREAS by act of Assembly every woman servant haveing a bastard is to serve two yeares, and late experiente shew that some dissolute masters have gotten their maides with child, and yet claime the benefitt of their service, and on the contrary if a woman gott with child by her master should be freed from that service it might probably induce such loose persons to lay all their bastards to their masters; *it is therefore thought fitt and accordingly enacted, and be it enacted henceforward* that each woman servant gott with child by her master shall after her time by indenture or custome is expired be by the churchwardens of the parish where she lived when she was brought to bed of such bastard, sold for two yeares, and the tobacco to be imployed by the vestry for the use of the parish.

MEN SERVANTS GETTING ANY BASTARD CHILD . . .

WHEREAS by the present law of this country the punishment of a reputed father of a bastard child is the keeping the child and saving the parish harmlesse, and if it should happen the reputed father to be a servant who can noe way accomplish the penalty of that act, *Be it enacted by the authority aforesaid* that where any bastard child is gotten by a servant the parish shall take care to keepe the child during the time of the reputed fathers service by indenture or custome, and that after he is free the said reputed father shall make satisfaction to the parish.

NEGRO WOMEN'S CHILDREN . . .

WHEREAS some doubts have arrisen whether children got by any English-man upon a negro woman should be slave or ffree, *Be it therefore enacted and declared by this present grand assembly,* that all children borne in this country shalbe held bond or free only according to the condition of the mother, *And* that if any christian shall committ ffornication with a negro man or woman, hee or shee soe offending shall pay double the ffines imposed by the former act.

April 1691

. . . For prevention of that abominable mixture and spurious issue which hereafter may encrease in this dominion, as well by negroes, mulattoes, and Indians intermarrying with English, or other white women, as by their unlawfull accompanying with one another, *Be it enacted by the authoritie afore-said, and it is hereby enacted,* that for the time to come, whatsoever English or other white man or woman being free shall intermarry with a negroe, mulatto, or Indian man or woman bond or free, shall within three months after such marriage be banished and removed from this dominion forever, and that the justices of each respective countie within this dominion make it their perticular care, that this act be put in effectuall execution. *And be it further enacted by the authoritie aforesaid, and it is hereby enacted,* That if any English woman being free shall have a bastard child by any negro or mu-latto, she pay the sume of fifteen pounds sterling, within one moneth after such bastard child shall be born, to the Church wardens of the parish where she shall be delivered of such child, and in default of such payment she shall be taken into the possession of the said Church wardens and disposed of for five yeares, and the said fine of fifteen pounds, or whatever the woman shall be disposed of for, shall be paid, one third part to their majesties for and towards the support of the government and the contingent charges thereof, and one other third part to the use of the parish where the offence is committed, and the other third part to the informer, and that such bastard child be bound out as a servant by the said Church wardens untill he or she shall attaine the age of thirty yeares, and in case such English woman that shall have such bastard child be a servant, she shall be sold by the said church wardens, (after her time is expired that she ought by law to serve her master) for five yeares, and the money she shall be sold for divided as is before appointed, and the child to serve as aforesaid. . . .

October 1705

And be it enacted . . . That if any woman-kind, or maiden of the age of twelve years or upwards, and under the age of sixteen years, shall contrary to the will or consent of her parent or guardian, and without publication of the banns, as aforesaid, consent and agree in her marriage with any person whatsoever; that then the next of kin to such woman-kind, or maiden, to whom the inheritance should descend or come, shall have right to enter upon and take possession of all the lands, tenements, hereditaments, and all other real estate whatsoever, which the said woman-kind, or maiden, at the time of her said marriage and agreement, had in possession, reversion, or remainder; and have, hold, occupy, and enjoy the same, to him, and the representatives of his stock, with all the immunities and privileges thereto belonging, during the coverture: And that after the determination thereof, the said lands, tenements, hereditaments, and other real estate, and also the possessions, reversions, and remainders thereupon, with all the rights, immunities, and privileges thereto belonging, shall then immediately vest, remain and be in the said woman so agreed and married, as aforesaid, and her heirs, or such person or persons as should have enjoied the same, if this act had never been made, other than the person with whom she shall so consent in marriage; with power to them, and every of them, to re-enter and take possession of the same; any thing herein contained, to the contrary thereof, in any-wise, notwithstanding.

A Puritan Parson Goes A-Courting

In colonial America one often had to go about finding a mate more than once. These documents concern the three courtships and marriages of the Reverend Michael Wigglesworth of Boston (1631–1705), best known perhaps for his poem, "The Day of Doom." Wigglesworth often seems to fit the still popular stereotype of the joyless, repressive, and self-repressed Puritan. But these selections are not intended to present him as the typical Puritan—if such a being can even be said to have existed. Puritanism was a culture which contained styles of self-loathing as well as a rich idiom of love and devotion. The Wigglesworth revealed here represents at most just one type of Puritan sensibility (Anne Bradstreet, p. 103, can be seen as representing a very different one). These documents, moreover, reflect a sequence of courtships over a span of nearly forty years and thus reveal something about the different considerations that were involved in making a marriage under varying circumstances and at different stages in one's life. The first consists of selections from Wigglesworth's diary, written as a young man just embarking upon adulthood and marriage. The second, coming when Wigglesworth was nearly fifty and after his first wife's death, is an unsuccessful attempt by Increase Mather, the leading minister of Massachusetts Bay Colony, to dissuade him from a contemplated marriage. The third, written when Wigglesworth was almost sixty and again a widower with small children, is a letter trying to persuade a widow (one of several he approached with the proposition) to marry him.

THE DIARY OF MICHAEL WIGGLESWORTH

February 14, 1653

. . . Now that I am to goe out into the world I am affraid, nay I know I shall lose my heart and my affections, I can do nothing for god receiv

"The Diary of Michael Wigglesworth, 1653–1657," Edmund S. Morgan, ed., *Transactions, 1942–1946*, XXXV (Colonial Society of Massachusetts), pp. 323, 394, 404–7. Reprinted by permission of Colonial Society of Massachusetts.

nothing from him but tis a snare unto me. why Lord thou art the guide of my youth into thy hands I commit my spirit, thou art my whole trust giue me to make the soe continually, let me walk in the light of thy countenance all the day long catervatim opprimer iniquitatum multitudinibus ipsiss. hoc die.

February 15, 1653

Pride I feel still again and again abounding, self-admiration, though destroying my self daly. god gracious and bountifull in bestowing in directing me and mine, but I unthankfully wickedly making gods gifts subservient to my vain glory. ah Lord I am vile, I desire to abhor my self (o that I could!) before the for these things. *I find such unresistable torments of carnal lusts or provocation unto the ejection of seed that I find my self unable to read anything to inform me about my distemper because of the prevailing or rising of my lusts. This I have procured to my self. God hath brought this to my eye this day Thou hast destroyed thy self but in me is thy help Lord let me find help in thee though I have destroyed my self by my iniquity. . . .*

July 9, 1654

After I was come safe home the next day I addrest my self to write to New Haven concerning the whole transaction of this business. when I was doing so there comes to my hand a letter of my mothers declaring that they had propounded a business of the like nature there in my behalf, and that I was now engaged in a sute there, and therefore to see that issued before I look't any further. This report did fill my spirit suddenly with marvellous sorrow and perplexity more then I wel knew how to bear; insomuch that I fear'd least the violence of it should overthrow my bodily health. I was affraid my withdrawing should seem contempt of the party who was of great note and birth and piety, and cast shame upon my friends who had motion'd such a thing as from me (though they had given some occasion and just pretence for my withdrawing) and dishonour upon the name and gospel of my god which I profess. These straits set me upon consideration of my own ways, and mourning for my own pride and self-overweening and rashness &c. And upon meditating much off such things as might stay my heart, and it pleased god to enable me to pray to him and seek him earnestly for to set me at liberty from such thraldom as I had brought my self into through my folly . . . .

April 17, 1655

I ventured out to wethersfield hooded. whence I had a hors brought me according to agreement on munday and on Tuesday I set forth for the Bay. The motives that hasten'd me were these. 1. I found my ilnes continue and no means there to help me. 2ly I conceived journeying might do me good as much as physick, if I could keep from could. 3. To redeem the spring time for marrying or taking physick, or both. God brought me thorow comfortably in 2 daes from springfield to Roxbury, much bettered (though wearied) with my journey. staying a day in the Bay and consulting with Mr Alcock (who advized to proceed with the busines of marriage In the 1st place) I reach't Rowley on the saturday.

On munday ensueing I dined and discoursed with Mr Rogers about the great busines. He could by noe means concur with the other physicians in advizing first to marriage and afterward to taking physick, for many reasons by him alledged; but thought it meet 1. to rectify the habit of my body and afterward to proceed. I was distressed at the hearing of his opinion, because it stil made the case more difficult. . . . My own weakness (which formerly perplexed me at such times) setting in with Mr Rogers his scruples did much trouble me, and caus me to questeon, whither it were my way to marry, before the use of more means, and to run such a hazzard as that of my life and health without an apparent necessity, before I had tryed the utmost that physick could doe. I repaired to Mr Alcock with all speed again to speak with him and object unto him for my farther satisfaction.

1: He told me that he hoped my diseas might be cured by physick; but It would be a long and teadious and far more difficult cure, then he hoped it would be by marriage, and astringent cordials afterward. . . .

2: He told me divers experiences of the success of this cours in like distempers. An example of one just affected like my self before his marriage, who was grievously perplexed with it, yet went on with it and did very wel after, and hath divers children living at this day. And so of divers others who have taken this cours with good success.

3: He told me that mine was not vera Gon: as he could prove. . . .

4ly. He told me that which made me so fearful, made him fearless, and gave him the more hopes, that marriage would take away the caus of that distemper, which was naturalis impulsus seu instinctus irresistibilis.

These things together with the consideration. 1. of my unsettled condition wherein I cannot attend rules of Physick with any conveniency. 2ly off the great charge and expences I must be at for a continued cours of Physick and diet better than ordinary. 3ly of my inability with comfort and honesty to live long as I am single. 4ly off the little hopes to prevayl against rebellious nature, which is disquieted rather than overcome by physick in statu presenti. These things make it pretty clear to me that god calleth to a speedy change of my condition, which I therefore desire to attend as a duty that god calleth unto, leaving my life and health in his hands. And oh! that I had a meek spirit to submit to his good pleasure. A beleiving heart! and a judicious mind to see clearly that this is my way at all times. . . .

May —, 1655

I was troubled to think that they were not willing to have the wedding before the election. . . . Yet here again providence appeared sweetly in bowing their spirits to issue it within a fourtnight, and so before the Election; And all things we found conspiring to further our intendment, Taylors ready to do the work in time, merchants ready to take provisions for shopp commoditys, &c. blessed be god! who worketh all our works in us and for us. . . .

I was somewhat perplexed also at my return into the bay after my contraction, concerning the lawfulness of marrying with a Kinswoman, because the mothers sister is forbidden; now sister in scripture language is put for a Kinswoman sometimes. I spent some time about it and the Lord gaue me comfortable satisfaction in this point also, that my scruple was Invalid.

May 18, 1655

At the time appointed with fear and trembling I came to Rowley to be marryed. The great arguments unto me were, 1: Physicians counsel: 2ly the institution of marryage by god himself for the preservation of purity and chastity, which with most humble and hearty prayers I have begged and stil wil beg of the Lord. so that I went about the business which god call'd me to attend And consummated it now is by the will of god May 18. 1655./ oh Lord! let my cry come up unto thee for all the blessings of a marryed estate, A heart sutable thereto, chastity especially thereby, and life and health if it be thy will. oh crown thy own ordinance with thy blessing, that it may appear it is not in vain to wait upon thee in the wayes of thy own appointment *I feel the stirrings and strongly of my former distemper even after the use of marriage the next day which makes me exceeding afraid. I know not how to keep company with my dearest friend but it is with me as formerly in some days already.* oh pitty the poorest and vilest of thy creatures for the Lords sake, And let not thy servants be a curs each to other but a blessing in this new relation.

INCREASE MATHER TO MICHAEL WIGGLESWORTH, MARCH 8, 1679

Reverend Sir,—Since I saw you the last in B. one that doth unfeignedly desire your welfare hath bin with mee, expressing grief of heart with reference unto a matter wherein yourselfe is concerned. I owe you that respect (& much more) as to informe you what I have bin told. The Report is, that you are designing to marry with your servant mayd, & that she is one of obscure parentage, & not 20 years old, & of no Church, nor so much as Baptised. If it be as is related, I would humbly entreat you (before it be too late) to consider of these arguments in opposition: 1. For you to doe this, which will be a grief of heart to your dear Relations, if it be not a matter which God doth command to be done (for no man will deny but one ought rather to grieve his friends, than to provoke the Lord) is not advisable. Now I hear that they are much troubled at your intended proceedings, & I suppose there is no divine precept requiring your marrying with such an one. Is it not then better to desist? 2. I doubt that considering her youth, & your age, & great bodily infirmities, such a change of your condition, if that which is intimated by the Holy Apostle, 1 Cor. 7, 3, should be attended, your days would be shortned, & consequently the 5th Commandment broken. 3. Such general Rules as those, Phil. 4, 8, doe concern as all christians, so eminently Ministers of Christ. And doubtless it will *male audire* for you to doe this thing, yea, I fear it will leave a blott upon your Name after you shall cease to be in this world. 4. The ministry will be blamed, which wee should be very carefull to prevent. 2 Cor. 6, 3. The mouths of carnal ones will be opened, not onely to censure you, but your brethren in the ministry will be condemned also. The world will say, theres such an one Hee was as justified a man as any of them, & yet wee see unto what his affections have carried him. 5. I am afraid that if you should proceed, that Rule, 2 Cor. 6, 14, will be transgressed. It useth to be said *nube pari*, but to marry with one so much your Inferior on all accounts, is not *nubere pari.* And to take one that was never baptised into such neerness of Relation, seemeth contrary to the Gospell; especially for a Minister of Christ to doe it. The like never was in N. E. Nay, I question whether the like hath bin known in the christian world. 6. Doth not that Script. 1 Tim. 3, 11, with others of the like importance, prohibit such proceedings?

Thus have I made bold to suggest my thoughts unto you. And if I had not respected the interest of Religion, & your credit & comfort, I should have bin wholly silent in a matter that concerns another & not me, further than as I am bound to seeke your welfare, & doe what I may to prevent trouble from coming upon my neighbor, & brother, especially such an one, whose Name hath bin, & I hope may still be, of precious esteem with the Lord's people.

Though your affections should be too far gone in this matter, I doubt not but if you put the object out of your sight, & looke up to the Lord Jesus for supplies of grace, you will be enabled to overcome these Temptations. The Lord be with you, I am

Yours unfeignedly,

3/8/1679.   Increase Mather.

MICHAEL WIGGLESWORTH TO MRS. AVERY, MARCH 23, 1691

Mrs. Avery   ⎫
& my very kind friend. ⎬

I heartily salute you in ye Lord with many thanks for yor kind entertainment when I was with you March 2d. I have made bold once more to visit you by a few lines in ye inclosed paper, not to prevent a personal visit, but rather to make way for it, which I fully intend the beginning of ye next week if weather and health Prevent not, craving the favor that you will not be from home at that Time, yet if yor occasions cannot comply with that Time, I shall endeavor to wait upon you at any other Time that may suit you better. Not further to trouble you at this Time, but only to present ye inclosed to yor serious thoughts, I commend both it & you to ye Lord & wait for an Answer from Heaven in due season, meanwhile I am & shall remain,   Yo^r True Friend & wel—wisher,

MICHAEL WIGGLESWORTH.

Maldon March 23, 1691.

I make bold to spread before you these following considerations which Possibly may help to clear up yor way before your return an answer unto ye Motion which I have made to you, I hope you will take them in good Part, and Ponder them seriously.

1st. I have a great perswasion that ye motion is of God, for diverse Reasons.

As first that I should get a little acquaintance with you by a short & transient visit having been altogether a stranger to you before, and that so little acquaintance should leave such impressions behind it, as neither length of Time, distance of Place, nor any other objects could wear off, but that my thoughts & heart have been toward you ever since.

2ly. That upon serious, earnest and frequent seeking of God for guidance & Direction in so weighty a matter, my thoughts have still been determined unto and fixed upon yo^rself as the most suitable Person for me.

3ly. In that I have not been led hereunto by fancy (as too many are in like cases) but by sound Reason & judgment, Principally Loving and desiring you for those gifts & graces God hath bestowed upon you, and Propounding ye Glory of God, the adorning and furtherance of ye Gospel. The spiritual as wel as outward good of myself and family, together with ye good of your self & children, as my Ends inducing me hereunto.

2ly. Be Pleased to Consider, that although you may Peradventure have offers made you by Persons more Eligible, yet you can hardly meet with one that can love you better, or whose love is built upon a surer foundation, or that may be capable of doing more for you in some respects than myself. But let this be spoken with all humility, & without ostentation. I can never think meanly enough of myself.

3ly. Whither there be not a great sutableness in it for one that hath been a Physician's wife to match with a Physician, By this means you may in some things & at some Times afford more help than another, & in like manner receive help, get an increase of skill, and become capable of doing more that way hereafter if need should be.

4ly. Whither God doth not now invite you to ye doing of some more Eminent Service for him, than you are capable of doing in yor Present Private capacity? and whither those many Emptyings from vessel to vessel & great afflictions that have befaln you might not be sent with a design to fit you for further service, & to losen you from yᵉ Place & way you have been in?

5ly. Whither yᵉ enjoyment of Christ in all his ordinances (which at present cannot be had where you are) be not a thing of that weight that may render this motion at this time somewhat more considerable?

6ly. Consider, if you should continue where you are whither yᵉ looking after & managing of your outward Business & affairs may not be too hard for you, and hazzard your health again?

7ly. If God should exercise you with sickness again whither it were not more comfortable and safe to have a neer and dear friend to take care of you and yours at such a Time, especially now when yoʳ dear mother is gone to Heaven.

8ly. This following summer is Likely to be full of Troubles (unless God prevent beyond the expectation of man) by reason of our Indian and French Enemyes: now whither it may not be more comfortable and safe to get neerer yᵉ heart of the Country, than to continue where you are & to live as you do?

9ly. The consideration of yᵉ many afflictions, losses & Bereavements which have befallen you, as it hath affected my heart with deep sympathy, so it hath been no small inducement to me to make this motion, hopeing that if God should give it acceptance with you I might be a friend & a Comforter to you instead of your many lost relations; and I hope upon trial you would find it so.

10ly. As my Late wife was a means under God of my recovering a better state of Health; so who knows but God may make you instrumental to Preserve & Prolong my health & life to do him service.

Obj. As to that main objection in respect to my Age, I can say nothing to that, But my Times are in the hands of God, who as he hath restored my health beyond expectation, can also if he Please Prolong it while he hath any service for me to do for his Name. And in yᵉ mean time, if God shall Please and yourself be willing to Put me in that Capacity, I hope I shall do you as much Good in a little time as it is Possible for me to do, & use some endeavours also to Provide for yoʳ future, as wel as Present, welfare, as God's Bounty shall enable me; for true love cannot be idle.

Ob. And for yᵉ other objection from yᵉ number of my children & difficulty of guiding such a family. 1st. the Number may be lessened if there be need of it.

2ly. I shall gladly improve my authority to stengthen yours (if God shall so Perswade your heart) to do what lieth in me to make the burden as light & comfortable as may be. And I am perswaded there would be a great suitableness in our tempers, spirits, Principles, & consequently a sweet and harmonious agreement in those matters (& in all other matters) betwixt us, and indeed this Perswasion is a Principle thing which hath induced me to make this motion to yoʳself & to no other.

Finally that I be not over tedious, I have great hope, that if God shall Perswade you to close with this motion, the Consequents will be for yᵉ furthurance of ye Gospel, for ye Comfort of us both, & of both our familyes & that ye Lord will make us mutual helpers & Blessings to each other, & that we shall enjoy much of God together in such a Relation, without which no relation can be truly sweet.

Courtship Among the High Virginia Gentry

By the early years of the eighteenth century, Virginia had developed a landed gentry. With its great expanses of land, the New World enabled some men—but fewer than myths suggest—to amass vast plantations, construct fine, almost baronial estates, and thereby set themselves up as colonial aristocrats even though they had no titles of nobility. But at the same time as they turned themselves into a gentry in the New World, forming an elite at the top of a society that as the century progressed developed a hierarchical complexity reminiscent of that of the mother country, they were made painfully aware of their standing as mere provincials in a broader Anglo-Atlantic world. Accordingly they looked to London—the metropolitan center—for the cultural cues and the social acceptance that could distinguish them as something more than wealthy colonial nabobs.

William Byrd II (1674–1744) was a quintessential early-eighteenth-century Virginia aristocrat. He was the son of a man who had parlayed a decent inheritance, a good marriage, political connections, and a shrewd business and political sense into enough wealth to establish himself as one of Virginia's wealthiest planters. Byrd spent much of his youth in England, where he acquired the tastes and habits of an English gentleman. But at his father's death in 1705 he returned to Virginia, took control of the Byrd interests and estate, and built Westover as the seat of a family dynasty that has endured through more than two centuries. He lived on as a Virginia squire and Anglo-American cosmopolite until he died in 1744, leaving a vast estate.

Just as the Wigglesworth materials permit us to probe into the processes of courtship and marriage within the cultural and social setting of Puritan New England, so these materials give us a glimpse into the cultural traditions of the "great family" that began in the eighteenth-century-Virginia tidewater aristocracy. They permit us to take a reading of the character of a man who may have been unique and idiosyncratic in some ways but who was nonetheless the product of a particular cultural style and social class and to observe that character responding to courtship in three rather different situations. We see Byrd the young Virginia gentleman selecting a suitable mate, Byrd the wealthy provincial widower spurned in his attempt to make an alliance with an English heiress, and Byrd the patriarch condemning the suit of his daughter.

THE CORRESPONDENCE OF WILLIAM BYRD II

William Byrd to Lucy Parke [Fidelia], ca. 1705–6

What woud some lovers give for this lucky occasion of beginning a billet doux? The moment I begin to write, I am entertaind with the cooing of 2 amorous turtles. Were I capable of understanding their language, as well as a certain philosopher did once upon a time, I would be their interpreter, and tell you a long story of the tender reproaches they make to one another. But tho I know as little of what these lovers say, as some translaters do of what their authors write, yet like them I venture to guess at their meaning. They talk of nothing but the dearest of all subjects love, and abound with expressions of tenderness to one another. One complains of too much coldness in her mate, and of the huge inequality of their passions. Another is full of reproaches to his mistress, for discovering too much distinction to his rival. A third tells his fears, least the summer shou'd end too soon, and too hastily conclude the intrigue. Another again like an unreasonable woman that has bin twice marry'd, is continually upbraiding her last gallant, with the exceeding kindness of her first. With such tender moans as these they spend their happy days, & reconcile all their murmuring quarrels with cooing, and billing.

I cant forbear envying these innocent lovers for the blessing they injoy of being always together; while I, poor I must lament the want of my dear, dear turtle for many days. Pray have the goodness to help me bear this misfortune, by all the instances of kindness, you can show; by gracious looks, and gracious actions when I am with you, by tender thoughts and tender letters when I am from you. Such expressions of favour on your side, and a good stock of patience and forbearance on mine, may perhaps enable me to out-live the uneasiness of our separation. . . .

Thus my dear Fidelia I have given you an account of the state of love amongst other people. I need not tell you how th[o]roughly I feel it my self, because I have mentiond it before, and fear least the repetition of it shoud prove sickly & mawkish to your stomach. However pray do me the justice to believe, that as those people have most honesty, most virtue, & most courage, that say least of it, so I have the most tender passion in the world for you, tho perhaps I dont stuff my letters, with those fond flourishes, with which the common herd of lovers spoil a great deal of

Maude H. Woodfin and Marion Tinling, eds., *Another Secret Diary of William Byrd of Westover,* *1739–1741* (Richmond, 1942), pp. 218–23, 303–5, 322–24, 357–59, 381–85. Reprinted by permission of the editors.

paper. But I leave my actions to speak for me, which are always the best vouchers in the world, and which will always convince you, that I am faithfully and intirely your Veramour.

William Byrd to Daniel Parke, ca. 1705–6

Since my arrival in this country I have had the honour to be acquainted with your daughters, and was infinitely surpriz'd to find young ladys with their accomplishments in Virginia. This surprize was soon improv'd into a passion for the youngest for whom I have all the respect and tenderness in the world. However I think it my duty to intreat your approbation before I proceed to give her the last testimony of my affection. And the young lady her self whatever she may determine by your consent will agree to nothing without it. If you can entertain a favourable opinion of my person, I dont question but my fortune may be sufficient to make her happy, especially after it has been assisted by your bounty. If you shall vouchsafe to approve of this undertakeing I shall indeavour to recommend my self by all the dutifull regards to your Excellency and all the marks of kindness to your daughter. Nobody knows better than your self how impatient lovers are, and for that reason I hope youll be as speedy as possible in your determination which I passionately beg may be in favour of your &c.

William Byrd to Sabina Smith, July 2, 1717

. . . If you cou'd look into my heart, you'd beleive that I love you without any mean Regard to your Fortune; I bless my Stars my circumstances are not so low, nor my Avarice so high as to require it. But if Sabina were mistress of no more than the Linnen that covers her agreable person, she wou'd be altogether as enchanting, and I as passionate as now. She may please to remember, that I sigh't for her at a time when her Fortune cou'd be no part of the Temptation. I beseech you dont do that Injustice to your own Charms, as to imagin, I cou'd have any other Reason but them for my Inclination. Alas when a heart is fir'd wth so generous a Flame as mine, twill detest all low considerations. But to give you the plainest argument that my tenderness has no motive but your most engageing Person, I declare, that I wou'd even marry you tho your Geoler shou'd be so hard hearted as to deny his Consent. and then t'is a plain case, you wou'd not be worth one spendid shilling If an act so very heroique be not sufficient to convince you I must pronounce you more unbeleiveing than a free think[er]. I know not what the discerning Sabina may Judge of this offer, but I vow I think in this covetous age, tis a handsome thing to love a Damsel well enough, to marry her with nothing but her good Qualitys. However I wou'd not desire this unless I knew my own Fortune sufficient to make you easy without any addition from yours. as violent as my Passion is for you, I wou'd not ask you to descend in your circumstances below the Post of your Education for my sake: but wou'd be always ready to sacrifice the dearest & most darling of my Inclinations to your happiness. This is true so help me Love, and Heaven.

Adieu.

Sabina Smith to William Byrd, July 4, 1717

I must acknowledge the very civil offer which you had the goodness to make me, but can't in conscience accept of it. I thank you nevertheless for your great Generosity, which is all a poor Damsel can do under my Circumstances of Obedience. I need not urge to Veramour the duty of the 5th Commandmant, which by the good leave of Constitution I will religiously observe. Neither ought you to preach up Rebellion against a Parent, in one that I'm confident you wou'd not teach to rebel against a Husband. I don't question but Veramours circumstances are sufficient to recommend him to a good Fortune in a more regular way. When a Man is in condition to go to market fairly, tis surely as unpardonable to steal a Wife, as any other valuable thing. But if you shou'd be averse to proceed in the forms with me, the utmost I can do, is to wish you may have all the happy terms you desire with some Nymph more deserving. However I am so much obliged to you for the over-value you are pleas'd to set upon my qualifications, that I shou'd be ungratefull if I did not wish you happy in marriage as well as in every other concern of life. Adieu.

William Byrd to Sabina Smith, July 5, 1717

. . . I beseech you . . . my Dear Sabina, continue to repose in me this most endearing Confidence. And may I suffer all the Pains of disappointed Love, if either vanity or levity, negligence or inadvertency tempt me to betray you. Then Madam as to the Indulgence you have been pleas'd to allow my letters, it shall never be abus'd. I will be carefull both to write, and to send them with so much precaution, that no mortal with all the Eys of Argus, and the Ears of Envy, shall ever discover the secret. I trust no Servant to carry my Billets to the Post, but perform that faithfully with my own hand; I only fear that the frequency of their comeing that way may alarm your watchfull Family. I wou'd therefore propose to the lovely Sabina a securer method, of which I shall wait her opinion before I make the least advance towards putting it in practice. Trolly that liv'd with our freind the Prophetess, has been here to desire to wash my Linnen. She told me of her own accord, that she was not without hopes of haveing some business of the same kind from you. Now I know her to be very faithfull, and therefore if you'll give me leave, I will swear her to everlasting secrecy, and trust her to carry my Respects to you: and I beleive the same hand may be the safest way of conveying your Commands to me. I propose this the rather Madam, because I cant conceive how you manage the sending your letters to the Post without confideing in somebody, that may not possibly be so trusty as honest Trolly. . . . I intreat the Charming Sabina not to beleive, that I was tempting her to violate her duty to her Father, while I was only giveing her an Instance of the intire generosity of my Passion.

William Byrd to John Smith, February 18, 1718

. . . Judging it altogether unwarrantable to proceed any other way, I think it my duty to explane my circumstances to you, and humbly intreat your consent. And because affairs of this sort ought above all others to be manag'd with truth and honour, I shall venture to say nothing on this occasion, but what may be fairly consistent with both. According to this good Principle I must beg leave to assure you, that the Estate I have, tho it lye so far off as Virginia, is very considerable. I have there about 43000 acres of Land and 220 Negros at work upon it with a prodigi[ous] quantity of stock of every kind. Some part of this Land is let out to Tenants, and more will be leas't every year. But the usual method of that Country is to seat our own slaves upon it, and send the fruit of their Labour, consisting in Tob° and Naval stores, to England. We can therefore have no certain way of valuing our Estates by the year, but they produce more or less, according as the market happens to be for those Commoditys here. What I can tell you for certain, is, to show how much clear mony my Returns have yeilded the 3 years since I have been over. In the year 1715 they produc'd clear of all charge £1716:5—In the year 1716 they clear'd no more than £1535:14:11. But this year they will yeild more than £1800— as I can prove by the accounts of my merchants in the city that dispose of my Effects, Who are men of great integrity as well as of great substance. This mony comes clear into my Pocket after all charges are deducted, which is more than any Estate in England will yeild of £2000 p annum. I cou'd make about £400 a year more of my Returns if I wou'd take the trouble to dispose of them my self. There are besides several other advantages belonging to this kind of Estate, namely y^t in a few years the value of it will grow to be double what it is at this time, by the increase of the Inhabitants of the Country, and by the great distance from water carriage, all the Land lys that remains now to be taken up. Then I can always make Ten p cent of whatever mony I lay down for the customes of my Tob° for prompt Payment. I need not tell you Sir how vastly more advantagious this Estate wou'd be, if I shou'd live upon the place, because I cant harbour the least thought of ever carrying Mrs S. . . . over thither, in case I shou'd be so happy as to marry her. This whole Estate I shou'd be willing to settle upon this marriage, only reserving a liberty of charging it with the summ of £4000 whenever my 2 Daughters shou'd come to marry. I am wholly unacquainted Sir what Fortune you will please to give your Daughter, because my passion for her is too disinterested ever to suffer me to make that Inquiry. But whatever it be, I shall agree to have it settled after what manner you please. For I can assure you without affectation, that Interest is very far from being any motive to this address. As to my Family, which I think shou'd be only mention'd upon these occasions, I am descended from the Family of my name at Broxon in Cheshire where they have been seated for more than 20 Generations. Then Sir for my character, you wont expect I shall say any thing of that my self, I must leave it to those that know me best, amongst whome I shall only name my Lord Percevale and Mr Southwell, who are Persons of most unquestionable honour and veracity, & who have been long acquainted with my morals, my Temper, & my Education, and will not deceave you. But you need not confine your inquiry to them, since there are many persons of distinction to whome I have the honour to be perfectly known. To them I submit my character intirely, and am ready when you please to make out all the Facts relateing to my circumstances by undoubted testimony. I own Sir you may marry your Daughter to a better Estate, and to higher Quality: but there is nothing necessary to make her happy, which may not be compasst by my Fortune; especially after it hath been assisted by your generosity. However this I will venture to promise for my self, that if I have the honour to be accepted, the greatest pleasure I shall take in this world, will be to make your daughter happy, and to behave my self in such a manner, as may be most dutifull & most agreable to your self, I humbly recommend my self to your favour, begging that you will be pleas'd to approve my address, which will ever engage me to be with all possible Respect &c.—

William Byrd to Sir Edward Des Bouverie, May 10, 1718

. . . Had I thought it proper to acquaint you with my Affair with Mrs Smith, I wou'd have taken the open handsome way of waiting upon you my self, nor wou'd I for any reason whatsoever have carry'd with me a third Person to be witness to a story so much to that Ladys disadvantage. I can assure you the only reason why I did not go to you was, because I consider'd, that after a Lady has been graciously pleas'd to give a man Encouragement for more than a year together and after frankly declareing her Inclinations, if she think fit to change her mind in favour of a greater Estate, she must have something so wrong in her composition that I am not only easy under the loss of her, but even thank God for the disappointment. Neither indeed wou'd I have taken the trouble to open to you so Extraordinary scene, but that your comeing in so hostile a manner might have made my silence look like fear, which is a suspicion you know a Gentleman ought to avoid by all the methods of truth and Integrity. There is one thing Sir I wou'd beg of you in complement to your mistresses character, which is, that you will be pleas'd not to represent the story differently from what I told it, because as often as I shall hear it told wrong, I must be oblig'd for my own justification to tell it right, which for her sake I shou'd be unwilling to do. And that you may not by any defect of memory be led into a mistake of this kind I must beg leave to recount all the Principal Incidents of our story. Mrs Smith then did me the honour to hold a Private Correspondence with me for above a year together, without the Privity of her Father, dureing which time she receiv'd about 15 letters from me full of the most passionate expressions, and writ in a character altogether invisible, til her art and industry brought it to light. . . . In obedience to her Commands I did make my Proposals, but my Estate lying in another Country it was not agreable to Mr Smith, tho she was so good as to endeavour to perswade him to it by declareing she cou'd be happyer with me than with any body else. How odd soever her fancy might be in this business, she was pleas'd to write to 2 of her Relations to intreat them to interceed with her Father in my behalf. . . . I was to be trail'd on by the Daughter after the Father had refus'd me, & to confirm me in the hopes of her Favour, she was pleas'd after that to write me a very gracious letter, to let me know how fearfull she was lest her Father shou'd take some rash Resolution to dispose of her to some other Person, which she said she shou'd find hard to digest. She also instructed me at the same time to be sure to write in the Invisible Character, to make up my letters in a square figure, and direct them to her maid, that so they might not fall into the hands of the old Gentleman. According to these kind Instruments I afterwards wrote her 4 or 5 letters conceiv'd in the most tender terms which she was so good as to receive. Thus we continued in very good Intelligence til your Estate came to be propos'd, which made her alter her style, and resolve to sacrifice both her character & Inclination to her Interest. This Sir is a faithfull account of our story, the truth of which tis too much in my power to prove ever to be disputed, and supposeing it to be so, I must appeal to your cooler thoughts after marriage, whether this Lady has treated me with common honour or common Justice. Her own Father has already condemn'd her by thinking it proper to salute her with the reproachfull terms above mention'd, tho the good man at the same time notwithstanding this confession of his Daughters injustice to me, made no scruple to push on the treaty with you. I was sorry to hear from so good a Judge as your self, that most women now adays treat Gentlemen at this odd rate, but I have too good an opinion of the sex to be of your sentiments in this matter. However I assure you Sir I must own my self much oblig'd to Mrs Smith for being so charitable to me as to cure intirely the wounds of her Eys by the imprudence of her Behaviour in imitation of the Viper that cures by the Vertues of its flesh the dead bite of its teeth. This makes me as easy at least in missing her, as you can be in marrying of her, and I shall esteem it as just a complement to wish me joy upon looseing as to give it you upon gaining so extraordinary a Prize.

William Byrd to Evelyn Byrd, July 20, 1723

Considering the solemn promise you made me, first by word of mouth, & afterwards by letter, that you wou'd not from thence forth have any Converse of Correspondence with the Baronet, I am astonisht you have violated that protestation in a most notorious manner. The gracious audience you gave him the morning you left Towne, & the open conversations you have with him in the Country have been too unguarded, to be deny'd any longer. Tis therefore high time for me to reproach you with breech of duty & breach of faith, & once more to repeat to you, my strict & positive Commands, never more to meet, speak, or write to that Gentleman, or to give him an opportunity to see, speak, or write to You. I also forbid you to enter into any promise or engagement with him of marriage or Inclination. I enjoin you this in the most positive terms, upon the sacred duty you owe a Parent, & upon the blessing you ought to expect upon the Performance of it. And that neither he nor you may be deluded afterwards with Vain hopes of forgiveness, I have put it out of my power, by vowing that I never will. And as to any Expectation, you may fondly entertain of a Fortune from me, you are not to look for one brass farthing, if you provoke me by this fatal instance of disobedience. Nay besides all that, I will avoid the sight of you as of a creature detested. Figure then to your self my Dear Child how wretched you will be with a provokt father, & a disappointed Husband. To whome then will you fly in your distress, when all the world will upbraid you with haveing acted like an Ideot? & your conscience must fly in your face for haveing disobey'd an indulgent Parent. I think my self oblig'd to give you this fair warning, & to point out to you the Rocks upon which you will certainly shipwreck all your happiness in this world, unless you think fit to obey my orders. For God's sake then my dear child, for my sake, & for your own, survey the desperate Precipice you stand upon, & don't rashly cast your self down head long into Ruin. The idle Promises this man makes you will all vanish into smoke, & instead of Love he will slight & abuse you, when he finds his hopes of Fortune disappointed. Then you & your Children (if you shou'd be so miserable as to have any) must be Beggers, & then you may be assur'd all the world will deservedly dispise you, & you will hardly be pity'd so much as by Him who wou'd faign continue   &c.

William Byrd to Erranti, July 20, 1723

I am inform'd upon very good Evidence, that you have for some time taken the trouble to follow Amasia with your Addresses; that now at last you have play'd the wise part of a Knight Errant, & pursued Her into the Country with a pompous Equipage, that dos Her & your self much honour. What success these worthy steps have met with in the Girle, I know not: but they shall never meet with any in the Father. I fear your circumstances are not flourishing enough to maintain a Wife in much splendour, that has nothing, and just such a Fortune as that my Daughter will prove, if she Ventures to marry without my consent. You are deluded if you believe that any part of my Estate is settled upon Her, or that she has any thing independant of my Pleasure. I confess you have not deserv'd it from me, but I will however stand your Friend so far, as to assure you before hand, that Her Portion will be extreemly small if she bestows her self upon so clandestine a Lover. I have made my Will since I heard of your good intention towards me, & have bequeath'd my Daughter a splendid shilling, if she marrys any man that tempts her to disobedience. After giveing you this friendly warning, I hope you will have discretion enough to leave off so unprofitable a Pursuit, to which no tears on my Daughters part, or Intreatys on yours will ever be able to reconcile   &c.

A Philadelphia Tradesman Makes a Match

Benjamin Franklin needs little introduction. But so dazzling is the portrait of Franklin the scientist and sage, Franklin the revolutionary statesman, and Franklin the quintessential American success story that it obscures what Franklin was and expected to become when he went about choosing a wife. When he married Deborah Read in 1730 he was a young printer, hoping simply to establish himself and prosper in his trade and attain a respectable station in life. The selection from Franklin's autobiography, chosen almost in spite of Franklin's later success and fame, provides an account of how a poor but ambitious young tradesman in early-eighteenth-century Philadelphia went about making a marriage. The second selection was written after Franklin had retired from his printing business (though he still derived a handsome income from it) and had become a gentleman and respected civic leader. It shows Franklin the sage, a worldly and somewhat detached observer and satirist of the ways of the world, reflecting upon passion and marriage.

THE AUTOBIOGRAPHY OF BENJAMIN FRANKLIN

. . . I had made some courtship during this time to Miss Read. I had a great respect and affection for her, and had some reasons to believe she had the same for me; but as I was about to take a long voyage and we were both very young, only a little above eighteen, it was thought most prudent by her mother to prevent our going too far at present, as a marriage, if it was to take place, would be more convenient after my return, when I should be as I hoped set up in my business. Perhaps, too, she thought my expectations not so well founded as I imagined them to be. . . .

I had hitherto continued to board with Godfrey, who lived in part of my house with his wife and children, and had one side of the shop for his glazier's business. . . . Mrs. Godfrey projected a match for me with a relation's daughter, took opportunities of bringing us often together, till

The Autobiography of Benjamin Franklin, A Restoration of the "Fair Copy" by Max Farrand (Berkeley, 1949), pp. 45–46, 83–85. Reprinted by permission of the University of California Press.

a serious courtship on my part ensued, the girl being in herself very deserving. The old folks encouraged me by continued invitations to supper and by leaving us together, till at length it was time to explain. Mrs. Godfrey managed our little treaty. I let her know that I expected as much money with their daughter as would pay off my remaining debt for the printing house, which I believe was not then above a hundred pounds. She brought me word they had no such sum to spare. I said they might mortgage their house in the Loan Office. The answer to this after some days was that they did not approve the match; that on enquiry of Bradford they had been informed the printing business was not a profitable one, the types would soon be worn out and more wanted; that S. Keimer and D. Harry had failed one after the other, and I should probably soon follow them; and therefore I was forbidden the house, and the daughter shut up. Whether this was a real change of sentiment or only artifice, on a supposition of our being too far engaged in affection to retract and therefore that we should steal a marriage, which would leave them at liberty to give or withhold what they pleased, I know not. But I suspected the motive, resented it, and went no more. Mrs. Godfrey brought me afterwards some more favourable accounts of their disposition and would have drawn me on again, but I declared absolutely my resolution to have nothing more to do with that family. This was resented by the Godfreys, we differed, and they removed, leaving me the whole house, and I resolved to take no more inmates. But this affair having turned my thoughts to marriage, I looked round me and made overtures of acquaintance in other places, but soon found that the business of a printer being generally thought a poor one, I was not to expect money with a wife, unless with such a one as I should not otherwise think agreeable. In the meantime that hard-to-be-governed passion of youth had hurried me frequently into intrigues with low women that fell in my way, which were attended with some expense and great inconvenience, besides a continual risk to my health by a distemper, which of all things I dreaded, tho' by great good luck I escaped it.

A friendly correspondence as neighbours and old acquaintances had continued between me and Miss Read's family, who all had a regard for me from the time of my first lodging in their house. I was often invited there and consulted in their affairs, wherein I sometimes was of service. I pitied poor Miss Read's unfortunate situation, who was generally dejected, seldom cheerful, and avoided company. I considered my giddiness and inconstancy when in London as in a great degree the cause of her unhappiness, tho' the mother was good enough to think the fault more her own than mine, as she had prevented our marrying before I went thither and persuaded the match in my absence. Our mutual affection was revived, but there were now great objections to our union. That match was indeed looked upon as invalid, a preceding wife being said to be living in England; but this could not easily be proved because of the distance. And tho' there was a report of his death, it was not certain. Then, tho' it should be true, he had left many debts which his successor might be called upon to pay.

We ventured, however, over all these difficulties, and I took her to wife, Sept. 1, 1730. None of the inconveniencies happened that we had apprehended; she proved a good and faithful helpmate, assisted me much by attending the shop; we throve together and ever mutually endeavoured to make each other happy.

BENJAMIN FRANKLIN TO A FRIEND, JUNE 25, 1745

My dear Friend

I know of no Medicine fit to diminish the violent natural Inclinations you mention; and if I did, I think I should not communicate it to you. Marriage is the proper Remedy. It is the most natural State of Man, and therefore the State in which you are most likely to find solid Happiness. Your Reasons against entering into it at present appear to me not well-founded. The circumstantial Advantages you have in View by postponing it, are not only uncertain, but they are small in comparison with that of the Thing itself, the being *married and settled.* It is the Man and Woman united that make the compleat human Being. Separate, she wants his Force of Body and Strength of Reason; he, her softness, Sensibility, and acute Discernment. Together they are more likely to succeed in the World. A single Man has not nearly the Value he would have in the State of Union. He is an incomplete Animal. He resembles the odd Half of a Pair of Scissars. If you get a prudent, healthy Wife, your Industry in your Profession, with her good Economy, will be a Fortune suffient.

But if you will not take this Counsel and persist in thinking a Commerce with the Sex inevitable, then I repeat my former Advice, that in all your Amours you should *prefer old Women to young ones.* You call this a Paradox and demand my reasons. They are these:

1. Because they have more Knowledge of the World, and their Minds are better stor'd with Observations, their Conversation is more improving, and more lastingly agreeable.

2. Because when Women cease to be handsome they study to be good. To maintain their Influence over Men, they supply the diminution of Beauty by an Augmentation of Utility. They learn to do 1,000 Services small and great, and are the most tender and useful of all Friends when you are sick. Thus they continue amiable. And hence there is hardly such a thing to be found as an Old Woman who is not a good Woman.

3. Because there is no Hazard of Children, which irregularly produc'd may be attended with much Inconvenience.

4. Because thro' more Experience, they are more prudent and discreet in conducting an Intrigue to prevent Suspicion. The Commerce with them is therefore safer with regard to your Reputation. And with regard to theirs, if the Affair should happen to be known, considerate People might be

Leonard W. Labaree, ed., *The Papers of Benjamin Franklin*, vol. 3 (New Haven, 1961), pp. 30–31. Reprinted by permission of Yale University Press.

rather inclin'd to excuse an old Woman, who would kindly take care of a young Man, form his Manners by her good Counsels, and prevent his ruining his Health and Fortune among mercenary Prostitutes.

5. Because in every Animal that walks upright, the Deficiency of the Fluids that fill the Muscles appears first in the highest Part. The Face first grows lank and wrinkled; then the Neck; then the Breast and Arms; the lower Parts continuing to the Last as plump as ever: so that covering all above with a Basket, and regarding only what is below the Girdle, it is impossible of two Women to tell an old one from a young one. And as in the dark all Cats are grey, the Pleasure of corporal Enjoyment with an old Woman is at least equal, and frequently superior; every Knack being, by Practice, capable of Improvement.

6. Because the Sin is less. The debauching a Virgin may be her Ruin, and make her for Life unhappy.

7. Because the Compunction is less. The having made a young Girl *miserable* may give you frequent bitter Reflection; none of which can attend the making an old Woman *happy.*

8thly & lastly. They are *so grateful!!*

Thus much for my Paradox. But still I advise you to marry directly; being sincerely Your affectionate Friend.

Benjamin Franklin

A Quaker Wooing

annah Logan, the accomplished daughter of a prominent Quaker merchant in eighteenth-century Philadelphia, was much sought after. The selections below record the attempt of John Smith, an enterprising young merchant, to gain her hand in marriage. After much persistence he succeeded, triumphing over competition with a larger estate. This courtship took place within the confines of the sensibility of the Quaker gentry of the town and thus bears comparison with the courting style of the more profane but even more high-born William Byrd of the landed gentry, for, in both, courtship was pursued within an idiom of affection but gave due attention to more prudential considerations. When compared with Benjamin Franklin's courtship and advice, the selections reveal something of the differences of class and culture in the same city at roughly the same time. Before reading them, however, it might be helpful to examine the selection by George Fox (p. 79), laying out Quaker ideals about marriage and love.

HANNAH LOGAN'S COURTSHIP

Letter of John Smith to Hannah Logan

Phila., 12th mo: 5th, 1747–8.

DEAR FRIEND

According to the Sentiments I Entertain of Friendship, that part of it which can bear with the weakness, and put the best Construction upon the failings of One Another Manifests the truest and most Exalted height of that Celestial Virtue. Judge, then, what an Opinion I have of thy Generosity in the little Conversation we had last Evening together, when the distress of my mind was such that it was difficult for me to Convey any Idea of my thoughts, Yet Good nature, instead of Endeavouring to Encrease my Confusion, which Thousands of the Sex in such a circumstance would

Albert Myers, ed., *Courtship of Hannah Logan* (Philadelphia, 1904), pp. 144–49, 160, 169, 179.

have been glad to do, kindly Bore with my frailty. May Gracious Heaven put it in my power to Shew my Gratitude by Actions, which I really could not by words; and I Beg thee to Rest fully Assured that no freedom shall ever be miscontrued or turned to thy disadvantage.

I am now going to Tell thee some of the Inducements I had to fix my Affections unmoveably—as I believe they are, whether they should ever be Crown'd with Success or not—and herein I shall discover some weakness, but I have had too many Instances of thy Candour to suspect Severity, nor is there a thought in my Soul but what I could freely disclose to thee. It is now some years since first I conceived a very great Esteem for thy person from several opportunities I had of seeing thee. I knew my Circumstances in the world, nor any Accomplishments I had, did not promise Success in the Entertainment of that passion, and therefore used my utmost Efforts to Conquer it, and I thought the likeliest way to do it was to seek another object. I found one which appeared agreeable, but a very small Acquaintance quite overset my Scheme. I had been early, thro unmerited kindness, Tinctured with Religious Sentiments. I knew a fair outside did not Constitute happiness, and in short I saw but little else in that person; wherefore, without ever having given any occasion to Expect that I designed an offer of my person, I as willingly dropt my acquaintance as I had begun it. Soon after that I had some opportunities of Converse where thou was in Company, which much Enhanced my Esteem. I plainly saw that though the Cabinet was Exquisitely framed, the mind lodged in it far Excelled; and thus as it renewed and strengthened my former Regard, so it increased the difficulty I saw it was obtaining what I so much wished for. Many were the Racking thoughts occasioned by the different Sensations of desire and doubt. To Enumerate them would require much more time than thou would willingly spare for that purpose. I long bore that Inward Contest before I ever Disclosed it to any person, and believe I never should have done [so] at all, but in a Journey that I went with M. Lightfoot, as we were riding very seriously together, he told me he had found out a wife for me. I little Expected that he or anybody Else would have thought me a suitable match for her I had in View, but as He, mentioning thy name, soon perceived by the Confusion in my Countenance the scituation of my thoughts—and Added something to what he had said, that Affected me with some degree of hope—and he was at that time, and hath been ever since, very near and dear to me—from that time I thought Seriously about it, and when in any degree favoured with Access to the Throne of Grace, I spread my case there, and with the utmost Submission and Reverence, desired to be Led aright in so weighty an Affair. Many and frequent were my Applications of that Sort, and I often found returns of Satisfaction and peace in these Addresses, and sometimes a nearness and Sympathy with thy Exercises, in such an Affecting manner, that words cannot Convey an Adequate Idea of. Sometimes I have thought I accompanied thee in much weakness and dejection of mind—in poverty and distress of Soul, and great have been my Sorrows in that State, and frequent my Cries, when I was able to look toward the Holy Hill, that the Everlasting Arm might be underneath to Support and carry through all thy difficulties, and make Every Exercise truly profitable. These Tender Sympathies would look very foolish to those that are unacquainted with the frequent Afflictions that attend a truly Religious Life, but as I am very certain thou art not one of those, am therefore very free. . . .

I thought when I asked permission to wait upon thee at Stenton it seemd to put thee into a deep thought. I Concluded thy not absolutely denying my Request was out of pity, and durst I ask such a favour, I would Beg a line or two upon the Subject. I am afraid of coming least it should give thee more uneasiness, and know by omitting it I vastly Encrease my own. If my Generous friend would favour me with her Sentiments in writing, the Letter should either be immediately returned or destroyed to prevent its being ever known to any mortal but ourselves.

I conclude with Observing that Marriage is a Solemn thing, but where undertaken with upright, honest Intentions, and the Blessing of the Almighty Solemnly sought and had therein, it must certainly be the happiest State of Life. And I must tell thee that my views in desiring to have thee mine, are so far [from] being mercenary, that should thou Incline to an Alteration with respect to place of Residence, Manner of Living, Business or anything Else, this Inclination shall be punctually Complied with. I pray God to pour down his choicest Blessings upon thy head—and with the Salutation of the Tenderest Regard,

I Remain
Thy Truly Affectionate Friend,
JOHN SMITH.

January 8, 1748

Called at Stenton; found Company there, who soon departed. I intended to stay all night, and accordingly did so. Had an opportunity of Telling my mind to James & his wife separately. They treated me Civilly, referring me Entirely to their daughter, and the Old Gentleman told me if I was her Choice, he would give his Consent &c^a. I had some of the dear Creature's Company, but our Conversation was so much of the Ambiguous kind, that after a Loving & friendly parting I retired to Bed full of Doubt & perplexity, & Got but little Sleep. In how much pain is a situation between hope & Despair. . . .

February 10, 1748

I was in the morning very unwell, having had a poor night's rest; but thought perhaps the sight of my dear Hannah might be so like to cure me as anything else, wherefore I went to Germantown meeting, wch was silent, & after to Stenton, where I was very agreeably Entertained. Had in the Even^g my Charmer's Company till 10 o'clock, and it was more delightful to me than Ever, and gave me greater grounds of hope than I durst before Entertain, and the Old Gentleman treated me in a very Generous manner, advising me how to Court, to have perseverance &c^a, and acquainting me that he had said more to his daughter on my behalf than he had ever done on Tho. Crosby's, though he was to have £20,000 &c^a. . . .

March 1, 1748

Had some further Conversation with my Charmer, and a great deal with the Old Gentleman her father. He Enquired into my Circumstances, and I told him I was worth about 3000 pound clear Estate. He repeated his willingness to my having his daughter, and told me if I got her he would give me his Bills on his Brother for £750 Sterling, that she had already 500 acres of Land of her own, would have Two thousand pound more at his death, and One thousand more at her Mother's. He desired me to Acquaint him when I had any Grounds to hope, because he found himself declining, had a mind to Settle his Affairs, and would make me an Executor &c^a.

Courtship in Ballad and Broadside

Love and courtship have always been themes of song and sources of laughter. No less than codes of law or sermons, music and humor are two of the many means by which people interpret experience and cope with life. Moreover, they cut deeply into the social structure, providing forms of expression and cultural transmission for people who did not have the wherewithal for leaving diaries and letters. Folksong, like a prism, refracts experience, breaking it into clear and simple emotional shades which color the common and ordinary events of life with loftier, universal themes. Humor about the family, whether joke, tall tale, broadside, or caricature, is an equally revealing mode of expression. Humor (perhaps like deviance) often exists at the boundaries of norm and behavior and comments upon that which is commonplace, inescapable, or frightening. It thereby criticizes, mocks, or reinforces the conditions of family life. As entertaining as these pieces might be, they should not be read simply as relief from the documents that surround them. They should be approached as cultural gestures, as glosses upon the problems and procedures of love and courtship revealed in the preceding material. The few ballads and broadsides reproduced here are typical of the hundreds that have endured to this day or that folklorists have recovered. The last pieces in this group touch upon "bundling" or "tarrying," a courtship custom of the eighteenth century. The extent of the practice is unknown; direct evidence about it comes from only a few sources. But however widespread bundling might have been, these poems attest that it had a mythic existence which is perhaps as historically revealing as the practice itself.

THE AMOROUS SAILOR'S LETTER TO HIS SWEETHEART

> Bright was the morning, cool the air,
> Serene was all the sky,
> When on the waves I left my Fair,
> The centre of my joys;

Worcester, 1781.

Heaven and nature smiling were,
    Nothing was sad but I;
My Breast was fill'd with anxious care,
    Strange thoughts did me annoy.
Each rosy field sweet ardour spread,
    All fragrant was the shore;
Each River-God rose from his bed,
    And fighting own'd his power;
The curling waves they deck'd their head,
    Being proud of what they bore;
But my poor heart she carried,
    With her unto the shore.
Glide on, ye waters, bear these lines,
    Tell her I am distress'd,
Bear all my sighs, ye gentle winds,
    Waft them to her sweet breast;
Should Polly to others incline,
    My woes would be increas'd;
Tell her if e'er she proves unkind,
    I never can have rest.
Sweet lovely charmer, tho' I go
    To fight 'gainst France and Spain,
My heart I leave along with you,
    Till I return again;
And since my foes have forc'd me hence,
    From my sweet lovely dear;
Their cruelty I'll recompense,
    When them I do come near.
May Heaven forfend my sweetest love,
    From sorrow, grief and care:
May guardian Angels still preserve
    My charming Polly dear;
What though from you I am apart,
    I faithful will remain,
So fare you well, my pretty heart,
    Until we meet again.

The Answer

My dearest Johnny, since I find,
    You are faithful, just and true;
I vow forever I'll prove kind
    And constant unto you;
No rivals will I entertain,
    My Jewel to perplex;

I faithful will to you remain,
    And never will you vex.
May heavens preserve that gallant ship,
    Wherein my love does sail;
And while she rolls upon the deep,
    May you have gentle gales,
To waft you to the British shore,
    Unto your own true love,
And I forever shall adore,
    The heavenly powers above.

THE JOLLY ORANGE WOMAN

A Hearty buxom Girl am I,
    came from Dublin city,
I never fear'd a Man, not I,
    Though some say more's the pity;
Well, let them say so once again,
    I've got no cause to mind 'em;
I always fancy pretty Men,
    Whenever I can find 'em.
I'll never marry, no indeed,
    For marriage causes trouble;
And after all the priest has said,
    'Tis merely hubble bubble.
The Rakes will still be counted Rakes,
    Not Hymen's chains can bind 'em,
And so preventing all mistakes,
    I'll kiss where'er I find 'em.
The game of Wedlock's all a chance,
    Cry over or cry under,
Yet many folks to Church will dance,
    At which I often wonder.
Some fancy this, some fancy that,
    All hope the joy design'd 'em;
I'll have my whim, that's tit for tat,
    Wherever I can find 'em.
But what a silly Jade am I,
    Thus idly to be singing,
There's not one here my fruit to buy,
    Nor any to be flinging;
In pretty Men all pleasure dwells,
    All hope the joy design'd 'em.

Worcester, 1781.

So now I'll wheel to Saddler's Wells,
And there I'm sure to find 'em.

YOUNG ROGER

. . .

In rings and fine jewels you'll go,
He's healthy and wealthy withal,
He's proper, straight, comely and tall.
He will befriend you
And very well attend you
With servant to come to your call.
Therefore, dearest daughter, I solemnly vow
You shan't marry Roger that follows the plow.

A fig for young Willy the Squire,
A whore he will certainly keep.
    He'll revel and sport
    with women in court
While I in my chamber do weep,
Lamenting my sad overthrow.
Young Roger, he'll never do so.
Oh, the joys of a lover
I mean to discover,
Young Roger he loves me, I know.
Therefore, dearest Mother, I solemnly vow
I'll marry Roger that follows the plow.

Oh the plow is the staff of the nation
And finally prospers the throne.
    By every hand
    it fattens the land
And makes plenty, 'tis very well known.
Oh if I had now guineas in gold
As much as my apron could hold
Oh who could be quiet
To live without diet
Or who could live without food.
Therefore, dearest mother, I solemnly vow
I will marry Roger that follows the plow.

Dear daughter, since this is your judgement,
Your notion I do recommend,
    for a good honest man
    will save all he can

Eliphabet Mason, *The Complete Pocket Song Book* (Northampton, 1803), pp. 38–41.

While a rake he will willingly spend,
Abusing his family quite.
Dear daughter you're much in the right.
I will not deny you,
Let Roger stay by you
Since he is your joy and delight.
And when you are married I'll make it well known
I'll give Roger a plow and a farm of his own.

A NEW BUNDLING SONG

When a young man is enamored of a woman, and wishes to marry her, he proposes the affair to her parents (without whose consent no marriage, in this colony, can take place); if they have no objections, he is allowed to tarry with her one night, in order to make his court. At the usual time the old couple retire to bed, leaving the young ones to settle matters as they can, who having sat up as long as they think proper, get into bed together also, but without putting off their under garments, to prevent scandal. If the parties agree, it is all very well, the banns are published, and they married without delay; if not, they part, and possibly never see each other again, unless, which is an accident that seldom happens, the forsaken fair proves pregnant, in which case the man, unless he absconds, is obliged to marry her, on pain of excommunication.

Since bundling very much abounds,
In many parts in country towns,
No doubt but some will spurn my song,
And say I'd better hold my tongue;
But none I'm sure will take offence,
Or deem my song impertinence,
But only those who guilty be,
And plainly here their pictures see.
Some maidens say, if through the nation,
Bundling should quite go out of fashion,
Courtship would lose its sweets; and they
Could have no fun till wedding day.
It shant be so, they rage and storm,
And country girls in clusters swarm,
And fly and buz, like angry bees,
And vow they'll bundle when they please.
Some mothers, too, will plead their cause,
And give their daughters great applause,
And tell them, 'tis no sin nor shame,
For we, your mothers, did the same; . . .

Henry Stiles, *Bundling, Its Origin, Progress, and Decline in America* (Albany, 1884), pp. 70–71, 83–101.

You plead you're honest, modest too,
But such a plea will never do;
For how can modesty consist,
With shameful practice such as this?
I'll give your answer to the life:
"You don't undress, like man and wife."
That is your plea, I'll freely own,
But whose your bondsmen when alone,
That further rules you will not break,
And marriage liberties partake?
Some really do, as I suppose,
Upon design keep on some clothes,
And yet in truth I'm not afraid
For to describe a bundling maid;
She'll sometimes say when she lies down,
She can't be cumber'd with a gown,
And that the weather is so warm,
To take it off can be no harm:
The girl it seems had been at strift;
For widest bosom to her shift,
She gownless, when the bed they're in,
The spark, nought feels but naked skin.
But she is modest, also chaste,
While only bare from neck to waist,
And he of boasted freedom sings,
Of all above her apron strings.
And where such freedoms great are shar'd
And further freedoms feebly bar'd,
I leave for others to relate,
How long she'll keep her virgin state. . . .
But you will say that I'm unfair,
That some who bundle take more care,
For some we may with truth suppose,
Bundle in bed with all their clothes.
But bundler's clothes are no defence,
Unruly horses push the fence;
A certain fact I'll now relate,
That's true indeed without debate.
A bundling couple went to bed,
With all their clothes from foot to head,
That the defence might seem complete,
Each one was wrapped in a sheet.
But O! this bundling's such a witch
The man of her did catch the itch,
And so provoked was the wretch,
That she of him a bastard catch'd.

Ye bundle misses don't you blush,
You hang your heads and bid me hush.
If you wont tell me how you feel,
I'll ask your sparks, they best can tell. . . .
A vulgar custom 'tis, I own,
Admir'd by many a slut and clown,
But 'tis a method of proceeding,
As much abhorr'd by those of breeding.
You're welcome to the lines I've penn'd,
For they were written by a friend,
Who'll think himself quite well rewarded,
If this vile practice is discarded.

A NEW SONG IN FAVOUR OF COURTING

Adam at first was form'd of dust,
   As scripture doth record;
And did receive a wife call'd Eve,
   From his Creator Lord.

From Adam's side a crooked bride,
   The Lord was pleas'd to form;
Ordain'd that they in bed might lay
   To keep each other warm. . . .

This new made pair full happy were,
   And happy might remain'd,
If his helpmate had never ate,
   The fruit that was restrain'd.

Tho' Adam's wife destroy'd his life,
   In manner that was awful;
Yet marriage now we all allow
   To be both just and lawful.

But women must be courted first,
   Because it is the fashion,
And so at times commit great crimes
   Caus'd by a lustful passion.

And nowadays there are two ways,
   Which of the two is right,
To lie between sheets sweet and clean,
   Or sit up all the night?

But some suppose bundling in clothes
   Do heaven sorely vex;
Then let me know which way to go,
   To court the female sex.

Whether they must be hugg'd or kiss'd
　　When sitting by the fire
Or whether they in bed may lay,
　　Which doth the Lord require?

But some pretend to recommend
　　The sitting up all night;
Courting in chairs as doth appear
　　To them to be most right.

Nature's request is, grant me rest,
　　Our bodies seek repose;
Night is the time, and 'tis no crime
　　To bundle in your clothes.

Since in a bed a man and maid,
　　May bundle and be chaste,
It does no good to burn out wood,
　　It is a needless waste.

Let coats and gowns be laid aside,
　　And breeches take their flight,
An honest man and woman can
　　Lay quiet all the night.

But if there be dishonesty
　　Implanted in the mind,
Breeches nor smocks, nor scarce padlocks
　　The rage of lust can bind.

Kate, Nance and Sue proved just and true,
　　Tho' bundling did practise;
But Ruth beguil'd and proved with child,
　　Who bundling did despise.

Whores will be whores, and on the floor
　　Where many has been laid,
To sit and smoke and ashes poke,
　　Won't keep awake a maid.

Bastards are not at all times got
　　In feather beds we know;
The strumpet's oath convinces both
　　Oft times it is not so. . . .

Now unto those that do oppose
　　The bundling trade, I say
Perhaps there's more got on the floor,
　　Than any other way.

In ancient books no knowledge is
  Of these things to be got;
Whether young men did bundle then,
  Or whether they did not.

Since ancient book says wife they took,
  It don't say how they courted;
Whether young men did bundle then,
  Or by the fire sported. . . .

Since bundling is not a thing
  That judgment will procure;
Go on young men and bundle then,
  But keep your bodies pure.

MARRIAGE

The Ties That Bind: Marriage Contracts

Under certain circumstances, formal contracts preceded marriage. Today such contracts exist largely among the very rich, between Jacqueline Kennedy and Aristotle Onassis, for example, although some modern couples have used contracts to specify conditions of equality within a marriage by spelling out the particular tasks and obligations of each partner. Most people of the seventeenth and eighteenth centuries, especially when there was little property involved, did not bother to draw up formal contracts at the time of their marriage "settlement." Still it was a fairly widespread practice, one which reflects the complex economic stakes and familial relationships that could be involved in a marriage. In analyzing such materials it is helpful to ask who the various parties to the negotiation and contract were who, either named or unnamed, had a stake in it. What seems to have been the purposes of the contract, who or what was being protected, and what were the different interests involved and how were they balanced? What, finally, might explain the need for such contracts: the need to spell out possessions, lines for the descent of property, obligations in such legally binding ways? What functions, finally, did the family serve through these forms?

MARRIAGE CONTRACT OF JOHN FRENCH AND ELEANOR VEAZIE

A covenant of marriage being purposed and intended between John French and Eleanor Veazie of Braintree in New England, made and concluded this eighth day of July, Anno Domini one thousand six hundred and eighty-three, doe witness that the said John French doth preëngage unto the said Eleanor Veazie not to meddle with or take into his hand any part of her estate wherein she is invested by her former husband William Veazie or any otherwise, nor any wise weakening her right or claim to the same. The said John French doth hereby engage and covenant to pay

"Ancient Marriage Contract," *Mayflower Descendant* (Oct. 1858), p. 353.

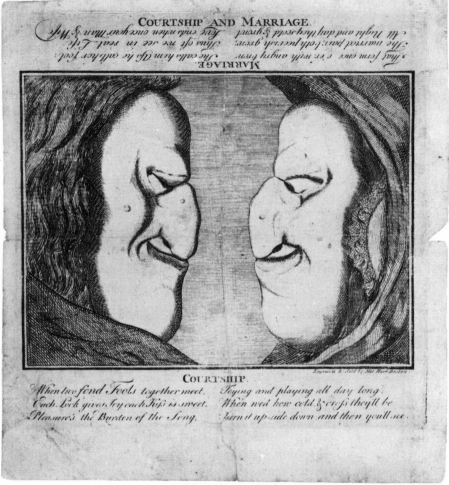

This type of print, commonly used before the nineteenth century, was called a broadside
or broadsheet. It was a self-sufficient single sheet. The "two-way" view in this drawing
was an old and favorite device to show the good and bad or virtue and vice of the same
subject. Courtship here is all smiles, but marriage (courtship upside down) is quite the
other. The print comes from Boston, circa 1750.

Used by permission of the American Antiquarian Society

to the said Eleanor Veazie after my decease four pounds per annum, annu-
ally, to be paid each year immediately insuing after the said John French's
decease, by his lawful Administrators, Executors or Assigns, at her dwelling
house, the specie of which payment shall be paid in cord word, porke,
beefe, malt or corne proportionably of each at price current. And that
shee the said Eleanor Veazie shall have, hold, possess and enjoy the new
end of the dwelling house, in which the said French now dwelleth with

the cellar appertaining, during the time of her widowhood. But the four pound annuity to bee and continue to her and her heirs or assigns during the terme of her natural life. To the true performance whereof the said John French doth hereunto set hand this eighth day of July Anno Domini one thousand six hundred eighty three. Before signing. And she shall have apples what she pleases for spending and a place for a garden plot.

Signed and concluded on
    before us   John French.
Samuel Tompson.
Ben. Tompson.

MARRIAGE CONTRACT OF JACOB MYGATT AND SARAH WHITING

Whereas I, Joseph Mygatt, of Hartford upon the River and in the jurisdiction of Connecticut in New England, have in the behalf of my son Jacob and at his request made a motion to Mrs. Susanna Fitch, in reference to her daughter Sarah Whiting, that my said son Jacob might with her good liking have free liberty to endeavor the gaining of her said daughter Sarah's affection towards himself in a way of marriage: now this present writing showeth that the said Mrs. Susanna Fitch having consented thereunto, I do hereby promise and engage that if God, in the wise disposition of His providence, shall so order it that my son Jacob and her daughter Sarah shall be contracted together in reference to marriage, I will pay thereupon unto my said son as his marriage portion the full sum of two hundred pounds sterling, upon a just valuation in such pay as shall be to the reasonable satisfaction of the said Mrs. Fitch, and so much more as shall fully equalize the estate or portion belonging to her said daughter Sarah. And I do further engage for the present to build a comfortable dwelling house for my said son and her daughter to live in by themselves, as shall upon a true account cost me fifty pounds sterling. And [I] will also give them therewith near the said house one acre of ground planted with apple trees and other fruit trees, which said house, land, and trees shall be and remain to my said son as an addition to his marriage portion, before mentioned, and to his heirs forever. And I do also further promise and engage that at the day of my death I shall and will leave unto him my said son and his heirs so much estate besides the dwelling house, ground, and trees, before given and engaged, as shall make the two hundred pounds, before engaged and to be paid [at] present, more than double the portion of the said Sarah Whiting. And for the true and sure performance hereof I do hereby engage and bind over my dwelling house and all my lands and buildings in Hartford, with whatsoever estate in any kind is therein and thereupon. And I do further engage that my daughter Mary's portion of one hundred pounds being first paid to her, I will leave to my said son and his heirs forever my whole estate at the day of my death, whatsoever it shall amount unto, and in what way, kind, or place soever it lies, he paying to my wife during her natural life twelve pounds a year, and allowing to her a dwelling entire to herself in the two upper rooms and cellar belonging to my now dwelling house, with the going of half the poultry and a pig for her comfort in each year during her said life; also allowing her the use of half the household stuff during her life, which she shall have power to dispose of to Jacob or Mary at her death, as she shall see cause. And I do further engage that the portion my said son shall have with her daughter Sarah shall (with the good liking of the said Mrs. Susanna Fitch and such friends as she shall advise with) be laid out wholly upon a farm for the sole use and benefit of my said son, her daughter, and their heirs forever. And upon the contraction in reference to marriage I do engage to jointure her said daughter Sarah in the whole estate or portion my son hath with her, laid out or to be laid out in a farm as aforesaid or otherwise, and in the thirds of his whole estate otherwise, to be to her sole and proper use and benefit during her life and after her death to their heirs forever. And lastly I do engage that the whole benefit of the Indian trade shall be to the sole advantage of my son Jacob, and do promise that I will during my life be [an] assistant and helpful to my said son in the best ways I can, both in his trading with the Indians, his stilling, and otherwise, for his comfort and advantage which I will never bring to any account with him; only I do explain myself and engage that in case my son Jacob shall depart this life before her daughter Sarah, and leave no issue of their bodies, then her said daughter Sarah shall have the full value of her portion left to her, not only for her life as before, but to her as her property to dispose of at her death as she shall see cause, and her thirds in all his other estate for her life, as is before expressed. It being also agreed and consented to that my wife after my decease and during her natural life shall have the use of two milch cows which my son Jacob shall provide for her, she paying the charge of their wintering and summering out of her annuity of twelve pounds a year. In witness whereunto, and to every particular on this and the other side, I have subscribed my name, this 27th of November, 1654.

Witnesses hereunto	The mark of
John Webster	J M
John Cullick	Joseph Mygatt
John Tallcott	

MARRIAGE GIFT OF RALPH WORMLEY
TO AGATHA STUBBINGS

To All to whom these presents shall come I Ralph Warmley of the Parrish and County of Yorke in Virginia gentleman send Greeting etc. Knowe

Susie Ames, ed., *County Court Records of Accomack-Northampton, VA, 1640–1645* (Charlottesville, 1973), pp. 433–34. Reprinted by permission of the University Press of Virginia.

Yee, That I the sayde Ralph Wormley For and in consideration of the unfayned love and affection That I beare unto Mrs. Agatha Stubbings late the wife of Luke Stubbinge of the County of Northampton gentleman deceased, And especially in Consideration of Matrimony intended presently (by gods grace) to bee solemnized betweene the sayde Ralph and the sayde Agatha doe by these presents give graunt confirme and endow, And by these presents have given graunted and in nature of a Free Joynture endowed unto Nathaniell Littleton Esquire and Phillip Taylor gentlemen Feoffees in trust For and on the behalfe of the sayde Agatha six Negro servaunts (Viz) Fower Negro men, and Two women, To say Sanio, and Susan his wife, and greate Tony, and his wife Dorothis, Tony the younger, and Will, Tenn Cowes, six Draught Oxen, two young Mares, two Feather Bedds and Furniture, sixe paire of sheets of Holland, two Dyaper table cloathes, two dozen of Napkins and Cubboard Cloath to it, two dozen of Napkins, Twelve pewter dishes, one dammaske table cloath, one Dozen of Napkins and cubboard Cloath to it, To have and to hold, the said Recited promisses and every parte thereof, unto her the sayde Agatha, and the heyres Lawfully ingendered between mee the said Ralph Wormley and shee the sayde Agatha whether Male or Female or both to bee equally devided after his decease Provided alwayes that the same and every parte thereof graunted as aforesaid shalbe and Remayne to the only use benifitt and behoofe of mee the said Ralph Wormley during my naturall Life, And in case I the said Ralph shall happen to depart this lyfe without issue begotten betweene mee the said Ralph and shee the said Agatha as aforesayde, Then the said demised promisses and every parte thereof with the proceeds and increase thereof shalbe and Remayne to the only use benifitt and behoofe of the sayde Agatha her heyres Executors or Administrators And For the true and reall performance of this deede and every parte and parcell thereof in manner and Forme aforesaid I the said Ralph Wormley doe bynde over unto the said Nathaniell Littleton Esquire and Phillip Taylor gentlemen the said Six Negroes and Six other Negroes, the sayde Tenn Cowes and other tenn Cowes, the sixe Oxen and other sixe oxten, one plantation and houses whereon I now live scituate at Yorke aforesaid Conteyning Five hundred Acres more or lesse according to the purchase lately made by mee of Jefery Power to bee all Lyable and Responsable For the full Assurance of makeing good the abovesaid Joynture for the use of the said Agatha her heyres Executors or Administrators as aforesaid In Witnes whereof I the sayde Ralph Wormley have hereunto sett my hand and Seale the second day of this instant July Annoque Domini 1645.

RALPH WORMELEY

The Ties That Bind: Marriage Ceremonies

All the colonies established civil or religious procedures for sanctifying marriage and binding the couple together in permanent union under the sanctions of legal matrimony. In colonies like Virginia and the Carolinas where Anglicanism was the established religion, marriage was considered a sacrament and conducted by a clergyman according to the prescriptions of the Book of Common Prayer. Puritan New England, maintaining a clear division between church and state on this matter, made marriage a civil ceremony, presided over by a magistrate rather than by a minister (see p. 76). The Society of Friends, or Quakers, as they came to be called, went even further than the Puritans in separating religious practices and institutions from worldly influences and civil authority. Harassed in England and persecuted and even executed in New England, the Quakers in their marriages recognized neither magistrate nor priest. Following forms laid down by George Fox, the founder of Quakerism, marriages among Friends were approved and solemnized by the whole "meeting," as a Quaker congregation was called. The formal ceremonies that gave a marriage a standing in law seem so commonplace that it is easy to neglect asking any historical questions of them. Why were marriages almost uniformly solemnized and the ties formalized as they were? What kinds of events were the ceremonies? Who participated, who was seen to have a concern in whether a marriage took place, and why? What kind of statement about the meaning of marriage does the act of formalization make?

Many people in seventeenth- and eighteenth-century America, however, were not in a position to enjoy the ministrations of clergy or magistracy. Settlement kept pressing into the backwoods, beyond the easy reach of ministers. Many couples consequently did not wait to have their unions blessed before "marrying" or "taking up" with each other. This problem was partly solved by having an itinerant minister marry couples and legitimize their offspring after they had set themselves up as a family or by the institution of the "common-law marriage," the granting of the rights and protections of legal marriage to couples who had lived together "as man and wife" for at least seven years. Still, the many couples beyond the easy reach of church or state were a problem, one which vexed some observers in ways that suggest a good deal about the significance attached to marriage formalities.

THE LAWS OF VIRGINIA

March 1661–62

NONE TO BE MARRYED BUT BY MINISTERS, NOR BY THEM BUT BY LYCENSE, OR PUBLISHING THE BANNES. (B)

THAT noe marriage be sollemnized nor reputed valid in law but such as is made by the ministers *(c)* according to the laws of England, and that noe ministers *(c)* marry any persons *(d)* without lycence from the governour or his deputy, or thrice publication of banes according to the prescription of the rubrick in *the (e)* comon prayer booke, which injoynes that if the persons to be marryed dwell in severall parishes the banes must be asked in both parishes, and that the curate of one parish shall not solemnize the matrimony untill he have a certificate from the curate of the other parish, that the banes have been there thrice published, and noe objection made against *the joyning the parties together, (f)* And if any minister shall contrary to this act marry any persons, he shall be fined tenn thousand pounds of tobacco, and any pretended marriage *hereafter (g)* made by any other then a minister be reputed null, and the children borne out of such marriage of the parents, be esteemed illegitimate and the parents suffer such punishment as by the laws *(h)* prohibiting ffornication ought to be inflicted.

THE FORM OF SOLEMNIZATION OF MATRIMONY

¶ *The laws respecting Matrimony, whether by publishing the Banns in Churches, or by Licence, being different in the several States, every Minister is left to the direction of those laws, in every thing that regards the civil contract between the parties.*

¶ *And when the Banns are published, it shall be in the following form:* I publish the Banns of Marriage between *M.* of ——, and *N.* of ——. If any of you know cause, or just impediment, why these two persons should not be joined together in holy Matrimony, ye are to declare it. This is the first [second *or* third] time of asking.

¶ *At the day and time appointed for Solemnization of Matrimony, the Persons to be married shall come into the body of the Church, or shall be ready in some proper house, with their friends and neighbours; and there standing together, the Man on the right hand, and the Woman on the left, the Minister shall say,*

DEARLY beloved, we are gathered together here in the sight of God, and in the face of this company, to join together this Man and this Woman

W. W. Hening, ed., *The Statutes at Large . . .* , III, pp. 49–51.
The Book of Common Prayer (New York, 1897), pp. 277–80.

in holy Matrimony; which is an honourable estate, instituted of God in the time of man's innocency, signifying unto us the mystical union that is betwixt Christ and his Church: which holy estate Christ adorned and beautified with his presence and first miracle that he wrought in Cana of Galilee, and is commended of Saint Paul to be honourable among all men: and therefore is not by any to be entered into unadvisedly or lightly; but reverently, discreetly, advisedly, soberly, and in the fear of God. Into this holy estate these two persons present come now to be joined. If any man can show just cause, why they may not lawfully be joined together, let him now speak, or else hereafter for ever hold his peace.

¶ *And also speaking unto the Persons who are to be married, he shall say,*

I REQUIRE and charge you both as ye will answer at the dreadful day of judgment when the secrets of all hearts shall be disclosed, that if either of you know any impediment, why ye may not be lawfully joined together in Matrimony, ye do now confess it. For be ye well assured, that if any persons are joined together otherwise than as God's Word doth allow, their marriage is not lawful.

¶ *The Minister, if he shall have reason to doubt of the lawfulness of the proposed Marriage, may demand sufficient surety for his indemnification: but if no impediment shall be alleged, or suspected, the Minister shall say to the Man,*

M. WILT thou have this Woman to thy wedded wife, to live together after God's ordinance in the holy estate of Matrimony? Wilt thou love her, comfort her, honour, and keep her in sickness and in health; and, forsaking all others, keep thee only unto her, so long as ye both shall live?

¶ *The Man shall answer,*

I will.

¶ *Then shall the Minister say unto the Woman,*

N. WILT thou have this Man to thy wedded husband, to live together after God's ordinance in the holy estate of Matrimony? Wilt thou obey him, and serve him, love, honour, and keep him in sickness and in health; and, forsaking all others, keep thee only unto him, so long as ye both shall live?

¶ *The Woman shall answer,*

I will.

¶ *Then shall the Minister say,*

WHO giveth this Woman to be married to this Man?

¶ *Then shall they give their troth to each other in this manner. The Minister, receiving the Woman at her father's or friend's hands, shall cause the Man with his right hand to take the Woman by her right hand, and to say after him as followeth.*

I   *M.* take thee *N.* to my wedded Wife, to have and to hold from this day forward, for better for worse, for richer for poorer, in sickness and in health, to love and to cherish, till death us do part, according to God's holy ordinance; and thereto I plight thee my troth.

¶ *Then shall they loose their hands; and the Woman with her right hand taking the Man by his right hand, shall likewise say after the Minister:*

I   *N.* take thee *M.* to my wedded Husband, to have and to hold from this day forward, for better for worse, for richer for poorer, in sickness and in health, to love, cherish, and to obey, till death us do part, according to God's holy ordinance; and thereto I give thee my troth.

¶ *Then shall they again loose their hands; and the Man shall give unto the Woman a Ring. And the Minister taking the Ring shall deliver it unto the Man, to put it upon the fourth finger of the Woman's left hand. And the Man holding the Ring there, and taught by the Minister, shall say,*

WITH this Ring I thee wed, and with all my worldly goods I thee endow: In the Name of the Father, and of the Son, and of the Holy Ghost. Amen.

¶ *Then, the Man leaving the Ring upon the fourth finger of the Woman's left hand, the Minister shall say,*

Let us pray.

OUR Father, who art in heaven, Hallowed be thy Name. Thy kingdom come. Thy will be done on earth, As it is in heaven. Give us this day our daily bread. And forgive us our trespasses, As we forgive those who trespass against us. And lead us not into temptation; But deliver us from evil. Amen. O ETERNAL God, Creator and Preserver of all mankind, Giver of all spiritual grace, the Author of everlasting life; Send thy blessing upon these thy servants, this man and this woman, whom we bless in thy Name; that, as Isaac and Rebecca lived faithfully together, so these persons may surely perform and keep the vow and covenant betwixt them made, (whereof this Ring given and received is a token and pledge,) and may ever remain in perfect love and peace together, and live according to thy laws; through Jesus Christ our Lord. *Amen.*

¶ *Then shall the Minister join their right hands together, and say,*

THOSE whom God hath joined together let no man put asunder.

¶ *Then shall the Minister speak unto the company.*

FORASMUCH as *M.* and *N.* have consented together in holy wedlock, and have witnessed the same before God and this company, and thereto have given and pledged their troth, each to the other, and have declared the same by giving and receiving a Ring, and by joining hands; I pronounce that they are Man and Wife, In the Name of the Father, and of the Son, and of the Holy Ghost. Amen.

¶ *And the Minister shall add this blessing.*

GOD the Father, God the Son, God the Holy Ghost, bless, preserve, and keep you; the Lord mercifully with his favour look upon you, and fill you with all spiritual benediction and grace; that ye may so live together in this life, that in the world to come ye may have life everlasting. *Amen.*

LETTERS TO QUAKERS ON MARRIAGE, 1660

. . . Though Enoch, Methuselah, and Lamech, and the holy men of God, their marriages God did not judge; but when the sons of those holy men, which were called the sons of God, went to the world for wives, they slew the spiritual birth in them, and quenched the holy spirit of God in them, and corrupted the earth, and filled it with cruelty, and followed the imaginations of their own hearts' lusts continually; insomuch that they grieved the Lord, and he repented that he made man. For he saw, all flesh had corrupted his way upon the earth, saving Noah, a just man, with his family, who walked with God, and did not join with the wickedness of the world. Therefore God destroyed the old world; and the beginning thereof was these bad marriages, as Jude and Peter saith, 'They followed strange flesh,' by which they came to be corrupted; and therefore God sent a flood, and destroyed the old world with its ungodly deeds. And there is your example, that marry with the world. Gen. vi.

And doth not the Lord say to the children of Israel, 'Thou shalt not give thy sons nor thy daughters in marriage with the heathen.' And were not such as did so, reproved by the Lord and his prophets? As ye may see through the scriptures. And doth not the apostle say, 'Be ye not unequally yoked together with unbelievers; for what fellowship hath light with darkness, or Christ with Belial, or a believer with an infidel?' For how many thousands of the Jews did the Lord destroy, who went and married with other nations, and pleaded liberty? And did not Phineas run one through, and his heathenish women? And so, must not all such be run through with the sword of the spirit of God? And the Lord said, 'Phineas hath turned mine anger away from the children of Israel,' when the Lord had destroyed twenty-four thousand of them. And doth not the world call such, bastard and hypocrite Quakers, and not faithful, that go to the world for a wife, and to the priests to be married? Oh! that ye should profess truth, and go from its power and life, and so corrupt yourselves, and to have no more esteem of your bodies, which God hath so honoured, and made them vessels of his mercy, to put his mercy into! and have no more esteem of God, his truth nor his people, but to esteem your affections and lusts above them all, and to make yourselves a talk and a laughing stock, by going into that, for which ye are judged of God, and of all his people, and of that of God in your own consciences also! And do not Friends buy burying-places, because they cannot give their dead bodies to the world, no more than Abraham could? And ye that profess yourselves to be quickened by Christ, and made alive by him, to give your bodies

George Fox, *A Collection of Many Select and Christian Epistles, Letters and Testimonies* (Philadelphia, 1831), II, pp. 180–81.

to them that are dead in sins and trespasses,—Oh, ye make yourselves ridiculous both to God's people and the world, and come under the judgment of both, and of God and the scriptures, to be such as follow strange flesh, and corrupt the earth, like the old world! Ye bring burthens upon the just. But God will shorten your days, as he did the old world's, except ye repent; as ye may read, Gen. vi. And therefore mind God's ordinance, and then ye will know God's joining by his spirit and by his power. And be not corrupted with them, that follow strange flesh, and corrupt themselves, that creep among you, and would be called by your name, which the priests and the world call bastard Quakers. And therefore keep the gospel order, which is the power of God, (before the devil was,) and the government of Christ Jesus, which destroys the devil and all his works. . . .

For the right joining in marriage is the work of the Lord only, and not the priests or magistrates; for it is God's ordinance, and not man's. And therefore Friends cannot consent, that they should join them together. For we marry none, it is the Lord's work, and we are but witnesses. But yet, if a Friend through tenderness have a desire that the magistrate should know it, (after the marriage is performed in a public meeting of Friends and others, according to the holy order and practice of Friends in truth throughout the world, and according to the manner of the holy men and women of God of old,) he may go and carry a copy of the certificate to the magistrate; Friends are left to their freedom herein. But for priests or magistrates to marry or join any in that relation, it is not according to the scripture; and our testimony and practice hath been always against it. It was God's work before the fall, and it is God's work only in the restoration.

Let not any go disorderly together in marriage, contrary to the practice of the holy men of God, who declared it in the assemblies of the righteous, when they took one another, all things being clear, and they both being free from any other, in respect to marriage. And when any take one another in marriage, let there not be less than a dozen Friends and relations present, (according to your former order,) having first acquainted the men's meeting, and that they have clearness and unity with them; and then it may be recorded in a book. And if any walk contrary to the order of truth herein, let some be appointed to speak to them, and give notice thereof to the next meeting.

And all that are widows, who have children, and do intend to marry, let inquiry be made, what she hath done for her children, (if there be no will made,) then let such part of her late husband's estate be set out for the children, as is equal and according to truth; and what they can do more afterwards, let them do it also. And where there is a will made, let those legacies and portions be improved and secured (before their marriage) for the children of the deceased, with what more they can do for them. And then, when these things are done, let them be recorded in a book at the next Quarterly Meeting.

And all men that hunt after women, from woman to woman; and also women, whose affections run sometimes after one man, and soon after to another, and so hold one another in affection, and so draw out the affections one of another; and after a while leave one another, and go to others, and then do the same things there; these doings are more like Sodom than saints, and are not of God's moving nor joining, where they are not to be parted. For marriage is God's ordinance, and God's command one to another, and in that is felt the power of God.

And if any go together in marriage, having declared it at Friends' meetings, if the magistrates do cast them into prison, because they are not married according to the national law, or by a priest, all the men Friends and women Friends in the meeting, (or twelve of them) may set their hands to a paper and send it to the justices, it being done in truth and righteousness, and according to the scriptures of truth. As Boaz declared his taking of Ruth in the town-gate; and Jacob when he was married, Laban called in his kindred; and other examples you may see in the scriptures, who did marry, and had no ring, nor priest neither to marry them.

Now, no man ought to speak to a woman concerning marriage before that he hath spoken to her father and mother, and have their consent; and if she have no father or mother, but guardians and trustees, then they must speak to them, if she be under age, that they may have their consent, and so proceed accordingly, as Abraham's servant did concerning Isaac's wife. And you are to see that all widows do make provision for their children before they are married to another, according to truth and righteousness.

And you are to see, that every man and woman are free from all entanglements with any other woman or man before they are married; and if they have been engaged, you must have a certificate under the hands of the person that they have been entangled with to discharge them; so that all things may be done in peace, and unity, and righteousness, according to the truth that is in every man and woman. And if the young man or young woman's relations be of the world, they must have their consent, and a certificate from them. And if the man or woman comes from beyond sea, or out of another country, ye must have a certificate from the men and women's meetings there, how they have lived, and whether they are free from all other persons, by any engagement, covenant, or contract concerning marriage; and if they are not clear, they must answer that, and be cleared by a certificate under their hands, before they proceed any further.

And if any man should defile a woman he must marry her, if she be a beggar, though he have never so many hundreds; for he must fulfil the law of God, for the law of God commands it, that he must marry her, and condemn his action, and clear God's truth. But no such marriages, where the bed is defiled, we bring into our men and women's meetings; but some Friends (if such a thing happen) draw up a certificate, and they to set their hands to it, that they will live faithfully together as man and wife, and fulfil the law of God.

And this I write, if ever such a thing should happen; but I hope that

Friends will be careful, and keep in the fear of the Lord, that they may have an esteem of the Lord's truth, and their own bodies, and of the honourable marriage, where the bed is undefiled.

And when any marriages is to be propounded, let it be laid before the women's meeting first. And after they have declared it there, if they do know any thing of the man or the woman, that it should not proceed so far as to the men's meeting, then let two or three women go to the men's meeting, that some of the men and women may have a distinct meeting concerning it, and let them end it before it comes to the men's meeting; and if there be no such occasion of any such meeting, let two or three women go along with them to the men's meeting. And so after Friends have taken their names, and places of abode, let two women of the women's meeting be nominated, and two men of the men's meeting, that if any one have any thing to say against the couple before the next meeting they may speak to them; and if there should appear any thing, they may end it before they come to the meeting. And if there be nothing, when they come the second time again to the women's meeting, the woman may go along with them to the men, and testify that they know nothing against their proceedings. And likewise the men, that are appointed to inquire out to make the like report, (and let the man and the woman always appear together, when they lay their intentions of marriage.) So then the thing is left to the men to give their judgment and advice to the couple that are to be married, all things being clear, and nothing appearing to the contrary; and their fathers, and mothers, or guardians, or overseers being satisfied, then they may have their liberty to appoint a meeting where they please, in some public meeting-place, where their relations and Friends may be present, and there get a certificate ready drawn up, with the day of the month, place, and year, how that such a couple did take one another in the presence of God, and in the presence of his people, who had laid their said intentions so often before them; and all things being found clear, according to the law of God and the practice of the holy men, recorded in the scriptures of truth, to live together in christian, honourable marriage, according to God's ordinance and his joining, to be help-meets together as long as they live.

"REMONSTRANCE PRESENTED TO THE COMMON'S HOUSE OF ASSEMBLY OF SOUTH CAROLINA, NOV. 1767"

And no *Marriage Licence* can be obtain'd but in *Charlestown*—And there ev'ry Person must repair to get Married, that would marry judicially and according to Law—for We have not Churches wherein to publish Banns,

Richard J. Hooker, ed., *The Carolina Backcountry on the Eve of the Revolution: The Journal and Other Writings of Charles Woodmason, Anglican Itinerant* (Chapel Hill, 1953), pp. 224–26. Copyright 1969 The University of North Carolina Press. Published for the Institute of Early American History and Culture, Williamsburg.

or Ministers to Marry Persons, Wherefrom, the Generality marry each other, which causes the vilest Abominations, and that Whoredom and Adultery overspreads our Land. Thus We live and have liv'd for Years past as if without God in the World, destitute of the Means of Knowledge, without *Law* or *Gospel, Esteem,* or Credit. For, We know not even the Laws of this Country We inhabit for where are they to be found, but in the Secretarys Office in Charlestown? The Printing a Code of the Laws, hath been long petitioned for, often recommended by the *Crown,* and delineated in the *presentments of Grand Juries,* as a Matter long wanting, and of the utmost Consequence: But like all other their Presentments, it lyes *totally unregarded.*

Of what Service has been—Of what Use are the Parish Churches of *Prince George, Prince Frederic* and *St. Mark,* to the Inhabitants of Williamsburgh Great and Little Pedee, Lynchs Creek, Waccamaw, the Congarees, Waxaws, Waterees, Saludy, Long Canes, Ninety Six, or Broad River! Places and Settlements containing Fifty thousand Souls? These Fabrics were plac'd where they are, to serve some Local Occasion, or particular Persons or Purposes; But are not (at least at present) of the least Benefit to the Back Country: What Church can We repair too for Divine Service, nearer than *Dorchester* or *Charlestown?* Several Parishes being now destitute of Ministers, and no effectual Plan settled for their being properly supplied.

It is notorious, That thro' the Want of Churches and Ministers, New Sects have arisen, now greatly prevail, especially those call'd *New Lights.* Prophaneness and Infidelity abound—Ignorance, Vice, and Idleness prevail—And to the Great Indifference shewn by all Ranks to promote the Interests of Religion and Vertue, it is in Great Measure owing that such few Checks have been given to the *Villains* and *Outlaws,* who have devour'd Us. For, the Common People hardly know the first Principles of Religion: And so corrupt are their Morals, that a Reformation of Manners among them *in our Time* is more to be wish'd for than expected.

Thro' want of Churches and Ministers, many Persons go into the *North* Province, there to be Married, by Magistrates; Which hath encouraged many of our Magistrates (so venal are they) for to take on them also to solemnize Marriages—And this, without any previous Publication of Banns or any Sett Form, but each after his own Fancy, which occasions much Confusion, as they ask no Questions, but couple Persons of all Ages, and ev'ry Complexion, to the Ruin, and Grief of many families. Their Example have been followed by the Low Lay Teachers of ev'ry petty Sect, and also copied by *Itinerant* and Stragling Preachers of various Denominations, who traverse the Back Country, (sent this Way from *Pennsylvania* and *New England,* to poison the Minds of the People)—From these irregular Practices, the sacred Bond of Marriage is so greatly slighted, as to be productive of many Great and innumerable Evils. For many loose Wretches are fond of such Marriages; On Supposition, that they are only Tempor[ar]y, or *Durante Placito;* Dissoluble, whenever their Interests or Passions incite them to Separate. Thus they live *Ad Libitum;* quitting each other at Pleasure, Inter-Marrying Year after Year with others; Changing from Hand to Hand as they remove from Place to Place, and swapping away their Wives and Children, as they would Horses or Cattle. Great Scandal arises herefrom to the Back Country, and Loss to the Community: For the Issue of such are too often expos'd deserted, and disown'd: Beggars are hereby multiplied—Concubinage establish'd (as it were) *by Law;* The most sacred Obligations are hereby trampled on, and Bastardy, Adultery, and other heinous Vices become so common, so openly practic'd and avow'd as to lose the Stigma annex'd to their Commission: These are some of the Main Roots from whence the reigning Gangs of Horse Theives have sprung up from.

The Good Marriage Extolled

R ecipes for a good marriage, works that lay out guidelines for the
conduct of marriage partners who want marital bliss, did not origi-
nate with the twentieth century. Designed to get people to adopt
a particular kind of marital behavior, writings of this genre should be approached warily as guides to behavior within actual marriages. Still, prescip-
tive literature about marriage is a particularly good source for probing
the complex relationship between family behavior and belief. Moral guide-
books seem to proliferate when behavior appears to many of those living
at the time to be changing in particularly baffling and troublesome ways.
As a species of reform literature, a moral guidebook attempts to bring
behavior back into line with some norms. It singles out practices which
seem particularly threatening and tries to impose either the traditional
moral order or a newly invented one upon them. In examining such texts
historically, we need to look at the author's state of mind, at the language
employed—tone, imagery—at the ideas or practices extolled and condemned, the form the argument takes, and the sanction or inducements mar-
shaled to persuade the audience to act as the writer wants it to.

This selection, Benjamin Wadsworth's *Well-Ordered Family,* can be approached as a kind of Puritan marriage manual. Wadsworth wrote in 1712,
two decades after Massachusetts Bay Colony had lost the charter of government which had enabled it to conduct itself as a Bible Commonwealth
and when the piety which it ultimately depended upon for its order seemed
at a particularly low ebb, especially when compared to the spiritual standards of the founding generations. It is instructive to examine this attempt
to delineate the well-ordered family in the context of the New Haven legal
code and the behavior revealed in the court records of the two selections
that follow.

THE DUTIES OF HUSBANDS AND WIVES

The Duties of Husband and Wives. Concerning the Duties of this Relation,
we may assert a few things; and then draw some inferences therefrom.
Concerning *Husband* and *Wife* we may therefore assert.

Benjamin Wadsworth, *The Well-Ordered Family, or, Relative Duties* (Boston, 1712), pp. 22–
47.

Tis their duty to cohabit or dwell together with one another. By God's own Ordinances Husband and Wife are brought into the nearest Union and Relation to each other; God's Word calls them one *flesh*. . . . *A man shall leave his Father and his Mother, and shall cleave to his Wife; and they shall be one flesh.* . . . *They twain shall be one flesh.* Being thus nearly *United,* surely they should *dwell together.* . . . The Greek word signifies, to *dwell in an house together,* or keep house together. If one house can't hold them, surely they're not affected to each other as they should be. Indeed men's necessary Occasions often call them abroad, and sometimes (Seamen especially) to be absent for many weeks or months together; and when necessity requires such an absence of Husbands from their Wives, there ought to be a willing compliance with the call of Providence. But they should not separate nor live apart, out of disgust, dislike, or out of choice; but should *dwell together* as constantly, as their necessary affairs will permit. *Let not the Wife depart from her Husband, and let not the Husband put away his Wife.* . . . The Duties of Husband and Wife one to another, oblige them to dwell together as much as may be: *To avoid fornication, let every man have his own wife; and let every woman have her own husband. Let the Husband render unto the Wife due benevolence, and likewise also the Wife to the Husband. The Wife hath not power of her own body, but the Husband; and likewise also the Husband hath not power of his own Body, but the Wife: Defraud not one the other, that Satan tempt you not for your incontinency.* Thus tis plain from Scripture, that Husband and Wife ought to dwell together; if therefore they quarrel and so live separate from each other, then they sin very greatly, they act quite contrary to God's plain commands. If any have thus done, they ought heartily to repent of it, and fly to the Blood of Jesus for pardon.

They should have a very great and tender love and affection to one another. This is plainly commanded by God. *Husbands love your wives, even as Christ also loved the Church.* That is, with a great, steady, constant, operative love. . . . This duty of love is mutual; it should be perform'd by each, to each of them. They should endeavour to have their affections really, cordially and closely knit, to each other. If therefore the *Husband* is *bitter against his Wife,* beating or striking of her (as some vile wretches do) or in any unkind carriage, ill language, hard words, morose, peevish, surly behavior; nay, if he is not kind, loving, tender in his words and carriage to her; he then shames his profession of Christianity, he breaks the Divine Law, he dishonours God and himself too, by this ill behaviour. The same is true of the *Wife* too. If she strikes her Husband (as some shameless, impudent wretches will), if she's unkind in her carriage, give ill language, is sullen, pouty, so cross that she'l scarce eat or speak sometimes; nay if she neglects to manifest real love and kindness, in her words or carriage either; she's then a shame to her profession of Christianity, she dishonours and provokes the glorious God, tramples his Authority under her feet; she not only affronts her Husband, but also God her Maker, Lawgiver and Judge, by this her wicked behaviour. The indisputable Authority, the plain Command of the Great God, requires Husbands and Wives, to have and manifest very great affection, love and kindness to one another. They should (out of Conscience to God) study and strive to render each others life, easy, quiet and comfortable; to please, gratifie and oblige one another, as far as lawfully they can. When therefore they contend, quarrel, disagree, then they do the Devils work, he's pleas'd at it, glad of it. But such contention provokes God, it dishonours him; it's a *vile example* before Inferiours in the Family; it tends to prevent *Family Prayer.* . . . The *Heathen* at their *Marriage Festivals*, were wont to take the gall out of the Beast to be sacrificed; intimating that there should be no *bitterness in that Relation.* They should be so mutually kind and loving, as to delight in each others company; if the contrary prevails, many mischiefs ensue. Though they should *love* one another as has been said, yet let this caution be minded, that they dont love inordinately, because death will soon part them.

They should be chaste, and faithful to one another. The Seventh Commandment requires this. *Thou shalt not commit Adultery.* So the Apostle tells us, the man must have *his own wife,* and the Woman *her own Husband.* They must have nothing to do with any but their *own. Rejoyce with the wife of thy youth,* . . . *let her Breasts satisfie thee at all times, and be thou ravish'd always with her love. And why wilt thou my Son, be ravish'd with a strange woman, and imbrace the bosome of a stranger? This is the will of God, even your Sanctification, that ye should abstain from fornication; that every one of you, should know how to possess his vessel in sanctification and honour.* As for Christians, their Bodies as well as Souls belong to Christ, and that by special dedication. Tis therefore a most vile aggravated wickedness in those that call themselves Christians (tis bad in any, but worse in them) to commit *fornication* or *adultery. Know ye not that your bodies are the members of Christ? Shall I then take the members of Christ, and make them the members of an harlot? God forbid.* There's a solemn Covenant between *Husband & Wife,* God is witness of it, and observes when any treacherously break it. And he himself will avenge such wickedness.

The Husband and Wife *should be helpful to each other.* The Lord said, it is not good that the man should be alone, I will make *an help meet for him.* The Wife should be a meet help to her Husband; he also should do what he can, to help forward her good and comfort. They should do one another all the good they can.

As to Outward Things. If the one is sick, pained, troubled, distressed; the other should manifest care, tenderness, pity, compassion, & afford all possible relief and succour. . . . Husband & Wife should bear one anothers burthens, sympathize with each other in trouble; affording to each other all the comfort they can. They should likewise unite their prudent counsels and endeavours, comfortably to maintain themselves, and the Family under their joint care. *He that provides not for his own especially them of his own house;* he hath denied the faith, and is worse than an Infidel. . . . The Husband should indeavour, that his Wife may have Food and Raiment suitable for her. He should contrive prudently, and work diligently, that his Family, and his Wife particularly, may be well provided for. The Wife also in her place should do what she can, that they may have a comfortable support.

The Apostle requires that *wives be faithful in all things, keepers of the home,* and *that they guide the house* (manage matters well within doors) *give none occasion to the adversary to speak reproachfully:* he condemns those that are Idle, wandring from house to house, and not idle only, but tatlers also, and busie bodies, speaking things which they ought not. When Women go idling and tatling abroad, neglecting their household affairs; the Apostle says, they give occasion to the adversary to speak reproachfully. They expose the profession of Christianity to reproach, by their idleness, as well as by their being tatlers and busie bodies, therefore diligence in business is part of the Wives' duty, as well as the Husbands'.

They should be helpful to each other *As to Spiritual Things.* They can't show greater love or kindness, than by prudently, earnestly, dilligently indeavouring each others spiritual everlasting welfare. Therefore if one of them seems to have little or no regard to Religion; the other should by serious counsels, and a godly example, indeavour to win him or her over to the saving knowledge and practice of the truth. . . . Surely, then, if Husbands that call themselves Christians, are vain, wicked, ungodly; their pious Wives (if such they have) should by a meek whining Conversation, indeavour their spiritual and eternal Good. Husbands also that are pious, should indeavour the like, as to the spiritual everlasting Welfare of their Wives. Art thou willing, O man, that the Wife of thy bosome should perish in Hell for ever? Art thou willing, O Woman, that thy Husband should perish in Hell for ever? If not, then by prudent counsels, cautions, exhortations, and a winning, obliging heavenly carriage, indeavour to further each other in those ways of Holiness which lead to Eternal Glory. Indeavour to live, *as heirs together of the Grace of life.*

Husband and Wife *should be patient one towards another.* If Husband and Wife are both truly pious, yet neither of them is perfectly holy. It may be through Satans Temptations, and their own Corruptions, such words and actions may sometimes happen, as may be displeasing and offensive to each other: now in such Cases, a patient forgiving, forbearing spirit, is very needful. Tis the duty of Christians in general, with all lowliness, meekness and long suffering, to forbear one another in love. . . . Much more then is it the duty of Husband and Wife, to be of a patient, forbearing, forgiving spirit to one another; for God has made them one *flesh.* You therefore that are Husbands & Wives, dont aggravate each others faults; dont aggravate every error or mistake, every wrong or hasty word, every wry step, as though it were a wilful designed intollerable crime; for this would soon break all to pieces: but rather put the best constructions on things they'l bear, and bear with and forgive one anothers failings: don't let every indiscreet word and action, make a flame, breach or broil between you. If you have any regard to the Glory of God, to the Honour of our dear Lord Jesus, then carefully avoid strife and contention; live and love as God commands you: You are one *flesh* by his Law, live as becomes *such,* If a man's head, hand, foot is uneasy or pained, he is not for beating it, or cutting it off, but useth means for its ease and recovery. So if some uncomfortable things happen between you, dont let them set you on scolding, quarrelling, fighting; don't let them make you cross, sullen, humoursome, to get pouting alone, not to speak or be spoken to; don't let them make you live separately, nor lodge separately neither: for if it once comes to this, Satan has got a great advantage against you, and tis to be fear'd he'l get a greater.

Wives are part of the House and Family, and ought to be under the Husband's Government: they should *Obey their own Husbands*. Though the Husband is to rule his Family and his Wife yet his Government of his Wife should not be with rigour, haughtiness, harshness severity; but with the greatest love, gentleness, kindness, tenderness that may be. Though he governs her, he must not treat her as a Servant, but as his own *flesh:* he must love her as himself. He should make his government of her, as easie and gentle as possible; and strive more to be lov'd than fear'd; though neither is to be excluded. On the other hand, Wives ought readily and chearfully to obey their Husbands. *Wives submit your selves to your own Husbands, be in subjection to them.*

Those Husbands are much to blame, who dont carry it lovingly and kindly to their Wives. O man, if thy Wife be not so young, beautiful, healthy, well temper'd and qualify'd as thou couldst wish; if she brought not so much Estate to thee, or cannot do so much for thee, as some other women brought to or have done for their Husbands; nay, if she does not carry it so well to thee as she should yet she is thy Wife, and *the Great God Commands thee to love her,* not to be bitter, but kind to her. What can be more plain and express than that? *Let every one of you in particular, so love his Wife even as himself.* How vile then are those, who dont love their Wives, can't abide to be with them, loathe their Company, hate them, call them vile names, curse them, reproach, defame and belie them; beat and strike them. Will some, vex, fret, fling and threaten as though they would rend all to pieces before them; so that their Wives can scarce even have a quiet hour with them? Such Husbands carry it more like bruits, than what becomes men; they deserve sharp reproof and severe punishment too. O man, it may be thou art idle, lazy, dost take no care to provide Necessaries for thy Wife and Family; but instead of this, dost take to Tipling, Gaming, Ill Company, dost tarry out very late and unseasonably, and then comest home drunk, vomiting, or raging like a furious beast; if tis so, thou art exceeding vile and wicked. But possibly thou dost not run this great length of wickedness, yet if thou dost purposely grieve and vex thy Wife, twit her of any deformities, or unwilful Infirmities, twit her of her mean Parentage, mean or vicious Relations, dost twit her of her Poverty when she came to thee, of her mean abilities of body or mind; or if thou at any time strivest purposely to displease, fret or provoke her, then thou are base, vile and wicked in so doing: For herein thou dost not only abuse a Woman, a Creature, part of thy self; but thou dost affront and provoke the Great God, in trampling his Holy Laws under thy feet. . . .

Those Wives are much to blame who dont carry it lovingly and obediently to their own Husbands. O Woman, if thy Husband be not so young, beautiful, healthy, so well temper'd and qualified as thee couldst wish; if he has not such abilities, riches, honours, as some others have; if he does not carry it so well as he should; yet he's thy Husband, and the Great God Commands thee to love, honour and obey him. Yea, though possibly thou hast greater abilities of mind than he has, wast of some high birth, and he of a more mean Extract, or didst bring more Estate at Marriage than he did; yet since he is thy Husband, God has made him thy Head, and set him above thee, and made it thy duty to love and reverence him. If therefore thou dost hate or despise him, revile or dishonour him, or disobey his lawful Commands; if thou dost usurp authority over him, much more if thou lift up thy hand to strike him (as some shameless wretches will), then thou dost shamefully transgress the plain Commands of the Great God: thou dost trample his Authority under thy feet. Nay, if thou dost twit thy Husband of his mean birth, abilities, Estate, Relations (if they are mean) if thou dost by being cross, pouty, sullen, humoursome, put the Family out of order, and so grieve and displease thy Husband; if thou dost so vex, fret, contend, that he can scarce have any quiet in the house, or comfort in thy Company, then thou sinnest very greatly indeed. If thou art proud and haughty, and aspirest to spend more, or live higher, than thy Husbands Incomes will allow of; and so causest contention in the Family, this is a very great crime in thee: For the man to labour and toil hard, to venture Estate and Person too, to get money; and for the Woman foolishly and prodigally to spend what's thus gotten, is very blame-worthy indeed. Thou shouldst be a meet help to thy Husband, but if thou dost carry thy self like a spend-thrift, like a fret & scold; thou art rather a cross and tryal to him. . . . O Woman, great is thy wickedness, if thou dost so carry thy self as to deserve such a Character as this: If thou dost carry it basely and wickedly to thy Husband, thou dost not only abuse man, but thou dost affront God himself, in trampling on his Holy Commands. It may be thy discontent, fretting, scolding, quarrelling, makes thy Husband weary of the house, he can't abide to be at home, he has no quiet nor peace there; this makes him idle away his time, get into bad company, stay out late at nights, take to Tippling, Gaming, and other ill practices; which tend to bring shame, poverty, misery on him, on thy self and Family. Has not thy ill undutiful carriage, been a great occasion of thy Husband's naughtiness? If it has, though this wont excuse him, yet it greatly condemns thee.

Marriages in Court

C ourt records, increasingly available in published form, open an especially revealing window upon colonial society. It is, to be sure, a
window that presents a rather skewed view of life. Still, sooner
or later in colonial times most matters of individual and social life—birth,
death, and taxes, the disposition of property, relations among families
and between neighbors, brushes with law and authority—turned up in court.
Equally important, it is largely through court proceedings that we can
find much trace of ordinary people—as principals, witnesses, or subjects—
and observe them acting as family members, neighbors, participants in a
social and economic order, and, perhaps, as citizens. The documents that
follow, taken from the Essex, Massachusetts, county court in the last half
of the seventeenth century, touch upon marital problems ranging from
desertion and abuse to illegal marriage and "insufficiency" (impotence).

SALEM QUARTERLY COURT, 1676–1682

June 1676

Henry Jackman, complained of for living from his wife in an uncivil
and disorderly way, was admonished for attempting to marry and ordered
to return speedily to his wife upon the penalty which the law requires. . . .

Edward Peggey, aged about thirty years, deposed that he being bound
for England, Henery Jackman "desired me to carey a Letter for him to
his wife which acording to his desire i ded and when I came to deliuer it
to ye wife of Henery Jackman shee asked me how hur husband did taking
up a Littell Child into her aremes saing though my hosband is ashamed
of me he nede not bee ashamed of his Child with maney other wordes
to that purpos and she desired me to carry hur a Letter to hur husband
wich this deponent did and deLiuerd it to him then I was informed that
he kept Compeney with ye dafter of goodman Stanton that Liueth at brushe

Records and Files of the Quarterly Courts of Essex County, Massachusetts (Salem, Mass., 1913–
1921) VI, pp. 172–73, 194–96, 297–98, 386–87; VII, pp. 216–18, 356–57.

hille I went to his hous and tould ye maid that Henery Jackman was a maried man in England She semed to me to be troubled wishing that she had neuer seene him and since ye deponent see ye aboue said Henery in person and bought a saruant maid of dockter waldon of boston and it was reported that he bought hur with an intent to marey hur I hearing of it went to him and tould him that I would acquaint the magstraits ore Goufernor with it and I haue not senn him since tell this very day seing him by accedent I called to him and he would giue me no answar but after wardes he came to Mr Gedneys where I was I asked him wether he was maried he answared that it may be hee was or to that porpos.". . .

July 1676

Edward Berry and Betteris his wife, presented for not living together as man and wife, were ordered to live together according to God's ordinance within one fortnight upon penalty of 5li. fine. . . .

Betterice Berry's petition, concerning not living with her husband Edmond Berry: "I can proue by Testimony verbally & also by writing under his hand ye conditionall coven^t made Between us before o^r marriage, ye wch Coven^t at ye Tyme of o^r marriage was acknowledged before ye honored Major Hathorne; & likewise I can make proofe by John Glouer whom he employed to come to me as a Friend to speake in his behalf; that ye sd Edm. Berry desired nothing of my estate he desired nothing but my person; but alas how he carried it to me afterwards I know ye Towne & Country hath rung of it, & that it cannot otherwise be but yor worships must of necessity haue heard of his base, brutish & Inhumane carriage to me being truly such as was Impossible for any poore woman specially a woman of my Age to liue with such a person & this I can bring proof of to ye honord Court that he did tell Jno Glouer that if I would not giue up ye writings that were made between us he would make me weary of my life & so indeed I found it; & so at Length with his consent we parted; & now I haue declared myself as breifly as I could; & doe desire to ly at ye mercy of ye court, for what euer I suffer I am not able to liue with such a Tyrant."

Christopher Waller, aged about fifty-seven years, deposed that having been in discourse with Goodman Plummer, the former husband of Betterice Berry, he told deponent that he lived as comfortably with her as a man could desire and if he had sought all the world over he could not have had a better wife. Deponent also knew that she lived comfortably with both husbands, but he heard Edmond Berry say to her that she should never live a quiet hour with him unless she burned the writings, etc.

Elizabeth Price, aged about sixty years, and Elizabeth White, aged about seventy years, testified that being at the house of Edward Berry and being sensible of Goodwife Berry's want to help and conveniences they asked him whether he were willing that she should leave him and go elsewhere. He replied yes, with all his heart.

June 1677

Edmond Bery, for being distempered with drink and for abusive carriages and speeches to his wife, was fined.

Bettorice Berry's petition: "It being not unknowne to this honored Court how it hath bin with me in respect of my wofull condition with liueing with my husband Edmond Berry, who in regard of his most bitter, Inhumane & most ill becomeing carriage to me, as many of my neighbors can give Testimony. I was compelled to goe away from him; liueing where I could gett harbor. ye honord Court upon Information hereof, compelld me upon ye penalty of Fiue pounds to liue with him againe wch as ye Lord knowes to my unexpressable sorrow hath bin now for about a Twelue month, as by Testimony Sufficient may speake for me & what shall a poor woman doe in the Case; if ye Lord doth not wonderfully help; as for matter of substance, I haue nothing of him neither haue I euer had but a very small matter euer since I was his wife, for such was & still is his absurd manner in eating his victualls, as takeing his meat out of ye pickle; & broyleing it upon ye coales, & this he would tell me I must eate or else I must fast so that if I had not reserved to my self a Little of myne owne I must haue perisht; neither will he allow me any necessary about house for decencey or that wch is absolutely needfull but am compelled to borrow of my neighbors; by wch it is evident that he exactly goes about to verifie what he hath reported; namely that he will haue my estate or elce he will make me weary of my Life; now ye honord Major Hathorne Knowes ye contract that was made between vs before marriage & acknowledgd before him; howeuer in hopes of my more comfortable liueing with him was willing to bring into yᵉ house what I could, & did doe it; although to be sure ill bestowed upon such a person, as you may please to Judge of him in part what he is by one late Expression of his to me who when I brought to him a cup of my owne Sugar & Beare (for he will allow me nothing of his owne) and dranke to him useing these words) come husband lett all former differences be buried & trod under Foote; why should we not liue in Loue & unity as other Folks doe, he replied to me againe, Thus; Thou old cheating Rogue; The Divell take thee if thou doest not bring me Forth this Court; but such like direfull expressing towards me are not rare with him; wch although my hard portion & very Tedious to beare, yet was rather willing to groane under it then to make a publique discovery of his wicked; & brutish carriage to me; but surely ye Lord brings him forth, & ye grand Jury had cognissance of his Impious behavior towards me & by theire act is he now presented & it is but rationall that I should speake something before yoʳ worships for yᵉ clearing up of myne owne Innocency, & also since ye Thing is brought forth to lay open my grievances before you although god knowes my mind was rather to haue borne my affection & haue waited upon him who is yᵉ perswader of yᵉ heart, with my poor prayers to my good god in hopes of ye worke of his grace upon his heart

& soule; whereby he might be brought to see ye evill of his wayes & so to carry it to me as becomes an honest man to his wife; but ye Lord in mercy Looke upon me; I am now past hopes of him; & ye onely wise god direct you what to doe with me in this my wofull case, for I am not onely continually abused by my husband, with most vile, threatening & opprobrious speeches but also his son who liues in howse with him hath in his Father's presence threatened me to throw me downe head long downe ye staires; & not onely so but he hath broken up my chest & taken away a part of that Little wch I had."

Deborah Winter, aged about thirty-one years, testified that she had heard Edmond Berry use very reproachful terms to his wife, as bad as possibly could be spoken and when she was sick he would also then most terribly revile her. He had said that he desired it for her good and he did not care if there were a fire in the south field and she in the middle of it.

Abigail White, aged about seventy-two years, testified that Berry called his wife Jezebell, cheating rogue, etc., and told her that he could not abide her, and bade her begone. Also that his wife had proffered to do what she could for him, such as to dress his victuals, wind his quills, etc., and she would entreat him to be quiet, but he was angry because she would not join her estate to his. Also when she was sick, he said that she should have nothing of him because he had nothing of hers. Deponent had tried to persuade him to live quietly with his wife but he said it was too late.

Abigail Gray, aged about twenty-one years, deposed that when his wife was sick in bed and the nurse at the same time was in bed with her, Goodman Berry asked for cider. The nurse said that she should rise and get him some. Goody Berry said he had had enough already, and he replied that he would have some more or he would pull her in pieces. . . .

January 1678

Bridget, wife of Thomas Oliver, presented for calling her husband many opprobrious names; as old rogue and old devil, on Lord's days, was ordered to stand with her husband, back to back, on a lecture day in the public market place, both gagged for about an hour with a paper fastened to each of their foreheads, upon which their offence should be fairly written. Upon request of Mary West, daughter of said Thomas, who paid 20s., he was released. . . .

November 1681

A warrant having been issued from Hon. Maj. Danill Denison for Mr. Edward Woodman's appearance, personally or by his attorney, to answer a complaint against him brought by Mr. Francis Wainewright for illegally marrying Symond Wainwright and Sara Gilbert against the mind and without the consent of said Francis, court declared that said Woodman's preceeding in marrying the aforesaid persons was illegal and unwarrantable, and advised and required him to forbear such practices in the future and ordered him not to join any persons in marriage until he received commission from the General Court. . . .

Nathaniell Roper, John Pearce and Samuell Graves testified that they were with Simon Wainewright at Newberry at Mr. Woodman's house. The latter asked if Simon were published according to law and they said they saw his publishment the last Lord's day upon the meeting house door and read it and it stood all day. He asked if it was put up by his father's order and they answered that they knew nothing to the contrary. . . .

Rebeca Poore, aged about fifty years, and Judeth Daues, aged about twenty years, deposed that when he married them, Mr. Woodman asked Simon if he had his father's consent and he said he had, and if he thought there would be any question about it he would have brought the consent under his father's hand. The three men present said that Simon's father ordered the publishment. Then Mr. Woodman asked if the maid had the consent of her friends and the men replied that her mother was dead and her father had many years ago gone out of the country, so that there was no one who had the disposing of her. . . .

Mr. Woodman declared that the reason he did not ask Simon and his bride why they came to him to be married when they had magistrates in their own town was because he supposed that being court time, they were away from home. . . .

Letter of Edward Woodman, sr., dated Newbury, Nov. 22, 1681, and addressed to "The worshipfull mager generall denesen, this p^{r}sent:"

"Much honored S^r it is known to y^{r}selfe that I ly under y^r warrant to make my appearanc at Salem Court thes lins to y^r worship are to desire that I may be relest of that warant which I Conseu y^{r}self and m^r wainwright may doe my resons of my desir are ferst Conserning my marying of Simon wainwright I haue sent you a coppy of the eudenc that is upon oth in the hands of the much honored magor Saltingstall with which he sems to be well satisfied with this adision to it that the why I ded not demand of Simon why he was not maryed at Ipswedg was that my fancy deseued mee that was the generall Court wicke and Concluded in my own brest that thay mest thayr sesone and put themselfs upon a Jory to newbery Conserning other ground of my proseding the Evedenc under oth may giue y^r worshep I hop satisafcksion to enter a descors any forther Concerning my power to mary which haue ben without question I thinke this twenty years or whether It was my duty to haue sued for a new Comesion euery year if thar be such a law expresly or inclusively I must confes my Ignorenc thar in nither haue any heigh or low minded me of such a thing the which if I had known but sospicsions of such a thinge I should not haue sued for such an unprofitabell Comision but haue quickly layd asid the worke which have Cost me many a bottle of sacke and liker when frends and aquaintanc haue ben Conserned in Case I was parsionale present with ye worshep I question not but I shuld giue you satisfecksion as that you might by the entrust you haue in m^r wainwright perswd him to withdraw his Complaint and for my owne part I still hearby asur y^r worshep that henc forth I will not mary any what euer thay be but resiue what pour soe euer I haue into thayr hands that gaue what more may be said I shall refer to my frend trostoram Coffen whom I haue sent to y^r worshep in my behalfe forther to debat the Case and to bring the result under y^r worsheps hand if you ples soe fare to fauer mee."

June 1682

Katheren Ellenwood, complaining of her husband Ralph Ellenwood's insufficiency, was given her apparel and what estate she brought with her, and court declared the marriage annulled. . . .

Mary Houghton deposed concerning what Ralph Ellenwood told her in his house one night when she sat up later than usual. He said he thought there were witches not far off, etc.

Ruth Haskins, wife of Roger Haskins, testified that Katherin Ellenwood, being a near neighbor, was to her knowledge a woman of civil carriage in word and action.

Danil Weld and Richard Knott, chirurgeon, testified that they were ordered by court to report upon Ellinwood's condition, etc.

Abigal Ston, wife of John Ston, testified that Katharin Elenwood lived near her one year, and Elizabeth Hoopper testified to the same and that Katharin was a civil person, etc.

David Perkins and his wife Elizebeth Perkins testified that she lived near them one year, etc.

John Ricards and his wife Elizabeth Richards testified to the good character of Katharine, etc.

Mary Horton testified that Katherine lived in one room of the house in which deponent lived and that she was a civil woman.

The Saga of a Seventeenth-Century Marriage

This selection, consisting of court documents stretching over nearly twenty years, bears upon the marital life of Lawrence and Rachel Halfield Clenton. It is a complicated and confusing set of materials: names are not always spelled the same way, personal pronouns are used ambiguously, and the dimension of time is not always clear. (In the first deposition, for example, Lawrence Clenton refers to Rachel as his wife while talking about her actions and events that happened before they were married.) Still, the richness of the yield justifies the trouble it may take to sort out the facts—who was related to whom and in what ways—and reconstruct the story of their marriage. It not only provides us with a case study of the continuing brush of one marriage with legal authority, it also reveals something of the conditions, pressures, and problems that played across the marital relations of the less well off in seventeenth-century America.

The first two (and longest and most confusing) entries concern a suit brought by one Thomas White, guardian of Rachel Halfield Clenton's mother, Martha, against one Robert Cross, master of Lawrence Clenton. The suit concerns some money that Rachel gave to Clenton to buy himself out of indentured servitude to Cross and against which White made a claim. From what can be pieced together out of the depositions in the case, what appear to be the relationships between White, Rachel, and Martha and between Cross and the other principals in the case? How can we explain and interpret how and why the marriage was made, what it was that might have led Rachel and Lawrence to enter into it? Once made, as the subsequent entries indicate, the marriage had a history as troubled as its beginnings. In considering the complaints brought by the authorities against Rachel and Lawrence, and by Rachel against Lawrence, we need to ask how and why the Clentons continued to show up in court. What were the actions that brought them there, and how might we explain why the complaints were disposed of in the ways that they were?

RACHEL HALFIELD AND LAWRENCE CLENTON

November 1666

Tho. White, guardian to Martha Halfield, widow, v. Robt. Cross, sr.

Lawrence Clenton testified, Nov. 27, 1666, that he received 21 li. of his wife to give to his master Crose for his time, and the latter was very unwilling to take the money, but desired him to keep it and procure him a servant, for a servant was of more consequence than the money. Deponent was very urgent for his freedom and so his master went with him to Rachell Hefield to know whether he had obtained the money honestly. His wife told his master that he need not question it, as she gave it to him and it was her own to give. Then he delivered the money to his master and received 46s. 4d. in money of him, which deponent laid out for his own use. . . .

Robert Lord, marshal of Ipswich, aged thirty-four years, deposed that being at the honored Major's house before both of the magistrates, Rachell said that her mother gave her the money before she was married. . . .

Thomas Fiske deposed that he heard Rachell Harfild acknowledge that the gold which she gave Clenton was not given to her by her mother but that it was in her custody as were the other goods of her mother and she thought that she could dispose of it according to her pleasure. Further that Clenton lent his dame twenty shillings. . . .

Willeam Durgi, aged about thirty-two years, deposed that as servant of Goodman Booshop, he was ordered by his master to go with Ratchell Haffelde's cow's calf and bringing it to the door, the old woman came forth and asked whether or not Rachell had bought that cow and deponent told her that she had paid four pieces of gold. Then the old woman said it was well, for she had given her all her money to dispose of as she saw occasion. At that time she was "not verie sencable." . . .

Richard Huton deposed that he heard Rachell Harfield say to Robert Crose, sr., concerning Clenton, "this is the man that you said was worth gold but it is not his fair Lookes that will maintain me.". . .

Richard Brabrook, aged fifty-four years, deposed that being a tenant of the farm called Haffeild's farm, he had occasion often to be with Rachell Haffeeld, now wife of Lawranc Clenttonn, to whom he had to pay the rent, and the goods always passed in her name either to master or merchant. Further, that about three years since her mother gave her thirty-one or two pieces of gold, because, said Rachell, her brothers-in-law had her portion in their hands and she doubted whether she should get it because she lived with her mother. . . .

Records and Files of the Quarterly Courts of Essex County, Massachusetts (Salem, Mass., 1913–1921), III, pp. 371–75, 456–58; IV, pp. 14–15, 257, 269, 324–25; V, pp. 223, 267, 312; VI, pp. 137, 196, 206, 278, 338–39, 375; VII, 303–7; VIII, 157, 181, 187, 353.

Willeam Nellsonn, aged about thirty-one years, deposed that having occasion to go to Goody Clentton's house for some corn due him, he found her very sad, weeping and crying, and said that her brother White went about to undue her in every way. She said that he would have her say that she stole the money or that her husband stole it, and he had tried to get away from her all that she had. This was the time when Tho. Whit took away the cow from Goodman Graves, etc. . . .

November 1667

Tho. White, guardain of Martha Haffeild v. Robert Crosse. Review. For withholding or refusing to deliver 21li. in gold, which was illegally taken from said Martha. . . .

Ruth White, aged about thirty years, deposed that being at her mother's house at Ipswich two or three days before Larranc Klenton and Rachell Haftell were examined before the Worshipful Magistrates about the money, she heard her say that she did not care for Klenton. But after she had heard Robert Cros, sr., speak before the magistrates in Laurance's commendation, telling about what rich friends he had in Ingland, deponent could not dissuade Rachell from keeping company with him. . . .

Johana Fiske, aged about thirty-five years, deposed that she heard Laranc Clenton say that his master Cross and he had agreed for his time for less, but said Cross got him into the parlor with a bottle of liquir between them, etc. . . .

Laurence Clenton, aged twenty-four years, deposed that his master did not know that he had money of his wife to buy his time until he had had it some time. Also that his master would not take it until he had proved that he came honestly by it, and when deponent's wife declared that she gave it to him to buy out the three and a half years' time that they might marry, etc. Also that his brother White declared before two magistrates in the Major's house that her mother gave his wife twelve pieces of gold when she gave his brother White and brother Coy twelve pounds each, all of which was affirmed before an audience of at least forty people. . . .

Richard Brabrooke, aged about fifty years, deposed that Goodman Crose's son and daughter would have turned Rachell Clenton out of doors to provide for herself, had it not been for Robert Crose, sr. . . .

Rachell Clenton deposed that Robert Crose, sr., solicited her to be married to Larrence Clenton and labored hard with the Worshipful Mr. Simonds to marry them, that he said he was a man who deserved a maid worth a bushel of gold and Cross himself would give her a better portion than her father did. Crose also sent his son to persuade her to be married to Clenton, and that the latter said that he had an uncle worth thousands and he would be his heir, so that he had fifty pounds in gold to come in Capt. Pearse, that he had a mother at Boston and other lies to delude her, etc. . . .

James Foord, aged about twenty six years, deposed that at the time of the examination, Robert Crose, sr., was to return the money to Elder Whipple and Mr. Richard Hubberd, which was published upon Ipswich meeting house door. Also that Crose called Clenton his right hand man, and Capt. Breeden had told Crose that Clenton had good friends in England. . . .

Ruth White, aged about thirty years, deposed that at the examination, Goodman Crosse and his brother Andrewes urged Rachell to give a definite answer as to whether she would marry Clenton, and at last Major Denison reproved them and bade them go out of doors and woo maids there but not in his house. Deponent went to her mother's house and remained there fearing that they would intice Rachell, her sister, etc. . . .

Petition of Rachell (her mark) Clinton: That she had been for two years under great suffering occassioned by the dealings of her brother, Thomas White; that the 30li. left her by her father was put first into her brother, Richard Coy's hands for improvement, thence into White's hands, and it had been kept from her thirteen years, both interest and principle; that now she is destitute of money and friends; that whereas she formerly lived with her mother in a small cottage in Ipswich, where she cared for her mother who was unable to care for herself, her said mother had been taken from her to said White's house, also the household stuff, and the cottage, which was built for petitioner's mother and herself and given by will by her mother, while she was in her right mind, to said Rachell, had been unlawfully sold and the estate disposed of as White pleased; that she asks the favor of the court "that shee may not be forced to wander from house to house like an Indian or bruit beast;" that she was willing to work but had not been able to because she had been made almost devoid of common reason, etc.

March 1667

Rachell Clenton, complaining to Mr. Symonds of John Clark's lying with her, and upon trial denying it, was ordered to be whipped.

March 1668

Lawrance Clenton surrendered his right and interest in the will of his mother-in-law Martha Halfield to Thomas Fiske of Wennam as feoffe in trust for Rachell Clenton, his wife.

Will of Martha Hallfield, widow of Richard Halfield, was proved by Daniell Warner and Samuell Younglove, sr. Richard Hubbard, who was named as executor, refused to serve, and Thomas White was appointed administrator. Said White was allowed charges of 21li. 2s. for care of his mother and other expenses.

June 1670

Laurence Clenton, for attempting to abase Mary Knoulton, was sentenced to be severely whipped with twenty stripes well laid on, to pay costs to Tho. Knoulton and to remain in prison until payment be made. Said Clenton was ordered to allow his wife 2s. per week toward her maintenance, to carry it himself to her, to live with her, as duty binds him, and at least to lodge with her one night in a week. He was also to bring a certificate from his wife or from Seargt. White to the Worshipfull Major Denison that he had fulfilled this order, otherwise to be sent to the house of correction.

September 1671

Upon a complaint of Rachell Clenton that her husband Laurance Clenton had not observed the order of Salem court by paying his wife 2s. per week, court ordered that he be sent to the house of correction and to remain there until he paid his wife 40s. for the time past and is to pay her 2s. per week for the future. He was to be sent to the house of correction again if he did not observe this order. She was enjoined to entertain him as her husband whenever he comes upon penalty of being sent to the house of correction.

May 1672

Laurance Clenton was discharged, his presentment not being proved. . . . Presented for not living with his wife. Also for taking 16s. for three and a half days' work at Mr. Baker's, in painting a room, with his dinner every day.

May 1674

Rachell Clenton, presented for not living with her husband, complained that he did not provide for her. Court ordered that Larance Clenton should every week, or at least once a fortnight, bring to his wife 2s. per week, for neglect of which he was to be sent to the house of correction.

March 1676

Laurance Clenton, complained of for not living with his wife, was ordered to live with her as man and wife ought to do, and when necessarily absent, he should pay her 18d. per week in corn. She was ordered to follow her work as she ought upon penalty of being sent to the house of correction.

September 1676

Mary Greely, presented for fornication, was sentenced to be whipped. . . . Presented for fornication with Laurence Clenton.

April 1677

Laurance Clenton, being the reputed father of the child of Mary Greely, was ordered to pay 20d. per week in corn toward the keeping of the child every week or at least by the month.

September 1677

Lawrance Clenton and Mary Woodden, bound over for fornication, confessed, and he was ordered to be severely whipped. . . .

Jonas Gregory, the whipper, for abusing the court, in not performing the duty of his office upon Lawrence Clenton, was sentenced to be whipped.

November 1677

John Foard and Rachell Clinton, convicted by their own confession of unlawful familiarity and much cause of suspicion of uncleanness and other evil practices, and deserving to be severely whipped, consedring that they have suffered a hard imprisonment above a week, they were bound to good behavior and ordered not to come to each other by night or day unless in the company of some other discreet person, under penalty of being imprisoned. Also ordered that by paying their fee to the keeper of the prison at Salem, and to the keeper and constable of Ipswich, they should immediately be set at liberty. . . . Nathaniell Rust, constable, deposed that he went to Clenton's house upon order of Major General Denison and found Ford in bed, etc., and by the bedside was a glass bottle with some liquor in it, and he ordered Rachell Clenton and John Ford to go along with him to the Major General's. Larenc Clenton testified to the same. . . .

Examination of John Ford and Rachel Clinton, Nov. 24, 1677, before Daniel Denison: that she gave him a napkin and a piece of stuff and kersey, and that he paid for them because she was his wife. He understood that she was divorced last court and she said she so understood it, but they had never lived together, etc.

November 1678

Lawrance Clenton was ordered to pay to Rachell, his wife, one peck of corn a week. . . . Petition dated September 25, 1678, of Rachell, wife of Laranc Clinton: that her husband was ordered by the court to allow her 2s. per week for her maintenance, about ten years ago, and she had never received more than ten pounds in all, and upon her asking for a divorce on Nov. 6th last, court declared that it could not be done but ordered her husband to pay her 50s. upon demand, which she had never received. She asked for assistance, as she had suffered the loss of her estate by her husband and is now altogether neglected by him.

April 1679

Laurance Clenten was ordered to serve Arthur Abott until the end of June next for his charges about the child of Mary Grely set by the court.

September 1680

Rachell Clenton, desiring that her husband provide for her, was allowed 20s., she to demand no more of him.

To a Dear and Loving Husband

In New no less than old England, poetry was a much prized art. Puritans, to be sure, had a rather chastened view of the muse and condemned literary elegance and vain display that seemed to celebrate the poet rather than the true Author of all things. Still, they regarded (and avidly read) poetry rightly used as a powerful instrument of Divine Truth. This selection consists of two love poems by Anne Bradstreet (1612–1672), the New World's first and best-known poet, daughter of one governor of Massachusetts Bay Colony and wife of another.

TO MY DEAR AND LOVING HUSBAND

If ever two were one, then surely we.
If ever man were loved by wife, then thee;
If ever wife was happy in a man,
Compare with me, ye women, if you can.
I prize thy love more than whole mines of gold
Or all the riches that the East doth hold.
My love is such that rivers cannot quench,
Nor ought but love from thee, give recompense.
Thy love is such I can no way repay,
The heavens reward thee manifold, I pray.
Then while we live, in love let's so persevere
That when we live no more, we may live ever.

A LETTER TO HER HUSBAND, ABSENT UPON PUBLIC EMPLOYMENT

My head, my heart, mine eyes, my life, nay, more,
My joy, my magazine of earthly store,
If two be one, as surely thou and I,

John W. Ellis, *Works of Anne Bradstreet in Prose and Verse* (Boston, 1867), p. 394.
Ellis, op. cit., p. 395.

How stayest thou there, whilst I at Ipswich lie?
So many steps, head from the heart to sever,
If but a neck, soon should we be together.
I, like the Earth this season, mourn in black,
My Sun is gone so far in's zodiac,
Whom whilst I 'joyed, nor storms, nor frost I felt,
His warmth such frigid colds did cause to melt.
My chilled limbs now numbed lie forlorn;
Return, return, sweet Sol, from Capricorn;
In this dead time, alas, what can I more
Than view those fruits which through thy heat I bore?
Which sweet contentment yield me for a space,
True living pictures of their father's face.
O strange effect! now thou art southward gone,
I weary grow the tedious day so long;
But when thou northward to me shalt return,
I wish my Sun may never set, but burn
Within the Cancer of my glowing breast,
The welcome house of him my dearest guest.
Where ever, ever stay, and go not thence,
Till nature's sad decree shall call thee hence;
Flesh of thy flesh, bone of thy bone,
I here, thou there, yet both but one.

Marriage Among the Virginia Gentry

T his selection returns to the Byrds for a look at the marriage of a Virginia aristocrat. It is taken from Byrd's secret diary and reveals some of the details of his relationship with his first wife, Lucy Parke Byrd (see p. 46 for their courtship). It also permits us to view an upper-class marriage within the broader context of the preoccupations and activities that made up the daily routine of a wealthy Virginia planter.

THE SECRET DIARY OF WILLIAM BYRD OF WESTOVER

April 7, 1709

I rose before 6 o'clock and read two chapters in Hebrew and 250 verses in Homer's *Odyssey* and made an end of it. I said my prayers devoutly. I ate milk for breakfast. I danced my dance. The men began to work this day to dig for brick. I settled my accounts and read Italian. I reproached my wife with ordering the old beef to be kept and the fresh beef used first, contrary to good management, on which she was pleased to be very angry and this put me out of humor. I ate nothing but boiled beef for dinner. I went away presently after dinner to look after my people. When I returned I read more Italian and then my wife came and begged my pardon and we were friends again. I read in Dr. Lister again very late. I said my prayers. I had good health, good thoughts, and bad humor, unlike a philosopher. . . .

April 9, 1709

I rose at 5 o'clock and read a chapter in Hebrew and 150 verses in Homer. I said my prayers devoutly and ate milk for breakfast. My wife and I had another scold about mending my shoes but it was soon over by her submission. I settled my accounts and read Dutch. I ate nothing but cold roast beef and asparagus for dinner. In the afternoon Mr. Custis

Louis B. Wright and Marion Tinling, eds., *The Secret Diary of William Byrd of Westover, 1709–1712* (Richmond, 1941), pp. 18–19, 107, 210–11, 296–97, 377, 461–63. Reprinted by permission of the editors.

complained of a pain in his side for which he took a sweat of snakeroot. I read more Dutch and took a little nap. In the evening we took a walk about the plantation. My people made an end of planting the corn field. I had an account from Rappahannock that the same distemper began to rage there that had been so fatal on the Eastern Shore. I had good health, good thoughts and good humor, thanks be to God Almighty. I said my prayers. . . .

November 2, 1709

I rose at 6 o'clock and read a chapter in Hebrew and some Greek in Lucian. I said my prayers and ate milk for breakfast, and settled some accounts, and then went to court where we made an end of the business. We went to dinner about 4 o'clock and I ate boiled beef again. In the evening I went to Dr. [Barret's] where my wife came this afternoon. Here I found Mrs. Chiswell, my sister Custis, and other ladies. We sat and talked till about 11 o'clock and then retired to our chambers. I played at [r-m] with Mrs. Chiswell and kissed her on the bed till she was angry and my wife also was uneasy about it, and cried as soon as the company was gone. I neglected to say my prayers, which I should not have done, because I ought to beg pardon for the lust I had for another man's wife. However I had good health, good thoughts, and good humor, thanks be to God Almighty. . . .

July 30, 1710

I rose at 5 o'clock and wrote a letter to Major Burwell about his boat which Captain Broadwater's people had brought round and sent Tom with it. I read two chapters in Hebrew and some Greek in Thucydides. I said my prayers and ate boiled milk for breakfast. I danced my dance. I read a sermon in Dr. Tillotson and then took a little [nap]. I ate fish for dinner. In the afternoon my wife and I had a little quarrel which I reconciled with a flourish. Then she read a sermon in Dr. Tillotson to me. It is to be observed that the flourish was performed on the billiard table. I read a little Latin. In the evening we took a walk about the plantation. I neglected to say my prayers but had good health, good thoughts, and good humor, thanks be to God. This month there were many people sick of fever and pain in their heads; perhaps this might be caused by the cold weather which we had this month, which was indeed the coldest that ever was known in July in this country. Several of my people have been sick, but none died, thank God. . . .

February 5, 1711

I rose about 8 o'clock and found my cold still worse. I said my prayers and ate milk and potatoes for breakfast. My wife and I quarreled about her pulling her brows. She threatened she would not go to Williamsburg if she might not pull them; I refused, however, and got the better of her, and maintained my authority. About 10 o'clock we went over the river and got to Colonel Duke's about 11. There I ate some toast and canary. Then we proceeded to Queen's Creek, where we all found all well, thank God. We ate roast goose for supper. The women prepared to go to the Governor's the next day and my brother and I talked of old stories. My cold grew exceedingly bad so that I thought I should be sick. My sister gave me some sage tea and leaves of [s-m-n-k] which made me mad all night so that I could not sleep but was much disordered by it. I neglected to say my prayers in form but had good thoughts, good humor, and indifferent health, thank God Almighty. . . .

April 30, 1711

I rose at 5 o'clock and said a short prayer and then drank two dishes of chocolate. Then I took my leave about 6 o'clock and found it very cold. I met with nothing extraordinary in my journey and got home about 11 o'clock and found all well, only my wife was melancholy. We took a walk in the garden and pasture. We discovered that by the contrivance of Nurse and Anaka Prue got in at the cellar window and stole some strong beer and cider and wine. I turned Nurse away upon it and punished Anaka. I ate some fish for dinner. In the afternoon I caused Jack and John to be whipped for drinking at John [Cross] all last Sunday. In the evening I took a walk about the plantation and found things in good order. At night I ate some bread and butter. I said my prayers and had good health, good thoughts, and good humor, thank God Almighty. The weather was very cold for the season. I gave my wife a powerful flourish and gave her great ecstasy and refreshment. . . .

December 31, 1711

I rose about 7 o'clock and read a chapter in Hebrew and six leaves in Lucian. I said my prayers and ate boiled milk for breakfast. The weather continued warm and clear. I settled my accounts and wrote several things till dinner. I danced my dance. I ate some turkey and chine for dinner. In the afternoon I weighed some money and then read some Latin in Terence and then Mr. Mumford came and told me my man Tony had been very sick but he was recovered again, thank God. He told me Robin Bolling had been like to die and that he denied that he was the first to mention the imposition on skins which he certainly did. Then he and I took a walk about the plantation. When I returned I was out of humor to find the negroes all at work in our chambers. At night I ate some broiled turkey with Mr. Mumford and we talked and were merry all the evening. I said my prayers and had good health, good thoughts, and good humor, thank God Almighty. My wife and I had a terrible quarrel about whipping Eugene while Mr. Mumford was there but she had a mind to show her authority before company but I would not suffer it, which she took very ill; however for peace sake I made the first advance towards a reconciliation which I obtained with some difficulty and after abundance of crying. However it spoiled the mirth of the evening, but I was not conscious that I was to blame in that quarrel.

January 1, 1712

I lay abed till 9 o'clock this morning to bring my wife into temper again and rogered her by way of reconciliation. I read nothing because Mr. Mumford was here, nor did I say my prayers, for the same reason. However I ate boiled milk for breakfast, and after my wife tempted me to eat some pancakes with her. Mr. Mumford and I went to shoot with our bows and arrows but shot nothing, and afterwards we played at billiards till dinner, and when we came we found Ben Harrison there, who dined with us. I ate some partridge for dinner. In the afternoon we played at billiards again and I won two bits. I had a letter from Colonel Duke by H-1 the bricklayer who came to offer his services to work for me. Mr. Mumford went away in the evening and John Bannister with him to see his mother. I took a walk about the plantation and at night we drank some mead of my wife's making which was very good. I gave the people some cider and a dram to the negroes. I read some Latin in Terence and had good health, good thoughts, and good humor, thank God Almighty. I said my prayers.

WILLIAM BYRD TO JOHN CUSTIS

London, 13th December, 1716

When I wrote last I little expected that I should be forced to tell you the very melancholy news of my dear Lucy's death, by the very same, cruel distemper that destroyed her sister. She was taken with an insupportable pain in her head. The doctor soon discovered her ailment to be the small-pox, and we thought it best to tell her the danger. She received the news without the least fright, and was persuaded she would live until the day she died, which happened in 12 hours from the time she was taken. Gracious God what pains did she take to make a voyage hither to seek a grave. No stranger ever met with more respect in a strange country than she had done here, from many persons of distinction, who all pronounced her an honor to Virginia. Alas! how proud was I of her; and how severely am I punished for it. But I can dwell no longer on so afflicting a subject, much less can I think of anything else, therefore, I can only recommend myself to your pity, and am as much as any one can be, dear brother, your most affectionate and humble servant,

W. Byrd.

George Washington Custis, *Recollections and Private Memoirs of George Washington* (New York, 1859), pp. 32–33.

Between Wife and Husband

These documents bear upon the issue of power and responsibility within marriage. The first selection consists of some letters between Deborah and Benjamin Franklin (It might be useful to look at them in conjunction with the account of their courtship on page 53.) As historical documents, letters are not simply repositories of fact and idea; they are also acts, and in the gestures family letters make, in their tone and style of address as well as in their more obvious content, they often reveal something of the character of the relationship between family members. As Benjamin Franklin made his ascent into more elevated social and intellectual circles, Deborah remained behind, helping manage his affairs just as she had when he was a striving young printer—she served, for example, as bookkeeper for the firm. Though he appears to have retained affection for her, Franklin nonetheless turned to more cosmopolitan women for emotional sustenance and intellectual companionship. These letters, full as they are of the "news" of daily life, reveal a good deal about the relationship between Deborah and Benjamin Franklin. Theirs, of course, was just one marriage between two particular people and should not be viewed as necessarily typical of the times. Nonetheless, the letters, as artifacts of that marriage, provide an example of how such material might be used to investigate marriages of the past.

Abigail and John Adams possessed one of the famous "good" marriages of American history. Like most men of affairs, John Adams was away from home much of the time, and Abigail took over essential control of the family's economic enterprises, freeing her husband to devote himself to matters of state. Unlike Deborah Franklin, Abigail—self-taught but well educated—served as one of her husband's most important intellectual companions. Moreover, she did not hesitate to express (albeit always in private correspondence) her ideas on matters well beyond the family circle. This selection consists of Abigail's famous plea to "remember the ladies" and John's response to that plea, a response that she did not consider entirely adequate, for in a letter to Mercy Otis Warren, a friend with an even more forceful personality, she complained that he had been "very sausy" in his reply.

BENJAMIN FRANKLIN

A Poem to My Wife

Of their Chloes and Phillisses Poets may prate,
  I sing my plain Country Joan,
Now twelve Years my Wife, still the Joy of my Life,
  Blest Day that I made her my own,
          My dear Friends,
  Blest Day that I made her my own.

Not a Word of her Face, her Shape, or her Eyes,
  Of Flames or of Darts shall you hear;
Tho' I Beauty admire 'tis Virtue I prize,
  That fades not in seventy Years,
          My dear Friends

In Health a Companion delightfull and dear,
  Still easy, engaging, and Free,
In Sickness no less than the faithfullest Nurse,
  As tender as tender can be,
          My dear Friends

In Peace and good Order, my Houshold she keeps,
  Right Careful to save what I gain,
Yet chearfully spends, and smiles on the Friends
  I've the Pleasures to entertain,
          My dear Friends

She defends my good Name ever where I'm to blame,
  Friend firmer was ne'er to Man giv'n,
Her compassionate Breast feels for all the Distrest,
  Which draws down the Blessing from Heav'n,
          My dear Friends

Am I laden with Care, she takes off a large Share,
  That the Burthen ne'er makes to reel,
Does good Fortune arrive, the Joy of my Wife
  Quite doubles the Pleasures I feel,
          My dear Friends

In Raptures the giddy Rake talks of his Fair,
  Enjoyment shall make him Despise,
I speak my cool sense, that long Experience
  And Enjoyment have chang'd in no wise,
          My dear Friends

Leonard W. Labaree, ed., *The Papers of Benjamin Franklin* (New Haven, 1959–1978), IV, pp. 17–18, VII, p. 352, XIII, pp. 43–46, XVIII, pp. 90–92, XXI, pp. 303, 402–03. Reprinted by permission of Yale University Press.

Were the fairest young Princess, with Million in Purse,
  To be had in Exchange for my Joan,
She could not be a better Wife, mought be a Worse,
  So I'd stick to my Joggy alone,
                    My dear Friends,

  I'd cling to my lovely ould Joan.

DEBORAH AND BENJAMIN FRANKLIN, CORRESPONDENCE, 1756–1774

To Deborah Franklin

Easton, Saturday Morning, Nov. 13, 1756.

My Dear Child,

I wrote to you a few days since, by a special messenger, and inclosed letters, for all our wives and sweethearts; expecting to hear from you by his return, and to have the northern newspapers and English letters, per the packet; but he is just now returned without a scrap for poor us. So I had a good mind not to write to you by this opportunity; but I never can be ill-natured enough, even when there is the most occasion. The messenger, says he left the letters at your house, and saw you afterwards at Mr. Dentie's and told you when he would go, and that he lodged at Honey's, next door to you, and yet you did not write; so let Goody Smith, give one more just judgment, and say what should be done to you; I think I wont tell you that we are well, nor that we expect to return about the middle of the week, nor will I send you a word of news; that's poz. My duty to mother, love to the children, and to Miss Betsey and Gracey, &c. &c. I am, Your *loving* husband,

B. FRANKLIN

PS. I have *scratched out the loving words,* being writ in haste by mistake, when I *forgot I was angry.*

From Deborah Franklin

Feb the 10, [1765]

I am set down to Confab a littel with my dear child as it Semes a Sorte of a hollow day for we have an ox arosteing on the river and moste pepel semes plesd with the a fair but as I partake of none of the divershons I stay at home and flatter myself that the next packit will bring me a letter from you.

By the laste packit thair was a letter from mr. Jackson to you the poste Came in laite att night I did not know hough to ackte as you had not sed aney thing to me a bought what I shold due with the letters had it a bin direckted to the Speker I shold a sent it to Mr. Fox but in the morning Billey Franklin Came to town and he and Mr. Galloway Came and [read?]

The Rebecca Nurse house in Salem, Massachusetts, built about 1675. Parts were added in later years. The basic structure would have been for a family of modest means. Rebecca Nurse herself was one of the Salem "witches."   *Samuel Chamberlain*

The "buttery" from the Tristram Coffin house in Massachusetts, about 1675. All the "appliances" were handmade, although not necessarily by the inhabitants, and show what historians mean when they speak of the family economy of this time (and for at least another century and a half) as "household production."

Samuel Chamberlain

The "spinning room" with spinning wheel and loom in Rebecca Nurse house. Another illustration of the "household economy."

Samuel Chamberlain

the letter thay sed tha wold write to you as I supose Billey did for he did not stay in town maney minites as he had letters to send. He had not heard the packi[t] was cumin when he lefte home which was the reson he maid no stay.

We have nothing stiring amoungst us but phamlits [pamphlets] and Scurrilitey but I have never sed or dun aney thing or aney of our famely you may depend on it nor shall we. All our good friends Cole [call] on us as yousall [usual] and we have bin asked ought but I have not gon but Salley has within this mounth but Shee was att Billeys all moste seven weeks.

This day the man is a puting up the fier plases that Came from London the darke one is in the parler. I am in hopes the harthes will be laid the wather will begin to be wormer and the Sun Stronger. The plasterer is a finishing the lathing of the stair Cases and I am a geting the lore parte of the house clened ought readey for the laying the kitching flore all this a bought the house.

Now a littel of what hapens Dr. Whit of Jermanton deyed this week. Mr. Plumsted in comin from N York had liked to be drounde he fell in seven times he gave a man ten pounds to pul him over the river on a bord leyin flat doune. He was in that Condishun for two owers but got home well and not aney Cold as I hear of. Now for a verey good pees of *news* our Governer gave in money for the poor ten pounds and fortey Cord of wood which is worth Sixtey pounds and more as it is sold now you donte know hough everey bodey loves him and we think our Governer is a kingbird. Salley is well and will write this time. Our Nabor Thomsons is verey well and our other friends. My love to Mrs. Stephenson to our Polley to Mr. and Mrs. Strahan and their whole famely and all of our friends.

Feb. 17

Sens I wrote the above our Cusin Antoney Willkison deyed verey sudenly. I had not herd that he was unwell tell his man Came for me he was dead he sed I have not seen my Cusin sense as the wather is so verey sever and slepey. On Freyday I got a man to helpe Gorge to Cute and Clear a way the Ise att the street dore and a bought the pump and [guter?]. It was near three feet thick. I never knew such a winter in my time but I am in hopes the worste of the wather is over. For severel day Gorge and my selef have bin att the New house a geting the roomes readey for the painter as Mr. Hadock ses he hopes he shall get to worke in march. I shall get the harthes Laid and if verey Cold wather is then we Can make a fier to prevent the painte reseveing aney dommaig. I only wish I was remouefed then I hope to be more relieved but I have not one ower my one att this time as a reporte is got aboute that you air arived in London and our friends all Come to know for them selves. The Mr. Whortons have all bin to inquier Hugh Robertes, Abel James and maney more.

Feb. the 21

Yisterday the letters by the packit Came and I had flattered my self that I shold a heard that you was arived att laste but it was not so but I hope by nexte packit that I shal heare that you air safe and well. Salley writes so I leve to her to tell hough Billey duse for I donte know wather he knew that the packit is to saile so soon as nexte Satterday. Coll. Bouquet has Cold Several times to see us as Cap. Orrey thay air bouth verey well. This morning is so verey Cold that I Can hardly hold a pen in my hand so shall write to you agen as soon as posabel. Brother and Sister is well not one word of Mr. Foxcrofte but the Suthren poste is not Com in nor has the Virjaney maile for more than two munthes. Mr. Mickill leyes dead now he was walking out his dore the day before he deyed.

Sense I wrote the a bove Mr. Hall Came in with the mareyland papear no Virjaney maile. Mr. Hall desiers to be remembered to you my love to Mrs. Stephenson it wold be needles to menshon names as everey bodey desiers to be remember to you. I am my Deareste Childe youre afeckshonet wife

D FRANKLIN

From Deborah Franklin

Auguste the 31 1769

My Deareste Child

I have but time to tell you that yister day our Dear littel Boy was Caireyed to Christe Church and was baptised by the Name of Benj Franklin. His Unkill and Ante stood for him Mr. Banton as procksey for you and I was well aneuef to stand for my self. I have the pleshuer to tell you that Salley is thank to god as well as we have resen to expeckte her to be and is in a way of makeing a fine nuerse. I thinke it wold be plesed to see houghe much plesher Billey takes in him and thinkes he is a verey fine child he is. I am much hurreyed at this time but this I muste to say. Mr. Petter proformed his offis he was so verey kind to cole on us and saw Salley and is verey kinde to her. Mr. Beach had a fine tortol cume in but Sundays we dresed it to diner. The pason from Burlinton came with them. Mr. Wharton the father dined with us Mr. Banton and pason Petters. One Jentelman of Mr. Beaches maid the whole companey. Everey one semed much plesed and the younk Jentelman behaved verey well and gives everey bodey hapey that have seen him. I am in hope to write by the nexte Packit. Mr. Brenmer is a passaig[er] as is Capt. Elvess and his son is on Bord all so the two Elves have seen your son and is to tell you aboute him. I donte say as it wold not be thoute possbel he is a fine lim[b]ed child but is verey spair and dilicat some thinke he is darke eyes sume sez blaik eyed but thay is verey prittey. He is verey good and quiet and if it shold plees god to spair him I think much in pleshuer of him. Be so kind as to give my love to good mrs. Stephenson and to Polley to Mr. and Mrs. Strahan to Mr. and Mrs. Weste Capte. Orrey Mr. Gombes.

I beleve all our children will write but thay air oute to dine to gather
and tomorrow we air to dine tomorrow with Mr. Hopkinson if I am well
aneuef to dine abrod. So I write today leste I not write to morrow you
will see hough in Conneckted staet I write. Have or had you seen Mr.
Foxcrofte I hope he is well supose you have seen the Commet that is
seen in this plase. I have not seen it but our children have seen it. I am
your afeckshonet wife

D FRANKLIN

I shold a told you that he was dresed in his christening sute and looked
verey well in them and will thanke you for them.

[*In Sally Bache's Hand:*] Mama desires me to tell you that yesterday, she
was well enough to dine abroad with us at Mr. F: Hopkinsons—and that
yesterday also she recd. a few Lines from you by Capt. Keys, and that
she knew nothing of Capt. Osborns sailing.

To Deborah Franklin

London, May 1. 1771

My dear Child,

I wrote to you per Capt. Osborne, and have since received yours of
Jan. 14. per Cousin Benezet, and of March 7. per the Packet.

The Bill on Sir Alexander Grant for £30 which you so kindly sent me
inclos'd, came safe to hand. I am obliged too to Mr. Hall for enabling
you on a Pinch to buy it. But I am sorry you had so much Trouble about
it; and the more so, as it seems to have occasioned some Disgust in you
against Messrs. Foxcrofts for not supplying you with Money to pay for
it. That you may not be offended with your Neighbours without Cause, I
must acquaint you with what it seems you did not know, that I had limited
them in their Payments to you, to the Sum of Thirty Pounds per Month,
for the sake of our more easily settling, and to prevent Mistakes. This
making 360 Pounds a Year, I thought, as you have no House Rent to
pay yourself, and receive the Rents of 7 or 8 Houses besides, might be
sufficient for the Maintenance of your Family. I judged such a Limitation
the more necessary, because you never have sent me any Account of your
Expenses, and think yourself ill-used if I desire it; and because I know
you were not very attentive to Money-matters in your best Days, and I
apprehend that your Memory is too much impair'd for the Management
of unlimited Sums, without Danger of injuring the future Fortune of your
Daughter and Grandson. If out of more than £500 a Year, you could have
sav'd enough to buy those Bills it might have been well to continue purchasing them: But I do not like your going about among my Friends to borrow
Money for that purpose, especially as it is not at all necessary. And therefore
I once more request that you would decline buying them for the future.
And I hope you will no longer take it amiss of Messrs. Foxcrofts that
they did not supply you. If what you receive is really insufficient for your
Support, satisfy me by Accounts that it is so, and I shall order more.

I am much pleased with the little Histories you give me of your fine Boy, which are confirm'd by all that have seen him. I hope he will be spared, and continue the same Pleasure and Comfort to you, and that I shall ere long partake with you in it. My Love to him, and to his Papa and Mama. Mrs. Stevenson too is just made very happy by her Daughter's being safely delivered of a Son: the Mother and Child both well. Present my affectionate Respects to Mrs. Montgomery, with Thanks for her most obliging Present. It makes a nice Bag for my Ivory Chessmen. I am, as ever, Your affectionate Husband

B FRANKLIN

To Deborah Franklin

Sept. 10, 1774

It is now nine long Months since I received a Line from my dear Debby. I have supposed it owing to your continual Expectation of my Return; I have feared that some Indisposition has rendered you unable to write; I have imagined any Thing rather than admit a Supposition that your kind Attention towards me was abated. And yet when so many other Old Friends dropt a Line to me now & then at a Venture, taking the Chance of finding me here or not as it might happen, why might I not have expected the same Comfort from you, who used to be so diligent and faithful a Correspondent, as to omit scarce any Opportunity?

This will serve to acquaint you that I continue well, Thanks to God.— It would be a great pleasure to me to hear that you are so. My Love to our Children, and believe me ever

Your affectionate Husband

B Franklin

I recommend the Bearer Mr. Westley to your Civilities

William to Benjamin Franklin

December 24, 1774

Hon'd Father:

I came here on Thursday last to attend the funeral of my poor old mother, who died the Monday noon preceding. Mr. Bache sent his clerk express to me on the occasion, who reached Amboy on Tuesday evening, and I set out early the next morning, but the weather being very severe and snowing hard, I was not able to reach here till about 4 o'clock on Thursday afternoon, about half an hour before the corpse was to be moved for interment. Mr. Bache and I followed as chief mourners; your old friend H. Roberts and several other of your friends were carriers, and a very respectable number of the inhabitants were at the funeral. I don't mention the particulars of her illness, as you will have a much fuller account from Mr. Bache than I am able to give. Her death was no more than might be reasonably expected after the paralytick stroke she received some time ago, which greatly affected her memory and understanding. She told me when I took leave of her on my removal to Amboy, that she never expected to see you unless you returned this winter, for that she was sure she should not live till next Summer. I heartily wish you had happened to have come over in the fall, as I think her disappointment in that respect prayed a good deal on her spirits. . . . Your dutiful son,

Wm. Franklin

ABIGAIL AND JOHN ADAMS CORRESPONDENCE, 1776

Abigail to John Adams

Braintree, March 31, 1776

I wish you would ever write me a Letter half as long as I write you; and tell me if you may where your Fleet are gone? What sort of Defence Virginia can make against our common Enemy? Whether it is so situated as to make an able Defence? Are not the Gentery Lords and the common people vassals, are they not like the uncivilized Natives Brittain represents us to be? I hope their Riffel Men who have shewen themselves very savage and even Blood thirsty; are not a specimen of the Generality of the people.

I am willing to allow the Colony great merrit for having produced a Washington but they have been shamefully duped by a Dunmore.

I have sometimes been ready to think that the passion for Liberty cannot be Eaquelly Strong in the Breasts of those who have been accustomed to deprive their fellow Creatures of theirs. Of this I am certain that it is not founded upon that generous and christian principal of doing to others as we would that others should do unto us.

Do not you want to see Boston: I am fearfull of the small pox, or I should have been in before this time. I got Mr. Crane to go to our House and see what state it was in. I find it has been occupied by one of the Doctors of a Regiment, very dirty, but no other damage has been done to it. The few things which were left in it are all gone. Cranch has the key which he never delivered up. I have wrote to him for it and am determined to get it cleand as soon as possible and shut it up. I look upon it a new acquisition of property, a property which one month ago I did not value at a single Shilling, and could with pleasure have seen it in flames.

The Town in General is left in a better state than we expected, more oweing to a percipitate flight than any Regard to the inhabitants, tho some individuals discovered a sense of honour and justice and have left the rent of the Houses in which they were, for the owners and the furniture unhurt, or if damaged sufficient to make it good.

Others have committed abominable Ravages. The Mansion House of your President is safe and the furniture unhurt whilst both the House and Furniture of the Solisiter General have fallen a prey to their own merciless party. Surely the very Fiends feel a Reverential awe for Virtue and patriotism, whilst they Detest the paricide and traitor.

L. H. Butterfield, ed., *Adams Family Correspondence* (Cambridge: Massachusetts Historical Society, 1963), I, pp. 369–70, 381–83. Reprinted by permission of the publisher.

I feel very differently at the approach of spring to what I did a month ago. We knew not then whether we could plant or sow with safety, whether when we had toild we could reap the fruits of our own industery, whether we could rest in our own Cottages, or whether we should not be driven from the sea coasts to seek shelter in the wilderness, but now we feel as if we might sit under our own vine and eat the good of the land.

I feel a gaieti de Coar to which before I was a stranger. I think the Sun looks brighter, the Birds sing more melodiously, and Nature puts on a more chearfull countanance. We feel a temporary peace, and the poor fugitives are returning to their deserted habitations.

Tho we felicitate ourselves, we sympathize with those who are trembling least the Lot of Boston should be theirs. But they cannot be in similar circumstances unless pusilanimity and cowardise should take possession of them. They have time and warning given them to see the Evil and shun it.—I long to hear that you have declared an independancy—and by the way in the new Code of Laws which I suppose it will be necessary for you to make I desire you would Remember the Ladies, and be more generous and favourable to them than your ancestors. Do not put such unlimited power into the hands of the Husbands. Remember all Men would be tyrants if they could. If perticuliar care and attention is not paid to the Laidies we are determined to foment a Rebelion, and will not hold ourselves bound by any Laws in which we have no voice, or Representation.

That your Sex are Naturally Tyrannical is a Truth so thoroughly established as to admit of no dispute, but such of you as wish to be happy willingly give up the harsh title of Master for the more tender and endearing one of Friend. Why then, not put it out of the power of the vicious and the Lawless to use us with cruelty and indignity with impunity. Men of Sense in all Ages abhor those customs which treat us only as the vassals of your Sex. Regard us then as Beings placed by providence under your protection and in immitation of the Supreem Being make use of that power only for our happiness.

John Adams to Abigail

April 14, 1776

You justly complain of my short Letters, but the critical State of Things and the Multiplicity of Avocations must plead my Excuse.—You ask where the Fleet is. The inclosed Papers will inform you. You ask what Sort of Defence Virginia can make. I believe they will make an able Defence. Their Militia and minute Men have been some time employed in training them selves, and they have Nine Battallions of regulars as they call them, maintained among them, under good Officers, at the Continental Expence. They have set up a Number of Manufactories of Fire Arms, which are busily employed. They are tolerably supplied with Powder, and are successfull and assiduous, in making Salt Petre. Their neighbouring Sister or rather Daughter Colony of North Carolina, which is a warlike Colony, and has several Battallions at the Continental Expence, as well as a pretty good Militia, are ready to assist them, and they are in very good Spirits, and seem determined to make a brave Resistance.—The Gentry are very rich, and the common People very poor. This Inequality of Property, gives an Aristocratical Turn to all their Proceedings and occasions a strong Aversion in their Patricians, to Common Sense. But the Spirit of these Barons, is coming down, and it must submit.

It is very true, as you observe they have been duped by Dunmore. But this is a Common Case. All the Colonies are duped, more or less, at one Time and another. A more egregious Bubble was never blown up, than the Story of Commissioners coming to treat with the Congress. Yet it has gained Credit like a Charm, not only without but against the clearest Evidence. I never shall forget the Delusion, which seized our best and most sagacious Friends the dear Inhabitants of Boston, the Winter before last. Credulity and the Want of Foresight, are Imperfections in the human Character, that no Politician can sufficiently guard against.

You have given me some Pleasure, by your Account of a certain House in Queen Street. I had burned it, long ago, in Imagination. It rises now to my View like a Phoenix.—What shall I say of the Solicitor General? I pity his pretty Children, I pity his Father, and his sisters. I wish I could be clear that it is no moral Evil to pity him and his Lady. Upon Repentance they will certainly have a large Share in the Compassions of many. But let Us take Warning and give it to our Children. Whenever Vanity, and Gaiety, a Love of Pomp and Dress, Furniture, Equipage, Buildings, great Company, expensive Diversions, and elegant Entertainments get the better of the Principles and Judgments of Men or Women there is no knowing where they will stop, nor into what Evils, natural, moral, or political, they will lead us.

Your Description of your own Gaiety de Coeur, charms me. Thanks be to God you have just Cause to rejoice—and may the bright Prospect be obscured by no Cloud.

As to Declarations of Independency, be patient. Read our Privateering Laws, and our Commercial Laws. What signifies a Word.

As to your extraordinary Code of Laws, I cannot but laugh. We have been told that our Struggle has loosened the bands of Government every where. That Children and Apprentices were disobedient—that schools and Colledges were grown turbulent—that Indians slighted their Guardians and Negroes grew insolent to their Masters. But your Letter was the first Intimation that another Tribe more numerous and powerfull than all the rest were grown discontented.—This is rather too coarse a Compliment but you are so saucy, I wont blot it out.

Depend upon it, We know better than to repeal our Masculine systems. Altho they are in full Force, you know they are little more than Theory. We dare not exert our Power in its full Latitude. We are obliged to go fair, and softly, and in Practice you know We are the subjects. We have only the Name of Masters, and rather than give up this, which would compleatly subject Us to the Despotism of the Petticoat, I hope General Washington, and all our brave Heroes would fight. I am sure every good Politician would plot, as long as he would against Despotism, Empire, Monarchy, Aristocracy, Oligarchy, or Ochlocracy.—A fine Story indeed. I begin to think the Ministry as deep as they are wicked. After stirring up Tories, Landjobbers, Trimmers, Bigots, Canadians, Indians, Negroes, Hanoverians, Hessians, Russians, Irish Roman Catholicks, Scotch Renegadoes, at last they have stimulated the [women] to demand new Priviledges and threaten to rebell.

The Marriages of Negro Dick, a Slave

S lave families lived under conditions and within constraints faced by no one else. (See p. 314 for nineteenth-century documents concerning the slave family.) Unlike indentured servants, who were forbidden to marry, slaves were often allowed and indeed sometimes even encouraged to marry. But slave marriages had no standing in law; they took place at the master's sufferance and were constantly subject to disruption by the sale or transfer of one or both of the partners. Few things have been more hidden from history than the slave family. Only in the last decade have historians begun to uncover it and to argue that any adequate understanding of the Afro-American experience under slavery has to build upon knowledge of the slave family. Materials for the seventeenth and eighteenth centuries are especially sparse (and of a scattered demographic kind that does not lend itself easily to inclusion in a volume of this kind). The selection here needs to be approached somewhat warily. It is the story an old man (who obviously relished the role of raconteur), looking back over nearly half a century, told to an English traveler who was at once captivated and shocked by what he heard. Still, the document does suggest something of the fragility and variety of marriage under slavery, as well as something of the mores of eighteenth-century society.

THE STORY OF DICK THE NEGRO

I was born at a plantation on the Rappahanoc river. It was the pulling of corn time, when 'squire Musgrove was governor of Virgina. I have no mixed blood in my veins. I am no half and half breed: no chestnut sorrel of a mulatto; but my father and mother both came over from Guinea.

When I was old enough to work, I was put to look after the horses. 'Squire Sutherland had a son who rode every fall to look at a plantation on James river, which was under the care of an overseer. Young master could not go without somebody on another horse to carry his saddle bags, and I was made his groom.

John Davis, *Personal Adventures* (London, 1817), pp. 89–92.

This young chap, Sir (here Dick winked his left eye), was a trimmer. The first thing he did on getting out of bed was to call for a julep; and I honestly date my own love of whiskey from mixing and tasting my young master's juleps. But this was not all. He was always upon the scent after game, and mighty ficious when he got among the negur wenches. He used to say, that a likely negur wench was fit to be a queen; and I forget how many queens he had among the girls on the two plantations.

The young 'squire did not live long. He was for a short life and a merry one. He was killed by a drunken negur man, who found him over ficious with his wife. The negur man was hanged alive upon a gibbet. It was the middle of summer, the sun was full upon him, the negur lolled out his tongue, his eyes seemed starting from their sockets, and for three long days his only cry was water! water! water!

The old gentleman took on to grieve mightily at the death of his son; he wished that he had sent him to Britain for his education, but after-wit is of no use; and he followed his son to that place where master and man, planter and slave, must all at last lie down together.

The plantation and negurs now fell to the lot of a second son, who had gone to Edinburgh to learn the trade of a doctor. He was not like 'squire Tommy, he seemed to be carved out of different wood. The first thing he did on his return from Britain, was to free all the old negur people on the plantation, and settle each on a patch of land. He tended the sick himself, gave them medicine, healed their wounds, and encouraged every man, woman, and child to go to a meetinghouse, that every Sunday was opened between our plantation and Fredericksburgh. Every thing took a change. The young wenches, who, in master Tommy's time, used to put on their drops, and their bracelets, and ogle their eyes, now looked down like modest young women, and carried their gewgaws in their pockets till they got clear out of the woods. He encouraged matrimony on the plantation, by settling each couple in a log-house, on a wholesome patch of land; hired a schoolmaster to teach the children, and to every one that could say his letters, gave a Testament with cuts. This made me bold to marry, and I looked out sharp for a wife. I had before quenched my thirst at any dirty puddle; but a stream that I was to drink at constant I thought should be pure,—and I made my court to a wholesome girl, who had never bored her ears, and went constantly to meeting.

She was daughter to old Solomon the carter, and by moonlight I used to play my banger under her window, and sing a Guinea love-song that my mother had taught me. But I found that there was another besides myself whose mouth watered after the fruit. Cuffey, one of the crop hands, came one night upon the same errand. I am but a little man, and Cuffey was above my pitch; for he was six foot two inches high, with a chew of tobacco clapped above that. But I was not to be scared because he was a big man, and I was a little one, I carried a good heart, and a good heart is every thing in love.

Cuffey, says I, what part of the play is you acting? Does you come after

Sal? May be, says he, I does. Then, says I, here's have at you, boy; and I reckoned to fix him by getting the finger of one hand into his ear, and the knuckles of the other into his eye. But the whore-son was too strong for me, and after knocking me down upon the grass, he began to stamp upon me, and ax me if I had yet got enough. But Dick was not to be scared; and getting his great toe into my mouth, I bit it off and swallowed it. Cuffey now let go his hold, and it was my turn to ax Cuffey if he had got enough. Cuffey told me he had, and I walked away to the quarter.

My master the next day heard of my battle with Cuffey. He said that I ought to live among painters and wolves, and sold me to a Georgia man for two hundred dollars. My new master was the devil. He made me travel with him hand-cuffed to Savannah; where he disposed of me to a tavern-keeper for three hundred dollars.

I was the only man-servant in the tavern, and I did the work of half a dozen. I went to bed at midnight, and was up an hour before sun. I looked after the horses, waited at table, and worked like a new negur. But I got plenty of spirits, and that I believed helped me.

The war now broke out, and in one single year I changed masters a dozen times. But I knowed I had to work, and one master to me was just as good as another. When the war ended, I was slave to 'squire Fielding, at Annapolis, in Maryland. I was grown quite steady, and I married a house-servant, who brought me a child every year. I have altogether had three wives, and am the father of twelve children; begot in lawful wedlock, but this you shall hear.

My wife dying of a flux, I was left to the management of my children; but my master soon saved me that trouble, for directly they were strong enough to handle a hoe, he sold the boys to Mr. Randolph at Fairfax, and the girls to 'squire Barclay of Port Tobacco. It was a hard trial to part with my little ones, for I loved them like a father; but there was no help for it, and it was the case of thousands besides myself.

When a man has been used to a wife, he finds it mighty lonesome to be without one; so I married a young girl who lived house-servant to a tavern-keeper at Elk Ridge landing. It is a good twenty-five miles from Annapolis to the landing place; but a negur never tire when he go to see his sweetheart, and after work on Saturday night, I would start for Elk Ridge, and get to my wife before the supper was put away.

I was not perfectly satisfied with my new wife; I had some suspection that she gave her company, when I was away, to a young mulatto fellow. If her children had not been right black and ugly like myself, I should have suspected her vartue long before I had a real cause. It troubled me to be tricked by a young girl, but I stripped her of all her clothing. Fine feathers make fine birds; and I laughed to think how she would look the next Sunday.

I now said to myself that it was right foolish for an old man to expect constancy from a young girl, and I wished that my first wife had not got her mouth full of yellow clay.

Memorials to a Marriage

This selection consists of the epitaphs for a husband and wife from the Virginia gentry of the eighteenth century. Epitaphs, of course, are intended to provide a tangible memorial of and to the dead. In this sense, much like formal portraits, they often provide an idealized picture of their subject, one expressing and accentuating what those left behind considered most essential and best about the character and life of the departed. They thus often embody the ideals of personal and family life, indicating the qualities associated with the good husband and father or the good wife and mother. Sometimes an epitaph also shows the relative place of those qualities amid others that are also singled out in celebration of an exemplary life.

JUDITH AND MANN PAGE

Sacrae et Piæ memoriæ
Hoc monumentum positum doloris
ab Honorato Mann Page Armigero
charissimæ suæ conjugis
Judithæ
In ipso aetatis flore Decussae
Ornatissimi Ralphi Wormeley
de Argo Middlesessiæ
Armigeri
Nec non Virginiani secretarii quondam Meritissimi
Filiæ dignissimæ
Lectissimæ dilectissimæque fœminæ
Quae vixit in Sanctissimo Matrimonio
quatuor annos totidemque menses
Utriusque Sexus unum Superstitem
reliquit

Epitaphs of Gloucester and Mathews Counties in Tidewater Virginia Through 1865 (Richmond, 1959), pp. 55–56.

Ralphum et Mariam
vera Patris simul et Matris ectypa
Habuitque tertium Mann Nominatum
vix quinque dies videntem
Sub hoc Silenti Marmore Matre sua inclusum
Post cujus partum tertiodie
Mortalitatem pro Immortalitate
commutavit
Proh dolor!
Inter uxores amantissima
Inter Matres fuit optima
Candida Domina
Cui Summa comitas
cum venustissima suavitate morum et sermonum
Conjuncta
Obiit duodecimo die Decembris
Anno Millesimo Septingentesimo decimo Sexto
Aetatis Suæ vicesimo Secundo

TRANSLATION: *To the sacred and most pious memory of his most beloved wife, Judith, cut down in the very flower of her age, this monument of grief was erected by the Honourable Mann Page Esquire. She was a most worthy daughter of the very illustrious Ralph Wormeley of County Middlesex, Esquire, formerly also a most deserving Secretary of Virginia. She was a most excellent and choice lady who lived in the state of most holy matrimony for four years and as many months. She left one survivor of each sex, Ralph and Maria, true likenesses together of Father and Mother. She also had a third named Mann, who, scarcely five days surviving, under this silent marble was enclosed with his Mother. On the third day after his birth she exchanged mortality for immortality. Alas, grief! She was a most affectionate wife, the best of Mothers, and an upright mistress of her family, in whom the utmost gentleness was united with the most graceful suavity of manners and conversation. She died on the 12th day of December in the year one thousand seven hundred and sixteen and the twenty-second of her age.*

Here lie the remains of the Honourable Mann Page Esq[r].

One of his Majesties Council of this Collony
of Virginia
who departed this Life the 24th Day of January 1730
in the 40th Year of his Age.

He was the only Son of the Honourable Mathew Page Esq[r]
who was likewise a member of his Majestys Council.

His first wife was Judith Daughter of Ralph Wormley Esq[r]
Secretary of Virginia;
By whom he had two sons and a Daughter.

He afterwards married Judith Daughter of the Hon[ble]
Robert Carter Esq[r]
President of Virginia
with whom he lived in the most tender reciprocal affection

For twelve Years
Leaving by her Five Sons and a Daughter

His publick Trust he faithfully Discharged
with
Candour and Discretion
Truth and Justice.

Nor was he less eminent in his Private Behavior
for he was
A tender Husband and Indulgent Father
A gentle Master and a faithful Friend
Being to All
Courteous and Benevolent Kind and Affable

This Monument was Piously Erected to His Memory
By His mournfully Surviving Lady.

PARENTS AND CHILDREN: CHILDREN AND PARENTS

The Birth and Death of Children—and Mothers

In the seventeenth and eighteenth centuries, the impending birth of a child was not a cause of unmitigated joy. More women between twenty and forty died in childbirth than for all other reasons combined. And in the colonies as a whole, probably not many more than two thirds of the children born survived their first year. These selections reflect how deeply this threat of mother and infant death cut into colonial consciousness and suggest how some colonists tried to cope with the fact and fear of it. The first selection is a poem Anne Bradstreet addressed to her husband in anticipation of childbirth; the second a poem for her son upon the death of his wife in childbirth. The third contains the sentiments Michael Wigglesworth confided to his diary when his wife lay in labor and while their infant child struggled to survive.

BEFORE THE BIRTH OF ONE OF HER CHILDREN

All things within this fading world hath end,
Adversity doth still our joys attend;
No ties so strong, no friends so dear and sweet,
But with death's parting blow is sure to meet.
The sentence past is most irrevocable,
A common thing, yet oh, inevitable.
How soon my Dear, death may my steps attend,
How soon't may be thy lot to lose thy friend,
We both are ignorant, yet love bids me
These farewell lines to recommend to thee,
That when that knot's untied that made us one,
I may seem thine, who in effect am none.
And if I see not half my days that's due,
What nature would, God grant to yours and you;
The many faults that well you know I have
Let be interred in my oblivious grave;

John W. Ellis, ed., *Works of Anne Bradstreet in Prose and Verse* (Boston, 1867), p. 393.

If any worth or virtue were in me,
Let that live freshly in thy memory
And when thou feel'st no grief, as I no harms,
Yet love thy dead, who long lay in thine arms.
And when thy loss shall be repaid with gains,
Look to my little babes, my dear remains.
And if thou love thyself, or loved'st me,
These O protect from step-dame's injury.
And if chance to thine eyes shall bring this verse,
With some sad sighs honour my absent hearse;
And kiss this paper for thy love's dear sake,
Who with salt tears this last farewell did take.

TO THE MEMORY OF MY DEAR DAUGHTER-IN-LAW, MRS. MERCY BRADSTREET, WHO DECEASED SEPT. 6, 1669, IN THE 28 YEAR OF HER AGE

And live I still to see relations gone,
And yet survive to sound this wailing tone;
Ah, woe is me, to write thy funeral song,
Who might in reason yet have lived long,
I saw the branches lopped the tree now fall,
I stood so nigh, it crushed me down withal.
My bruised heart lies sobbing at the root,
That thou, dear son, hath lost both tree and fruit.
Thou, then on seas sailing to foreign coast,
Was ignorant what riches thou hadst lost.
But ah, too soon those heavy tidings fly,
To strike thee with amazing misery;
Oh, how I sympathize with thy sad heart,
And in thy griefs still bear a second part;
I lost a daughter dear, but thou a wife,
Who loved thee more (it seemed) than her own life.
Thou being gone, she longer could not be,
Because her soul she'd sent along with thee.
One week she only passed in pain and woe,
And then her sorrows all at once did go;
A babe she left before she soared above,
The fifth and last pledge of her dying love,
Ere nature would, it hither did arrive,
No wonder it no longer did survive.
So with her children four, she's now at rest,
All freed from grief (I trust) among the blest;

Ellis, op. cit., pp. 407–8.

She one hath left, a joy to thee and me,
The heavens vouchsafe she may so ever be.
Cheer up, dear son, thy fainting bleeding heart,
In Him alone that caused all this smart;
What though thy strokes full sad and grievous be,
He knows it is the best for thee and me.

THE DIARY OF MICHAEL WIGGLESWORTH

May 16, 1656

February 20 toward night being wednesday my wife began to travail, and had sore paines. The nearnes of my bed to hers made me hear all the nois. her pangs pained my heart, broke my sleep the most off that night, I lay sighing, sweating, praying, almost fainting through wearines before morning. The next day. the spleen much enfeebled me, and setting in with grief took away my strength, my heart was smitten within me, and as sleep departed from myne eyes so my stomack abhorred meat. I was brought very low and knew not how to pass away another night; For so long as my love lay crying I lay sweating, and groaning. I was now apt to be hasty and impatient, but the Lord made me desirous to stoop to his wil (if he should take away her whom he had given, much more) if he should onely prolong her pains (himself supporting) and in time restore her. Being brought to this the Lord gaue some support to my heart. After about midnight he sent me the glad tidings of a daughter that and the mother both living; after she had been in paines about 30 houres or more. oh Let the Lord be magnifyd who heareth the poor chatterings of his prisoners; who wil lay no more than he enableth to bear. 2 Lessons the Lord hath taught me by this. 1. If the evil of sorrow be so great how evil then in [is?] sin the caus off it. 2. If the dolours of child-bearing be so bitter (which may be onely a fatherly chastizement) then how dreadful are the pangs of eternal death.

After our child was about a Fourtnight old it was much afflicted with a sore mouth, which continued near 3 weeks, accompanyd with griping and loosnes and sore hips.

shee had in this time 2 pittiful nights, especially the one of them. At that time 2 things I desir'd of the Lord. 1. A heart to subject my wisdom and wil to his touching the childs life or Extremity. he knows what is best, and is as tenderly affected as I, and much more. 2. That I may maintain good thoughts of god while he afflicts amare deum castigantem I haue giuen up my daughter to him with all my heart desiring she may be his, rejoycing he hath giuen me a child to giue up to him. And shall he not

"The Diary of Michael Wigglesworth, 1653–1657," Edmund S. Morgan, ed., *Transactions, 1942–1946*, XXXV (Colonial Society of Massachusetts), pp. 415–16. Reprinted by permission of Colonial Society of Massachusetts.

do with his own as he will, either to afflict it or take it to himself. His glory is better than the eas of the creature, and yet his glory shall be coincident with our good.

After this the Lord mercifully recovered it, and it is now grown and come to a quarter old. Friday May 16.

The Well-Ordered Family, or, Relative Duties

Just as the colonials had a clear vision of the ideal marriage, so they also possessed a clear ideal of the well-ordered family, of the relations, duties, and decorum between parents and children that would provide the order and harmony they cherished in family life. The first document, taken from an eighteenth-century version of the etiquette book, sets out the decorum that governed the bearing of "good" children toward their parents. The second selection is again taken from Benjamin Wadsworth's guidebook on family relations. Though clearly a Puritan and New England source, the selection nonetheless presents an ideal of the well-ordered family that was probably the standard one for the Anglo-American world of the seventeenth and eighteenth centuries. What values seem to govern the ideal of family order? What are the things that to Wadsworth make up the well-ordered family, and what does he single out as threats to it?

THE SCHOOL OF GOOD MANNERS

Twenty Mixt Precepts

1. Fear God and believe in Christ.
2. Honour the King.
3. Reverence thy Parents.
4. Submit to thy Superiors.
5. Despise not thy Inferiors.
6. Be Courteous with thy Equals.
7. Pray Daily and Devoutly.
8. Converse with the Good.
9. Imitate not the Wicked.
10. Hearken diligently to Instruction.
11. Be ever desirous of Learning.
12. Love the School.
13. Be always Neat and Cleanly.
14. Study Virtue and Embrace it.

The School of Good Manners (Boston, 1768), pp. 3–5.

15. Provoke no Body.
16. Love thy School Fellows.
17. Please thy Master.
18. Let not Play entice thee.
19. Refrain thy Tongue.
20. Covet future Honour, which only Virtue and Wisdom can procure.

Of Children's Behaviour when at Home

1. Make a Bow always when you come Home, and be immediately uncovered.
2. Be never covered at Home, especially before thy Parents or Strangers.
3. Never Sit in the Presence of thy Parents without bidding, tho' no Stranger be present.
4. If thou passest by thy Parents, at any Place where thou seest them, when either by themselves or with Company, Bow towards them.
5. If thou art going to speak to thy Parents, and see them engaged in discourse with Company, draw back and leave thy piece until afterwards; but if thou must speak, be sure to whisper.
6. Never speak to thy Parents without some Title of Respect, *viz.* Sir, Madam, &c. according to their Quality.
7. Approach near thy Parents at no time without a Bow.
8. Dispute not, nor delay to Obey thy Parents Commands.
9. Go not out of Doors without thy Parents leave, and return within the Time by them limited.
10. Come not into the Room where thy Parents are with Strangers, unless thou art called, and then decently; and at bidding go out; or if Strangers come in while thou art with them it is Manners, with a Bow, to withdraw.
11. Use respectful and courteous, but not insulting or domineering Carriage or Language towards the Servants.
12. Quarrel not nor contend with thy Brethren or sisters, but live in love, peace & unity.
13. Grumble not nor be discontented at any thing thy Parents appoint, speak or do.
14. Bear with Meekness and Patience, and without Murmuring or Sullenness thy Parents Reproofs or Corrections: Nay, tho' it should so happen that they be causeless or undeserved.

THE DUTIES OF CHILDREN TO THEIR PARENTS

Children should love their parents. Parents and Children should love mutually, love one another; if they don't, they're without *natural affection,* which is

Benjamin Wadsworth, *The Well-Ordered Family, or, Relative Duties* (Boston, 1712), pp. 90–102.

mention'd among the worst crimes of Heathens. . . . If Children dulely consider, they'll find they have abundant cause to *love* their Parents, they are very base and vile if they neglect it. Unless they *love* their parents, they can't do other duties which they owe to them, as they should.

Children should fear their Parents. God requires that *every person* should *fear* his Parents, not only his *Father,* but also his *Mother.* Yes, the *Mother* is here mention'd first possibly because Persons are more apt to disregard their *Mothers,* tho they stand in some aue of their *Fathers.* But the great God of Heaven bids *Children fear their Parents,* if therefore they fear them not, they rebel against God.

Children should Reverence and Honour their Parents. . . . This is one of those commands which the great God uttered immediately with his own Mouth. . . . It becomes Children of what *Age, Sex, Quality* or *Dignity* so ever to show respect and reverence to their Parents, both in *Words* and *Gestures.* And wo unto them that despise, contemn or abuse their Parents. *He that smiteth Father or Mother shall surely be put to Death,* Exod. 21.15 Twas not death, a capital crime, nearly to smite another person; but God's law made it a capital crime, for any to smite Father or Mother. *So, Lev. 20.9. He that curseth Father or Mother shall surely be put to death. Prov. 20.17. The eye that mocketh at his Father, or despiseth to obey his Mother; the Ravens of the valley shall pick it out, and the young Eagles shall eat it.* That is, such an one shall come to shamefull and untimely Death; die so shamefully, as that the birds of prey should feast up on him. Children therefore should take heed that they dont dare to *Mock* at Parents or despise to obey them. . . . Persons are often more apt to *despise a Mother* (the weaker vessel, and frequently most indulgent) than *Father;* yet if any man does despise his Mother, God calls him a *fool* for it; God counts him, and will treat him, as a vile, scandalous wicked Person. If Parents are grown *Old, Crazy, Infirm, Sickly;* able to do little or no business but need much tendance; if they're weak or shatter'd in the abilities of their minds; nay if they're chargeable with evident sinful failings & infirmities; yet Children should *not despise* them, but *honor* them still. Tho Children should hate their sins; yet they should honor & love their Persons. Noah's Drunkenness was a great Sin in him, yet twas base for his *Son* to *Mock* or *Jear* at him (as Ham probably did) and twas commendable in Shem and Japhet to cover and hide as far as lawfully they could, what might expose their Father to further shame or contempt. . . .

Children should give diligent heed, to the wholesome instructions and Counsels of their Parents. . . .

Children should patiently wear, and grow better by, the needful chastisements and Corrections their Parents give them. . . .

Children should be faithful and obedient to their Parents. They should be faithful to their interest, and not wrong them in their Estates. It may be some Children are apt to think, that what's their Fathers is theirs; and so will make bold to take almost what they please of their Fathers Estates, without their Fathers leave; and will spend, give or game away the same as they list. . . . And as Children should be *faithful* to their Parents interest, so they should *obey their commands*. That is, in all *Lawful* things; for if Parents bid their Children *Lie, Steal, Swear Falsely*, or do any thing that's Sinful, they ought not to obey them therein. God is our supream Lawgiver and Judge, therefore if any should bid us act contrary to his Laws, we ought not to obey them therein. We must never displease Christ, to please any Person whatsoever. But Children should obey their Parents, in all lawful things. Children, if you find your hearts ready to rise and rebel against your Parents; then read these plain commands of God now mentioned, wherein your Maker requires you to obey your Parents. In this case (as well as in a thousand more) endeavor to impress an awful sense of God's Authority on your Consciences. When you disobey the lawful commands of Parents, you disobey God himself. . . . Oh Children, consider these things, they are not light or small matters; lay them seriously to heart. It may be your Parents bid you go to work, bid you do these or those things; but you wont, you disregard what they say. It may be you idle away your time, you'l be abroad very late on Nights, very unseasonably; you'll get into ill Company, frequent Taverns, take to Gaming and other ill practices, and all this quite contrary to the plain commands of your Parents. Is it so? If it is, then you disobey and rebel against God himself. Tis no small evil you're guilty of; you greatly provoke the Holy God, you're in the way to ruine. When children are stubborn and disobedient to Parents, they're under awful symptoms of terrible ruine. When Children are disobedient to Parents, God is often provoke'd to leave them to those Sins, which bring them to great shame and misery in this World, as weall as to endless Plagues in the other. . . . Alas, Children, if you once become disobedient to Parents, you dont know what vile abominations God may leave you to fall into. When Persons have been brought to die at the Gallows for their crimes, how often have they confess'd that *Disobedience to Parents* led them to those crimes? As for my own part, except what's openly irreligious and profane, scarce anything is more grating and roiling to me, than to see Children rude, sawcy, unmannerly, and disobedient to their Parents. . . .

Children should be very willing and ready to support and Maintain their Indigent Parents. If our Parents are Poor, Aged, Weak, Sickly, and not able to maintain themselves; we are bound in duty and conscience to do what we can, to provide for them, nourish, support, and comfort them. . . . Indeed, Children should not be coveteous & Niggardly in supplying their Parents; but (if able) they should readily afford what may suffice, be enough and sufficient for them. For if they dont requite and relieve their Parents; they are *not Pious*, they neglect what's *Good & acceptable to God*. In a word, it's vile and abominable in Children, to suffer their helpless Parents to want what's for their necessity and comfort, if they are able to supply them. What care did our Parents take of us when we were little things, when we could not *do* and *speak* for ourselves? How often and how long a time, did they *feed* & *clothe* us? And they did it gladly and cheerfully. How tender were they of us, in our Sickness & Wants; how ready to do all they could for our welfare. Surely we can't sufficiently requite them; we should think nothing too much that we can do, for their real comfort. We dont deserve food for ourselves, if we are not willing to grant part of it to our Parents, if they need it. Let us consider what has been offer'd, from the plain word and law of God; and be quickened hereby to do our duty to our Parents, as long as they and we shall be continued in the World.

Child Nurture

C hildren are more than simply the biological offspring of parents; they also embody the culture of the families they are born into or into which they are placed. In the past, as now, parental responsibility was not confined to providing the physical care and protection needed for survival and growth. (The human young are the only mammals that require such an extensive period of physical care and protection.) Parents were also expected to endow their children with the habits and beliefs—less "personality" than "character," to use a favorite term of the nineteenth century—that society (or at least its official spokesmen) wanted its citizens to possess. In the seventeenth century no less than in the twentieth, commentators often traced the worrisome and criminal behavior of individuals, as well as social disorder in general, to the alleged failures of the family to produce the right kind of habits and beliefs in its young. The public sermons of colonial divines—particularly the Jeremiads that implored the entire society to reform its sinful ways—invariably contained dire warnings about the evil consequences of the decline of family order. Almost three centuries later, more than one analyst of the 1960s traced the rebelliousness of youth and the apparent hedonism of the youth culture to a generation nurtured according to the seemingly permissive precepts of John Dewey and Dr. Benjamin Spock. The practices, ideals, methods, and worries about child nurture thus furnish a perspective not only on the family itself but also on the junction between family forms and functions and the society and culture of which the family is a part.

The broadest responsibilities of parenthood—and concern about whether they are being met adequately—have remained much the same over the past four centuries. How people have construed the goals and methods of child nurture—that is, the type of child to be produced—has been as subject as anything else to variations of time, place, and culture. Perhaps childhood itself, as some historians maintain, is the relatively recent invention of the sixteenth and seventeenth centuries. An array of evidence— the application to adults of terms which later were reserved for children, the lack of special places for children in the household and distinct institutions for their nurture, the absence of a notion of a psychology unique to children, children's dress, and how they were represented in paintings—argues that before about 1650 children after infancy were regarded and treated as miniature adults rather than as a special category of being, to be isolated from the adult world and nurtured in a special way. However children are viewed—as, for example, sinful creatures, full of unredeemed traits and appetites, who have to be controlled if not remolded, or as pure and uncorrupted beings who have to be protected and nurtured in their innocence—can influence how the goals and methods of child-rearing are defined and how responsibility for molding the character of children is apportioned between mother and father. In addition, ideas of the child and childhood are often fraught with implications for how the family itself and its functions are construed and for how the boundaries between the family and the world outside it are defined.

The documents that follow all address the methods and goals of child-rearing in seventeenth- and eighteenth-century America. The first is the poem adumbrating her life as a mother that Anne Bradstreet wrote as a preface to a set of meditations bequeathed to her children. The next document describes how Cotton Mather (1663–1728), for forty years New England's most noted, influential, and prolific minister, went about bringing up his children. This is followed by some advice about child nurture offered by the Reverend John Witherspoon (1723–1794), a Scottish Presbyterian who came to the colonies in 1768 as president of Princeton College. Though a pious Calvinist in religion, Witherspoon was a staunch Whig in politics who, drawing upon the precepts of Locke and others, vigorously supported the American Revolution. The next selection contains the account John Heckewelder (1743–1823), son of a Moravian minister and himself a missionary to the Indians of Ohio and Pennsylvania, gave of some Indian child-rearing practices. The last selection is a famous piece of mythmaking. It is taken from Parson Weems's renowned 1804 biography of George Washington. One of the earliest examples of the hagiography that so rapidly turned the leaders of the Revolution into godlike Founding Fathers, this selection addresses the role that in Weems's eyes family nurture played in creating the "Father of his Country." (See page 276 for a later version of the Washington myth, one which stresses the influence of his mother, Mary Washington.) In examining these documents it might be useful to ask how each defines the goals of child nurture and to whom are given various responsibilities for it. What idea of the child is implied by the goals and by the methods employed, described, or suggested? To what extent is child-rearing intended to create a particular kind of behavior or particular kind of person, and to what extent are the methods designed to change or enhance the child's given nature? To what extent do the goals of child nurture center on the child itself, and to what extent are they directed to needs other than those of the child?

IN REFERENCE TO HER CHILDREN, 23 JUNE, 1659

I had eight birds hatched in one nest,
Four cocks there were, and hens the rest.
I nursed them up with pain and care,
Nor cost, nor labour did I spare,
Till at the last they felt their wing,
Mounted the trees, and learned to sing;
Chief of the brood then took his flight
To regions far and left me quite.
My mournful chirps I after send,
Till he return, or I do end:
Leave not thy nest, thy dam and sire,
Fly back and sing amidst this choir.
My second bird did take her flight,
And with her mate flew out of sight;
Southward they both their course did bend,
And seasons twain they there did spend,
Till after blown by southern gales,
They norward steered with filled sails.
A prettier bird was no where seen,
Along the beach among the treen.
I have a third of colour white,
On whom I placed no small delight;
Coupled with mate loving and true,
Hath also bid her dam adieu;
And where Aurora first appears,
She now hath perched to spend her years.
One to the academy flew
To chat among that learned crew;
Ambition moves still in his breast
That he might chant above the rest,
Striving for more than to do well,
That nightingales he might excel.
My fifth, whose down is yet scarce gone,
Is 'mongst the shrubs and bushes flown,
And as his wings increase in strength,
On higher boughs he'll perch at length.
My other three still with me nest,
Until they're grown, then as the rest,
Or here or there they'll take their flight,
As is ordained, so shall they light.
If birds could weep, then would my tears

John W. Ellis, ed., *Works of Anne Bradstreet in Prose and Verse* (Boston, 1867), pp. 400–402.

Let others know what are my fears
Lest this my brood some harm should catch,
And be surprised for want of watch,
Whilst pecking corn and void of care,
They fall un'wares in fowler's snare,
Or whilst on trees they sit and sing,
Some untoward boy at them do fling,
Or whilst allured with bell and glass,
The net be spread, and caught, alas.
Or lest by lime-twigs they be foiled,
Or by some greedy hawks be spoiled.
O would my young, ye saw my breast,
And knew what thoughts there sadly rest,
Great was my pain when I you bred,
Great was my care when I you fed,
Long did I keep you soft and warm,
And with my wings kept off all harm,
My cares are more and fears than ever,
My throbs such now as 'fore were never.
Alas, my birds, you wisdom want,
Of perils you are ignorant;
Oft times in grass, on trees, in flight,
Sore accidents on you may light.
O to your safety have an eye,
So happy may you live and die.
Meanwhile my days in tunes I'll spend,
Till my weak lays with me shall end.
In shady woods I'll sit and sing,
And things that past to mind I'll bring.
Once young and pleasant, as are you,
But former toys (no joys) adieu.
My age I will not once lament,
But sing, my time so near is spent.
And from the top bough take my flight
Into a country beyond sight,
Where old ones instantly grow young,
And there with seraphims set song;
No seasons cold, nor storms they see;
But spring lasts to eternity.
When each of you shall in your nest
Among your young ones take your rest,
In chirping language, oft them tell,
You had a dam that loved you well,
That did what could be done for young,
And nursed you up till you were strong,
And 'fore she once would let you fly,

She showed you joy and misery;
Taught what was good, and what was ill,
What would save life, and what would kill.
Thus gone, amongst you I may live,
And dead, yet speak, and counsel give:
Farewell, my friends, farewell adieu,
I happy am, if well with you.

SOME SPECIAL POINTS, RELATING TO THE EDUCATION OF MY CHILDREN

I. I pour out continual Prayers and Cries to the God of all Grace for them, that He will be a Father to my Children, and bestow His Christ and His Grace upon them, and guide them with His Councils, and bring them to His Glory,

And in this Action, I mention them distinctly, every one by Name unto the Lord.

II. I begin betimes to entertain them with delightful Stories, especially *scriptural* ones. And still conclude with some *Lesson* of Piety; bidding them to learn that *Lesson* from the *Story*.

And thus, every Day at the *Table*, I have used myself to tell a *Story* before I rise; and make the *Story* useful to the *Olive Plants about the Table*.

III. When the Children at any time accidentally come in my way, it is my custome to lett fall some *Sentence* or other, that may be monitory and profitable to them.

This Matter proves to me, a Matter of some Study, and Labour, and Contrivance. But who can tell, what may be the Effect of a *continual Dropping?*

IV. I essay betimes, to engage the Children, in Exercises of Piety; and especially *secret Prayer*, for which I give them very plain and brief *Directions*, and suggest unto them the *Petitions*, which I would have them to make before the Lord, and which I therefore explain to their Apprehension and Capacity. And I often call upon them; *Child, Don't you forgett every Day, to go alone, and pray as I have directed you!*

V. Betimes I try to form in the Children a Temper of *Benignity*. I put them upon doing of Services and Kindnesses for one another, and for other Children. I applaud them, when I see them Delight in it. I upbraid all Aversion to it. I caution them exquisitely against all Revenges of Injuries. I instruct them, to return good Offices for evil Ones. I show them, how they will by this *Goodness* become like to the Good GOD, and His Glorious CHRIST. I lett them discern, that I am not satisfied, except when they have a Sweetness of Temper shining in them.

Worthington Chauncey Ford, ed., *Diary of Cotton Mather, 1681–1724*, Collections of the Massachusetts Historical Society, 7th Series, 2 vols. (Boston, 1911–12), vol 1, pp. 534–37. Reprinted by permission of Massachusetts Historical Society.

VI. As soon as tis possible, I make the Children learn to *write*. And when they can *write*, I employ them in Writing out the most agreeable and profitable Things, that I can invent for them. In this way, I propose to fraight their minds with *excellent Things,* and have a deep Impression made upon their Minds by such Things.

VII. I mightily endeavour it, that the Children may betimes, be acted by Principles of *Reason* and *Honour.*

I first begett in them an high Opinion of their Father's Love to them, and of his being best able to judge, what shall be good for them.

Then I make them sensible, tis a Folly for them to pretend unto any Witt and Will of their own; they must resign all to me, who will be sure to do what is best; my word must be their Law.

I cause them to understand, that it is an *hurtful* and a *shameful* thing to do amiss. I aggravate this, on all Occasions; and lett them see how *amiable* they will render themselves by well doing.

The *first Chastisement,* which I inflict for an ordinary Fault, is, to lett the Child see and hear me in an Astonishment, and hardly able to beleeve that the Child could do so *base* a Thing, but beleeving that they will never do it again.

I would never come, to give a child a *Blow;* except in Case of *Obstinacy;* or some gross Enormity.

To be chased for a while out of *my Presence,* I would make to be look'd upon, as the sorest Punishment in the Family.

I would by all possible Insinuations gain this Point upon them, that for them to learn all the brave Things in the world, is the bravest Thing in the world. I am not fond of proposing *Play* to them, as a Reward of any diligent Application to learn what is good; lest they should think *Diversion* to be a better and a nobler Thing than *Diligence.*

I would have them come to propound and expect, at this rate, *I have done well, and now I will go to my Father; He will teach me some curious Thing for it.* I must have them count it a *Priviledge,* to be taught; and I sometimes manage the Matter so, that my Refusing to teach them Something, is their *Punishment.*

The *slavish* way of *Education,* carried on with raving and kicking and scourging (in *Schools* as well as *Families,*) tis abominable; and a dreadful Judgment of God upon the World.

VIII. Tho' I find it a marvellous Advantage to have the Children strongly biased by Principles of *Reason and Honour* (which, I find, Children will feel sooner than is commonly thought for:) yett I would neglect no Endeavours, to have *higher Principles* infused into them.

I therefore betimes awe them with the *Eye* of God upon them.

I show them, how they must love JESUS CHRIST; and show it, by doing what their Parents require of them.

I often tell them of the *good Angels,* who love them, and help them, and guard them; and who take Notice of them: and therefore must not be disobliged.

Heaven and *Hell,* I sett before them, as the Consequences of their Behaviour here.

IX. When the Children are capable of it, I take them *alone,* one by one; and after my Charges unto them, to fear God, and serve Christ, and shun Sin, *I pray with them* in my Study and make them the Witnesses of the Agonies, with which I address the Throne of Grace on their behalf.

X. I find much Benefit, by a particular Method, as of *Catechising* the Children, so of carrying the *Repetition* of the public Sermons unto them.

The Answers of the *Catechism* I still explain with abundance of brief *Quaestions,* which make them to take in the Meaning of it, and I see, that they do so.

And when the Sermons are to be *Repeated,* I chuse to putt every *Trust,* into a *Quaestion,* to be answered still, with *Yes,* or, *No.* In this way I awaken their *Attention,* as well as enlighten their *Understanding.* And in this way I have an Opportunity, to ask, *Do you desire such, or such a Grace of God?* and the like. Yea, I have an Opportunity to demand, and perhaps, to obtain their *Consent* unto the glorious Articles of the *New Covenant.* The Spirit of Grace may fall upon them in this Action; and they may be siez'd by Him, and Held as His *Temples,* thro' eternal Ages.

LETTERS ON EDUCATION

. . . The next thing I shall mention as necessary, in order to the education of children, is, to establish as soon as possible an entire and absolute authority over them. This is a part of the subject which requires to be treated with great judgment and delicacy. I wish I may be able to do so. Opinions, like modes and fashions, change continually upon every point; neither is it easy to keep the just middle, without verging to one or other of the extremes. On this, in particular, we have gone in this nation in general, from one extreme, to the very utmost limits of the other. In the former age, both public and private, learned and religious education, was carried on by mere dint of authority. This, to be sure, was a savage and barbarous method, and was in many instances terrible and disgusting to the youth. Now, on the other hand, not only severity, but authority, is often decried; persuasion, and every soft and gentle method is recommended, on such terms as plainly lead to a relaxation. . . .

I have said above, that you should "establish, as soon as possible, an entire and absolute authority." I would have it early, that it may be absolute, and absolute, that it may not be severe. If parents are too long in beginning to exert their authority, they will find the task very difficult. Children, habituated to indulgence for a few of their first years, are exceedingly impatient of restraint; and if they happen to be of stiff or obstinate tempers, can

John Witherspoon, "Letters on Education," in Witherspoon, *Works* (Philadelphia, 1802), vol. IV, pp. 133–41.

hardly be brought to an entire, at least to a quiet and placid submission; whereas, if they are taken in time, there is hardly any temper but what may be made to yield, and by early habit the subjection becomes quite easy to themselves.

The authority ought also to be absolute, that it may not be severe. The more complete and uniform a parent's authority is, the offences will be more rare, punishment will be less needed, and the more gentle kind of correction will be abundantly sufficient. We see every where about us examples of this. A parent that has once obtained, and knows how to preserve authority, will do more by a look of displeasure, than another by the most passionate words, and even blows. It holds universally in families and schools, and even the greater bodies of men, the army and navy, that those who keep the strictest discipline give the fewest strokes. I have frequently remarked that parents, even of the softest tempers, and who are famed for the greatest indulgence to their children, do, notwithstanding, correct them more frequently, and even more severely, though to very little purpose, than those who keep up their authority. The reason is plain. Children, by foolish indulgence, become often so forward and petulant in their tempers that they provoke their easy parents past all endurance, so that they are obliged, if not to strike, at least to scold them, in a manner as little to their own credit as their childrens profit.

There is not a more digusting sight, than the impotent rage of a parent who has no authority. Among the lower ranks of people, who are under no restraint from decency, you may sometimes see a father or mother running out into the street after a child who is fled from them, with looks of fury and words of execration, and they are often stupid enough to imagine, that neighbors or passengers will approve them in this conduct, though in fact it fills every beholder with horror. There is a degree of the same fault to be seen in persons of better rank, though expressing itself somewhat differently. Ill words and altercations will often fall out between parents and children before company; a sure sign that there is defect of government at home or in private. The parent, stung with shame at the misbehaviour or indiscretion of the child, desires to persuade the observers that it is not his fault, and thereby effectually convinces every person of reflection that it *is*.

I would therefore recommend to every parent to begin the establishment of authority much more early than is commonly supposed to be possible: that is to say, from about the age of eight or nine months. You will perhaps smile at this; but I do assure you from experience, that by setting about

A "token" was usually a small book or even a single sheet broadside such as this and was often used as a gift for children. "Token" also meant something like augury or message. Children's presents were often moralistic and didactic until at least the middle of the nineteenth century. This broadside token comes from Boston, about 1731.

American Antiquarian Society

A
Token for Children.

That they may know to avoid the Evil,
and chuse the Good.

'MONGST all the Wonders I have read,
   There's none so wondrous great,
As is that Love of GOD to Man,
   The Gospel doth relate,
The Father, Son, and Holy Ghost,
   Together did combine,
To save th' Elect of Adam's Race,
   By Mysteries Devine.
Let us adore the God of Grace,
   Who when we were undone,
In Pity and paternal Love
   Most freely gave his Son.
Let us adore the Son of God;
   Our Saviour, let us prize;
Who freely gave himself, for us,
   To be a Sacrifice.
Adore the Holy Spirit too,
   That makes us to embrace
The Offers of a Saviour dear,
   And Tenders of his Grace.
By Sin we sold away our God,
   Our Souls, our Heav'n; and then,
It cost the Lord his Life and Blood,
   To buy them back again.
In th' Letter of his Testaments,
   Deep Mysteries are found;
To which his dear Embassadors
   Are sent, for to expound.
In ev'ry Sermon, we do hear,
   Soundeth from above;
Sent down from our ascended Lord,
   In Token of his Love.
'Tis with Heav'n's Voice our Pulpits ring,
   (Oh, let it not displease us!)
The Voice that minds us of our Need,
   And bids us come to JESUS.
Famished Soul! Dost thou want Bread,
   And fain wouldst it obtain?
To Jesus come, He'll give thee Bread,
   That shall thy Life sustain.
Dost thou want Drink, in parching Heat,
   Thee to refresh and chear?
Then look to Christ on high; he'll give
   Thee Living Waters here.
Dost thou want Cloathing? Go to Christ;
   He will choice Raiment bring;
He'll put the Wedding Garment on,
   Shall shine before the King.
Dost want an House to harbour in,
   T' shelter thee from Storms?
Christ is an Habitation sure;
   Will shield thee from all Harms.
Dost thou want Riches? Go to Christ;
   He'll make thee rich indeed:
Hast in thy Purse this Pearl of Price,
   'Twill answer all thy Need.
Dost thou want Honour? Go to Christ,
   He will Honour bring;
   He'll make thee, to be Son,
   To the King.

Dost thou want healing? Bring to Christ
   Thy Sickness and thy Sore;
And he will perfect healing give,
   And Life for evermore.
But if for want of Pleasures here,
   Thou sadly dost complain?
Get into Christ and then thou shalt
   Rivers of Pleasures gain.
Or dost thou heav'nly Wisdom lack?
   Of Christ be not afraid;
He Wisdom liberally gives;
   And he doth not upbraid.
And when thou know'st not what to do,
   To Christ, thy Friend betake thee;
And he has promis'd thee, he will
   Not fail thee, nor forsake thee:
Doth Guilt upon thee Horror bring,
   That thou canst not endure?
He'll give thee Pardon thro' his Blood,
   And thou may'st sleep secure.
Vex'd with Sins Filthiness art thou,
   Then let thy Saviour know;
He'll purge, and purify, and make
   Thee whiter then the Snow.
Art thou with Hardness sore oppress'd;
   And wouldest be releas'd,
Then come to Christ; He'll soften thee,
   And he will give thee Rest.
Art proud; then come and learn of Christ,
   And he will make thee lowly:
Doth Sin prevail, yet come to Christ,
   And he will make thee holy.
Wouldst have Affliction sanctify'd,
   When thou dost feel the Rod,
It is but going for't by Faith,
   Unto the Son of GOD.
Dost feel thou want'st the Feet of Faith,
   To Christ thou canst not go,
Bewail thy want; and cry to GOD,
   That Faith he may bestow.
Wait on him duly in his House,
   And daily in thine own;
Faith is His Gift; which he'll bestow,
   On ev'ry chosen One.
This oft proclaimed joyful Sound,
   Blessed are they that mind;
Blessed are they that seek Christ's Grace;
   For they shall Glory find.
Now Christ stands knocking at our Door,
   And fain would enter in:
We keep him out, while we prefer
   Th' World, Satan, Flesh and Sin.
If we neglect our Day of Grace,
   We may cry, knock, and call:
And Christ will say, Depart from me;
   I know you not at all.
Children! May these few Lines you move,
   Christ to embrace, while young;
You'll ne're repent that you have read,
   Or I have writ this Song.

BOSTON: Printed and Sold at the Heart and Crown in Cornhill. 1731.

it with prudence, deliberation, and attention, it may be in a manner completed by the age of twelve or fourteen months. Do not imagine I mean to bid you use the rod at that age; on the contrary, I mean to prevent the use of it in a great measure, and to point out a way by which children of sweet and easy tempers may be brought to such a habit of compliance, as never to need correction at all; and whatever their temper may be, so much less of this is sufficient than upon any other supposition. This is one of my favourite schemes; let me try to explain and recommend it.

Habits, in general, may be very early formed in children. An association of ideas is, as it were, the parent of habit. If, then, you can accustom your children to perceive, that your will must always prevail over theirs, when they are opposed, the thing is done, and they will submit to it without difficulty or regret. To bring this about, as soon as they begin to shew their inclination by desire or aversion, let single instances be chosen now and then (not too frequently) to contradict them. For example, if a child shews a desire to have any thing in his hand that he sees, or has any thing in his hand with which he is delighted, let the parent take it from him, and when he does so, let no consideration whatever make him restore it at that time. Then at a considerable interval, perhaps a whole day is little enough, especially at first, let the same thing be repeated. In the mean time, it must be carefully observed, that no attempt should be made to contradict the child in the intervals. Not the least appearance of opposition, if possible, should be found between the will of the parent and that of the child, except in those chosen cases when the parent must always prevail.

I think is necessary that those attempts should always be made and repeated at proper intervals by the same person. It is also better it should be by the father than the mother or any female attendant, because they will be necessarily obliged, in many cases, to do things displeasing to the child, as in dressing, washing, &c. which spoil the operation; neither is it necessary that they should interpose, for when once a full authority is established in one person, it can easily be communicated to others, as far as is proper. Remember, however, that mother or nurse should never presume to condole with the child, or shew any signs of displeasure at his being crossed; but, on the contrary, give every mark of approbation, and of their own submission to the same person. . . .

There is a great diversity in the temper and disposition of children, and no less in the penetration, prudence, and resolution of parents. From all these circumstances difficulties arise, which increase very fast as the work is delayed. Some children have naturally very stiff and obstinate tempers, and some have a certain pride, or if you please, greatness of mind, which makes them think it a mean thing to yield. This disposition is often greatly strengthened in those of high birth, by the ideas of their own dignity and importance, instilled into them from their mother's milk. I have known a boy not six years of age, who made it a point of honour not to cry when he was beat, even by his parents. Other children have so strong passions, or so great sensibility, that if they receive correction they will cry immoderately, and either be, or seem to be, affected to such a degree, as to endanger their health or life. Neither is it uncommon for the parents in such a case to give up the point, and if they do not ask pardon, at least they give very genuine marks of repentance and sorrow for what they have done.

I have said this is not uncommon; but I may rather ask you, whether you know any parents at all, who have so much prudence and firmness as not to be discouraged in the one case, or to relent in the other? At the same time it must always be remembered, that the correction is wholly lost which does not produce absolute submission. Perhaps I may say it is more than lost, because it will irritate instead of reforming them, and will instruct or perfect them in the art of overcoming their parents, which they will not fail to manifest on a future opportunity. It is surprising to think how early children will discover the weak side of their parents, and what ingenuity they will shew in obtaining their favour or avoiding their displeasure. I think I have observed a child in treaty or expostulation with a parent, discover more consummate policy at seven years of age, than the parent himself, even when attempting to cajole him with artful evasions and specious promises. On all these accounts, it must be a vast advantage that a habit of submission should be brought on so early, that even memory itself shall not be able to reach back to its beginning. Unless this is done, there are many cases in which, after the best management, the authority will be imperfect; and some in which any thing that deserves that name will be impossible. . . .

Let us now proceed to the best means of preserving authority, and the way in which it ought to be daily exercised. I will trace this to its very source. Whatever authority you exercise over either children or servants, or as a magistrate over other citizens, it ought to be dictated by conscience, and directed by a sense of duty. Passion or resentment ought to have as little place as possible; or rather, to speak properly, though few can boast of having arrived at full perfection, it ought to have no place at all. Reproof or correction given in a rage, is always considered by him to whom it is administered, as the effect of weakness in you; and therefore the demerit of the offence will be either wholly denied or soon forgotten. I have heard some parents often say, that they cannot correct their children unless they are angry; to whom I have usually answered, Then you ought not to correct them at all. Every one would be sensible, that for a magistrate to discover an intemperate rage in pronouncing sentence against a criminal, would be highly indecent. Ought not parents to punish their children in the same dispassionate manner? Ought they not to be at least equally concerned to discharge their duty in the best manner, in the one case as in the other?

He who would preserve his authority over his children, should be particularly watchful of his own conduct. You may as well pretend to force people to love what is not amiable, as to reverence what is not respectable. A

decency of conduct, therefore, and dignity of deportment, is highly service-
able for the purpose we have now in view. Lest this, however, should be
mistaken, I must put in a caution, that I do not mean to recommend keeping
children at too great a distance, by an uniform sternness and severity of
carriage. This, I think, is not necessary, even when they are young; and
it may, to children of some tempers, be very hurtful when they are old.
By and bye you shall receive from me a quite contrary direction. But by
dignity of carriage, I mean parents showing themselves always cool and
reasonable in their own conduct; prudent and cautious in their conversation
with regard to the rest of mankind; not fretful or impatient, or passionately
fond of their own peculiarities; and though gentle and affectionate to their
children, yet avoiding levity in their presence. . . .

That this may not be carried too far, I would recommend every expression
of affection and kindness to children when it is safe; that is to say, when
their behavior is such as to deserve it. There is no opposition at all between
parental tenderness and parental authority. They are the best supports
to each other. It is not only lawful, but will be of service, that parents
should discover the greatest fondness for children in infancy, and make
them perceive distinctly with how much pleasure they gratify all their innocent inclinations. This, however, must always be done when they are quiet,
gentle, and submissive in their carriage. Some have found fault with giving
them, for doing well, little rewards of sweet-meats and play-things, as tending to make them mercenary, and leading them to look upon the indulgence
of appetite as the chief good. This, I apprehend, is rather refining too
much; the great point is, that they be rewarded for doing good, and not
for doing evil. When they are cross and froward, I would never buy peace,
but force it. Nothing can be more weak and foolish, or more destructive
of authority, than where children are noisy and in an ill-humour, to give
them or promise them something to appease them. When the Roman em-
perors began to give pensions and subsidies to the northern nations to
keep them quiet, a man might have foreseen, without the spirit of prophecy,
who would be master in a little time. The case is exactly the same with
children. They will soon avail themselves of this easiness in their parents,
command favours instead of begging them and be insolent when they
should be grateful. . . .

It is a noble support of authority, when it is really and visibly directed
to the most important end. My meaning in this, I hope, is not obscure.
The end I consider as most important is, the glory of God in the eternal
happiness and salvation of children. Whoever believes in a future state,
whoever has a just sense of the importance of eternity to himself, cannot
fail to have a like concern for his offspring. This should be his end, both
in instruction and government; and when it visibly appears that he is under
the constraint of conscience, and that either reproof or correction are
the fruit of sanctified love, it will give them irresistible force. I will tell
you here, with all the simplicity necessary in such a situation, what I have
often said in my course of pastoral visitation in families, where there is

in many cases, through want of judgment as well as want of principle, a great neglect of authority: "Use your authority for God, and he will support it. Let it always be seen that you are more displeased at sin than at folly. What a shame is it, that if a child shall, through the inattention and levity of youth, break a dish, or a pane of the window, by which you may lose the value of a few pence, you should storm and rage at him with the utmost fury, or perhaps beat him with unmerciful severity; but if he tells a lie, or takes the name of God in vain, or quarrels with his neighbours, he shall easily obtain pardon; or perhaps, if he is reproved by others, you will justify him, and take his part."

You cannot easily believe the weight that it gives to family authority, when it appears visibly to proceed from a sense of duty, and to be itself an act of obedience to God. This will produce coolness and composure in the manner; it will direct and enable a parent to mix every expression of heart felt tenderness, with the most severe and needful reproofs. It will make it quite consistent to affirm, that the rod itself is an evidence of love, and that it is true of every pious parent on earth, what is said of our Father in heaven, "Whom the Lord loveth he chasteneth, and scourgeth every son whom he receiveth. If ye endure chastening, God dealeth with you as with sons; for what son is he whom the Father chasteneth not? But if ye are without chastisement, whereof all are partakers, then ye are bastards and not sons." With this maxim in your eye, I would recommend, that solemnity take the place of, and be substituted for severity.

CUSTOMS OF THE INDIAN NATIVES

It may justly be a subject of wonder, how a nation without a written code of laws or system of jurisprudence, without any form or constitution of government, and without even a single elective or hereditary magistrate, can subsist together in peace and harmony, and in the exercise of the moral virtues; how a people can be well and effectually governed without any external authority; by the mere force of the ascendancy which men of superior minds have over those of a more ordinary stamp; by a tacit, yet universal submission to the aristocracy of experience, talents and virtue! Such, nevertheless, is the spectacle which an Indian nation exhibits to the eye of a stranger. . . . It is in a great degree to be ascribed to the pains which the Indians take to instil at an early age honest and virtuous principles upon the minds of their children, and to the method which they pursue in educating them. . . .

The first step that parents take towards the education of their children, is to prepare them for future happiness, by impressing upon their tender minds, that they are indebted for their existence to a great, good and

John Heckewelder, "The History, Manners, and Customs of the Indian Natives Who Once Inhabited Pennsylvania and the Neighboring States," *Transactions of the American Philosophical Society* (Philadelphia, 1819), I, pp. 98–102.

benevolent Spirit, who not only has given them life, but has ordained them for certain great purposes. That he has given them a fertile extensive country well stocked with game of every kind for their subsistence, and that by one of his inferior spirits he has also sent down to them from above corn, pumpkins, squashes, beans and other vegetables for their nourishment; all which blessings their ancestors have enjoyed for a great number of ages. That this great Spirit looks down upon the Indians, to see whether they are grateful to him and make him a due return for the many benefits he has bestowed, and therefore that it is their duty to show their thankfulness by worshipping him, and doing that which is pleasing in his sight.

This is in substance the first lesson taught, and from time to time repeated to the Indian children, which naturally leads them to reflect and gradually to understand that a being which hath done such great things for them, and all to make them happy, must be good indeed, and that it is surely their duty to do something that will please him. They are then told that their ancestors, who received all this from the hands of the great Spirit, and lived in the enjoyment of it, must have been informed of what would be most pleasing to this good being, and of the manner in which his favour could be most surely obtained, and they are directed to look up for instruction to those who know all this, to learn from them, and revere them for their wisdom and the knowledge which they possess; this creates in the children a strong sentiment of respect for their elders, and a desire to follow their advice and example. . . .

When this first and most important lesson is thought to be sufficiently impressed upon children's minds, the parents next proceed to make them sensible of the distinction between good and evil; they tell them that there are good actions and bad actions, both equally open to them to do or commit; that good acts are pleasing to the good Spirit which gave them their existence, and that on the contrary, all that is bad proceeds from the bad spirit who has given them nothing, and who cannot give them any thing that is good, because he has it not, and therefore he envies them that which they have received from the good Spirit, who is far superior to the bad one.

This introductory lesson, if it may be so called, naturally makes them wish to know what is good and what is bad. This the parent teaches him in his own way, that is to say, in the way in which he was himself taught by his own parents. It is not the lesson of an hour nor of a day, it is rather a long course more of practical than of theoretical instruction, a lesson, which is not repeated at stated seasons or times, but which is shown, pointed out, and demonstrated to the child, not only by those under whose immediate guardianship he is, but by the whole community, who consider themselves alike interested in the direction to be given to the rising generation.

When this instruction is given in the form of precepts, it must not be supposed that it is done in an authoritative or forbidding tone, but, on the contrary, in the gentlest and most persuasive manner: nor is the parent's authority ever supported by harsh or compulsive means; no whips, no punishments, no threats are even used to enforce commands or compel obedience. The child's *pride* is the feeling to which an appeal is made, which proves successful in almost every instance. A father needs only to say in the presence of his children: "I want such a thing done; I want one of my children to go upon such an errand; let me see who is the *good* child that will do it!" This word *good* operates, as it were, by magic, and the children immediately vie with each other to comply with the wishes of their parent. If a father sees an old decrepid man or woman pass by, led along by a child, he will draw the attention of his own children to the object by saying: "What a *good* child that must be, which pays such attention to the aged! That child, indeed, looks forward to the time when it will likewise be old!" or he will say, "May the great Spirit, who looks upon him, grant this *good* child a long life!"

In this manner of bringing up children, the parents, as I have already said, are seconded by the whole community. If a child is sent from his father's dwelling to carry a dish of victuals to an aged person, all in the house will join in calling him a *good* child. They will ask whose child he is, and on being told, will exclaim: what! has the *Tortoise*, or the *little Bear* (as the father's name may be) got such a *good* child? If a child is seen passing through the streets leading an old decrepid person, the villagers will in his hearing, and to encourage all the other children who may be present to take example from him, call on one another to look on and see what a *good* child that must be. And so, in most instances, this method is resorted to, for the purpose of instructing children in things that are good, proper, or honourable in themselves; while, on the other hand, when a child has committed a *bad* act, the parent will say to him: "O! how grieved I am that my child has done this *bad* act! I hope he will never do so again." This is generally effectual, particularly if said in the presence of others. The whole of the Indian plan of education tends to elevate rather than depress the mind, and by that means to make determined hunters and fearless warriors. . . .

This method of conveying instruction is, I believe, common to most Indian nations; it is so, at least, amongst all those that I have become acquainted with, and lays the foundation for that voluntary submission to their chiefs, for which they are so remarkable. Thus has been maintained for ages, without convulsions and without civil discords, this traditional government, of which the world, perhaps, does not offer another example; a government in which there are no positive laws, but only long established habits and customs, no code of jurisprudence, but the experience of former times, no magistrates, but advisers, to whom the people, nevertheless, pay a willing and implicit obedience, in which age confers rank, wisdom gives power, and moral goodness secures a title to universal respect. All this seems to be effected by the simple means of an excellent mode of education, by which a strong attachment to ancient customs, respect for age, and the love of virtue are indelibly impressed upon the minds of youth, so that these impressions acquire strength as time pursues its course, and as they pass through successive generations.

LIFE OF WASHINGTON

His father fully persuaded that a marriage of virtuous love comes nearest to angelic life, early stepped up to the *altar* with glowing cheeks and joy sparkling eyes, while by his side, with soft warm hand, sweetly trembling in his, stood the angel form of the lovely Miss Dandridge.

After several years of great domestic happiness, Mr. Washington was separated, by death, from this excellent woman, who left him and two children to lament her early fate.

Fully persuaded still that *"it is not good for man to be alone,"* he renewed, for the second time, the chaste delights of matrimonial love. His consort was Miss Mary Ball, a young lady of fortune, and descended from one of the best families in Virginia.

From his intermarriage with this charming girl, it would appear that our Hero's father must have possessed either a very pleasing person, or highly polished manners, or perhaps *both; for,* from what I can learn, he was at that time at least 40 years old! while she, on the other hand, was universally toasted as the belle of the Northern Neck, and in the full bloom and freshness of love-inspiring sixteen. This I have from one who tells me that he has carried down many a sett dance with her; I mean that amiable and pleasant old gentleman, John Fitzhugh, Esq. of Stafford, *who* was, all his life, a neighbour and intimate of the Washington family. By his first wife, Mr. Washington had two children, both sons—Lawrence and Augustin. By his second wife, he had five children, four sons and a daughter—George, Samuel, John, Charles, and Elizabeth. Those *over delicate* ones, who are ready to faint at thought of a second marriage, might do well to remember, that the greatest man that ever lived was the son of this second marriage!

Little George had scarcely attained his fifth year, when his father left Pope's creek, and came up to a plantation which he had in Stafford, opposite to Fredericksburg. The house in which he lived is still to be seen. It lifts its low and modest front of faded red, over the turbid waters of Rappahannock; whither, to this day, numbers of people repair, and, with emotions unutterable, looking at the weatherbeaten mansion, exclaim, *"Here's the house where the Great Washington was born!"*

But it is all a mistake; for he was born, as I said, at Pope's creek, in Westmoreland county, near the margin of his own roaring Potomac.

The first place of education to which George was ever sent, was a little

Mason L. Weems, *The Life and Character of George Washington* (Cambridge, 1962), pp. 7–12, 17–18.

"The Frank Confession" was the title for this print that appeared in the early editions of Weems's *Life of Washington*. The incident of the little hatchet and the cherry tree was the most famous (but unsubstantiated) tale told to children about Washington's exemplary life.

"old field school," kept by one of his father's tenants, named Hobby; an honest, poor old man, who acted in the double character of sexton and schoolmaster. On his skill as a gravedigger, tradition is silent; but for a teacher of youth, his qualifications were certainly of the humbler sort; making what is generally called an A. B. C. schoolmaster. Such was the preceptor who first taught Washington the knowledge of letters! Hobby lived to see his young pupil in all his glory, and rejoiced exceedingly. In his cups—for, though a *sexton,* he would sometimes drink, particularly on the General's birth-days—he used to boast, that *" 'twas he, who, between his knees, had laid the foundation of George Washington's greatness."*

But though George was early sent to a schoolmaster, yet he was not on that account neglected by his father. Deeply sensible of the *loveliness* and *worth* of which human nature is capable, through the *virtues* and *graces* early implanted in the heart, he never for a moment, lost sight of George in those all-important respects.

To assist his son to overcome that selfish spirit which too often leads children to fret and fight about trifles, was a notable care of Mr. Washington. For this purpose, of all the presents, such as cakes, fruit, &c. he received, he was always desired to give a liberal part to his play-mates. To enable him to do this with more alacrity, his father would remind him of the love which he would hereby gain, and the frequent presents which would in return be made *to him;* and also would tell of that great and good God, who delights above all things to see children love one another, and will assuredly reward them for acting so amiable a part.

Some idea of Mr. Washington's plan of education in this respect, may be collected from the following anecdote, related to me twenty years ago by an aged lady, who was a distant relative, and when a girl spent much of her time in the family.

"On a fine morning," said she, *"in the fall of 1737, Mr. Washington, having little George by the hand, came to the door and asked my cousin Washington and myself to walk with him to the orchard, promising he would show us a fine sight. On arriving at the orchard, we were presented with a fine sight indeed. The whole earth, as far as we could see, was strewed with fruit: and yet the trees were bending under the weight of apples, which hung in clusters like grapes, and vainly strove to hide their blushing cheeks behind the green leaves. Now, George, said his father, look here, my son! don't you remember when this good cousin of yours brought you that fine large apple last spring, how hardly I could prevail on you to divide with your brothers and sisters; though I promised you that if you would but do it, God Almighty would give you plenty of apples this fall. Poor George could not say a word; but hanging down his head, looked quite confused, while with his little naked toes he scratched in the soft ground. Now look up, my son, continued his father, look up, George! and see there how richly the blessed God has made good my promise to you. Wherever you turn your eyes, you see the trees loaded with fine fruit; many of them indeed breaking down, while the ground is covered with mellow apples more than you could ever eat, my son, in all your life time."*

George looked in silence on the wide wilderness of fruit; he marked the busy humming bees, and heard the gay notes of birds, then lifting his eyes filled with shining moisture, to his father, he softly said, *"Well, Pa, only forgive me this time; see if I ever be so stingy any more."*

Some, when they look up to the oak whose giant arms throw a darkening shade over distant acres, or whose single trunk lays the keel of a man of war, cannot bear to hear of the time when this mighty plant was but an acorn, which a pig could have demolished: but others, who know their value, like to learn the soil and situation which best produces such noble trees. Thus, parents that are *wise* will listen well pleased, while I relate how moved the steps of the youthful Washington, whose single worth far outweighs all the oaks of Bashan and the red spicy cedars of Lebanon. Yes, they will listen delighted while I tell of their Washington in the days of his youth, when his little feet were swift towards the nests of birds; or when, wearied in the chace of the butterfly, he laid him down on his grassy couch and slept, while ministering spirits, with their roseate wings, fanned his glowing cheeks, and kissed his lips of innocence with the fervent love which makes *the Heaven!*

Never did the wise Ulysses take more pains with his beloved Telemachus, than did Mr. Washington with George, to inspire him with an *early love of truth.* "Truth, George," (said he) "is the loveliest quality of youth. I would ride fifty miles, my son, to see the little boy whose heart is so *honest,* and his lips so *pure*, that we may depend on every word he says. O how lovely does such a child appear in the eyes of every body! His parents doat on him; his relations glory in him; they are constantly praising him to their children, whom they beg to imitate him. They are often sending for him, to visit them; and receive him, when he comes, with as much joy as if he were a little angel, come to set pretty examples to their children.

"But, Oh! how different, George, is the case with the boy who is so given to lying, that nobody can believe a word he says! He is looked at with aversion wherever he goes, and parents dread to see him come among their children. Oh, George! my son! rather than see you come to this pass, dear as you are to my heart, gladly would I assist to nail you up in your little coffin, and follow you to your grave. Hard, indeed, would it be to me to give up my son, whose little feet are always so ready to run about with me, and whose fondly looking eyes and sweet prattle make so large a part of my happiness: but still I would give him up, rather than see him a common liar."

"Pa, (said George very seriously) do I ever tell lies?"

"No, George, I *thank God* you do not, my son; and I rejoice in the hope you never will. At least, you shall never, from me, have cause to be guilty of so shameful a thing. Many parents, indeed, even compel their children to this vile practice, by barbarously beating them for every little fault; hence, on the next offence, the little terrified creature slips out a *lie!* just to escape the rod. But as to yourself, George, you know I have *always* told you, and now tell you again, that, whenever by accident you do any thing wrong, which must often be the case, as you are but a poor little boy yet, without *experience* or *knowledge*, never tell a falsehood to conceal it; but come *bravely* up, my son, like a *little man*, and tell me of it: and instead of beating you, George, I will but the more honour and love you for it, my dear."

This, you'll say, was sowing good seed!—Yes, it was: and the crop, thank God, was, as I believe it ever will be, where a man acts the true parent, that is, the *Guardian Angel*, by his child.

The following anecdote is a *case in point.* It is too valuable to be lost, and too true to be doubted; for it was communicated to me by the same excellent lady to whom I am indebted for the last.

"When George," said she, "was about six years old, he was made the wealthy master of a *hatchet!* of which, like most little boys, he was immoderately fond, and was constantly going about chopping every thing that came in his way. One day, in the garden, where he often amused himself hacking his mother's pea-sticks, he unluckily tried the edge of his hatchet on the body of a beautiful young English cherry-tree, which he barked so terribly, that I don't believe the tree ever got the better of it. The next morning the old gentleman finding out what had befallen his tree, which, by the by, was a great favourite, came into the house, and with much warmth asked for the mischievous author, declaring at the same time, that he would not have taken five guineas for his tree. Nobody could tell him any thing about it. Presently George and his hatchet made their appearance. *George,* said his father, *do you know who killed that beautiful little cherry-tree yonder in the garden?* This was a *tough question;* and George staggered under it for a moment; but quickly recovered himself: and looking at his father, with the sweet face of youth brightened with the inexpressible charm of all-conquering truth, he bravely cried out, *"I can't tell a lie, Pa; you know I can't tell a lie. I did cut it with my hatchet."*—*Run to my arms, you dearest boy,* cried his father in transports, *run to my arms; glad am I, George, that you killed my tree; for you have paid me for it a thousand fold. Such an act of heroism in my son, is more worth than a thousand trees, though blossomed with silver, and their fruits of purest gold."* . . .

Thus pleasantly, on wings of down, passed away the few short years of little George's and his father's *earthly* acquaintance. Sweetly ruled by the sceptre of REASON, George almost adored his father; and thus sweetly *obeyed* with all the cheerfulness of LOVE, his father doated on George. . . . And though very different in their years, yet parental and filial love rendered them so mutually dear, that the old gentleman was often heard to regret, that *the school took his little companion so much from him*—while George, on the other hand, would often quit his playmates to run home and converse with his more beloved father.

But George was not long to enjoy the pleasure or the profit of such a companion; for scarcely had he attained his tenth year, before his father was seized with the gout in the stomach, which carried him off in a few days. George was not at home when his father was taken ill. He was on a visit to some of his cousins in Chotank, about twenty miles off; and his father, unwilling to interrupt his pleasures, for it was but seldom that he visited, would not at first allow him to be sent for. But finding that he was going very fast, he begged that they would send for him in all haste . . . he often asked if he was come, and said how happy he should be, once more to see his little son, and give him his blessing before he died. But alas! he never enjoyed that last mournful pleasure; for George did not reach home until a few hours before his father's death, and then he was speechless! The moment he alighted, he ran into the chamber where he lay. But oh! what were his feelings when he saw the sad change that had passed upon him! when he beheld those eyes, late so *bright* and *fond,* now reft of all their lustre, faintly looking on him from their hollow sockets, and through swelling tears, in mute but melting language, bidding him a LAST, LAST FAREWELL! . . . Rushing with sobs and cries, he fell upon his father's neck . . . he kissed him a thousand and a thousand times, and bathed his clay-cold face with scalding tears.

O happiest youth! Happiest in that love, which thus, to its enamoured soul strained an aged an[d] expiring sire. O! worthiest to be the founder of a JUST and EQUAL GOVERNMENT, lasting as thy own deathless name! And O! happiest old man! thus luxuriously expiring in the arms of such a child! O! well requited for teaching him that LOVE OF HIS GOD (*the only fountain of every virtuous love*) in return for which he gave thee ('twas all he had) *himself*—his *fondest company*—his *sweetest looks and prattle.* He now gives thee his little strong embraces, with artless sighs and tears; faithful to thee still, his feet will follow thee to thy grave: and when thy beloved corse is let down to the stones of the pit, with streaming eyes he will rush to the brink, to take *one more* look, while his bursting heart will give thee its last trembling cry. . . . *O my father! my father!*

Orphans and Apprentices

Children firmly under the dominion of parents, to be controlled and provided with the skill or property needed to establish them as independent adults—that was the ideal. But the death of one or both parents often made it impossible to meet this ideal. The documents below, taken from seventeenth-century laws and court records from New York, Maryland, and Virginia, bear on the problem of the orphan, the need to ensure that parentless children who were too young to care for themselves were provided for and protected. They also indicate the problems the death of parents posed for children and society, as well as the means used to meet those problems. But orphans were not the only young people who lived outside parental supervision. Large numbers of boys and girls from ten or twelve years on (those we today would still designate as children) were placed by parents or guardians as servants or apprentices in other households. Thus, though the household—rather than the individual—was the basic social unit in colonial America, it was a good deal more "open" than most families of twentieth-century America, a structure that often routinely included people other than biologically related parents and offspring.

LAWS OF VIRGINIA

December 1656

CONCERNING orphans estates, *Be it from henceforth enacted,* That all wills and testaments be firme and inviolable, but in case the executors or overseers refuse to execute their trust, then the estates disposed of by will to be liable to such rules as are laid down for the management of estates of persons intestate.

That noe accounts be allowed on orphans estates, but they to be educated vpon the interest of the estate, if it will beare it, according to the proportion of their estate, But if the estate be so meane and inconsiderable that it

W. W. Hening, ed., *The Statutes at Large* . . . , II, pp. 416–17; IX, p. 212.

will not reach to a free education then that orphan be bound to some manuall trade till one and twenty yeares of age, except some ffriends or relations be willing to keep them with the increase of that small estate, without diminution of the principall, which whether greate or small allways to returne to the orphans at the yeares appointed by law.

That all cattell, horses and sheep be returned in kind by the guardians, according to age and number, whereat he received them, as all household stuff, lumber and the like to be prized in money, And by the guardians to be paid in the country comodity (whatsoever it shall be) to the orphans as it is then currant in the country and in the perticular place where the orphan's estate is managed.

That the court take able and sufficient security for orphans estates, and enquire yearly of the security, & if the court sees cause, to have it changed or called in and placed as the court shall think best, The said court also to enquire whether orphans be kept and maintained and educated according as their estates will beare, And if they find any notorious defect to remove the orphans to other guardians, As also for those that are bound apprentices to change their master if he vse them rigourously or neglect to teach them his trade.

That such orphans as are not bound apprentices shall after seaventeen yeares of age have the produce of their owne labours and industry and to dispose of as they list, besides the maintenance from their guardians, Allwaies provided that nothing be infringed.

That no more be allowed to guardians for collecting of debts due to the estate then what is allowed vsually by merchants to their ffactors or attorneys, or rather that so much in the hundred be appointed as shall seem reasonable to the courts.

February 1727

Be it enacted . . . That if it should happen, that the parent or parents of any child or children, upon due proof before the court of the county wherein such parent or parents inhabit, shall be adjudged incapable of supporting and bringing up such child or children, by reason of his, her, or their idle, dissolute, and disorderly course of life, or that they neglect to take due care of the education and instruction of such child or children, in christian principles, that then it shall and may be lawful, upon certificate from the said court, to and for the churchwardens of the said parish, where such child or children shall inhabit to bind out, or put out to service or apprentice, such child or children, for such time or term, and under such covenants, as hath been usual and customary, or the law directs in the case of orphan children.

BONDS OF APPRENTICESHIP, 1655–1705

Kent County, Maryland, 1655

Theese pᵣsents witneseth That wheareas Andrew Hansonn hath dessessed and left unto his wiffe Annicak Hanson foure small children and bige with child with the fifth And beeinge altogather unable hauinge no estate left for the maintenance of her selfe and Children and beeinge constrained for want of abillitie to disposse of sume of them to sume Christian freinds, for theire maintenance and subsistanc I doe by theese pᵣsents acknowledge freely to bestowe and giue Hance Hansonn my oldest sonne unto Joseph Weeckes, who doth by theese pᵣsents acknowledge a free acceptance of him, And doth faithfuly p̄mis and bind himselfe to tacke care and p̄uide for him for such thinges as shall bee any wayes Conuenient and nessessarie for his maintenance and breedinge as alsoe to beestow such Education and learninge upon him as reedinge in the English tounge writeinge of a good legable hand and castinge of Accoumpt in foure seuerall rules of Arethmaticke as the aforesayd Hance Hanson shall bee any wayes capable to learne, which learinge is to bee made good unto him duringe his abode and continuanc with the sayd Weeckes

In Consideration of the aforesayd Weeckes his freindly or otherwayes fatherly care Charge and Education of the sayd Hance Hanson hee is to continue and remaine with him to bee wholy at his disposinge when or whearesoeuer or about what lawfull imploymᵗ soeuer either by [   ] aforesayd Weecks his Executᵣˢ or Assignes shall [   ] the day of this pᵣsent date untill hee shall bee twenty *one yeares of* agge which beeinge at pᵣsent nine yeares of agge. . . .

Signed sealed and deliūed
   in the pᵣsents of
      Tho: Hill Claꝛ of Kent
      Isa Iliue
      The marke of
      John ✝ Salter

The marke of
Annicak **X** Hanson
The marke of
Hance **X** Hanson

Talbott County, Maryland, 1666

To the Worshipfull Commissioners for Talbott County thᵉ humble petition of Mary Woodley and Sarah Wallis.

Shewith That whereas our Father Law Alexander Ray did severall all times abuse your Petitioners as by theire Complnᵗ made to this Court Appeare, and hath all this time turned them out of his house, soe that your petitioners haue noe abiding place the premisses Considered your petitioners humbly Craue that wee may haue Liberty to Choose our Gaur-

Kent County Court Proceedings, 1648–1655 (Annapolis, 1975), pp. 28–29; *Talbott County Court Proceedings, 1662–1674* (Annapolis, 1975), pp. 392–93; *Charles County Court Proceedings, 1666–1668* (Annapolis, 1975), pp. 106–7; *Kent County Court Proceedings, 1668–1671* (Annapolis, 1975), p. 247; *Kent County Court Proceedings, 1656–1662* (Annapolis, 1975), p. 290; *New-York Historical Society Collections* (New York, 1886), pp. 18, 574–75, 608–9.

dian our selues and that our Father in Law Alexander Ray aboue said shall deliver our Estate that doth belong to uss Into our said Gardians hands and your petitioner Shall Ever Pray

Whereas the aboue said Orphants haue petitioned for to Choose A Gardian, the Court haue granted it, and appoynted William Goodin to bee theire Gardian, and also to haue theire Estates deliuered into his Custody, with Two Barills of Corne they haueing made Choice of the said Goodin for theire Gardian; its also ordered that the said Goddin Putt in security to bee accomptable for what Estate is delivered him to the Court when hee shalbe Called thereto.

Charles County, Maryland, 1667

Ordered That th[e] youngest girle of Arthur Turner latelie dec[d] about a monthe old be put out to George Taylors wife Susannah Taylor who is to nurse th[e] same and to find it all necessaries for Cloathing, diet, &c and to be allowed one Thousand Sixe hundred pounds of tobaccoe p̄ añ for th[e] same in manner as followeth viz[t], That if th[e] Child die anie time within halfe a yeare then the Allowance to be but for halfe a yeare and if it die anie time within a yeare after th[e] halfe yeare then she is to have th[e] whole yearelie allowance

Authur Turner eldest Sonne of Arthur Turner latelie dec[d] came into th[e] C[rt] and chose Cap. Josias Fendall for his Guardian

James Turner Second Sonne of the said Arthur made choice of his Godfather M[r] Walter Beane for his Guardian.

Ordered That Edward Turner be bound apprentice to James Bowling untill he come to th[e] age of one and twentie yeares

Ordered That Anne Turner be bound Apprentice to M[r] William Marshall untill she come to th[e] age of 16 yeares, and afterwards to remaine with him untill her age of one and twentie yeares unlesse she marrie before such age.

Kent County, Maryland, 1668

Bee it knowne unto all men by these presents that I John Dabb of the Island of Kent for diuers good Causes and Consideraĉons me Thereunto moueing doe bind ouer my Daughter Sarah Dabb unto m[r] Morgan Williams and his wiffe for and during the Terme of Foure yeares to serue them in such occasions as they shall require and in Consideration whereof the Said Williams is to finde her meate drincke washing and Lodging and Cloths for the true performance of the premises I bind my selfe my heires Executors Administrat[rs] or Assignes In witnes whereof I haue hereunto sett my hand the 30th June 1668   John ✤D Dabb
                                                                                            his marke

Kent County, Maryland, 1658

Nicolas Pickard & Mary Baxter hath moued this Court, to haue George Crouch, The sonn of Geo: Crouch decedent, Lefte in th[e] Custody of Nico: Pickard aforesd.

The Courte doth therefore order, By & with th^e Concent of th^e said Nicolas Pickard & Mary Baxter, That the sd Geo: Crouch bee & Remaine in th^e Custody of the sd Pickard & that all th^e Childes Cattle shall remaine wth Nico: Pickard, And hee to haue th^e halfe of th^e Male increase From this time Forward, For Keepinge the s^d Child, & putinge him to scoole & Furnishinge th^e Childe wth other Nescessaries soe longe till Just occation be mayd Appeare as Law povides For Orphants in such Cases
Testis me John Cowrsey Clk.

New York, 1697

Recorded for Nathaniel Marston, ye 24th. day of August, 1697.

This Indenture Wittnesseth that Nathaniel Lynus by and with the Consent of his Parents hath put himselfe and by these Presents doth Voluntarily and of his own free will and Accord put himselfe Apprentice to Nathaniel Marston of New Yorke Barber to learn his Art Trade or Mystery and after the manner of An Apprentice to Serve from ye Date hereof till the full Terme of Seaven Years be Compleat and Ended During all which Terme the Said Apprentice his Said Master Nathaniel Marston and Mistriss Margarett Marston faithfully Shall Serve his Secretts keep his Lawfull Commands Gladly Everywhere obey he Shall do no Damage to his Said Master Nor See it to be done by others without letting or Giving Notice thereof to his Said Master he Shall not waste his Said Masters goods nor lend them Unlawfully to Any he Shall not Committ Fornication Nor Contract Matrimony within the Said Terme; Att Cards Dice or any other unlawfull Game he shall not play whereby his Said Master may have Damage with his own goods Nor the Goods of others During the Said Terme without Lycense from his Said Master he Shall Neither buy nor Sell he Shall not absent himselfe Day nor Night from his Masters Service without his Leave. Nor haunt Ale houses Taverns or Playhouses but in all things as a faithfull Apprentice he shall behave himselfe towards his Said Master and all his During the Said Terme. And the said Master his Said Apprentice in the Same Art which he Useth by the best means that he Can Shall teach or Cause to be taught and Instructed finding unto him meat Drinke, Apparell Lodging and washing fitting for an Apprentice During the Said Terme. And for the true Performance of all and Every of the Said Covenants and Agreements Either of the Said Parties binde themselves unto the other. . . .

Nathaniel Lynus

Signed Sealed and Delivered in the Presence of us

William White,
the marke of x Damascus White,
Jno. Basford.

New York, 1705

This Indenture Wittnesseth that Phillip Lyon Aged fourteen years or thereabouts being fatherless and motherless of his own free and Voluntary

Will hath placed and by these presents doth put bind and place himself A Servant and apprentice unto Hendrick Van Bael of the City of New York Merch^t and as a Servant and Apprentice with him the Said Hendrick Van Bael to dwell from the day of the date of these presents untill the full end and Term of Seaven Years from thence Next Ensueing & fully to be Compleat and Ended during which time and Term the Said Phillip Lyon Shall the Said Hendrick Van Bael his Master well and faithfully Serve in all Such Lawfull business as the Said Phillip Lyon Shall be put unto According to his power With Ability and honesty & Obediently in all things Shall behave himself towards the Said Hendrick Van Bael during the Term aforesaid. And the Said Hendrick Van Bael for his part Covenanteth promiseth and agreeth that he the Said Hendrick Van Bael Shall teach and Instruct or Cause to be taught and Instructed his Said Servant and Apprentice to read and write the English Tongue and Shall find and allow unto his Said Servant and Apprentice Sufficient Apparrell meat drinke washing and lodging and all other Nessessary's meet and Convenient for Such a Servant during the Terme aforesaid.

The Passing of Generations

Childhood is not a permanent state, and as children and parents both age, the relationship between them changes. When colonial children established themselves in adulthood and their parents aged or became widowed, parental authority and control diminished and often parents passed their last years almost as dependent upon one or more of their children as the children once had been dependent upon them. These documents all touch upon this generational process. What do the wills reveal of the complexity colonial families and their possessions could take on? What do they indicate about how fathers or other heads of households maintained or relinquished control over property and the family? How could a will permit a parent to ignore death and influence the behavior and fortunes of those left behind? Other documents touch upon the problems of the care of infirm or aged parents. As Benjamin Wadsworth enjoined in the first document in this part (p. 133), children were obliged to support their parents in their declining years. But as some of the court materials suggest, parents could not always count on moral precept and the goodwill of their children. The last selection contains the final gesture of respect Benjamin Franklin bestowed upon his parents.

COURT RECORDS, 1682–1715

Ipswich Quarterly Court, 1682

Thomas Laiton and Frances Burrell were ordered at the last Ipswich court to sell enough land of the widow Mary Davis to pay her son-in-law, Thomas Ivory, for past maintenance of said Mary, and in the future in the time of her age and weakness at the rate of 4s. per week during her life. They were also impowered to bring suit for any rents or debts due to her, which should be used to defray the expense of maintenence of said Mary Davis. . . .

Petition of John Daves, inhabitant of Lynn, brother-in-law of Thomas

Records and Files of the Quarterly Courts of Essex County, Massachusetts (Salem, Mass., 1913–1921), VIII, pp. 346–47.

Ivory, and son of Mrs. Mary Davis, that according to court order Mr. Thomas Laughton, sr., and Francis Burrell, sr., had sold five and a quarter acres of land which said Ivory accepted for the time past, but would not accept the 4s. per week for the future; that said John did not know that Ivory was going to that court at Ipswich which was not fair dealing; that his mother should be maintained by the estate and by her children, which are but two, petitioner and Thomas Ivory's now wife; that petitioner was and is willing to bear two parts to Ivory's one; "and am willing to doe my utmost for my honrd mother. And as I am the son I was willing to p^{r}serue the estate together while my mother liued if possible and soe haue posessed ye Inheritance of my father, of wch lands my brother might expect a third part or pay for it after my mothers decease. And yor petitioner hath the land by lease from my mother when shee was of good understanding & that for her life time, at a certayn rate per yeer which your now petition^r paid yeerly, soe as y^t Thomas Ivory owneth he received fourteen pounds & twelve shillings in this fowre yeers that he declared hee had maintained my mother, yor petitioner was willing & is willing to Joyne with his brother Iuory to maintaine o^r mother two parts for one with him, and hath proffred him that if hee be weary yor now petition^r would take his mother & keepe her: aloe hath proffred to referr the matter concerning his mothers maintainance to two Indifferent men or more & will be bound to stand unto & doe as they should appoynt but nothing wilbe accepted, but the land wch is yor petition^{rs} by lease taken away, of which yor poore petition^r is enforced to complayne for in this way yor poore petition^r shalbe quickly bereaued of y^t wch he had good hopes to Injoy as the Inheritance of his father whereupon hee hath laid out a great deal to make a comfortable place of abode and now is greatly spoyled of his intentions and good subsistance & Thomas Iuory my brother hath given under his hand that he was fully satisfyed for all things concerning my mother to this foure yeers last past, & that therein he hath receiued neere fifteen pounds of mee wherefore yor poore petition^r is enforced to Implore this Honord Courts fauo^r that hee may not be driuen out of the Inheritance of his father, But that they both as children may be ordered to doe their duty, and the Inheritance of o^r father remayne together according to our deceased fathers intention."

York County Court of General Sessions, July 5, 1715

Upon reading the petion of Nicho Gillison Setting forth that Sometime Since he Through his great Imprudence & Ignorence without any maner of Reserve did give & Convey his Estate unto his three Sons vizt Nicholas, Joseph & Ichabod Gillison, That is to say the Moiety or halfe part thereof unto the sd Nicholas & the other Moiety to be Equally divided between the sd Joseph & Ichabod, whereby he is reduced to very Miserable Circumstances in his Old age being unable to Labour. Its Considered by the

Court that the sd Nicholas Gillison Junior, Joseph Gillison & Ichabod Gilli-son provide for the maintainence & Subsistence of their aged father & mother in proportion. vizt The sd Nicholas to be at one halfe the Charge & the sd Joseph & Ichabod the other halfe Equally so far as the Estate given them by their sd father will Extend.

The Petition of Nicholas Gellison
Most humbly Sheweth—

That whereas Your petitioner someime since threw great improducence, ignarance, and [inadvertency?], without any [means?] of [*word illeg.*] did convey one half of his Estate unto his Eldest Son, and after that, the other half unto his two other Sons, whereby your petitioner is miserably impover-isht and like to be a Town charge—

Most humbly Supplicates, considering my infirmity and weakness in these my advanced yeares, that your Worships would please to cause Such Suit-able maintenance out of my Said Estate from my respective Sons, both for me and my wife, as you in your prudence Shall See meet—and your petitioner Shall Ever pray &ct   his

                                         Nicholas /\ Gellison
                                                  mark.]

THE WILL OF MARTHA EMONS

I, *Martha Emons*, of Boston, widow, being sicke & weake in body, but of p^rfect memory, make this my last will. Debts to be paid. I give vnto my sone, *Obadiah Emons*, all that my messuage tenem^t. or dwelling house, with the land thereto belonging, wherein he now dwelleth, being in Boston. Vnto my sone, *Samuel Emons*, my dwelling house wherein I now live, wth. the land thereto belonging, situate in Boston. Vnto my sone, *Joseph Emons*, £20, to be paid him by my executo^rs, at such times as the ou^rseers to this my will shall judg meet, (that is to say) when he doth take such good corses as to live orderly & to follow the Trade of a Cordwaine^r. & is clear of such debts as he now owes by following the imploy he now hath taken up. Vnto my Sone, *Benjamin Emons*, Foure score pounds, to be paid him by my executo^rs, as followeth, £60 thereof in such pay as will p^rduce him lether & other things wch he may need. I will that the £20 given my Sone, *Benjamin*, by his fathers will, be paid to him, in the moneth of June, wch shall be in the year 1667, by my executo^rs; & for the £60 aforesaid, to be paid vnto him £40, by my sone, *Obadiah*, out of the value of the house I have hereby bequeathed him, & £20 by my sone, *Samuel*, out of the value of the house I have bequeathed him, & £20 by *Obadiah*, & £10 by *Samuel*, to pay the said *Benjamin* in June 1668; the other £30 to be paid in specie in the moneth of June thence next ensuing; the other £20 to be paid my sone, *Benjamin,* to make up the sume of Fourscore pounds to be paid vnto him by the value thereof, of my goods, viz. that Fether bed wch he best liketh, with the Bolster & pillow, the new Cou^rled, a paire of Blankets, Curtins, hangings, the bedstead I now ly on, Two paier of my best sheets, a paire of pillow beers, my Silver Beker & Silver Spoon; & of other my goods, as pewter, Brasse & old bedding, to make up the value of £20; said goods to be paid him when he receives the legacie of £20, aforesaid, given him by the will of his father or soone^r if his occasions cale for it, & the plate & bedding immedyatly after my Decease. Vnto my son, *Samuel,* my Cloth Gound to make him a sute, & to his wife my best cloth petticote. To my dau. *Alice Emons,* my Turkey moehaire coate & my finest paire of new pillowbers. Vnto my grandsone, *Thomas,* 40^s·; vnto my Grand Dau. *Martha Emons,* my Gold ring & my silue^r bodkin; to my grandson, *Samuel,* my Silver wine cup & Dram cup; vnto my grand dau. *Mary,* 20^s, to be paid her in pewter; to my grand dau. *Elizabeth* 10^s· to buy her a silue^r spoon. Vnto my grandson, *Samuel Crab,* £18, to be paid him by my executo^rs when he shall be 20 years of age; vnto my Kinswoman, *Martha Winsor,* £8, to be paid vnto her at her age of 21, or day of Marriage, wch of them shall first be, & my hire Calliminco gound, & my old Moehaire petticoate & a red taminy petticoate & a new cloth wastcoate, wch lyeth in my chest, & a sute of my linning complete, (except a white Apron) & my bible & box. To Goodman *Prat,* of Charlestowne, 10^s; vnto my Kinswoman, *Hannah Winsor,* Two platters to be paid her at her Marriage. Vnto Goodwife, *Cop,* & goodwife, *Goold,* 10^s apeece; vnto my loving neighbo^rs Goodwife *Stanes* & goodwife *Winsor,* each of them, a dresing of my best, after that my dau. *Alice* hath take her choice. My will is, that such of my waring lining not disposed of, my dau^rs to Devid between them. My will is, that my Sone, *Samuel,* shall have the refuse of such implem^ts in my house wch he shall desier, paying for it as it is prized. Vnto my sons, *Obadiah & Samuel,* all my goods, Debts & estate not hereby bequethed, to be devided between them, whom I make joint executo^rs of this my last will & testament. I intreat my loving friends, *Mr John Wiswell* & *Mr William English* to be overseers, whom I do hereby also impower, that in case my executo^rs be remisse in p^rforming this my will, that then, upon such neglect, they shall have power over the before bequeathed dwelling houses to dispose of them for time, till my debts & legacies be paid, anything before expressed to the Contrary there of notwithstanding. Vnto my before named friends, *Mr Wiswell* & *Mr English,* 40^s· a peece for theire paines. I have here vnto set my hand & seale the second day of April in the year above written. In Case my houshold goods & debts will not amount to pay my debts & legacies hereby ordered & bequeathed, then the same shall be made up & paid by my executo^rs out of the Value of the houses respectively, hereby to them bequeathed, *Obadyah* paying two parts & *Samuel* one part thereof.

Martha Emons

THE WILL OF THOMAS MAKEPEACE

I, *Thomas Makepeace,* being weake in body but of Competent & good memory, doe by this my Last will, dispose of my temporal estate in manner following. Vnto *Thomas Makepeace,* mine eldest sonne, (beyond ye seas) & to his heyrs for euer, the debt of £50, which hee oweth mee (for which end I have torne off the seale of his bill) & no more, because I haue giuen him his portion formerly, vizt. ye house & land in England (he being the heyre to it) which he hath longe possessed. Unto my sone, *William Makepeace,* y^t my house in Boston, wherein my sonne in Law, *Lawrence Willis,* now dwelleth, wth y^t peece of Land as I haue now staked out to it, I say, I giue the same to him, my sd sonne *W^m* & to his heyres foreuer, hee to enter upon the same at the death of my dau. *Mary Willis,* & not before; besides this, I freely giue vnto my said sonne, *William,* a debt due to mee from *Thomas Terry,* of Blocke Island, being three pound odd money. Vnto *Hannah,* mine eldest dau., the wiffe of *Stephen Hoppin,* of Thomsons Island, & to her heires foreuer, £5, to be payed her, or her order, wth In one yeare affter my death. Vnto my dau. *Mary,* the wife of *Lawrance Willis* of Boston, that house in Boston wherein shee wth her sd Husband now dwells, during her life only. And at her death, her brother, *William,* shall haue ye same. Also, unto my dau. *Mary,* & to her heires foreuer one debt owing to mee from *Jno Willis,* of Bridgewatter, senio^r, & also one debt due to me from his sonne, *Jno Willis,* of ye same towne afores^d, Junior. Vnto my dau. *Hester,* ye wife of *John Browne,* of Malborrough, & to her heyrs foreuer, £5, to bee pd w^thin one yeare affter my decease, also to her & her heyrs, y^t debt her sd husband owes me. Vnto my dau. *Waytawhile,* the wiffe of *Josiah Cooper,* of Boston, £5, [to be pd, as before.] Vnto my Grand Children, *Delieurance, Jno. Stephen, Hannah, Sarah, Thomas, Oppertunity, Joseph* & *Benjamen Hoppin,* (they being the nine children) of my Dau. *Hannah,* the wife of *Stephen Hoppin,* aboue sayed, to each, £10, which sayed Legacies the male Children shall receiue as they come to the age of 21, & the females, at 18, or day of marriage, which shall happen first, with this exception, Relating to *Stephen,* only, That if my Executo^rs shall, when he comes to 21 yeares of age, Find him to persist on in his wild & wastfull courses, then they shall pay him (of his sd Legacy of £10) Only 10 shillings p^r Anumm till hee be well reformed, & then, & not before, they shall pay him the residue he hath not receaued of the sayed tenne pounds. Vnto my Grand Children, vizt. *Elizabeth, Joseph, Sarah, Mary,* & *John Browne,* they being the fiue Children of my dau. *Hester,* ye wife of *Jno. Browne,* vnto cach £10, males at 21, females at 18 or day of marriage. Vnto my Grand Children, *Elizabeth* & *Thomas Cooper,* the two Children of my daughter *Waitawhile,* the wife of *Josiah Cooper,* £10, to be paid them as all the other my Grand Children aboue mentioned. It hath pleased God to take away *Thomas Cooper,* one of ye children aboue named, my will is, y^t if shee be now wth child, that child to injoy ye ten pound. If any of my Grandchildren dye before the age & time afforesd, theire Legacies shall bee pd. by an equall deuision amongst all their bretheren & systers as they from time to time come to the Age & time abouesd. Vnto my kinswoman, *Mary*, the wife of *Jn⁰. Pearce*, of Rhoad Island & to her heires foreuer, £3, to bee payd in one yeare affter my death.

Vnto my wiues three dau⁵. vizt. *Mary*, yᵉ wife of *James Dennis*, of Boston; to *Martha*, yᵉ wife of *Joseph Walters*, of Milford; vnto *Mary*, yᵉ wife of *Emanuell Sprinckfeild*, in old England, vnto each, & theire heires 50ˢ. to bee payd in one yeare affter my death. I also Freely Giue them such debts as any of theire respective husbands oweth mee. I Appoynt *Elizabeth*, my wife, & my sonne in Law, *Josiah Cooper*, of Boston, & my dau. *Waiteawhile*, his wife, (or the surviuors of them) to bee my Executoʳs & Executrexes, to pay sd. Legacies, either by selling my houses & Lands or any other waies as they in theire best discretion shall see to bee most Conduceable to all ends & purposes beforesd. All debts due mee being Receaued & all debts owing by mee being payed, my wiues third pt of the whole being deducted, and the Afforesd Legacies being pd or secured, my will is, that the Remaindeʳ of my estate bee deuided into three equall parts or shares to yᵉ proppeʳ vse of my executoʳs, vizᵗ. one third pᵗ thereof to bee *Elizabeths*, my wiues, the other two third pᵗˢ. to bee *Waitawhile*, my Daughter, & *Josiah Cooper*, her husband. If any of the Executors shall dye, theire shares giuen them of the remaindeʳ of my estate shall Fall into the hands of the Surviueoʳs or Surviueoʳ of my sd Executoʳs to bee his or hers and his or her heires foreuer. I giue vnto my sonne in Law, *Abell Langly*, 50ˢ· to be pd him as yᵉ like legacies Abousayed.

Thomas Makepeace

BENJAMIN FRANKLIN'S MEMORIAL TO HIS PARENTS

Josiah Franklin
And Abiah his wife
Lie here interred.
They lived lovingly together in wedlock
Fifty-five years
Without an estate or any gainful employment,
By constant labour and industry,
With God's blessing,
They maintained a large family
Comfortably;
And brought up thirteen children,
And seven grandchildren
Reputably.
From this instance, Reader,

The Autobiography of Benjamin Franklin, A Restoration of the "Fair Copy" by Max Farrand (Berkeley, 1949), p. 33. Reprinted by permission of the University of California Press.

Be encouraged to diligence in thy calling,
And distrust not Providence.
He was a pious and prudent man,
She a discreet and virtuous woman.
Their youngest son,
In filial regard to their memory,
Places this stone.

J. F. born 1655—Died 1744—AEtat. 89.
A. F. born 1667—Died 1752——85.

SELECTED BIBLIOGRAPHY
FOR PART ONE

Bailyn, Bernard. *Education in the Forming of American Society.* Chapel Hill: University of North Carolina Press, 1960.

Benson, Mary S. *Women in Eighteenth-Century America: A Study of Opinion and Social Usage.* New York: Columbia University Press, 1935.

Demos, John. *Little Commonwealth: Family Life in Plymouth Colony.* New York: Oxford University Press, 1970.

Earle, Alice M. *Home Life in Colonial Days.* New York: Macmillan, 1910.

Frost, William J. *The Quaker Family in Colonial America.* New York: St. Martin's Press, 1973.

Greven, Philip J., Jr. *Four Generations: Population, Land, and Family in Colonial Andover, Massachusetts.* Ithaca, N.Y.: Cornell University Press, 1970.

——. *The Protestant Temperament: Patterns of Child Rearing, Religious Experience, and the Self in Early America.* New York: Knopf, 1977.

Laslett, Peter. *The World We Have Lost.* New York: Scribner's, 1965.

Morgan, Edmund S., ed. *The Puritan Family.* New York: Harper & Row, 1966.

——. *Virginians at Home: Family Life in the Eighteenth Century.* Williamsburg, Va.: Colonial Williamsburg, Inc., 1952.

Spruill, Julia Cherry. *Woman's Life and Work in the Southern Colonies.* Chapel Hill: University of North Carolina Press, 1938.

Stone, Lawrence. *The Family, Sex, and Marriage in England, 1500–1800.* New York: Harper & Row, 1977.

Tate, Thad W., and David L. Ammerman, eds. *The Chesapeake in the Seventeenth Century: Essays on Anglo-American Society.* Chapel Hill: University of North Carolina Press, 1979.

Part Two

TESTING THE LIMITS OF LIFE
1820–1900

Introduction

However momentous for other chronologies, the year 1800 and its "Jeffersonian revolution" have little meaning for changes in the family. There does seem to have been a watershed in family history, or at least in American expression about family life, about 1820–30. Interest in the family heightened, intensity of concern about its future increased, and Americans spoke of challenges as well as opportunities to perfect family life; yet these may only indicate changes that were largely by-products of increased literacy and printing and of a general "crisis of the spirit" about the time of the nation's fiftieth birthday in 1826.

According to the census of 1800 the population of the United States was beyond 5 million, heavily concentrated east of the Appalachians, although the western boundaries of the nation were at the Mississippi. In national origins and races the country already was extraordinarily diverse, but by head count the population was overwhelmingly from the British Isles. By 1900, the population was almost twenty times larger, beyond 90 million. These people lived across 3,000 miles with an unprecedentedly similar culture. America's borders were now continental, with coast-to-coast lines of settlement, communication, and transport. Outside the cities, however, there were only a few hundred miles of paved roads. The Indians, that old dread of families, had not only been defeated—a few small uprisings were to come—but on the way to near-decimation of body and spirit. Millions of ex-slaves had been free for a generation, but black families lived now under new tyrannies of Jim Crow and sporadic lynch law. America's ethnic revolution was under way, accompanying industrial and urban explosions, with all three changes sweeping Americans "old" and "new" into fearful diversity.

All these alterations had momentous consequences for families. If a grown man in 1800 had also been alive and mature in 1700, he probably would have found little that was different in daily family life. Vary this hypothesis to have him contrast 1900 with the year 1800, and the man would probably be dumbfounded by family routines of 1900 and, even more, astonished at what families thought of themselves and how they envisioned their future. True, the majority, the remaining rural families of 1900, would be less trans-

formed than city folk, but they were probably almost as troubled in spirit about the rapid pace of change. When Appalachia was "discovered" about 1890 it was taken as a remnant of a lost past; no traveler in 1800 would have thought of it that way or would even have had to discover it.

What in family life by 1900 was not in question? In the remotest communities, country newspapers and family religious magazines repeated the national sense of family disruption. Although the notion of the family in disarray had been sounded before, by 1900 the old family enemies, godlessness and materialism, were more varied, more subtle, more pervasive. Family confidence in moral righteousness was far more difficult, for few families by 1900 were not increasingly dependent on the materialism, money, and manufactures of a boisterous industrial capitalism. Rail though parents and their ministers might about loss of family independence and corruption of individual character, the devil was too often an invisible, unacknowledged member of the household, gnawing from within in the family's ambitions, appetites, and aspiration for amplitude.

Relevant major categories of daily life by about 1900–1910 show that throughout American society (a range of classes that was itself very different from what it had been in 1800) family style and outlook had been transformed in only a few generations. Simply and generally, there were factories and cities, technology and science, secularism and "ethnicity." These changes have to be juxtaposed, however, against the family world 1607–1820, and not merely against an earlier America, but a European-American family style, call it, cautiously, "traditionalist." About 1830, Tocqueville had already caught the quickening of American family life when he observed that in the United States the family in its aristocratic and Roman—i.e., full patriarchal—sense no longer existed. In 1910 the formal and practical daily authority of parents over children and of husbands over wives was probably still dominating, but the age-old bases of that power were eroding rapidly.

By 1900, for prime example, changes in the nature and place of work and an ever-expanding world of ready-made products were dramatically altering the character of the family as a self-sufficient economic unit. Unlike the "family economy" of the farmers, artisans, and shopkeepers of an earlier day, centered in the household itself, that of the new industrial world now sent husbands and often children and wives as well out into mills and factories to earn the wages needed to sustain the family. There the work itself was different: more mechanized, more noisy, more crowded, with ever-greater "division of labor," more scheduled and "rationalized," syncopated not by seasons and the rhythms of nature but by the clock, often harder, and, above all, unrelenting within 60 to 70 hours of at least a six-day work week. In sum, work was now at odds with the older pace of domestic hand labor as well as with the "culture" of the traditional household. The separation between household and work place was equally—though differently—severe for families of the more comfortable classes, which sent their husbands out into an increasingly bureaucratized business world while their wives remained at home, managing the "sacred sphere" and trying to preserve it as a refuge from an outside world that impinged upon it in new and baffling ways.

By 1900, families of all kinds, including those still on the farm, were increasingly turning to the machine age for the "goods" that supported family life. Dishes, cutlery, pots and pans, canned foods and packaged goods, flour or meal for bread, and countless other things needed in the home came increasingly from outside the family, made or grown not in the neighborhood, but hundreds or a thousand miles away. The steam combines of 1890 would soon give way to gasoline motors, and the sales catalogs in prairie and plains houses showed other devices that had already nudged America's rural world toward the machine age. Horses and their vehicles still dominated country and town transport, but not for long. By 1904 there was an electric subway in New York to challenge the horsecars and the steam "elevateds," and there were also electric trolleys and traction cars. By 1910 the chug and spit of automobiles and trucks were heard and talked of everywhere, and the black ribbons of hardtop highways began to unroll for family ease, reward, and pleasure. The great American rail network was already near completion by 1900, and its effects on the family's daily provisioning and shipping were profound. The rail system also created opportunities impossible for the families of 1800. The young of the comfortable could easily attend faraway colleges and schools; families could visit cities for shopping or "expositions" (Chicago '93, St. Louis '04, San Diego '15, San Francisco '15); the well-off could "escape the heat" at a "vacation spot." All this meant "wider horizons."

Family health care? Still grave and constant threats, especially the annual perils of epidemics, but professional doctors and nurses, antiseptics and anesthesia, and at least scattered decent hospitals all contributed to a fifty-percent increase over 1800 in average life expectancy at birth. Hygiene and safety for city families (35 percent of the population by 1900)? Still filth and terror for most but also ice delivery and garbage removal, underground main-line sewers, uniformed full-time police and firemen, and electric street lighting. "Outside agencies"? Up to 1800, beyond the home and family perhaps only a church, but by 1900, churches, schools (with a burgeoning education bureaucracy), intrusive town, county, city and state governments with boards of health, bureaus of licenses, inspectors of this, supervisors of that. Symbols and sources of daily authority and "models" of behavior? Still, by 1900, father, mother, older sisters and brothers, and the minister (priests too, now, and rabbis) but also clubs, guilds, unions, Wheels, Alliances, Vereins (for Germans), Bunds (for Polish Jews), Sokols (for Bohemians), auxiliaries, leagues, and, for youth in peril, the dreaded ways of the "streets": gangs, toughs, and organized full-time crime and prostitution.

Where these and other deep changes in family life were not yet experienced by 1900, they were anticipated with a mixture of desire and dread. Help, on the one hand; loss of control or independence, corruption, and interference on the other. When Henry Adams at about this time began to write about nineteenth-century America he thought of its culture as energy and force, largely centripetal and veering beyond control. In general outline, at least, the century of changes in the family fit Adams's cultural metaphors. There was universal agreement about a loosening of family authority and ties to tradition. Everyone felt both a push and a pull at the hearth outward from small to larger worlds and from intimacy to impersonalism, from emphasis on surviving to searches for surfeit of energy and success.

This cultural restlessness had earlier given rise in the 1830s and '40s to what John Higham has characterized as a feeling of "boundlessness," the sense that America had shed the traditions and conditions with which the Old World had shackled the spirit. Because of this freedom and the seemingly inexhaustible bounty "Nature and Nature's God" had bestowed upon the nation, what the human will could achieve was limitless. Though intoxicating to some—Ralph Waldo Emerson's earliest statement of the credo bestowed almost Godlike capacities on the self-reliant American—it was terrifying to others, and by the middle decades of the century the exuberance was muted, giving way to what David Brion Davis has called a "search for limits" and what Robert Wiebe, in a related context, has spoken of as a somewhat later "search for order." Such themes are also apt for describing the overall, contrasting tendencies of the family in pursuit of power and opportunity and yet yearning for predictability, roots, continuity, control, and—Wiebe's word—"order." Novelists from Hawthorne on recurrently caught the dilemmas and pains of Americans afire with visions of the "orgiastic future," as Scott Fitzgerald would call it.

Every individual in the family was primed for power and wealth. In the campaign for a stranglehold on life there was no dearth of coarser appetites and the worldliest ambitions. But at the same time, along with the crude dynamics of (as later expressed) "the world is your oyster" and "the sky's the limit," there were the search for stasis, the yearning for familial peace, Christian perfection, and pure love, an other-world of "this too shall pass away" and "this day shalt thou be with me in paradise." Daily contraries and contradictions, absolute and demanding. Impossible? Not the World or the Word. Both. The American Way.

It was not, to be sure, a universal way. By condition or culture many in nineteenth-century America—Indians, blacks, both enslaved and freed, many non-English speaking and non-Protestant immigrants, the less skilled industrial workers, for example—were only at its edge or fell outside it. Nonetheless, the dominant or "official" culture by which those who regarded themselves as the "best Americans" perceived and judged such groups, and against which "outsiders" and "newcomers" had to define themselves, was created from the array of ideas and anxieties arranged around the World and the Word.

Viewed in the light of these two great beacons of life, various aspects of the "official" American cult of the family in the nineteenth century became comprehensible. After 1820 Americans made a religion of domesticity, casting supernal light around mother, child, and home. Childhood was invented as a distinct and lengthening stage of life, innocent and pure, or at least purifiable, of sin. Tended by holy mothers, the child would save the republic. Sermon, tract, manual, poem, story, primer, oration, hymn, sampler—the artifacts of these cults are countless. All express the type of feeling that powerful "escapist" fantasies pay to disturbing, contrary fact: a sentimentality, a pretense that there was no conflict, an easy and spurious release from the genuine emotional dilemma of serving World or Word. The American family and home were perfect or could be made perfect, refuges for innocence and fortresses of the rectitude needed to cope with and judge the world. Guilt and shame made it necessary to pretend that Christian and virtuous republican families did not do what they did and had to do if children were to win the world. In fact, the family deliberately nurtured the very hungers for the world that the "spirituality" of its otherworldly Christianity affected to despise.

Noteworthily, the American father was the least enshrined figure in the sentimental cults. He could not, of course, be left out. But how to deal with him? There were countless advice and conduct books on the paragon father. And who, in print, was not deferential to the paternal authority? But as the world-shaker, world-maker, bringer-home-of-the-bacon, good provider (the more the better), the "man of the world" (precisely), he had to be urged to remember his roles, to return to his duties, not to lose his place in the minds, hearts, and prayers of his family. Implicitly he was, too often, too much of that world out there beyond the "family shrine." Out there, the hope was he would be "man enough" to best it, yet "manly" enough to wrest well with it morally. How could he not be tainted by the world outside the home? And how would he seem at home when it was his crude man's world outside that the mother was to keep at bay? Suspect? An enemy? Indeed, by the end of the century it had become necessary to include lessons in fathering as one of the biggest, if touchiest, tasks of the saintly super-mother.

Until about 1870, tension within the family between the World and the Word was in the literal terms of the age-old struggle between Mammon and God, of the worldliness of business or frivolity in conflict with Christian, otherworldly perfection. By 1900, these terms had not disappeared, but word and world also had other, more secular, meanings. The Christian's sin-ridden World, ever-near apocalypse, became a gentler moral synonym like "unworthy," and the saving Word of God, of Christ, and of the Scriptures had become "charac-

ter." By 1900 Jesus was still the Christ but he was then, even more, the paramount figure of character and "high-mindedness."

Despite the official hallowing of family and home, civil war seems to have raged on American hearths. Memoirs, stories, dramas, letters, diaries, and legal and police records are full of the hostilities over property, patrimony, precedence, and other sibling rivalries; not "good enough" marriages; family financial support, career choices, required or secret departures and desertions. The world in fact pulled family members in contrary ways and into conflict with each other. The American's creed said, "Where there's a will, there's a way." "Success!" Change is the law of life. "Go West." Pull up roots and bootstraps. Be better than fathers and other than yesterday. The Word from the Bible, the ancients of 1776, and the writer-doyens of the domesticity cult warned, "Honor thy father and mother," "Be thou then perfect," "Let us have peace," "Love eternal, ever-healing." And what of the "old homestead," "home sweet home," "old folks at home," "my old Kentucky home"? Renditions of the "lost home" theme seem countless. How could families fight in or quarrel over the home or abandon the family "seat" or send forth the children bravely yet have "home" too? The nostalgia and sentimentality of the songs: home never left your memory and feelings! Yet, whatever the hankering for home, tens of millions of Ishmaels, of nomads, wandering from sea to shining sea were lost to the World.

With family and home, despite the pretensions of the religion of domesticity, in fact so short or thin a presence, so at bay before the world, how did family culture "hang on" or try to compensate for the disruptions the family itself had inspired by setting loose the world-killer instinct in breasts of the American young? It is essential to appreciate how deeply America by 1870 differed from the society of the past. Home to many was no longer a real and perennial place. For one notable thing, it moved—and often. The "seat" was abandoned. Back there might be a place, good for a nostalgic foray in genealogy or even one visit, if time and money permitted. The weight of the generations had been dismissed or abandoned. Left were faded photographs and family trees in the front of the old Bible. Grandparents, parents, brother, and sister were seldom in one place or locatable—only somewhere, perhaps, in the dark fields of the republic. Progeny moved, and the statistics of the century on that meaning of "mobility" are astonishing. There were no telephones to "reach out and touch someone." Popular lore has it that the rare telegram announced only a distant, sudden, unanticipated family disaster. There was the occasional letter and chance of word-of-mouth news, however paltry, to stir memories of family, but family and home as on-the-spot, life-long receivers, translators, and transmitters of the messages of conscience and culture had disappeared.

The nomad could, at best, carry "family" and "home" within. If "family" *controlled it was largely through what was called "character," "conscience," "ideals," "high-mindedness." These words became the litany of the family cult as the nineteenth century wore on. Implanting them became the very purpose of the family, beset as it was by the future and by the omnipresent, disruptive struggle of World with Word. Proper nurture of the idealized, unspoiled, open-to-everything child would "internalize" the Word and yield "character." Its ideals would steer the Ishmael safely through the temptations of this American world. The rules of the road of life, learned at the hearth, were not, however, as rationalistic or abstract as their expression in hymns and samplers may make them seem. Powerful feelings of guilt, shame, remorse, and anxiety from memories of the distant all-loving, all-wise mother and of the observant, justice-dispensing father kept the gyroscopic morality machines going: succeed squarely and be succored by conscience; think or act falsely and be flailed by it. "Remember thy father and mother" indeed!*

Of course, the moral gyroscope was seldom strong enough against the American world and one's own appetite. When a critic told Sigmund Freud that people did not do the terrible things or think the unthinkable thoughts Freud had recorded, because God had given man a conscience, Freud answered that God had done very uneven work. Inevitably, the parents of the nineteenth century not only did uneven work but, more tellingly, contradictory work; they preached and instilled God, love, and family but inspired simultaneously godlessness, aggression, and internecine strife. The private debacle and social explosion created a long record of pathology. That is too simply described as hypocrisies. The American who made his real estate "killing" in the morning and lunched with his "brothers" at the YMCA board meeting or Rotary, or who observed the Christian Sunday with a Klan membership card in his pocket, was "conflict-ridden." He went through and came out of the nineteenth century with at least two souls burning in his breast. Earlier in American history, the Christian Word and the World's maxims had coexisted, if clumsily, within him. The American record is, of course, full of stories of the excesses of spirituality or venality which either of the souls could inspire when coexistence failed or when the family controls broke down. But the nineteenth century immeasurably heightened the stakes of the great American game of a world to win, for everyone. Space, land booms, slaves traded; Indian and Civil wars; oil, steel, and coal; plank roads, canals, and railroads; rivers, deserts, mountains (NATURE); the frontier (western, urban, professional, scientific, technological). All this meant, "Conquer We Must." To this the Word added, too often as echo, "For our cause, it is just."

WESTWARD AND ONWARD THE COURSE OF FAMILIES

The nineteenth century began portentously with the doubling of our geography through the purchase of Louisiana in 1803. The years continued with a flood of Americans westward and culminated with the announcement after the Census of 1890 that the frontier was closed. This extraordinary conquest of a continent within one hundred years deeply impressed American historians. Starting with its presentation in 1893, the "frontier theory" of Frederick Jackson Turner influenced for the next fifty years the history of America's families as much as it affected other research. According to the school of Turner, life on the frontier demanded improvisation and self-reliance and encouraged treating persons for their "true worth" and performance, not rank. This life democratized family relations as it did other American institutions. Fathers and sons had to develop comradery rather than command, and women had to be respected and given the vote. The frontier thus liquidated patriarchal ties and other vestiges of the traditional hierarchical worlds that immigrants from Europe, Asia, and Africa had known. Turner also argued that readily available free land in the West provided a "safety valve" for Americans who could not "make it" in settled areas. Hard-pressed families could take off for a fresh start and greater opportunities in the West.

By now the "Turner thesis" has largely succumbed to the accumulated criticism of its contradictory claims and the ambiguity of its key ideas of "frontier," "democracy," and "individualism." It now seems clear that the "democratization" of the family and other institutions depended on more than the frontier or the West; that Turner and his followers exaggerated the extent of economic opportunity the frontier provided; that, as the nineteenth century wore on, millions of farm and rural folk sought their opportunities on the urban and industrial "frontiers" rather than through the safety valve of free or cheap land.

Nonetheless, as both fact and symbol, the West did contribute to the extraordinary roaming of Americans in the nineteenth century. In East and West, on the land and in towns and cities, Americans moved with a frequency contrasting dramatically with how, for centuries, the villages of Europe and Asia had bound families to place. In a style of nomadism (recorded in the notations of birthplaces in the manuscripts of the federal censuses), American families changed locations, dwellings, crafts and callings, and churches with astonishing frequency. Although moving often, families at least tried to stay in an allied calling. Over two generations, a family's members might try the rural careers of independent farmer, farm laborer, rural town merchant, itinerant mechanic, livery stableman, windmill or insurance salesman, teacher, preacher, and farm-reform lecturer.

The first selection in this section, from the Strong family records, suggests what stresses moving entailed and the chart allows us to reconstruct the specific moves of one family over several generations. The ceaseless movement across the nation as well as in vocations is also heavily chronicled in American folklore and literature. Two pieces here, a popular ballad that went through as many versions as there were frontiers, and a portion of Hamlin Garland's autobiography supplement each other and express some of the strains in family relations and expectations that accompanied moving on. Was there something peculiarly American in a positive desire to be "a rolling stone," to be free of roots and ties, time and culture? How often, we need to ask, was moving as much the result of dream or fantasy as it was an economic or demographic necessity, as though to move was a personal destiny or an imperative of culture?

Whatever the allure of "heading west" or "moving on," settling in was a shock. Much had to be learned afresh, like what in a new locale was safe to eat, and much lore and technique from the forsaken area had to be abandoned or forgotten. Several memoirs here of Western settlers should recreate their hopes and need for innovations and yet the simultaneous yearning for the tried and tested. Try to recall the successive details of family routine and imagine how much of this management was altered by changing the family seat. Think of a new terrain, new climate and cycle of seasons, new crops, new game animals, new fuels, possibly less water, and the effects of all of these on daily family order and customs. Add to these the strain in making the family safe from white marauders, Indians, or wild animals.

"Going West" often meant a family giving up the people and convenience of a settled culture. Out where it was fresh, there were no over-the-fence neighbors, no clan of relatives or dropping-in visitors, no roads, no detailed maps, no dependable mail or local newspaper or other "essential" services, and no minister or church to sanctify baptism, marriage, and other turning points of life.

Despite all the evidence of how much it meant to Americans to make a fresh start, they could not transcend much of the past. Parents not only remembered but were *conditioned* by their past, both its facts and fantasies. Even if their children were born on the new worlds of the frontiers, they had their lessons and conditioning from their remembering parents. Indeed, families did not want to reject all of the past, especially if a family sought principally economic opportunity in moving. How, indeed, did the exposure to the new and strange affect desires to remember, to hang on, conserve and, to *sanctify* the new life in traditional ways?

ONE FAMILY'S MOVES

To Nathan Strong Sr.

Dear and Much esteemed Parents. I sit down to inform you of my health which is very poor this winter. I have not been able to do but a little work this winter I have been to Doren Stevens to finish a job I commenced in the fall but was not able to finish it yet but hope. This week your stack of hay was burnt up Last week I bought Mother shers the price was nine shillings. Mr. Bulen had no shoes would fit her tremens he was deranged through his sickness declaring he was in Hell Eld. Lothrop preach the funeral sermon Mary Ann Stone washed last monday and took cold and settled on her lungs and she died on Friday and was buried today She was Shelie Ann school mate. Yesterday was our covenant meeting and it was a good one today we had a communion season it was truly a pleasant time to me. Mrs. Dolitle has been sickly to the south

I often dream of you that you are a keeping house and I am living with you but I am mistaken I waked a few nights ago calling Mother but she did not hear me but I find it a comfort to dream of those I love I may never see you again as death is on every side but I want to be prepared for the change that I may meet my Judge with joy and not with grief. I should like to know how you prosper in religion at the domain Be assured that I should like to have a letter from my father although I am unworthy of it

Jan 6 I have been to Blodgets to day and they are all well Issac has got judgement against Mr. Stevens the old man put his property out of his hands has secured him for the judgement but he is afraid of damages. Jan 12 I have been to meeting to day and we had preaching would have done you good to hear it. Elder Lothrop he preaches better and better he is very much engaged this winter there will be a donation held for Eld. L a week from next thursday night Nathan and myself are on the committee and we meet tomorow night to make arrangements for the part it is to be held at the temperence house. It is sickly in town this winter Mr. Pulcifer is not expected to live he has the consumption there is a good many sick here there are needy and they beg all to do clothing they can and make it [unintelligible] for children and knit stockings and bed quilts and make comforters they bought a piece of coton and made sheets and pilow cases of it I joined last Friday we meet every week at Mrs. Fisks there is a great many that are destitute Sarah is not much better but she is very anxious to go to the domain and Nathan has made up his mind to go if he can be excepted there.

Betsy Strong

"Strong Family Papers" in Ceresco, Wisconsin Papers (manuscript). State Historical Society of Wisconsin, Madison, Wisconsin.

JOURNEYS OF THE STRONG FAMILY

NAME	BIRTHPLACE	BIRTH DATE	ARRIVAL AT CERESCO	DEATH OR DEPARTURE
Nathan Strong, Sr.	Granville, N.Y.	5/2/1782	7/31/1844	
Sarah Strong	Caldwell, R.I.	3/5/1790	" "	
Cynthia H. Strong	Vineyard, Vt.	11/17/1822	" "	3/28/1846
Phebe Ann Strong	" "	7/31/1824	9/28/1844	Departed
Betsy Strong	" "	6/3/1807	2/18/1845	
William D. Strong	Vineyard, Vt.	8/24/1808	9/28/1844	Departed
Eunice Strong	Mealome, N.Y.	12/28/1812	" "	Died, 12/2/1847
Harriett N. Strong	" "	5/23/1832	" "	
Henry V. Strong	Greenfield, Ind.	1/17/1837	" "	
Ann Eliza Strong	P. Prairie, Wis.	10/20/1840	" "	
Cynthia A. Strong	Paris, Wis.	2/27/1843	" "	Died, 8/10/1846
Alice A. Strong	Ceresco, Wis.	8/26/1845	" "	
Nathan Strong, Jr.	Vineyard, Vt.	11/11/1813	2/18/1845	Departed
Sarah Strong	? , S.C.	3/2/1816	" "	Died, 9/10/1845
Lewis G. Strong	Greenfield, Ind.	10/29/1836	" "	Departed
Benj. F. Strong	Coldwater, Mich.	9/4/1838	" "	Departed
Sarah A. Strong	P. Prairie, Wis.	9/10/1840	" "	Died, 10/19/1845
Jas. E. Strong	" "	1/22/1842	" "	Departed
Emily Strong	Ceresco, Wis.	7/21/1845	" "	

Membership record of Ceresco Community, a utopian group established in 1844 in present-day Ripon, Wisconsin. From Strong Family records, *loc. cit.*

A BALLAD ABOUT MOVING

Rolling Stone

Since times are so hard, I'll tell you, my sweetheart,
I'm 'bout to leave off my plow and my cart.
And down to Kentucky Genoa we'll go,
To better our fortunes as other folks do,
Whilst here we must labour each day in the field,
The winter destroys all the summer can yield.

O Collin, I've seen with a sorrowful heart,
You long have neglected your plow and your cart,
O, your sheep now at random disorderly run,
Your Sunday's new waistcoat goes every day on:
Stick close to your farm or you'll suffer a loss,
For the stone that is rolling can gather no moss.

"Rolling Stone" in Eliphabet Mason, *Complete Pocket Song Book* (1803), pp. 344–47.

Dear wife, don't be talking of stones nor of moss,
Or think by our going you will suffer a loss,
For there we can have as much land as we please,
Drink brandy and whiskey and live at our ease:
Whilst here we must labour each day in the field,
The winter destroys all the summer can yield.

O Collin, pray hear me, I think you are wrong,
The lands in those parts are not bought with a song,
In purchasing whiskey I am almost in despair,
It must be of cash, a great consequence there:
Stick close to your farm or you'll suffer a loss,
For the stone that is rolling can gather no moss.

We've houses we've lands, we've harrows we've plows,
We've sheep we have horses, we've heifers we've cows,
Besides a good barn that stands in our yard,
We'll turn into cash and we need not fare hard:
Whilst here we must labour each day in the field,
The winter destroys all the summer can yield.

Your Genesee's land Kentucky to clear,
Will cost you both labour and money a year,
You've cows, sheep and heifers and all things to buy,
You'll hardly get suited before that you die:
Stick close to your farm or you'll suffer a loss,
For the stone that is rolling can gather no moss.

There's a house and a barn and a plenty of land,
We can have ready clear'd without doubt at our hand,
Besides heifers and sheep are not very dear,
We can feast upon buffalo half of the year:
Whilst here we must labour each day in the field,
The winter destroys all the summer can yield.

I wish I'd a purse of ten thousand bright crowns,
And a store of good lots in the best of our towns,
O, then we'd remove and we'd wish for good luck,
We'd ride on the banks of the pleasant Kentuck:
The poor must be humbled or suffer a loss,
For the stone that is rolling can gather no moss.

Your argument I know is not without right,
Yet I must go there for I long to be great.
In less than a year in a coach you will ride,
In coaches and stages with Collin you'll glide:
Whilst here we must labour each day in the field,
The winter destroys all the summer can yield.

O Collin remember those lands of delight,
Infested by indians who murder by night,
Your house may be plunder'd and burnt to the ground,
Your wife and your children lie mangled around:
Stay here or you'll certainly suffer a loss,
For the stone that is rolling can gather no moss.

Dear wife you've convinc'd me I'll urge you no more,
I never once thought of your dying before,
My children I love altho' they are but small,
My dear wife I do value as much as them all:
We'll stick to our farm and prevent every loss,
For the stone that is rolling can gather no moss.

We'll set all our thoughts on farming affairs,
To make our corn grow and our appletrees bear,
'Tis contentment upbraided contentment to know,
So you to your distaff and I to my plow:
We'll stick to our farm and prevent every loss,
For the stone that is rolling can gather no moss.

FATHER SELLS THE FARM

Green's Coulee was a delightful place for boys. It offered hunting and coasting and many other engrossing sports, but my father, as the seasons went by, became thoroughly dissatisfied with its disadvantages. More and more he resented the stumps and ridges which interrupted his plow. Much of his quarter-section remained unbroken. There were ditches to be dug in the marsh and young oaks to be uprooted from the forest, and he was obliged to toil with unremitting severity. There were times, of course, when field duties did not press, but never a day came when the necessity for twelve hours' labor did not exist.

Furthermore, as he grubbed or reaped he remembered the glorious prairies he had crossed on his exploring trip into Minnesota before the war, and the oftener he thought of them the more bitterly he resented his up-tilted, horse-killing fields, and his complaining words sank so deep into the minds of his sons that for years thereafter they were unable to look upon any rise of ground as an object to be admired.

It irked him beyond measure to force his reaper along a steep slope, and he loathed the irregular little patches running up the ravines behind the timbered knolls, and so at last like many another of his neighbors he began to look away to the west as a fairer field for conquest. He no more thought of going east than a liberated eagle dreams of returning to its narrow cage. He loved to talk of Boston, to boast of its splendor, but to

Hamlin Garland, *A Son of the Middle Border* (New York, 1914), pp. 42–46.

live there, to earn his bread there, was unthinkable. Beneath the sunset lay the enchanted land of opportunity and his liberation came unexpectedly.

Sometime in the spring of 1868, a merchant from LaCrosse, a plump man who brought us candy and was very cordial and condescending, began negotiations for our farm, and in the discussion of plans which followed, my conception of the universe expanded. I began to understand that "Minnesota" was not a bluff but a wide land of romance, a prairie, peopled with red men, which lay far beyond the big river. And then, one day, I heard my father read to my mother a paragraph from the county paper which ran like this, "It is reported that Richard Garland has sold his farm in Green's Coulee to our popular grocer, Mr. Speer. Mr. Speer intends to make of it a model dairy farm."

This intention seemed somehow to reflect a ray of glory upon us, though I fear it did not solace my mother, as she contemplated the loss of home and kindred. She was not by nature an emigrant,—few women are. She was content with the pleasant slopes, the kindly neighbors of Green's Coulee. Furthermore, most of her brothers and sisters still lived just across the ridge in the valley of the Neshonoc, and the thought of leaving them for a wild and unknown region was not pleasant.

To my father, on the contrary, change was alluring. Iowa was now the place of the rainbow, and the pot of gold. He was eager to push on toward it, confident of the outcome. His spirit was reflected in one of the songs which we children particularly enjoyed hearing our mother sing, a ballad which consisted of a dialogue between a husband and wife on this very subject of emigration. The words as well as its wailing melody still stir me deeply, for they lay hold of my sub-conscious memory—embodying admirably the debate which went on in our home as well as in the homes of other farmers in the valley,—only, alas! our mothers did not prevail.

It begins with a statement of unrest on the part of the husband who confesses that he is about to give up his plow and his cart—

> Away to Colorado a journey I'll go,
> For to double my fortune as other men do,
> *While here I must labor each day in the field*
> *And the winter consumes all the summer doth yield.*

To this the wife replies:

> Dear husband, I've noticed with a sorrowful heart
> That you long have neglected your plow and your cart.
> Your horses, sheep, cattle at random do run,
> And your new Sunday jacket goes every day on.
> *Oh, stay on your farm and you'll suffer no loss,*
> *For the stone that keeps rolling will gather no moss.*

But the husband insists:

> Oh, wife, let us go; Oh, don't let us wait;
> I long to be there, and I long to be great,
> While you some fair lady and who knows but I
> May be some rich governor long 'fore I die,
> *Whilst here I must labor each day in the field,*
> *And the winter consumes all the summer doth yield.*

But wife shrewdly retorts:

> Dear husband, remember those lands are so dear
> They will cost you the labor of many a year.
> Your horses, sheep, cattle will all be to buy,
> You will hardly get settled before you must die.
> Oh, stay on the farm,—etc.

The husband then argues that as in that country the lands are all cleared to the plow, and horses and cattle not very dear, they would soon be rich. Indeed, "we will feast on fat venison one-half of the year." Thereupon the wife brings in her final argument:

> Oh, husband, remember those lands of delight
> Are surrounded by Indians who murder by night.
> Your house will be plundered and burnt to the ground
> While your wife and your children lie mangled around.

This fetches the husband up with a round turn:

> Oh, wife, you've convinced me, I'll argue no more,
> I never once thought of your dying before.
> I love my dear children although they are small
> And you, my dear wife, I love greatest of all.

> Refrain (both together)
> We'll stay on the farm and we'll suffer no loss
> For the stone that keeps rolling will gather no moss.

This song was not an especial favorite of my father. Its minor strains and its expressions of womanly doubts and fears were antipathetic to his sanguine, buoyant, self-confident nature. He was inclined to ridicule the conclusions of its last verse and to say that the man was a molly-coddle—or whatever the word of contempt was in those days. As an antidote he usually called for "O'er the hills in legions, boys," which exactly expressed his love of exploration and adventure.

This ballad which dates back to the conquest of the Allegheny mountains opens with a fine uplifting note,

> Cheer up, brothers, as we go
> O'er the mountains, westward ho,
> Where herds of deer and buffalo
> Furnish the fare.

and the refrain is at once a bugle call and a vision:

> Then o'er the hills in legions, boys,
> Fair freedom's star
> Points to the sunset regions, boys,
> Ha, ha, ha-ha!

and when my mother's clear voice rose on the notes of that exultant chorus, our hearts responded with a surge of emotion akin to that which sent the followers of Daniel Boone across the Blue Ridge, and lined the trails of Kentucky and Ohio with the canvas-covered wagons of the pioneers.

A little farther on in the song came these words,

> When we've wood and prairie land,
> Won by our toil,
> We'll reign like kings in fairy land,
> Lords of the soil!

which always produced in my mind the picture of a noble farm-house in a park-like valley, just as the line, "We'll have our rifles ready, boys," expressed the boldness and self-reliance of an armed horseman.

The significance of this song in the lives of the McClintocks and the Garlands cannot be measured. It was the marching song of my Grandfather's generation and undoubtedly profoundly influenced my father and my uncles in all that they did. It suggested shining mountains, and grassy vales, swarming with bear and elk. It called to green savannahs and endless flowery glades. It voiced as no other song did, the pioneer impulse throbbing deep in my father's blood. That its words will not bear close inspection today takes little from its power. Unquestionably it was a directing force in the lives of at least three generations of my pioneering race. Its strains will be found running through this book from first to last, for its pictures continued to allure my father on and on toward "the sunset regions," and its splendid faith carried him through many a dark vale of discontent.

FIRST SEASONS ON THE FRONTIER

Like most men, my dear father should never have married. Though his nature was one of the sweetest I have ever known, and though he would at any call give his time to or risk his life for others, in practical matters

Anna Howard Shaw, *The Story of a Pioneer* (New York, 1915), pp. 27–38, passim.

he remained to the end of his days as irresponsible as a child. If his mind turned to practical details at all, it was solely in their bearing toward great developments of the future. To him an acorn was not an acorn, but a forest of young oaks.

Thus, when he took up his claim of three hundred and sixty acres of land in the wilderness of northern Michigan, and sent my mother and five young children to live there alone until he could join us eighteen months later, he gave no thought to the manner in which we were to make the struggle and survive the hardships before us. He had furnished us with land and the four walls of a log cabin. Some day, he reasoned, the place would be a fine estate, which his sons would inherit and in the course of time pass on to their sons—always an Englishman's most iridescent dream. That for the present we were one hundred miles from a railroad, forty miles from the nearest post-office, and half a dozen miles from any neighbors save Indians, wolves, and wildcats; that we were wholly unlearned in the ways of the woods as well as in the most primitive methods of farming; that we lacked not only every comfort, but even the bare necessities of life; and that we must begin, single-handed and untaught, a struggle for existence in which some of the severest forces of nature would be arrayed against us—these facts had no weight in my father's mind. Even if he had witnessed my mother's despair on the night of our arrival in our new home, he would not have understood it. . . .

We faced our situation with clear and unalarmed eyes the morning after our arrival. The problem of food, we knew, was at least temporarily solved. We had brought with us enough coffee, pork, and flour to last for several weeks; and the one necessity father had put inside the cabin walls was a great fireplace, made of mud and stones, in which our food could be cooked. The problem of our water-supply was less simple, but my brother James solved it for the time by showing us a creek a long distance from the house; and for months we carried from this creek in pails, every drop of water we used, save that which we caught in troughs when the rain fell.

We held a family council after breakfast, and in this, though I was only twelve, I took an eager and determined part. I loved work—it has always been my favorite form of recreation—and my spirit rose to the opportunities of it which smiled on us from every side. Obviously the first thing to do was to put doors and windows into the yawning holes father had left for them, and to lay a board flooring over the earth inside our cabin walls, and these duties we accomplished before we had occupied our new home a fortnight. There was a small saw-mill nine miles from our cabin, on the spot that is now Big Rapids, and there we bought our lumber. . . . Nothing is more comfortable than a log cabin which has been carefully built and finished; but for some reason—probably because there seemed always a more urgent duty calling to us around the corner—we never plastered our house at all. The result was that on many future winter mornings we awoke to find ourselves chastely blanketed by snow, while the only warm spot in our living-room was that directly in front of the fireplace, where great logs burned all day. Even there our faces scorched while our spines slowly congealed, until we learned to revolve before the fire like a bird upon a spit. . . .

It was too late in the season for plowing or planting, even if we had possessed anything with which to plow, and, moreover, our so-called "cleared" land was thick with sturdy tree-stumps. Even during the second summer plowing was impossible; we could only plant potatoes and corn, and follow the most primitive method in doing even this. We took an ax, chopped up the sod, put the seed under it, and let the seed grow. The seed did grow, too—in the most gratifying and encouraging manner. Our green corn and potatoes were the best I have ever eaten. But for the present we lacked these luxuries.

We had, however, in their place, large quantities of wild fruit—gooseberries, raspberries, and plums—which Harry and I gathered on the banks of our creek. Harry also became an expert fisherman. We had no hooks or lines, but he took wires from our hoop-skirts and made snares at the ends of poles. My part of this work was to stand on a log and frighten the fish out of their holes by making horrible sounds, which I did with impassioned earnestness. When the fish hurried to the surface of the water to investigate the appalling noises they had heard, they were easily snared by our small boy, who was very proud of his ability to contribute in this way to the family table.

During our first winter we lived largely on cornmeal, making a little journey of twenty miles to the nearest mill to buy it; but even at that we were better off than our neighbors, for I remember one family in our region who for an entire winter lived solely on coarse-grained yellow turnips, gratefully changing their diet to leeks when these came in the spring. . . .

On every side, and at every hour of the day, we came up against the relentless limitations of pioneer life. There was not a team of horses in our entire region. The team with which my brother had driven us through the wilderness had been hired at Grand Rapids for that occasion, and, of course, immediately returned. Our lumber was delivered by ox-teams, and the absolutely essential purchases we made "outside" (at the nearest shops, forty miles away) were carried through the forest on the backs of men. Our mail was delivered once a month by a carrier who made the journey in alternate stages of horseback riding and canoeing. . . .

Naturally, our two greatest menaces were wild animals and Indians, but as the days passed the first of these lost the early terrors with which we had associated them. We grew indifferent to the sounds that had made our first night a horror to us all—there was even a certain homeliness in them—while we regarded with accustomed, almost blasé eyes the various furred creatures of which we caught distant glimpses as they slunk through the forest. Their experience with other settlers had taught them caution; it soon became clear that they were as eager to avoid us as we were to shun them, and by common consent we gave each other ample elbow-

The white man with a camera did not have many opportunities to capture scenes of
Indian life in unconquered villages. Most photographs of live Indians thus date from
after their conquest. These pictures of two Indian families from southern Idaho in the
1890s show two different stages of Indian accommodation to white culture. In the first

picture, the family is in tribal dress but poses in the white-family formal studio style of the period. In the second picture, again like whites, the family is dressed to the nines for a sitting, but now in store-bought white clothing.   *National Archives*

room. But the Indians were all around us, and every settler had a collection of hair-raising tales to tell of them. . . .

In my first encounter with them . . . mother had to meet her unwelcome guests supported only by her young children. She at once prepared a meal, however, and when they arrived she welcomed them calmly and gave them the best she had. . . . They were quite sober, and though they left without expressing any appreciation of her hospitality, they made her a second visit a few months later, bringing a large quantity of venison and a bag of cranberries as a graceful return. . . .

Our second encounter with the Indians was a less agreeable experience. There were seven "Marquette warriors" in the next group of callers, and they were all intoxicated. Moreover, they had brought with them several jugs of bad whisky—the raw and craze-provoking product supplied them by the fur-dealers—and it was clear that our cabin was to be the scene of an orgy. . . .

By dawn, however, the whisky was all gone, and they were in so deep a stupor that, one after the other, the seven fell from their chairs to the floor, where they sprawled unconscious. When they awoke they left quietly and without trouble of any kind. They seemed a strangely subdued and chastened band; probably they were wretchedly ill after their debauch on the adulterated whisky the traders had given them.

During our first year there was no school within ten miles of us but this lack failed to sadden Harry or me. We had brought with us . . . a box of books, in which, in winter months, when our outdoor work was restricted, we found much comfort. They were the only books in that part of the country, and we read them until we knew them all by heart. Moreover, father sent us regularly the *New York Independent,* and with this admirable literature, after reading it, we papered our walls. Thus, on stormy days, we could lie on the settle or the floor and read the *Independent* over again with increased interest and pleasure. . . .

When the advantages of public education were finally extended to me, at thirteen, by the opening of a school three miles from our home, I accepted them with growing reluctance. The teacher was a spinster forty-four years of age—and the only genuine "old maid" I have ever met who was not a married woman or a man. She was the real thing, and her name, Prudence Duncan, seemed the fitting label for her rigidly uncompromising personality. I graced Prudence's school for three months, and then left it at her fervid request. I had walked six miles a day through trackless woods and Western blizzards to get what she could give me, but she had little to offer my awakened and critical mind. My reading taught me more than Prudence knew—a fact we both inwardly admitted and fiercely resented from our different viewpoints. Beyond doubt I was a pert and trying young person. I lost no opportunity to lead Prudence beyond her intellectual depth and leave her there, and Prudence vented her chagrin not alone upon me, but upon my little brother. I became a thorn in her side, and one day, after an especially unpleasant episode in which Harry also figured, she plucked me out, as it were, and cast me for ever from her. From that time I studied at home, where I was a much more valuable economic factor than I had been in school.

FRONTIER DEMANDS ON THE FAMILY

One of the most painful things in the Western States and Territories is the extinction of childhood. I have never seen any children, only debased imitations of men and women, cankered by greed and selfishness, and asserting and gaining complete independence of their parents at ten years old. The atmosphere in which they are brought up is one of greed, godlessness, and frequently of profanity. Consequently these sweet things seem like flowers in a desert.

Except for love, which here as everywhere raises life into the ideal, this is a wretched existence. The poor crops have been destroyed by grasshoppers over and over again, and that talent deified here under the name of "smartness" has taken advantage of Dr. H. in all bargains, leaving him with little except food for his children. Experience has been dearly bought in all ways, and this instance of failure might be a useful warning to professional men without agricultural experience not to come and try to make a living by farming in Colorado.

My time here has passed very delightfully in spite of my regret and anxiety for this interesting family. I should like to stay longer, were it not that they have given up to me their straw bed, and Mrs. H. and her baby, a wizened, fretful child, sleep on the floor in my room, and Dr. H. on the floor downstairs, and the nights are frosty and chill. Work is the order of their day, and of mine, and at night, when the children are in bed, we three ladies patch the clothes and make shirts, and Dr. H. reads Tennyson's poems, or we speak tenderly of that world of culture and noble deeds which seems here "the land very far off," or Mrs. H. lays aside her work for a few minutes and reads some favorite passage of prose or poetry, as I have seldom heard either read before, with a voice of large compass and exquisite tone, quick to interpret every shade of the author's meaning, and soft, speaking eyes, moist with feeling and sympathy. These are our halcyon hours, when we forget the needs of the morrow, and that men still buy, sell, cheat, and strive for gold, and that we are in the Rocky Mountains, and that it is near midnight. But morning comes hot and tiresome, and the never-ending work is oppressive, and Dr. H. comes in from the field two or three times in the day, dizzy and faint, and they condole with each other, and I feel that the Colorado settler needs to be made of sterner stuff and to possess more adaptability. . . . This is not Arcadia. "Smartness," which consists in over-reaching your neighbor in every fashion which is not illegal, is the quality which is held in the greatest

Isabella Bird, *A Lady's Life in the Rocky Mountains* (New York, 1879), pp. 67–69.

As frontier houses went, this Texas dwelling from about 1830 was probably uncommonly spacious and refined even when some later additions are subtracted. The house was near enough to trees to be made of wood. Farther west or north the first dwelling of a frontier family might be of stone or sod or skins. *Amon Carter Museum, Fort Worth, Texas*

repute, and Mammon is the divinity. From a generation brought up to worship the one and admire the other little can be hoped.

HOMESTEADING AND THE FAMILY

When I read of the hard times among the Denver poor, I feel like urging them every one to get out and file on land. I am very enthusiastic about women homesteading. It really requires less strength and labor to raise plenty to satisfy a large family than it does to go out to wash, with the added satisfaction of knowing that their job will not be lost to them if they care to keep it. Even if improving the place does go slowly, it is that much done to stay done. Whatever is raised is the homesteader's own, and there is no house-rent to pay. This year Jerrine cut and dropped

Elinore Pruitt Stewart, *Letters of a Woman Homesteader* (New York, 1914), pp. 214–17.

enough potatoes to raise a ton of fine potatoes. She wanted to try, so we let her, and you will remember that she is but six years old. We had a man to break the ground and cover the potatoes for her and the man irrigated them once. That was all that was done until digging time, when they were ploughed out and Jerrine picked them up. Any woman strong enough to go out by the day could have done every bit of the work and put in two or three times that much, and it would have been so much more pleasant than to work so hard in the city and then be on starvation rations in the winter.

To me, homesteading is the solution of all poverty's problems, but I realize that temperament has much to do with success in any undertaking, and persons afraid of coyotes and work and loneliness had better let ranching alone. At the same time, any woman who can stand her own company, can see the beauty of the sunset, loves growing things, and is willing to put in as much time at careful labor as she does over the washtub, will certainly succeed; will have independence, plenty to eat all the time, and a home of her own in the end. . . .

You'd think I wanted you to homestead, wouldn't you? But I am only thinking of the troops of tired, worried women, sometimes even cold and hungry, scared to death of losing their places to work, who could have plenty to eat, who could have good fires by gathering the wood, and comfortable homes of their own, if they but had the courage and determination to get them.

DEMOCRACY AND THE FAMILY

By the 1820s America was not only a place, it had also become an idea of a new order—Democracy—growing in the New World. An object of great curiosity, it brought many Europeans to American shores for a first-hand look at the beast. The most insightful, far-ranging, and rigorous of these attempts to assess this new world was Alexis de Tocqueville's classic, *Democracy in America,* first published in 1835 by the French aristocrat who was intrigued by democracy. Convinced that "the advent of Democracy as a governing power . . . universal and irresistible, was at hand," Tocqueville came to America to find, as he put it, "the image of democracy itself." In this selection he considered what America's "equality of condition," rampant "spirit of commerce," and "puritanical religion" did to the family, to paternal authority, and to relations among the sexes, and in so doing he pointed to themes and conditions echoed in many subsequent documents in this volume.

The materials in this section are intended neither to illustrate nor to refute Tocqueville's depiction of the democratic family—or even to suggest that it is necessarily valid to attribute the changes that might have come over families in the nineteenth century to "the principle of democracy." (Tocqueville's single-minded pursuit of the "image of democracy" led him to many perceptive observations about the United States, but it also led him to trace everything he saw to the workings of his peculiar notion of democracy.) The documents that follow Tocqueville's views are intended, instead, as materials that permit further exploration of some of the issues raised by him. The first two selections are drawn from letters between family members. They reveal a good deal about parental authority, the way it was exercised, and some of the strain against it. The letters also suggest something of the complex play of command, sentiment, and piety in family relationships. In the first set, Joshua Wilson, a Presbyterian minister in Cincinnati, Ohio, and his wife, Sarah, try to guide their son, George, as he prepares himself for adulthood. The second set, coming from the family of a planter-physician in eastern North Carolina, concerns a daughter's marriage, subsequent disownment, and attempt to become reconciled with her parents. (See also the letter of Elias Nason [p. 216] for an indication of how some of the new conditions of American life worked to bring about a reversal of some roles, forcing sons to take on some of the responsibilities traditionally associated with paternal authority.) The next selection about sources of sexual inequality is taken from the autobiography of Elizabeth

Cady Stanton (1815–1902), an ardent abolitionist and one of the earliest and most persistent advocates of women's rights. It is followed by excerpts from *The Woman's Bible,* which she prepared in her attack against the religious doctrines she came to consider the ultimate source of women's inequality in America.

INFLUENCE OF DEMOCRACY ON THE FAMILY

It has been universally remarked that in our time the several members of a family stand upon an entirely new footing towards each other; that the distance which formerly separated a father from his sons has been lessened; and that paternal authority, if not destroyed, is at least impaired.

Something analogous to this, but even more striking, may be observed in the United States. In America the family, in the Roman and aristocratic signification of the word, does not exist. All that remains of it are a few vestiges in the first years of childhood, when the father exercises, without opposition, that absolute domestic authority which the feebleness of his children renders necessary and which their interest, as well as his own incontestable superiority, warrants. But as soon as the young American approaches manhood, the ties of filial obedience are relaxed day by day; master of his thoughts, he is soon master of his conduct. In America there is, strictly speaking, no adolescence: at the close of boyhood the man appears and begins to trace out his own path.

It would be an error to suppose that this is preceded by a domestic struggle in which the son has obtained by a sort of moral violence the liberty that his father refused him. The same habits, the same principles, which impel the one to assert his independence predispose the other to consider the use of that independence as an incontestable right. The former does not exhibit any of those rancorous or irregular passions which disturb men long after they have shaken off an established authority; the latter feels none of that bitter and angry regret which is apt to survive a bygone power. The father foresees the limits of his authority long beforehand, and when the time arrives, he surrenders it without a struggle; the son looks forward to the exact period at which he will be his own master, and he enters upon his freedom without precipitation and without effort, as a possession which is his own and which no one seeks to wrest from him.

It may perhaps be useful to show how these changes which take place in family relations are closely connected with the social and political revolution that is approaching its consummation under our own eyes.

There are certain great social principles that a people either introduces everywhere or tolerates nowhere. In countries which are aristocratically constituted with all the gradations of rank, the government never makes

Alexis de Tocqueville, *Democracy in America,* trans. Henry Reeve (New York, 1889), vol. 2, pp. 202–8.

a direct appeal to the mass of the governed; as men are united together, it is enough to lead the foremost; the rest will follow. This is applicable to the family as well as to all aristocracies that have a head. Among aristocratic nations social institutions recognize, in truth, no one in the family but the father; children are received by society at his hands; society governs him, he governs them. Thus the parent not only has a natural right but acquires a political right to command them; he is the author and the support of his family, but he is also its constituted ruler.

In democracies, where the government picks out every individual singly from the mass to make him subservient to the general laws of the community, no such intermediate person is required; a father is there, in the eye of the law, only a member of the community, older and richer than his sons. . . .

Although the legislation of an aristocratic people grants no peculiar privileges to the heads of families, I shall not be the less convinced that their power is more respected and more extensive than in a democracy; for I know that, whatever the laws may be, superiors always appear higher and inferiors lower in aristocracies than among democratic nations.

When men live more for the remembrance of what has been than for the care of what is, and when they are more given to attend to what their ancestors thought than to think themselves, the father is the natural and necessary tie between the past and the present, the link by which the ends of these two chains are connected. In aristocracies, then, the father is not only the civil head of the family, but the organ of its traditions, the expounder of its customs, the arbiter of its manners. He is listened to with deference, he is addressed with respect, and the love that is felt for him is always tempered with fear.

When the condition of society becomes democratic and men adopt as their general principle that it is good and lawful to judge of all things for oneself, using former points of belief not as a rule of faith, but simply as a means of information, the power which the opinions of a father exercise over those of his sons diminishes as well as his legal power.

Perhaps the subdivision of estates that democracy brings about contributes more than anything else to change the relations existing between a father and his children. When the property of the father of a family is scanty, his son and himself constantly live in the same place and share the same occupations; habit and necessity bring them together and force them to hold constant communication. The inevitable consequence is a sort of familiar intimacy, which renders authority less absolute and which can ill be reconciled with the external forms of respect.

Now, in democratic countries the class of those who are possessed of small fortunes is precisely that which gives strength to the notions and a particular direction to the manners of the community. That class makes its opinions preponderate as universally as its will, and even those who are most inclined to resist its commands are carried away in the end by its example. I have known eager opponents of democracy who allowed their children to address them with perfect colloquial equality.

Thus at the same time that the power of aristocracy is declining, the austere, the conventional, and the legal part of parental authority vanishes and a species of equality prevails around the domestic hearth. I do not know, on the whole, whether society loses by the change, but I am inclined to believe that man individually is a gainer by it. I think that in proportion as manners and laws become more democratic, the relation of father and son becomes more intimate and more affectionate; rules and authority are less talked of, confidence and tenderness are often increased, and it would seem that the natural bond is drawn closer in proportion as the social bond is loosened.

In a democratic family the father exercises no other power than that which is granted to the affection and the experience of age; his orders would perhaps be disobeyed, but his advice is for the most part authoritative. Though he is not hedged in with ceremonial respect, his sons at least accost him with confidence; they have no settled form of addressing him, but they speak to him constantly and are ready to consult him every day. The master and the constituted ruler have vanished; the father remains.

PARENTS *V.* A SON

Sarah Wilson to George Wilson, September 5, 1817

I was very much pleased with your letter of August 12 because it not only let us know that you were pursuing your studies in peace and happiness, but that you wrote from a sense of duty. Nothing can be more gratifying to me than to see you acting from a sense of duty. Your duty to God first should occupy your mind, that will lead you to the relative duties incumbent upon you. My dear, I feel a deep anxiety about you, I hope you are doing yourself credit, and preparing for future usefulness in life. The years of sixteen, seventeen and eighteen is a very critical period in a young man's life, his judgement is unformed, his views is false in almost every thing that surrounds him and yet what an age of confidence, of self-conceit, how seldom is the eye turned to heaven or ear open to the admonitions of experience, wisdom, or friendliness. Even the' remonstrances of conscience, the reproofs of paternal authority, the counsels and intreaties of maternal tenderness are scarcely heard amidst the turbulence of youthful passings and incitements to irregularities. My heart aches while with mingled emotions of hope and fear for you I thus pour forth its sensations. Nothing but the guidance of heaven can steer you safely through the perils which you are exposed to from without or within. I hope you read your Bible. It will make you wise unto salvation, there you may find directions for your conduct in all the affairs of life. . . . I long very much to see you, it seems a long time since we parted but the kind letters we have received from you and your uncle and couzin has in some measure lessened the pain of absence. Nothing but the desire I have for your improvement, the good opinion I formed of your cousin David, the confidence I had in your uncle that he would endeaver to protect you from evil could have reconciled me to so long an absence from you at this time of life. I hope you may be enabled to feel sufficiently grateful to your uncle and family for so great a kindness, and I trust my dear you will try to repay their kindness with every mark of respect and affection in your power.

Joshua Wilson to George Wilson, January 2, 1823 (on his 20th birthday)

The first seven years of your life were spent in as high a state of innocence and love as falls to the lot of any who are not sanctified by the spirit of Grace. Unable to conduct your education in the domestic circle on account of daily interruptions you were committed to tutors and professors until you chose for yourself a professional study, to which, I hope, you are now making successful proficiency. In this situation your parents still watch over you with many a pang but the anxiety of mental vigilence is soothed by the knowledge they possess of the patronage with which you are favored in the ability and friendship of Mr. and Mrs. Pope. . . . In the ardour and inexperience of youth you cast your wishful eyes over the theatre of life, while all the kingdoms of the world and the glory of them spring up to the view of your bewildered imagination; yet in the clamberings of thought you may fancy yourself mounting through all the grades of wealth and popularity, from the humble attitude of a junior apprentice of the law to the presidential chair of our confederated Empire.

Joshua and Sally Wilson to George Wilson, November 23, 1823

We presume you are already informed that your letter of the 28th was duly received. The delicate and important subject suggested for our consideration form a sufficient reason for some delay that we might not give advice in a matter of such moment without meditation, prayer, and serious conference. It would be very unreasonable for us to attempt to restrain the lawful and laudable desires of our children, all we ought do is to endeavor to direct and regulate their innocent wishes and curb and conquer those which are vicious. Nor are we ignorant of the great advantages which frequently result from virtuous love and honorable wedlock. But there is a time for all things, and such are the fixed laws of nature that things are only beautiful and useful when they occupy their own time and place. Premature love and marriage are often blighted by the frosts of adversity and satiety leaving hasty lovers to droop in the meridian of life and drag out a miserable existence under the withering influence of disappointment and disgust. . . . We do not say you have been hasty but we wish you to reflect seriously upon this question. Is not the whole affair premature? We know from experience and observation that schemes which appear reasonable and desirable at the age of twenty wear a very different aspect at twenty five. We think it probable that greater maturity, more experience in business and a larger acquaintance with the world might change your views and feelings. Besides we are not sure that you have sufficiently considered the weighty responsibility. We feel no disposition to place any insuperable barrier in your way. Our advice is that you give the subject that consideration which its importance demands, that you unite with us in praying for divine direction, that every thing be done deliberately, decently, orderly, honorably and devoutly.

Joshua and Sally Wilson to George Wilson, December 9, 1823

Your letter of Nov 18 has been duly received. On its contents we have meditated with deep solicitude. . . . You seem confident that your decision is not premature nor hasty. Here we feel compelled to demur and beg you to weigh the matter again. You express a hope that before great length of time we shall have an opportunity of receiving Miss B much to our satisfaction. Dear George, it will not be any satisfaction to us to see you place a lady in a more precarious condition than you found her and this we are sure would be the case if marriage with this young lady should take place shortly. We must remind you of a pledge given in your former letter and insist upon its obligation, that you marry no woman without the prospect of supporting her in a suitable manner. Think of the circumstances in which she has been educated, of the circle of society in which she has been accustomed to move, of her delicate constitution and refined sensibility and then imagine to yourself her disappointment upon entering into a poor dependent family occupying an indifferent tenement without the means of affording a comfortable lodging or decently accommodating her friends. She has been accustomed to see you in agreeable aspect of the scholar and a gentleman and she has seen your father also in flattering circumstances. . . . We do not say things to discourage you but to show you the necessity of prudence in your plans, diligence in your studies and such application to business as will afford a reasonable prospect of success before you become the head of a family.

Joshua Wilson to George Wilson, May 11, 1824

Never since the death of your dear sister Sally have I been so completely overwhelmed with sorrow as I was in the hour of our last separation. Always when you left home before I still considered you one of my family and in some senses under my paternal direction. I still thought that after a few months' absence you would return home and mingle again with your brothers and sisters as a child. It still appeared possible to me that an opening might present itself for your success in business where we could see you frequently and witness both the state of your health and your progress in your profession. From your earliest infancy I had been offering up prayers to God that you might in the days of your youth be made a new creature, that before you graduated from parental jurisdiction you might be girded with truth and shielded with faith. But when I saw the hour of your departure arrive, the moment of adieu present and then past—when I reflected how little I was able to do for you, that you were gone only to return as a visitor and that perhaps at long intervals you were going to live among strangers exposed to every temptation incident to youth and above all that notwithstanding all the instructions, warnings, invitations, and opportunities with which you had been favored you were yet in a state of nature, unrenewed, unsanctified, unprepared for death and a judgment to come—my heart sank within me and I hastened into solitude to give vent to my feelings before Holy Jesus Christ who only could afford me consolation and support.

Joshua Wilson to George Wilson, March 30, 1825

It is now after midnight, I am in my office, spending the hours usually consecrated to repose in deep affliction. Your dear sister Amanda is lying sick in your grandmother's room. Your brother Henry, whom I believe you love and whom I hope you will still love, poor wayward, unhappy Henry is lying on the bed where you and he used to slumber together in a deep state of intoxication and your dear dear mother is in the dining room distracted with grief. Here I sit in melancholy silence indulging many a sad and sorrowful reflection. Nothing is more painful to me at this moment than the state of my own heart. It seems petrified, chilled to the very center. Could I weep, could I pray, could I feel one soft affection, my distress would be mitigated, but alas I seem grasped and crushed by the hand of desolation. My judgment indeed tells me that the desolation is not yet complete, that God is yet long suffering, gracious and merciful and that his grace can reclaim the prodigal and save the chief of sinners. I see also many rich blessings temporal and spiritual of which I am not yet deprived. . . . O God of Mercy permit me, help me to offer up at least one prayer for my wretched son. George, can you pray? If you can, pray for your lost brother, pray to him who came to seek and save the lost. My mind recurs to past scenes, I am over the history of my life, especially the part I have spent in the character of a father, and the retrospect makes me tremble. Such defects in family instruction, such blunders in family government, such improprieties in example, no wonder that I am left to witness some of the dreadful results of my own mismanagement, of my own unfaithfulness. I should instantly sink into a state of desperation were it not for the hope of salvation through the power and merit of the Son of God. And is it not strange that a person in my present situation should have such a hope? You, who are accustomed to think of me with affection and perhaps to admire some traits in my character, may possibly suppose that I am carrying this subject of self-crimination to a great extreme but I tell you George, I see sin enough in my conduct simply as a father to ruin the universe if it were charged to all created intelligences. But my children are not innocent. My dear Henry lies before me the voluntary victim of an evil heart surcharged with the poison of infidelity and over come by the example of wicked companions. O George, if you were a Christian you could assist me with your counsel and prayers. But if you can not pray for me I hope you can sympathize with me and never, o never forget the pangs of your affectionate mother whose heart is bleeding at every pore.*

A DAUGHTER *V.* HER PARENTS

Edenton, N.C., 19 August 1846

My dear Daughter,

. . . . It certainly requires great talents, as well as great goodness and philosophy, *to be a good house-keeper.* It requires great industry, patience, good nature, self-denial, vigilance & care to qualify a lady for the duties of such an office: and she who does not possess all these qualities in an *eminent degree* ought never to undertake it. The interests connected with it are so important, the duties it imposes so sacred, and the exposure, toil & privation it calls for, so perilous & trying that I sometimes feel surprised that it is not totally abandoned. . . . Certainly, my dear, if it is not managed with great ability, sobriety, & good sense, the duty of house-keeping is dirty, demoralising & debasing in a high degree. It sours & exasperates the temper, disquiets the mind & fosters the most trouble-some and tormenting passions. It confines one to a series of low pursuits, a course of filthy drudgery, & disgusting slovenliness that leave but little time for study or quiet mediation & very little for improving conversation or refined society; & it is altogether unsuited to moral & religious enjoy-ment. It keeps one in perpetual agitation, anxiety, and apprehension & has no pleasures equal to the pains, the toil, the privations and the suffering which it is almost sure to impose. It may be said, with great truth, that there are few of your sex who possess the ability, the virtue & the grace to give dignity to such an occupation, or to invest it with charms sufficiently attractive to win the regard of sober, sensible, & reflecting minds. Yet, *there are such;* and they alone are destined to bless & adorn the social state, to grace the domestic scene, to soften & sweeten the labors of active and busy life. I will draw you a picture of such a house-keeper, in some future communication.

You must remember, my daughter, what I have said to you, *on a certain subject.* I would not *acknowledge* myself to be *engaged,* affianced, to any man not in a condition to give me a comfortable & respectable support—to

---

*Five months later George died, remaining to the end an unconverted Christian.—Ed.

Norcom Family Letters (North Carolina Division of Archives and History). Reprinted by permission.

place me beyond the chance of want or poverty. I, my dear, could *never never* ratify such an engagement were you to make it. Everything, therefore, in relation to this matter must be *conditional.* It cannot be positive, for, however meritorious a man may be, & how high he might be in my opinion or esteem, I could not sanction his connexion with a daughter of mine, in the "Holy Estate" with the prospect of poverty & wretchedness before her.

Treat the man who honors you with his partiality & preference with candor, politeness—nay, with kindness, *but let him not hope,* if he is inconsiderate enough to wish it, to draw you into a situation in which you would be less comfortable than you are in your father's dwelling, or less comfortable than you could be among your friends, in your present condition. W—— is a meritorious and respectable young man, an honour to his family, & worthy of general esteem; and had I a fortune, my daughter, to give you, or the means of making you independent, I see nothing in his character to object to. But his inability to support a family, *as long as it lasts,* is an insurmountable objection, & of the probability of its removal no correct opinion can *now* be formed. Time alone can instruct us on the subject. Pray be prudent, my daughter, and do nothing in your absence from us, that *you would not do in the presence of* your father,

Ja Norcm

Cincinnati, July 4, 1848

My *dear, dear* Mother,

Now that my heart is *bleeding* and *rent with anguish*—suffering all that the human heart *can* suffer, will you not *forever* bury the past, and give me if you can *some* consolation. You have lost children, Dear Mother—*darling infants*—and one advanced to maturity and you suffered beyond endurance. *I* too *thought* I felt the stroke keenly, but Oh God what are my sufferings *now* compared to those. My misery is what *yours once was* Dear Mother, and you can feel for me I hope in my present affliction. Heaven has taken from us our *darling little* boy. Yesterday we buried him. 'Tis more than I can bear, for God never sent so lovely a creature to any human being—and to think that you had never loved him. Mother— our little Angel—the darling of our hearts for whom every thought and wish was garnered up—our only child, our only infant, our *Idol*—oh that you have seen him *once,* once, only, you could not have helped loving him. I pray God to give me strength to endure it. Kind friends come around to console me but oh, tis only in prayer that I find relief for my troubled soul. I pray that we may meet his little spirit in Heaven and may God help us to keep our vows. Two more weeks of such suffering as the past, I feel, would carry me to my grave. I could not endure it. Day and night I watched by the little sufferer and oftener prayed to have him spared to us—but now he is an angel with God and free from all pain. Oh, that we had been married under different circumstances—all friendly—that some of you could have been with us at this trying time. Ask Pa to forgive and forget all. If I could be with you once again, My Dear Parents, I would prove by my devotion to you both, how sincerely I regret the pain I occasion you, and that we could not have been married with your consent—for now I can appreciate all your motives and understand your feelings. If it be not pleasant to you to have me—of my husband I will not do it, but if you could throw aside your prejudice—forget the past and know him as he *now is* and *has been* since I married him, your feelings I'm sure would change, for no one ever had a kinder or better husband—nor one who would strive as he does to make a wife comfortable and happy. May the day come soon when we will all meet in friendship and love—Brother Wistan, too, must forget all. I freely forgive him for what he *caused me* to suffer—I would like to hear from him, and have him come and see us— We are keeping house, but to stay in it long would kill me—for ten thousand recollections of my child present themselves that almost drive me mad. In a few days we shall sell out—break up house-keeping and leave Cincinnati for a few weeks. I feel that we must have some relief—some change—or heaven only knows what would become of me. We shall go to Illinois and Michigan to visit Mr. Marmor's relations and when we return, *board.* I could only keep house on my return on one condition—that you will let Sister come and live with us for a year or two, that is if it be her wish. How I would love for one or both of you to come and see me. Cannot brother Wistan bring sister. Traveling over the mountains would be of benefit to him this summer. I heard from you all a few weeks since through Fletcher Skinner who spent several evenings with us and how I wished then you could see Johnny, my little darling who was looking so lovely, but *delicate* from teething—he died from cutting eight teeth all at once, but under the hands of one of the most skillful Physicians in the City. He had every attention—and with but one thing we reproach our-selves—that we did not remain in the mountains with him this summer. I think sometimes he might have born his sufferings there—but he is gone now. My darling boy and we are left to mourn him. We placed his little body in a lead box—in the private family vault of one of our friends in the city—that when we left Ohio we might carry him to Norfolk where we design settling. Two of his dear little curls I send you—one for Sister. Will you keep them, Mother, for my sake and my child's sake, for you had only to see him once to have loved him. If you would like it I will send you one of his pictures and a ring made of his hair. Just one month ago I was upon the eve of sending you some little presents in Johnny's name, as presents from him, but I did not know how you would receive them and hesitated. Now I wish I had sent them. Will you write to me immediately dear Mother—for it would give me such comfort and consola-tion to hear from you. . . .

Always your affectionate daughter
Mary Matilda

A DAUGHTER'S INEQUALITY

. . . Our parents were as kind, indulgent, and considerate as the Puritan ideas of those days permitted, but fear, rather than love, of God and parents alike, predominated. Add to this our timidity in our intercourse with servants and teachers, our dread of the ever present devil, and the reader will see that, under such conditions, nothing but strong self-will and a good share of hope and mirthfulness could have saved an ordinary child from becoming a mere nullity.

The first event engraved on my memory was the birth of a sister when I was four years old. It was a cold morning in January when the brawny Scotch nurse carried me to see the little stranger, whose advent was a matter of intense interest to me for many weeks after. The large, pleasant room with the white curtains and bright wood fire on the hearth, where panada, catnip, and all kinds of little messes which we were allowed to taste were kept warm, was the center of attraction for the older children. I heard so many friends remark, "What a pity it is she's a girl!" that I felt a kind of compassion for the little baby. True, our family consisted of five girls and only one boy, but I did not understand at that time that girls were considered an inferior order of beings. . . .

When I was eleven years old, two events occurred which changed considerably the current of my life. My only brother, who had just graduated from Union College, came home to die. A young man of great talent and promise, he was the pride of my father's heart. We early felt that this son filled a larger place in our father's affections and future plans than the five daughters together. Well do I remember how tenderly he watched my brother in his last illness, the sighs and tears he gave vent to as he slowly walked up and down the hall, and, when the last sad moment came, and we were all assembled to say farewell in the silent chamber of death, how broken were his utterances as he knelt and prayed for comfort and support. I still recall, too, going into the large darkened parlor to see my brother, and finding the casket, mirrors, and pictures all draped in white, and my father seated by his side, pale and immovable. As he took no notice of me, after standing a long while, I climbed upon his knee, when he mechanically put his arm about me and, with my head resting against his beating heart, we both sat in silence, he thinking of the wreck of all his hopes in the loss of a dear son, and I wondering what could be said or done to fill the void in his breast. At length he heaved a deep sigh and said: "Oh, my daughter, I wish you were a boy!" Throwing my arms about his neck, I replied: "I will try to be all my brother was."

Then and there I resolved that I would not give so much time as heretofore to play, but would study and strive to be at the head of all my classes and thus delight my father's heart. All that day and far into the night I pondered the problem of boyhood. I thought that the chief thing to be

Elizabeth Cady Stanton, *Eighty Years and More* (New York, 1895), pp. 20–25.

done in order to equal boys was to be learned and courageous. So I decided to study Greek and learn to manage a horse. Having formed this conclusion I fell asleep. My resolutions, unlike many such made at night, did not vanish with the coming light. I arose early and hastened to put them into execution. They were resolutions never to be forgotten—destined to mold my character anew. As soon as I was dressed I hastened to our good pastor, Rev. Simon Hosack, who was always early at work in his garden.

"Doctor," said I, "which do you like best, boys or girls?"

"Why, girls, to be sure; I would not give you for all the boys in Christendom."

"My father," I replied, "prefers boys; he wishes I was one, and I intend to be as near like one as possible. I am going to ride on horseback and study Greek. Will you give me a Greek lesson now, doctor? I want to begin at once."

"Yes, child," said he, throwing down his hoe, "come into my library and we will begin without delay."

He entered fully into the feeling of suffering and sorrow which took possession of me when I discovered that a girl weighed less in the scale of being than a boy, and he praised my determination to prove the contrary. . . . The old grammar which he had studied in the University of Glasgow was soon in my hands, and the Greek article was learned before breakfast.

Then came the sad pageantry of death, the weeping of friends, the dark rooms, the ghostly stillness, the exhortation to the living to prepare for death, the solemn prayer, the mournful chant, the funeral cortège, the solemn, tolling bell, the burial. How I suffered during those sad days! What strange undefined fears of the unknown took possession of me! For months afterward, at the twilight hour, I went with my father to the new-made grave. Near it stood two tall poplar trees, against one of which I leaned, while my father threw himself on the grave, with outstretched arms, as if to embrace his child. At last the frosts and storms of November came and threw a chilling barrier between the living and the dead, and we went there no more. . . .

I kept up my lessons at the parsonage and made rapid progress. I surprised even my teacher, who thought me capable of doing anything. I learned to drive, and to leap a fence and ditch on horseback. I taxed every power, hoping some day to hear my father say: "Well, a girl is as good as a boy, after all." But he never said it. When the doctor came over to spend the evening with us, I would whisper in his ear: "Tell my father how fast I get on," and he would tell him, and was lavish in his praises. But my father only paced the room, sighed, and showed that he wished I were a boy; and I, not knowing why he felt thus, would hide my tears of vexation on the doctor's shoulder.

Soon after this I began to study Latin, Greek, and mathematics with a class of boys in the Academy, many of whom were much older than I. For three years one boy kept his place at the head of the class, and I always stood next. Two prizes were offered in Greek. I strove for one and took the second. How well I remember my joy in receiving that prize. There was no sentiment of ambition, rivalry, or triumph over my companions, nor feeling of satisfaction in receiving this honor in the presence of those assembled on the day of the exhibition. One thought alone filled my mind. "Now," said I, "my father will be satisfied with me." So, as soon as we were dismissed, I ran down the hill, rushed breathless into his office, laid the new Greek Testament, which was my prize, on his table and exclaimed: "There, I got it!" He took up the book, asked me some questions about the class, the teachers, the spectators, and, evidently pleased, handed it back to me. Then, while I stood looking and waiting for him to say something which would show that he recognized the equality of the daughter with the son, he kissed me on the forehead and exclaimed, with a sigh, "Ah, you should have been a boy!"

INEQUALITY IN THE SCRIPTURES

From the inauguration of the movement for woman's emancipation the Bible has been used to hold her in the "divinely ordained sphere," prescribed in the Old and New Testaments.

The canon and civil law; church and state; priests and legislators; all political parties and religious denominations have alike taught that woman was made after man, of man, and for man, an inferior being, subject to man. Creeds, codes, Scriptures and statutes, are all based on this idea. The fashions, forms, ceremonies and customs of society, church ordinances and discipline all grow out of this idea. . . .

The Bible teaches that woman brought sin and death into the world, that she precipitated the fall of the race, that she was arraigned before the judgment seat of Heaven, tried, condemned and sentenced. Marriage for her was to be a condition of bondage, maternity a period of suffering and anguish, and in silence and subjection, she was to play the role of a dependent on man's bounty for all her material wants, and for all the information she might desire on the vital questions of the hour, she was commanded to ask her husband at home. . . . No wonder the majority of women stood still, and with bowed heads, accepted the situation.

Listening to the varied opinions of women, I have long thought it would be interesting and profitable to get them clearly stated in book form. To this end six years ago I proposed to a committee of women to issue a Woman's Bible, that we might have women's commentaries on women's position in the Old and New Testaments. It was agreed on by several leading women in England and America and the work was begun, but from various causes it has been delayed, until now the idea is received

Elizabeth Cady Stanton, *The Woman's Bible* (New York, 1898), pp. 7–9, 16–23.

with renewed enthusiasm, and a large committee has been formed, and we hope to complete the work within a year. . . .

Genesis ii: 21–25.

21 And the Lord God caused a deep sleep to fall upon Adam, and he slept; and he took one of his ribs, and closed up the flesh thereof.

22 And the rib which the Lord God had taken from man, made he a woman, and brought her unto the man.

23 And Adam said, This is now bone of my bone, and flesh of my flesh: she shall be called Woman, because she was taken out of man.

24 Therefore shall a man leave his father and his mother, and shall cleave unto his wife; and they shall be one flesh.

25 And they were both naked, the man and his wife, and were not ashamed.

As the account of the creation in the first chapter is in harmony with science, common sense, and the experience of mankind in natural laws, the inquiry naturally arises, why should there be two contradictory accounts in the same book, of the same event? It is fair to infer that the second version, which is found in some form in the different religions of all nations, is a mere allegory, symbolizing some mysterious conception of a highly imaginative editor.

The first account dignifies woman as an important factor in the creation, equal in power and glory with man. The second makes her a mere afterthought. The world was in good running order without her. The only reason for her advent being the solitude of man.

There is something sublime in bringing order out of chaos; light out of darkness; giving each planet its place in the solar system; oceans and lands their limits; wholly inconsistent with a petty surgical operation, to find material for the mother of the race. It is on this allegory that all the enemies of women rest their battering rams, to prove her inferiority. Accepting the view that man was prior in the creation, some Scriptural writers say that as the woman was of the man, therefore, her position should be one of subjection. Grant it, then as the historical fact is reversed in our day, and the man is now of the woman, shall his place be one of subjection? . . .

The equal position declared in the first account must prove more satisfactory to both sexes; created alike in the image of God—The Heavenly Mother and Father.

Thus, the Old Testament, "in the beginning," proclaims the simultaneous creation of man and woman, the eternity and equality of sex; and the New Testament echoes back through the centuries the individual sovereignty of woman growing out of this natural fact. Paul, in speaking of equality as the very soul and essence of Christianity, said, "There is neither Jew nor Greek, there is neither bond nor free, there is neither male nor female; for ye are all one in Christ Jesus." With this recognition of the feminine element in the Godhead in the Old Testament, and this declaration of the equality of the sexes in the New, we may well wonder at the contemptible status woman occupies in the Christian Church of to-day. . . .

It is evident that some wily writer, seeing the perfect equality of man and woman in the first chapter, felt it important for the dignity and dominion of man to effect woman's subordination in some way. To do this a spirit of evil must be introduced, which at once proved itself stronger than the spirit of good, and man's supremacy was based on the downfall of all that had just been pronounced very good. This spirit of evil evidently existed before the supposed fall of man, hence woman was not the origin of sin as so often asserted.

FROM FARMS TO FACTORIES

Changes in family beliefs and attitudes are very difficult to document adequately. We can be more confident about evidence of changes in the physical setting and material conditions of family life such as a shift from living on farms and in houses to a life in mills and tenements. In the nineteenth century, probably the most wrenching change in the setting of American family life was the move from farm to industrial work and from life in the countryside to a city or to a town with an increasingly city-style life.

How this great transformation affected family structure, conduct, and attitude is still debatable, in good degree because the millions of families involved left little or no direct record. Later selections will deal with some principal characteristics of family life in the industrial city after 1880. The dates of the pieces here are earlier and the documents have been chosen to suggest some of the difficulties in the transition of Americans from the farm to the mill.

Millions of the native-born eventually made the move, but millions more went into factories and cities directly after landing in America as immigrants from the "old country." By 1850 during the great wave of Irish and German migrations to America, much of Europe was still far more rural and traditionalist than the American countryside. By then the American farm and landed life were long past feudalism and were capitalistic and "modern" in a dedication to freedom and risk and to markets, profits, innovation, and self-improvement. Despite self-flattering and often crippling delusions to the contrary, generations of American farm families before the industrial era were used to "getting and spending" and to bitter squabbles and litigation about land tenure, prices, contracts, and interest. Could this mean that the native-born rural American found the pace, lingo, and "market relationships" of the city and factory more familiar or easier to deal with than did peasant immigrants, especially those from remoter eastern and southern Europe who knew little or nothing of producing for large and distant markets, of expanding their acreage as a speculation in land prices, and of other tendencies of America's commercial agriculture?

What does the picture of New England farm life already suggest of problems in the 1850s? What was their origin? Why would New Englanders leave their farms if the life was satisfying and profitable? What does the Nason letter from a "savvy" son giving advice to a farm family at home suggest about the "old order" of fathers managing family affairs? Why might those Nasons still on the land have been considering the move to the mill? How much were such families shoved by ambition or pulled by business and population pressures? Suppose the Nasons considered moving from an old farm in trouble to new lands in the West. How might prospects have differed for the place and power of the father as family head and "provider," or for the departure of the children from the home?

Were early labor contracts for mill work like those sampled here the first market relationships that American rural folk had known? Had they ever before seen a contract or heard of a cash obligation? What about wills, mortgages, documents of indenture, papers relative to slavery, promissory notes, ledgers, and accounts with merchants in eighteenth- and seventeenth-century farm life? For the mill owners, do the workers in the contracts seem to the employer only "hands" (a revealing old term of the time)? What does the hiring of an entire family for mill work suggest about the organization, labor force, and demands of the work itself, about the setting and the outlook of the owner?

The selection from Harriet Robinson draws attention to the most famous American attempt in the early nineteenth century to combine work in the mill and the "new discipline" of machine-tending with idealized conditions of family and Christian life. Lowell, Massachusetts, organized in 1826, although unique even in America, became an international model of the benignity of the new factory order, but the experiment there lasted for only about a generation. In the 1840s the mills started to use newly arrived immigrants and developed familiar labor conflicts. Even in its early days, however, Lowell was heavily paternalistic and authoritarian in its concern with the moral and religious life of its young women workers. Yet it had a large and particular charm in attracting simple girls "of good family" for a few years of "residence." Why? What did it seem to offer the families in the way of "all this and heaven too"? The Lowell experiment raises a question often asked at the time and recurrently since. Are "ideal family" relationships compatible with the industrial work day, whether capitalist or socialist, and the atmosphere, pace, rhythm, rewards, and penalties intrinsic to factories? How much say or "responsibility" should fatherlike factory owners have for the lives of their workers outside the factory? Conversely, if daily life outside the factory is left entirely to private family choice, how may the family ideal of love and mutuality conflict with the factory style of work dictated by the machine and management routines? And how might families with troubles of their own making, such as drunkenness or frequent pregnancies, find it difficult to send their members to the mills for an effective workday?

FARM LIFE IN ANTE-BELLUM NEW ENGLAND

There is probably no better exponent of the farmer's life than the farmer's home. We propose to present the portrait of such a home, and, while

"Farming Life in New England," *Atlantic Monthly*, 2 (August 1858), pp. 334–41.

we offer it as a just outline of the farmer's home generally, in districts removed from large social centres, we gladly acknowledge the existence of a great multitude of happy exceptions. But the sketch:—A square, brown house; a chimney coming out of the middle of a roof; not a tree nearer than the orchard, and not a flower at the door. At one end projects a wood-shed and wagon-cover, occupied at night by hens; beyond the wood-shed, a hog-pen, fragrant and musical. Proceeding no farther in this direction, we look directly across the road, to where the barn stands, like the hull of a great black ship-of-the-line, with its port-holes opened threateningly upon the fort opposite, out of one of which a horse has thrust his head for the possible purpose of examining the strength of the works. An old ox-sled is turned up against the wall close by, where it will have the privilege of rotting. This whole establishment was contrived with a single eye to utility. The barn was built in such a manner that its deposits might be convenient to the road which divides the farm, while the sty was made an attachment of the house for convenience in feeding its occupants.

We enter the house at the back door, and find the family at dinner in the kitchen. A kettle of soap-grease is stewing upon the stove, and the fumes of this, mingled with those that were generated by boiling the cabbage which we see upon the table, and by perspiring men in shirt-sleeves, and by boots that have forgotten or do not care where they have been, make the air anything but agreeable to those who are not accustomed to it. This is the place where the family live. They cook everything here for themselves and their hogs. They eat every meal here. They sit here every evening, and here they receive their friends. The women in this kitchen toil incessantly, from the time they rise in the morning until they go to bed at night. Here man and woman, sons and daughters, live, in the belief that work is the great thing, that efficiency in work is the crowning excellence of manhood and womanhood, and willingly go so far into essential self-debasement, sometimes, as to contemn beauty and those who love it, and to glory above all things in brute strength and brute endurance.

Here we are ready to state the point and the lesson of our discussion:— The real reason for the deterioration of agriculture in New England is to be found in the fact, that the farmer's life and the farmer's home, generally, are unloved and unlovable things, and in the multitude of causes which have tended to make them so. . . . It is not strange that the country grows thin and the city plethoric. It is not strange, that mercantile and mechanical employments are thronged by young men, running all risks for success, when the alternative is a life in which they find no meaning, and no inspiring and ennobling influence.

Yet what is the position of the mother in the New England farmer's home? The farmer is careful of every animal he possesses. The farm-yard and the stall are replenished with young, by creatures for months dismissed from labor, or handled with intelligent care while carrying their burden; because the farmer knows that only in this way can he secure improvement, and sound, symmetrical development, to the stock of his farm. In this he is a true, practical philosopher. But what is his treatment of her who bears his children? The same physiological laws apply to her that apply to the brute. Their strict observance is greatly more imperative, because of her finer organization; yet they are not thought of; and if the farmyard fail to shame the nursery, if the mother bear beautiful and well-organized children. Heaven be thanked for a merciful interference with the operation of its own laws! Is the mother in a farmhouse ever regarded as a sacred being? Look at her hands! Look at her face! Look at her bent and clumsy form! Is it more important to raise fine colts than fine men and women? Is human life to be made secondary and subordinate to animal life? Is not she who should receive the tenderest and most considerate ministries of the farmer's home, in all its appointments and in all its service, made the ceaseless minister and servant of the home and all within it, with utter disregard of her office? To expect a population to improve greatly under this method is simply to expect miracles; and to expect a farmer's life and a farmer's home to be attractive, where the mother is a drudge, and secures less consideration than the pets of the stall, is to expect impossibilities.

Another cause which has tended to the deterioration of the farmer's life is its solitariness. The towns in New England which were settled when the Indians were in possession of the country, and which, for purposes of defence, were settled in villages, have enjoyed great blessings; but a large portion of agricultural New England was differently settled. It is difficult to determine why isolation should produce the effect it does upon the family development. The Western pioneer, who, leaving a New England community, plants himself and his young wife in the forest, will generally become a coarse man, and will be the father of coarse children. The lack of the social element in the farmer's life is doubtless a cause of some of its most repulsive characteristics. Men are constituted in such a manner, that constant social contact is necessary to the healthfulness of their sympathies, the quickness of their intellects, and the symmetrical development of their powers. It matters little whether a family be placed in the depths of a Western forest, or upon the top of a New England hill; the result of solitude will be the same in kind, if not in degree.

ESCAPING THE MILLS

Dear Parents,

I have been for some time expecting a letter from home. I have been very anxious as you must suppose to know how you prosper and as there is now a P.O. at your elbow I see no reason why my wish should not be gratified. . . . Bliss was over here the other day from Stow. He wants to have William come to him. He says he will give him his tuition and board is but $1.50. If I can get the money to pay for his board at the first of

"Elias Nason to His Parents," March 9, 1835, in *Elias Nason Papers*, American Antiquarian Society, Worcester, Massachusetts. Reprinted by permission.

April I think I shall send him to Stow. He is now studying Latin and making very good progress. Edward comes up to see me almost every day. He likes his place very well. He goes to meeting with me and attends the Sunday School. I have made no arrangements with Mr. Marshall the man with whom he works about his staying. He is now on trial. I think some of taking him to school with me in the spring. Edward is a good boy and a smart boy I think. He wants a black silk handkerchief. I bought him a good pair of boots in Boston for which I gave $3.50. I bought Mary a Book for which I gave the same. Mary is going to school and studying Latin etc. She is complaining that you do not write to her. I believe that all the children are well satisfied with their places and that they are all doing well. I have not received an answer from Grafton yet. I wrote out nearly a fortnight ago. I feel anxious to go to Grafton and it is probable that I shall have a large school there. If I go there I shall come home at the first of April and perhaps William will come with me as his term closes then. Do you think of leaving Unionville in the spring? If you [desire] a good place, perhaps you had better go, for I don't much like that long house exceedingly well. Perhaps Mr. A. Eames would like to accommodate you. But if I did move I would look out for a respectable and a convenient house. You said something about breaking up housekeeping. I would not do that. You have kept house so long and have considerable furniture and the children will want a house to visit you know. And there seems to be a little disgrace attached to breaking up of housekeeping as if folks were not able to keep house. I would not put any of the children into the mill. Factories are talked about as schools of vice in all circles here. And it is a hard thing for small children to be confined in a tight close room all the day long. It affects their growth, makes them pale and sickly and the company with which they associate is of the lowest order. There is no establishment in the country conducted better than that at Unionville. It is a factory still and nothing has ever touched my pride so much as to have it said that my sister worked in a *Cotton Mill.* Mary says the girls where she boards frequently speak of Factory girls as the very *lowest* but we know that they are not so. Some of them are as good, as intelligent, as fair as any girls in the community. And I pity from my soul the thousands in our country that are reduced to the necessity of laboring in a Factory for a livelihood. God has spread out the various professions in life before us in order that we may have a choice which we will pursue. We have a perfect right then to choose that which is most agreeable to our wishes. We may act in accordance to his will in any of them and fit our selves for his kingdom hereafter. But in as much as some of the different employments are conducive to goodness—to improvement than others, it becomes us to choose those which are most favorable to virtue and intelligence. Now a cotton factory is the last place to which I should put children for improvement either in manners, goodness, or intelligence. I hope therefore you will put Ann out at some good place and perhaps Charles—He is old enough to earn his living on a farm—and keep Susan at home. Eliza is old enough to manage for herself. Wm. and Edward I want to educate and I think I can do it if I have my health. Susan and Father and Mother can live together in a small house or tenement—and if Father's health is good he can support a small family without difficulty. I spoke to Mason about some money before I came. He said then he would let me have some but he has since written that he can not let me have any. You must be just as frugal as possible till I get upon my feet and then I shall work with all my might and whatever I make shall be devoted to the good of the family. I wish father could have all the money he gets for his work and let me have it to clear out from here with. Let all the debts out there go. I wish to have this affair turn out creditably. I think that I shall make $100 before next commencement and this will set me on my feet again. Perhaps you can borrow some money from some of your nearest neighbors—not telling them what it is for until next August. But I wish you to write me about every week to know how things move and what your intentions are.

FAMILY LABOR CONTRACTS

A m[emorandum] of an agreement made and entered into by and between Jesse S. _____ of Thompson in the County of Windham and State of Connecticut. Labourer on the one part and Slater & Howard of Dudley in the County of Worcester and State of Massachusetts Woolen manufacture on the other part. Witnesseth said S _____ on his part agree to work for said Slater & Howard one year from the first day of April next with his family *viz* my son Joseph at six shilling per week. My son William at ten shillings per week and my son Lyman seventeen shillings per week for myself—four dollars per week the whole amt. . . . to be payable at the expiration of one year. I also agree for myself and family to work faithfully for said Slater & Howard at any branch of business they may think most to their benefit and I also agree for myself and family at all times while in their employ to abide to the order and rules of this said Slater & Howard in their establishment.

Said Slater & Howard agree to pay unto said S for himself and family the above mentioned sums as above . . . at the expiration of one year that is to say after that rate for all the time the said S and family may work. The said Slater & Howard agreed to find a dwelling house for said S and family to dwell in and said S paying said Slater & Howard the sum of twenty-five dollars at the expiration of this contract as witness our hand dated at Dudley February 18th, A.D. 1823.

"Letters and Miscellaneous Papers, 1824–1837," *Slater Papers,* Vol. XXVI, Baker Library, Harvard Graduate School of Business Administration.

Dennis Rier of Newbury Port has this day engaged to come with his family to work in our factory on the following conditions. He is to be here about the 20th of next month and is to have the following wages per week:

Himself	$5.00
His son Robert Rier, 10 years of age	.83
Daughter Mary, 12 years of age	1.25
Son William, 13 years of age	1.50
Son Michael, 16 years of age	2.00
	10.58
His sister, Abigail Smith	2.33
Her daughter Sally, 8 years of age	.75
Son Samuel, 13 years of age	1.50
	4.58

House rent to be from $20. to $30. Wood cut up $2. per cord.

THE FACTORY BOARDING HOUSE

In 1831, under the shadow of a great sorrow which had made her four children fatherless—the oldest but seven years of age—my mother was left to struggle alone; and, although she tried hard to earn bread enough to fill our hungry mouths, she could not do it, even with the help of kind friends. And so it happened that one of her more wealthy neighbors, who had looked with longing eyes on the one little daughter of the family, offered to adopt me. But my mother, who had had a hard experience in her youth in living amongst strangers, said, "No; while I have one meal of victuals a day, I will not part with my children." I always remembered this speech because of the word "victuals," and I wondered for a long time what this good old Bible word meant.

My father was a carpenter, and some of his fellow workmen helped my mother to open a little shop, where she sold small stores, candy, kindling-wood, and so on, but there was no great income from this, and we soon became poorer than ever. Dear me! I can see the small shop now, with its jars of striped candy, its loaves of bread, the room at the back where we all lived, and my oldest brother (now a "D.D.") sawing the kindling-wood which we sold to the neighbors.

That was a hard, cold winter; and for warmth's sake my mother and her four children all slept in one bed, two at the foot and three at the head,—but her richer neighbor could not get the little daughter; and, con-

"Rier Family Document, December, 1814," *Plant and Poignaud Papers,* Town Library, Lancaster, Massachusetts.

Harriet Robinson, *Loom and Spindle* (Boston, 1892), pp. 25–28.

trary to all the modern notions about hygiene, we were a healthful and a robust brood. We all, except the baby, went to school every day, and Saturday afternoons I went to a charity school to learn to sew. My mother had never complained of her poverty in our hearing, and I had accepted the conditions of my life with a child's trust, knowing nothing of the relative difference between poverty and riches. And so I went to the sewing school, like any other little girl who was taking lessons in sewing and not as a "charity child," until a certain day when something was said by one of the teachers, about me, as a "poor little girl,"—a thoughtless remark, no doubt, such as may be said to-day in "charity schools." When I went home I told my mother that the teacher said I was *poor,* and she replied in her sententious manner, "You need not go there again."

Shortly after this my mother's widowed sister, Mrs. Angeline Cudworth, who kept a factory boarding-house in Lowell, advised her to come to that city. She secured a house for her, and my mother, with her little brood and her few household belongings, started for the new factory town. . . .

When we reached Lowell, we were carried at once to my aunt's house, whose generous spirit had well provided for her hungry relations; and we children were led into her kitchen, where, on the longest and whitest of tables, lay, oh, so many loaves of bread!

After our feast of loaves we walked with our mother to the Tremont Corporation, where we were to live, and at the old No. 5 (which imprint is still legible over the door), in the first block of tenements then built, I began my life among factory people. My mother kept forty boarders, most of them men, mill-hands, and she did all her housework, with what help her children could give her between schools; for we all, even the baby three years old, were kept at school. My part in the housework was to wash the dishes, and I was obliged to stand on a cricket in order to reach the sink!

My mother's boarders were many of them young men, and usually farmers' sons. They were almost invariably of good character and behavior, and it was a continual pleasure for me and my brothers to associate with them. I was treated like a little sister, never hearing a word or seeing a look to remind me that I was not of the same sex as my brothers. I played checkers with them, sometimes "beating," and took part in their conversation, and it never came into my mind that they were not the same as so many "girls." A good object-lesson for one who was in the future to maintain, by voice and pen, her belief in the equality of the sexes!

I had been to school constantly until I was about ten years of age, when my mother, feeling obliged to have help in her work besides what I could give, and also needing the money which I could earn, allowed me, at my urgent request (for I wanted to earn *money* like the other little girls), to go to work in the mill. I worked first in the spinning-room as a "doffer." The doffers were the very youngest girls, whose work was to doff, or take off, the full bobbins, and replace them with the empty ones.

I can see myself now, racing down the alley, between the spinning-frames, carrying in front of me a bobbin-box bigger than I was. These mites had to be very swift in their movements, so as not to keep the spinning-frames stopped long, and they worked only about fifteen minutes in every hour. The rest of the time was their own, and when the overseer was kind they were allowed to read, knit, or even to go outside the mill-yard to play. . . .

The working-hours of all the girls extended from five o'clock in the morning until seven in the evening, with one-half hour for breakfast and for dinner. Even the doffers were forced to be on duty nearly fourteen hours a day, and this was the greatest hardship in the lives of these children. For it was not until 1842 that the hours of labor for children under twelve years of age were limited to ten per day; but the "ten-hour law" itself was not passed until long after some of these little doffers were old enough to appear before the legislative committee on the subject, and plead, by their presence, for a reduction of the hours of labor.

I do not recall any particular hardship connected with this life, except getting up so early in the morning, and to this habit, I never was, and never shall be, reconciled, for it has taken nearly a lifetime for me to make up the sleep lost at that early age. But in every other respect it was a pleasant life. We were not hurried any more than was for our good, and no more work was required of us than we were able easily to do.

Most of us children lived at home, and we were well fed, drinking both tea and coffee, and eating substantial meals (besides luncheons) three times a day. We had very happy hours with the older girls, many of whom treated us like babies, or talked in a motherly way, and so had a good influence over us. And in the long winter evenings, when we could not run home between the doffings, we gathered in groups and told each other stories, and sung the old-time songs our mothers had sung, such as "Barbara Allen," "Lord Lovell," "Captain Kid," "Hull's Victory," and sometimes a hymn. . . .

And we told each other of our little hopes and desires, and what we meant to do when we grew up. For we had our aspirations; and one of us, who danced the "shawl dance," as she called it, in the spinning-room alley, for the amusement of her admiring companions, discussed seriously with another little girl the scheme of their running away together, and joining the circus. Fortunately, there was a grain of good sense lurking in the mind of this gay little lassie, with the thought of the mother at home, and the scheme was not carried out.

There was another little girl, whose mother was suffering with consumption, and who went out of the mill almost every forenoon, to buy and cook oysters, which she brought in hot, for her mother's luncheon. The mother soon went to her rest, and the little daughter, after tasting the first bitter experience of life, followed her. Dear Lizzie Osborne! little sister of my child-soul, such friendship as ours is not often repeated in after life! Many pathetic stories might be told of these little fatherless mill-children, who worked near their mothers, and who went hand in hand with them to and from the mill.

THE FAMILY CIRCLE

One aspect of the family cult in nineteenth-century America was an old tendency to classify people in society-at-large with familial or marital nomenclature. "Bachelor" or "spinster" were used to characterize or identify persons in newspapers and legal documents, and these figures also became well known in song and story. When all the terms for family types in daily use at the time are assembled, scarcely anyone in America, with or without near relations, lacked a familial identity. The description of even political events like the Civil War as a "fratricidal struggle" has particular poignancy in its implication that, however divided, America remained one big family. One recent writer on the events leading to the war views the political rhetoric during the crises, e.g., "a house divided against itself cannot stand," as particularly effective because it used family imagery and stirred people to believe that valued family relations and ideals in the "house" of the Union were threatened.

These documents express some of the folklore about a few of the figures in the American national family circle. The first piece, on a family gathering, reveals the sense of ties and respect across generations despite the ties being deeply tried by geography and time. The idea of periodic family *reunions*, which was far less well known (or necessary) in Europe, should also imply tendencies that broke the American family circle.

Following this piece is, in effect, a gallery of figures of the American family circle: the spinster aunt, single man/bachelor; and stepchild. What do the texts of these poems, songs, and stories reveal of assumptions about the advantages and disadvantages of being married or "familial"? How could we deduce from these popular expressions generalizations about the family ideal in American society? How much idealization, nostalgia, or even ritualized skepticism about family ties do these portraits reveal? Nostalgia and sentimentality always try to hide something behind either affection or disdain. What sense of society lurked behind the ideal of every American being somehow "familied," even if only by title?

THE FAMILY REUNION.

Family reunions were popular enough to be depicted in prints after the Civil War. This lithograph from 1871 incorporates much familiar sentiment and imagery from such occasions. *American Antiquarian Society*

FAMILY REUNION

Wednesday, November 7, 1860, is a day whose pleasant memories will long be fresh in the hearts of the descendants of the late DAVID L. DODGE.

The *Eightieth* Anniversary of the birthday of Mrs. SARAH CLEVELAND DODGE, his wife, brought together a large number of her descendants, to rejoice in the goodness of that kind Providence which had spared her for so many years, with such good health, unimpaired faculties, and cheerful spirits.

The gathering was at an early hour of the evening, at the house of her son WILLIAM E. DODGE, in Madison Avenue, New York. Each family was represented in part, and with its branches occupied a distinct portal of the room, while the venerable Lady was seated in an arm chair at the head of the parlour, where her eye could rest upon the entire group. At eight o'clock, her son WILLIAM E. DODGE called the assembly to order; and standing beside his Mother, spoke briefly as follows: . . .

When Parliament is convened, one of the ministers of the Queen is privileged to read her royal address to her subjects. To me it is a greater

A Family Gathering of the Descendants of Mrs. Sarah Cleveland Dodge, on her 80th Birthday, November 7, 1860 (New York, 1861), pp. 4–27, passim.

honour, on this occasion, to be my Mother's minister, and read the address she has written for her descendants:

Welcome, my children and grandchildren dear.
I rejoice that you have assembled here,
To join in praise and thanksgiving with me,
On this joyful day of jubilee—
To Him who has lengthened out my days,
I owe unbounded songs of praise.
He early sought my soul to claim,
to trust Him, and revere His name.
Kindly He led me through various ways,
And His mercy has followed me all my days.
In dangers known; unknown; still plainly I've seen
That my God's preserving care ever has been:
From languishing on the bed of pain,
He raised me to health and strength again:
He has given me children, kind and dear,
A progeny numerous, as exemplified here;
For those loved ones He has been pleased to call home
I will not mourn—to them, soon I shall come.—
And now, my Beloved, I turn to you;
Are not your praises also due?
For your Heavenly Father's richer grace,
Shown *you* above myriads of our race:
They born in lands as dark as night,
Trained with no ray of Gospel light;
Your birth has been in this favoured land,
Where blessings abound on every hand;
With parents kind to guide your way,
Lest in devious paths, your feet should stray:
God's holy Word they taught to revere,
Which shows the way of Salvation so clear;
To seek the Lord, most earnest its call,
Since Jesus has died, to rescue us all.—
I rejoice, my descendants, so many are led,
To trust in the Saviour who suffered and bled;
Yet fain do I hope that they all will submit,
And cast down their Idols at Jesus's feet;
Let go their hold on this world's transient joys,
For a treasure in Heaven, where nothing alloys.
A damper is cast o'er our pleasures to-day,
That so many dear ones are far, far, away.
Out of sight, yet still we are with them in *heart,*
And to hear of their welfare, true joy doth impart.

They are just as near Heaven—*there* at last may *we*
   meet,
Where Love will be perfect, and Communion sweet.

After the reading of these lines of welcome: by request,—WILLIAM DODGE
PORTER presented some statistics of the family:

The Descendants of David L. and Sarah C. Dodge are then as follows:
children, 7; grandchildren, 57; great-grandchildren, 27; 91 of the direct
descendants: and if to these we add 29 who have intermarried into the
family, there are 120 in all. Not one of this entire number has ever brought
dishonour upon the name of his ancestors; and of the 95 now living, 51
are professors of religion. Of the remaining 44, there are 25 still under
13 years of age, who we have faith to believe, will be brought early into
the fold of the Saviour . . . and I am sure that each one here to-night,
will cordially unite with me in saying, as the sincere prayer of our hearts:

> DEAR GRANDMOTHER, on this your festal day,
> When *eighty* years at length have rolled away
> Since first you came to earth; we here would prove
> The heart-felt tribute of our earnest love.
>
> We bless our God that he has spared your life,
> 'Mid scenes of care, and toil, and anxious strife,
> To this good, green, old age; may it be given
> To prove, indeed, a stepping-stone to heaven.
>
> We come to-night, with hearts that would set forth
> Our gratitude for all your Christian worth:
> Both child and grandchild; e'en the little one,
> Whose feet the race of life have just begun.
>
> We still revere the memory of him,
> Who, long in Heaven, feels not the power of Sin.
> *David, our Sire;* the man by God approved,
> Dwells with that Saviour, whom so long he loved.
>
> We know, *ten years ago* you crossed that line
> Which separates Eternity from Time;
> And yet we pray that many days be given,
> Before you wing your flight from Earth to Heaven.
>
> *Four Daughers* loved, await you in *that* home;
> They have gone first; and you will follow soon—
> *Sarah*—then *Susan*—*Mary*—*Julia* last;
> From earthly toil, to heavenly rest they passed.
>
> Only one left, and she on foreign shore,
> Expects to meet her mother *here* no more:
> *Elizabeth*—but she, we know, will pray
> That God may keep you; though so far away.

Two sons, the staff of your declining years,
Often have caused you happiness—not tears—
David and *William;* and they still will prove,
The comfort of that mother whom they love.

God bless you ever, is our earnest prayer
At home, abroad, always, and everywhere;
In health or sickness; here; in heaven above,
Where, sorrows ended, all will e'er be love.

And when the scenes of life are fading fast,
May Jesus be your solace to the last;
And then with dear ones who have gone before,
In that blest world all meet, *to part no more.*

BUT SHALL WE ALL BE THERE, with happy end?
Is Christ, *our* hope, *our* trust, *our* DEAREST friend?
If so, then welcome Death: soon shall we be
Praising Emmanuel through eternity.

MR. NORMAN WHITE, a Son-in-Law, being called upon, said:

I had not expected to make any remarks upon this occasion; but I need no urging, for my heart is full. This gathering is one of intense interest. Here we see a venerable Lady surrounded by her descendants; and although I am not a descendant, yet she has been to me a very dear Mother, and none present, I am sure, feel a deeper or warmer love for her.

She is the Mother of another Mother, with whom I lived for more than a quarter of a Century in the greatest happiness; and to whom I have been indebted, more than to any other human being; for, from her wise counsels and holy life, I derived daily instruction. Her lovely, unselfish character endeared her to all her friends. She is not here. Her work is done, and she has gone to her rest.

But here are her children; and I am most happy to embrace this occasion to say, that, to their beloved Mother's teaching and gentle influence, they are largely indebted for a measure of happiness which has rarely been exceeded.

The instructions received from her Parents in the morning of life, were imparted to her own children; and I now present them to their honoured Grandmother, as children who, by their filial respect and love, as well as by their rectitude of conduct, have done much to promote my own happiness, and also the happiness of their lamented Mother.

The following letter from Rev. CHARLES CLEVELAND of Boston, the only surviving Brother of Mrs. Dodge, and now in his *eighty-ninth* year, was received on her birthday:

MY BELOVED SISTER:—Should you live until to-morrow, you will have passed *eighty* years of your pilgrimage through a world of sin and of many trials. Soon will *you* and your *brother* reach a most glorious home, to be forever with Him, whom we love as the chiefest among ten thousands;

nor shall we see Him as "through a glass darkly," but *face to face*. Yes, blessed be God, Who hath in so many years given us to discover, in a happy measure, a dawning sense of His glorious attributes, as shining in the face of Jesus Christ. Blessed be God, manifested in the flesh, who hath given us the heart-comforting assurance, that, among the *many* mansions prepared for His blood-washed flock, *one* is prepared for each of *us*. How sweet the promise, "where I am, there shall also my servants be." In this world of perpetual change, each revolving year numbering its thousands passing to their long home, *our* lives are still most wonderfully protracted.

MY AUNT

My aunt! my dear unmarried aunt!
    Long years have o'er her flown;
Yet still she strains the aching clasp
    That binds her virgin zone;
I know it hurts her,—though she looks
    As cheerful as she can;
Her waist is ampler than her life,
    For life is but a span.

My aunt! my poor deluded aunt!
    Her hair is almost gray;
Why will she train that winter curl
    In such a spring-like way?
How can she lay her glasses down,
    And say she reads as well,
When, through a double convex lens,
    She just makes out to spell?

Her father—grandpapa! forgive
    This erring lip its smiles—
Vowed she should make the finest girl
    Within a hundred miles;
He sent her to a stylish school;
    'T was in her thirteenth June;
And with her, as the rules required,
    "Two towels and a spoon."

They braced my aunt against a board,
    To make her straight and tall;
They laced her up, they starved her down,
    To make her light and small;

Oliver Wendell Holmes, "My Aunt," *The Poetical Works of Oliver Wendell Holmes* (Boston, 1886), p. 4.

"The Grandmother's Gift" and "The Grandfather's Advice" are prints by the same firm and are typical images of the American "family circle." The grandfather's advice is, unsurprisingly, the greatest of the domestic homilies for children, and a grandmother's gift such as is shown was commonly a book of moral tales, cautionary poems, or religious exhortations.
American Antiquarian Society

THE GRANDFATHER'S ADVICE.

Honor thy Father and thy Mother

They pinched her feet, they singed her hair,
    They screwed it up with pins;—
O never mortal suffered more
    In penance for her sins.

So, when my precious aunt was done,
    My grandsire brought her back;
(By daylight, lest some rabid youth
    Might follow on the track;)
"Ah!" said my grandsire, as he shook
    Some powder in his pan,
"What could this lovely creature do
    Against a desperate man!"

Alas! nor chariot, nor barouche,
    Nor bandit cavalcade,
Tore from the trembling father's arms
    His all-accomplished maid.
For her how happy had it been!
    And Heaven had spared to me
To see one sad, ungathered rose
    On my ancestral tree.

REVERIES OF A BATCHELOR

Smoke—Signifying Doubt.

A wife?—thought I;—yes, a wife!

And why?

And pray, my dear sir, why not—why? Why not doubt; why not hesitate; why not tremble?

Does a man buy a ticket in a lottery—a poor man, whose whole earnings go in to secure the ticket,—without trembling, hesitating, and doubting?

Can a man stake his batchelor respectability, his independence, and comfort, upon the die of absorbing, unchanging, relentless marriage, without trembling at the venture?

Shall a man who has been free to chase his fancies over the wide-world, without lett or hindrance, shut himself up to marriage-ship, within four walls called Home, that are to claim him, his time, his trouble, and his tears, thenceforward forever more, without doubts thick, and thick-coming as Smoke?

Shall he who has been hitherto a mere observer of other men's cares, and business—moving off where they made him sick of heart, approaching whenever and wherever they made him gleeful—shall he now undertake

Ik Marvel, *Reveries of a Batchelor* (New York, 1851), pp. 19–28.

administration of just such cares and business, without qualms? Shall he, whose whole life has been but a nimble succession of escapes from trifling difficulties, now broach without doubtings—that Matrimony, where if difficulty beset him, there is no escape? Shall this brain of mine, careless-working, never tired with idleness, feeding on long vagaries, and high, gigantic castles, dreaming out beatitudes hour by hour—turn itself at length to such dull taskwork, as thinking out a livelihood for wife and children?

Where thenceforward will be those sunny dreams, in which I have warmed my fancies, and my heart, and lighted my eye with crystal? This very marriage, which a brilliant working imagination has invested time and again with brightness, and delight, can serve no longer as a mine for teeming fancy: all, alas, will be gone—reduced to the dull standard of the actual! No more room for intrepid forays of imagination—no more gorgeous realm-making—all will be over! . . .

For a poor hunter of his kind, without traps or snares, or any aid of police or constabulary, to traverse the world, where are swarming, on a moderate computation, some three hundred and odd millions of unmarried women, for a single capture—irremediable, unchangeable—and yet a capture which by strange metonymy, not laid down in the books, is very apt to turn captor into captive, and make game of hunter—all this, surely, surely may make a man shrug with doubt!

Then—again,—there are the plaguey wife's relations. . . . Last, and worst, is some fidgety old uncle, forever too cold or too hot, who vexes you with his patronizing airs, and impudently kisses his little Peggy!

——That could be borne, however: for perhaps he has promised his fortune to Peggy. Peggy, then, will be rich:—(and the thought made me rub my shins, which were now getting comfortably warm upon the fire-dogs.) Then, she will be forever talking of *her* fortune; and pleasantly reminding you on occasion of a favorite purchase,—how lucky that *she* had the means; and dropping hints about economy; and buying very extravagant Paisleys. . . .

She will be provokingly silent when you hint to a tradesman, that you have not the money by you, for his small bill;—in short, she will tear the life out of you, making you pay in righteous retribution of annoyance, grief, vexation, shame, and sickness of heart, for the superlative folly of "marrying rich."

——But if not rich, then poor. Bah! the thought made me stir the coals; but there was still no blaze. The paltry earnings you are able to wring out of clients by the sweat of your brow, will now be all *our* income; you will be pestered for pin-money, and pestered with your poor wife's-relations. . . .

Perhaps she is ugly;—not noticeable at first; but growing on her, and (what is worse) growing faster on you. . . .

Perhaps Peggy is pretty enough—only shrewish.

——No matter for cold coffee;—you should have been up before.

What sad, thin, poorly cooked chops, to eat with your rolls! . . .

Again, Peggy is rich enough, well enough, mild enough, only she doesn't care a fig for you. She has married you because father, or grandfather thought the match eligible, and because she didn't wish to disoblige them. . . .

But, again, Peggy loves you;—at least she swears it, with her hand on the Sorrows of Werter. . . .

You never fancied when you saw her buried in a three volume novel, that it was anything more than a girlish vagary; and when she quoted Latin, you thought innocently, that she had a capital memory for her samplers. . . .

You hint at broken rest and an aching head at breakfast, and she will fling you a scrap of Anthology—in lieu of the camphor bottle—or chant the αἰαῖ αἰαῖ, of tragic chorus.

——The nurse is getting dinner; you are holding the baby; Peggy is reading Bruyère.

The fire smoked thick as pitch, and puffed out little clouds over the chimney piece. I gave the fore-stick a kick, at thought of Peggy, baby, and Bruyère.

I WISH I WERE SINGLE AGAIN

I wish I were single, oh then, oh then!
I wish I were single, oh then!
When I was single my pockets did jingle,
And I wish I were single again.

When I was single, oh then, oh then!
When I was single, oh then!
I liv'd at my ease and I went where I pleas'd,
And I wish I were single again.

I married a wife, oh! then, oh then!
I married a wife, oh! then!
I married a wife, she's the plague of my life,
And I wish I were single again.

And now I am married, oh! then, oh! then!
And now I am married, oh! then!
If I go any where, my wife's sure to be there,
And I wish I were single again.

When my wife died, oh! then, oh! then!
When my wife died, oh! then!
When my wife died, I'll be hanged if I cried,
So glad to be single again.

"I Wish I Were Single Again," music and lyrics by J. C. Beckel, 1871.

I went to the funeral, oh! then, oh! then!
I went to the funeral, oh! then!
The music did play, and I danced all the way,
So glad to be single again.

I married another, oh! then, oh! then!
I married another, oh! then!
I married another, she's worse than the tother!
And I wish I were single again.

Now all ye young men, oh! then, oh! then!
Now all ye young men, oh! then!
Be kind to your first, or the last will prove worse!
And you'll wish for the old one again.

THE STEPCHILD

The Blind Girl

"They tell me, father, that tonight
You wed another bride,
And that you'll clasp her in your arms
Where my poor mother died.

"They say her name is Mary, too,
The name my mother bore.
Oh, tell me, is she kind and true
As the one you loved before?

"And is her step so soft and low,
Her voice so sweet and mild,
And do you think that she will love
Your blind and only child?

"Please, father, do not bid me come
To greet your loving bride.
I could not meet her in the room
Where my poor mother died.

"Her picture's hanging on the wall,
Her books are lying near;
And there's the harp her fingers touched;
And there's her vacant chair—

William Tyler, "The Blind Girl," in H. M. Belden, *Ballads and Songs Collected by the Missouri Folklore Society*, University of Missouri Studies (Columbia, Mo., 1940), p. 276.

"The chair whereby I've often knelt
To say my evening prayer.
Oh! father, it would break my heart.
I could not meet her there.

"I love you, but I long to go
To yon bright world so fair
Where God is true, and I am sure
There'll be no blind ones there.

"Now let me kneel down by your side
And to our Savior pray
That God's right hand may shield you both
Through life's long dreary way.

"My prayers are ended now, dear pa.
I'm tired now," she said.
He picked her up all in his arms
And laid her on the bed.

And as he turned to leave the room
A joyful cry was given.
He heard, and caught the last sweet smile—
His blind child was in heaven.

They laid her by her mother's side
And raised a marble fair,
And but engraved these simple words:
"There'll be no blind ones there."

COURTSHIP

Many nineteenth-century Americans courted under circumstances and in a style that were very different from those that had characterized courtship in colonial times. Economic and demographic conditions had greatly reduced the ability of parents to control the timing of their children's marriages or to influence their choice of a mate. For most families, the holdings were too small, the children surviving to adulthood too many, the life expectancy of parents too long, and available land and the money to buy it too scarce for parents to give their progeny sufficient patrimonies and dowries to set up their own households. This not only limited parents' economic leverage over their children, it also drove many young men (and, to a lesser extent, young women) away from home to do their courting beyond the view or control of their parents. (See the Wilson and Norcom letters in previous sections.)

As liberating as these new circumstances might have been, they also posed some new problems, as the diary of Lucien Boynton (1808–78) suggests. Deciding when to marry and then choosing the right mate were not easy. Should a young man wait until his prospects were sure? But how could one be certain of his prospects in the fast-changing life of mid-nineteenth-century America? What of the argument that in the absence of parental controls, "early marriages" were necessary to keep young men on the path of virtue? Many courting couples were relative strangers to each other. Without the traditional fuller knowledge about a swain or sweetheart's previous life and family, how could one know if the other really did possess the qualities of a good wife or husband?

Although prudential considerations—whether a mate was of the appropriate class or a young man's prospects were sufficient—still played a part in the decisions leading to marriage, courtship centered far more than previously on the notion of "marrying for love." The idea of romantic love—unlike that found in many of the colonial documents—underplayed sexual attraction if it did not deny it altogether. (The existence and power of the "baser passions" were, of course, fully acknowledged in the innumerable seductions and betrayals of romantic fiction as well as the recourse of scions of gentility to bordellos and the favors of "low" women.) Instead, the rituals and language of proper courtship reflected an ideal of "elevated" love, love aspiring to the purity that a true lady—chaste, refined, delicate and spiritual—and a true gentleman—manly and properly worshipful of pure womanhood—extolled in each other. (The extreme of this style of courtship was achieved by the couple in the 1890s who sought medical advice to help them overcome the impotence that afflicted the husband when he first faced the prospect of "defiling" the pure young woman he had successfully courted.)

Proper courtship was complex and generated many rules, which tried to "enlist the affections" without crossing the bounds of propriety, that revealed "manly" or "refined" character while maintaining barriers against "coquetry" or "deceit," that intensified feeling without provoking dangerous and illicit passions. But as the documents in this section indicate, it was often a troublesome etiquette. How did a couple like Miss Kemper and Mr. Nelson balance emotional intensity with restraint and "elevate" their affections to the appropriate plane? How did one distinguish between artifice and real affection, or, did the very recourse to "devices" reveal a lack of character? Did the "rules of honor" that Catharine Beecher discussed in her *Truth Stranger Than Fiction* (a book championing the cause of a young woman whose affections, Beecher thought, a prominent Yale professor had solicited falsely and then betrayed), and that Richard Wells tried to codify in his 1892 book of manners, protect a young lady or merely reveal her entrapment in the ideal of purity? More broadly, how do both the conventions and the complexities of genteel courtship relate to the attitudes toward sexuality and the cult of the home reflected in the documents in later sections?

COURTSHIP OF LUCIEN BOYNTON

Monday. 11. Don and Lady went to Newark on Thursday last, and myself with Miss Jacques and Miss Piper on Saturday. . . . The meeting of so many cousins far from their native home was very agreeable, and to me attended with many interesting associations and reflections. But however interested I was in this meeting of cousins and however well pleased I was with their society, I soon found that my interest began to concentrate in a single individual, a person who came from Wilmington along with us, and that my pleasure was dependant more and more upon a single source. This being observed by my cousins, they seemed to take every occasion to encourage it, which together with the clearly expressed evidence which I had, that the object of my interest, was in a similar situation with respect to myself, led me on till I at length found, that I was not only happy but miserable. Or, in the language of Romance, Poetry, and the fine arts, I was—in—love. . . .

Trifling aside, I find that in such social visits where some are gay, some thoughtless, and all lively and cheerful, I am apt too much to forget

Solon J. Buck, ed., "The Journal of Lucien C. Boynton," *Proceedings of the American Antiquarian Society*, new series, vol. 43 (Oct. 1933), pp. 338–49. Reprinted by permission.

the more solemn matters of life, the high duties to God and men, for which I ought to live . . . and I am resolved to guard against it in the future. . . .

[*April*] 5. I find I have formed an acquaintance which troubles me a little. After the formation of a pretty warm friendship, I find a defect of early education, which somewhat surprises me. The question is whether, accomplishments, good natural talents, and a warm heart in a companion, will sufficiently compensate for this defect. Then whether this acquaintance possess these.

May 4. How may we know when a lady is artful (as the phrase is)? Answer. When a lady sees that a gentleman is becoming partial to her there are a thousand little acts and sayings and allusions, that are peculiarly adapted to encourage this partiality. If she understands these well, and is skillful and ready in the use of them, she may be called artful, yet such a person is not necessarily a coquette. She may in this way, seek to secure the affection of the person she loves.

If however we meet with a lady who possesses and practices this skill or art, we may I think infer as follows.

1. That she possesses considerable natural talents: else she could not perform the part so successfully.

2. That she has practiced these arts considerably toward others. For skill in art is acquired only by practice.

3. You cannot put confidence in such a person. For (1) you know not how far she is sincere in what she says and does, or how far it is mere art. And (2) she has become so accustomed to practice this art on others, you may not be sure she will entirely cease for you.

4. There is some reason to expect, that such a person has not strict and well-established moral principles. For the art even requires the violation of strict morality. . . .

June 29. Miss Carry Jacques and Miss S. L. Piper have been here at Cousin's all the past week on a visit, and I of course have done nothing by way of study. The week has left a painful vacancy in my mind, and the "Blues" seem to be already gathering around me. My soul feels as though it had been feeding on wind and vapor. . . .

The above visit was attended with some circumstances a little painful at the time, but ending on the same ground where we were at first, or perhaps a little more positive ground, respecting Miss Piper. . . .

Saturday [*July*] *6th*. [*Wilmington.*] Walked up the Brandywine this morning with S. L. P. Full reconciliation. Free conversation as to circumstances of each. Correspondence agreed upon. Returned home with Mr. Graves. Felt my affections increased. . . .

Saturday 13. [*Newark.*] Received letter from S. L. in answer to mine of Wednesday. Confidence and affection increased. . . .

Wednesday 17. S. L. came to Newark on Monday and returns with me to Wilmington tomorrow. Some things in her manner to the other gentlemen, and toward me much astonished me, and are somewhat unaccountable. It gave me much pain during her visit, and unless she can explain it satisfactorily, I now think it will be decisive with me.

18. Rode to Wilmington to day with Miss Piper and took along with us Mr. Adams, who has sons here at Newark in school and who resides in Philadelphia. Started 5 o'clock A.M. conversed with Mr. Adams among other things . . . of marriage and celibacy, early marriages &c. He thinks that a man ought to marry to be happy. Is in favor of early marriages. Miss Piper very attentive after arriving at Wilmington. Left her somewhat coldly, enough to signify that something was wrong. . . .

Saturday August 17. [*Newark.*] In about two weeks after S. L. left Newark I wrote her a letter mentioning some objectionable things in her conduct at last visit, and signifying that unless a reasonable explanation could be given, it would be decisive with me. Received a conciliatory answer in which a pretended reason was given, but as it is mere pretence does not at all excuse her conduct. . . .

S. is a remarkable person in many respects. She possesses some qualities which if they were real and founded in a good heart, and regulated by good moral principles, would be very valuable. Indeed, if she was what she has sometimes seemed to me to be, and in addition had a well educated mind, and virtuous and industrious habits and some other things, I should value her higher than any earthly object. But now her exceptionable qualities are such as to put to the foil all her excellancies. She has all the leading qualities of a coquette. Her art in certain traits of character, and feelings is very remarkable; but her plans and schemes are very imprudent and foolish and such as will not fail to expose her very soon wherever she may go. But I have reason to believe that she is naturally unprincipled and selfish. She will sacrifice anything, no matter what, to the object she may have in view which may be merely the gratification of vanity. Yet I have no doubt but her object in her intercourse with me has been from the first to gain me if possible. . . . I have long regarded her as a very improper person for me, in most respects and do now consider it a most fortunate circumstance, that my eyes were opened and I receded as soon as I did. I think the Lord permitted me thus to be led away, for the purpose of teaching me my frailty and the importance of looking to him, in all things. After some time I came so much to myself as to make it a subject of prayer. . . .

December 3d. Newark. Miss Piper came to Newark the Thursday before I went to the city and is here still at Mr. Graves. . . . Has explained many things which I considered as exceptionable toward me, and which made her appear to me to possess some very undesirable traits of character. Though I think her very censurable in many respects yet I am persuaded that she is less so than I supposed, and that I have done her injustice. The concessions she has made, her forbearance in view of the plainness and severity of my language, have been such as to indicate, what I consider some very good traits of character and that she has some regard for me. . . .

Saturday May 8 [*1841*]. Received a letter last Saturday bringing intelligence calculated to affect me not a little on account of its nature and its being so sudden and unexpected. My friendship for L had been upon the whole increasing for the last six months, though because I thought I saw important faults in her I had withheld a very strong expression of it. I intended to have visited the North last Fall but circumstances were such as to render it almost impossible. My desire to remain here another year without visiting the North together with my previous apparent neglect in writing her so seldom &c., I suppose, led her to conclude that she could not depend on me and perhaps had little to hope. She therefore perhaps encouraged attention from other sources as much as possible and was successful. . . . I, as yet know no particulars concerning her marriage which I suppose is consummated before now. If she took the step chiefly on account of my delinquency in the expression of my attachment and desire, I can blame her only for not having previously given me some intimation of it. However, the chief fault, I suppose was with me and the circumstances in which I have been placed. The intelligence affected me somewhat for a few days, but does not much now. It has been ordered by Providence and is of course all for the best. . . .

LOVE LETTERS

James A. Nelson to Judith S. Kemper

April 7th 1835

Miss Kemper

You may be a little surprised at this *cold* address, when I assure you it is far below the temperature of my present feelings.

But my present object is not to write a *Love Letter*—(If I can help it), all I intend, is to express my feelings, and lay open before you my future prospects, with that *frankness* and *candour,* which I have ever found to be a distinctive characteristic of yourself, and which I hope will continue to mark not only your, but my future course.

I know you have not been aware of the high estimation in which you have been held by me, almost from our earliest acquaintance, and which continued to rise higher and higher the farther our acquaintance was extended.

A sense of *Duty,* not less than a *constitutional diffidence* (which, however *unmanly* it may appear, I must confess I inherit), has hitherto induced me to *conceal,* rather than cherish my affections for you— And except so far as personal interview might have occasionally afforded an opportunity for expressing the feelings of my heart by offices of kindness, the same causes would have operated to produce the same effect, and my feelings would have been known only to myself, had I not been almost *compelled* to unbosom

Nelson-Kemper Letters, Joseph Regenstein Library, University of Chicago. Reprinted by permission.

myself to *one* whom I shall ever feel safe in making my confident, and been *assured* by him, that they were *reciprocated*— One great obstacle to my addressing you in the character of a *Suitor* being thus removed; it only remains to explain the *other*, viz. A sense of *Duty*— Happy would it be for us if *inclination* could always be made to coincide with *duty*, but alas! how often it is the reverse, particularly to those who *would* deviate from the path of rectitude— Hitherto I have acted from, what I conceived to be, a sense of *Duty*, both to myself and You; to myself I owed it, not to cherish hopes which *might be blasted;* to you, not to excite expectations, which it might not be in my power to fulfill— Think not from this that my affections are vibrating between You and any other *earthly* object, No!— without *You*, the World would be to me a *"void immense"*—

As *children* are *apt* to do; I have often looked around me upon the whole circle of my acquaintance, in search of *One* whom, *All* things considered, I would be *willing* (were I prepared) to take for a *Wife*, and my eye has invariably found a uniform *blank*, untill it rested upon *You*.

In some of these reveries, All the young ladies of my acquaintance have been, one by one, thrown into the ballance and weighed *against myself*, and *all found wanting*, with One single exception, and *then*, to my no little discomforture, I felt the Scale turn *against me*.

The cause of my great deficiency, I learned, without much elaborate investigation, to be this, viz. *Immaturity*— I am young in years, and still younger in *knowledge*, and still *feebler* in pecuniary resources— I have indeed completed my Collegiate course, but that is only a *preparatory step*, to the study of a Profession— And so far as I know, I am intirely destitute of the means of support, *other* than the assistance of a *generous Father*, who, with comparatively limited means, has four younger sons and a young daughter to support. My education and Profession (if I ever get it) will be all the fortune I ever expect or *desire*— All that prevents me from, at once, renouncing my dependence, and working my own way through the studies of a Profession, is, that instead of three years, it would require perhaps *twice* that time, and put farther off that long wished for Day, when I could set me down, with a *Companion* at my side— My present arrangements are to study *Medicine*, with an Uncle who lives in Richmond, Va., though my Mother has many objections to my going to a slave state, and particularly to Richmond; her health has been rather delicate for the last year, and having been from home so much, I considered it my duty to comply with her wishes, and remain at home during the winter— She is now much better, If she can be persuaded to leave home, I will take her with me to Va., where she will be surrounded by her, and Father's nearest relations. . . .

And *now*, whàt shall I subscribe myself?! I have thrown open to you my *whole heart*, I therefor leave it to your own *good sense* to supply the ellipsis, and subscribe myself— Yours &-ᶜ.

James A. Nelson

Judith S. Kemper to James A. Nelson

April 18, 1835

Dear Friend

(For, after the disclosures you have made, I think I am safe in thus addressing you;) I rec'd yours of the seventh inst. with mingled emotions of hope and fear, on the 17th. I had received one from our mutual friend S. a few days before, in which he told me that I might expect one from you soon. You may well suppose that I awaited with anxiety, the arrival of that, which was to give hope, life, and energy, to those feelings which had been lurking in my breast, unknown till recently, to all but myself; or to crush and blight them forever. I succeeded in concealing them for eight or ten months, and should still have done so, had not my roommates, this winter, compelled me to avow them, or do worse. This very avowal seemed to strengthen them, and I felt that I had done myself an injustice, in doing *any thing* that would confirm my attachment to *yourself*, when I had *no* reason to hope that that attachment was in any degree reciprocated. Although I could never have forgotten you, yet I was *determined* to live down those feelings, and not to let them render me unhappy. But when your letter came I found, to my no small gratification, that I had a much greater share of your affections, than I had ever even allowed myself to *hope* for—for I cannot doubt your candor.

You say, in the commencement, that you do not wish to write a "love-letter"? neither do I; if by this we are to understand what is often meant by this expression. I do dislike very much the lovesick trash, that I have sometimes seen on paper; and I hope to be able to avoid it, at all times. It is not necessary, in order to express the feelings of the heart. We have been provided with purer, more ennobling language by which to convey our ideas; and it is our duty to strive to elevate the affections, as much as any other quality of our minds—for it can be done. . . .

I read your letter to mother (for I considered it my duty to do so) and asked her, what answer I should send you. She said, you were a stranger to her, and that she could not advise me one way or the other; but that I must act according to my own judgment. She is extremely solicitous for the welfare of her daughters—anxious that they should do well in every thing; but especially in affairs of this kind; she therefore advised me to be cautious. I told her that I felt perfectly safe, with regard to you, and had no doubt that she would be satisfied, when she would become acquainted with you. There is a case of the same nature, pending between one of my sisters, and another gentleman, whom mother has never seen, and if she were like some mothers, she would object entirely. But she does not. I think you will not disapprove of my consulting her; for I owe her all that a daughter can owe one of the best of mothers.

I hope you will not fail in your promised visit; and allow yourself sufficient time, to have several days to spend with us. You will receive a hearty welcome. I think you will be pleased with our neighborhood, for it is very pleasant, and *our* location is delightful.

When I bade you farewell last fall, just as I was leaving Oxford, I felt that I should probably never see you again, and almost wished, that I never had seen you; for there was a feeling inspired within my bosom that I could not conceal from myself, if I did from others, and that I could not flatter myself was also awakened in yours. I have seen many others, both before and since my first acquaintance with yourself; but *you* are the standard by which I have compared them all; and no one has come up to it. I have not yet seen anyone whom I would prefer before you, everything being taken into consideration. In every one there has been something lacking, or some objection which I never met with, when thinking of you. But these things have never troubled me very much; I always felt that I was young enough to think much of them, and too young to let them trouble me; also that I had need of more time to improve myself, in almost every branch of knowledge. . . .

You speak of a want of pecuniary resources. My good father used to say, he did not wish to see his children set out in the world, with a fortune in their hands, but that he would much rather see them have to make it by their own industry and economy; and then they would know how to enjoy it. If I should ever accept your hand, I want it to be, not for what you have, but for what you are—*for yourself alone.* I am but a plain farmer's daughter, who has left to his children a good name, and enough of this world's goods to support us comfortably, if we continue to use that industry and economy which he taught us from our infancy. . . .

It is now almost a year since I first went to Oxford, and since that time I have experienced greater changes, than ever before. While there I passed my time very pleasantly, and I hope profitably. I found many warm and valuable friends, and expect to look back with pleasure on the time spent in their society—there too, I added something, to my small stock of knowledge. You were the first stranger to whom I was introduced in the place. It was done by Mrs. Irwin, almost immediately after our arrival. She spoke of you, before you came in, in the highest terms; but little did I think then, what was to be the issue of that introduction; I did not even imagine, that in less than a year, upon an acquaintance of three or four months, I should be penning you such a letter as this. You will doubtless recollect the time, and I wish you would recall it, and think of it. I love to dwell upon the scenes of bygone days; and *now,* I shall indulge this inclination, and let memory recall the seasons, though few and short, that I passed where you were. I have not hitherto, suffered myself to think of them, when I could avoid it—but the propensity was too strong to be always resisted. I have sometimes tried to reason myself out of the belief, that my affection for you, was any thing more than a *common friendship;* but I could not do it—the conviction would force itself upon me, that it was *something stronger* than friendship. Oxford very soon connected my name with *another,* without any just cause—I knew it was groundless, and therefore let it give me no trouble. I always consoled myself with the thought that they were mistaken, with regard to my choice at least, notwithstanding I valued and esteemed him as a friend and enjoyed his society very much, yet I could not forget you.

COURTING MANNERS FOR LADIES

In reference to the interests of women, the rules of honor have especially been brought to bear on those points where she is at once most defenceless, and most susceptible to suffering. It is in *the affections* that woman is exposed to the most suffering, and here, too, is where she most needs protection.

By the construction of nature, by the ordinance of Providence, by the training of the family and school, by the influence of society, and by the whole current of poetry and literature, woman is educated to feel that a happy marriage is the summit of all earthly felicity, and yet by a fantasy of custom, it has become one of the most disgraceful of all acts for a woman to acknowledge that she is seeking to attain this felicity. On the contrary, she is trained to all sorts of concealments and subterfuges, to make it appear as if it was a matter to which she is perfectly indifferent, and such is the influence of custom and high cultivation, that the more delicate, refined, and self-respecting a woman becomes, the more acute is the suffering inflicted, by any imputation of her delicacy in this respect.

It is owing to this, that the most stringent rules of honor are maintained in this direction. A man of high honor not only avoids everything that would tempt a woman to manifest an interest which cannot be returned, but he scrupulously avoids every thing that would involve her in any such suspicion. There is a certain amount and style of intercourse, that any lady can accept without any implication that is derogatory. There is another amount and style of intercourse which no lady can receive without the implication, either that she is dishonestly encouraging approaches merely to gratify a mean vanity, or that she is willing to accept an offer of marriage; or, at least, is willing to be influenced to such a result.

COURTING MANNERS FOR MEN

A Lady's Position

A lady's choice is only negative—that is to say, she may love, but she cannot declare her love; she must wait. It is hers, when the time comes, to consent or to decline, but till the time comes she must be passive. And whatever may be said in jest or sarcasm about it, this trial of a woman's patience is often very hard to bear.

Catharine E. Beecher, *Truth Stranger Than Fiction* (New York, 1859), p. 23.
Richard Wells, *Manners, Culture and Dress* (Springfield, Mass., 1891), pp. 225–35.

A Gentleman's Position

A man may, and he will learn his fate at once, openly declare his passion, and obtain his answer. In this he has great advantage over the lady. Being refused, he may go elsewhere to seek a mate, if he be in the humor; try his fortune again, and mayhap be the lucky drawer of a princely prize.

To a gentleman seeking a partner for life, we would say—look to it, that you be not entraped by a beautiful face.

Conduct of a Gentleman toward Ladies

A gentleman whose thoughts are not upon marriage should not pay too exclusive attentions to any one lady. He may call upon all and extend invitations to any or all to attend public places of amusement with him, or may act as their escort on occasions, and no one of the many has any right to feel herself injured. But as soon as he neglects others to devote himself to a single lady he gives that lady reason to suppose he is particularly attracted to her, and there is danger of her feelings becoming engaged.

Conduct of a Lady toward Gentlemen

Neither should a young lady allow marked attentions from any one to whom she is not especially attracted, for several reasons: one, that she may not do an injury to the gentleman in seeming to give his suit encouragement, another, that she may not harm herself in keeping aloof from her those whom she might like better, but who will not approach her under the mistaken idea that her feelings are already interested. A young lady will on no account encourage the address of one whom she perceives to be seriously interested in her unless she feels it possible that in time she may be able to return his affections. The prerogative of proposing lies with man, but the prerogative of refusing lies with woman; and this prerogative a lady of tact and kind heart can and will exercise before her suitor is brought to the humiliation of a direct offer. She may let him see that she receives with equal favor attentions from others, and she may check in a kind but firm manner his too frequent visits. She should try, while discouraging him as a lover, to still retain him as a friend.

A young man who has used sufficient delicacy and deliberation in this matter, and who, moreover, is capable of taking a hint when it is offered him, need not go to the length of a declaration when a refusal only awaits him. . . .

Trifling with a Man's Feelings

Some young ladies pride themselves upon the conquests which they make, and would not scruple to sacrifice the happiness of an estimable person to their reprehensible vanity. Let this be far from you. If you see clearly that you have become an object of especial regard to a gentleman, and do not wish to encourage his addresses, treat him honorably and humanely, as you hope to be used with generosity by the person who may engage your own heart. Do not let him linger in suspense; but take the earliest opportunity of carefully making known your feelings on the subject. This may be done in a variety of ways. . . .

Let it never be said of you, that you permit the attentions of an honorable man when you have no heart to give him; or that you have trifled with the affections of one whom you perhaps esteem, although you resolve never to marry him. It may be that his preference gratifies and his conversation interests you; that you are flattered by the attentions of a man whom some of your companions admire; and that, in truth, you hardly know your own mind on the subject. This will not excuse you. Every young woman ought to know the state of her own heart; and yet the happiness and future prospects of many an excellent man have been sacrificed by such unprincipled conduct. . . .

Proposal of Marriage

The mode in which the avowal of love should be made, must of course, depend upon circumstances. It would be impossible to indicate the style in which the matter should be told. The heart and the head—the best and truest partners—suggest the most proper fashion. Station, power, talent, wealth, complexion; all have much to do with the matter; they must all be taken into consideration in a formal request for a lady's hand. If the communication be made by letter, the utmost care should be taken that the proposal be clearly, simply, and honestly stated. Every allusion to the lady should be made with marked respect. Let it, however, be taken as a rule that an interview is best; but let it be remembered that all rules have exceptions. . . .

"Asking Papa"

When a gentleman is accepted by the lady of his choice, the next thing in order is to go at once to her parents for their approval. In presenting his suit to them he should remember that it is not from the sentimental but the practical side that they will regard the affair. Therefore, after describing the state of his affections in as calm a manner as possible, and perhaps hinting that their daughter is not indifferent to him, let him at once frankly, without waiting to be questioned, give an account of his pecuniary resources and his general prospects in life, in order that the parents may judge whether he can properly provide for a wife and possible family. . . .

All lovers cannot afford to present their lady-loves with diamond rings, but all are able to give them some little token of their regard which will be cherished for their sakes, and which will serve as a memento of a very happy past to the end of life. The engagement ring should be worn upon the ring finger of the right hand.

WIVES AND HUSBANDS

The self-consciousness that in the nineteenth century overtook almost every aspect of family life could not ignore marriage itself. The literature devoted to the "duties and relations" of husbands and wives was enormous, affecting almost every aspect of American culture and exempting few aspects of marital life from scrutiny. Countless domestic novels focused on the attempts of couples (especially wives) to withstand the forces from within and without that threatened to corrupt marriage and subvert its true purposes. Gift books, newspapers, the religious quarterlies, magazines like *Godey's Lady's Book*, the *Ladies' Repository*, and *The Southern Ladies' Companion* were filled with sketches of exemplary wives, poems and songs extolling "perfect love," and various pieces promoting "just" views of the matrimonial state. Manuals like William A. Alcott's *The Young Wife* and *The Young Husband* proposed to instruct couples with a detail that seemed to leave no aspect of married life open to chance or instinct. Treatises on birth control and numerous moral and medical texts brought questions of marital sexuality into open though carefully guarded and circumspect discussion. Lecturers (both male and female) coursed the country offering various kinds of marital advice. Often they set aside special times for private consultation, offering what we now would call a kind of marriage counseling.

A particular ideal of "wedded bliss" (invoked here in two of the most popular wedding songs, "Oh, Promise Me," and "O Perfect Love") framed the literature on marriage, an ideal composed of all the elements to be found in the codes of genteel courtship and in the cult of domesticity. (See pages 235 and 271.) In one way or another, the literature invoked the ideal of "refined," "elevated," and "disinterested" love and portrayed the ideal home as a peaceful, harmonious refuge from the hostile and unpredictable world of temptation, power, and money. But at the same time the discussion of marital relations was often deeply troubled. A counterpoint to the invocation of love, harmony, and refuge was a scarcely muted sense of turmoil, conflict, and confusion. (Note the lithographic portrayal of the "Seven Stages of Matrimony.")

One major source of confusion was sexuality, attested to here by Sylvester Graham's prescription for the proper "sexual economy" in marriage, by Robert Dale Owen's argument for birth control, and by one husband's struggle with "the most dangerous of all our passions." For a sex reformer like Graham, who developed a vegetarian whole-grain diet as a device for keeping "stimulants" from "exciting" uncontrollable appetites, sexual-

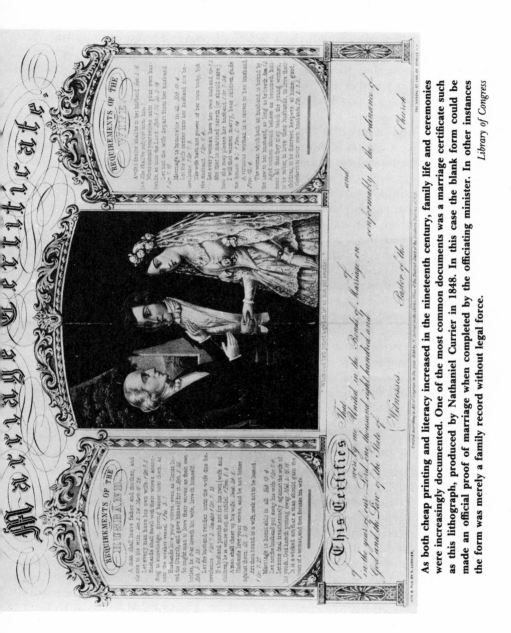

As both cheap printing and literacy increased in the nineteenth century, family life and ceremonies were increasingly documented. One of the most common documents was a marriage certificate such as this lithograph, produced by Nathaniel Currier in 1848. In this case the blank form could be made an official proof of marriage when completed by the officiating minister. In other instances the form was merely a family record without legal force.

Library of Congress

ity provided the nightmare image of the inner forces that plagued a population of solitary "individuals" outside traditional restraints. Though Graham
was a figure at the fringes of society, his notion of a carefully controlled
and limited "sexual economy" was picked up and endorsed by more widely
read marriage advisers like William Alcott. What was it that lay behind
this fear of sexuality, the sense of its essential destructiveness, even within
marriage? To what extent might it have been a corollary to the cult of
pure womanhood? To what extent might it have served as a metaphor
for broader concerns about purity and the need, in such a tumultuous
world, for new forms of self-discipline and control? Many who might not
have shared a Graham-like terror of sexual pleasure were concerned about
other consequences of marital sexuality. Robert Dale Owen (1801–77),
marriage reformer and son of the Scottish industrialist who founded the
utopian community of New Harmony in Indiana in 1824, was one of the
first Americans openly to proclaim the morality of forms of birth control
other than abstinence. Critics argued that artificial means of limiting conception opened the way to immorality and promiscuity. To what extent
did Owen's view of sexuality share or depart from the assumptions of
his critics? What, next, do the letters from a Confederate general away
from home, and the attitudes toward childbearing expressed by Willis and
Harriet Williams, suggest about the anxieties and strains that might have
led people to try to limit conception? How do these arguments and conditions compare with those of the twentieth century, the century that completed the birth-control revolution? (See pages 469–86.)

The uneasiness to be found in much of the writings about marriage in
the middle decades of the nineteenth century goes well beyond fears of
pregnancy and the nightmares of moralists about the evils of unbridled
sensuality. Even within many of the writings—especially those by women—
extolling true womanhood and idealizing the wife's role within the "sacred
sphere," there was often an undercurrent of discontent. (See Elizabeth
Cady Stanton's *Woman's Bible* [page 210] and the Fourierist argument [page
339] for more explicit challenges to the cult of domesticity.) In spite of
all the "happy endings" in the novels of writers like Catharine Sedgwick,
Eliza Southwick, and Caroline Hentz, there were countless portraits of
women as the victims of their husbands' moral and economic failures or
of their aggressive "lust" and "appetites." The irony that Charlotte Perkins
Gilman's "Wedded Bliss" was written during a marriage that soon dissolved
suggests that some women may have found the pedestal so carefully constructed for them over the century excessively anchoring. (See her later
critique of woman's lot in the home, page 459). Moreover, we need to
ask why the portraits of women who served as moral and spiritual ballast
to a predatory, grasping society contained a sense of grievance and pain
for their selfless sacrifice and suffering. How are we to interpret the depiction of "Woman's Everyday Life," and the injunction in the *Ladies' Repository*
that the wife, under all circumstances, must maintain her "cheerfulness"?
What do Harriet Williams's bouts of depression and self-doubt as she strug-

gled to be a "good wife" and Charlotte Howard Gilman's awakening to what marriage really entailed suggest of strains that the life of the aspiring classes imposed on their marital relations? How might the high ideal of marriage and home as a refuge have been itself a source for some of the confusion and conflict revealed in the documents in this section?

DUTIES OF YOUNG WIVES

The Young Wife

TABLE OF CONTENTS

Chapter I. General Remarks.
Objects of marriage. Duties of a wife. Her importance as an educator. Why.

Chapter II. Submission.
A common error abroad. Real object of woman. In what respects she is to submit to her husband. Bible doctrine on this subject. Physical inferiority. Concession must be made. Leaving home. Anecdote of a married couple. Caution to the young wife.

Chapter III. Kindness.
Effects of kindness on brute animals—on savages—on children. Case of a father. Effects of kindness on servants and slaves—on a husband. Opinion of Solomon. A new era. Its results to woman. Counsel. Beautiful extracts.

Chapter IV. Cheerfulness.
Influence of cheerfulness. Opinion of the Journal of Health. Dr. Salgues' opinion. Interesting anecdote. Evils of a want of cheerfulness. Story of Alexis and Emilia. Reflections.

Chapter V. Confidence.
Duty of confidence. Married women not always wives. Confiding in gossips. Fault in education. A bad husband not to be given up. Experiment in trusting. We should have but few secrets.

Chapter VI. Sympathy.
Scripture doctrine. Miss Edgeworth's opinion—Dr. Rush's. Effects of sympathy. Disposition to vex each other. A caution. Sympathy the first step to improvement.

Chapter VII. Friendship.
Few real friends. Parents not always true friends to children. Anecdote. Stormy period of life. Necessity of a friend. Arrangement of Providence. Woman sent as the friend of man. Wives the truest friends. Four qualifications for this office. Religion considered. Enemies sometimes friends.

William A. Alcott, *The Young Wife, or, The Duties of the Wife in the Marriage Relation* (Boston, 1838), pp. 6–13.

Chapter VIII. Love.

Is it necessary for love to decline after marriage? Internal love increases. Means of increasing it. Doing good to others makes us love them. Anecdotes; the little girl—the deist. Love, a matter within our own control. General rule. Cautions.

Chapter IX. Delicacy and Modesty.

Many forms of immodesty. A quotation. Modesty in matrimony. Unchaste language. Example to the husband. Specimens of bad examples.

Chapter X. Love of Home.

Paul's opinion. Effects of "gadding." Anecdote. Dislike of home. Error in female education. Importance of loving home. A picture drawn by Solomon. Two pictures by Abbott. Effects of loving home on the family. Hints to the reader. The Family Monitor.

Chapter XI. Self-Respect.

A principle. Self-respect should be early cultivated. An anecdote.

Chapter XII. Purity of Character.

Explanation of the term. Impurity of character very common. Case of Lucius and Emilia. Seduction. The consequences. Several hints.

Chapter XIII. Simplicity.

Simplicity a virtue. Very rare. Simplicity of language. Story of Mrs. L. Simplicity of conduct.

Chapter XIV. Neatness.

Great importance of neatness. Want of it. Effects on the husband. Neatness in small matters. Structure of the skin. Necessity of bathing. Effect of neatness on morals. Effect of example. Difficulties considered. How to train a husband to slovenliness. Want of neatness in little things.

Chapter XV. Order and Method.

Order, heaven's first law. Importance to the housekeeper. Book-learning. Prejudices against it. Story of Fidelia. Consequences of disorder.

Chapter XVI. Punctuality.

Punctuality lengthens life—is indispensable. Its influence on others. Various forms of punctuality. Anecdote. Reflections. Case of the farmer. The wife's excuses. Real state of the case. Appeal to those whom it concerns.

Chapter XVII. Early Rising.

The young wife should rise early. Means of forming the habit. Retire early—with a quiet stomach—a quiet mind. Resolve strongly. Early training. Mr. and Mrs. Clifford. Samuel Sidney. Reflections.

Chapter XVIII. Industry.

An ancedote. Motives to industry. Bible examples of this virtue.

Chapter XIX. Domestic Economy.

Economy a word of broad meaning. Much of this chapter anticipated. Servants—their general employment to be regretted. Spirit of the times—illustrated by an anecdote.

American nobles. Servants cannot always be dispensed with. Seven reasons for avoiding them, if possible. 1. They are unnecessary. 2. Costly. 3. Break in upon the order of families. 4. Create distinctions in society. 5. Are bad teachers. 6. Practice anti-republican. 7. It is unchristian. Waste of time in cookery. What useful cookery is. Other wasteful practices. Morning calls. General remarks. An anecdote.

Chapter XX. Domestic Reform.
Present state of things. Female ignorant of domestic concerns. A great mistake in education. Nature of the mistake. Cause of the pecuniary distress of our country. Examples of ministers. Change or reform necessary. How it is to be effected. By whom begun. The young wife to begin it. She should begin immediately. One serious difficulty. How to overcome it. Gradual reformation. Rapid progress, ultimately. Book learning. How far books are useful. "The Frugal Housewife." "Bread and Bread-making."

Chapter XXI. Sobriety.
Definition of the term. Something more than temperance. Tea drinking. Effects of tea and coffee. Physiology of their effects. Nervous excitement—compared with intoxication. Proofs of the author's views. Sobriety at feasts. Sobriety in company. Other forms of sobriety.

Chapter XXII. Discretion.
Paul's estimate of the importance of discretion. Opinions of Gisborne. Various forms of indiscretion. Danger of extremes. What true purity is. A word of caution to the indiscreet.

Chapter XXIII. Scolding.
Many kinds of scolds. Internal scolding. Intermittent scolds. Periodical scolding. Other forms of scolding. Hints over the husband's shoulder.

Chapter XXIV. Forbearance.
Perfection not to be expected. Maxim of a philosopher. Spirit of forbearance a pearl of great price. Cases where forbearance is required. Triumphing, "I told you so." Comparisons. Joking. Saying of Salzman.

Chapter XXV. Contentment.
Value of contentment. Why it is especially valuable to the young wife. Duty to her own family and others. Duty to God.

Chapter XXVI. Habits and Manners.
Little things. Setting out in life. Important to set out right. Difficulty with some husbands. How to manage. Eugene and Juliet. General principles.

Chapter XXVII. Dress.
Opinion of Paul. Real objects of dress. Modesty. Dress should regulate our temperature. Frequent change—why useful. General rule. A painful sight. Nature of profuse perspiration, or sweating. Material of dress. Objections to cotton. Fashion of dress. Compression

of the lungs—its evils. Sympathies. Moderate indulgence. Hiding defects by dress. Dress of the husband.

Chapter XXVIII. Health.
Purity of the air in our apartments. Purity of clothing—furniture—cellars—drains—wells, &c. Personal cleanliness. Its expense not to be considered. Various modes of exercise. Household labor. Exercise in the open air. Walking. Riding. Health, in our own keeping. The husband's health. General remarks.

Chapter XXIX. Attending the Sick.
Attending the sick should be a part of female education. Objections to this view considered. Reasons why females should be thus trained. Their native qualifications for this office. Their labor cheaper. They have stronger sympathies. Application of the principle to the case of the young wife.

Chapter XXX. Love of Infancy and Childhood.
What the love of childhood is. Frequent want of it. Dr. Gregory's opinion—Mr. Addison's. Great gulf fixed between children and adults. Love of childhood favorable to mental improvement—to the happiness of the wife—to the happiness of her husband—to religious improvement. Example of the Saviour. How to elicit this love, when it is wanting. Remarks on faith. What faith can enable us to accomplish.

Chapter XXXI. Giving Advice.
Advice of females in regard to business. Why it is often undervalued. Objections answered. How far advice is applicable. Advice in manners and morals. Advice in religion.

Chapter XXXII. Self-Government.
Difficulties of self-government. Meaning of the term. Error in education. What is to be done? Motive to be present. Directions how to proceed. Cooperation of the husband. The results happy.

Chapter XXXIII. Intellectual Improvement.
Anecdote of Mrs. H. Course of study after marriage. Much of it excellent. Cooperation of the husband and wife. Nature of education. Difficulties of studying in married life. They may be overcome. Importance of system. Evils of a want of it. Anecdote. Chemistry. Its importance illustrated. Terrible consequences of ignorance in housewifery. Much poisoning in the community. Study of other sciences. Anatomy and physiology. A few books recommended. Collateral topics of study. Knowledge necessary to benevolent effort. Study of the subject of education. Errors. Theory and experience.

Chapter XXXIV. Social Improvement.
Anecdote of Alcibiades. Intention of the Creator. Marriage of course a social state. Morning calls. Evening visits. Excitements. Balls and theatres. Visiting in the afternoon. Social advantages of large families. Visiting by large companies. Topics of conversation. Scandal. Opposition of human nature to the gospel. Reading at social meetings. An important caution.

Chapter XXXV. Moral and Religious Improvement.
Doing good. Many forms of doing good. Philosophy of doing good. Associated effort. How to select societies. Individual charitable effort. The poor. The ignorant. The

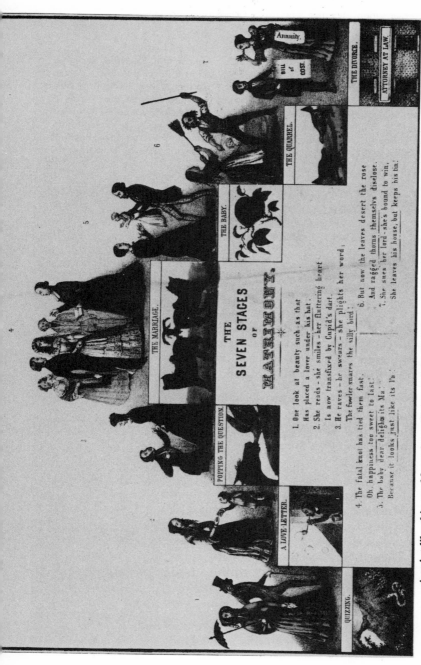

A print like this would not have illustrated the literature of domesticity in the nineteenth century; It addresses men, particularly those who, for one reason or other, resisted the pressures to "take the plunge." The print belongs to a large body of popular pictures between the pornographic-salacious and the respectable. It might have been found in better saloons and barbershops or in racier clubs and restaurants, the dens of resistance to the religion of domesticity.

American Antiquarian Society

vicious. The sick. Caution in regard to visiting the sick. Prayer as a means of improvement. Self-examination. Reading. The Bible. Other useful books.

Chapter XXXVI. Moral Influence on the Husband.

Mode of female influence on the husband. Mr. Flint's encomium. Examples of female influence. Wife of Jonathan Edwards—of Sir James Mackintosh. True position of woman in society. Serious error of some modern writers. A caution. Making haste to be rich. A species of mania. Its extent and evils. How the young wife is concerned with it. What she can do to remove it. Agur's prayer—seldom used in modern times. Particular modes of female influence. Office seeking. How to dissuade from it. Exposures to intemperance. Female consistency. Female piety. Its effects on the husband—compared with amiableness and beauty. Apparent objection to the writer's views. Woman's prerogative.

MARRIAGE SONGS AND POEMS

O Perfect Love

O perfect Love, all human thought transcending,
Lowly we kneel in prayer before thy throne,
That theirs may be the love which knows no ending,
Whom thou for evermore dost join in one.

O perfect Life, be thou their full assurance
Of tender charity and steadfast faith,
Of patient hope, and quiet, brave endurance,
With childlike trust that fears nor pain nor death.

Grant them the joy which brightens earthly sorrow;
Grant them the peace which calms all earthly strife,
And to life's day the glorious unknown morrow
That dawns upon eternal love and life.

Oh, Promise Me

Oh, promise me that some day you and I
Will take our love together to some sky
Where we can be alone, and faith renew,
And find the hollows where those flowers grew,
Those first sweet violets of early spring,
Which come in whispers, thrill us both, and sing
Of love unspeakable that is to be;
Oh, promise me! oh, promise me!

Oh, promise me that you will take my hand,
The most unworthy in this lonely land,

"O Perfect Love," music by Joseph Barnby, lyrics by Dorothy Frances Gurney, 1883.
"Oh, Promise Me," music by Reginald DeKoven, lyrics by Clement Scott, 1889.

And let me sit beside you, in your eyes,
Seeing the vision of our paradise,
Hearing God's message while the organ rolls
Its mighty music to our very souls;
No love less perfect than a life with thee;
Oh, promise me! oh, promise me!

Wedded Bliss

"O COME and be my mate!" said the Eagle to the Hen;
"I love to soar, but then
I want my mate to rest
Forever in the nest!"
Said the Hen, "I cannot fly,
I have no wish to try,
But I joy to see my mate careering through the sky!"
They wed, and cried, "Ah, this is Love, my own!"
And the Hen sat, the Eagle soared, alone.

"O come and be my mate!" said the Lion to the Sheep;
"My love for you is deep!
I slay, a Lion should,
But you are mild and good!"
Said the Sheep, "I do no ill—
Could not, had I the will—
But I joy to see my mate pursue, devour, and kill."
They wed, and cried, "Ah, this is Love, my own!"
And the Sheep browsed, the Lion prowled, alone.

"O come and be my mate!" said the Salmon to the Clam;
"You are not wise, but I am.
I know sea and stream as well;
You know nothing but your shell."
Said the Clam, "I'm slow of motion,
But my love is all devotion,
And I joy to have my mate traverse lake and stream and ocean!"
They wed, and cried, "Ah, this is Love, my own!"
And the Clam sucked, the Salmon swam, alone.

ON CHASTITY

Whatever . . . may be thought of marriage as a divine institution, authorized and enjoined by the sacred Scriptures, be assured, my young friends,
that marriage—or a permanent and exclusive connection of one man with

Charlotte Perkins Gilman, *In the World* (New York, reprinted, 1974), pp. 157–58.
Sylvester Graham, *A Lecture to Young Men on Chastity* (Boston, 1841), pp. 74–83, 181–89.

one woman—is an institution founded in the constitutional nature of things, and inseparably connected with the highest welfare of man, as an individual and as a race! And so intimately associated are the animal and moral sensibilities and enjoyments of man, that, besides the physical and social evils which result from illicit commerce between the sexes, the chaste and delicate susceptibilities of the moral affections are exceedingly depraved, and the transgressor renders himself incapable of those pure and exalted enjoyments which are found in connubial life, where perfect chastity has been preserved. . . .

Let it ever be remembered, however, that no conformity to civil institutions—no ostensible observance of civil law, can secure a man from the evils which result from the violation of the constitutional laws of his nature. The mere fact that a man is married to one woman, and is perfectly faithful to her, will by no means prevent the evils which flow from venereal excess, if his commerce with her transgresses the bounds of that connubial chastity which is founded on the real wants of the system. Beyond all question, an immeasurable amount of evil results to the human family from sexual excess within the precincts of wedlock. Languor, lassitude, muscular relaxation, general debility and heaviness, depression of spirits, loss of appetite, indigestion, faintness and sinking at the pit of the stomach, increased susceptibilities of the skin and lungs to all the atmospheric changes, feebleness of circulation, chilliness, headache, melancholy, hypochondria, hysterics, feebleness of all the senses, impaired vision, loss of sight, weakness of the lungs, nervous cough, pulmonary consumption, disorders of the liver and kidneys, urinary difficulties, disorders of the genital organs, spinal diseases, weakness of the brain, loss of memory, epilepsy, insanity, apoplexy;—abortions, premature births, and extreme feebleness, morbid predispositions, and early death of offspring,—are among the too common evils which are caused by sexual excesses between husband and wife.—(See Note C.)

It is, therefore, impossible to lay down a precise rule, which will be equally adapted to all men, in regard to the frequency of their connubial commerce. But as a general rule, it may be said to the healthy and robust, it were better for you not to exceed, in the frequency of your indulgences, the number of months in the year; and you cannot habitually exceed the number of weeks in the year, without in some degree impairing your constitutional powers, shortening your lives, and increasing your liability to disease and suffering; if indeed you do not thereby actually induce disease of the worst and most painful kind; and at the same time transmit to your offspring an impaired constitution, with strong and unhappy predispositions.

Let no one demur at this. Remember, my young friends, the end of your organization! Recollect that the *final cause* of your organs of reproduction—the propagation of your species—requires but seldom the exercise of their function!—and remember that the higher capabilities of man qualify him for more exalted and exalting pleasures than lie within the precincts of sensual enjoyment!—and remember, also, that by all we go beyond the real wants of nature, in the indulgence of our appetites, we debase our intellectual and moral powers, increase the carnal influences over our mental and moral faculties, and circumscribe our field of rational acquisition and ennobling pleasures.

Who, then, would yield to sensuality, and forego the higher dignity of his nature, and be contented to spend his life and all his energies in the low satisfactions of a brute! when earth and heaven are full of motives for noble and exalting enterprise?—and when time and eternity are the fields which lie before him, for his achievements of virtue, and happiness, and immortality, and unperishing glory?

Note C

The evils arising from excesses between man and wife, are very far greater than is apprehended by even those who suffer them. It is no uncommon thing for a young couple to enter into wedlock in good health, and in due time to be blessed with one and perhaps two or three healthy and vigorous children; and afterwards they will have, in succession, two, three, four or five feeble and puny offspring, which will either be still-born, or survive their birth but a few months, or at longest, but two or three years; and very probably during this time there will be several early abortions; and all the while the unfortunate wife will be afflicted with great debility and extensive functional derangement, and almost constantly suffer those numerous and distressing pains and ailments which result from sexual excesses. Very frequently, also, the husband becomes severely afflicted with distressing consequences. Besides those named in the text, debility, inflammation, swelling and excruciating pain of the spermatic cords, and also of the testicles, resulting, perhaps, in the necessity for castration, and sometimes in death, are often the fruits of connubial intemperance. . . .

Physiological science teaches us that . . . instead of encouraging those who have large organs of amativeness, to indulge more frequently in venereal passion, we ought rather, if possible, to ascertain and rigorously pursue those plans of physical, mental and moral education, by which the organization, the propensities and the habits of man, shall be brought into strict accordance with the constitutional purposes of his sexual faculties. For it is entirely certain that no degree of development and energy of the organ of amativeness will prevent the pernicious effects of too frequent sexual indulgence.

The following case is by no means a solitary one. . . . Mr. S., a respectable mechanic, came to me for advice concerning his health. . . . "I married," said he, "seven years ago, at the age of twenty-six. At the time of my marriage, as before, I was very vigorous and athletic. My habits were active, and my employment in the open air. My sexual propensity and power were exceedingly great, and my indulgence, as I now learn, was excessively intemperate. During the first four years of my connubial life, my health remained tolerably good, but was gradually impaired. At the age of thirty-one, I began to be affected with pain in the spermatic cords, extending to the thighs and also over the loins; pains in the neck of the bladder and in the kidneys, attended with excessive discharges of urine; and severe contractions alternating with great relaxation of the spermatic cords. I soon became excessively nervous, and suffered indescribably. I put myself under medical prescription, but without benefit. My symptoms continually became worse and worse; and I was in a short time so emaciated and so feeble, that I was obliged to keep my bed. I then put myself upon a diet of coarse wheaten crackers and water, and in the course of six weeks was able to leave home and to journey. I found that animal food aggravated all my symptoms, and therefore I continued, during my absence from home, to live strictly on vegetable food, and in six months I gained sixty-four pounds in weight.

"My two first children are living and healthy, and appear to possess a good constitution. Since these, we have had five puny children, all of which are dead. Of these five, four were twins. One pair of the twins were still-born, and the other pair died soon after birth. My wife for the last four or five years has been continually feeble and sickly, and suffered a great deal."

ON BIRTH CONTROL

Among the various instincts which contribute to man's preservation and well-being, the instinct of reproduction holds a distinguished rank. It peoples the earth; it perpetuates the species. Controlled by reason and chastened by good feeling, it gives to social intercourse much of its charm and zest. Directed by selfishness or governed by force, it is prolific of misery and degradation. Whether wisely or unwisely directed, its influence is that of a master principle, that colours, brightly or darkly, much of the destiny of man.

This instinct, then, may be regarded in a two-fold light: *first,* as giving the power of reproduction; *second,* as affording pleasure.

And here, before I proceed, let me recall to the reader's mind, that it is the province of rational beings to bear UTILITY strictly in view. Reason recognizes the romantic and unearthly reveries of Stoicism, as little as she does the doctrines of health-destroying and mind-debasing debauchery. She reprobates equally a contemning and an abusing of pleasure. She bids us avoid asceticism on the one hand, and excess on the other. In all our inquiries, then, let reason guide us, and let UTILITY be our polar star. . . .

Upon this distinction of the instinct in its two-fold character, rests the present discussion. It sometimes happens—nay, it happens every day and

Robert Dale Owen, *Moral Physiology, or, A Brief and Plain Treatise on the Population Question* (London, 1859), pp. 9–21, 29, 36–39.

hour—that mankind obey its dictates, not from any calculation of consequences, but simply from animal impulse. Thus many children that are brought into the world owe their existence, not to deliberate conviction in their parents that their birth was really desirable, but simply to an unreasoning instinct, which men in the mass have not learned either to resist or control.

It is a serious question—and surely an exceedingly proper and important one—whether man can obtain, and whether he is benefited by obtaining, control over this instinct. IS IT DESIRABLE, THAT IT SHOULD NEVER BE GRATIFIED WITHOUT AN INCREASE TO POPULATION? OR, IS IT DESIRABLE, THAT, IN GRATIFYING IT, MAN SHALL BE ABLE TO SAY WHETHER OFFSPRING SHALL BE THE RESULT OR NOT!

To answer these questions satisfactorily, it would be necessary to substantiate, that such control may be obtained without injury to the physical health, or violence to the moral feelings; and also, that it should be obtained without any real sacrifice of enjoyment; or, if that cannot be, with as little as possible. . . .

It is no question—never can be a question—whether there shall be a restraint to population or not. There MUST be; unless indeed we find the means of visiting other planets, so as to people them. In the nature of things, there must be a check, of some kind, at some time. The only question is, what that check shall be—whether, as heretofore, the check of war, want, profligacy, misery; or a "moral restraint," suggested by experience, and sanctioned by reason. . . .

What would be the probable effect, in social life, if mankind obtained and exercised a control over the instinct of reproduction?

My settled conviction is—and I am prepared to defend it—that the effect would be salutary, moral, civilizing; that it would prevent many crimes, and more unhappiness; that it would lessen intemperance and profligacy; that it would polish the manners and improve the moral feelings; that it would relieve the burden of the poor, and the cares of the rich; that it would most essentially benefit the rising generation, by enabling parents generally more carefully to educate, and more comfortably to provide for, their offspring. I proceed to substantiate these positions.

And first, let us look solely to the situation of married persons. Is it not notorious, that the families of the married often increase beyond what a regard for the young beings coming into the world, or the happiness of those who give them birth, would dictate? In how many instances does the hard-working father, and more especially the mother of a poor family, remain slaves throughout their lives, tugging at the oar of incessant labour, toiling to live, and living only to die; when, if their offspring had been limited to two or three only, they might have enjoyed comfort and comparative affluence! How often is the health of the mother—giving birth, every year, perchance, to an infant—happy, if it be not twins!—and compelled to toil on, even at those times when nature imperiously calls for some relief from daily drudgery—how often is the mother's comfort, health, nay, her life, thus sacrificed! Or when care and toil have weighed down the spirit, and at last broken the health of the father, how often is the widow left, unable with the most virtuous intentions to save her fatherless offspring from becoming degraded objects of charity, or profligate votaries of vice! . . .

It may be, that some sticklers for orthodox morality will still demur to the positions I defend. They will perhaps tell me, as the committee of a certain society in this city lately did, that the power of preventing conceptions "holds out inducements and facilities for the prostitution of their daughters, their sisters and their wives."

Truly, but they pay their wives, their sisters, and their daughters, a poor compliment! Is, then, this vaunted chastity a mere thing of circumstance and occasion? Is there but the difference of opportunity between it and prostitution? Would their wives, their sisters, and their daughters, if once absolved from the fear of offspring, become prostitutes—sell their embraces for gold, and descend to a level with the most degraded? In truth, they slander their own kindred; they libel their own wives, sisters, and daughters. If they spoke truth—if fear were indeed the only safeguard of their relatives' chastity, little value should I place on a virtue like that, and small would I esteem his offence who should attempt to seduce it. . . .

Among the modes of preventing conception which may have prevailed in various countries, that which has been adopted, and is now practised by the cultivated classes on the continent of Europe, by the French, the Italians, and, I believe, by the Germans and Spaniards, consists of complete withdrawal, on the part of the man, immediately previous to emission. *This is, in all cases, effectual.* It may be objected, that the practice requires a mental effort and a partial sacrifice. I reply, that, in France, where men consider this (as it ought ever to be considered, when the interests of the other sex require it,) a *point of honour, all* young men learn to make the necessary effort; and custom renders it easy, and a matter of course. As for the sacrifice, shall a trifling (and it is but a very trifling) diminution of physical enjoyment be suffered to outweigh the most important considerations connected with the permanent welfare of those who are the nearest and dearest to us; Shall it be suffered to outweigh the risk of incurring heavy and sacred responsibilities, ere we are prepared to fulfill them? Shall it be suffered to outweigh a regard for the comfort, the well-being—in some cases, the *life* of those whom we profess to love?—The most selfish will hesitate deliberately to reply in the affirmative to such questions as these. A cultivated young Frenchman, instructed as he is, even from his infancy, carefully to consult, on all occasions, the wishes and punctiliously to care for the comfort and welfare, of the gentler sex, would learn almost with incredulity, that, in other countries, there are men to be found, pretending to cultivation, who were less scrupulously honourable on this point than himself. You could not offer him a greater insult than to presuppose the possibility of his forgetting himself so far, as thus to put his own momentary gratification, for an instant, in competition with the wish or the well-being of any one to whom he professed regard or affection. . . .

I knew personally and intimately for many years a young man of strict honour, in whose sincerity I ever placed confidence, and who confided to me the particulars of his situation. He was just entering on life, with slender means, and his circumstances forbade him to have a large family of children. He, therefore, having consulted with his young wife, practised this restraint, I believe for about eighteen months, and with perfect success. At the expiration of that period, their situation being more favourable, they resolved to become parents; and in a fortnight after, the wife found herself pregnant. My friend told me, that though he felt the partial privation a little at first, a few weeks' habit perfectly reconciled him to it; and that nothing but a deliberate conviction that he might prudently now become a parent, and a strong desire on his wife's part to have a child, induced him to alter his first practice. . . .

I add another instance. A short time since, a respectable and very intelligent father of a family, about thirty-five years of age, who resides west of the mountains, called at our office. Conversation turned on the present subject, and I expressed to him my conviction, that this check was effectual. He told me he could speak from personal experience. He had married young, and soon had three children. These he could support in comfort, without running into debt or difficulty; but, the price of produce sinking in his neighbourhood, there did not appear a fair prospect of supporting a large family. In consequence, he and his wife determined to limit their offspring to three. They have accordingly employed the above check for seven or eight years; have had no more children; and have been rewarded for their prudence by finding their situation and prospects improving every year. He confirmed an opinion I have already expressed, by stating, that custom completely reconciled him to any slight privation he might at first have felt. . . .

I may add, that *partial* withdrawal is not an infallible preventive of conception.

Other modes of prevention have been employed,* but this is at once the most simple and the most efficacious; the only one, or nearly so, employed by the cultivated among European nations; and the only one I here venture to recommend. From all I have heard, as well from physicians as from private individuals, it is, as regards health, at the least perfectly innocent; it has been even said to produce upon the human system an effect similar to that of temperance in diet; but whether there be truth in

---

* One of these modes, the sponge, has been zealously recommended. I do not allude to it in the text, because I believe it to be of doubtful efficacy; and, more certainly, physically disagreeable in its effects; and because I feel convinced, that the selfish of either sex will adopt *no* expedient, while the well-disposed will adopt the best in preference.

I also pass over all allusion to the BAUDRUCHE, which is every way inconvenient, and is chiefly used to guard against syphilis. I do not write to facilitate, but, on the contrary, effectually to prevent, the degrading intercourse of which it is intended to obviate the penalty.

this hypothesis I know not. As regards any moral impropriety in its use, enough, methinks, has already been said to convince all except those who *will* not be convinced, that to employ it in all cases where prudence or the well-being of our companions requires it, is an act of practical virtue.

It may be said, and said truly, that this check places the power chiefly in the hands of the man, and not where it ought to be, in those of the woman. She, who is the sufferer, is not secured against the culpable carelessness, or perhaps the deliberate selfishness, of him who goes free and unblamed whatever may happen. To this the reply is, that the best and only effectual defence for women is to refuse connection with any man *void of honour*. An (almost omnipotent) public opinion would thus be speedily formed; one of immense moral utility, by means of which the man's social reputation would be placed, as it should be, in the keeping of women, whose moral tact and nice discrimination in such matters is far superior to ours. How mighty and beneficent the power which such an influence might exert, and how essentially and rapidly it might conduce to the gradual, but thorough extirpation of those selfish vices, legal and illegal, which now disgrace and brutify our species, it is difficult even to imagine.

THE GENERAL TO HIS LADY

Camp Jones, Va., Sept. 11th, 1861

My dear Wife

. . . Honey, altho' writing that you were in better health and spirits than for some time, your letter left me more sad and depressed than any you have written for a long time. The thought that you had been suffering as you must have been, made me feel very sad indeed. Oh! Darling, and I have to reproach myself for it. Honey, the same that causes you so much trouble is my stumbling block in this world. When I think I am getting better it rises up and stares me in the face to my great mortification, for I do feel humbled and mortified to think that the most dangerous of all our passions and the most sinful when indulged, should be the one that I cannot conquer. But I will toil on in the good road and see if it cannot be overcome in thought as well as act. It is the greatest curse it seems to me that could have been laid on man.

Camp Fisher, Va., Feb. 21st, 1862

My dear Wife

I found Dorsey's cradle in my room and I think I shall let it stay. It will only remind me still more forcibly of what happiness I did enjoy and how cheerless I am. I wish I had but one room. Oh! darling, did we not spend seven happy weeks together. They were as so many days, but I shall not forget them soon. . . .

William W. Hassler, ed., *The General to His Lady: The Civil War Letters of William Dorsey Pender to Fanny Pender* (Chapel Hill, 1966), pp. 57–58, 114, 201–2. Copyright 1965 The University of North Carolina Press. Reprinted by permission.

However much darling I miss you—and I can assure you it is more than you will believe—I do not regret taking you away from here. I am more convinced than ever that it is no place for ladies. I am perfectly astonished at Capt. Scales allowing his wife to remain here particularly in her condition. Please let me know of your hopes, as to your condition on the day you left Richmond turned out to be as you thought, or if it was a false alarm. I sincerely hope it was bona fide, for we all have enough to contend with in these times even when we are free from continuous nausea and have to look forward to nine months of pain and general ill feeling. . . .

Camp Gregg, Va., March 10th, 1863

My dear little Wife

I received your letter of the 6th today, and I can assure you its contents gave me anything but pleasure. Indeed I did sincerely hope that you had escaped this time, but darling it must be the positive and direct will of God that it should be so, for would you not have supposed that it were next thing to an impossibility? I know it would look like mockery for me to say try to bear it as cheerful as possible. I who have none of the pains or troubles, but indeed my solicitude for you is next thing to the actual condition itself. The Lord be kind to you and bring you through it with as much comfort as under the circumstances could be expected.

Honey you cannot give me credit for the sorrow I felt today when I read your letter. But let me hope it is not so. If you are not positively certain, would it not be well to use Dr. Powell's prescription, for if you only use three of the pills and take the baths three days, there could be no harm done if you are as you write. It comes in a season of the year when you would like to be able to enjoy yourself, and when I hoped that you would be able to go from home somewhere and have a nice time. God bless you and he only knows what I would do for you if the doing of it would do you any good. I am very anxious to go to see you more by a great deal than ever. Would a few days visit to you do you good? I am almost tempted to ask for a leave, but I do not think it would be granted. . . .

A WIFE'S TRAVAIL

Harriet Williams to Willis R. Williams

Oct. 23, 1862

. . . I received two letters—one on Tuesday and the other Thursday. I was glad to hear the Dr. thinks he can cure you. I had rather hear that than anything else. We are all well, the children look hearty and well. Honey I'm sorry my letter made you think and feel sad for above all things

Willis R. Williams Papers, Southern Historical Collection, Library of the University of North Carolina, Chapel Hill. Reprinted by permission.

I want you cheerful. Honey I have never regretted my marriage, you have always been kind and loving to me and I hope you will continue so, now that I am kept alive. If you treat me cold it will soon bend my poor withering form and consign me to my mother dust. I don't expect to live long, neither do I crave it. The children are small and will soon forget me and then Willis you will be free to go and stay and your troubles will be lighter. Some wives are nothing but trouble and I am one, I am not fit for anything but to have children and that is nothing but trouble and sorrow. Willis, I don't write this to make you sad but I can't help it. It seems as if there is a band or harness about my heart, poor weak creature that I am. . . .

Harriet Williams to Willis R. Williams

Jan. 26, 1867

Being alone today, Sunday, I could not forgo the pleasure of writing to my husband. It affords me comfort and happiness to write and receive letters from you. Honey, I don't think I ever felt so lonely as I have since you left. It seems as if I could never become happy and contented while you are away. Honey, I won't say any more about it for fear you will have the bleus, but you know I am compelled to have them when you are gone. In the week I don't find time to be sad but Sundays there is nothing else for me to do. . . .

I have not seen anything of my *monthlies* yet and I am afraid your goings to Raleigh and comings home again will make me suffer, for I am afraid you left more behind than you and I wished. Honey, you know I hate to even think of such a thing and if it is so, I expect nothing but the bleus all the time, for I have prayed that I might never have another baby. I took a cup of hot ginger tea and it was very strong but I have not seen anything yet. It may be that I have taken so much cold, but I am very much affraid that such is not the case. If it is we must make the best of it we can.

I have not seen or heard anything from Delia. She must be sick or she would have come. The negroes have kept me in wood and lightwood ever since you left and seem willing to do what they can. They commenced hauling dirt yesterday and seem to work and don't stay at the house half as long as the negroes did last year. I think if they keep on we will make more than Brown did. Mrs. Jordan asked me if I was going to send daughter to Miss Sallie Ann. I told her I did not see how I could possibly send daughter and she agreed with me and said I could not do without her. But honey I think I can teach her grammar, geography and writing, but as for arithmetic I don't think I am capable of teaching daughter but Bob and Tom I will do my best. I have a school every morning. Bob has almost forgotten his multiplication table but I intend to make him learn it before he gets clear of it. I think Tom will be a smart boy. He is very studious for a little boy and minds me so well. I sent a quarter to Falkland and bought him a spelling book Tuesday. I will be bothered about the boys but as soon as I get through I will take them to their studies again. Honey, you know I am willing to do all I can, and I know you will do the same. When you come home you can improve daughter in arithmetic. That will not take much of your time. What on earth is the matter with you. I looked for a letter Monday but did not get one and you wrote every mail when you were gone before. It makes me very uneasy about you. For heaven's sake write me if you are sick. I want to hear from you and if you are not I am all anxiety about you. I am always dreaming something and a few nights ago I dreamed you had disease, please write what is the matter.

Willis R. Williams to Harriet Williams

Jan. 31, 1867

Yours of the 26th came to hand today, which made me both sorrowful and joyful at the same time. Glad that all are well and sorry to see you so sad and melancholy. I wrote you yesterday so I hope you get both these letters at once. I was never in better health in my life, my bowels are very good, digestion never better, so your dreams were not correct. I have been having bad dreams but you know I never put the slightest faith in any such thing. I am glad the negroes have gone to work, hope they will do well.

Now, suppose you may be off, but I hardly belive it, tho' I never was hopeful that you not have more children. You come of a breed too prolific to stop at your age and if it's the lord's will why we must submit to it. . . .

EVERY-DAY MARRIAGE LIFE

"QUICKLY. 'Look you, I keep his house, and I wash, wring, bake, scour, dress meat, and drink, make the beds, and do all myself.'
"SIMPLE. ' 'Tis a great charge to come under one body's hand.' "

KIND reader, it is no fancy sketch that I am going to give you. It is drawn from life in all its reality; and in every city, village, county-town, and neighborhood, its truthfulness will be recognized. It is the every-day life of woman—woman in her domestic character—we intend portraying. Yes, woman, it is here, when thou art true to the nature thy Maker hath given thee, thou excellest, and art honored; long-suffering, full of humble and generous affections, sacrificing thyself to the happiness of those thou lovest, and grateful to Heaven that of the two penalties the severest falls upon thee. Thy love is, indeed, the cynosure of life; never wandering from the one point, never faltering, never failing.

A young man arrives at an age when he thinks it time for him to get married, and settle down. He has a respectable education, and wants a woman who is his equal. He looks about him, and makes a choice. She is a girl well educated, reared by careful parents, and is, in the truest

"Every-day Life of Woman," *Ladies' Repository*, XI (Oct. 1851), pp. 365–66.

sense, a lady. She is intelligent, loves books, possesses a refined and delicate taste, and is, in all points, well fitted to be the mistress of a cheerful, happy home. She becomes his wife; is industrious, and ambitious to do as much as she can toward a living. May be they are not very well off as to the things of this world, and both are equally ambitious to accumulate a comfortable property; and the husband soon becomes avaricious enough to allow the woman of his love to become his most devoted drudge. Her life is thenceforth one of the most unremitting toil. It is nothing but cook and bake, wash dishes, thrash about among pots and kettles, wash and iron, churn, pick up chips, draw water, and a thousand other things "too tedious to mention."

The result is, the husband soon owns the house he lives in, and something besides; takes his ease when he chooses, reads and improves his mind, and becomes important in community. But the cares of his faded, broken-down wife know no relaxation. The family enlarges, and she, poor woman, has enough to do without finding time to increase her stock of knowledge, or to watch the progress of the minds of her children. It is, therefore, no fault of hers that they are growing up with characteristics and habits of a doubtful tendency. There is always the measles, the hooping-cough, worm fever, or summer complaint, or something of that sort, in the family; and Will is constantly breaking his head, and bruising his knees, and cutting his fingers; and Ned and Sue are invariably in need of soap and water. And when the little, noisy, mischievous, yet beloved flock are safely tucked away for the night in trundle-beds and cribs, how many stockings there are out at the heels and toes; how many jackets out at the elbows, and trowsers out at the knees! What a variety of cross-grained holes in frocks, and how many buttons, and hooks, and eyes off—all to sigh over, and be mended!

The only wonder is, that the mother does not sink within this circle of everlasting drudgery, which deprives her of the privilege of relaxation for a day, and the time which she would gladly devote to the maternal education of her children. She is occupied, from morning till night, in one unending round of duties and cares—mistress, mother, and maid of all work. Her mind, though craving knowledge, can not seek it; for she is generally too much fatigued by the exertions of the day to seek it after the noisy little group are out of the way, and she has done darning and patching. Husband comes in now, and reads from some book or newspaper. He wonders why she is so little interested, and, may be, very gently, hints at her deficiencies in this respect. Yes, amid all these cares and this drudgery, he would have her satisfied and happy, sit by his side like Klopstock's Meta, "looking so still in his sweet face."

In the morning, as soon as the birds begin their songs, the little flock are out of bed. Then come the washings and dressings; the busy mother needs twenty hands, since as many wants are poured in upon her distracted ears. It's "Mother, where's my jacket?" "Mother, I can't get the knot out of my shoe-string," or "I've broke my shoe-string;" "Mother, I want a pin;" "Mother, Ned is spattering me with soap-suds;" "Mother, mayn't I wear my pink dress or my new apron?" By this time the baby wakes, and opens his infantile battery of screams. In scolding Ned—the naughty rogue, so full of fun and frolic—and helping the rest, and quieting the baby, the minutes fly. Husband comes in, with,

"Goodness, wife, an't breakfast ready yet? It's ten minutes past eight. I've been waiting for more than an hour."

"You forget that I have all the children to see to, and the baby is very fretful this morning," replies the wife.

Silenced but not convinced, the husband is quite as apt to take the newspaper and sit down, as he is to take the baby from the arms of his oppressed and tender wife, so that she can hurry his breakfast. When it is ready, and they are seated at the table, wife must, as usual, pour out the coffee with the baby in her arms, too much fatigued to enjoy her breakfast. "My dear," says husband, "seems to me the coffee is not quite as clear as usual, the steak is a little too rare or overdone, or the hash is not seasoned quite right." Not that he means to complain; for he knows how desirous she is to please him, ever to say a word intentionally to wound her feelings. But these slight hints to an overtasked woman, amid her gentle but imperious demands, are often irritating to the feelings, and call out many a sharp, caustic reply, of which she repents in five minutes after.

Thus many a woman breaks and sinks beneath the wear and tear of the frame and the affections. She rallies before the world, and "her children rise up and called her blessed," and she is blessed in conscious attempts to discharge her duty; but cares eat away at her heart; the day presses on her with new toils; the night comes, and they are unfulfilled; she lies down in weariness, and rises with uncertainty; her smiles become languid and few, and her husband wonders at the gloominess of his home. When he married, he thought the chosen of his heart his equal in intelligence, but now she is far his inferior. Poor soul! I wonder she ever had courage to even think of a book—she who must care for body and soul, day and night; who must pray for, teach, guide, and rule her own household. . . .

Now, this is certainly wrong; and the foundation of all this wrong is principally in that avaricious spirit which makes the dollar the standard of respectability. The money expended for help in the house looks so large to some men, that, so long as their meals are cooked, their shirts, cravats, and collars are in order, not a button off, their stockings darned, etc., they don't trouble themselves about the circumstances under which these things have been done.

MARRIAGE CONDUCT

Perhaps you remember a young couple, who, a few years ago, found themselves at your house on a happy visit, away east in one of our smallest

Elizabeth True, "Married Life," *Ladies' Repository*, XI (April 1851), pp. 204–5.

states, and who, before they left, took the marriage vow upon themselves, and were by you pronounced husband and wife, in the name of the holy Trinity.

Having reminded you of this circumstance—in this way introducing myself to you as one of that newly wedded pair—perhaps you will give me the liberty to say something of married life to the ladies who read the Repository. What I have to say will be more appropriate to young ladies yet unmarried than to others; for to others my thoughts will have become familiar by their own experience.

The particular feature in the disposition and expression of the wife and the mother of which I wish to speak is *uniform cheerfulness.* When we are living alone in the world—in other words, when we are not necessarily connected with and surrounded by those who watch our countenances as they would thermometers, that would indicate to them the temperature of the air they must breathe—we may sometimes indulge an inclination to look upon the somber pages of this life's book, so that our faces shall, for a little time, contract some of their shades without troubling any one. But when we come to be seated where a husband looks us in the face every time he looks up, and children are turning their reading eyes to us from either side, it is then we can have no time to indulge in melancholy, though, for variety's sake, it might sometimes be sweet to us.

I do not suppose that any of the readers of the Repository can be so uncultivated as to have a tendency to fits of ill-nature; so that it is not in such feelings that I am saying the wife will have no opportunity to indulge. Neither do I speak of mute, weeping fits; for any woman, however young, must see that such behavior would greatly mar, if not utterly destroy, sooner or later, the peculiar happiness of the husband and wife, parents and children, in their organized capacity. I only wish to say, that she who enters the marriage relation, and thus becomes a vital organ in the family constitution, must calculate upon a vigorous cultivation of her own feelings, which shall result in perpetual cheerfulness. She can hardly be allowed the natural expression of her full heart, as her family friends are called away by death, and the home of her childhood made desolate; for she will see that, while she indulges her grief in outward expression, the current of joy which flows through her own house is fast diminishing. One child says, "Mother, what makes you look so sad?" and another says, "I can not eat, if you don't, mother;" while the husband, by his looks, seems to entreat that his wife may have no more sorrow. And, indeed, I do not wonder that the husband and children feel uneasy and unhappy when the wife and mother is in sadness; for I remember that, when I have been a mere boarder in a family, my contentment and happiness there depended more than half upon the cheerfulness of her who, for the time, was "the mother of us all." How can a woman make her family happy—and, in so saying, we ask, How can she be happy herself?—unless at the outset, when she enters the marriage state, she resolves upon living strictly for others? And while she is living for others, they are learning to live for her. There is more than one case in which he or she who will lose life shall save it.

But while she who is wife and mother resolves upon being always cheerful for her family's sake, which must be, perhaps, sometimes in despite of her own first impulses, she is doing the greatest favor to herself. She acquires the habit of catching a view at once of the clearest and brightest touches of the picture of any of the dispensations which she and her family may be called to live under; and though sometimes there may be a good deal of darkness in some of them, so that the living souls with whom she is united do almost sink in sorrow, she can sing and rejoice among them, and before they are aware they will be joining in with the song of an angel. By this means she not only raises up those who live in her heart and in her life when they are cast down, but she is herself saved from the wearing and destroying influence of grief and gloom. And in giving herself this cultivation, little does she know what future solitary hours she is preparing to make comfortable to herself, when her dearest ones shall have been separated from her by that something which intervenes between this world and the world of immortality.

A PLANTER'S BRIDE

I was not selfish, and even urged Arthur to go to hunt and to dinner parties, although hoping that he would resist my urging. He went frequently, and a growing discomfort began to work upon my mind. I had undefined forebodings; I mused about past days; my views of life became slowly disorganized; my physical powers enfeebled; a nervous excitement followed; I nursed a moody discontent, and ceased a while to reason clearly. Woe to me had I yielded to this irritable temperament! I began immediately, on principle, to busy myself about my household. The location of Bellevue was picturesque—the dwelling airy and commodious; I had, therefore, only to exercise taste in external and internal arrangement to make it beautiful throughout. I was careful to consult my husband in those points which interested him, without annoying him with mere trifles. If the reign of romance was really waning, I resolved not to chill his noble confidence, but to make a steadier light rise on his affections. If he was absorbed in reading, I sat quietly waiting the pause when I should be rewarded by the communication of ripe ideas; if I saw that he prized a tree which interfered with my flowers, I sacrificed my preference to a more sacred feeling; if any habit of his annoying me, I spoke of it once or twice calmly, and then bore it quietly if unreformed; I welcomed his friends with cordiality, entered into their family interests, and stopped my yawns, which, to say the truth, was sometimes an almost desperate effort, before they reached eye or ear.

This task of self-government was not easy. To repress a harsh answer, to confess a fault, and to stop (right or wrong) in the midst of self-defence,

Charlotte (Howard) Gilman, *Recollections of a Southern Matron* (New York, 1852), pp. 296–98.

in gentle submission, sometimes requires a struggle like life and death; but these *three* efforts are the golden threads with which domestic happiness is woven; once begin the fabric with this woof, and trials shall not break or sorrow tarnish it.

Men are not often unreasonable; their difficulties lie in not understanding the moral and physical structure of our sex. They often wound through ignorance, and are surprised at having offended. How clear is it, then, that woman loses by petulance and recrimination! Her first study must be self-control, almost to hypocrisy. A good wife must smile amid a thousand perplexities, and clear her voice to tones of cheerfulness when her frame is drooping with disease, or else languish alone. Man, on the contrary, when trials beset him, expects to find her ear and heart a ready receptacle; and, when sickness assails him, her soft hand must nurse and sustain him.

I have not meant to suggest that, in ceasing to be a mere lover, Arthur was not a tender and devoted husband. I have only described the natural progress of a sensible, independent married man, desirous of fulfilling all the relations of society. Nor in these remarks would I chill the romance of some young dreamer, who is reposing her heart on another. Let her dream on. God has given this youthful, luxurious gift of trusting love, as he has given hues to the flower, and sunbeams to the sky. It is a superadded charm to his lavish blessings; but let her be careful that when her husband

> "Wakes from love's romantic dream,
> His eyes may open on a sweet esteem."

Let him know nothing of the struggle which follows the first chill of the affections; let no scenes of tears and apologies be acted to agitate him, until he becomes accustomed to agitation; thus shall the star of domestic peace arise in fixedness and beauty above them, and shine down in gentle light on their lives, as it has on ours.

HOME AND MOTHER

In the nineteenth century cheaper and improved printing, increasing literacy, and better transportation helped spread American inquiry about the family. By 1850 a torrent of books, magazines, stories, reports, poems, pictures, sermons, and manuals had made home and mother the paramount themes in an American cult of domesticity. Part of what Gordon Wood has called "a social and cultural transformation as great as any in American history," the cult changed the mother into the moral and spiritual guardian of the American Republic. Saving souls and creating virtuous citizens had long been a responsibility of the family, but traditionally the father as head of household and surrogate for God the father had been responsible for this missionary work. By 1850 many appeals still urged him to meet his solemn duties. But the same literature also confessed that the father's preoccupation with the world of money and power outside the home had made the mother the principal overseer of the home, the "ark of the nation." The concern that she be a paragon was not confined to the writings of idea-mongering moralists but was echoed in personal letters, diaries, memoirs, autobiographies, parents' letters, and organization reports in newspapers and magazines. The result of precept and practice was to make concerns for "home," "mother," and child-rearing (see below) into staples of American popular culture that have not diminished since.

The first selection here from this immense record is a popular memoir of George Washington's mother. In it the reader found the qualities most desirable in American mothers. It is also one example of how history at the time was combed to create a large gallery of heroines and saints to inspire American mothers in their sacred missions. The piece by Catharine Beecher and Harriet Beecher Stowe (both from the Beecher line of moralist-commentators) further defines the tasks of motherhood and homemaker. Given the call to perfection on the hearth, writers had to work on mothers to convert them, prevent their backsliding, and enlarge their faith and capacity for the holy task. What does this piece also imply men and women are *failing* to do or to understand? Is there any implication that home life, *per se*, has failed women?

The literary assault on mothers, after 1830, to get on with their work used every form of the printed and spoken word and produced generations of songs and poetry, some of the most familiar of which are reprinted here for thematic analysis. How far the cult of home could be carried is

FOUR SEASONS OF LIFE: CHILDHOOD

FOUR SEASONS OF LIFE: YOUTH

In the nineteenth century family ideals of harmony and happiness were derived from the Bible, but increasingly also from the supposedly reassuring lessons of nature. Good family life was depicted as being ruled by nature's own wisdom and pace. Artificial and distorting dress, diet, amusements, and manners were attacked as unnatural. The natural

THE FOUR SEASONS OF LIFE: MIDDLE AGE

FOUR SEASONS OF LIFE: OLD AGE

was not fallen and imperfect but simple and beneficent. Nature had only to be set free by love and simplicity among family members for virtue to appear. For everything there was a season and each season, as shown here, suggested the proper family style and order. *Library of Congress* implicit in the white man Stephen Foster's lyrics ascribing to slaves longings for a world of the home that few of them ever had known.

If any one person presided over the cult of domesticity, it was Sarah Josepha Hale, editor of the magazine *Godey's Lady's Book,* an unofficial organ of the cult. Her verse in praise of the home, like her admired poem here, found its way into numerous newspapers and ladies' and home magazines.

Like verse, pictures and prints with home themes were published in millions of copies and incalculable variety. At mid-century the cheaper technology of reproducing pictures enticed the craft-businessmen Currier and Ives to form a firm that in 75 years produced more than 7,000 lithographs that yielded millions of reproductions in magazines and books, advertisements and calendars across the continent. Included here is one of the favorite Currier and Ives series, four prints on the "seasons of life" which clearly associated life at its best with domestic settings and the family. Analysis of the particular elements in each picture and of implicit transitions from one to another should evoke many of the ideals of home life, especially of what the home affords for each "season." There are also parallels between the series and the four seasons of the year, an old metaphor that the home and mother cults employed, setting forth for each cycle of life the pleasant expectations that harmony with nature would produce.

The cult of home and mother also turned the home into the front line of the attempt to "evangelize" the nation and place the republic on the firm foundation of a population of saved (Protestant) Christians. The basic Christian elements of the proper household included Bible reading, daily family prayers, strict observance of the sabbath as a day of rest and reflection, Sunday school and church attendance at least once every Sunday, and emphasis on the religious aspects of national holidays and feast days (including the rediscovery—or creation—of Thanksgiving Day during the Civil War to recapture or rekindle the piety of the original Pilgrims).

"Saving souls" was not simply the minister's task. Beyond defining the home generally as a spiritual haven both to correct and to resist the erring world outside, evangelical domesticity charged parents to work ceaselessly on themselves and the young to ready them as early as possible for "adoption into the family of Christ." The home was to become, in effect, "a nursery of piety," where parents examined children ceaselessly for the signs of repentance and grace that signaled a spirit ripe for conversion. Gone was the earlier passivity associated with the idea of "waiting God's time" and the belief that conversion was an event of young adulthood. Children were urged from the earliest years to seek salvation, and parents stood ever ready to help them to their "surrender" to Christ. New genres of evangelical literature and organizations like mothers' associations to help them in the task grew astonishingly. From several of the more notable outside auxiliaries there are samples here of the armory for the Christian battle in the home. Organizations like the American Tract Society and the American Sunday-School Union produced tens of millions of free or inexpensive books giving guidance to the reformed Christian life. Home weeklies like the *Youth's Companion* specialized in pieces, ostensibly by parents, usually entitled "Memoir of . . ." or "Memorial of . . ." These were accounts of child prodigies of piety used to show parents "the way" and to stimulate a competitive home capitalism in the manufacture and display of finished souls. Critics of the home evangelist mission, especially of work on small children (and we are often confronted with reports of "triumphs" with infants under two years) complained that conversion wracked children or wrecked them. Sometimes, the parents' pressure forced children to a knowingly false or imperfect conversion just to end their travail or please the parents.

Often the young models of Christian perfection were "too good for this world," and it is worth discussing how and why spiritual proficiency frequently came with such frail little bodies. Also worth investigating is why saving a child's soul seemed so much more urgent than saving an adult's. The high rates of child mortality and the continuing threat to mothers of death in childbirth? The compounding of the pain of losing a child with the knowledge that the death of a child unconverted precluded eventual "reunion" in heaven? The convention of the pious but sickly or ailing child produced such famous figures as "Little Eva" in *Uncle Tom's Cabin* (1851), itself basically a tale of families caught up in slavery. Her deathbed scene was a staple of local and traveling theater groups until the end of the century, long after the urgency of the novel's antislavery had been lost.

The version here of the perfect little Christian, Nathan Dickerman, was created or described from life by G. D. Abbott and incorporated in a guidance book of the 1830s by his brother John S. C. Abbott. Nathan seems to have been so effective a model for families that he recurrently appeared in the Christian home literature for almost a generation after 1830. He was the paragon child every parent should yearn to create before death struck and it would be too late to save the child's soul.

The same American homes and mothers that were called to such lofty, spiritual tasks were, puzzlingly, also expected to create energetic, world-embracing, success-conquering heroes of America's commercial and frontier life. How did the two family ethics coexist? One model of life came from the otherworldly Word of God, and the other (however disguised) was a tribute to the ostensibly fallen and tempting world of man. What price did conflict between World and Word within the Christian home exact from parents and children? Did a double character bred in the home have anything to do with America's exhausting *intensity*, its ferocious, moralistic Indian and Civil wars, the obsessions of its racism, the cheating and gouging of land booms and that gallery of possessed and forlorn American types whom Melville captured at mid-century in his American portraits in *The Confidence Man*? Were the cults of home and mother sentimental and nostalgic "covers" for the very appetites that the cults were supposed to help curb? Or were the cult ideals just as "real" and "sincere" as the worldliness ethic but deeply contradictory to it and making Americans divided and "driven" personalities? Was there not ultimately something peculiarly American—hypocrisy is too simple a description—to reach for the spirit while wrenching the workaday world out of other hands and into one's own?

GEORGE WASHINGTON'S MOTHER

In that genuine and judicious kindness lies the secret of the power always maintained by this venerated mother over the minds of her offspring. If she assumed the right to direct the actions of others, her daily life exhibited such powers of self-control and self-denial as convinced her children, by more irresistible evidence than mere words would convey, of the justice and disinterestedness by which she was habitually actuated.

That she rendered their home, simple, nay even humble, though it might be, endearing to her children, is proved in some degree, by the frequency and pleasure with which, as we gather from much incidental testimony, the happy band that once rejoiced in the comfort and security of her well-ordered abode, in after years revisited the maternal roof. Indeed, we are expressly informed, upon the best authority, that an interdiction of the innocent amusements and relaxations, a taste for which is so natural to the young, formed no part of the system of juvenile training practised with such preëminent success by Mrs. Washington.

She never rendered necessary restraint and discipline needlessly distasteful or repulsive by ascetic sternness or harsh compulsion. The power that sometimes gently coerced the subjects of her guidance was a *moral suasion* far more effective and beneficial than influences such as those can ever exert.

Of all the mental qualities of this celebrated woman, perhaps none was more constantly illustrated in her life than her native *good sense,* the practical effects of which were infinitely more useful and precious to her children than she could possibly have rendered volumes of theoretical precept, however philosophical and profound.

To her possession of this unpretending, but invaluable characteristic, emphatically, her illustrious son was indebted for the education that formed the basis of his greatness.

This it was that taught the great WASHINGTON those habits of application, industry, and regularity, that were of such essential service to him, alike in the camp and in the cabinet, and which so materially contributed to render his character a perfect model, bequeathed to successive ages.

This it was, that, by inculcating and enforcing habitual temperance, exercise, and activity, strengthened and developed the wonderful physical powers that were rivalled only by the indomitable will and stupendous wisdom of her son.

Margaret Conkling, *Memoirs of the Mother and Wife of Washington* (Auburn, N.Y., 1850), pp. 22–26, 71–72.

To his mother Washington owed the high value he attached to *"the only possession of which all men are prodigal, and of which all men should be covetous":* and from her early instructions he imbibed that *love of truth* for which he was remarkable, and which is so pleasingly and forcibly illustrated in some of the favorite anecdotes of our childhood.

Trained to unvarying respect for the truths of revealed religion, in which she was herself a firm believer, and rigidly regardful of the dictates of an enlightened conscience, her gifted son was indebted to Mrs. Washington for his quick moral sense, and the unflinching adhesion to principle that so strongly marked every act of his public and private life.

The noble friend and pupil of Washington, and others among her numerous panegyrists, have likened the mother of the "Hero" to a Spartan matron. With due deference to the high source whence the comparison emanated, it seems scarcely just to her who was its subject. Her life reminds us, rather, of those celebrated women whose names are recorded with grateful affection and respect by St. Paul, in his Epistles—those heroic, self-sacrificing friends and champions of early Christianity, and its devoted advocates, who were "succorers of many," who scorned not to "bestow much labor" upon the temporal necessities of the Apostle and his fellow-martyrs, and who even "laid down their own necks" for them! Mrs. Washington was a CHRISTIAN MATRON, who derived her ideas of parental authority and government from the same BOOK, wherein she sought her own rules of life; and she was as much superior to a Spartan mother, as are the inspired principles of our blessed religion to the heathen teachings which exalted mere physical courage above the highest virtues of humanity!

Her Name and her Fame are the priceless inheritance, not of her native country alone, but of every land that boasts a knowledge of the glorious achievements of the immortal *Champion of Liberty!*

Her name will be revered, and her memory cherished, when those of mighty empires and world-renowned sovereigns shall have sunk forever into the whirlpool of Oblivion: unsullied, unobscured by the supremacy of power and the lapse of ages, they will beam forth resplendent in the sanctified lustre of MORAL GRANDEUR.

At the feet of the proud daughter of the Ptolemies, the conquerors of the world laid down their crowns, yet Clio, faithful to the truth, withholds the meed of honor from the coward soul that could not brave adversity. The history of Christina, the royal Swedish wanderer, scarce serves, at best, to "point a moral," and awakens no more exalted sentiment than one of pitying regret. Maria Theresa, despite her many and exalted excellencies, sacrificed some of woman's first, best duties on the altar of ambition. And who will demand either love or veneration for the memory of England's greatest Queen, renowned as much for her most unfeminine faults, as for her boasted masculine virtues.

Imagination may pall in the contemplation of mere charms of person,— even though unrivalled,—when associated with the moral cowardice of the famous Egyptian Queen; we may regard profound erudition without respect, when allied with the undisciplined instincts and uncontrolled passions of the celebrated daughter of the Great Gustavus; or hear with indifference, tributes to the religious enthusiasm and regal heroism of the Empress-King; or turn with unsympathizing dislike from the haughty, indomitable, relentless Elizabeth; but when shall the daughers of Columbia be weary of imbibing the benign and hallowed influences inseparably associated with the pure and sacred name of MARY WASHINGTON?

The combined qualities of her consistent, elevated, conscience-illuminated character, constitute a *perfect whole,* that most beautifully and strikingly illustrates alike the *Woman* and the *Christian,* in the highest and most comprehensive sense of those expressive words.

Enshrined in the *Sanctuary of Home,* her sublime example is the peerless boast of her country; and it shall but brighten as it recedes with revolving years.

WOMAN'S TRUE PROFESSION

The authors of this volume, while they sympathize with every honest effort to relieve the disabilities and sufferings of their sex, are confident that the chief cause of these evils is the fact that the honor and duties of the family state are not duly appreciated, that women are not trained for these duties as men are trained for their trades and professions, and that, as the consequence, family labor is poorly done, poorly paid, and regarded as menial and disgraceful.

To be the nurse of young children, a cook, or a housemaid, is regarded as the lowest and last resort of poverty, and one which no woman of culture and position can assume without loss of caste and respectability.

It is the aim of this volume to elevate both the honor and the remuneration of all the employments that sustain the many difficult and sacred duties of the family state, and thus to render each department of woman's true profession as much desired and respected as are the most honored professions of men.

When the other sex are to be instructed in law, medicine, or divinity, they are favored with numerous institutions richly endowed, with teachers of the highest talents and acquirements, with extensive libraries, and abundant and costly apparatus. With such advantages they devote nearly ten of the best years of life to preparing themselves for their profession; and to secure the public from unqualified members of these professions, none can enter them until examined by a competent body, who certify to their due preparation for their duties.

Woman's profession embraces the care and nursing of the body in the critical periods of infancy and sickness, the training of the human mind

Catharine Beecher and Harriet Beecher Stowe, *The American Woman's Home* (New York, 1869), pp. 13–19.

in the most impressible period of childhood, the instruction and control of servants, and most of the government and economies of the family state. These duties of woman are as sacred and important as any ordained to man; and yet no such advantages for preparation have been accorded to her, nor is there any qualified body to certify the public that a woman is duly prepared to give proper instruction in her profession. . . .

During the upward progress of the age, and the advance of a more enlightened Christianity, the writers of this volume have gained more elevated views of the true mission of woman—of the dignity and importance of her distinctive duties, and of the true happiness which will be the reward of a right appreciation of this mission, and a proper performance of these duties. . . .

What, then, is the end designed by the family state which Jesus Christ came into this world to secure?

It is to provide for the training of our race to the highest possible intelligence, virtue, and happiness, by means of the self-sacrificing labors of the wise and good, and this with chief reference to a future immortal existence.

The distinctive feature of the family is self-sacrificing labor of the stronger and wiser members to raise the weaker and more ignorant to equal advantages. The father undergoes toil and self-denial to provide a home, and then the mother becomes a self-sacrificing laborer to train its inmates. The useless, troublesome infant is served in the humblest offices; while both parents unite in training it to an equality with themselves in every advantage. Soon the older children become helpers to raise the younger to a level with their own. When any are sick, those who are well become self-sacrificing ministers. When the parents are old and useless, the children become their self-sacrificing servants.

Thus the discipline of the family state is one of daily self-devotion of the stronger and wiser to elevate and support the weaker members. Nothing could be more contrary to its first principles than for the older and more capable children to combine to secure to themselves the highest advantages, enforcing the drudgeries on the younger, at the sacrifice of their equal culture.

Jesus Christ came to teach the fatherhood of God and consequent brotherhood of man. He came as the "firstborn Son" of God and the Elder Brother of man, to teach by example the self-sacrifice by which the great family of man is to be raised to equality of advantages as children of God. For this end, he "humbled himself" from the highest to the lowest place. He chose for his birthplace the most despised village; for his parents the lowest in rank; for his trade, to labor with his hands as a carpenter being "subject to his parents" thirty years. And, what is very significant, his trade was that which prepares the family home, as if he would teach that the great duty of man is labor—to provide for and train weak and ignorant creatures. Jesus Christ worked with his hands nearly thirty years, and preached less than three. And he taught that his kingdom is exactly opposite to that of the world, where all are striving for the highest positions. "Whoso will be great shall be your minister, and whoso will be chiefest shall be servant of all."

The family state then, is the aptest earthly illustration of the heavenly kingdom, and in it woman is its chief minister. Her great mission is self-denial, in training its members to self-sacrificing labors for the ignorant and weak: if not her own children, then the neglected children of her Father in heaven. She is to rear all under her care to lay up treasures, not on earth, but in heaven. All the pleasures of this life end here; but those who train immortal minds are to reap the fruit of their labor through eternal ages.

To man is appointed the out-door labor—to till the earth, dig the mines, toil in the foundries, traverse the ocean, transport merchandise, labor in manufactories, construct houses, conduct civil, municipal, and state affairs, and all the heavy work, which, most of the day, excludes him from the comforts of a home. But the great stimulus to all these toils, implanted in the heart of every true man, is the desire for a home of his own, and the hopes of paternity. Every man who truly lives for immortality responds to the beatitude, "Children are a heritage from the Lord: blessed is the man that hath his quiver full of them!" The more a father and mother live under the influence of that "immortality which Christ had brought to light," the more is the blessedness of rearing a family understood and appreciated. Every child trained aright is to dwell forever in exalted bliss with those that gave it life and trained it for heaven.

SONGS AND POEMS OF HOME AND PARENTS

O Happy Home

O happy home, where Thou art loved the dearest,
Thou loving Friend and Saviour of our race,
And where among the guests there never cometh
One who can hold such high and honored place!
O happy home, where each one serves Thee, lowly,
Whatever his appointed work may be,
Till every comman task seems great and holy,
When it is done, O Lord, as unto Thee!

O happy home, where Thou art not forgotten,
When joy is overflowing, full, and free;
O happy home, where every wounded spirit
Is brought, Physician, Comforter, to Thee.
Until at last, when earth's days' work is ended,
All meet Thee in the blessed home above,

"O Happy Home," music by Joseph Barnby, lyrics by Carl J. P. Spitta, n.d.

From whence Thou comest, where Thou hast ascended,
Thy everlasting home of peace and love!

The Picture That Is Turned Toward the Wall

Far away beyond the glamour of the city and its strife,
There's a quiet little homstead by the sea,
Where a tender, loving lassie used to live a happy life,
As contented in her home as she could be;
Not a shadow ever seem'd to cloud the sunshine of her youth,
And they thought no sorrow could her life befall,
But she left them all one evening and their sad hearts knew the truth,
When her father turned her picture to the wall.

CHORUS

There's a name that's never spoken and a mother's heart half broken,
There is just another missing from the old home, that is all,
There is still a mem'ry living, there's a father unforgiving,
And a picture that is turned toward the wall.

Where Is My Wandering Boy Tonight?

Where is my wandering boy tonight,
The boy of my tenderest care;
The boy that was once my joy and light,
The child of my love and prayer?

Once he was pure as morning dew,
As he knelt at his mother's knee;
No face was so bright, no heart more true,
And none was so sweet as he.

O, could I see you now, my boy,
As fair as in olden time;
When prattle and smile made him a joy,
And life was a merry chime.

Go for my wandering boy, tonight!
Go search for him where you will!
But bring him to me, with all this blight,
And tell him I love him still!

CHORUS

O, where is my boy tonight?
My heart o'erflows,

"The Picture That Is Turned Toward the Wall," music and lyrics by Charles Graham, 1891.
"Where Is My Wandering Boy Tonight?," music and lyrics by Reverend Robert Lowry, 1877.

For I love him, he knows;
O, where is my boy tonight?

Over the Hill to the Poor House

What no! it can't be that they've driven
Their father, so helpless and old,
Oh, God, may their crime be forgiven,
To perish out here in the cold,
Oh, Heav'ns, I am sadden'd and weary,
See the tears how they course down my cheeks!
Oh, this world it is lonely and dreary,
And my heart for relief vainly seeks.

Ah me! on that old doorstep yonder,
I've sat with my babes on my knee,
No father was happier or fonder,
Than I of my little ones three,
The boys, both so rosy and chubby,
And Lilly with prattle so sweet!
Oh, God knows how their father has loved them,
But they've driven him out in the street.

REFRAIN
For I'm old and I'm helpless and feeble,
The days of my youth have gone by,
Then over the hill to the poor house,
I wander alone there to die.

Home Sweet Home

'Mid pleasures and palaces though I may roam,
Be it ever so humble, there's no place like home;
A charm from the sky seems to hallow us there,
Which, seek thro' the world, is ne'er met elsewhere.

An exile from home, splendor dazzles in vain,
Oh, give me the lowly thatched cottage again;
The birds singing gaily, that come at my call;
Give me them, with that peace of mind, dearer than all.

To thee, I'll return, overburdened with care,
The heart's dearest solace will smile on me there.
No more from that cottage again will I roam,
Be it ever so humble, there's no place like home.

"Over the Hill to the Poor House," music by David Braham, lyrics by George L. Catlin, 1874.
    "Home Sweet Home," music by Henry Rowley Bishop, lyrics by John Howard Payne, 1823.

CHORUS
Home! Home! Sweet, sweet home!
There's no place like home,
There's no place like home.

Old Folks at Home

Way down upon the Swanee river,
Far, far away,
There's where my heart is turning ever;
There's where the old folks stay.
All up and down the whole creation,
Sadly I roam,
Still longing for the old plantation,
And for the old folks at home.

All 'round the little farm I wander'd,
When I was young;
Then many happy days I squander'd,
Many the songs I sung.
When I was playing with my brother,
Happy was I,
Oh, take me to my kind old mother,
There let me live and die.

One little hut among the bushes,
One that I love,
Still sadly to my mem'ry rushes,
No matter where I rove.
When shall I see the bees a-humming,
All 'round the comb?
When shall I hear the banjo strumming,
Down in my good old home.

CHORUS
All the world is sad and dreary
Ev'rywhere I roam,
O darkies, how my heart grows weary,
Far from the old folks at home.

My Old Kentucky Home

The sun shines bright on the old Kentucky home,
'Tis summer, the darkies are gay;
The corntop's ripe and the meadow's in the bloom,
While the birds make music all the day;
The young folks roll on the little cabin floor,

"Old Folks at Home," music and lyrics by Stephen Foster, 1851.
"My Old Kentucky Home," music and lyrics by Stephen Foster, 1851.

All merry, all happy, and bright;
By'n'by hard times come a-knocking at the door,
Then, my old Kentucky home, good night!

They hunt no more for the 'possum and the 'coon,
On the meadow, the hill, and the shore;
They sing no more by the glimmer of the moon,
On the bench by the old cabin door;
The day goes by like a shadow o'er the heart,
With sorrow where all was delight;
The time has come when the darkies have to part,
Then, my old Kentucky home, good night!

The head must bow and the back will have to bend,
Wherever the darky may go;
A few more days and the trouble all will end,
In the fields where the sugar-canes grow;
A few more days for to tote the weary load,
No matter, 'twill never be light;
A few more days till we totter on the road,
Then, my old Kentucky home, good night!

CHORUS
Weep no more, my lady,
Oh! weep no more today!
We will sing one song for the old Kentucky home,
For the old Kentucky home, far away.

SARAH J. HALE

Home

Where burns the loved hearth brightest,
  Cheering the social breast?
Where beats the fond heart lightest,
  Its humble hopes possessed;
Where is the smile of sadness
  Of meek-eyed patience born,
Worth more than those of gladness
  Which mirth's bright cheek adorn?
Pleasure is marked by fleetness
  To those who ever roam;
While grief itself has sweetness,
  At Home! dear Home!

Sarah J. Hale, "Home," *The American Ladies' Magazine*, VIII (August 1835), p. 464.

EUGENE FIELD

Father's Letter

I'm going to write a letter to our oldest boy who went
Out West last spring to practise law and run for president;
I'll tell him all the gossip I guess he'd like to hear,
For he hasn't seen the home-folks for going on a year!
Most generally it's Marthy does the writing, but as she
Is suffering with a felon, why, the job devolves on me—
So, when the supper things are done and put away to-night,
I'll draw my boots and shed my coat and settle down to write. . . .

These are the things I'll write him—our boy that's in the West;
And I'll tell him how we miss him—his mother and the rest;
Why, we never have an apple-pie that mother doesn't say:
"He liked it so—I wish that he could have a piece to-day!"
I'll tell him we are prospering, and hope he is the same—
That we hope he'll have no trouble getting on to wealth and fame;
And just before I write "good-by from father and the rest,"
I'll say that "mother sends her love," and that will please him best.
. . .

For when *I* went away from home, the weekly news I heard
Was nothing to the tenderness I found in that one word—
The sacred name of mother—why, even now as then,
The thought brings back the saintly face, the gracious love again
And in my bosom seems to come a peace that is divine,
As if an angel spirit communed awhile with mine;
And one man's heart is strengthened by the message from above,
And earth seems nearer heaven when "mother sends her love."

REDEEMING THE FAMILY

I went out to speak to him; and saw a venerable old man, whose long
hoary hair and deeply wrinkled countenance commanded more than common respect. He was resting his arm and head upon the gate, the tears
were streaming down his cheeks. On my approach, he made a low bow,
and said,

"Sir, I have brought you a letter from my daughter; but I fear you will
think us very bold in asking you to take so much trouble."

"By no means," I replied, "I shall be truly glad to oblige you and any
of your family in this matter."

Eugene Field, "Father's Letter," *The Poems of Eugene Field* (New York, 1915), pp. 249–50.
Reverend Leigh Richmond, "The Dairyman's Daughter," *The Publications of the American Tract Society* (New York, 1826), vol I, pp. 4–6.

I desired him to come into the house, and then said,

"What is your occupation?"

"Sir, I have lived most of my days in a little cottage, six miles from here. I have rented a few acres of ground and kept a few cows, which, in addition to my day labour, has been my means of supporting and bringing up my family."

"What family have you?"

"A wife now getting very aged and helpless; one son, and one daughter; for my other poor dear child is just departed out of this wicked world."

"I hope, for a better."

"I hope so too; poor thing, she did not use to take to such good ways as her sister; but I do believe that her sister's manner of talking with her before she died, was the means of saving her soul. What a mercy it is to have such a child as mine is! I never thought about my own soul seriously till she, poor girl, begged and prayed me to flee from the wrath to come."

"How old are you?"

"Turned seventy, and my wife is older; we are getting old and almost past our labour; but our daughter has left a good place, where she lived in service, on purpose to come home and take care of us and our little dairy. And a dear, dutiful, affectionate girl she is."

"Was she always so?"

"No, Sir; when she was very young, she was all for the world, and pleasure, and dress, and company. Indeed we were all very ignorant, and thought if we took care for this life, and wronged nobody, we should be sure to go to heaven at last. My daughters were both wilful, and, like ourselves, were strangers to the ways of God and the word of his grace. But the eldest of them went out to service, and some years ago she heard a sermon preached; and from that time she became quite an altered creature. She began to read the Bible, and became quite sober and steady. The first time she came home afterwards to see us, she brought us a guinea which she had saved from her wages, and said, as we were getting old, she was sure we should want help; adding, that she did not wish to spend it in fine clothes, as she used to do, only to feed pride and vanity. She would rather show gratitude to her dear father and mother; and this, she said, because Christ had shown such mercy to her.

"We wondered to hear her talk, and took great delight in her company, for her temper and behaviour were so humble and kind, she seemed so desirous to do us good both in soul and body, and was so different from what we had ever seen her before, that careless and ignorant as we had been, we began to think there must be something real in religion, or it never could alter a person so much in a little time.

"Her younger sister, poor soul, used to laugh and ridicule her at that time, and said her head was turned with her new ways. 'No sister,' she would say, 'not my *head*, but I hope my *heart* is turned from the love of sin to the love of God. I wish you may one day see, as I do, the danger and vanity of your present condition.'

"Her poor sister would reply, 'I do not want to hear any of your preaching: I am no worse than other people, and that is enough for me.'—'Well sister,' Elizabeth would say, 'if you will not hear me, you cannot hinder me from praying for you, which I do with all my heart.'

"And now, Sir, I believe those prayers are answered. For when her sister was taken ill, Elizabeth went to wait in her place and take care of her. She said a great deal to her about her soul, and the poor girl began to be so deeply affected, and sensible of her past sin, and so thankful for her sister's kind behaviour, that it gave her great hopes indeed for her sake. When my wife and I went to see her as she lay sick, she told us how grieved and ashamed she was of her past state; but said, she had a hope, through grace, that her dear sister's Saviour would be her Saviour too; for she saw her own sinfulness, felt her own helplessness, and only wished to cast herself upon Christ as her hope and salvation.

"And now, Sir, she is gone, and I hope and think her sister's prayers for her conversion to God have been answered. The Lord grant the same for her poor father and mother's sake likewise."

THE PIOUS CHILD

The Scriptures declare that the preaching of Christ crucified is the powerful instrument which God uses in convincing of sin, and leading to penitence and gratitude. And the history of the church in all ages has shown that the story of a Saviour's love and death will awaken contrition and melt the heart, when all other appeals are in vain. Your child will listen, with tearful eye, while you tell of the Saviour's elevation in heaven; of his becoming man; of the sufferings and persecution of his life; and of his cruel death upon the cross. And when you tell your child that it was God who thus became manifest in the flesh, and suffered these indignities, that he might redeem his sinful creatures from woe, you will convey to the tender mind such an idea of God's kindness, and the ingratitude of sinners, as nothing else can produce. . . .

Any person will be interested, in turning over the pages of almost any pious child's biography, to witness how strong the impression which a Saviour's love produces upon the heart. Even under the most adverse circumstances, the youthful heart has found its way, unguided and alone, to repose in the bosom of the Saviour. Not a few instances have occurred, in which parents who have not been accustomed to give prominency to the Saviour in their instructions, have been surprised to find that Jesus Christ is the sympathizing friend to whom a child, in sickness and in suffering, has most affectionately clung. God in Christ has attractions which nothing else can have.

John S. C. Abbott, *The Mother at Home* (New York, 1834), pp. 142–45.

The growth in the nineteenth century of the idea that all little children were angels was reflected in tombstone art and inscriptions. This child's gravestone from Mt. Auburn cemetery in Cambridge, Massachusetts, exemplifies both visual image and literary idea of the pure child by using the age-old Christian symbol of the lamb to make its point. The inscription reads: "Our Baby/ A grave with myrtle overgrown,/ A lock of hair is all we own/ Of what was once our baby fair./ This little golden lock of hair./ We guard that grave with jealous care/ And kiss this tiny lock of hair,/ And though the tears will dim our eyes,/ Our lips shall murmur 'God is wise.' "

When little Nathan Dickerman was asked, "What do you love to think about most when you are in pain?" "The Lord Jesus Christ," he answered.

At another time, his biographer records, "Nathan is very sick to-night. His heart is beating most violently and rapidly, while the pulse can hardly be perceived at the wrist. But he says he is more happy than usual. I asked him, why? He replied, 'Because my Saviour is nearer.' " . . .

The remembrance of what the Saviour suffered sustained him in all his sufferings. Redeeming love was the theme of his sweetest meditations.

One day, some one was mentioning in the room that his disease was of such a nature that he would probably die suddenly. Nathan heard it, and, rising up in the bed, clasped his hands together, and repeated the verse,

> 'Jesus can make a dying bed
>   Feel soft as downy pillows are,
> While on his breast I lean my head,
>   And breathe my soul out sweetly there.'

"And after sitting a few moments in silence, he added another:

> 'Jesus, my God, I know his name,
>   His name is all my trust;
> Nor will he put my soul to shame,
>   Nor let my hope be lost.'

'Is'nt that a good hope, ma?' "

We might open almost any memoir of early piety in illustration of this principle. And indeed every one who is familiar with the characteristics of devotional feeling, as they are exemplified in the mind of a child, must have observed the wonderful adaptation of religious truth to our weakness and frailty.

Let parents, therefore, imitate the Apostles, and preach to their children a suffering Saviour. Show them God in Christ, reconciling the world to himself. This is the simplicity of the Gospel.

CHILD-REARING: THE MISSION
SO SACRED

The nineteenth century was the great age of the middle-class or bourgeois family, the time of its triumph as an ideal and of its self-confidence in its strength as an institution. Since, unlike Europe, America had neither aristocratic nor peasant traditions, we find little other than various bourgeois ideals among its dominant whites. Such families were inextricably tied to the marketplace and unabashedly devoted to "success," "betterment," and "prosperity," all the while professing ideas of mutual respect and affection and seeking comfort and happiness in the home.

Dedicated as it was to "improvement," the American family came to dote on and worry ceaselessly about its children. In the great American stir about child nurture after about 1830, we find the predecessors of our child-guidance professionals. Their names, once almost as famous as Dr. Spock's, are now forgotten. If their books are read, it is only for historical interest. Both the advice and the procedures used with children now seem quaint and "dated" for we now know a great deal that is more reliable about child development. Even more, we have radically shifted the focus of our concern for children. These earlier "experts" were unabashedly moralists and often fervently religious. Even the first American treatises on pediatrics, as the selection from Dr. Dewees shows, indicate that the primary mission was moral. Concern for the child's physical well-being and happiness, even for mother's milk and safe medicines, were ancillary to "training" the child as a determinedly moral man or woman, a model citizen, and a pious, observant Christian. The child of 1850 existed to become an adult, and within the child-rearing literature of the time there are only occasional harbingers of later ideals of a childhood carefree and happy for its own sake. Familiar figures from American lore like the ten-year-old "little man" who enterprisingly sold lemonade or newspapers en route to becoming master of a mill or who performed some heroic or patriotic act are other indications of how childhood was scanned for intimations of adulthood. Families who put their young children to work probably had little notion that they had any destiny other than becoming grown-up breadwinners and as quickly as possible.

No issue in the swelling literature of advice and commentary matched the importance of obedience and absolute parental control. Could there indeed be a true "family" unless children obeyed and copied parents? Could children become adults capable of surviving the temptations and dangers of adulthood without a character fixed by carefully nurtured habits of obedience? In a society so unencumbered by traditional restraints, the responsibilities for social order that family nurture had to carry seemed all the greater. What were the consequences for individuals and society in an America filled with such opportunities "for evil as well as good," of a breakdown of the stable, ordered, deferential family? As much as parents might celebrate America for its opportunities, they also feared it—with good reason—for its capacity to corrupt or dissolve their idealized but fragile family ties.

The custody case here suggests some of the issues in defining parenthood at the time and in apportioning status and responsibilities between the claimants to the children. How does the judge view the parents' roles? How does he find the priority between the mother and the guardian? What does he discern as the good of the child? Who *controls,* and for what approved purpose?

There follow two documents from before 1850 on the issue of corporal punishment, the seeming ultimate expression of control and obedience. The pseudonymous author of "A Case of Conviction" was Francis Wayland (1796–1865), one of America's foremost educators and moral philosophers. In his early years Wayland was still influenced by the orthodox, if ebbing, Christian ideas of the sinfulness of unrepentant infants and the obduracy of their will in a contest, before God, with his "surrogate," the father of the family. Parents were enjoined to "break the will" and to correct every display of fractiousness, sexuality, and even playfulness lest the child be lost to sin and Satan.

This graphic "true life" testimony was like many accounts in the moral and religious magazines for the home in the 1830s and 1840s. Compare it however with the newer discipline described in a chapter from *Home,* Catharine Sedgwick's best-selling novel of 1835. This "Glimpse at Family Government" (revealing words) shows what was announced by many commentators as a more rational, realistic, and effective scheme of family order, control, and punishment. What seem to be Mr. Barclay's guiding assumptions about the psychology of his child? Was the boy a sinner? Was he "merely a child" and in error? How does the father view his role? How psychologically did this punishment work, for both child and father? What were the trade-offs as between the quick, severe whipping we might anticipate from an "old-fashioned father" and the new methods for treating little Wallace's "moral disease" of temper?

Together, the Wayland and Sedgwick pieces reveal the forms and practices of parental authority in transition. The persisting worry, with or without beatings or breaking the will, was how to assure an effective parental stamp on the young. Why parents thus begin to doubt or question themselves seems a more interesting question than whether they would be psychologically or physically severe. It is also wise to remember that law and the courts in the 1840s often justified (or refused intervention against) fathers who beat wives and children.

A selection of short excerpts from some famous names in nineteenth-century child-nurture literature also dwell on the issues of discipline and obedience. Notice how the views change generation by generation. They are given here in chronological order of publication. The persisting questions are: "What is a child?" "What does he exist for?" "What is a good parent?" "What are a parent's duties to himself, to his children, to society, to God?" "What can reasonably be expected of children?" "What are the reasons for strict or 'permissive' behavior toward them at different times of life?"

The group of "experts" begins with Lydia M. Child, a favorite home writer of stories, poems, and advice in the 1830s and 1840s. In the next decade there appeared the weightier work of the theologian Horace Bushnell. His *Views of Christian Nurture* (1847) is a landmark in the philosophical debate about the nature and possibilities of children. Bushnell played a major role in modifying the old Calvinist view of the innate depravity and the probable damnation of most infants. Writing after two generations of intense controversy, Bushnell argued that depravity was only a tendency in the child and that proper and tender nurture could offset it in infancy and early years. Not every expression of energy and zest, for example, was proof of devilish stirrings; thus his chapter on play.

A generation later Jacob Abbott published the book represented here. He was a famous son of another distinguished New England line of moralists and ministers and had been a successful writer on child nurture since the 1830s. *Gentle Measures* is the first major American book on child-rearing to make use of "the teachings of science" and to substitute observation and fact for abstract arguments about the child's "essence." Despite this new emphasis in Abbott, the distance between him and Kate Douglas Wiggin in the 1890s is greater than may seem implicit in Abbott's invocation of science. For Wiggin, the child was all potential for good, if nurture did not turn it wrong. The very title of her book should suggest her general emphasis, and it helps us to know of her support for the kindergarten and child-study movements and in other innovations in childhood education. This book was one of the gospels of what was called the "new education," putting the child and childhood at the center of inquiry and effort rather than the adult or his wishes. For many the issue by 1890 had become the rights of childhood against the claims of adulthood. How does that measure the distance since Lydia Child's day?

DEWEES ON PEDIATRICS

Part I

The physical treatment of children, in its details, is almost infinitely diversified; for custom, prejudice, and speculation, have imposed regulations,

Dr. William P. Dewees, *A Treatise on the Physical and Medical Treatment of Children*, 8th ed. (Philadelphia, 1842; first edition, 1826) Part I, pp. ix–xiii; Part II, pp. i–vi.

which, in their extent, are neither sanctioned by reason nor experience, for, were these to be the foundation, much less difference would be found in the education of children than at present exists.

The education we are now considering, consists in the development of the physical and moral powers of man; consequently, that scheme which does this in the most perfect manner, must be the best—but much discrepancy prevails, in what the scheme should consist. . . .

It will be seen, by the arrangement of our subject, that it is our opinion, that the physical treatment of children should begin, as far as may be practicable, with the earliest formation of the embryo: it will, therefore, necessarily involve the conduct of the female even before her marriage, as well as during the period of pregnancy. It will also be obvious, that the various contingencies which may affect her, as well in health, as in disease, must also exert an influence upon the fœtus. To the mother, then, we have addressed a few directions that she may be enabled to contribute to the healthful stamina of her child, about to be born.

We would not, however, positively say, with some, that every man is nothing more nor less, than that which his mother has made him; nor that to her care, alone, he is indebted for a vigorous constitution; nor to her neglect that he must solely attribute a feeble frame: yet we dare advance, that very much depends on her either to ensure the one, or prevent the other. . . .

As the influence of the maternal constitution upon the embryo must be admitted, we have thought it proper to suggest, how much a woman owes it to herself, as well as to society, that she enter not into the marriage state while labouring under such disqualifications as will be sure to entail debility, or disease upon her offspring; we have, therefore, directed our first chapter to this object.

To constitute a mother, in the best sense of the term, much more is required than giving birth to progeny—it requires qualities both rare and estimable; it exacts a patient endurance of fatigue, and anxious solicitude, as well as a submission to privations, which nothing will render supportable, but that love of offspring which a kind Providence has so generally, and so deeply implanted in the female heart. Thus, the toil and danger of child-birth; the fatigue and anxiety of nursing, and the responsibility of education, exclusively for a time devolve upon the female. Can the attempt, then, to diminish the first, to relieve the second, and divide the third, be unacceptable? . . .

The general simplicity of the diseases of children, renders their management more easy, as well as more certain than those of adults; their complaints are almost always acute, and of the *sthenic* kind; hence the necessity and success of evacuations,* in almost all of them. . . .

The experience of every day would prove, how well children support long-continued evacuations, did we not turn our eyes from the useful lesson.

* Cleaning out the bowels.—Ed.

Who has not witnessed the long continuance of diarrhœa, without producing even weakness, much less death? And who has not seen a profuse salivation, of even months' continuance, during the agony of teething, without even robbing the little sufferer's cheeks of their bloom? Would this obtain with the adult? No! He would, perhaps, die by the first; and certainly emaciate by the second.

We are well aware of the importance of the views now under consideration; we shall, therefore, advance nothing in support of them, that does not appear corroborated by our own experience. For to us there are no positions in medicine more clear, than that there are few of the diseases of childhood which will not yield to well directed evacuations: and, that when not thus treated, they become not only obstinate, but often formidable. We are also equally persuaded, that could this view of the character of the diseases of children gain the ascendency in the minds of parents, much less difficulty would be experienced in the treatment of them, and, consequently, fewer would be called to an untimely grave.

It is well known to almost every parent, that danger may await the sudden stoppage of a diarrhœa, or incipient dysentery by the use of astringents; and many have had reason to remember, with much sadness of heart, the improper drying up of the discharge from excoriated ears, especially during dentition; yet in each of these instances, did we yield to the popular belief, that nearly all the diseases of childhood are of the asthenic kind, the early exhibition of laudanum, or some other astringent, would be proper in the first, and some drying application necessary in the second.

Besides, it has been but too generally believed that the disorders of the internal organs of children have no distinctive signs, by which we can determine, or fix, either the particular part attacked, or the precise nature of the affection. From this we must dissent; for we are of opinion, that we can by a careful examination of symptoms determine the seat of the complaint; and by the particular state of the pulse, at least determine its general character; that is, whether it be a disease of too much, or too little action; and this is the main point of investigation; for it at once enables us to adapt the remedies to the general state of the diathesis. . . .

Part II

The diseases of childhood have not, until lately, sufficiently engaged the attention of physicians, though they have strongly claimed it. It would be difficult to explain satisfactorily, the causes of this indifference; it may, however, we believe, chiefly be ascribed to the following facts: 1st, To the practice of midwifery being confined almost exclusively to women, until within the last fifty or sixty years; by which the physician was thus prevented from seeing many of the diseases of children. 2dly, In Great Britain, especially, to a by-law of the Royal College of Physicians, "by which its fellows are compelled to exclude themselves from practising midwifery," thereby operating like the first cause. 3dly, To a belief that the diseases of childhood are obscure, or even unintelligible. 4thly, To parents supposing that nurses and old women are more conversant with these diseases than the most enlightened physician; by which they are deprived of the opportunity of studying them with as much diligence and accuracy as they deserve. . . . We are far from entertaining such opinions; and we are most anxious, so far as our feeble efforts may have power, to banish them from the minds; not only of the medical practitioner, but from all who may entertain them—for they are unworthy of the one, and painful to the other. . . .

How many parents have had reason to repent of the neglect of a slight hoarseness, of perhaps even several days' continuance, which terminated in a few hours after it had fully developed its character, in death; and how many, who, perhaps, in some measure aware of its tendency, had relied upon a feeble administration of antimonial wine, or a little of the expressed juice of the onion, when nothing but the prompt application of active remedies, could, even in its commencement, have subdued the disease.

GUARDIANSHIP

APPEAL from chancery.

A. S. J. Alston died in the state of Tennessee, in 1834, having by his will appointed his brother, James J. Alston, guardian of his children. The guardian qualified, and the children, with their mother, resided with him until the winter of 1840, when their mother, who had in the meantime intermarried with Foster, the plaintiff in error, and removed to Holly Springs, in the state of Mississippi, went with an armed force to the house of the guardian, and forcibly took possession of the children, and brought them to the residence of the mother in this state, where Foster and wife obtained letters of guardianship.

The depositions of several witnesses were taken on both sides in the progress of the proceeding. On the part of the guardian, Philip W. Alston, his brother, was examined, who stated that his brother, A. S. J. Alston, was living with his brother James J. Alston at the time of his death; that, when his recovery was despaired of, he made his will, and by it left his brother the guardian of his children; that, having given his watch to the deponent, and made a similar bequest to Ruffin Smith, he addressed James J. Alston in these words—"And what must I give you? I give you my children. You have been a father to me, and you will be a father to them." That he also commended his children to the care of his mother; that he requested his wife (now Mrs. Foster) to live with Elizabeth P. and James J. Alston as long as she could, and added, in the form, not of a request, but an injunction, that in the event of her ceasing to live with the said James J. and Elizabeth P. Alston, she was not to take the children away from them; and not to take more than one child at a time on a visit to herself, and then for no longer a period than three or four weeks, saying, "this I do not request of you, but I command it. . . ."

"Foster and Wife, Appellants, *v.* Alston," *Missouri (6 How)*, 1842, p. 459.

Mr. Justice Turner delivered the opinion of the court. . . .

What is this court, under these circumstances, called on to do? It is in proof that these children are fond of their mother; and, after trying both situations—first with their uncle, grand-mother and aunt, and then with their mother and step-father—decidedly prefer remaining with their mother, expressing at the same time an affectionate regard for their grand-mother. Does this show illegal restraint, the very thing or ingredient necessary to give this court the right to change their custody? I think not.

But what are we called on to do with these children, by the petitioner, the testamentary guardian? To tear these tender female children, aged nine and ten years, from the care and custody of a fond, devoted and capable *mother,* and place them under the care of a *bachelor uncle,* residing some seventy-five miles from their mother. To state the proposition would seem to decide it. Let every mother, let every father answer this question.

We respect the rights and the feelings of the guardian. He may yet be *the guardian* of these infants, and prove himself worthy, as he no doubt is, of the trust confided to him by a dying brother. Let him manage their estate, if he chooses, in Tennessee, and watch over their personal interests and welfare also; but let him cease to complain that he is, by the highest authority of the state, relieved from a duty he is, in the nature of things, incapable of performing. For, at best, if he were to obtain the custody of these children, he would have to select his mother, or his sister, or some other female, to take charge of and superintend their persons, instead of their mother.

The first error committed, in relation to these children, was, in not allowing them to go home with their *mother* when she obtained a *home* by her intermarriage with her present husband. No one can say that Mrs. Foster did wrong in contracting a second marriage. No person had a right to deny her that right. Their mother's home should be the children's home, until circumstances occur to establish, before a court of justice, that the interest of the child requires a separation from their natural protectors. Mrs. Foster, after remaining in widowhood some three or four years, thought proper to take another husband. And who did she take to be her husband, and to be the father of her orphan children? A minister of the gospel of Christ—the friend, and pastor, and instructor, and the very inmate of the Alston family. If there were any thing wrong or imprudent in this her choice, who should share the blame but the head of that family, by whose authority he was a chosen inmate and daily associate, and the divine instructor of that family? But we see nothing wrong, so far, in this second marriage.

Mr. Chief Justice SHARKEY dissenting,

The first question which naturally presents itself is, as to the right or power of the father over his children, as contrasted with that of the mother, for I consider the whole question reduced to a naked abstract question of law. Amongst the various authorities introduced, none have gone so far as to deny the superior claims of the father to the control of his children.

We are informed by the first elementary books we read, that the authority of the father is superior to that of the mother. It is the doctrine of all civilized nations. It is according to the revealed law and the law of nature, and it prevails even with the wandering savage, who has received none of the lights of civilization. The father is considered the head and governor of the family. He controls even the mother, and must of necessity control the children. Some writers, I am aware, have contended for the equal authority of the mother, on the ground of her superior affection for her offspring. Their efforts to prove that the law should be so, are of themselves evidence that it is otherwise, and the warmer attachment of the mother, instead of proving the error in the law, may serve to prove its policy. We are all aware that children must be brought up under a proper state of discipline. Faults must be corrected, and errors avoided. A system of training must be adopted which is often repugnant to the wishes of the child. Which is best calculated to do these things, the doting, partial mother, with whom every fault is a virtue, every wish a command, or the less partial father, who looks to future welfare, rather than the gratification of childish folly? I am sensible that there are kind offices which none can so well discharge as a mother, but these are not inconsistent with the father's superior authority; and that his authority is superior in controlling the destiny and custody of his children, is manifest from the statute which authorizes him to appoint a guardian by will or deed. This he may do, notwithstanding the mother be living.

BREAKING THE WILL

Mr. Editor,

I offer for the perusal of your readers, the simple narration of a trifling incident which has in a few days occurred in my own family. . . .

My youngest child is an infant about 15 months old, with about the intelligence common to children of that age. It has for some months been evident, that he was more than usually self willed, but the several attempts to subdue him, had been thus far relinquished, from the fear that he did not fully understand what was said to him. It so happened, however, that I had never been brought into collision with him myself, until the incident occurred which I am about to relate. Still I had seen enough to convince me of the necessity of subduing his temper, and resolved to seize upon the first favorable opportunity which presented, for settling the question of authority between us.

On Friday last before breakfast, on my taking him from his nurse, he began to cry violently. I determined to hold him in my arms until he ceased. As he had a piece of bread in his hand, I took it away, intending to give

A Plain Man [Francis Wayland], "A Case of Conviction," *American Baptist Magazine* (October 1831), pp. 35–38.

it to him again after he became quiet. In a few minutes he ceased, but when I offered him the bread he threw it away, although he was very hungry. He had, in fact, taken no nourishment except a cup of milk since 5 o'clock on the preceding afternoon. I considered this a fit opportunity for attempting to subdue his temper, and resolved to embrace it. I thought it necessary to change his disposition, so that he would receive the bread *from me*, and also be so reconciled to me that he would *voluntarily* come to me. The task I found more difficult than I had expected.

I put him into a room by himself, and desired that no one should speak to him, or give him any food or drink whatever. This was about 8 o'clock in the morning. I visited him every hour or two during the day, and spoke to him in the kindest tones, offering him the bread and putting out my arms to take him. But throughout the whole day he remained inflexibly obstinate. He did not yield a hair's breadth. I put a cup of water to his mouth, and he drank it greedily, but would not touch it with his hands. If a crumb was dropped on the floor he would eat it, but if *I* offered him the piece of bread, he would push it away from him. When I told him to come to me, he would turn away and cry bitterly. He went to bed supperless. It was now twenty-four hours since he had eaten any thing.

He woke the next morning in the same state. He would take nothing that I offered him, and shunned all my offers of kindness. He was now truly an object of pity. He had fasted thirty-six hours. His eyes were wan and sunken. His breath hot and feverish, and his voice feeble and wailing. Yet he remained obstinate. He continued thus, till 10 o'clock A.M. when hunger overcame him, and he took from me a piece of bread, to which I added a cup of milk, and hoped that the labor was at last accomplished.

In this however I had not rightly judged. He ate his bread greedily, but when I offered to take him, he still refused as pertinaciously as ever. I therefore ceased feeding him, and recommenced my course of discipline.

He was again left alone in his crib, and I visited him as before, at intervals. About one o'clock Saturday, I found that he began to view his condition in its true light. The tones of his voice in weeping were graver and less passionate, and had more the appearance of one bemoaning himself. Yet when I went to him, he still remained obstinate. You could clearly see in him the abortive efforts of the will. Frequently he would raise his hands an inch or two, and then suddenly put them down again. He would look at me, and then hiding his face in the bedclothes weep most sorrowfully. During all this time I was addressing him, whenever I came into the room, with invariable kindness. But my kindness met with no suitable return. All I required of him was, that he should come to me. This he would not do, and he began now to see that it had become a serious business. Hence his distress increased. He would not submit, and he found that there was no help without it. It was truly surprising to behold how much agony so young a being could inflict upon himself.

About three o'clock I visited him again. He continued in the state I have described. I was going away, and had opened the door, when I thought that he looked somewhat softened, and returning, put out my hands, again requesting him to come to me. To my joy, and I hope gratitude, he rose up and put forth his hands immediately. The agony was over. He was completely subdued. He repeatedly kissed me, and would do so whenever I commanded. He would kiss any one when I directed him, so full of love was he to all the family. Indeed, so entirely and instantaneously were his feelings towards me changed, that he preferred me now to any of the family. As he had never done before, he moaned after me when he saw that I was going away.

Since this event several slight revivals of his former temper have occurred, but they have all been easily subdued. His disposition is, as it never has been before, mild and obedient. He is kind and affectionate, and evidently much happier than he was, when he was determined to have his own way. I hope and pray that it may prove that an effect has been produced upon him for life.

And now, Mr. Editor, let me say that I should not have taken the trouble of writing, nor given you the trouble of reading this apparently trifling detail, but for some lessons of practical improvement, which it has suggested to my own mind. . . .

I. From this incident, which is in every respect literal fact, without any embellishment, parents may learn the intensity of the obstinacy of children. When they find their children stubborn, they need not be surprised. Let them hold out in a mild yet firm course of discipline until this obstinacy is subdued. This is real kindness. There can be no greater cruelty than to suffer a child to grow up with an unsubdued temper. Let us strive, by the grace of God, to cure the evil as early as possible. I do not make these remarks, by way of telling how much better I govern my family than other people. I believe no such thing. Far from it. God has seen fit to call me to bring up a child of unusually unyielding temper. I have related the effect of this method of treatment, in the hope that it might be an encouragement to those who may be required to undergo a similar trial.

II. But secondly, I could not avoid looking upon the whole of this little incident, as illustrative of the several steps in the ordinary progress of a sinner's conversion.

1. I remarked that my child was about 15 months old, and yet I had never been obliged thus to treat him before. The fact is, I had never before required anything of him, which was directly contrary to his will. Hence there had never occurred anything to test the question, whether he was disposed to consider my will or his own as of supreme authority. But as soon as a case occurred, which brought him and myself into direct and naked collision, his disposition was revealed in an instant. How unyielding that spirit of disobedience was, I have already related. . . .

2. It will be remembered, that I offered my child food, and he would not take it. I offered to receive him to my arms, if he would renounce his will to me, and evince it by simply putting forth his arms to come to

me. I would not force him to come, nor would I treat him with favor until he submitted. I was right and he was wrong. He might at any moment have put an end to the controversy. He was therefore inflicting all this misery voluntarily upon himself.

Here several things are to be observed.

1. The terms I offered him were perfectly kind. I was willing to pass by all that he had done, if he would only evince a right disposition. 2. I could offer no other terms. To have received him on any other terms would have been to allow that his will was to be my rule of action, and whenever he set out to have his own way, I must have obliged my whole family to have conformed in all their arrangements to his wishes. He must have been made the centre of the whole system. A whole family under the control of a child 15 months old! How unjust this would have been to all the rest, is evident. Besides, my other children and every member of my family would have been entitled to the same privilege. Hence there would have been as many supreme wills as there were individuals, and contention to the uttermost must have ensued.

Again, suppose I had subjected all my family to this infant's caprice, and had done so whilst he remained under my roof, how could I have afflicted him with a more grievous curse? He would soon have entered a *world where other and more powerful beings than he* would have opposed his will, and his disposition which I had cherished must have made him miserable as long as he lived.

Or again, if all this had been done, he could not have been made happy. He did not *know enough* to be able to secure his own happiness. Had I let him do as he pleased, he would have burnt and scalded himself a dozen times a day and would very soon have destroyed his life. Seeking, therefore, his good, and the good of the family, I could do nothing else than I did. Kindliness to him as much as to them, taught me not to yield to him on any other terms than a change of disposition.

On the contrary, by yielding to me, my whole family has been restored to order; he is happier by far than he has ever been before, and he is acquiring a disposition which will fit him for the wide world, which, if he lives, he will enter upon.

So, to apply all this to the case of a sinner, *God* can offer a sinner *no other terms than repentance.* To yield to the sinner's will, and save him without the unconditional surrender of his will, would be to make the sinner's will the centre of the moral universe. How would you like amoral government founded on your neighbor's caprice? It would be to throw down the government of law, and make this universe a hell.

A GLIMPSE AT FAMILY GOVERNMENT

The family were assembled in a back parlor. Mrs. Barclay was at some domestic employment, to facilitate which Martha had just brought in a

Catharine M. Sedgwick, *Home* (Boston, 1835), pp. 15–27.

tub of scalding water. Charles, the eldest boy, with a patience most *unboyish*, was holding a skein of yarn for grandmama to wind; Alice, the eldest girl, was arranging the dinner-table in the adjoining room; Mary, the second, was amusing the baby at the window; Willie was saying his letters to Aunt Betsey;—all were busy, but the busiest was little Haddy, a sweet child of four years, who was sitting in the middle of the room on a low chair, and who, unobserved by the rest, and herself unconscious of wrong, was doing deadly mischief. She had taken a new, unfinished, and very precious kite belonging to her brother Wallace, cut a hole in the centre, thrust into it the head of her pet Maltese kitten, and was holding it by its fore paws and making it dance on her lap; the little animal looking as demure and as formal as one of Queen Elizabeth's maids of honor in her ruff. At this critical juncture Wallace entered in search of his kite. One word of prefatory palliation for Wallace. The kite was the finest he had ever possessed; it had been given him by a friend, and that friend was waiting at the door, to string and fly it for him. At once the ruin of the kite, and the indignity to which it was subjected, flashed on him, and perhaps little Haddy's very satisfied air exasperated him. In a breath he seized the kitten, and dashed it into the tub of scalding water. His father had come in to dinner, and paused at the open door of the next room. Haddy shrieked— the children all screamed—Charles dropped grandmama's yarn, and, at the risk of his own hand, rescued the kitten; but seeing its agony, with most characteristic consideration, he gently dropped it in again, and thus put the speediest termination to its sufferings.

The children were all sobbing. Wallace stood pale and trembling. His eye turned to his father, then to his mother, then was riveted on the floor. The children saw the frown on their father's face, more dreaded by them than ever was flogging, or dark closet with all its hobgoblins.

"I guess you did not mean to, did you, Wally?" said little Haddy, whose tender heart was so touched by the utter misery depicted on her brother's face, that her pity for him overcame her sense of her own and pussy's wrongs. Wallace sighed deeply, but spoke no word of apology or justification. The children looked at Wallace, at their father, and their mother, and still the portentous silence was unbroken. The dinner-bell rung. "Go to your own room, Wallace," said his father. "You have forfeited your right to a place among us. Creatures who are the slaves of their passions, are, like beasts of prey, fit only for solitude."

"How long must Wallace stay up stairs?" asked Haddy, affectionately holding back her brother who was hastening away.

"Till he feels assured," replied Mr. Barclay, fixing his eye sternly on Wallace, "that he can control his hasty temper; at least so far as not to be guilty of violence towards such a dear good little girl as you are, and murderous cruelty to an innocent animal;—till, sir, you can give me some proof that you dread the sin and danger of yielding to your passions so much that you can govern them. The boy is hopeless," he added in a low voice to his wife, as Wallace left the room.

"My dear husband! Hopeless at ten years old, and with such a good, affectionate heart as his? We must have patience."

A happy combination for children is there in an uncompromising father and an all-hoping mother. The family sat down to table. The parents were silent, serious, unhappy. The children caught the infection, and scarcely a word was said above a whisper. There was a favorite dish on the table, followed by a nice pudding. They were eaten, not enjoyed. The children realized that it was not the good things they had to eat, but the kind looks, the innocent laugh, and cheerful voice, that made the pleasure of the social meal.

"My dear children," said their father, as he took his hat to leave them, "we have lost all our comfort to-day, have not we?"

"Yes, sir—yes, sir," they answered in a breath.

"Then learn one lesson from your poor brother. Learn to dread doing wrong. If you commit sin, you must suffer, and all that love you must suffer with you; for every sin is a violation of the laws of your Heavenly Father, and he will not suffer it to go unpunished."

If Mr. and Mrs. Barclay had affected their concern, to overawe and impose on their children, they would not have been long deceived; for children, being themselves sincere, are clearsighted. But they knew that the sadness was real; they felt that it was in accordance with their parents' characters and general conduct. They never saw them ruffled by trifles. Many a glass had been broken, many a greasy knife dropped, many a disappointment and inconvenience incurred, without calling forth more than a gentle rebuke. These were not the things that moved them, or disturbed the domestic tranquillity; but the ill temper, selfishness, unkindness, or any moral fault of the children, was received as an affliction.

The days passed on. Wallace went to school as usual, and returned to his solitude, without speaking or being spoken to. His meals were sent to his room, and whatever the family ate, he ate. For the Barclays took care not to make rewards and punishments out of eating and drinking, and thus associate the duties and pleasures of a moral being with a mere animal gratification. "But ah!" he thought, as he walked up and down his apartment, while eating his pie or pudding, "how different it tastes from what it does at table!" and though he did not put it precisely in that form, he felt what it was that "sanctified the food." The children began to venture to say to their father, whose justice they dared not question, "How long Wally has stayed up stairs!" and Charles, each day, eagerly told how well Wallace behaved at school. His grandmother could not resist her desire to comfort him; she would look into his room to see "if he were well," "if he were warm enough," or "if he did not want something." The little fellow's moistening eye and tremulous voice evinced his sensibility to her kindness, but he resolutely abstained from asking any mitigation of his punishment. . . .

Two weeks had passed when Mr. Barclay heard Wallace's door open, and heard him say, "Can I speak with you one minute before dinner, sir."

"Certainly, my son." His father entered and closed the door.

"Father," said Wallace, with a tremulous voice but an open, cheerful face, "I feel as if I had a right now to ask you to forgive me, and take me back into the family."

Mr. Barclay felt so too, and kissing him, he said, "I have only been waiting for you, Wallace; and, from the time you have taken to consider your besetting sin, I trust you have gained strength to resist it."

"It is not consideration only, sir, that I depend on; for you told me I must wait till I could give you *proof;* so I had to wait till something happened ·to try me. I could not possibly tell else, for I always do resolve, when I get over my passion, that I never will get angry again. Luckily for me—for I began to be horribly tired of staying alone—Tom Allen snatched off my new cap and threw it in the gutter. I had a book in my hand, and I raised it to send at him; but I thought just in time, and I was so glad I had governed my passion, that I did not care about my cap, or Tom, or any thing else. 'But one swallow doesn't make a summer,' as Aunt Betsey says; so I waited till I should get angry again. It seemed as if I never should; there were provoking things happened, but somehow or other they did not provoke me—why do you smile, father?"

"I smile with pleasure, my dear boy, to find that one fortnight's resolute watchfulness has enabled you so to curb your temper that you are not easily provoked. . . . There is no telling, Wallace, how much good may be done by a single right action, nor how much harm by a single wrong one."

"I know it, sir; I have been thinking a great deal since I have been up stairs, and I do wonder why God did not make Adam and Eve so that they could not do wrong."

"This subject has puzzled older and wiser heads than yours, my son, and puzzled them more than I think it should. If we had been created incapable of sin, there could have been no virtue. Did you not feel happier yesterday after your trial, than if it had not happened?"

"O yes, father; and the strangest of all was, that after the first flash, I had not any bad feelings towards Tom."

"Then you can see, in your own case, good resulting from being free to do good or evil. You certainly were the better for your victory, and, you say, happier. It is far better to be virtuous than sinless—I mean, incapable of sin. If you subdue your temper, the exercise of the power to do this will give you a pleasure that you could not have had without it."

"But if I fail, father?" Wallace looked in his father's face with an expression which showed he felt that he had more than a kingdom to gain or lose.

"You cannot fail, my dear son, while you continue to feel the worth of the object for which you are striving; while you feel that the eye of God is upon you; and that, not only your own happiness, but the happiness of your father, and mother, and brothers, and sisters—of our *home,* depends on your success. . . . You have manifested a virtuous resolution; and you not only have my forgiveness, and my entire sympathy, but I trust you have the approbation of your Heavenly Father. Come, come along to your mother; take her happy kiss, and then to dinner. We have not had one right pleasant dinner since you have been up stairs."

"Stop one moment, father." Wallace lowered his voice as he modestly added, "I don't think I should have got through it alone, but every day I have prayed to God to help me."

"You have not been alone, my dear son," replied his father, much moved, "nor will you ever be left alone in your efforts to obey God; for, you remember, Jesus has said, 'If a man keep my words, my Father will love him, and we will come unto him and make our abode with him.' God, my son, is present in every dictate of your conscience, in every pure affection and holy emotion of your soul.". . .

The dinner-bell sounded, and Wallace was heard running down stairs before his mother, his heels as light as his heart. The children, jumping up behind and before him, shouted out his welcome. Grandmama wiped her eyes, and cleared her voice to say, "Dear me, Wally, how glad we all are to see you!" Even Aunt Betsey looked smiling, and satisfied, and unprovokable for an hour to come. . . .

The process was slow but sure. It required judgment, and gentleness, and, above all, patience on the part of the parents; but every inch of ground gained was kept. The children might not appear so orderly as they whose parents are like drill-sergeants, and who, while their eyes are on the fugelman, appear like little prodigies; but, deprived of external aid or restraint, the self-regulating machine shows its superiority.

THE SOVEREIGN PARENT

One parent should never allow a child to do what the other has forbidden; no expression of disapprobation concerning management should ever be made by either party, except when alone. A young child ought never to suspect it is possible for his parents to think differently concerning what relates to his education. . . . The child not being old enough to understand the reasons why his parents differ, cannot receive any good from the discussion. Implicit obedience is the first law of childhood. The simple belief that their parents know what is best, is all the light children have to follow, at first. If they see their parents do not agree between themselves as to what is right, it naturally weakens their confidence, and makes them uncertain which they ought to obey. . . . It is hardly possible to exaggerate the bad effects of discord between parents; and the blessed influence of domestic union may well be compared to a band of guardian angels protecting innocence from all evil things.

If your marriage has been an unfortunate one—if the influence of a father may not be trusted—or if he delights in thwarting your well-meant

Lydia M. Child, *The Mother's Book* (Boston, 1831), pp. 50–51.

endeavors—I know not what to say. If patience, humility and love cannot win him to a sense of duty, the only thing you can do, is to redouble your vigilance for the good of your children, and as far as possible withdraw them from his influence. Until it becomes an imperious duty, never speak of a parent's errors; unless there is great danger of their being imitated, let a thick veil rest upon them. But why should I dwell upon a case so unnatural, so wretched, and so hopeless? If such be your unhappy lot, pray to God, and he will give you light to make the path of duty clear before you. He alone can help you.

CHILDREN AT PLAY

There is a very sublime reason for the play state of childhood which respects the moral and religious well-being of manhood, and makes it important that we should have our first chapter of life in this key. Play is the symbol and interpreter of liberty, that is, Christian liberty; and no one could ever sufficiently conceive the state of free impulse and the joy there is in it, save by means of this unconstrained, always pleasurable activity, that we call the play of children. . . . One of the first duties of a genuinely Christian parent is, to show a generous sympathy with the plays of his children; providing playthings and means of play, giving them play-times, inviting suitable companions for them, and requiring them to have it as one of their pleasures, to keep such companions entertained in their plays, instead of playing always for their own mere self-pleasing. Sometimes, too, the parent, having a hearty interest in the plays of his children, will drop out for the time the sense of his years, and go into the frolic of their mood with them. They will enjoy no other play-time so much as that, and it will have the effect to make the authority, so far unbent, just as much stronger and more welcome, as it has brought itself closer to them, and given them a more complete show of sympathy. . . .

If . . . we can bear with adult Christians, who are much in the world, and, forgetting themselves often, fall into moods of real disinclination to their duty, are we to set it down as some total evidence against the piety of a child, that, by mere exuberance of life, he is occasionally hurried away from sacred things, into matters of play? Nothing is more unjust. Why should we require it of a child to be perfect, when we do not require it of a man? And if we tolerate inconstancy of feeling or impulse in one, why not a much less worldly and deliberate inconstancy in the other? . . .

Drawing the question to a closer point, suppose the child, having so many evidences of piety in his dispositions, to be found at some kind of play in the family prayers, or that he rushes out from such prayers, in a manner that indicates eagerness and an emancipated feeling, or that he sometimes shows uneasiness in the hours of public worship on Sunday,

Horace Bushnell, *Views of Christian Nurture* (Hartford, Conn., 1847), pp. 291–99.

or gives manifest tokens, in the morning, of a desire to escape from it, is it then to be set down, in your parental remonstrances with him, that he has, of course, no love to God, or the things of religion? By no means.

SCIENCE AND NURTURE

In order rightly to understand the true nature of that extraordinary activity which is so noticeable in all children that are in a state of health, so as to be able to deal with it on the right principles and in a proper manner, it is necessary to turn our attention somewhat carefully to certain scientific truths in respect to the nature and action of force in general which are now abundantly established, and which throw great light on the true charac-

Pictures like this for family use, which encouraged children to play piano or to draw rather than pray or meditate, became common only after the Civil War when "frivolity" was no longer so condemned. This charming scene of perfect parents at work shows the new "gentle measures" that could use childish curiosity and talent to good moral effect.   *American Antiquarian Society*

Jacob Abbott, *Gentle Measures in the Management and Training of the Young* (New York, 1871), pp. 151, 167–73.

ter of that peculiar form of it which is so characteristic of childhood, and is, indeed, so abundantly developed by the vital functions of almost all young animals. . . .

COMMON MISTAKE

We make a great mistake when we imagine that children are influenced in their activity mainly by a desire for the objects which they attain by it. It is not the ends attained, but the pleasurable feeling which the action of the internal force, issuing by its natural channels, affords them, and the sense of power which accompanies the action.

Parents very often do not understand this, and are accordingly continually asking such foolish questions as, "George, what do you wish to climb over that fence for, when there is a gate all open close by?". . .

The children, if they understood the philosophy of the case, might answer, "We don't climb over the fence at all because we wish to be on the other side of it; or scramble up the bank for the sake of any thing that is on the top of it; or run about to different places because we wish to be in the places particularly. It is the internal force that is in us working itself off, and it works itself off in the ways that come most readily to hand.". . .

The whole subject of the reception and the storing up of force from the sun by the processes of vegetable and animal life, and the subsequent liberation of it in the fulfillment of the various functions of the animal system, is full of difficulties and mysteries. It is only a very simple view of the *general principle* which is presented in these articles. . . . It will teach them, among other things, the following practical rules:

PRACTICAL RULES

1. Never find fault with children for their incapacity to keep still. You may stop the supply of force, if you will, by refusing to give them food; but if you continue the supply, you must not complain of its manifesting itself in action. After giving your boy his breakfast, to find fault with him for being incessantly in motion when his system has absorbed it, is simply to find fault with him for being healthy and happy. . . .

2. In encouraging the activity of children, and in guiding the direction of it in their hours of play, we must not expect to make it available for useful results, other than that of promoting their own physical development and health. At least, we can do this only in a very limited degree. . . . In the *child* the mode of action must change every few minutes. He is made tired with five minutes' labor. He is satisfied with five minutes' rest. . . . He is not to be blamed for this seeming capriciousness.

3. Parents at home and teachers at school must recognize these physiological laws, relating to the action of the young, and make their plans and arrangements conform to them. . . . What children call play, must be regarded not simply as an indulgence, but as a necessity for them. . . . The mothers of young children at home are often at a loss by what

means to effect this purpose, and many are very imperfectly aware of the desirableness, and even the necessity, of doing this. . . . It will, however, be a great point gained for her when she once fully comprehends that the *tendency* to incessant activity, and even to turbulence and noise, on the part of her child, only shows that he is all right in his vital machinery, and that this exuberance of energy is something to be pleased with and directed, not denounced and restrained.

CHILDREN'S RIGHTS

It is the age of independent criticism. The child problem is merely one phase of the universal problem that confronts society. It seems likely that the rod of reason will have to replace the rod of birch. Parental authority never used to be called into question; neither was the catechism, nor the Bible, nor the minister. How should parents hope to escape the universal interrogation point leveled at everything else? In these days of free speech it is hopeless to suppose that even infants can be muzzled. We revel in our republican virtues; let us accept the vices of those virtues as philosophically as possible. . . .

The mother who is most apt to infringe on the rights of her child (of course with the best intentions) is the "firm" person, afflicted with the "lust of dominion." There is no elasticity in her firmness to prevent it from degenerating into obstinacy. It is not the firmness of the tree that bends without breaking, but the firmness of a certain long-eared animal whose force of character has impressed itself on the common mind and become proverbial. . . .

We must not expect children to be too good; not any better than we ourselves, for example; no, nor even as good. Beware of hothouse virtue.

CHILDHOOD IDEALIZED

The Children's Hour

Between the dark and the daylight,
    When the night is beginning to lower,
Comes a pause in the day's occupations,
    That is known as the Children's Hour.

I hear in the chamber above me
    The patter of little feet,
The sound of a door that is opened,
    And voices soft and sweet.

Kate Douglas Wiggin, *Children's Rights* (Boston, 1892), pp. 19–21.
Henry Wadsworth Longfellow, "The Children's Hour," *The Complete Poetical Works of Henry Wadsworth Longfellow* (Boston, 1922), pp. 255–56.

From my study I see in the lamplight,
    Descending the broad hall stair,
Grave Alice, and laughing Allegra,
    And Edith with golden hair.

A whisper, and then a silence:
    Yet I know by their merry eyes
They are plotting and planning together
    To take me by surprise.

A sudden rush from the stairway,
    A sudden raid from the hall!
By three doors left unguarded
    They enter my castle wall!

They climb up into my turret
    O'er the arms and back of my chair;
If I try to escape, they surround me;
    They seem to be everywhere.

They almost devour me with kisses,
    Their arms about me entwine,
Till I think of the Bishop of Bingen
    In his Mouse-Tower on the Rhine!

Do you think, O blue-eyed banditti,
    Because you have scaled the wall.
Such an old mustache as I am
    Is not a match for you all!

I have you fast in my fortress,
    And will not let you depart,
But put you down into the dungeon
    In the round-tower of my heart.

And there will I keep you forever,
    Yes, forever and a day,
Till the walls shall crumble to ruin,
    And moulder in dust away!

THE BLACK FAMILY UNDER SLAVERY AND AFTER

Most enslaved Afro-Americans—like most free Americans of the nineteenth century—lived in separate families centered around monogamous couples. But the slaves lived under conditions no other Americans faced. They were property and could be bought and sold, seized in payment of a master's debts, transferred and inherited. This single fact meant that whatever surface or deeper similarities slave families might have had to the families of free whites, they were nonetheless different, though it is still unclear just what kind of family order the slaves did create. (Some contemporary writers, as well as more recent scholars, using the bourgeois family as the model, have argued that the slaves' family condition was pathological if their families even existed.) There was the continuing threat and frequent fact of separation by sale or inheritance. In addition, husbands and wives often belonged to different owners and lived apart, meeting whenever the husband had a "pass" to visit his wife. Slavery established particular constraints and mores surrounding pre- and post-marital sexuality, and it profoundly affected the work and familial roles of men and women. Finally, there was the master's ultimate authority and power, his all but unchecked ability to intervene in slave families in ways that disrupted the relationships between husbands and wives and parents and children. Although slave children were partly under the supervision of parents or other kin, they nonetheless were the possession of the master, whose needs and will could always supersede that of any parent.

Both masters and slaves attached great importance to marriage and stable families—though for very different reasons. The "good" master encouraged marriage among his slaves out of a combination of motives. (Actual treatment varied enormously, ranging from sadistic brutality to benevolent kindness.) Subscribing fully to general domestic ideals and a special brand of paternalism, he was concerned about the well-being and happiness of his "slave family" and probably felt some responsibility to "civilize" those he thought of as members of a heathen and inferior race. The family was also considered a mechanism of control; slaves in the family state, the argument went, were less "wild," more content, and thus better workers and, because of their ties to their families, less likely to run away. The slaves put rather different stock in their familial order and looked to it as a cushion against the conditions of slavery. Several recent studies, in fact, have shown that the slave family—extending across time and space and incorporating a vast array of real and "fictive" kin—provided slaves with a supportive and protective community. Along with slave religion, it

The photographic record of nineteenth-century slaves, especially in the rural South, is sparse. An extremely rare and early photograph is this portrait of five generations of a recently emancipated black family from the Smith plantation near Beaufort, South Carolina, circa 1864. Like family portraits of other groups, it both records its subject and intrudes upon it, producing a self-conscious and possibly idealized image of the family as its members and perhaps the photographer want it to be captured on film.

Library of Congress

often gave the slaves the psychological and cultural space they needed to preserve their sense of identity and self-esteem.

But no matter how much slaves or masters might cherish them, slave families had little standing or protection in law, as the first two documents reveal. Taken from North Carolina and Kentucky court decisions, they suggest some of the problems raised by the slave family's virtual legal nonexistence.

The second set of documents represents some of the kinds of material that do exist about slave family life. There are a few letters from slaves concerning the breakup of their families; an 1863 interview by a federal commission of Robert Smalls, as escaped slave; interviews with elderly former slaves conducted as a WPA project in the 1930s; and letters from Lucy Chase, a New England missionary who went in 1863 to the Sea Islands off the Georgia and South Carolina coasts to work with the freed slaves. All these sources pose special problems beyond those that any historical document would present. The WPA narratives are recollections of people in their eighties and nineties whose memories are filtered through decades of subsequent black-white experience. The documents containing the words of slaves themselves were mostly produced in the presence or through the intercession of masters and whites. Under these circumstances, blacks usually took care to reveal only those things about themselves that they wanted to reveal and often told the master and white man only what they wanted to hear. ("Puttin' on old massa" it was called.). Moreover, most whites, whether Southerners who were surrounded by slaves or Northerners sympathetic to the "plight of the African," filtered their perceptions and questions about slave behavior and mores through firmly held cultural images and racial stereotypes. They saw slaves as an exotic and somewhat mysterious people, mired by race or condition in sensuality and superstition, and they judged slave family "feelings" and behavior against the ideas of virtue, purity, and discipline embedded in the cult of domesticity.

Problematic as such sources are, they reveal a good deal about the looming presence of the master's power over his property as well as the strength of the slaves' familial ideals and ties and the resiliency of the family even under conditions of servitude.

Other documents in this section suggest something of the role that ideas of the family played in the bitter controversy over slavery. Beginning in the early 1830s, abolitionists mounted a vehement attack against slavery as the most heinous of sins and demanded its end. Soon their onslaught against the "peculiar" institution inspired an equally impassioned defense of it. Both sides employed in their arsenal of arguments the images and values of the cult of the home. Abolitionist tracts and the atrocity-filled narratives of ex-slaves featured the breakup of slave families on the auction block and condemned slavery as a "system of universal concubinage," which trammeled the marriage bond and reduced the female slave to the helpless victim of her master's lust. The defenders of slavery, on the other hand, portrayed the plantation as one vast family in which the childlike, ignorant, and dependent blacks found care and protection under the kindly paternalism of "massa" and the Christian benevolence of his wife.

The next selection is from Harriet Beecher Stowe's *Uncle Tom's Cabin.* Far and away the most effective piece of antislavery literature, the novel was as much an expression of the cult of domesticity as it was a product of the antislavery impulse. Marshaling the conventions of sentimental and domestic fiction—death and separation, maternal love and sacrifice—Mrs. Stowe, much like Alex Haley later in *Roots,* centered her novel on what the institution did to slaves as family members. She portrayed the slaves, not as abstract victims or members of an alien and different race and culture but as husbands and wives and mothers and fathers whose suffering, love, and concern for each other and their children was identical to that of the white mothers and fathers to whom she addressed the novel.

The selection by George Fitzhugh (1806–81), a Virginia lawyer who was the most intellectually rigorous of the proslavery apologists, employs familial ideas as part of the general argument that the "chattel" slaves of the South were better off than the "wage" slaves of northern and European factories.

Transition from slavery to freedom removed the threat of forced separation from most black families and provided black marriages with legal standing. In the first three years following the close of the Civil War, tens of thousands of black men and women rushed to give legal sanction and protection to the marriages they had made under slavery. But emancipation opened few lasting opportunities to the freedmen, and for the rest of the century and after they faced the unrelenting and largely successful attempt of white society to defeat their efforts to secure at least the white level of economic gains and civil rights that freedom was supposed to mean. Throughout the later parts of the century the vast majority of the blacks continued as agricultural laborers for white planters, comprising a kind of black peasantry made up of tenant farmers and sharecroppers.

At the same time, a group of black craftsmen, artisans, small businessmen, educators, and preachers did emerge to lead the drive for what was widely refered to as "race progress." The final document here is an 1882 address by Alexander Crummell, a minister and black spokesman in Washington, D.C. He extolled black pride and self-help before one of the mission societies set up to aid the freedmen and reflects two dimensions of the black experience after emancipation. Crummell's piece is at once a description of the families of the black peasantry and a rallying cry in the campaign for black self-improvement. In his attitude toward those he describes and in the familial virtues and models he extols, Crummell raises questions about the reach of the familial ideals of the dominant white culture and about the extent to which class and race fostered different familial forms and perceptions. In this respect, it might be useful to compare Crummell's view of the black peasantry with Lucy Chase's views of blacks (p. 323) and with the way middle-class reformers like Loring Brace (p. 383) or Jacob Riis (p. 402) perceived the "other half."

SLAVE CHILDREN IN COURT

A man and female slave intermarried, with the consent of the owners, in the form usual among slaves; afterwards, the male slave was emancipated, and purchased his wife; they then had born to them one child; the female slave was then emancipated, and, still living as man and wife, but without any further ceremony passing between them, they had several other children; it *was Held* that neither the first nor the others of these children were legitimate; so as to take as tenants in common with legitimate children of the father by a second marriage.

PEARSON, C. J.   A slave, being property, has not the legal capacity to make a contract, and is not entitled to the rights or subjected to the liabilities incident thereto. He is amenable to the criminal law, and his person (to a certain extent) and his life, are protected. This, however, is not a concession to him of civil rights, but is in vindication of public justice, and for the prevention of public wrongs. Marriage is based upon contract; consequently the relation of "man and wife" cannot exist among slaves. It is excluded, both on account of their incapacity to contract, and of the paramount right of ownership in them, as property. This subject is discussed in *State* v. *Samuel*, where it is held, that a slave is a competent witness for or against another slave, towards whom she sustained the relation of wife, in a certain sense of the term, on the ground that the relation was not that of "man and wife" in its legal sense, and did not embrace any of the civil rights incident to marriage.

In *Alvaney* v. *Powell*, it is held where a mother and children are emancipated, a child begotten and born while the mother had no husband, was entitled to the same share of her estate, as the children who were begotten and born while she had a husband; on the ground "that in regard to slaves, even after they become free negroes, there is no necessity growing out of grave consideration of public policy, for the adoption of the stern rule of the common law." A bastard shall be deemed *nullius filius;* to have no parents, and not even be considered the child of the mother who gave it birth; and in contemplation of law there is no difference between the case of slaves who enter into the qualified relations of "man and wife" by the express permission of their owners, and that of those who "take up" with each other, from a mere impulse of nature, in obedience to the command, "multiply and replenish the earth," for the law does not recognise either relation so as to give to it any effect in respect to civil consequences. On the other hand, there is in moral contemplation, and in the nature of man, a wide distinction between the cohabitation of slaves, as "man and wife," and an indiscriminate sexual intercourse; it is recognized among slaves, for as a general rule, they respect the exclusive rights of fellow slaves who are married. Such marriages are permitted and encouraged by owners, as well in consideration of the happiness of the slaves and

Howard v. *Howard, 51 North Carolina* (Dec. 1858), pp. 235–40.

their children, as because, in many ways, their interests, as masters, is thereby promoted. Hence a married couple is permitted to have a "cabin and a patch off to themselves," and where they belong to different persons, the man, at stated times, is allowed "to go to his wife's house." The relation is so far favored in the administration of the criminal law, as to allow to it the effect of drawing into application the rule, that when a person finds one in the act of adultery with his wife, and instantly kills him, it is but manslaughter, because of the legal provocation. This result, however, is not attributable to any civil right, growing out of the relation, but to the fact that, to a certain extent, it has its origin in nature; and a violation of the right which is peculiar to it, in that respect, excites the *furor brevis,* whether the relation was entered into with or without the legal capacity, and the ceremonies and forms necessary to make a marriage valid for civil purposes. . . .

Thus far the line is established by these three cases. We are now to run further, and fix another landmark. In *Alvaney* v. *Powell, supra,* the Court was not called on to decide whether the children, after being emancipated with their mother, were to be considered as legitimate, or illegitimate; the purpose of the case being answered by holding that they all stand on the same footing; because, in either view, they were entitled to succeed to their mother and to each other, both, according to our laws, and the laws of Canada. Nor are we now at liberty to decide it, because the facts of this case do not present it. Both parents were slaves when the relation was entered into. Afterwards, the father was emancipated, and bought the mother, and *held her as his slave,* at the birth of the lessor, Frances. This presents a question, in many respects, different from that of the *status* of a child born while both parents were slaves, and lived together as man and wife; for the relation of master and slave is wholly incompatible with even the qualified relation of husband and wife, as it is supposed to exist among slaves, and the idea that a husband may own his wife as property and sell her, if he chooses, or that a parent may own his children and sell or give them away as chattels, and that the wife or the children, are, nevertheless, entitled to any of the civil rights incident to those relations, involves, a legal absurdity. The relations are repugnant; and as that of master and slave is fixed and recognised by law, the other cannot exist; and it follows that the lessor, Frances, does not take as one of the heirs of her father.

The other lessors are in a condition still more unfortunate; for, while relieved from the incongruity, which is involved in the case of their sisters, but the fact, that their mother, at the time of their birth, was free, yet, that circumstance caused them to be unlawfully begotten. Their parents, having become free persons, were guilty of a misdemeanor in living together as man and wife, without being married, as the law required; so that, there is nothing to save them from the imputation of being "bastards."

Our attention was called by *Mr. Moore* to *Girod* v. *Lewis,* where it is held that, "a contract of marriage, legal and valid by the consent of the master and moral assent of the slave, from the moment of freedom, although dormant during the slavery, produces all the effects which result from such contracts among free persons." No authority is cited, and no reason is given for the decision, except the suggestion that the marriage, being dormant during the slavery, is endowed with full energy from the moment of freedom. We are forced to the conclusion, that the idea of civil rights being merely *dormant* during slavery, is rather a fanciful conceit, (we say it with respect) than the ground of a sound argument. It may be, that in Louisiana, the marriage relation is greatly affected by the influence of religion, and the mystery of its supposed dormant rights, is attributable to its divine origin. If so, the case has no application, for, in our courts, marriage is treated as a mere civil institution.

To the suggestion, that as the qualified relation of husband and wife between slaves is *not unlawful,* and ought, in fact, to be encouraged, upon the ground of public policy, so far as it comports with a right of property, emancipation should be allowed to have the effect of curing any defect arising from the non-observance of the prescribed form and ceremonies, and the absence of a capacity to contract, as there is plenary proof of consent, which forms the essence of the marriage relation; the reply is:

The relation between slaves is essentially different from that of man and wife joined in lawful wedlock. The latter is indissoluble during the lives of the parties, and its violation is a high crime; but with slaves it may be dissolved at the pleasure of either party, or by a sale of one or both, dependant on the caprice or necessity of the owners. So the union is formed, and the consent given in reference to this state of things, and no ground can be conceived of, upon which the fact of emancipation can, not only draw after it the qualified relation, but by a sort of magic, convert it into a relation of so different a nature. In our case, the emancipation of the father could not draw after it the prior relation, because the mother was not then free, and, in fact, afterwards became his slave. So the relation was not connected with the *status* of the parties in a way to follow as an incident. Suppose, after being free, the father had married another woman, could he have been convicted of bigamy, on the ground that a woman, who was his slave, was his wife? Or, after both were freed, would the penalty of the law have attached, if either had married a third person, living the other? Certainly not; because the averment of a prior, lawful marriage could not be supported, and yet, if the marriage followed the emancipation as an incident, it would present an instance of a marriage relation, which either is at liberty to dissolve at pleasure.

A SLAVE MARRIAGE IN COURT

Chief Justice WHEAT delivered the opinion of the court. . . .

Stephen and Cynthia Kyler filed their petition in equity against Dunlap and Arnold, and obtained an injunction inhibiting the sale of Cynthia under

Kyler v. *Dunlap,* 18 B Monroe (Kentucky) (Dec. 1857), pp. 561–69.

the executions. The petition averred, in substance, that one Joseph Kyler, who had once owned Stephen, and manumitted him, purchased Cynthia because she was the wife of Stephen, and being desirous to secure to Cynthia her freedom after his death, consulted a lawyer on the subject of emancipating Cynthia, who was unwilling to leave this State, and having been advised by the lawyer that under the existing constitution of Kentucky Cynthia could not be emancipated and remain in this state; and the lawyer having advised Joseph Kyler that the only way he could secure Cynthia to Stephen for a wife, whilst she remained in Kentucky, was to make a bill of sale or deed conveying her to Stephen to be held by him as a wife.

A deed expressing a nominal consideration, was executed by Joseph Kyler to Stephen Kyler, conveying Cynthia to Stephen in fee, after reserving a life estate to Cynthia in the grantor, and the deed was regularly recorded in the office of the clerk of the Garrard county court. The deed contains a clause stipulating for a warranty, by the grantor, to Stephen against all claims to Cynthia.

Dunlap and Arnold answered the petition, justifying the levy of the executions on Cynthia, and attested that she was subject to Stephen's debts, and denying that it was the intention of the grantor, Kyler, to place Cynthia under the plaintiff, Stephen, as a wife merely, and not as property; that Stephen did not merely take a naked title to Cynthia upon trade recognizing the right to freedom in her, or the enjoyment of the rights of a free woman. They also state that Stephen held her as property, upon the lease of the deed of gift, which he had accepted.

We do not deem it necessary to examine or comment upon all the grounds assumed by the counsel of Stephen and Cynthia, as we apprehend the claim to her exemption from the debts mentioned in the executions levied upon her must turn upon the effect of the deed from Joseph Kyler to Stephen.

We remark, that the deed is an absolute one upon its face, and passed the title in Cynthia to Stephen and by the laws of Kentucky slaves are subject to execution for the debts of their owner, just as any other personal property is subject.

To exempt Cynthia from this category it is insisted that she was held by Stephen not as property, but as a wife merely, under a trust created by parol at the time the deed was made. It is also insisted that it is legal for Stephen to hold his wife by virtue of the 6*th section of article* 1, *chapter* 93, *title slaves, &c., Revised Statutes, page* 628. That section is in these words: "No free negro shall be capable of acquiring, in fee, or holding or owning for any length of time, as hirer, or otherwise, any slave, other than the husband, wife, parent, or descendant of such free negro."

This section evidently was never intended to protect slave property from execution; it only permits free negroes to have an interest and property in certain relatives, but expressly prohibits them from acquiring in fee, holding, or owning, for any length of time as hirer or otherwise, any slave, other than the husband, wife, parent, or descendant of such free negro.

Article 10, *section* 1, *of the Constitution of Kentucky,* speaking of the general assembly, among other things says, "they shall pass laws to permit owners of slaves to emancipate them, saving the rights of creditors, and to prevent them from *remaining in this state after they are emancipated.*". . . These extracts . . . show that Cynthia has not been emancipated according to the laws of this state, and that any attempt to do so, by a pretended sale of her to her husband, to be held by him only as his wife, is a mere attempt to evade the statutes of this commonwealth on the subject of free negroes, and obviously at war with the policy of the laws of this commonwealth. . . .

That Cynthia is a slave we have no doubt whatever, and there is a little room to doubt that Stephen took the absolute fee simple title to her as property, and as his slave by the deed referred to in the pleadings of the parties. The deed is absolute on its face, and conveys the fee simple title to Cynthia, reserving the use of her to the grantor for life.

We have seen that Cynthia is a slave, and although the laws of this state give a recognition to marriages between free negroes, yet marriages between free negroes and slaves is not recognized but to very limited extent.

It is now contended by Stephen and Cynthia, that Cynthia, if a slave, was not subject to execution emanating from the office of a justice of the peace. By our statutes slaves are declared personal property, and we know of no provision in any statute which prohibits a constable from levying an execution upon and selling slaves.

"DEAR MASTER": LETTERS FROM SLAVES

Jones Borough Nov^{br} 16 1834

Dr Master

Your Servant James trobles you with this scrap the object of which is to inform you that your Servant Jim together with his fellow Servants are all well except two of the women who have been lately been confined. The . . . grand & principal object is to get Master to be so kind as to inquire about my Sister Francis and request my Sister to inform me her Situation how many children she has where she is living with her husband is living with and in fine how she is getting a long in the world also wither my father is living or dead & if dead how long since his decease and wither Dear Hope my cozen she used to work about town a Taylors is still living in town and how she is & wither my old godfather Robin Edmonson is still alive if you should see Anthony my cozen please remember me to him and his family your servant James is also desirous of returning to his place of Nativity and if you (Master) should return in the spring if you will be so kind to your servant as to order him sent on your servant

Mrs. George P. Colman, ed., *Virginia Silhouette: Contemporary Letters Concerning Negro Slaves in the State of Virginia* (Richmond, 1934), pp. 35–40. Reprinted by permission of The Dietz Press, Inc.

will ever reverence and obey his master your James wishes you to read this to his old ecquantance to all of which he wishes to be remembered and particularly Gaberil Toney Benjamin King your Servant James also would inform his master that he together with his fallow Servants are getting along peacible and in a way that he hopes will afford Master pleasure when he may see cause to return to Missori

if Master cannot make it convenient to see my sister he will oblige his Jim by Inclosing this to my sister and as she will see the principal object of this has been to inquire after I hope she answer my inquiries herself

from you obt Servant

James Hope

St. Louis, Oct. 24th 1842

Dear Master—

We, two of your humble Servants have come to the conclusion to write you a few lines upon a subject that has given us much pain, which will be more keenly felt if you will not grant their humble request. We hope and pray that you will not think hard of us in so doing, as we are in much distress, and write the very feelings of our hearts.

About two weeks ago M[r] Jones, a neighbour of M[r] Bundlett in Texas, called with a letter from M[r] Bundlett saying that we must come on with M[r] Jones. As we had been here a long time and had become much attached to the place (our Husbands being here) and as we hated the idea of going to Texas, M[r] Jones was kind enough to let us remain till March, before which time he expected to hear from you on the subject. Our object in writing dear Master is this: We can't bear to go to Texas with a parcel of strangers—if you were there we should go without saying a word, but to be separated from our husbands forever in this world would make us unhappy for life. We have a great many friends in this place and would rather be sold than go to Texas.

In making this request, dear Master, we do not do it through any disrespect (for you have always been kind to us) but merely because we shall be happier here with our friends and Husbands. We don't think there will be the least difficulty in getting ourselves sold, together with our children from whom we hope you will not separate us. Ersey has six children, the youngest of which is about six weeks old, a fine little Girl. Susan has two Boys, the eldest nearly three years old, and the youngest eight months. We hope dear Master and Mistress that you will not let us go to Texas, but grant us our humble petition. We are both well, also our children. If you conclude to sell us, please write to any one of the following gentlemen, with your terms, with whom you are acquainted. Edward Bates, Andrew Elliott, R. H. Graham or W[m] G. Pettus Remember us kindly to Mistress and her children and the Servants & children.

Yours truly

Susan (Sukey)

& Ersey

SLAVE FAMILY CUSTOMS

Q: What generally in the City leads a man to take a wife among the colored people?

A: I will tell you what made me get a wife. My idea was to have a wife to prevent me running around—to have somebody to do for me and to keep me. The colored men in taking wives always do so with reference to the service the women will render.

Q: Do the colored men fall in love very often?

A: No, sir; I think not.

Q: How do the colored men regard the marriage relation—as taken upon themselves for their whole life?

A: Yes, sir; if a woman loses her husband she mourns for him and will not marry again for a year and a half, unless she is driven to it by want, and must have somebody to help her.

Q: Suppose a man takes a wife and finds that she is ill-tempered and will not help him;—that she is lazy and idle—does he not consider himself privileged to change her? . . .

A: Not among the City people. With them you hardly ever find a husband will separate from his wife except he finds her going with another man. In that case he goes to his wife's master and complains and the two masters make a separation.

Q: In relation to that matter of a woman going with another man—how is that? does it occur frequently?

A: No, sir; it never happens unless a woman stands in actual need and she does this to help herself. Sometimes a woman gets a lazy man.

Q: Have not colored women a good deal of sexual passion?

A: Yes, sir.

Q: Are they not carried away by their passion to have intercourse with men?

A: Yes, sir; but very few lawful married women are carried away if their husbands can take care of them.

Q: How is it with the young women?

A: They are very wild and run around a great deal.

Q: What proportion of the young women do not have sexual intercourse before marriage?

"American Freedman's Inquiry Commission Interviews" (Washington, 1863), printed in John Blassingame, *Slave Testimony* (Baton Rouge, 1977), pp. 374–77.

A: The majority do, but they do not consider this intercourse an evil thing. This intercourse is principally with white men with whom they would rather have intercourse than with their own color.

Q: Do they do this for money?

A: The majority of the young girls will for money.

Q: At what age do the colored girls begin to have intercourse with white men?

A: I have known them to as young as twelve years.

Q: What proportion of the colored girls join the Church?

A: Most all the girls join the Church. Generally between 15 and 16 years of age they go through a certain probation and are admitted as members. No matter how bad a girl may have been as soon as she joins the Church she is made respectable.

Q: Does this joining the Church make a difference in their conduct?

A: Yes, sir; the change is very great—as great as between the sunshine and a hail-storm. She stops all this promiscuous intercourse with men. The rules of the Church are strict about it.

Q: In relation to the obedience of a child for his parents—does a colored child feel bound to obey his parents?

A: Yes, sir; they are very strict about that.

Q: Which parent do they regard the most?

A: The mother; they would be inclined to obey the mother.

Q: Do they have much affection for each other—the different members of a family?

A: Yes, sir; their love is strong. The country people regard their relations more than city people; they often walk fifteen miles on Saturday night to see a cousin.

Q: When they say "parents," what do they mean by the word?

A: They mean relations in general; the same that they mean when they say "family."

SLAVE NARRATIVE

Massa Hawkins am good to he niggers and not force 'em work too hard. Dere am as much diff'ence 'tween him and old Massa Black in de way of treatment as 'twixt de Lawd and de devil. Massa Hawkins 'lows he niggers have reason'ble parties and go fishin', but we'uns am never tooken to church and has no books for larnin'. Dere am no edumcation for de niggers.

Slave Narrative Collection, Federal Writers' Project (Washington, D.C., 1936), *Texas Narratives,* pt. 4, pp. 174–78.

Dere am one thing Massa Hawkins does to me what I can't shunt from my mind. I knows he don't do it for meanness, but I allus holds it 'gainst him. What he done am force me to live with dat nigger, Rufus, 'gainst my wants.

After I been at he place 'bout a year, de massa come to me and say, "You gwine live with Rufus in dat cabin over yonder. Go fix it for livin'." I's 'bout sixteen year old and has no larnin', and I's jus' igno'mus chile. I's thought dat him mean for me to tend de cabin for Rufus and some other niggers. Well, dat am start de pestigation for me.

I's took charge of de cabin after work am done and fixes supper. Now, I don't like dat Rufus, 'cause he a bully. He am big and 'cause he so, he think everybody do what him say. We'uns has supper, den I goes here and dere talkin', till I's ready for sleep and den I gits in de bunk. After I's in, dat nigger come and crawl in de bunk with me 'fore I knows it. I says, "What you means, you fool nigger?" He say for me to hush de mouth. "Dis am my bunk, too," he say.

"You's teched in de head. Git out," I's told him, and I puts de feet 'gainst him and give him a shove and out he go on de floor 'fore he know what I's doin'. Dat nigger jump up and he mad. He look like de wild bear. He starts for de bunk and I jumps quick for de poker. It am 'bout three feet long and when he comes at me I lets him have it over de head. Did dat nigger stop in he tracks? I's say he did. He looks at me steady for a minute and you's could tell he thinkin' hard. Den he go and set on de bench and say, "Jus wait. You thinks it am smart, but you's am foolish in de head. Dey's gwine larn you somethin'."

"Hush yous big mouth and stay 'way from dis nigger, dat all I wants," I say, and jus' sets and hold dat poker in de hand. He jus' sets, lookin' like de bull. Dere we'uns sets and sets for 'bout an hour and den he go out and I bars de door.

De nex' day I goes to de missy and tells her what Rufus wants and missy say dat am de massa's wishes. She say, "Yous am de portly gal and Rufus am de portly man. De massa wants you-uns fer to bring forth portly chillen."

I's thinkin' 'bout what de missy say, but say to myse'f, "I's not gwine live with dat Rufus." Dat night when him come in de cabin, I grabs de poker and sits on de bench and says, "Git 'way from me, nigger, 'fore I busts yous brains out and stomp on dem." He say nothin' and git out.

De nex' day de massa call me and tell me, "Woman, I's pay big money for you and I's done dat for de cause I wants yous to raise me chillens. I's put yous to live with Rufus for dat purpose. Now, if you doesn't want whippin' at de stake, yous do what I wants."

I thinks 'bout massa buyin' me offen de block and savin' me from bein' sep'rated from my folks and 'bout bein' whipped at de stake. Dere it am. What am I's to do? So I 'cides to do as de massa wish and so I yields.

When we'uns am given freedom, Massa Hawkins tells us we can stay and work for wages or share crop de land. Some stays and some goes. My folks and me stays. We works de land on shares for three years, den moved to other land near by. I stays with my folks till they dies. . . .

I never marries, 'cause one 'sperience am 'nough for dis nigger. After what I does for de massa, I's never wants no truck with any man. De Lawd forgive dis cullud woman, but he have to 'scuse me and look for some others for to 'plenish de earth.

FAMILY TIES, SLAVE AND FREE

March 4, 1864

Our young Ary, one of our clothing-room assistants, pines for a young child she was forced to leave behind her when she ran away and which died, soon after she left it. She looked long, and fondly, one day, at a child's skirt, saying, "Once that belonged to some dear little baby." She told us her story, one day. "Young Master was the father of my baby, and he was very fond of it. He made me dress it clean, three times a day, and he was never tired of playing with it and calling it pet names. One day the nurse put it in a tub of water and got a grit in its eye, and I thought he'd go mad about it. We always played together from the time we were little children. Old Master was the richest man in Virginia. He's all outdoors secesh. His sons were Union and Anti-Slavery. Oh, how he would quarrel with them, and swear to them! He'd make his daughters kiss the bible, every morning, and say they would not give anyone a rasher of meat. I've seen ten cargoes of negroes sold on his plantation, at once. They came and tied young Master's hands and feet together, and took him off to the war. He used to write to me, and a young lady who was in love with his brother used to read me his letters." "Did your Master's sisters know how intimate you were with him?" I asked. "Oh, yes, indeed," she said, "and they were all as fond of me as he was, and of the baby too. The baby was very white, and looked just like him. When the cavalry came and took off young Master's brother, I had gone to the point, four miles, and got a woman to mind my baby while I was gone. Master's brother rode up to me and said, 'Don't go back Ary—I'll take charge of the child. It shall go to my house, hurry to the Union Army.' And the next thing I knew, in four weeks, the baby's father wrote me that baby had died. He said I must not grieve, that it was a great deal better off now than it would be with me. That he should try very hard to get to the Union, but he was afraid he could not. That if I found any-body I loved, I must marry him, and try to be happy. He used to say he should go mad if I left him. He always stood up for the North, and found fault with the South. His

H. L. Swint, ed., *Dear Ones at Home: Letters from the Contraband Camps* (Nashville, 1966), pp. 55–56, 121–22, 242–43. Reprinted by permission of Vanderbilt University Press.

mother came from the North. O, baby could walk, and could say almost any-thing. He would not let me have any-thing to do with colored men; he said they weren't good enough for me. He was my cousin, and he named the baby for his uncle."

July 1, 1864

The positive influence for good that emanates from the zealous friends who have made their home in Sabletown is marked in its results upon the reverential, receptive people. It seems like a well-regulated realm there. Forty couples, over whom "The Matrimonial" had never "been read," because no state law could make it binding, were married in the church, while we were there, and were feasted at the Mission-house with huge slices of rich, frosted wedding cake, and lemonade without stint. The Superintendent of Contrabands united with one of the energetic teachers in compelling all living as man and wife to take the choice of separation or marriage. Many unwillingly assented to marriage, while others indicate a full appreciation of the necessity, propriety, and dignity of the ceremony. It was a strangely picturesque and impressive sight to see, in the twilight, the neatly dressed couples, moving from their various quarters and drawing near our doorway. Old men and women, hand in hand, coming up to their "bridal." "Take her by the hand," one old man said as he led his wife forward. Everyone had an air of serious modest reserve. Some were young enough to blush, and all seemed to say, "This is our marriage day." After the ceremonies in the church, the newly married were invited to the house, where the great cakes were cut for them and the air was sweetened by the magnolias and brilliantly illuminated by the kerosene. Our good friends anticipate immediate and wholesome results from the occasion. The colored people easily assume the responsibilities, proprieties, and graces of civilized life. As a class, their tastes are comely, though they are acquainted with filth. I fancy they see the moral significance of things quite as readily as white people. Eighty other applicants urged their claim to enter the pale too late to make preparations for them, but in a week they will promise faithfulness to each other and each will have a gift of a candle in its stick. The candle will be lighted that it may shine on their new way.

1869

I don't know whether I have told you Laura Spicer's story. She was sold from her husband some years ago, and he, hearing she was dead, married again. He has had a wavering inclination to again unite his fortunes with hers; and she has been persistent in urging him to do so. A few days ago she received a letter from him in which he said, "I read your letters over and over again. I keep them always in my pocket. If you are married I don't ever want to see you again." And yet, in some of his letters, he says, "I would much rather you would get married to some good man, for every time I gits a letter from you it tears me all to pieces.

The reason why I have not written you before, in a long time, is because your letters disturbed me so very much. You know I love my children. I treats them good as a Father can treat his children; and I do a good deal of it for you. I was very sorry to hear that Lewellyn, my poor little son, have had such bad health. I would come and see you but I know you could not bear it. I want to see you and I don't want to see you. I love you just as well as I did the last day I saw you, and it will not do for you and I to meet. I am married, and my wife have two children, and if you and I meets it would make a very dissatisfied family."

Some of the children are with the mother, and the father writes, "Send me some of the children's hair in a separate paper with their names on the paper. Will you please git married, as long as I am married. My dear, you know the Lord know both of our hearts. You know it never was our wishes to be separated from each other, and it never was our fault. Oh, I can see you so plain, at any-time, I had rather anything to had happened to me most that ever have been parted from you and the children. As I am, I do not know which I love best, you or Anna. If I was to die, today or tomorrow, I do not think I would die satisfied till you tell me you will try and marry some good, smart man that will take good care of you and the children; and do it because you love me; and not because I think more of the wife I have got than I do of you. The woman is not born that feels as near to me as you do. You feel this day like myself. Tell them they must remember they have a good father and one that cares for them and one that thinks about them every day—My very heart did ache when reading your very kind and interesting letter. Laura I do not think that I have change any at all since I saw you last.—I thinks of you and my children every day of my life. Laura I do love you the same. My love to you *never* have failed. Laura, truly, I have got another wife, and I am very sorry, that I am. You feels and seems to me as much like my dear loving wife, as you ever did Laura. You know my treatment to a wife and you know how I am about my children. You know I am one man that do love my children. You will please make a [one word illegible] of the thing."

UNCLE TOM'S CABIN

Mrs. Bird was a timid, blushing little woman, of about four feet in height, and with mild blue eyes, and a peach-blow complexion, and the gentlest, sweetest voice in the world; as for courage, a moderate-sized cock-turkey had been known to put her to rout at the very first gobble, and a stout house-dog, of moderate capacity, would bring her into subjection merely by a show of his teeth. Her husband and children were her entire world, and in these she ruled more by entreaty and persuasion than by command

Harriet Beecher Stowe, *Uncle Tom's Cabin* (New York and Boston, n.d.), pp. 66–74.

or argument. There was only one thing that was capable of arousing her, and that provocation came in on the side of her unusually gentle and sympathetic nature; anything in the shape of cruelty would throw her into a passion, which was the more alarming and inexplicable in proportion to the general softness of her nature. Generally the most indulgent and easy to be entreated of all mothers, still her boys had a very reverent remembrance of a most vehement chastisement she once bestowed on them, because she found them leagued with several graceless boys of the neighborhood, stoning a defenseless kitten. . . .

On the present occasion, Mrs. Bird rose quickly with very red cheeks, which quite improved her general appearance, and walked up to her husband, with quite a resolute air, and said in a determined tone:

"Now, John, I want to know if you think such a law as that is right and Christian?"

"You won't shoot me, now, Mary, if I say I do!"

"I never could have thought it of you, John; you didn't vote for it?"

"Even so, my fair politician."

"You ought to be ashamed, John! Poor, homeless, houseless creatures! It's a shameful, wicked, abominable law, and I'll break it, for one, the first time I get a chance; and I hope I *shall* have a chance, I do! Things have got to a pretty pass, if a woman can't give a warm supper and a bed to poor, starving creatures, just because they are slaves, and have been abused and oppressed all their lives, poor things!"

"But, Mary, just listen to me. Your feelings are all quite right, dear, and interesting, and I love you for them; but, then, dear, we mustn't suffer our feelings to run away with our judgment; you must consider it's not a matter of private feeling—there are great public interests involved—there is such a state of public agitation rising, that we must put aside our private feelings."

"Now, John, I don't know anything about politics, but I can read my Bible; and there I see that I must feed the hungry, clothe the naked, and comfort the desolate; and that Bible I mean to follow.". . .

Now, if the truth must be told, our senator had the misfortune to be a man who had a particularly humane and accessible nature, and turning away anybody that was in trouble never had been his forte; and what was worse for him in this particular pinch of the argument was, that his wife knew it, and, of course, was making an assault on rather an indefensible point. . . . So he had recourse to the usual means of gaining time for such cases made and provided; he said "ahem," and coughed several times, took out his pocket-handkerchief, and began to wipe his glasses. Mrs. Bird, seeing the defenseless condition of the enemy's territory, had no more conscience than to push her advantage.

"I should like to see you doing that, John—I really should! Turning a woman out of doors in a snow-storm, for instance; or, may be you'd take her up and put her in jail, wouldn't you? You would made a great hand at that!". . .

"Mary! Mary! My dear, let me reason with you."

"I hate reasoning, John—especially reasoning on such subjects. There's a way you political folks have of coming round and round a plain right thing; and you don't believe in it yourselves, when it comes to practice. I know *you* well enough, John. You don't believe it's right any more than I do; and you wouldn't do it any sooner than I."

At this critical juncture, old Cudjoe, the black man-of-all-work, put his head in at the door, and wished "missis would come into the kitchen"; and our senator, tolerably relieved, looked after his little wife with a whimsical mixture of amusement and vexation, and, seating himself in the armchair, began to read the papers.

After a moment, his wife's voice was heard at the door, in a quick, earnest tone—"John! John! I do wish you'd come here a moment."

He laid down his paper, and went into the kitchen, and started, quite amazed at the sight that presented itself: A young and slender woman, with garments torn and frozen, with one shoe gone, and the stocking torn away from the cut and bleeding foot, was laid back in a deadly swoon upon two chairs. There was the impress of the despised race on her face, yet none could help feeling its mournful and pathetic beauty, while its stony sharpness, its cold, fixed deathly aspect, struck a solemn chill over him. He drew his breath short, and stood in silence. His wife, and their only colored domestic, old Aunt Dinah, were busily engaged in restorative measures; while old Cudjoe had got the boy on his knee, and was busy pulling off his shoes and stocking, and chafing his little cold feet. . . .

"Poor creature!" said Mrs. Bird, compassionately, as the woman slowly unclosed her large, dark eyes, and looked vacantly at her. Suddenly an expression of agony crossed her face, and she sprang up, saying, "O, my Harry! Have they got him?"

The boy, at this, jumped from Cudjoe's knee, and, running to her side, put up his arms. "O, he's here, he's here!" she exclaimed.

"O, ma'am!" said she, wildly, to Mrs. Bird, "do protect us! don't let them get him!"

"Nobody shall hurt you here, my poor woman," said Mrs. Bird, encouragingly. "You are safe; don't be afraid."

"God bless you!" said the woman, covering her face and sobbing; while the little boy, seeing her crying, tried to get into her lap.

With many gentle and womanly offices, which none knew better how to render than Mrs. Bird, the poor woman was, in time, rendered more calm. A temporary bed was provided for her on the settle, near the fire; and, after a short time, she fell into a heavy slumber, with the child, who seemed no less weary, soundly sleeping on her arm; for the mother resisted, with nervous anxiety, the kindest attempts to take him from her; and, even in sleep, her arm encircled him with an unrelaxing clasp, as if she could not even then be beguiled of her vigilant hold.

Mr. and Mrs. Bird had gone back to the parlor, where, strange as it may appear, no reference was made, on either side, to the preceding conversation. . . . Dinah looked in to say that the woman was awake, and wanted to see missis.

Mr. and Mrs. Bird went into the kitchen, followed by the two eldest boys, the smaller fry having, by this time, been safely disposed of in bed.

The woman was now setting up on the settle, by the fire. She was looking steadily into the blaze, with a calm heart-broken expression, very different from her former agitated wildness.

"Did you want me?" said Mrs. Bird, in gentle tones. "I hope you feel better now, poor woman!". . .

"You needn't be afraid of anything; we are friends here, poor woman! Tell me where you came from, and what you want," said she.

"I came from Kentucky," said the woman. . . .

"Were you a slave?" said Mr. Bird.

"Yes sir; I belonged to a man in Kentucky."

"Was he unkind to you?"

"No, sir; he was a good master."

"And was your mistress unkind to you?"

"No, sir—no! my mistress was always good to me."

"What could induce you to leave a good home, then and run away, and go through such dangers?"

The woman looked up at Mrs. Bird, with a keen, scrutinizing glance, and it did not escape her that she was dressed in deep mourning.

"Ma'am," she said, suddenly, "have you ever lost a child?"

The question was unexpected, and it was a thrust on a new wound; for it was only a month since a darling child of the family had been laid in the grave.

Mr. Bird turned around and walked to the window, and Mrs. Bird burst into tears; but, recovering her voice, she said:

"Why do you ask that? I have lost a little one."

"Then you will feel for me. I have lost two, one after another—left 'em buried there when I came away; and I had only this one left. I never slept a night without him; he was all I had. He was my comfort and pride, day and night; and, ma'am, they were going to take him away from me— to *sell* him down south, ma'am, to go all alone—a baby that had never been away from his mother in his life! I couldn't stand it, ma'am; I knew I never should be good for anything, if they did; and when I knew the papers were signed, and he was sold, I took him and came off in the night, and they chased me—the man that bought him, and some of mas'r's folks—and they were coming down right behind me, and I heard 'em. I jumped right on to the ice; and how I got across, I don't know, but, first I knew, a man was helping me up the bank.". . .

"How come you to tell me you had a kind master?" he [the senator] suddenly exclaimed, gulping down very resolutely some kind of rising in his throat, and turning suddenly round upon the woman.

"Because he *was* a kind master; I'll say that of him, any way; and my mistress was kind; but they couldn't help themselves. They were owing money; and there was some way, I can't tell how, that a man had a hold on them and they were obliged to give him his will. I listened, and heard him telling mistress that, and she begging and pleading for me, and he told her he couldn't help himself, and that the papers were all drawn; and then it was I took him and left my home, and came away. I knew 'twas no use of my trying to live, if they did it; for 't 'pears like this child is all I have."

"Have you no husband?"

"Yes, but he belongs to another man. His master is real hard to him, and won't let him come to see me, hardly ever; and he's grown harder and harder upon us, and he threatens to sell him down south—it's like I'll never see *him* again!"

"I say, wife, she'll have to get away from here, this very night. That fellow will be down on the scent bright and early to-morrow morning; if 't was only the woman, she could lie quiet till it was over; but that little chap can't be kept still by a troop of horse and foot, I'll warrant me; he'll bring it all out, popping his head out of some window or door. A pretty kettle of fish it would be for me, too, to be caught with them both here, just now! No; they'll have to be got off to-night."

"To-night! How is it possible—where to?"

"Well I know pretty well where to," said the senator, beginning to put on his boots, with a reflective air; and stopping when his leg was half in, he embraced his knee with both hands, and seemed to go off in deep meditation.

"It's a confounded awkward, ugly business," said he, at last, beginning to tug at his boot-straps again, "and that's a fact!" After one boot was fairly on, the senator sat with the other in his hand, profoundly studying the figure of the carpet. "It will have to be done, though, for aught I see—hang it all!" and he drew the other boot anxiously on, and looked out of the window.

Now, little Mrs. Bird was a discreet woman—a woman who never in her life said, "I told you so!" and, on the present occasion, though pretty well aware of the shape her husband's meditations were taking, she very prudently forbore to meddle with them, only sat very quietly in her chair and looked quite ready to hear her liege lord's intentions, when he should think proper to utter them. . . .

"Your heart is better than your head, in this case, John," said the wife, laying her little white hand on his. "Could I ever have loved you, had I not known you better than you know yourself?" And the little woman looked so handsome, with the tears sparkling in her eyes, that the senator thought he must be a decidedly clever fellow, to get such a pretty creature into such a passionate admiration of him; and so, what could he do but walk off soberly, to see about the carriage. At the door, however, he stopped a moment, and then coming back, he said, with some hesitation:

"Mary, I don't know how you'd feel about it, but there's that drawer full of things—of—of—poor little Henry's." So saying, he turned quickly on his heel, and shut the door after him.

His wife opened the little bedroom door adjoining her room, and, taking the candle, set it down on the top of a bureau there; then from a small recess she took a key, and put it thoughtfully in the lock of a drawer, and made a sudden pause, while two boys, who, boylike, had followed close on her heels, stood looking, with silent, significant glances, at their mother. And oh! mother that reads this, has there never been in your house a drawer, or a closet, the opening of which has been to you like the opening again of a little grave? Ah! happy mother that you are, if it has not been so.

DEFENDING SLAVERY

The chief and far most important enquiry is, how does slavery affect the condition of the slave? One of the wildest sects of Communists in France proposes not only to hold all property in common, but to divide the profits, not according to each man's input and labor, but according to each man's wants. Now this is precisely the system of domestic slavery with us. We provide for each slave, in old age and in infancy, in sickness and in health, not according to his labor, but according to his wants. The master's wants are more costly and refined, and he therefore gets a larger share of the profits. A Southern farm is the beau ideal of Communism; it is a joint concern, in which the slave consumes more than the master, of the coarse products, and is far happier, because although the concern may fail, he is always sure of a support; he is only transferred to another master to participate in the profits of another concern; he marries when he pleases, because he knows he will have to work no more with a family than without one, and whether he live or die, that family will be taken care of; he exhibits all the pride of ownership, despises a partner in a smaller concern, "a poor man's negro," boasts of "our crops, horses, fields and cattle;" and is as happy as a human being can be. And why should he not?—he enjoys as much of the fruits of the farm as he is capable of doing, and the wealthiest can do no more. Great wealth brings many additional cares, but few additional enjoyments. Our stomachs do not increase in capacity with our fortunes. We want no more clothing to keep us warm. We may create new wants, but we cannot create new pleasures. The intellectual enjoyments which wealth affords are probably balanced by the new cares it brings along with it.

There is no rivalry, no competition to get employment among slaves, as among free laborers. Nor is there a war between master and slave. The master's interest prevents his reducing the slave's allowance or wages

George Fitzhugh, *Sociology for the South* (Richmond, 1854), pp. 242–47.

This exterior and first-floor plan of "Belle Grove," a major antebellum plantation house in Louisiana, suggests that high comfort and generations of lavish living were the common standards of the slave masters. But such houses were rare. Most were built at the end of the slave-owning period, and even rooms like these might be furnished sparsely or shabbily. In the vast area of thirteen slave states, there were only about two thousand slaveholding establishments that we would call plantations, with great acreage and more than a hundred slaves. Most of the stories about great houses of the slave South were part of the myth of the lost cause invented about 1880 to dignify defeat with the fantasy of a noble civilization, complete with palaces, ruined by the Yankee barbarian conqueror.

Floor plans from Louisiana Plantation Homes, *copyright © 1965 by Professor W. Darrell Overdyke. Used by permission of Architectural Book Publishing Co.*

in infancy or sickness, for he might lose the slave by so doing. His feeling for his slave never permits him to stint him in old age. The slaves are all well fed, well clad, have plenty of fuel, and are happy. They have no dread of the future—no fear of want. A state of dependence is the only condition in which reciprocal affection can exist among human beings—the only situation in which the war of competition ceases, and peace, amity and good will arise. A state of independence always begets more or less of jealous rivalry and hostility. A man loves his children because they are weak, helpless and dependent. He loves his wife for similar reasons. When his children grow up and assert their independence, he is apt to transfer his affection to his grandchildren. He ceases to love his wife when she becomes masculine or rebellious; but slaves are always dependent, never the rivals of their master. Hence, though men are often found at variance with wife or children, we never saw one who did not like his slaves, and rarely a slave who was not devoted to his master. "I am thy servant!" disarms me of the power of master. Every man feels the beauty, force and truth of this sentiment of Sterne. But he who acknowledges its truth, tacitly admits that dependence is a tie of affection, that the relation of master and slave is one of mutual good will. Volumes written on the subject would not prove as much as this single sentiment. It has found its way to the heart of every reader, and carried conviction along with it. The slaveholder is like other men; he will not tread on the worm nor break the bruised reed. The ready submission of the slave, nine times out of ten, disarms his wrath even when the slave has offended. The habit of command may make him imperious and fit him for rule; but he is only imperious when thwarted or crossed by his equals; he would scorn to put on airs of command among blacks, whether slaves or free; he always speaks to them in a kind and subdued tone. We go farther, and say the slaveholder is better than others—because he has greater occasion for the exercise of the affections. His whole life is spent in providing for the minutest wants of others, in taking care of them in sickness and in health. Hence he is the least selfish of men. Is not the old bachelor who retires to seclusion, always selfish? Is not the head of a large family almost always kind and benevolent? And is not the slaveholder the head of the largest family? Nature compels master and slave to be friends; nature makes employers and free laborers enemies.

The institution of slavery gives full development and full play to the affections. Free society chills, stints and eradicates them. In a homely way the farm will support all, and we are not in a hurry to send our children into the world, to push their way and make their fortunes, with a capital of knavish maxims. We are better husbands, better fathers, better friends, and better neighbors than our Northern brethren. The tie of kindred to the fifth degree is often a tie of affection with us. First cousins are scarcely acknowledged at the North, and even children are prematurely pushed off into the world. Love for others is the organic law of our society, as self-love is of theirs.

BLACK WOMEN OF THE RURAL SOUTH

The truth is, "Emancipation Day" found her a prostrate and degraded being; and, although it has brought numerous advantages to her sons, it has produced but the simplest changes in her social and domestic condition. She is still the crude, rude, ignorant mother. Remote from cities, the dweller still in the old plantation hut, neighboring to the sulky, disaffected master class, who still think her freedom was a personal robbery of themselves, none of the "fair humanities" have visited her humble home. The light of knowledge has not fallen upon her eyes. The fine domesticities which give the charm to family life, and which, by the refinement and delicacy of womanhood, preserve the civilization of nations, have not come to *her*. She has still the rude, coarse labor of men. With her rude husband she still shares the hard service of a field-hand. Her house, which shelters, perhaps, some six or eight children, embraces but two rooms. Her furniture is of the rudest kind. The clothing of the household is scant and of the coarest material, has ofttimes the garniture of rags; and for herself and offspring is marked, not seldom, by the absence of both hats and shoes. She has rarely been taught to sew, and the field labor of slavery times has kept her ignorant of the habitudes of neatness, and the requirements of order. Indeed, coarse food, coarse clothes, coarse living, coarse manners, coarse companions, coarse surroundings, coarse neighbors, both black and white, yea, every thing coarse, down to the coarse, ignorant, senseless religion, which excites her sensibilities and starts her passions, go to make up the life of the masses of black women in the hamlets and villages of the rural South. . . .

I have two or three plans to offer which, I feel assured, if faithfully used, will introduce widespread and ameliorating influences amid this large population.

The *first* of these is specially adapted to the adult female population of the South, and is designed for more immediate effect. I ask for the equipment and the mission of "sisterhoods" to the black women of the South. I wish to see large numbers of practical Christian women, women of intelligence and piety; women well trained in domestic economy; women who combine delicate sensibility and refinement with industrial acquaintance— scores of such women to go South; to enter every Southern State; to visit "Uncle Tom's Cabin;" to sit down with "Aunt Chloe" and her daughters, to show and teach them the ways and habits of thrift, economy, neatness, and order; to gather them into "Mothers' Meetings" and sewing schools; and by both lectures and "talks" guide these women and their daughters into the modes and habits of clean and orderly housekeeping.

There is no other way, it seems to me, to bring about this domestic revolution.—We can not postpone this reformation to another generation.

Alexander Crummell, *Africa and America: Addresses and Discourses* (Washington, 1891), pp. 66–81.

Postponement is the reproduction of the same evils in numberless daughters now coming up into life, imitators of the crude and untidy habits of their neglected mothers, and the perpetuation of plantation life to another generation. No, the effect must be made immediately, in *this* generation, with the rude, rough, neglected women of the times.

Let me state just here definitely what I want for the black girls of the South:

1. I want boarding-schools for the *industrial training* of one hundred and fifty or two hundred of the poorest girls, of the ages of twelve to eighteen years.

2. I wish the *intellectual* training to be limited to reading, writing, arithmetic, and geography.

3. I would have these girls taught to do accurately all domestic work, such as sweeping floors, dusting rooms, scrubbing, bed making, washing and ironing, sewing, mending, and knitting.

4. I would have the trades of dressmaking, millinery, straw-platting, tailoring for men, and such like, taught them.

5. The art of cooking should be made a specialty, and every girl should be instructed in it.

6. In connection with these schools, garden plats should be cultivated, and every girl should be required, daily, to spend at least an hour in learning the cultivation of small fruits, vegetables, and flowers.

I am satisfied that the expense of establishing such schools would be insignificant. As to their maintenance, there can be no doubt that, rightly managed, they would in a brief time be self-supporting. Each school would soon become a hive of industry, and a source of income. But the *good* they would do is the main consideration. Suppose that the time of a girl's schooling be limited to *three*, or perchance to *two* years. It is hardly possible to exaggerate either the personal family or society influence which would flow from these schools. Every class, yea, every girl in an outgoing class, would be a missionary of thrift, industry, common sense, and practicality. They would go forth, year by year, a leavening power into the houses, towns, and villages of the Southern black population; girls fit to be thrifty wives of the honest peasantry of the South, the worthy matrons of their numerous households.

FAMILIES IN UTOPIA

The first half of the nineteenth century—like the 1960s and the 1970s—witnessed the founding of numerous "alternative communities" within the United States. Attempting to provide their adherents with a sacred or secular version of heaven on earth, these experiments tried to counter the presumed evils and disorders of existing society with a life that consciously departed either from the institution of private property or from monogamy. These societies derived from a wide variety of often highly idiosyncratic religious and secular doctrines and took a number of different forms: Some preserved the basic outlines of separate families, while others deliberately obliterated the "natural" family order; some insisted upon total celibacy, while others promoted forms of "purified" but promiscuous sexual mingling. But all reflected a belief that human beings by their own will, whether because of spiritual conversion or the application of universal truths, could achieve moral and social perfection in this life.

The selections here are taken from the Shakers, the Fourierists, and the Mormons, three very different communitarian groups that commanded more followers and probably more attention than most other groups. The United Society of Believers in Christ's Second Appearing, or Shakers, was founded by Ann Lee (1732–84), a member of an English Quaker sect, who had a revelation that the foundation of all evil lay in the cohabitation and carnal congress of the sexes. (She had come to believe that the death of all her children in infancy was a divine punishment for her carnality.) Proclaiming herself Mother Ann Lee, the person in which the second coming of Christ would occur, she brought her small band of followers to the New World in 1774 to escape persecution and live a life according to her doctrines of separation from the world, dissolution of the "natural" family, and total celibacy. After her death, Shakerism, under the leadership of Father Joseph Meacham and Mother Lucy Wright, grew and developed its permanent doctrines and institutions. Between 1787 and 1810, a dozen Shaker villages (lasting into the twentieth century) were established, drawing their members from ordinary families converted during the "second Great Awakening" that swept Western New England and the Ohio Valley around the turn of the eighteenth century. The villages were organized around "families" of a divine rather than natural order. Each family composed of roughly equal numbers of men and women and organized in exactly parallel institutions, was presided over by an eldress and an elder, reflecting the dual nature of the Divine Headship. Total celibacy was enforced and the relations among the sexes carefully scrutinized, arrangements reflected in the selections from the Shaker "Constitution" printed in this section.

The next two documents come from Brook Farm, a community set up in Massachusetts in 1842 by a transcendentalist minister, George Ripley. It was reorganized according to the "doctrine of association" developed by Charles Fourier, an eccentric French silk salesman who offered his "law of passional attraction" as the scientific truth that would revolutionize society. Fourier's writings offered a meticulously detailed blueprint, spelling out the organization of work, living arrangements, and even the architecture for a "phalanx," his term for a properly constructed "association." Resting upon a complex mathematical calculus that divided the human constitution into twelve "passions," Fourierism projected a society that combined complete individualism with perfect order and total harmony. When Albert Brisbane (largely through a series of articles in Horace Greeley's *New York Tribune* in 1842) brought the doctrine of association to the attention of Americans, he left out many of the most extreme elements, especially Fourier's obliteration of conventional marriage. The doctrine struck a responsive chord, and within three years more than twenty associations were started. (The Strong family materials, pages 183, come from their membership in the Wisconsin phalanx.) In the selections here a defender of the doctrine compares the plight of women under the existing scheme of "isolated households" with the promise of association, while Charles Lane, who tried a number of different brands of communalism, queries whether marriage and association are in any way compatible.

The last documents in this section concern the Mormon practice of "plural wives," or polygamy, as it was usually called. In upstate New York in 1830, Joseph Smith (1806–44) discovered a set of mysterious golden plates that told of an ancient Christian civilization and foretold the coming of a new prophet who would set up Christ's kingdom in the New World. Translating the plates into the Book of Mormon and proclaiming himself the new prophet, Smith organized the Church of Jesus Christ of Latter-Day Saints, or Mormons. Facing opposition and persecution from the outset, the Mormons moved westward, first to Kirkland, Ohio, and to Independence, Missouri. Driven from Missouri and hounded out of Ohio, they established the model city of Nauvoo, Illinois, which by 1844 contained nearly 15,000 believers. After Smith and his brother were killed by a mob outraged at Mormon doctrine, hints of bizarre marital arrangements, and Smith's autocratic if not dictatorial rule, the Mormons, under their new prophet, Brigham Young (1801–77) began their long trek to Utah, where they hoped to set up the new Zion, free of interference from Babylon, as they referred to the outside world. In Utah in 1852, Young, pointing to a revelation Smith supposedly had had in 1842, proclaimed the doctrine of "celestial marriage," which declared the taking of plural wives the highest, most spiritual form of matrimony. The doctrine rested in large part on the idea of preexistent souls, sanctified spirits waiting to pass through a period of temporal existence encased in human bodies on their way to the celestial kingdom. Thus, according to Mormon theology, with plural wives and the progeny they could produce, a Mormon saint could surround himself with a vast family of souls, "sealed" to him for all eternity. The first Mormon document here consists of selections from an exposition by Orson Pratt, Young's chosen spokesman of the new doctrine of "celestial marriage" to the Mormon faithful.

No practice or doctrine of Mormonism inspired greater hostility than its polygamy. For nearly forty years (until the Mormon hierarchy in 1890 bowed to pressure and the continual arrest of its leaders and declared it would no longer sanction marriages contrary to civil law), there was a flood of angry denunciations and exposés, much of it by or built upon the tales of refugees and apostates from Mormonism. The second Mormon document, taken from *The Women of Mormonism* (published in 1881), is representative of the genre, an exposé that reveals as much about the familial ideas and anxieties of the critics as it does about Mormonism.

The historical significance of these challenges to the familial practices and ideas of the American mainstream in the nineteenth century does not lie in the number of adherents the utopian schemes gained or in how widely their doctrines were accepted. Rather, they stand as extensions of, commentaries on, or criticisms of the ideas and practices at the center of the culture. Do these documents from the fringe reflect concerns and conditions that one finds underlying more accepted or "official" views of the family? At what points do they seem to depart from and thus expose the limits of orthodox and conventional views? To what extent do the various utopians seem to share the ideals, the concerns, or language of the mainstream and to what extent do they offer a counter vision? Asking such questions of these documents can expand our view of the spectrum of anxieties, images, and concerns covered by the idea of the family in nineteenth-century America.

THE SHAKERS

The General Organization of Society

In societies of Believers which are sufficiently large to admit of it, the order of God requires a regular organization of families in order to accommodate and provide for the different circumstances of individuals in temporal things, and also for the advancement of spiritual travel in the work of regeneration, and the universal good of all the members, composing such society.
2. The orders, rules and regulations in each family, concerning things spiritual and temporal, should be such as are adapted to the protection, benefit and increase, of the numbers gathered therein.

Reprinted in Edward Deming Andrews, *The People Called Shakers* (New York, 1963), pp. 253, 266. Reprinted by permission of Dover Publications, Inc.

3. *The families should be of different classes, or grades, as to order, government and arrangement in things spiritual and temporal, adapted to the different situations and circumstances of members in society, and should be denominated—1st or center family, generally called the Church of the society,—2nd. Family, 3rd., 4th, etc.—or the name of each, may be such as is adapted to local circumstances, but their respective places in point of order, should be gradual and progressive.*

4. *The different orders and families, should in no wise have uncontrolled access to each other, by their communications either verbal or written, but all written communications and visits with each other, should be by the liberty of the Elders therein; and without such liberty, members should never go from one, to the other of said families.*

5. *The Church or center family, and as far as is practicable, each family that is gathered into order, should have a lot of Elders & Eldresses and a lot of Deacons and Deaconnesses or Trustees, each lot of which should contain four or more persons, two of each sex.*

6. *The Church or center family, should be composed of such members, as are free from any involvements with those without, and such as are prepared by a previous privilege in families that are back, (where those who come in, over the age of thirteen, should be first proved), to advance into a further degree of gospel order, in a forward family, and a closer spiritual work of purification, and it would be well, if all could come in at the gathering order, and be measurably proved, before they advance further.*

7. *None should be gathered into the Church or first family, who cleave unto their natural kindred of Fathers, Mothers, brothers, sisters, husbands, or wives, houses or land; none should be gathered into this order, but such as may by obedience stand spotless before the Lord. . . .*

Orders Concerning Intercourse Between the Sexes

The gospel of Christ's Second Appearing, strictly forbids all private union between the two sexes, in any case, place, or under any circumstances, in doors or out.

2. *One brother and one sister, must not be together, alone, at any time, longer than to do a short and necessary duty or errand; and must not have private talk together at all, which they desire to have unknown to the Elders. Neither should brethren and sisters touch each other unnecessarily.*

3. *Brethren and sisters must not work together, except on special occasions, and then by liberty from the Elders.*

4. *Brethren and sisters may not make presents to each other in a private manner.*

5. *Brethren and sisters may not write for each other nor to each other, without liberty from the Elders.*

6. *If brethren and sisters need instruction in reading, writing, or music, or any other branch of literature or science, they must receive it from those of their own sex, or by such persons as the Elders may appoint.*

7. *Brethren and sisters may not pass each other on the stairs.*

8. *Brethren and sisters may not shake hands together.*

9. *It is contrary to order for Believers to offer to shake hands with apostates; and if brethren shake hands with women of the world, or if sisters shake hands with men of the world, they must open it to their Elders before attending meeting.*

BROOK FARM OBSERVED

Of about seventy persons now assembled there, about thirty are children sent thither for education; some adult persons also place themselves there chiefly for mental assistance; and in the society there are only four married couples. With such materials it is almost certain that the sensitive and vital points of communication cannot well be tested. A joint-stock company, working with some of its own members and with others as agents, cannot bring to issue the great question, whether the existence of the marital family is compatible with that of the universal family, which the term "Community" signifies. This is now the grand problem. By mothers it has ever been felt to be so. The maternal instinct, as hitherto educated, has declared itself so strongly in favor of the separate fire-side, that association, which appears so beautiful to the young and unattached soul, has yet accomplished little progress in the affections of that important section of the human race—the mothers. With fathers, the feeling in favor of the separate family is certainly less strong; but there is an undefinable tie, a sort of magnetic *rapport*, an invisible, inseverable, umbilical chord [*sic*] between the mother and child, which in most cases circumscribes her desires and ambition to her own immediate family. All the accepted adages and wise saws of society, all the precepts of morality, all the sanctions of theology, have for ages been employed to confirm this feeling. This is the chief corner stone of present society; and to this maternal instinct have, till very lately, our most heartfelt appeals been made for the progress of the human race, by means of a deeper and more vital education. Pestalozzi and his most enlightened disciples are distinguished by this sentiment. And are we all at once to abandon, to deny, to destroy this supposed stronghold of virtue? Is it questioned whether the family arrangement of mankind is to be preserved? Is it discovered that the sanctuary, till now deemed the holiest on earth, is to be invaded by intermeddling skepticism, and its altars sacrilegiously destroyed by the rude hands of innovating progress? Here "social science" must be brought to issue.

The question of association and of marriage are one. If, as we have been popularly led to believe, the individual or separate family is in the true order of Providence, then the associative life is a false effort. If the associative life is true, then is the separate family a false arrangement. By the maternal feeling, it appears to be decided that the coexistence of both is incompatible, is impossible. So also say some religious sects. Social science ventures to assert their harmony. This is the grand problem now remaining to be solved, for at least, the enlightening, if not for the vital elevation of humanity. That the affections can be divided or bent with equal ardor on two objects, so opposed as universal and individual love, may at least be rationally doubted. History has not yet exhibited such phenomena in an associate body, and scarcely perhaps in any individual.

Charles Lane, "Brook Farm," *The Dial*, IV (Jan. 1844), pp. 351–57.

The monasteries and convents, which have existed in all ages, have been maintained solely by the annihilation of that peculiar affection on which the separate family is based. The Shaker families, in which the two sexes are not entirely dissociated, can yet only maintain their union by forbidding and preventing the growth of personal affection other than that of a spiritual character. And this in fact is not personal in the sense of individual, but ever a manifestation of universal affection. Spite of the speculations of hopeful bachelors and aesthetic spinsters, there is somewhat in the marriage bond which is found to counteract the universal nature of the affections, to a degree tending at least to make the considerate pause, before they assert that, by any social arrangements whatever, the two can be blended into one harmony. The general condition of married persons at this time is some evidence of the existence of such a doubt in their minds. Were they as convinced as the unmarried of the beauty and truth of associate life, the demonstration would be now presented. But might it not be enforced that the two family ideas really neutralize each other? Is it not quite certain that the human heart cannot be set in two places; that man cannot worship at two altars? It is only the determination to do what parents consider the best for themselves and their families, which renders the o'er populous world such a wilderness of selfhood as it is. Destroy this feeling, they say, and you prohibit every motive to exertion. Much truth is there in this affirmation. For to them, no other motive remains, nor indeed to any one else, save that of the universal good, which does not permit the building up of supposed self-good, and therefore, forecloses all possibility of an individual family.

These observations, of course, equally apply to all the associative attempts, now attracting so much public attention; and perhaps most especially to such as have more of Fourier's designs than are observable at Brook Farm. The slight allusion in all the writers of the "Phalansterian" class, to the subject of marriage, is rather remarkable. They are acute and eloquent in deploring Woman's oppressed and degraded position in past and present times, but are almost silent as to the future. In the meanwhile, it is gratifying to observe the successes which in some departments attend every effort, and that Brook Farm is likely to become comparatively eminent in the highly important and praiseworthy attempts, to render labor of the hands more dignified and noble, and mental education more free and loveful.

THE FAMILY AT BROOK FARM

And now for the particular things in your letters, which are the domestic relations, the position of women, and the education of children. Upon these points you have, I think, failed to grasp the theory of Association,

The Phalanx, I (Feb. 8, 1844), pp. 317–19.

both because it has not been sufficiently explained to you, and because you have taken a partial view of what has been said. It is generally necessary in public lectures and in conversation upon the subject, to select some single aspect of the doctrine and make it prominent otherwise we should not be understood. If we endeavored to state universal principles in their universality, but few minds could receive them. But the misfortune is that in thus dwelling upon a particular view of the great Truth, it is often supposed that we cannot take any other, so much are people accustomed to one-sided teaching. Thus, when we say, that the isolated household is a source of innumerable evils, which Association alone can remedy, the mind of the hearer sometimes rushes to the conclusion that we mean to destroy the home relations entirely, and that we leave out of our account all those delicate and beautiful affections which form so much of the best life of man, but which, in the present unfortunate situation of the world, are *possible* only to a minority, so small, that in a general view of Humanity, they cannot be so much as reckoned. When, too, we say, that the existing system of Education is wholly wrong, it is feared that we design some violence to the parental sentiment, or that, in your own words, we would give children "wholly up to the care of others, when only a mother can bear and forbear with a child, and yet love it." Now, my dear W., these are not our doctrines but your misconceptions of them. You say that we "war against Nature." We hold to the most implicit obedience to her, but it must be to the whole of Nature and every one of her promptings, and not to any one or two or more of them, to the exclusion of all the others, or any one of them. . . .

The isolated household is wasteful in economy, is untrue to the human heart, and is not the design of God, and therefore it must disappear, but the domestic relations are not so, however they may have been falsified and tarnished by what man has mixed with them. Of these relations the present position of woman is an essential part, and she can be raised out of that position only by purging them of what is alien to their essential character. Now, as we think, the pecuniary dependence which society estab-lishes for woman, is one of the most hurtful of these foreign elements, and we do not doubt that with its removal we shall see social relations generally rise to a degree of truth and beauty, to which they cannot at present attain. In the progress of society we see that the position of woman is a hinge on which all other things seem more or less to turn. In the savage state she is the drudge and menial of man; in the barbarous state she is his slave and plaything, and in the civilized state she is as you confess, his "upper servant." Society rises with the degree of freedom it bestows on woman, and it is only by raising her to "integral independence," and making her as she should be, and as God made her, the equal of Man, though not by making her precisely the same as Man as some mistaken reformers have wished, the world can be saved. You must not judge in matters of such importance from the few facts that your own personal knowledge may give you; your comparatively fortunate education, has shown you but little of the worst side of the world. A few days after I received your letter of September, I was driving through one of the richest parts of the State of New-York, where Nature seemed to have expended her utmost wealth for the benefit of man. I happened to turn my head and saw a middle aged woman bare-foot carrying around the hovel in which she lived, the food for some half dozen swine. "That," said I, "is the position of Woman in civilization." The few women who seem to fill their appropriate spheres are as nothing to the great majority, that toil in poverty, in degradation and in unhappiness, or even to those that drag out a short but wretched life, lost to all that renders life anything but a curse.

MORMON POLYGAMY EXPLAINED

. . . We read that those who do the works of Abraham, are to be blessed with the blessing of Abraham. Have you not, in the ordinances of this last dispensation, had the blessings of Abraham pronounced upon your heads? O yes, you say, I well recollect, since God has restored the everlasting Priesthood, that by a certain ordinance these blessings were placed upon our heads,—the blessings of Abraham, Isaac, and Jacob. Why, says one, I never thought of it in this light before. Why did you not think of it? Why not look upon Abraham's blessings as your own, for the Lord blessed him with a promise of seed as numerous as the sand upon the seashore; so will you be blessed, or else you will not inherit the blessings of Abraham.

How did Abraham manage to get a foundation laid for this mighty kingdom? Was he to accomplish it all through one wife? No. Sarah gave a certain woman to him whose name was Hagar, and by her a seed was to be raised up unto him. Is this all? No. We read of his wife Keturah, and also of a plurality of wives and concubines,—which he had,—from whom he raised up many sons. Here then, was a foundation laid, for the fulfilment of the great and grand promise, concerning the multiplicity of his seed. It would have been rather a slow process, if Abraham had been confined to one wife, like some of those narrow, contracted nations of Modern Christianity.

I think there is only about one-fifth of the population of the globe, that believe in the one-wife system; the other four-fifths believe in the doctrine of a plurality of wives. They have had it handed down from time immemorial, and are not half so narrow and contracted in their minds as some of the nations of Europe and America, who have done away with the promises, and deprived themselves of the blessings of Abraham, Isaac and Jacob. The nations do not know anything about the blessings of Abra-

Orson Pratt, "Celestial Marriage Explained," in *The Most Holy Principle: Vol. I: The Law and the Testimony* (Salt Lake City, 1974), pp. 28–33.

ham; and even those who have only one wife, cannot get rid of their covetousness, and get their little hearts large enough to share their property with a numerous family; they are so penurious, and so narrow and contracted in their feelings, that they take every possible care not to have their families large; they do not know what is in the future, nor what blessings they are depriving themselves of, because of the traditions of their fathers; they do not know that a man's posterity, in the eternal worlds, are to constitute his glory, his kingdom, and dominion.

Here, then, we perceive, just from this one principle, reasoning from the blessings of Abraham alone, the necessity,—if we would partake of the blessings of Abraham, Isaac and Jacob,—of doing their works; and he that will not do the works of Abraham, and walk in his footsteps, will be deprived of his blessings.

Again, let us look at Sarah's peculiar position in regard to Abraham. She understood the whole matter; she knew that unless seed was raised up to Abraham, that he would come short of his glory; and she understood the promise of the Lord, and longed for Abraham to have seed. And when she saw that she was old, and fearing that she should not have the privilege of raising up seed, she gave to Abraham, Hagar. . . .

. . . But again, there is another reason why this plurality should exist among the Latter-day Saints. I have already given you one reason, and that is, that you might inherit the blessings and promises made to Abraham, Isaac, and Jacob, and receive a continuation of your posterity, that they may become as numerous as the sand upon the seashore. There is another reason, and a good one, too. What do you suppose it is? I will tell you; and it will appear reasonable to every man and woman of a reflecting mind. . . .

. . . I have already told you that the spirits of men and women, all had a previous existence, thousands of years ago, in the heavens, in the presence of God; and I have already told you that among them are many spirits that are more noble, more intelligent than others, that were called the great and mighty ones, reserved until the dispensation of the fulness of times, to come forth upon the face of the earth, through a noble parentage that shall train their young and tender minds in the truths of eternity, that they may grow up in the Lord and be strong in the power of His might; be clothed upon with His glory; be filled with exceeding great faith; that the visions of eternity may be opened to their minds; that they may be Prophets, Priests, and Kings to the Most High God. Do you believe, says one, that they are reserved until the last dispensation, for such a noble purpose? Yes; and among the Saints is the most likely place for these spirits to take their tabernacles—through a just and righteous parentage. They are to be sent to that people that are the most righteous of any other people upon the earth; there to be trained up properly, according to their nobility and intelligence, and according to the laws which the Lord ordained before they were born. This is the reason why the Lord is sending them here, brethren and sisters; they are appointed to come and take their bodies here, that in their generations they may be raised up among the righteous. . . .

But then another question will arise; how are these things to be conducted? Are they to be left at random? Is every servant of God at liberty to run here and there, seeking out the daughters of men as wives unto themselves without any restrictions, law, or condition? No. We find these things were restricted in ancient times. Do you not recollect the circumstance of the Prophet Nathan's coming to David? He came to reprove him for certain disobedience, and told him about the wives he had lost through it; that the Lord would give them to another; and he told him, if he had been faithful, that the Lord would have given him still more, if he had only asked for them. Nathan the Prophet, in relation to David, was the man that held the keys concerning this matter in ancient days; and it was governed by the strictest laws.

So in these days; let me announce to this congregation, that there is but one man in all the world, at the same time, who can hold the keys of this matter; but one man has power to turn the key to enquire of the Lord, and to say whether I, or these my brethren, or any of the rest of this congregation, or the Saints upon the face of the whole earth, may have this blessing of Abraham conferred upon them; he holds the keys of these matters now, the same as Nathan, in his day.

A MORMON WIFE

TO THE
HAPPY WIVES AND MOTHERS OF AMERICA,
WHOSE HOMES ARE PROTECTED FROM INVASION BY THE
MAJESTIC ARM OF THE LAW;
TO THOSE TO WHOM THE WAIL OF THEIR FIRST-BORN
IS SWEETER THAN THE MUSIC OF THE SPHERES,
BECAUSE THAT BABE IS THE PLEDGE OF
THE UNITED AFFECTION OF
ONE MAN AND ONE WOMAN;
TO THOSE WHOSE CHILDREN DO NOT BRING WITH THEM A
BIRTHRIGHT OF SORROW, AND WHOSE MOTHER-
HOOD IS NOT A BADGE OF SHAME,
THIS BOOK IS APPEALINGLY DEDICATED BY SOME OF THE
WOMEN OF MORMONISM.

A First Wife's Story

Many friends who have heard me complain of the sorrows I have endured in polygamy, censure me deeply for having given my consent for my husband to take another wife. They say I could easily have prevented it if I

Jennie Frosieth, *The Women of Mormonism* (New York, 1881), pp. 57–65.

had been determined and threatened him with Gentile law, as it is only a few years, comparatively speaking, since he went into plurality. I will relate the facts just as they are, and people can see for themselves how utterly impossible it would have been for me to have acted any differently.

My husband was doing well in his business, and had frequently been counseled by various members of the priesthood, to avail himself of his privilege, and add to his family. It may not, perhaps, be understood by the Gentiles, that when a man shows signs of being prosperous, he is not given any peace until he has bound himself in the chains of polygamy. He is then a much greater slave to the priesthood, and not so likely to apostatize.

One day my husband announced to me that he had determined to live his religion, and take another wife. In one way I was not much surprised, for I knew the influences that had been brought to bear upon him continually for months, influences which could not be ignored without the possibilities of utter ruin. Besides, I had seen that blighting shadow destroy the peace of too many homes not to fear that it might also cast its baleful influence over mine; yet still I hoped that it might pass me by. We had lived together happily for fifteen years, and seven children had been born to us, four of whom were living. One of these children was a dearly loved, I may say, an idolized, little girl, who had been an invalid from her birth, and whom I had cherished like a delicate, rare, hot-house flower; another was a babe in arms; the rest were two stout hearty little boys, not old enough to do anything to help themselves.

When he told me of his intention to go into polygamy, he also said that he had been counseled to marry a certain woman. I had many reasons to regard this woman with special aversion. A year or two previous she had been a servant in my family, and in addition to a very high temper, she had annoyed and disgusted me by her efforts to attract the attention of my husband. He did not seem to notice her in the least at that time, and made no objections when I discharged her for an unkind action toward my little girl, whom she appeared to dislike extremely; and why, I never could imagine, for she was as sweet and gentle a little creature as ever lived. Subsequently, I heard that he had been advised by the church authorities to marry this woman, on purpose to humble me, because I was suspected of having more spirit and independence than was befitting a Mormon woman.

Well, it is no use repeating what I said to him. I knew that it would be in vain, for the decree had gone forth. It was like a drowning man clutching at a straw when I wept and prayed him to avert the disaster a little longer, if not altogether, and not to ruin our happy home. I reminded him of what we had been to each other for fifteen long years, and how I had forsaken all my friends for him; how I had tried to be an exemplary wife and a good mother to our children.

"It is well that you think of your children," was his reply, "for if you will not do your duty and consent for me to do mine, by living up to the privileges of a Latter-day Saint, they shall have neither food, clothing, nor shelter of my providing during the coming winter."

Gentile ladies who read this will perhaps think that my husband was a brute. On the contrary, he had been one of the best of husbands, and had never given me a rough word in fifteen years of married life, until he considered himself forced to "bring me to my senses," as the Mormons would say. None but those who have lived and suffered in it, can imagine the tyranny of Mormonism.

But what could I do? Could I see my innocent children, who had always been tenderly cared for, go hungry, naked, and homeless? I was not strong enough to do all my own household work, and I had a three months' old baby at my breast. I could not go out and earn their food and clothes. I could not bring myself to see them suffer, as I knew they must do, for I knew him well enough to be assured that he would carry out his threat; so I said, "Well, if you must take another wife, do so, but let it be any other woman in the world rather than the one you have named. You know how hateful she was to May, and how could I tolerate any one in the house that would be unkind to her? Choose any other woman in the city, and I will try to make the best of it."

He answered, "She it must be, and none other, and there need not be any trouble. You will keep your side of the house and mind your children, and I will make her keep hers."

"Henry," I said, "the day that woman enters this house will be the last day of domestic happiness for us."

"I cannot help it, Mary," he replied, "I am determined to live my religion; and if you know when you are well off, you will not make any fuss, but act like a sensible woman. There is nothing to prevent my leaving you without a penny, if I like, for you know that women, especially first wives, have no rights in this Territory, not even the right of dower. Do as you ought, and I will pledge myself that neither you nor the children shall ever want for anything; but make a fool of yourself, and you may go where you like, and do the best you can for them."

Again I ask, what could I do? Nothing. So I consented, went to the Endowment House, and gave as wife to my husband the woman that I most hated and despised of all women in the world. I saw her enter my house and take my place in the heart of the man for whom I had given up all I had held dear in this life. I know that, as a rule, the Gentile ladies consider the Mormon women weak, miserable creatures to bear what they do, but the sacrifices that many of us have made for our children will prove that we are not different from other women, at least in the matter of a mother's love.

I could tell you much more, but to what purpose? I could tell you how that woman's influence awakened and fostered all that was evil in my nature, how we together changed my kind, tender husband into a perfect brute, how the strong arm that had defended me for fifteen years came to be lifted against me, and how the death blow came to my little angel child in trying to save her mother from it, as she thought. But I ask again, to what purpose? It will not avail me anything, for there is neither law, justice, nor mercy for women in this Territory. It was not my intention to give any history of my sufferings in polygamy, I simply wanted to tell how I was coerced into giving my consent for my husband to enter it; and I will say this much, that Satan himself could not devise any worse tortures than women experience in the infernal system called "Celestial Marriage."

BREAKDOWN AND PATHOLOGY

The high ideals of nineteenth-century family life and the strength of the family code may well have increased the strain on family relations, since it was so difficult to live up to what was demanded. And that much was expected by "nice people" meant also that they were shocked when "respectability" cracked and bankruptcy, adultery, or insanity in a family was revealed. There were, of course, the "hopeless classes," probably the large majority of Americans by 1860, who lived relatively isolated and untutored lives, untouched, that is, by "instruction" and the literature of the family cult. Among the worst of these were the seemingly sizable numbers of unmarried or merely "common-law" couples and many bastard children. Such people were often viewed as sinners or irredeemably corrupt. At best, they were subjects for missionary work by clerics and teachers and anti-vice societies. "Uplift" was intended to bring them to "middle-class morality" and to inspire them with models of the pious, rational, and instructed families.

For Americans who tried to live strictly by the demanding family code, there is a relevant observation of psychiatry that holds that a person who seems excessive in enforcing a self-denying discipline may be covering conduct or wishes that contradict pretensions to purity. The family code in sex and morals deplored masturbation, premarital intercourse, adultery and infidelity, divorce, sexually curious and responsive wives, peacock husbands, lust in thought as well as deed, drink, immodest dress and "fancy" foods, smoking (even by men), disobedient children, prostitution, homosexuality, buying on credit, speculation, bankruptcy, failures to attend church and to observe family prayers and the sabbath, etc., etc. The code would be attacked later as "puritanical" or "Victorian," as "Comstockery" (after a New York anti-vice crusader), or as "provincial" and "unsophisticated." The strength of the moralism in the mid-nineteenth-century code probably helps explain the vigor of the counter-moralism against it in the twentieth.

The failure of the family ideal to control fully even its proponents was apparent in their indulgence in brothels, taverns, and gambling houses, or in their being lodged in an insane asylum. One of the achievements of the family code was to blot out the existence of those outside it by creating "nice" neighborhoods, policing city streets, and putting up walls of institutions, like jails or hospitals or asylums, to lock up and shut off aberrations from view. This "civilizing" encouraged illusions about the extent of the rationality and meliorability of the world and thus ill prepared comfortable and rationalistic people for dealing with the violence and irrationality of nineteenth- and twentieth-century life when they did erupt. The words spoken at the end of one of Ibsen's most shocking plays, "Good God, people don't do such things," express the filtering of the horrible that the family code attempted, almost, it seems, intentionally.

What happened across the tracks or down in the ghetto might be made to seem distant and manageable, but many nice families had "dirty little secrets" within their own circle and thus knew directly of the breakdown of their class pretensions or of pathology within it. Letters, diaries, and memoirs supplement police and newspaper reports to help the historian go beyond the veneer of respectability. Popular American novels and plays like Eugene O'Neill's *Long Day's Journey into Night* have also repeatedly recorded such figures as the alcoholic spinster sister, the cocaine-addict wife, the drunken husband, the pregnant unmarried daughter, the effeminate or homosexual son, the bankrupt or speculating brother, or the incestuous father.

The documents that follow reveal something of those Americans who either lived beyond or without the code or were tutored by the family code but were caught in violation of its rules or ideals. The aim here is not to assess the extent of "revolts" but to assay what people felt was at stake when breakdown or pathology appeared.

No family problem was more extensively pursued and exposed than "drink," or "demon rum" as it was revealingly termed. By the middle of the nineteenth century, the American consumption of alcohol and alcoholism from strong drink seem to have been prodigious. There really were poisons in alcohol and physical as well as moral decay were obvious however unamenable these were to control by the police or saloon-smashers. The one institution most often and most severely affected by alcohol in excess was the family. And the stronger and more "moral" the family ideal became, the more liquor seemed a threat. It is simple to understand how alcoholism badly affects family peace and amiability, income, health, social acceptance, employability, schooling, social aspirations, and so on. Clearly, alcohol was a problem when it brought loss of control over all the "baser appetites" that threatened family order. "Intemperance" quickly became a powerful metaphor for all the ills that beset family and society. Its status as a real pathology and as broader symbol reveals why alcohol was seen as such a threat to the cult of home and family.

The campaign against drink began in the 1820s and came in many forms. At first urging moderation by private choice and prohibiting only "ardent spirits," "temperance" by the 1840s had come to mean total abstinence. Organized largely by evangelical churches and, later, by allied groups like the Women's Christian Temperance Union (WCTU), the campaign used various tactics, ranging from efforts to inspire self-reformation—"taking the pledge"—to attempts to secure laws such as the Dow law in Maine restricting or totally prohibiting the manufacture, sale, and use of alcohol. (The worry about controlling "liquor" has still not died and goes on despite the failure of the "noble experiment" with national prohibition from 1920 to 1933.)

Apart from crusades, campaigns, and "politicking," the enthusiasm to
save the family particularly by redeeming the drunken husband produced
a huge and varied literature of salvation. From that record one of the
most famous in using the family theme was T. S. Arthur's novel of 1854,
Ten Nights in a Bar-Room and What I Saw There. Arthur was one of the country's
best selling "moral writers" of the mid-century, and his immensely popular
novel was soon converted into an even more celebrated melodrama. For
a half century it was repeatedly performed before thousands of audiences
in every part of the nation. By about 1910, however, it became a curio
or was even deliberately "played for laughs" as a set piece of American
old-fashioned melodrama. The play simplified the book but did not compromise the moral theme. The Morgan family featured in the play is only a
subplot in the novel but both book and play tried to make clear that nothing
threatened the family ideal more than drinking. And in the moral universe
of the play (and the age), just one drink implied the road to ruin and
perdition. From the extract from the play reprinted here, analyze the specific
ways in which drunkenness affects the family members and how it violates
the family code. What did it do to the mind and senses, to convince Christians that *any* alcohol was immoral?

In another popular genre, temperance songs, like the classic "Father,
Dear Father" and others reprinted here, dramatized alcohol's threat to
the family. A large repertory of such songs and hymns accumulated as
the anti-drink enthusiasm swept on. The temperance literature in pamphlet
and tract was also huge, much of it issued by organizations like the WCTU
and the Anti-Saloon League. One of the most famous pamphlets was Frances Willard's *Home Protection Manual* (1879). Again, the focus was on the
family as the principal victim of drink, but Willard depicted all America
at bay before alcohol and often saw restriction of alcohol as the "one
thing needful" that, if achieved by law, would totally secure America's
moral destiny.

The manual was intended to instruct Americans in political tactics to
end the threat of drink by granting women the ballot, at least to vote on
alcohol as a home, family, and thus peculiarly "women's issue." Such links
between a so-called "moral issue" and women's suffrage were to become
familiar with later reformers like Jane Addams (see pages 570ff.), who
were to generalize the connection between a better America and votes
for women. That this link was made illustrates the existence of conservative
or conserving aspects ("Save the family!") of what was too often seen as
merely the radical proposal to enfranchise women.

Two other notable examples of family breakdown were divorce and adultery. Although Protestant America in the main had long permitted divorce
by law, it was usually only for adultery and even *that* had to be weighed
against the lifelong sanctity of marriage. By the middle of the nineteenth
century, the family code ruled that since the sexual wrong (sometimes a
crime) of adultery was "unthinkable" for nice families, a divorce that
stemmed from it was a disgrace and marriage with a divorced person

a disaster. There was also a double standard at work. Despite the code condemning adulterous men *and* women, a husband charged with adultery was more difficult to shed than was an adulterous wife. Although divorce violated respectability, there are many divorce cases in the records, and study of them along lines of social class is worthwhile. One is presented here to try to demonstrate both the depth of the difficulty in obtaining a divorce and how much might be excused an erring husband in order to continue a marriage. Even violating racial lines (although common enough) might not bring divorce, as the Hansley case shows. We can only wonder about the consequences if the husband had sued the wife and charged the same wrongs against her with a black male as she claimed against him with his black mistress.

Adultery did not always lead to divorce, but when it came into the open it made one of the worst scandals, especially if it involved one of the moral grandees. Henry Ward Beecher was one of these paragons of respectability. A member of the famous Beecher family of divines, preachers, and moralists who march across the nineteenth century (Catharine Beecher and Harriet Beecher Stowe were his sisters), Beecher by 1860 was a national figure. Based in the pulpit of the well-to-do Plymouth Church in Brooklyn, New York, he was a much-sought commentator on the latest moral crisis of the republic and a source of respectable, even mildly reformist, opinion about public and private morality, theology and science.

Suddenly, in 1872, Beecher found himself the object of sensational public accusations by a husband that he was an adulterer and, as details accumulated, a hearty one at that. The woman involved was Mrs. Theodore Tilton, who with her accusing husband were members of Beecher's congregation. Mr. Tilton was a young writer and editor whom Beecher had helped but then cut off, partly because Tilton had become involved with Victoria Woodhull and her world of radicals, among them Susan B. Anthony. Woodhull, a militant feminist, advocated "free love" and the vote for women and ran for the Presidency of the United States in 1872. She was the first to publish the charges against Beecher. For nearly four years the scandal wore on, fully reported by a popular urban press now bold enough to treat the scandal openly and sensationally. The "Beecher-Tilton case" became *the* private scandal of the decade and one of the most revealing of the century to the social historian. Beecher's reputation lifted the case beyond the many common episodes of adultery up to that time. The accusations eventually had to come before his church, which conducted long and full hearings before fully exonerating him. A few years later the libel case over the accusations finally brought a hung jury.

What interests us here from the large record are Mrs. Tilton's portrait of what passed as a respectable marriage with a young man with a rising reputation and Beecher's tone and images of rectitude about marriage and other family matters. The full and long history of the entire sordid matter is a fine entry into the elaborate ethic of the age about the licit and illicit ways of sexuality. The titillation of the public by repeated scandals seems to have provided a "counterculture" to the world of respectability.

Divorce and adultery are usually merely breakdowns of family ties, but these can also have decidedly pathological aspects, such as an erring husband suffering from alcoholism. The nineteenth century had a nourished interest in and mounting study of "pathology" proper—that is, disease, violence, and bizarre disruptive behavior both within and around the family. Selections from the journal of the young Henry Ward Beecher record the workaday horrors among the "other Americans" of the 1830s. These are only short pieces, but combined with a large police and newspaper record of assault, mayhem, and murder within families across the century. This record casts another important light on the status and meaning of the family ideal of order and justice, what might be called its whistle-in-the-dark discipline. Sixty years after this Beecher peek at the "underworld," the family code had taken hold of respectable America. Of course, the peace was broken more often than pretended, one of the most notable instances being in Fall River, Massachusetts, in 1892 when "Lizzie" Borden was accused of taking an ax, first to her stepmother and then her father. The legendary trial that followed produced the selection here from the prosecuting attorney's closing summary of the state's case. What contrasts are drawn between how the Borden family appeared and its actual fate? Because she seemed so dutiful a daughter Lizzie was acquitted. What suggestion is there of a question like, "If this could happen in this fine family, then who is next?" What change would be necessary for Americans to be less surprised at the strong aggression and hostility fostered within respectable families like the Bordens?

The Borden case was part of a generation of shocks after 1890 to nice Americans about their society. There were not only private crimes and increasing defiance of their code by "Bohemians" and new immigrants but the general shock of recognition of the limited sway of the code amid slums, numbing poverty, giant strikes, sweatshops, civic and corporate corruption, the decadence of the rich, and the disdain of the poor for middle-class reform, "uplift," and assimilation.

FAMILY AND DRINK

Ten Nights in a Bar-Room

ACT II, SCENE IV

. . . *Enter* MORGAN, *door in flat.*

MOR: (C.) Here I am. In spite of my good resolutions, I find myself once more in the "Sickle and Sheaf." What hope is there left for poor Joe Morgan? Every sixpence I get only makes me the more anxious to reach

T. S. Arthur, *Ten Nights in a Bar-Room and What I Saw There* (Philadelphia, 1857), pp. 18–20, 29–31.

this house to obtain that which will keep me from thinking of my miserable home—my heart-broken wife and angel child. Here, Frank, give me some more rum. (*Staggering to bar,* L.) There—there is more money for you— take it.   (*Slaps money down on bar.*

FRANK: (*At bar.*) Father told me not to let you have any more liquor unless you could keep quiet.

MOR: Well, I'll keep quiet. I'll not disturb the *gentlemen* yonder. (*Points to* R. *table.*) Give me my glass; I'll sit here by myself. (*Sits* L.C.) Let a man once fall—no matter when, where or how much he may have suffered— the *good* people of this world raise their hands, set up the long, loud cry against him, and the poor inebriate dies—when a timely hand might have saved him. No matter—no matter! . . .   (*Laughs discordantly.*

Enter SLADE, L., *he goes behind bar.* FRANK *comes from it and exits* L.

SLADE: (*To* GREEN *and* WILLIE.) Good evening, gentlemen. I am glad to see you all looking so sociable, this evening. (*Sees* JOE.) Joe Morgan, what brings you here, like an evil star, to mar our happiness?

MOR: Oh, yes; I know I am an unwelcome guest! My presence displeases the refined miller—I beg your pardon—*landlord.* He has become ashamed of his old friend—haven't you?   (*Thumps the counter.*

SLADE: (*Coming from behind bar.*) Off with you, Joe Morgan! I won't put up with your insolence any longer! Leave my house and never show your face here again. I won't have such low vagabonds as you here. If you can't keep decent, and stay decent, don't intrude yourself upon respectable company.

MOR: A rumseller's decency. Poh! You were a decent man once, and a good miller, but that time is past and gone. Decency died out when you exchanged the calling of a miller for that of the rumseller. Decency! How like a fool you talk; as if it were any more decent to *sell* rum than to *drink* it!

SLADE: I've heard enough from you. (*Goes to bar—takes up a glass.*) Now, leave my house!

MOR: (R.) I won't!

SLADE: Won't you?—take that, then! (*Throws glass—it passes* MORGAN *out* R.

MARY *screams, runs in door in flat, with forehead bloody.*

MARY: Father! dear Father! They have killed me!   (*Falls* C.

(GREEN *and* WILLIE *rise from table.*

WILLIE: Who struck this child? Who did it?

MOR: Who?—curse him!—Simon Slade! Villain, your career of landlord shall be short; for here I swear, by the side of my murdered child, you shall die the death of a dog!

(*Piano music.* MORGAN *seizes* SLADE—*they struggle.* MORGAN *throws him into* L. *corner—rushes to get stool, and raises it to strike* SLADE—*is held back by* WILLIE *and* GREEN.

. . .

ACT IV, SCENE III.—MORGAN'S HOUSE

MORGAN *on floor* R. *of couch.* MARY *on couch* C., *asleep.* MRS. MORGAN *watching her,* L. *Slow music.*

MRS. M: Throughout the long, long night have I watched my suffering ones. Heaven only knows what is in store for me; yet I cannot bring my mind to believe that all that is truly noble and deserving in his nature should be destroyed. My poor child; how anxiously have I watched every movement of that sweet face. How I have longed for the morning sun to usher in its beams, and bring a gleam of joy to this almost broken heart!

MARY: (*Waking.*) Mother! Oh, how long I've been asleep! Is father awake?

MRS. M: He is still asleep, dear.

MARY: Oh, I wish he was awake—I want to see him so much. Try and wake him, mother, or shall I call him? Yes, I will! He's been asleep a long time. Father!

MOR: That voice! Where am I?   (*Awakes.*

MRS. M: You have been very ill, husband.

MARY: Oh, father, I'm so glad you're awake. I was afraid you were never going to look upon your little Mary ever again.

MOR: What can I do for you, my dear child?

MARY: I don't wish for anything, I only wanted to see you. You've always been good to me, haven't you, father?

MOR: Oh, no! I've never been good to any one.

MARY: You haven't been good to yourself, but you have always been good to me. Yes; and to poor mother too.

MOR: Don't, Mary! Don't say anything about that—say that I've been very bad. I only wish that I was as good as you are; I'd like to die then, and go right away from this wicked world. I wish there was no liquor to drink— no taverns—no bar-rooms—no anything—I only wish that I were dead!

MARY: Father! I want to tell you something.

MOR: What is it, Mary?

MARY: There will be no one to go after you any more.

MOR: Don't talk about that, Mary—I'm not going out in the evening any more, until you get well. Don't you remember, I promised?

MARY: Yes, I know, but——

MOR: What, dear?

MARY: I'm going away to leave you and mother; *(points upwards)* our Heavenly Father has called me.

MOR: What shall we do when you are gone? Let *me* die too.

MARY: You are not ready to go with me yet—you will live longer, that you may get ready. Haven't I tried to help you—oh, so many times, but it wasn't any use. You would go out. You would go to the tavern. It seemed almost as if you could not help it—maybe I can help you better father, after I die. I love you so much, that I'm sure the good angels will let me come to you, and watch over you always. Don't you think so, mother?

MRS. M: My dear child, you are not going to leave us?

MARY: Oh, yes I am! I dreamed something about pa while I slept. I thought it was night, and I was still sick—you promised not to go out again until I was well, but you did go out, and I thought you went over to Mr. Slade's tavern. When I knew this, I felt as strong as when I was well, and I got up and dressed myself, and started out after you—at last I came to Mr. Slade's tavern, and there you stood, father, in the door, and you were dressed so nice. You had on a new hat, and a new coat, and your boots were new, and shined ever so bright; I said, Oh! father, is this you? and then you took me up in your arms and kissed me, and said, Yes, Mary, this is your real father, not old Joe Morgan, but Mr. Morgan now. It seemed all so strange; for there wasn't any bar-room there any longer, but a store full of goods, and over the door I read your name, father. Oh, I was ever so glad that I awoke, and then I cried all to myself, for it was only a dream.

MOR: That dream, my dear child, shall become a reality; for here I promise that, with heaven's help, I will never go out at night again for a bad purpose!

MRS. M: Do you indeed promise that, husband?

MOR: Yes, wife, and more.

MARY: What?

MOR: I'll never go into a bar-room again!

MARY: Never?

MRS. M: Do you promise that too?

MOR: Yes; and what is still more, I will never drink another drop of liquor as long as I live.

MRS. M: Oh, husband, this is indeed happiness! Look! look at our dear child! Her eyes are fixed—she is dying!

MARY: Yes, mother; your Mary has lived long enough—the angels have heard little Mary's prayer! Father won't want any one to follow him, for he will be good, and sometime we shall all be together. Don't you remember the little hymn you taught me? It all comes in my mind now, although I had not thought of it before for a long time. Everything looks so beautiful around me; I don't feel any pain now. *(Kisses him.)* Good-bye, mother.

(Kisses her.

> We shall meet in the land where spring is eternal,
>   Where darkness ne'er cometh—no sorrow nor pain;
> Where the flowers never fade—in that clime ever vernal
>   We shall meet, and our parting be never again.

MARY *dies;* MORGAN *falls on the couch.* MRS. MORGAN *sobs over the body. Slow music.*

TEMPERANCE SONGS

Father, Dear Father, Come Home with Me Now

Father, dear father, come home with me now!
The clock in the steeple strikes one;
You said you were coming right home from the shop,
As soon as your day's work was done.
Our fire has gone out, our house is all dark,
And mother's been watching for you;
With poor brother Benny so sick in her arms,
Without you, oh, what can she do?
Come home! Come home! Come home!
Please, father, dear father, come home.

Father, dear father, come home with me now!
The clock in the steeple strikes two;
The night has grown colder and Benny is worse,
But he has been calling for you.
Indeed, he is worse, Ma says he will die,
Perhaps before morning shall dawn;
And this is the message she sent me to bring,
"Come quickly, or he will be gone."

"Father, Dear Father, Come Home with Me Now," music and lyrics by Henry C. Work, 1864.

Come home! Come home! Come home!
Please, father, dear father, come home.

Father, dear father, come home with me now!
The clock in the steeple strikes three;
The house is so lonely, the hours are so long,
For poor weeping mother and me.
Yes, we are alone, poor Benny is dead,
And gone with the Angels of light;
And these were the very last words that he said,
"I want to kiss Papa good night."
Come home! Come home! Come home!
Please, father, dear father, come home.

CHORUS

Hear the sweet voice of your own little child,
As she tearfully begs you to come!
Oh, who could resist this most pitiful pray'r,
"Please, father, dear father, come home!"

The Drunkard's Wife

In the midst of a meeting a woman arose
And a warning she uttered there,
For the girls in the bloom of their beautiful youth
Who were happy and free and fair.

Oh, I married a drunkard, dear girls, she exclaimed,
And was giddy and young and gay,
But like mist in the morning my joys took their flight
And thus swiftly they passed away.

Oh girls, she then pleaded, oh heed me well,
And listen while I my story tell,
Too late I had learned of my wasted life
The terrible fate of a drunkard's wife.

I have learned that the crown of all sorrow below
Which will crush and will blight the heart,
The poor wife of a drunkard is destined to know
And to writhe and to suffer the smart.
Though young, yet behold my hair is white
Made so by the scenes of one sad night.

Oh the sight, oh the sight of that terrible night,
She exclaimed in an anguished tone,
And the scenes of the past seemed to rush o'er her sight

"The Drunkard's Wife," music by L. L. Pickett, lyrics by M. W. Knapp, 1894.

As if reason they would dethrone.
With hands that were pale she hid her face
As if to conceal her deep disgrace.

The delirium tremens, oh girls, have you seen?
May God spare you the fearful sight
Of a husband insane by the demon drink
As he staggers toward home at night.
Oh take them away! I heard him scream,
It seems like a sad and awful dream.

On that night I was sitting beside my sick boy
And my two little girls at rest.
With a feeling of fear, that they both were unsafe,
Of my soul possessed.
I rushed to their room, and on the bed
I found they were mangled, cold and dead.

By the hands of their father they both had been slain
And the knife with their blood still red,
In the frenzy of drink and madness of shame
He still raved with his reason fled.
On me he then glared, his wretched wife
And then with a thrust he took his life.

Then I fell to the floor and was borne from the room,
A wreck since that night I've been,
And the boy that was left had a passion for drink,
The sad mark of his father's sin.
It chained him, though young, a hopeless slave,
And early he filled a drunkard's grave.

I beg of you girls, as you value your lives
From the drinker to turn aside,
And give heed to no plea, whatever it be
Of a drinker to be the bride.
To save from such sorrow as wrecked my life,
Oh never become a drunkard's wife.

Lips That Touch Liquor Shall Never Touch Mine

You are coming to court me, but not as of yore
When I hastened to answer your ring at my door,
For I trusted that he who stood waiting me then
Was the brightest and truest and noblest of men.
When your lips on mine imprinted farewell
They had never been soiled by the beverage of hell,

"Lips That Touch Liquor Shall Never Touch Mine," attributed to George W. Young, 1901.

But they come to me now with that terrible sign,
And the lips that touch liquor shall never touch mine.

I think of that night in the garden alone
When in whispers you told me your heart was my own,
That your love in the future should faithfully be
Never shared by no other, kept faithfully for me.
Oh sweet to my soul is that memory still
Of the lips that met mine when I murmured I will,
But now to that pressure no more I incline,
For the lips that touch liquor shall never touch mine.

Oh John, how it crushed me when first in your face
The pen of the Demon had written disgrace,
And turned me in silence and tears from the breath
All poisoned and fouled with the perfume of death.
It scattered the hopes I had treasured to last,
It ruined the future and darkened the past,
It shattered my idle and sullied the shrine,
For the lips that touch liquor shall never touch mine.

I loved you dearer than language can tell,
You saw it, you knew it, you proved it too well,
But the man whom I loved was far other than he
Who now from the barroom comes reeling to me.
In manhood and honor so noble and right,
Your heart was so true and your genius so bright,
Your soul was unstained, unpolluted by wine,
But the lips that touch liquor shall never touch mine.

You promised reform, but I trusted in vain,
The pledge was but made to be broken again,
And the lover so false to his promises now
Would not as my husband be true to his vow.
The word must be spoken that bids you depart,
Though the effort to speak it will shatter my heart,
In silence, with blighted affection I'll pine,
But the lips that touch liquor shall never touch mine.

If one spark of virtue within you remains,
Go fan it with prayers till it kindles again,
Resolve with God's help you in future will be
From wine, beer and whiskey unshackled and free,
And if you can conquer this foe of the soul,
In manhood and honor beyond its control,
This heart will again beat responsive to thine,
And your lips free from liquor be welcome to mine.

HOME PROTECTION BY LAW

"HOME PROTECTION" is the general name given to a movement already endorsed by the W.C.T. Unions of eight states, the object of which is to secure for all women above the age of twenty-one years the ballot as one means for the protection of their homes from the devastation caused by the legalized traffic in strong drink. . . .

It will be seen that, while the reason for seeking this added weapon in women's hands is in each case *that it may be used against the rum power, in defense of Home,* there is much latitude in the methods by which it is sought, as also in the extent to which the idea is carried out and in the progress which different states have made. . . .

About Petitions

Let us remember that, in giving prominence to this branch of work, we are but *transferring the crusade from the saloon to the sources whence the saloon derives its guaranties and safeguards.* Surely, this does not change our work from sacred to secular! Surely, that is a short-sighted view which says: "It was womanly to plead with saloon-keepers not to sell; but it is unwomanly to plead with law-makers not to legalize the sale and to give us power to prevent it." . . .

King Majority

Once more will the time-honored declaration be made to-day, by a thousand Fourth of July orators, that "the Americans are a free people." But I insist that we are governed by the most powerful king whose iron rule ever determined the policy, moulded the institutions, or controlled the destinies of a great nation.

So pervasive is his influence that it penetrates to the most obscure and distant hamlet with the same readiness, and there wields the same potency as in his empire's capital; nay (with reverence be it said), he is like Deity in that his actual presence is co-extensive with his vast domain. Our legislatures are his playthings, our congressmen his puppets, and our honored President the latest child of his adoption. We do not often call him by his name, this potentate of million hands and myriad voices; but, to my thinking, nothing is to day so vital to America as that we become better acquainted with our ruler. Let me then present to your thought his Majestic Highness KING MAJORITY, Sovereign Ruler of these United States.

King Alcohol

Permit me now to introduce a different character, who comes to the court of King Majority as chief ambassador from the empire of his Satanic Majesty. Behold! I show you the skelton at our patriotic banquet. It has a skull with straightened forehead and sickening smile; but bedecked with

Frances E. Willard, *Home Protection Manual* (New York, 1879), passim.

wreaths of vine, clusters of grape, and heads of golden grain—King Alcohol, present at court in radiant disguise. With a foaming beer-mug at his lips, he drinks the health of King Majority; and, placing at his feet a chest of gold labeled "Internal Revenue," he desireth conditions of peace.

The Question

Behold in these two figures the bewildering danger and the ineffable hope of the Republic! How can we rouse the stolid giant, King Majority? How light in those sleepy eyes the fires of a holy and relentless purpose? How nerve once more, with the resistless force that smote African slavery to death, the mighty sinews of the Republic's sleeping king? . . .

The Women of Illinois

Kind friends, I am not theorizing. I speak that I do know and testify what I have seen. Out on the Illinois prairies we have resolved to expend on voters the work at first bestowed upon saloon-keepers. We have transferred the scene of our crusade from the dram-shop to the council-room of the municipal authorities, whence the dram-shop derives its guaranties and safeguards. Nay, more. The bitter argument of defeat led us to trace the tawny, seething, foaming tide of beer and whiskey to its source; and there we found it surging forth from the stately capitol of Illinois, with its proud dome and flag of stripes and stars. . . . Among the many branches of our work, we gathered up 175,000 names of Illinois's best men and women (80,000 being the names of voters), who asked the legislature for a law giving women the ballot on the temperance question. In prosecuting our canvass for these names, we sent copies of our "Home Protection Petition" to every minister, editor, and postmaster in the state; also to all leading temperance men and women, and to every society and corporation from which we had anything to hope.

In this way our great state was permeated, and in most of its towns the petition was brought before the people. . . . Men have placed money in our hands to carry on the Home Protection work, saying: "The women of America must solve this problem. Our business relations, our financial interests, our political affiliations and ambitions have tied our hands; but we will set yours free, that you may rid us of this awful curse." . . .

Enter yonder saloon. See them gathered around their fiery or their foamy cups, according to the predominance in their veins of Celtic or of Teuton blood. What are they talking of, those sovereign citizens? The times have changed. It is no longer tariff or no tariff, resumption of specie payments, or even the behavior of our Southern brethren that occupies their thought. No. Home questions have come elbowing their way to the front. The child in the midst is also in the market-place, and they are bidding for him there, the politicians of the saloon. So skillfully will they make out the slate, so vigorously turn the crank of the machine, that, in spite of churches and temperance societies combined, the measures dear to them will triumph and measures dear to the fond mother heart will fail. Give her, at least, a fair chance to offset by her ballot the machinations which imperil her son. . . .

During past years the brave women who pioneered the equal suffrage movement, and whose perceptions of justice were keen as a Damascus blade, took for their rallying cry: "Taxation without representation is tyranny." But the average woman, who has nothing to be taxed, declines to go forth to battle on that issue. Since the Crusade, plain, practical temperance people have begun appealing to the same average woman, saying, "With your vote we can close the saloons that tempt your boys to ruin"; and behold! they have transfixed with the arrow of conviction that mother's heart, and she is ready for the fray. Not rights, but duties; not her need alone, but that of her children and her country; not the "woman," but the "human" question is stirring women's hearts and breaking down their prejudice to-day. . . .

Make Self-Interest Our Ally

The great majority of men who are in office desire to be re-elected. By fair means, if they can; but to be re-elected anyhow. Only in one way can they bring this to pass: by securing on their side old King Majority. If we furnish them with a constituency committed to the proposition "The saloon must go," then go it will, and on the double quick. Let the city council know that women have the ballot, and will not vote for them if they license saloons, and they will soon come out for prohibition. Let the sheriff, marshal, and constable know that their tenure of office depends on their success in executing the law thus secured, and their faithfulness will leave nothing to be desired. Let the shuffling justice and the truckling judge know that a severe interpretation of the law will brighten their chances of promotion, and you will behold rigors of penalty which Neal Dow himself would wince to see. . . .

Our hope for the entire suppression of the evils of intemperance is in the direction of prevention, rather than of cure. We may not hope to reform all the drinkers of the present; but, if we can prevent others from forming the habit, we shall soon free the country from its greatest curse and shame. If we remove these places of temptation from the streets, and take away the garb of respectability which a government license gives to the deadly traffic, the oncoming generation will be comparatively free from the evils which so oppress us. A great army of boys—innocent, bright, buoyant, and full of hope; just from their mothers' warm kiss and benediction—is now moving into the field, taking their first experience in contact with the world; and, unless these places of temptation are suppressed, great numbers of them will soon be swallowed up by this great vortex of ruin, which already has had too much of our best blood and brain. We ask that the people shall have the chance to say by vote whether the business of making drunkards, whose wives and children are to be covered with shame and crushed with poverty; whether the business which renders life and property insecure, piles up taxes, and corrupts public morals, shall be carried on in their midst; and we affirm that to deny the people this right *is oppression.*

For God and Home and Native Land

HOME PROTECTION PETITION.

ILLINOIS W. C. T. U.

To be Returned to ____, *at* ____, *by the* ____ *Day of* ____, *Without Fail.*
TO THE SENATE AND HOUSE OF REPRESENTATIVES OF THE STATE OF ILLINOIS:

Whereas, In these years of temperance work the argument of defeat in our contest with the saloons has taught us that our efforts are merely palliative of a disease in the body politic, which can never be cured until law and moral suasion go hand in hand in our beloved state; and
Whereas, The instincts of self-protection and of apprehension for the safety of her children, her tempted loved ones, and her home render woman the natural enemy of the saloons; *Therefore,* your petitioners, men and women in the State of Illinois, having at heart the protection of our homes from their worst enemy, the legalized traffic in strong drink, do hereby most earnestly pray your honorable body that, by suitable legislation, it may be provided that in the State of Illinois the question of licensing at any time, in any locality, the sale of any and all intoxicating drinks shall be submitted to and determined by ballot, in which women of lawful age shall be privileged to take part, in the same manner as men, when voting on the question of license.

DIVORCE DIFFICULTIES

This is a suit instituted by Ruth A. Hansley against her husband Samuel G. Hansley for a divorce *a vinculo matrimonii* [from the bonds (chains) of marriage—ed.] and for alimony. The parties were married in 1836 and lived together until August 1844; when the wife left her husband and went to reside with her brother in the same neighborhood and has lived there ever since.

The petition was filed on the 25th day of March 1845. It states, that the "petitioner lived for many years the wife of the said Samuel, enjoying much happiness, and fondly hoped to do so for many years yet to come, as she cheerfully fulfilled all the duties of an affectionate wife, until the conduct of her husband became so intolerable that it could no longer be endured: that, without any cause known to her, her husband took to drink,

James Iredell, ed., *Reports of Cases at Law Argued and Determined in the Supreme Court of North Carolina from August Term, 1849, to December Term, 1849* . . . (Raleigh, 1850), vol. 10, pp. 506–16, passim.

and, while in that state, would commit so many outrages against the modesty and decency of the petitioner, that she refrains from repeating them: that the influence of his intoxication would last sometimes for a month; all of which time the conduct of the said Samuel G. towards the petitioner would be intolerable; and the petitioner was often cruelly beaten by him, and his whole course of conduct towards her would be so entirely different from what she might have reasonably anticipated, that he rendered her life burdensome and too intolerable to be borne, from a habit so well calculated to destroy the reason, the affections and all the social relations of life, and to which the petitioner must attribute this brutal conduct of her said husband: that for weeks the said Samuel G. would absent himself from the petitioner during the whole night, although during the day time residing on the same farm, while so absenting himself; that it has come to the knowledge of the petitioner, that her husband did habitually, while so absenting himself from the petitioner, bed and cohabit with a negro woman named Lucy, belonging to him: that for some time previous to this fact coming to her knowledge with that degree of certainty, upon which she could rely, her suspicions were aroused, that such must be the fact; but that, not being able to prove the charge, and not being satisfied to abandon her husband until the proof could be clearly satisfactory to her own mind, the petitioner tried to endure, as long as it was reasonable for any wife to endure, the conduct of her husband; and that, during all the said time, her husband not only abandoned her bed entirely, and bedded with the said negro Lucy, but he deprived the petitioner of the control of all those domestic duties and privileges connected with the house, which belong to a wife, and placed the said Lucy in the full possession and enjoyment of those privileges and duties, and insulted the petitioner by openly and repeatedly ordering her to give place to the said negro, and saying that the petitioner was an incumbrance, and encouraged the said Lucy to treat her also: that, when the petitioner would no longer endure these things, and became entirely satisfied of the cause of such treatment, and of the truth of her previous suspicions, the petitioner abandoned her said husband: that, bedsides all this, her said husband, not satisfied with the treatment as above set forth, would go from home and take with him the keys of the house, and deprive the petitioner of food for two or three days at a time, and of every comfort, to which, as a wife, she was entitled: that often he would, at night, compel the petitioner to sleep in bed with said negro Lucy, when he would treat the said Lucy as his wife, he occupying the same bed with the petitioner and the negro Lucy: that from the cruel and severe treatment of her husband toward the petitioner, she was afraid to resist or to decline so occupying the same bed with her husband and the said negro woman: that, when it was not agreeable to her husband to permit the petitioner to occupy the house, he would often lock her out of doors and there compel her to remain, during the whole night, unprotected and exposed to all the trials incident to such a situation: that she, at length, abandoned the residence of her husband in August 1844, and has made her home with one of her brothers ever since: and that, since her knowledge of the adulterous conduct of her said husband with the said negro Lucy, the petitioner has not admitted him to conjugal embraces, and is resolved never again so to do."

The petition then sets out the husband's estate, with a view to alimony, and it prays for a divorce from the bonds of matrimony and for a suitable provision.

The answer admits, that, at one period the defendant was intemperate and in the habit of intoxication; but it states, that, for several years before his wife left him, he had been perfectly sober. The defendant also admits that he chastised his wife once: but he denies that he ever did so but at that time, or that that was a violent or severe beating: and he says, that he immediately regretted having done so, and acknowledged that he was wrong and made the most humble apologies to her therefor, which he thought reconciled her: but that on the same night she abandoned his house. The answer then denies all the other allegations of the libel specially. . . .

RUFFIN, C.[hief] J.[ustice] The divorce act requires all the material facts charged to be submitted to a jury, upon whose verdict and not otherwise, the Court is to decree. It excludes, by necessary implication, from the consideration of the jury, admissions in the pleadings, and, consequently, any made orally on the trial. The purpose is to prevent collusion. . . .

The Court, however, is of opinion that a sufficient case does not appear in the record to authorize a divorce *a vinculo matrimonii*, which is that granted and the only one prayed for. The jury, indeed, found that the defendant separated himself from his wife and lived in adultery with his slave; and, if there were any corresponding allegation in the libel, there would be a case to render the decree right. But we think there is no such allegation. There is such a want of precision as to the dates and order of events charged, that one cannot say exactly, how far the allegations were meant to extend. The only periods given are those of 1836 for the marriage, and August 1844, for the separation of the petitioner from her husband and going to live with her brother. Everything, stated in the libel, is stated as having occurred between those periods. There is no separation of the parties alleged until that in 1844, when the petitioner left her husband's house, and there is no allegation of any adultery by him after that event. As far as we can understand the petition . . . the grossness of his debaucheries, and the cruelty and indignity, with which he treated his wife, made her condition with him intolerable and authorized her to escape from his society and control. In such cases the third section of the act allows a divorce *a mensa et thoro* to be granted, so as to protect the wife from the efforts of the husband to force her to return. But those are not sufficient causes for a divorce from the bonds of matrimony, under the second section. That does not authorize such a divorce for cruelty, nor for every act of adultery, nor even for habitual adultery, provided the parties continue to live together. On the contrary, the words are, that when "either party

has separated him or herself from the other and is living in adultery,"
the injured person may be divorced *a vinculo*. In addition, the eighth section
enacts, that if the party complaining admitted the other either to conjugal
embraces or society, after knowledge of the criminal fact, it shall be a
bar to a suit for divorce for cause of adultery. Now, in the first place, it
is certain, upon the face of the libel, that the wife continued to live with
the husband, not only after she knew such circumstances, as created the
most violent presumption of his guilt, but after the actual knowledge of
it by being present and in the same bed at the fact. There is no statement
of any act of adultery, which we can say or suppose was posterior to those,
to which the wife was thus privy. As they took place before the separation
and she was privy to them, a divorce *a vinculo* cannot be founded on them
by themselves. We are far, however, from thinking those defaults of the
husband purged by the conduct of his wife. On the contrary she fully
accounts for her finally leaving his house, and divested that act of the
appearance of fault on her part. After such a separation, forced on her
by the debasing depravity, violence and other outrages of the husband,
she might well insist on any supervening criminality on his part. For, so
far from being precluded from making complaint of the repetition of the
fault, the guilt of the repetition, after such forbearance—not connivance—
on the part of the wife, would be aggravated beyond that of the first fault.
We shall hold, therefore, that she might insist on adultery with this slave,
supervening the separation thus forced on her. From the evidence respecting the child, about whom the petition would hardly have been silent, if
it had been born when it was filed, and from the findings of the jury, it
may be presumed, that in fact the criminal and disgraceful connexion between this man and his negro woman did continue after the petitioner
left him. If so, it is unfortunate that it should have been omitted in framing
the petition. That it is omitted, is quite clear; for, the petition gives no
account of the husband's life after the day the wife left him, excepting
only that he had not subsequently been admitted by her into conjugal
embraces. The finding of the jury, therefore, that the husband separated
himself from his wife and is living or afterwards lived in adultery, and
that she never admitted him into conjugal embraces after her knowledge
of that adultery, can have no influence on the decree, because it is incompatible with the petition, or, at least, is without any allegation in the petition
of such supervening adultery, to authorize it. That the existence of such
adultery in fact is indispensable, is clear from the words of the act "is
living in adultery" after the separation. But it is equally clear from the
reason of the thing. For, the law does not mean to dissolve the bonds of
matrimony and exclude one of the parties from marriage, until there is
no just ground to hope for a reconciliation. For that reason a divorce of
that kind is denied, when the parties give such evidence of the probability
of reconciliation, as to continue to live together. And even when there is
a separation, if the offending party should reform forthwith and lead a
pure life afterwards, the law does not look upon it as hopeless, that reconcili-

ation may in time follow the reformation. It may not be a case, indeed, in which the law will permit the husband to insist on a restoration of the conjugal rights of society and cohabitation, by compelling the wife's return. But, on the other hand, it is not a case of which it is past hope, that the wife may not, upon the strength of ancient affections, and a sense of duty and interest, be willing of herself, at some time, to partake of the society and share in the fate of her reformed husband; and, until that be past hope, or, at least, a continuing impurity of life, after separation, so far impairs the hope of reformation as to leave no just expectation of it, the law will not cut off the parties from the liberty of uniting. In the present case, there is nothing in the petition to shew, that the husband and his former paramour have ever seen each other since the day the wife left the premises. Consequently, the decree was erroneous, and the petition ought to have been dismissed, notwithstanding the verdict; which will be certified accordingly.

ADULTERY AMONG THE GENTEEL

Mr. Beecher's Denial

The publication of Mr. Tilton's statement . . . drew from Mr. Beecher the following emphatic denial of his assertions, and defence of Mrs. Tilton. . . .

I recognize the many reasons which make it of transcendent importance to myself, the church, and the cause of public morality, that I shall give a full answer to the charges against me. But having requested the Committee of Investigation [of the Plymouth Church—ed.] to search this matter to the bottom, it is to them that I must look for my vindication.

But I cannot delay for an hour to defend the reputation of Mrs. Elizabeth R. Tilton, upon whose name, in connection with mine, her husband has attempted to pour shame.

One less deserving of such disgrace I never knew. From childhood she has been under my eye, and since reaching womanhood she has had my sincere admiration and affection. I cherish for her a pure feeling, such as a gentleman might honorably offer to a Christian woman, and which he might receive and reciprocate without moral scruple. I reject with indignation every imputation which reflects upon her honor or my own.

My regard for Mrs. Tilton was perfectly well known to my family; when serious difficulties sprang up in her household, it was to my wife that she resorted for counsel; and both of us, acting from sympathy, and, as it subsequently appeared, without full knowledge, gave unadvised counsel which tended to harm.

I have no doubt that Mr. Tilton found that his wife's confidence and

Charles F. Marshall, *The True History of the Brooklyn Scandal* (Philadelphia, 1873), pp. 177–81, 189–95, passim.

reliance upon my judgment had greatly increased, while his influence had diminished, in consequence of a marked change in his religious and social views, which was taking place during those years. Her mind was greatly exercised lest her children should be harmed by views which she deemed vitally false and dangerous.

I was suddenly and rudely aroused to the reality of impending danger by the disclosure of domestic distress, of sickness, perhaps unto death, of the likelihood of separation, and the scattering of a family every member of which I had tenderly loved. The effect upon me of the discovery of the state of Mr. Tilton's feelings, and the condition of his family, surpassed in sorrow and excitement anything that I had ever experienced in my life. That my presence, influence and counsel had brought to a beloved family sorrow and alienation, gave, in my then state of mind, a poignancy to my suffering which I hope no other man may ever feel.

Even to be suspected of having offered, under the privileges of a peculiarly sacred relation, an indecorum to a wife and mother, could not but deeply wound any one who is sensitive to the honor of womanhood. There were peculiar reasons for alarm in this case on other grounds, inasmuch as I was then subject to certain malignant rumors, and a flagrant outbreak in this family would bring upon them an added injury, derived from these shameless falsehoods. . . .

Believing at the time that my presence and counsels had tended, however unconsciously, to produce a social catastrophe, represented as imminent, I gave expression to my feelings in an interview with a mutual friend. . . . Had I been the evil man Mr. Tilton now represents, I should have been calmer and more prudent. It was my horror of the evil imputed that filled me with morbid intensity at the very shadow of it. . . .

Is it conceivable, if the original charge had been what is now alleged, that he would have condoned the offence, not only with the mother of his children, but with him whom he believed to have wronged them? The absurdity, as well as the falsity of this story is apparent, when it is considered that Mr. Tilton now alleges that he carried this guilty secret of his wife's infidelity for six months, locked up in his own breast, and that then he divulged it to me, only that there might be a reconciliation with me. Mr. Tilton has since, in every form of language, and to a multitude of witnesses, orally, in written statements and in printed documents, declared his faith in his wife's purity.

After the reconciliation of Mr. Tilton with me, every consideration of propriety and honor demanded that the family trouble should be kept in that seclusion which domestic affairs have a right to claim as a sanctuary; and to that seclusion it was determined that it should be confined. . . .

I do not purpose to analyze and contest at this time the extraordinary paper of Mr. Tilton; but there are two allegations which I cannot permit to pass without special notice. They refer to the only two incidents which Mr. Tilton pretends to have witnessed personally: the one, an alleged scene in my house while looking over engravings; and the other a chamber scene in his own house. His statements concerning these are absolutely false.

Nothing of the kind ever occurred, nor any semblance of any such things. They are now brought to my notice for the first time.

To every statement which connects me dishonorably with Mrs. Elizabeth R. Tilton, or which in any wise would impugn the honor and purity of this beloved Christian woman, I give the most explicit, comprehensive and solemn denial.

HENRY WARD BEECHER.

Mrs. Tilton's Cross-Examination

The official report of the cross-examination of Mrs. Elizabeth R. Tilton before the Investigating Committee, as communicated to the press by the chairman of that committee, is given . . . as follows:

By Mr. HILL—You stated, I think, the date of your marriage in your former examination?

A: I believe so—1855. . . .

Q: Please state to the committee what Mr. Tilton's conduct was toward you in the early part of your married life, so far as personal attention was concerned, in sickness or in health?

A: I wish these gentlemen to understand that, to a very large extent, I take the blame upon myself of the indifference my husband has shown to me in all my life; at first I understood very well that I was not to have the attention that many wives have; I realized that his talent and genius must not be narrowed down to myself; that I made him understand also; to a very large extent I attribute to that the later sorrows of my life; I gave him to understand, that what might be regarded as neglect under other circumstances would not be regarded by me as neglect in him, owing to his business and to his desire to make a name for himself and to rise before the world.

Q: To what extent was that attention to outside matters carried by him to the neglect of his family?

A: At the birth of the first three children, I had very severe and prolonged sicknesses; but when he saw me, he never felt that I was sick, because on seeing him I always tried to seem well; I felt so desirous of his presence. It was charged upon me many a time by my mother and my brother: "When Theodore or the doctor comes, you are never sick." They said of me: "She has never a genius for being sick."

Q: Will you state just what attention your husband bestowed upon you in case of sickness during your confinement, or any other illness if you had them?

A: Well, I had no attention whatever, I may truthfully say, from him, any more than a stranger would give; I do not think it was from neglect so

much as from an inability on his part to understand that I was sick and
suffering; though, in fact, I was very seriously ill. . . .

EARLY MARRIED LIFE

Q. How much was he engrossed with actual business at this time?

A: Not very much; I always thought that if Theodore had more business
he would have less time for sentiment and romance.

Q: How much time did he spend in actual business as editor?

A: In the early years of his editorial life I think he was a pretty hard worker;
he never had his study at home then, and never wrote much at home. . . .

Q: You intimated that you thought it would be better if your husband
had been more fully occupied; will you explain further what you meant
by that remark?

A: He spent a great deal of his time at home in moods of dissatisfaction
with the surroundings, yearning and wanting other ministrations; there
was nothing in our home that satisfied him.

Q: Why was that?

A: It was on account of my domestic duties; I think it was because I could
not minister to him in the way he wanted me to—that is, in reading; his
life was largely literary, and I could not meet him there; I had three little
children, all about the same age, at that time. . . .

THE FIRST SEEDS OF DISCORD

Q: I want to ask you in regard to his attention to domestic wants—to the
needs of the family?

A: He did not know anything about them at all; I took charge of them
myself altogether; often he was critical about it, and I would say, "Well,
alone I can do no better; but with you I think I can do much better!"
and he would say, "I do not call upon you to go to the office to do my
work; this is yours—the other is mine."

Q: What was the character of his criticisms?

A: They were very unreasonable, indeed; he would speak to me harshly
and severely about any little extravagance, as he considered it; he was
very fastidious, and must have the best of everything; but he didn't realize
the cost.

Q: Do you mean that he found fault with your domestic management?

A: Yes, sir; with my management of my servants, and with my management
of the household matters generally.

Q: You speak of his referring to it harshly and severely; how did he treat
you in matters of that description?

A: I fail generally when I attempt to be severe, and, therefore, I do not think I can imitate or describe him; he would frequently make some very impulsive remark; I remember his taking me to task and scolding me severely before the butcher in regard to my dealings there; but directly after making a severe remark to me he would always apologize, and say that he was sorry; but the apology was in private; it is a sorry story, indeed.

Q: Were his demands extravagant?

A: Very much so; he was very particular with regard to his diet, and the table linen and his own apparel, and the glass and china must be very nice; but these things cost money, so that the expenses which we were subjected to were largely increased, while I would have liked very well to have had it different.

Q: Now, state to the committee what it was that first really disturbed your peace of mind in your family?

A: I think that first I was jealous of his attention to the ladies. . . .

COMMENTS ON MR. BEECHER'S FIRST VISITS

Q: When did he begin to talk with you, if at all, in regard to your association with and friendship for Mr. Beecher?

A: I think I had no personal visits from Mr. Beecher before 1866; that is the first that I remember seeing him very much.

Q: What was the criticism in regard to Mr. Beecher and yourself which Mr. Tilton made?

A: I would like to go back a little here, for I think it will show you my manner with Mr. Beecher; when I lived in Oxford street, that was the first of this taint with which Mr. ____ filled my husband's mind as early as 1865; Theodore then used to begin to talk to me about Mr. Beecher's wrong-doings with ladies with which he (Mr. Tilton) had heard from Mr. ____, and night after night, and day after day, he talked about Mr. Beecher; he seemed to be worried on that subject, so that when Mr. Beecher came to see me, Mr. Tilton immediately began to have suspicions; but in order that I might be perfectly transparent to my husband with respect to my interviews with Mr. Beecher whenever I was alone with him, I used to make a memorandum, and charge my mind with all the details of the conversation that passed between us, that I might repeat them to Mr. Tilton; it was so in regard to every gentleman who came to see me, and with whom I sat alone; I was very closely watched and questioned, but especially in regard to Mr. Beecher; I attributed those criticisms from Theodore to Mr. ____'s criticisms; I never had a visit from Mr. Beecher that I was not questioned; Theodore would question me till I thought I had told him all that we talked about, and, perhaps, a day or two afterward, I would throw out a remark which Mr. Beecher had made, and Theodore would say, "You didn't tell me that yesterday;" I would say: "I forgot it;" "You lie," he would say, "you didn't mean to tell me;" "Oh, yes, I did mean to tell you, but I forgot it;" for two or three years I tried faithfully to repeat to my husband everything that I said and did, till I found it made him more suspicious than ever; he believed that I left out many things purposely, while I was conscious of never meaningly omitting anything; I wanted Theodore to know everything that passed between us; I often said that if he would only come home and be there he would know all. . . .

THE FIRST CRIMINAL CHARGES

Q: When did his complaints against you change from the form of criticism to that of accusation, or something more than mere criticism?

A: In the latter part of the winter, and in the early sping of 1869–70 he began to talk to me, assuming that I had done wrong.

Q: In what respect?

A: With Mr. Beecher.

Q: Criminally?

A: Yes; I have been with him days and nights talking this matter over; but I would like to have you know that these conversations lasted for years, and that the change of his thought from the "old to the new," as he called it, was gradual; I used to think that his suspicions of me were caused by his not being at rest in his own mind. . . .

MR. TILTON'S ADMISSION TO HIS WIFE

MR. HILL—In July, 1870, had you any conversation with Mr. Tilton in regard to his own habits and his associations?

A: Yes, sir, I had.

Q: What was the character of this conversation?

A: He had always very freely opened his heart and his thoughts to me in all these conversations, for I think he never had a thought without telling me; no matter how much it hurt, he would tell it, and he made a great many disclosures to me of his life that summer.

Q: Did he make any confession to you of criminality with other ladies?

A: Yes, sir.

Q: And did you say that was about July, 1870?

A: Yes, sir.

Q: You have noticed his statement in which he says you confessed adultery to him about that time; and you say that the confession was the other way—from him to you?

A: It was; I do not mean that his confession at that time referred to one; his talk with me referred to several; it was the time when I was making up my mind what to do in regard to living with a person who had reached such a state, and in connection of those ideas he had grown into; he said he wished me to understand that when he was away from home on lecturing or anywhere visiting with friends, if he desired the gratification of himself he would do it.

Q: State what you refer to in your published statement, where you speak of your going to other people to correct impressions with reference to him, and finding that he had anticipated you?

A: The world was filled with slanders about him; he did not seem to know it; he thought everything came from me, and he said so; he declared that I was the originator of all this talk about him, and he insisted upon my correcting these impressions.

Q: Do you remember that that was in the summer of 1870?

A: Yes. I will give you one instance which occurred with Elizabeth so-and-so. Said he, "That woman has been talking against me, and I want you to go around and see her, and put an end to it." Well, I immediately did. The next day I put on my things and made a call on her, and said that I was surprised that she should add to the stories already in circulation—that I should have thought that she would have avoided doing it for my sake; and she said, "Mrs. Tilton, do you know why I didn't? Because the night before your husband had told stories of yourself to such and such a person, that came to me directly, and I was not going to allow an accusation of that character to stand against you." I found where I went not only the accusation, but the details which he has now published.

MR. SAGE—He was charging you with the same crime that he was committing himself?

A: Yes; and it was a very singular thing for him to do; I would go back from these calls utterly speechless; I could say no more to these people, and I said to him, "Theodore, what made you send me there?" He would deny that he had ever said any such things as were attributed to him; there was no talking with him; he was very unreasonable.

VIOLENT FAMILIES, 1835

Sydney, Ohio, 1833–34

Indictment, riot lodged against eight or ten young men and convicted and a wife also. Arose from wife of drunkard. For attending meeting, he

Henry Ward Beecher, *Journal*, Beecher Family Papers, Sterling Library, Yale University.

A scene from the 1870s of the final break in family ties. The consummate realism of these family occasions went with the themes of the "last farewell" and the "need to pay respects" and acknowledged the fragility of all earthly bonds.   *University of Kansas*

had abused her. Young men got up riot to dunk drunkard. That gave rise to indictment (by this drunkard, as in trial for riot he testified against young men). They said he swore falsely and tried him for perjury—all these young men then came up as witnesses against him. Next he brought civil action against them for damages for the beating and dunking.

Sunday Oct. 18, 1835, Cincinnati, Ohio

Conversed with Judge Holt on a number of criminal cases. *All* murderers who were convicted were so by Alcoholic Spirits. One in Clark County—child lost parents went to live with Uncle. Child became enfeebled with dysentery. Uncle came home drunk, ordered child to bring some 60 lbs. of goods for house. Child said would presently, his wife said child could not, enraged caught by arm, took ram-rod and beat child—cast to floor then told same again, child and wife again answered same, whipped again, cast to cradle, died that night.

Judge says three-fourths of crime by intemperance.

Another Case, Sydney, Ohio, 1835, Summer Term

Old man 80 years old. Son 35, hale and hearty for assault on father. Grand juryman testified, father and son at mill, son got drunk. Old man tried to tie up shirt of wagon, son became petulant, shoved him away and gave him a kick—said nothing—, went round to fore part of wagon, son came around, angry, struck him over head. He put both hands up and juryman got up, then and stopped him—asked old man if he hurt. "Some," said he, "but I should not care if this was first time but am used to it."

FAMILY VIOLENCE, 1890s

Prosecutor's Summation

In the midst of the largest city of this county, in the midst of his household, surrounded by people and houses and teams and civilization, in the midst of the day, right in that household, while they were attending to their household duties in the midst of their families, an aged man and an aged woman are suddenly and brutally assassinated. It was a terrible crime. It was an impossible crime. But it was committed. And very much, very much, Mr. Foreman, of the difficulty of solving this awful tragedy starts from the very impossibility of the thing itself. Set any human being you can think of, put any degraded man or woman you ever heard of at the bar, and say to them, "You did this thing," and it would seem incredible. And yet it was done; it was done. And I am bound to say, Mr. Foreman, and I say it out of a full heart, that it is scarcely more credible to believe the charge that followed the crime. I would not for one moment lose sight of the incredibility of that charge, nor ask you to believe it, unless you find it supported by facts that you cannot explain or deny. The prisoner at the bar is a woman, and a Christian woman, as the expression is used.

Edwin H. Porter, *The Fall River Tragedy* (Fall River, Mass., 1893), pp. 270–303, passim.

It is no ordinary criminal that we are trying to-day. It is one of the rank of lady, the equal of your wife and mine, of your friends and mine, of whom such things have never been suspected or dreamed before. I hope I may never forget nor in anything that I say here to-day lose sight of the terrible significance of that fact. We are trying a crime that would have been deemed impossible but for the fact that it was, and are charging with the commission of it a woman whom we would have believed incapable of doing it but for the evidence that it is my duty, my painful duty, to call to your attention. But I beg you to observe, Mr. Foreman and gentlemen, that you cannot dispose of the case upon that consideration. Alas, that it is so! But no station in life is a pledge or a security against the commission of crime, and we all know it. . . . The prisoner is a woman, one of that sex that all high-minded men revere, that all generous men love, that all wise men acknowledge their indebtedness to. It is hard, it is hard, Mr. Foreman and gentlemen, to conceive that woman can be guilty of crime. It is not a pleasant thing to reflect upon. But I am obliged to say what strikes the justice of every man to whom I am talking, that while we revere the sex, while we show our courtesies to them, they are human like unto us. They are no better than we; they are no worse than we. If they lack in strength and coarseness and vigor, they make up for it in cunning, in dispatch, in celerity, in ferocity. If their loves are stronger and more enduring than those of men, am I saying too much that, on the other hand, their hates are more undying, more unyielding, more persistent? We must face this case as men, not as gallants. You will be slow to believe it is within the capacity of a man to have done it. But it was done. You will be slower to believe that it was within the capacity of a woman to have done it, and I should not count you men if you did not, but it was done. It was done for a purpose. It was done by hatred. But who did it? You have been educated to believe, you are proud to recognize your loyalty, your fealty to the sex. Gentlemen, that consideration has no place under the oath you have taken.

. . .

We must now go into this establishment and see what manner of family this was. . . . It is useless to tell you that there was peace and harmony in that family. We know better. We know better. The remark that was made to Mrs. Gifford, the cloakmaker, was not a petulant outburst, such as might come and go. That correction of Mr. Fleet, at the very moment the poor woman who had reared that girl lay dead within ten feet of her voice, was not merely accidental. It went down deep into the springs of human nature. Lizzie Borden had never known her mother. She was not three years old when that woman passed away, and her youthful lips had scarcely learned to pronounce the tender word, mamma, and no picture of her lay in the girl's mind. And yet she had a mother—she had a mother. Before she was old enough to go to school, before she arrived at the age of five years, this woman, the choice of her father, the companion of her father, who had lost and mourned and loved again, had come in and had done her duty by that girl and had reared her, had stood in all the attitudes which characterize the tenderest of all human relations. Through all her childhood's sicknesses that woman had cared for her. When she came in weary with her sports, feeble and tired, it was on her breast that girl had sunk as have our children on the breast of their mothers. She had been her mother, faithful persevering, and had brought her up to be at least an honorable and worthy woman in appearance and manner.

This girl owed everything to her. Mrs. Borden was the only mother she had ever known, and she had given to this girl her mother's love and had given her this love when a child when it was not her own and she had not gone through the pains of childbirth, because it was her husband's daughter. And then a quarrel; what a quarrel. . . . You have worked round our father and have got a little miserable pittance of $1,500 out of him, and you shall be my mother no more. Am I exaggerating this thing? She kept her own counsel. Bridget did not know anything about it. She was in the kitchen. This woman never betrayed her feelings except when some one else tried to make her call her mother, and then her temper broke forth. Living or dead, no person should use that word mother to that poor woman unchallenged by Lizzie Borden. She had left it off herself; all through her childhood days, all through her young life Mrs. Borden had been a mother to her as is the mother of every other child to its offspring, and the time comes when they still live in the same house and this child will no longer call her by that name. Mr. Foreman, it means much. It means much. . . .

. . .

There may be that in his case which saves us from the idea that Lizzie Borden planned to kill her father. I hope she did not. But Lizzie Andrew Borden, the daughter of Andrew Jackson Borden, never came down those stairs. It was not Lizzie Andrew Borden, the daughter of Andrew Jackson Borden, that came down those stairs, but a murderess, transformed from all the thirty-three years of an honest life, transformed from the daughter, transformed from the ties of affections to the most consummate criminal we have read of in all our history or works of fiction. She came down to meet that stern old man. His picture shows that, if nothing more, even in death. That just old man, of the stern puritan stock, that most of you are from, gentlemen, that man who loved his daughters, but who also loved his wife, as the Bible commanded him to. And, above all, the one man in all this universe who would know who killed his wife. She had not thought of that. She had gone on. There is cunning in crime, but there is blindness in crime, too. She had gone on with stealth and cunning, but she had forgotten the hereafter. They always do. And when the deed was done she was coming downstairs to face Nemesis. There wouldn't be any question of what he would know of the reason why that woman lay in death. He knew who disliked her. He knew who could not tolerate her presence under the roof. He knew the discussion which had led up to the pitch of frenzy which resulted in her death, and she didn't dare to let him live, father though he was, and bound to her by every tie of affection. It is the melancholy, the inevitable attribute of crime that it is the necessary and fruitful parent of crime. . . .

. . .

I would not lift the weight of my finger to urge that this woman remarkable though she is, nervy as she is, brave as she is, cool as she is, should be condemned because grief, it may have been, but for other things in the case, drove back the tears to their source and forbade her to show the emotions that belong to the sex. But there are some things that are pregnant. My distinguished friend tells of the frequency of presentiments. They are frequent in the storybooks, Mr. Foreman. If they occur in real life they are usually thought of afterward. Did you ever hear one expressed beforehand? Tell me that this woman was physically incapable of that deed? My distinguished friend has not read female character enough to know that when a woman dares she dares, and when she will she will, and that given a woman that has that absolute command of herself . . . a woman whose courage surpassed that of any man I am talking to, I very humbly believe—tell me that she is physically incapable of this act? But those are trifles, Mr. Foreman. Those are trifles. Those are little chips that do not perhaps directly indicate which way the current flows. But there is more in the case than that. . . .

FAMILY, SOCIETY, AND STATE

Good family order makes good social order was a rule held as firmly in the nineteenth century as in the seventeenth and eighteenth or in the twentieth. But even in colonial life sometimes events led outside authorities to take on responsibilities that ordinarily fell to the family. Before the nineteenth century, communities acted in family matters mainly when death left children unprotected, and then only to place them firmly within families. By the 1840s and 1850s, however, broader kinds of outside intervention had begun to emerge. Public schools, of course, were beginning in many places to take on more of the tasks of education that families had done or that had taken place within family settings. In addition, as the case of Crouse *et al.* below asserted, the state had clear interests in the way children were raised and could even remove children from their natural families, either because the children themselves had become ungovernable or because the parents were deemed unfit to raise them.

A number of new institutions before the Civil War were designed to meet the problem of incompetent families and "wayward and homeless children." One of the earliest was the Children's Aid Society, founded in New York City in 1853 by Charles Loring Brace, a twenty-six-year-old clergyman who ran it for nearly forty years. The society first set up a boy's Industrial School, designed to give "street arabs" the skills and some of the moral influences they needed if they were to become "useful citizens." The society also pioneered the "free home" or "placing-out system" which put homeless children in the presumably morally superior homes out West, far from the evil influences of the urban environments they had previously inhabited. Another new way of providing for some children was legal adoption by those who could not have children, and by some who had recently "lost" a natural child. Adoption went beyond guardianship and gave the adopted child the same standing it would have had as a "child of the body." For children who had become "vicious" and turned to crime, the "reform school" was devised, a custodial institution designed not simply to remove the offenders from society and punish them but to bring about their "moral reformation."

The report extolling the Ohio Reform School (organized on the "cottage plan" and set in a pristine rural setting) raises the question of the extent to which these attempts to redress the evils of failed families themselves were based upon the assumptions that lay behind the sanctification of "the home." But the selection from Brace's *The Dangerous Classes of New York* (1872) indicates that although reformers subscribed to the idea of the sacredness of the home, their idea of it was based upon just one model, deviation from which justified breaking up other types of families. The last selection, an 1890s critique of the "placing-out system," questioned whether homes were in fact superior to institutions and carried the justification for interference close to where it was in the early decades of the twentieth century, the century of full-scale intervention in all aspects of family life.

THE REFORMATORY

. . . The House of Refuge is not a prison, but a school. Where reformation, and not punishment, is the end, it may indeed be used as a prison for juvenile convicts who would else be committed to a common gaol; and in respect to these, the constitutionality of the act which incorporated it, stands clear of controversy. It is only in respect of the application of its discipline to subjects admitted on the order of a court, a magistrate, or the managers of the Alms-house, that a doubt is entertained. The object of the charity is reformation, by training its inmates to industry; by imbuing their minds with principles of morality and religion; by furnishing them with means to earn a living; and, above all, by separating them from the corrupting influence of improper associates. To this end, may not the natural parents, when unequal to the task of education, or unworthy of it, be superseded by the *parens patria*, or common guardian of the community? It is to be remembered that the public has a paramount interest in the virtue and knowledge of its members, and that, of strict right, the business of education belongs to it. That parents are ordinarily entrusted with it, is because it can seldom be put into better hands; but where they are incompetent or corrupt, what is there to prevent the public from withdrawing their faculties, held, as they obviously are, at its sufferance? The right of parental control is a natural, but not an unalienable one. It is not excepted by the declaration of rights out of the subjects of ordinary legislation; and it consequently remains subject to the ordinary legislative power, which, if wantonly or inconveniently used, would soon be constitutionally restricted, but the competency of which, as the government is constituted, cannot be doubted. As to abridgment of indefeasible rights by confinement of the person, it is no more than what is borne, to a greater or less extent, in every school; and we know of no natural right to exemption from restraints which conduce to an infant's welfare. Nor is there a doubt of the propriety of their application in the particular instance. The infant has been snatched from a course which must have ended in confirmed depravity;

Ex Parte Crouse, 4 Wharton (Pa.) 9 (1838).

and, not only is the restraint of her person lawful, but it would be an act of extreme cruelty to release her from it.

ADOPTION, 1853

The People of the State of Wisconsin, represented in Senate and Assembly, do enact as follows:

SECTION 1.—Any inhabitant of this state may petition the county judge where he or she may reside, for leave to adopt a child not his or her own by birth.

SEC. 2.—If both, or either, of the parents of such child shall be living, they, or the survivor of them, as the case may be, shall consent in writing to such adoption; if neither parent be living, such consent may be given by the legal guardian of such child: if there be no legal guardian nor father nor mother, the next of kin of such child within the state, may give such consent, and if there be no such next of kin, the county judge may appoint some discreet and suitable person, to act in the proceedings as the next friend of such child, and give or withhold such consent.

SEC. 3.—If the child be of the age of fourteen years or upwards, the adoption shall not be made without his or her consent.

SEC. 4.—No petition by a person having a lawful wife shall be allowed unless such wife shall join therein; and no woman having a lawful husband shall be competent to present and prosecute such petition, unless the husband consent thereto.

SEC. 5.—If upon such petition, so presented and consented unto, as aforesaid, the county judge shall be satisfied of the identity and relations of the persons, and that of the petitioners, or in case of husband and wife, that the petitioners are of sufficient ability to bring up the child, and furnish suitable nurture and education, having reference to the degree and condition of its parents, and that it is fit and proper that such adoption shall take effect, he shall make a decree setting forth the said facts, and ordering that from and after the date of the decree, such child should be deemed and taken to all legal intents and purposes, the child of the petitioner or petitioners.

SEC. 6.—A child so adopted as aforesaid, shall be deemed for the purposes of inheritance and succession by such child, custody of the person, and right of obedience by such parent or parents by adoption, and all other legal consequences and incidents of the natural relation of parents and children, the same to all intents and purposes as if such had been born in lawful wedlock of such parent or parents by adoption, saving only that such child shall not be deemed capable of taking property expressly limited to the heirs of the body or bodies of such petitioner or petitioners.

Cited in Elinor Nims, *The Illinois Adoption Law and Its Administration* (Chicago, 1928), p. 121.

THE OHIO REFORM SCHOOL

[It is recommended that the state of Ohio] . . . provide an institution, such as all experience and the joint testimony of all, who have examined into this interesting subject, demonstrate to be the right one, we mean a *State Reform Farm*, where the mass of these unfortunate youths may be employed in agricultural, horticultural, and concomitant mechanical labors,—an institution without any semblance of a prison, and upon a system of labor, education, and discipline, for which, life *as it is*, and not as *life should not be*, forms the model.

Such a farm should consist of, at least, 2,000 acres. The land should be selected more with regard to health than its richness. The first cost of it should not exceed $20,000. Upon this farm the State should establish its principal reformatory school, under the system now in successful operation in Mettray, in France, modified according to the habits of life and domestic economy of this country. That system is called "the *family system*," as contradistinguished from the *big house cell* or *prison system*. Its main differences are—1st, That instead of one large building there are several detached ones, and each constituting one family, or household of 40 inmates, with a chief or *"father,"* and two sub-chiefs, or *"elder brothers,"* for each. 2nd, That all the various kinds of agricultural and a few of the more simple and more generally diffused mechanical trades form the source of employment. 3d, The establishment grows gradually and chiefly through the labor of the inmates. 4th, Its discipline is that of a family whose subsistence springs from labor, and officers as well as inmates are employed and work with each other; and, 5th, In its simplicity and studied adhesion to the kind of life led by the mass of the community, avoiding all experimenting in food, dress, lodgings, etc.

Such an institution, based upon the quantity of land suggested, might be started with one family of 40 boys; the building (and any common good farm house, or Swiss cottage, suits for it) being either already on the land, or to be erected at a cost not to exceed $2,000—and this one family taken from the Cincinnati institution, of the most able bodied and better disposed boys could build the houses for the second and so on, until the whole farm would gradually grow to the *model farm* of the State. The labor to be under the charge of the State Board of Agriculture. Such an institution appears to be just the thing wanted, for the following reasons.

The first and most prominent is, that divine law indicates the *family*, and its discipline dictated as it is by parental duty and enforced by parental love, as the institution where youth is best taken care of. Few, not more than one half per cent. of the population, happily ever require any other. The other should be as near the heaven-appointed institution as the nature of the case will admit of. Prisons are never of much use for educational and reformatory purposes, even for adults. To obviate the dire necessity

Commissioners of the Ohio Reform School, Annual Report, 1856 (Columbus, 1856), pp. 618–22.

of other existence, or, at least, to mitigate and diminish their extent, in other words to "stop the supplies" for crimes and prisons is the avowed and chief object of reform schools, houses of refuge and such like establishments, and, in view of this, it certainly seems to us a proposition too clear for argument, that the true way to accomplish this object is not a prison, but rather, an institution as much unlike it as possible. There are some boys and girls who are unfit for any other than prison life, but they are exceptions, and for them, and them only, prisons should be erected with most rigid discipline. And in this connection may we be allowed to state the well known fact, that nine-tenths of all the inmates of such establishments came there, because they either never enjoyed the sweet of a good family home, or the family influences surrounding them were bad. Does not that fact teach the unmistakable lesson, that the State, to reform such youths, must, in the means employed, come as near the idea of a well regulated, honest family, as is possible under the circumstances? Employment on a farm and instruction in its agricultural and simple mechanical labors, is universally admitted to be the best adapted for the purpose. Every institution we visited admitted this, and all of them used the land they could use, however little, with avidity. It affords variety of labors, and thereby the means to employ nearly every inmate usefully. "Boys are nearer to the ground than men," says a French proverb, whence may be argued with propriety, the general adaption of boys to the greater part of agricultural and horticultural labor.

The experience of all houses of refuge and similar institutions, teaches that the mass of the inmates of such establishments come from cities, and very frequently their mere removal is a reform in itself. Must not this fact at once suggest the idea, that the instruction and employment should be such as not to lead the youth after discharge right back to his haunts of vice? Confine him to mere mechanical or manufacturing employment, and he must after his discharge seek the cities to earn his livelihood. Habituate him to the life and labor of a farm, and he will, in nearly every case, continue so to live and labor when restored to society, and so the good influences commenced in the State institution will not be effaced.

DANGEROUS FAMILIES, 1870s

It is extraordinary, among the lowest classes, in how large a number of cases a second marriage, or the breaking of marriage, is the immediate cause of crime or vagrancy among the children. When questioning a homeless boy or street-wandering girl as to the former home, it is extremely common to hear "I couldn't get on with my step-mother," or "My step-father treated me badly," or "My father left, and we just took care of ourselves." These apparently exceptional events are so common in these

Charles Loring Brace, *The Dangerous Classes of New York* (New York, 1872), pp. 39–42.

classes as to fairly constitute them an important cause of juvenile crime. When one remembers the number of happy second marriages within one's acquaintance, and how many children have never felt the difference between their step-mother and their own mother, and what love and patience and self-sacrifice are shown by parents to their step-children, we may be surprised at the contrast in another class of the community. But the virtues of the poor spring very much from their affections and instincts; they have comparatively little self-control; the high lessons of duty and consideration for others are seldom stamped on them, and Religion does not much influence their more delicate relations with those associated with them. They might shelter a strange orphan for years with the greatest kindness; but the bearing and forbearing with the faults of another person's child year after year, merely from motives of duty or affection to its parent, belong to a higher range of Christian virtues, to which they seldom attain. Their own want of self-control and their tendency to jealousy, and little understanding of true self-sacrifice, combine to weaken and embitter these relations with step-children. The children themselves have plenty of faults, and have doubtless been little governed, so that soon both parties jar and rub against one another; and as neither have instincts or affections to fall back upon, mere principle or sense of duty is not enough to restrain them. What would be simply slights or jars in more controlled persons, become collisions in this class.

Bitter quarrels spring up between step-son and mother, or step-daughter and father; the other parent sometimes sides with the child, sometimes with the father; but the result is similar. The house becomes a kind of pandemonium, and the girls rush desperately forth to the wild life of the streets, or the boys gradually prefer the roaming existence of the little city-Arab to such a quarrelsome home. Thus it happens that step-children among the poor are so often criminals or outcasts.

It needs a number of years among the lower working-classes to understand what a force public opinion is in all classes in keeping the marriage-bond sacred, and what sweeping misfortunes follow its violation. Many of the Irish peasants who have landed here have married from pure affection. Their marriage has been consecrated by the most solemn ceremonies of their church. They come of a people peculiarly faithful to the marriage-tie, and whose religion has especially guarded female purity and the fidelity of husband and wife. At home, in their native villages, they would have died sooner than break the bond or leave their wives. The social atmosphere about them and the influence of the priests make such an act almost impossible. And yet in this distant country, away from their neighbors and their religious instructors, they are continually making a practical test of "Free-Love" doctrines. As the wife grows old or ugly—as children increase and weigh the parents down—as the home becomes more noisy and less pleasant,—the man begins to forget the vows made at the altar, and the blooming girl he then took; and, perhaps meeting some prettier woman, or hearing of some chance for work at a distance, he slips quietly away, and the deserted wife, who seems to love him the more the more false he is, is left alone. For a time she has faith in him and seeks him far and near; but at length she abandons hope, and begins the heavy struggle of maintaining her little family herself. The boys gradually get beyond her control; they are kept in the street to earn something for their support; they become wild and vagrant, and soon end with being street-rovers, or petty thieves, or young criminals. The girls are trained in begging or peddling, and, meeting with bold company, they gradually learn the manners and morals of the streets, and after a while abandon the wretched home, and break what was left of the poor mother's hope and courage, by beginning a life of shame.

FOSTER HOMES

It is very popular just now to advocate the placing of destitute children in families as rapidly as possible, instead of retaining them in institutions for any length of time. The advocates of this system seem to think that almost any home for a poor child is better than an institution. In the imaginations of these, the humblest country home has been glorified into a child-saving instrument of wonderful efficiency; and to put a wayward street Arab into one of these homes is nearly equivalent to saving it. Even ninety-eight per cent. of such children, it is sometimes claimed, are so saved,—a much higher per cent., by the way, than respectable, well-to-do families can show among their own children. . . .

Two things have been broadly asserted, which I propose to notice:

1. That good homes can readily be found for every homeless child; and

2. That a family, however humble it be, is the best place for every homeless child.

If these postulates are true, the logical sequence would be that no more institutions should be established for destitute children, and that those already in existence should be converted to some other uses. A few plain houses of reception, located in convenient places in each State, where the children could be gathered together, cleansed and reclothed, previous to being transferred to the homes that suitable agents had found in advance, would be all that would be necessary. It would be a farce to erect and maintain costly establishments, fitted up with kindergartens, school-rooms, chapels, etc., as many of the advocates of this system are doing, since the children would derive no benefit from them. But is there not an error in the premises? Can good homes be found so readily? and, if so, is it best to place every child in a family as soon as a home can be found? It remains yet to be proven that really good homes can be found as easily as is claimed. Not that there are no such homes, nor that good families

Lyman P. Alden, "The Shady Side of the Placing-out System," *Twelfth Annual Conference of Charities* (New York, 1896), pp. 201–7.

cannot readily be found to take all the attractive and good little children; but, unfortunately, this constitutes only a small part of the whole number who find their way to children's homes. The great majority are not particularly attractive in appearance, and, when first gathered from the streets and slumholes of society, have such habits that, as a rule, the best families do not care to assume the responsibility and risk of taking them into their homes. There are many exceptions to this, of course; and, perhaps with great care, more could be found who, believing in the value of every human soul, for the sake of the great Master would be willing to undertake the charge. But such families cannot be found by the wholesale. It is well known by all who have had charge of the binding out of children that the great majority of those who apply for children over nine years old are looking for cheap help; and while many, even of this class, treat their apprentices with fairness, and furnish them a comfortable home, a much larger number of applicants do not intend to pay a *quid pro quo,* but expect to make a handsome profit on the child's services, and, if allowed one, will evade, as far as possible, every clause in the contract,—furnishing poor food, shoddy clothing, work the child beyond its strength, send it to school but a few months, and that irregularly, and sometimes treat it with personal cruelty, though this, in a thickly settled country, is not likely to occur so frequently. . . .

But, admitting that fairly good homes, as they average in the country, can be found as fast as has been claimed, is it best that all children should be placed, even in such homes, as fast as they become dependent upon the public? There is no question that a good family is the most natural and the best place for men and women, as well as for children, as a rule. But it is not the best place for all. There are many exceptions to the rule. . . . The great majority of all the children thrown upon the public for support are from the lower stratum of society. They have inherited tendencies to wrongdoing more or less marked, or have acquired habits, through neglect and a bad environment, that unfit them to enter a respectable family, especially when there are children. If sent out at once, they are soon returned; or, if they remain, the probability is that these bad habits will cling to them and grow stronger. Before being sent out to homes, they need something more than a change of clothes and a good bath.

Skilful training and considerable time are necessary to eradicate these habits and build up a new character. If the ordinary family is unable to cope with physical ailments, how much less is it able to cope with vastly more complicated moral maladies! . . . There is a large number who, though peculiarities of disposition as well as bad habits unfit them, at first, to go out to homes, can be and have been so trained, in well-conducted institutions, that later they can be sent out with considerable probability of doing well. This change cannot be effected in three months, however, by any patent process yet invented. Time is a very important element. I can say that, while I have seen many bad children converted by institutional training into good children, and many children, who were obedient, orderly, and easily controlled in the institution, fall from grace after being placed in families, I do not remember a single instance where, after a patient and long-continued effort to save a child by institutional training without success, it was improved by being put in a family, although the experiment was frequently tried. . . .

SELECTED BIBLIOGRAPHY
FOR PART TWO

Barker-Benfield, G. J. *Horrors of the Half-Known Life: Male Attitudes Toward Women in Nineteenth-Century America.* New York: Harper & Row, 1977.

Berg, Barbara. *The Remembered Gate: Origins of American Feminism—the Woman and the City 1800–1860.* Fair Lawn, N.J.: Oxford University Press, 1978.

Blassingame, John W. *The Slave Community: Plantation Life in the Antebellum South.* New Haven: Yale University Press, 1972.

Brown, Herbert Ross. *The Sentimental Novel in America, 1789–1860.* Durham, N.C.: Duke University Press, 1940.

Cott, Nancy. *The Bonds of Womanhood: "Woman's Sphere" in New England, 1780–1835.* New Haven: Yale University Press, 1978.

Douglas, Anne. *The Feminization of American Culture.* New York: Knopf, 1977.

Dublin, Thomas. *Women at Work: The Transformation of Work and Community in Lowell, Massachusetts, 1826–1860.* New York: Columbia University Press, 1979.

Faragher, John. *Women and Men on the Overland Trail.* New Haven: Yale University Press, 1979.

Forgie, George B. *Patricide in the House Divided: A Psychological Interpretation of Lincoln and His Age.* New York: Norton, 1979.

Genovese, Eugene D. *Roll, Jordan, Roll: The World the Slaves Made.* New York: Pantheon, 1975.

Haller, John S. and Robin M. *The Physician and Sexuality in Victorian America.* Urbana: University of Illinois Press, 1974.

Jeffrey, Julie. *Frontier Women: The Trans-Mississippi West, 1840–1880.* New York: Hill & Wang, 1979.

Kuhn, Anne L. *The Mother's Role in Childhood Education: New England Concepts 1830–1860.* New Haven: Yale University Press, 1947.

Muncy, Raymond Lee. *Sex and Marriage in Utopian Communities: 19th Century America.* Bloomington: Indiana University Press, 1973.

Papashvily, Helen W. *All the Happy Endings.* Port Washington, N.Y.: Kennikat Press, 1971; reprint of 1956 ed.

Perry, Lewis. *Childhood, Marriage, and Reform: Henry Clarke Wright, 1797–1870.* Chicago: University of Chicago Press, 1980.

Pivar, David J. *Purity Crusade: Sexual Morality and Social Control, 1868–1900.* Westport, Conn.: Greenwood Press, 1973.

Scott, Anne Firor. *The Southern Lady: From Pedestal to Politics, 1830–1930.* Chicago: University of Chicago Press, 1970.

Sklar, Kathryn Kish. *Catharine Beecher: A Study in American Domesticity.* New Haven: Yale University Press, 1973.

Welter, Barbara. *Dimity Convictions: The American Woman in the Nineteenth Century.* Athens: Ohio University Press, 1976.

Wishy, Bernard. *The Child and the Republic: The Dawn of Modern American Child Nurture.* Philadelphia: University of Pennsylvania Press, 1968.

Part Three

BEYOND BIOLOGY

1890 to the Present

Introduction

In the summer of 1978, the world had the startling news of the birth in England of Louise Brown, ostensibly the first child conceived not in a mother's womb but in a laboratory. Because Mrs. Brown was unable to conceive normally, doctors had removed one of her eggs, fertilized it with the father's sperm in vitro, *and then implanted the minuscule fetus in the mother's womb for the eventual normal birth. This event came after decades of research on problems of sterility and human embryology. Like other medical and scientific "miracles" reported so frequently in the twentieth century, the birth gave hope to thousands of women who had despaired of bearing children. This "test-tube baby" also symbolized almost a century of extraordinary changes that brought human families beyond assumed biological limits both in creating children and in overcoming the vagaries of the human body in nurturing the young. More than ever, families and their destinies seemed acts of choice and consciousness.*

At the beginning of the twentieth century, Americans, like the rest of mankind, were subject to severe biological hazards in living within marriage until old age, in producing children, and in maintaining families through sickness and accidents. Following intercourse, despite rudimentary efforts to prevent or abort conception, men and women were at the mercy of their biology. Biology determined conception by chance, but chance also subjected both the fetus and its mother to nine months of perils to their health, often leading to miscarriage, stillbirth, or defective babies. After a birth, a vast range of mysterious ailments, disorders, and stresses had to be risked, determining whether the child and mother would survive the postpartum period. Despite growing demands by reformers after about 1880 to have only the "fit" breed (efforts generally known as "eugenics"), biology's sway meant that the genetically abnormal might produce, without prediction or control, mentally or physically deficient infants. Religion, law, custom, and ignorance did nothing or little to inhibit a mate's coupling with, for example, a menopausal woman or a syphilitic male to yield a dead, deformed, or irreversibly damaged child. If a physically normal infant was lucky enough not to be killed or abandoned at birth, and if parents made even a rudimentary attempt at a decent nurture during the first year or so of life, biology then gave other grim prospects. The "childhood diseases" appeared, brought on by poor diet, crude hygiene, ignorance (for example, that still waters could incubate killing mosquitoes), and undiscovered or uncontrollable germs or viruses. The common and dramatic disease tuberculosis, for example, was caused by a combination of these. Often such threats of biology to a family were increased by supposed preventives or palliatives like closed windows or increased warmth to treat fevers. Too many medicines were eventually found to be dangerous drugs or poisons. Ironically, in the frequent valleys of the shadow of death, very strong specific immunities could be acquired, but these did not lessen the fears or the high risks of other diseases. Life for most families was further discounted by few and poor doctors and crude, often septic, surgery.

Ignorance of how to control biological forces recurrently put nature on a rampage of so-called pandemics, and these disregarded class, race, or social standing. Every summer in the United States, and long into the twentieth century, brought terror about children and adults surviving diphtheria, typhoid, poliomyelitis, and other killers. Even today, despite use of vaccines, our annual "flu" epidemics remind us mildly of the low odds against disease with which American families lived only a half century ago.

The biology of disease had its social setting as well as its individual carriers. A communal water system could produce typhoid-laden water for an entire neighborhood or, because a neighborhood or town water pump was a meeting place for gossip among water fetchers, infection could pass from persons gathered around the pump or using the same dipper. Street filth, rodents, contaminated food at butcher shops and slaughterhouses, the paucity of health organizations, and the ineffectiveness or botching by charity workers (few as these were) gave social reinforcement to biological threats. Still, every year after 1900 that a child or adult survived and acquired more resistance against diseases (or knowledge of how to cure or avoid them) increased the chances to live beyond average life expectancy. Our evidence is not fully clear, but it is striking how many individuals already lived beyond 65 or 70 in the generations before 1900, probably demonstrating the obvious—that the longer one escaped death after surviving exposure to pathology, the resistances acquired favored further survival. Old age itself, furthermore, probably left people of 1900 less isolated and exposed to neglect or despair than in the world of 1980, because there were so fewer alternatives to staying with one's family and what care and comfort it could offer.

Despite the commonness of disease and death, by 1850 the odds on life had been slowly and steadily rising for almost a century. For reasons we do not yet understand, death rates in America and Atlantic Europe began to drop in the late 1700s from heights that had endured for centuries, possibly

In the late nineteenth century it was uncommon for American families with even modest means to live anywhere except in a house of their own. For the wealthy, the would-be prestigious and successful apartment houses had to match or exceed the amenities of some of the mansions then being built. The first luxury apartment house in New York City made use of the latest technology in lighting, heating, refrigeration, and indoor flush toilets.

millennia. Roughly simultaneous improvements in food and water supply and in rudimentary public sanitation and health care, the introduction of a potent if risky vaccine for smallpox, and possibly even the more benign cycles and nature of warfare markedly affected the general death rate and, with that, another index that later demographers would call "life expectancy at birth."

Insofar as statistics and the terminology itself are reliable, American children born about the year 1800, on a crude general average could expect to live about 35 years, the enduring level for centuries in the Atlantic world. The longer individuals survived beyond these 35 years, the more difficult is the historian's problem of defining and understanding the statistics of survival. Changes of immeasurable complexity, continuing from the late eighteenth century and in both biological and social conditions, by 1900 had raised the average

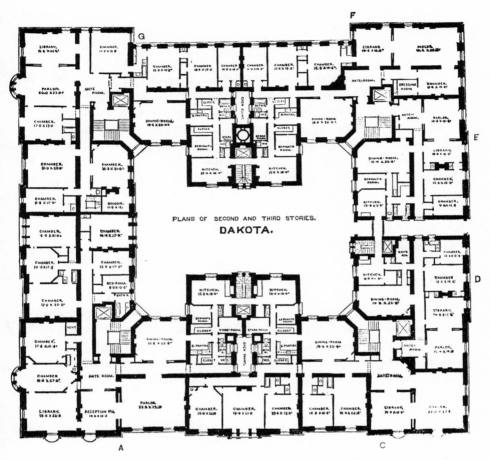

PLANS OF SECOND AND THIRD STORIES.
DAKOTA.

The Dakota opened in 1882 on 72nd Street facing Central Park, far north of the city's business district. The floor plan suggests the amplitude of the arrangements. Only the "finest," to whom its advertising was addressed, could afford it (as is still the case). Note particularly the number of W.C.s (water closets, or indoor flush toilets) and baths per apartment compared with what families of more modest means would expect today.

Library of Congress

life expectancy at birth for American children to about 47 years, an increase of a third in just one century and after eons of the lower unpierceable general limit of 35. From 1900 to 1980, within only four generations in the United States, that 47-year-average predicted limit had risen meteorically to an expectation at birth of about 74 years for males and females together.

The debate about bettering the economic, moral, and political situation of American families throughout this century too often diverts us from appreciating the weight of these radical changes in the biological or environmental conditions of life. What happened when, within about one lifetime after 1910, millions of family members suddenly began to live much longer and, while they lived, anticipated and demanded still longer lives? The incalculably strong lust for life aroused by hopes for the "conquest of cancer" or the overcoming of heart disease, cystic fibrosis, crib death, threats of birth defects, and so on has become a remarkable and powerful contemporary social force. Most of the resulting crusade for life (let alone the "good life") now represents deliberate decisions to alter the traditional biological and social foundations of the family.

Such decisions also imply the other main theme in recent family history, "intervention." This old word (as in "the intervention of God") now alerts us to self-conscious efforts not only to transcend biology as it had worked but also to weaken cultural sanctions against interference with the "sacred privacy of the hearth" or with the home as "every man's castle." By 1900 the massive raw facts of daily existence in the United States had already created demands for "intervention" from every quarter. The next census of 1910 showed the total population of the country from both resident and foreign-born sources soaring toward 100,000,000. Such unprecedented numbers of people in one nation, and steadily living longer, the radical novelty of concentrating millions of them within the one generation since 1880 in cities (many of them larger than any previously known in history), the growing sense of a single American community on a continental scale, the greater ease of rapid communication through telegraph and telephone and soon the "wireless," the spectacle of millions of people moving their work and homes almost constantly—all such changes in the scale and pace of life in the generation before 1914 deeply disturbed the making and maintaining of families, at least as most people still envisioned them. The ghetto immigrants, the "nice families" with their tidy houses, farmers on the prairies, migrant laborers, beleaguered blacks, and recently conquered Indians all felt this weight of America's size. The fears of bigness, of complexity, and of being swamped by this or that alien force were offset by prospects of pleasures and ease from a cascade of scientific and technological discoveries. But omnipresent increases of bureaucracies (public and private) and incessant ethnic, religious, and economic tensions bred a national sense that every tradition and habit in the family (and in everything else) were at discount, that as one writer put it, "everything was becoming a problem." Concurrent with the new "scientific" penchant for posing "problems," researchers and moralists fed a growing search for "solutions." Anxiety about the problems and the accompanying faith that there were solutions rapidly increased intervention in what was called the "private sphere" of the family, so much so that in recent generations the American family has been increasingly at bay. This has been depicted either as apocalypse (will the family survive at all?) or the crisis has been narrowed to specific problems (how a working mother affects her family's well-being). This permanent, almost ritualized, invocation of threats to family life has the multiplying effect that any intervention leads to further cries of disruption and still further intervention.

Much of the significant intervention since 1900 has taken place within families by their members' initiative. Families had to decide to take themselves beyond biology in considering the use of contraception or in washing more often, as teachers, nurses, and advertisements urged them to do. "Family planning," a phrase deriving from the contraception debate, became a metaphor for an entire range of decisions for a family trying to alter its inherited, traditional patterns of life.

The most dramatic break with biology within families came in the rapid spread of easy, safe, and effective birth-control techniques. Devices like the condom and pessary came into millions of homes after their first hushed-up appearance among the better-off. Within the family also this momentous step in defiance of law and biology now seems almost inevitably to have implied massive use of abortion once it was legally available. Birth control, broadly speaking, also meant successful attacks on sterility and impotence, including the emotional blocks to successful intercourse or conception. A planned baby, a wanted baby, heightened the importance that it arrive well and safely and thus stimulated decisions to use special diets for pregnant women and to make universally available safe milk and water. The precious and loved child led to the idea of "germ-free" diapers and the correct "formula" (precisely) for feeding the newborn. "Beyond biology" within the private confines of individual families signaled the startling success of the sulfa drugs and penicillin against the ravages of the "love diseases" themselves, syphilis and gonorrhea, that had so scarred countless marriages and offspring. Husbands and wives and, later, "singles" and "gays" went beyond the traditional biological basis of a marriage for producing children to have them, without shame, through adoption or foster parenthood. Most recently these tendencies to overcome merely biological parenthood have further broadened into what observers call "instant families" or "intentional families." Families and familial ideals are created by forming communes or by remaining unmarried while living together with or without offspring. Also, in reversal, some husbands with working wives now tend the hearth. Such changes in family structure by individual initiative include the great leaps since 1900, in the numbers of known divorces, desertions, annulments and separations.

Taken together, this diversification and innovation in family life have severely shaken the age-old family rules, so potent still as this century began, that "whom God hath brought together, let no man put asunder" and "be fruitful and multiply." By 1980, alternatives abounded against the old argument that marriage prevented sexual anarchy and that there could be no other formula for a union than the traditional legal and sanctified expression for sexual instinct. Similarly, the long period of care needed biologically by human offspring and the consequent need to protect hearth-tending wives and mothers from the outside world are no longer definitive or effective arguments for leaving women at home.

Intervention by individuals within families against the decrees of biological development or sociobiological norms have come with the growth outside the family of an immense bureaucratic world for promoting this or that familial ideal. Some of this change in organization and law often can be linked historically to some assumption about biology that has been proven wrong or transcendable. Notably, the arguments for free mass public education in America after about 1830 included rejection of the old notion that many children were innately incapable of significant intellectual accomplishment or a decent moral life. Locke and Rousseau had argued philosophically that all children had great potentialities for a full and happy life that a proper education could fulfill, and nineteenth-century research in physiology, neurology, and experimental psychology seemed to strengthen such claims. So, if parents in ignorance, poverty, or sloth stood against the school in fulfilling the child's destiny, Americans were increasingly armed to require attendance in the name of the "good of the child" and "for the sake of society." Soon after 1880, society generally set minimum years and competence for schooling; it attempted to lessen or abolish child labor and add more instruction; it required children at school to be inoculated against this or that disease. Such initiatives eventually formed a vast array of intervention by state or private organizations, with schooling being only one area of concern.

In another respect, the traditional arguments that a woman's place was in the home, that the American home was sacrosanct, that marriages were almost indissoluble, and that the male alone was to provide for his spouse and offspring—all these had somehow assumed biological and associated inferiorities, or at least a strikingly different "nature," for females. By 1900, each of these perennial postulates of patriarchy and mottoes of monogamy had already been challenged by unorthodox writers or in heterodox practices such as Mormon polygamy or the "Bohemian life." Less infuriating, but widely debated, the "new woman" was increasingly entering novel professions like social work and old ones like law and medicine. "Woman's-club types" were starting the Mother's Congress, the Child Study Association, the Campfire Girls, and innumerable other organizations calculated to aid or improve the home.

As the twentieth century moved on, early, sporadic breaks by both women and men with "proper" family roles became a steady and visible stream, moving far beyond mere calls for easier and more uniform divorce or for approving the mother who worked. Marriage styles and family modes thus developed into their current prodigious and extraordinarily tolerated diversity, but there were also remarkable continuity and dominance of conventional marriage despite ceaseless debate about what a family might be or what a family is for.

Whether asserting the novel or traditional, most documents about family life since 1900 suggest one common outstanding characteristic: the imperative of ideas. Increasingly, even the humblest American families seem to have become aware from books, newspapers, radio, movies, television, schools, churches, institutes—in short, their "culture"—that beyond their travail there exist ideas of the good, healthy, and happy for judging and altering their life. "Ideas," for example, make it legitimate to hold a cruel father, a frigid wife, or disrespectful children before some mirror of reason or happiness and try to change what we see. Such inspection guided by ideas encourages, in turn, both private innovation and more social intervention, such as the call in the 1960s for a national policy to strengthen black family ties. All these imperial ideas bring with them not only bureaucracy but hordes of family "experts" and "counselors," ranging from ministers to a variety of therapists to the syndicated columnist. And counseling often has become command or "take it or leave it": the compelling word of the family court judge, the public welfare caseworker, the financial screening office at the county hospital.

As the twentieth century began, the ideas about intervention in the family really concerned how both "halves" of society lived; the "other half" caught most of the headlines and, later, the historians. This was the millions of immigrant poor whose plight was documented and pleaded relentlessly by journalists like Jacob Riis. But there was also the other "other half," in the so-called "nice home" of at least relative comfort, security, and decent education. This other half was also being scrutinized and indicted. It was charged with drudgery, dullness, the hushed-up tyrannies of latter-day patriarchs, the waste of time and effort under unscientific management, and, soon, the hidden hostilities and pathology that early psychoanalysis discovered under that cover of repression called "respectability." Both halves, however, seemed to be failing to live up to the possibilities of the new age of "modern ideas." Both the "unspeakable" homes of the tenements and the "decent" homes of those who had "made it" were on trial, although the documents suggest double as well as common standards for assessing the family crises of the new century. The paradoxes and ironies replete in these early reports and debates continued through the century: The tenement homes of 1900 were a disgrace and a threat because they weren't American enough, but the seeming alternative, the nice American home, often was authoritarian or unscientific. Reformers argued for the right of family women to work as well as vote, but some radicals questioned whether the profit-driven and drudgery-laden worlds of industry and finance, of the degraded democracy in the bossed city or in the "millionaire's club" of the United States Senate, were worth any man's or woman's participation except with radical changes that only a few championed.

A half century later, such paradoxes persist as intervention grows. A few critics by the 1970s asked black and other minority families, who professedly wanted only as much chance as other Americans before them, to "look before they leap." Should their leaders, at least, not ask, "Chance for what?" Had affluence, education, "equal opportunity," and innumerable family programs since 1900 meant better or happier families for the 80 percent of Americans who in 1980 still lived within a marriage, having children, with a two-parent home? Put another way, beyond its own pieties in its earlier time and the later nostalgia about saving or joining it, was the good old family a transient form of culture, merely one way for human beings to manage scarce resources, restrict a feared sexuality, optimize slow hand labor, and rally to hold on to life against its general cheapness in nature and society? And for today, is what William Leuchtenburg has called the "troubled feast" of American life since 1945, going so far toward making work, goods, money, sex, education, health available to all, radically altering or even destroying the basic family unity that movements for family freedom and comforts once hoped to salvage?

Social freedom and fairer laws have also encouraged the "instant families" of flower children, communes, and gay or single parents. These people insist that the family is no longer to be a product of biological pressure or chance but a conscious act of freely given and reciprocated love. How much evidence is there on the frontiers of family forms that these ideals of love and respect have been any better fulfilled than under the traditional legal lifelong marriage with enforced family ties? Do the new ease and freedom to form and end "couples" raise such high expectations for their success that few families, legal or not, can hope adequately to fulfill them? Did the old ties of law, custom, and public opinion breed not only tyrannies but resignation, now lost or disappearing, to the "human" frailty and imperfections of mates and children? If love, not law, is to be the only bond of family life, can an absolute of love and "commitment" become, more easily than we imagine, coercive, however disguised? Do public welfare systems providing aid to dependent children in families in which there is only one breadwinner put an appreciable premium on mates remaining legally unmarried or on living apart so as to augment welfare income?

Such questions of the 1980s may involve only a minority of American families, perhaps 20 percent. But the figure, in fact, means almost ten million families, some forty million Americans. Will such figures grow, stabilize, or shrink as we try to peer ahead with the rather weak light we can obtain from family history since 1900? That complex chronicle is still too close for us to have mastered, but as it stands, it seems deeply ambiguous and thus moves us from the historian's basic question, "What happened?" to everyman's commonsense query, "Was it a good thing?"

NICE HOMES AND OTHER HALVES, 1890–1940

Creating and Coping with the "Other Half"

This group of four readings comes from the records of an extraordinary period of public investigation of American family life starting about the year 1890. Two tumultuous decades had already torn deeply at established family customs and ideas of work, responsibility, authority and independence. In addition to millions of lives now being spent in the urban-industrial world, after 1880 millions of immigrants brought families to America with unfamiliar customs, moral standards and religions. In too many ways, they did not "speak the same language" as those already here. Their numbers, their concentration in burgeoning cities, their poverty, their seeming differences shocked comfortable and educated observers like Jacob Riis, himself a Danish immigrant and thus of the so-called "older stock" of northwestern European immigrants. The shock brought deep misconceptions as well as compassion about how the other half lived. Indeed, one may question whether the "other half" was not in some measure the creation of Americans like Riis. Many of even his more well-intentioned errors became deeply embedded in public policies about housing, social work, school attendance, etc., and even more in "right-thinking" attitudes about work, crime, and poverty. Try to distinguish such errors in reading from this classic account but recall, too, Riis's goodwill.

The second piece is one of the early efforts to bring system and expertise to bear on the same phenomena that so upset moralists like Riis. What are the differences in assumptions, methods, conclusions, tone? The authors were Robert W. De Forest and Lawrence Veiller. The latter especially was to become an important figure in professional campaigns to better the housing of the poor. These efforts included formal training for disciplined, empirical investigation; exposure and publication for public view and debate; legislative hearings, studies, and testimony; electoral and other public agitation and pressures; and the enactment of adequate codes and laws with realistic inspection and enforcement.

By the year 1910 such methods had made governmental investigation a major feature of American life along with growing regulation and bureaucracy. In 1910 the United States Senate began to publish a noteworthy series of hearings in nineteen volumes incorporating detailed statistical studies of the family in industrial America. These contributed to a "condition of American question" reminiscent of the storm about the "condition of England" in that industrializing country more than three generations earlier. Why should so much of this concern have centered on the family? In transforming what President Theodore Roosevelt had sarcastically called "muckraking" into a respectable function of government and other agencies, investigations turned everything about the American family into a problem. And for every problem, given the new prestige and jargon of science, there was presumably a "solution." How have the perceptions, ever since, of family life as a series of problems and solutions complicated the conduct and expectations of families as well as the formulation of public policy about the family? What must be known? Who knows it? With what implication or effect?

The growing range of the routine, even ritual, of investigation is only suggested by the last selection from I. M. Rubinow's famous study of social insurance. By 1913 the United States was the last of the major countries of the Western world to adopt national programs of so-called social insurance after Bismarck's Germany established a model almost thirty years earlier. Rubinow's study also helped put the place of older Americans high among the most persistent and fastest growing problems of the family in this century. The simple fact was and remains that, relatively suddenly, millions lived longer while also working fewer years. With what effect on them and their families?

To appreciate the atmosphere and implications of the age of investigation we should list both the explicit and implicit "problems" and "solutions" to be found in these four selections. If we add to the ostensible problems of the families under scrutiny, our examination of the investigations, of the agencies appealed to and the public involved, how do the dimensions for understanding family life change? To comprehend the maze of conditions and purposes involved in probing the lives of the other half—or "two nations," or "third of a nation"; the titles vary as the twentieth century moves on—consider what visions of the idealized family lie behind these depictions. What made that family so desirable? With what historical, moral, or religious justifications? How could the phrase "other half" blind investigators as well as historians? How, for example, does positing the existence of another half affect the assessment made of one's own family or family "type"? Throughout these inquiries how expert or naïve, scientific or misled do each of the investigators seem about what they observe in other families, in their assumptions about "nice" families and in the prospects for changing family conditions? In other words, in every investigation, who is determining what, about and for whom, and with what vision of the future? And who is to give up what in order to attain something else?

THE LOWER OTHER HALF

Introduction

Long ago it was said that "one half of the world does not know how the other half lives." That was true then. It did not know because it did

Jacob Riis, *How the Other Half Lives* (New York, 1890), passim.

not care. The half that was on top cared little for the struggles, and less for the fate of those who were underneath, so long as it was able to hold them there and keep its own seat. There came a time when the discomfort and crowding below were so great, and the consequent upheavals so violent, that it was no longer an easy thing to do, and then the upper half fell to inquiring what was the matter. Information on the subject has been accumulating rapidly since, and the whole world has had its hands full answering for its old ignorance.

In New York, the youngest of the world's great cities, that time came later than elsewhere, because the crowding had not been so great. There were those who believed that it would never come; but their hopes were vain. Greed and reckless selfishness wrought like results here as in the cities of older lands. . . .

In 1869 there were 14,872 tenements in New York, with a population of 468,492 persons. In 1879 the number of the tenements was estimated at 21,000, and their tenants had passed the half-million mark. At the end of the year 1888, when a regular census was made for the first time since 1869, the showing was: 32,390 tenements, with a population of 1,093,701 souls. To-day we have 37,316 tenements, including 2,630 rear houses, and their population is over 1,250,000. A large share of this added population, especially of that which came to us from abroad, crowds in below Fourteenth Street, where the population is already packed beyond reason, and confounds all attempts to make matters better there. At the same time new slums are constantly growing up uptown, and have to be kept down with a firm hand. This drift of the population to the great cities has to be taken into account as a steady factor. It will probably increase rather than decrease for many years to come. At the beginning of the century the percentage of our population that lived in cities was as one in twenty-five. In 1880 it was one in four and one-half, and in 1890 the census will in all probability show it to be one in four. Against such tendencies, in the absence of suburban outlets for the crowding masses, all remedial measures must prove more or less ineffective. The "confident belief" expressed by the Board of Health in 1874, that rapid transit would solve the problem, is now known to have been a vain hope.

Workingmen, in New York at all events, will live near their work, no matter at what sacrifice of comfort—one might almost say at whatever cost, and the city will never be less crowded than it is. . . .

As emigration from east to west follows the latitude, so does the foreign influx in New York distribute itself along certain well-defined lines that waver and break only under the stronger pressure of a more gregarious race or the encroachments of inexorable business. A feeling of dependence upon mutual effort, natural to strangers in a strange land, unacquainted with its language and customs, sufficiently accounts for this. . . .

There is a church in Mulberry Street that has stood for two generations as a sort of milestone of these migrations. Built originally for the worship of staid New Yorkers of the "old stock," it was engulfed by the colored tide, when the draft-riots drove the Negroes out of reach of Cherry Street and the Five Points. Within the past decade the advance wave of the Italian onset reached it, and today the arms of United Italy adorn its front. . . . A map of the city, colored to designate nationalities, would show more stripes than on the skin of a zebra, and more colors than any rainbow. . . .

The Down Town Back Alleys

Down below Chatham Square, in the old Fourth Ward, where the cradle of the tenement stood, we shall find New York's Other Half at home, receiving such as care to call and are not afraid. Not all of it, to be sure, there is not room for that; but a fairly representative gathering, representative of its earliest and worst traditions. . . . Leaving the Elevated Railroad where it dives under the Brooklyn Bridge at Franklin Square, scarce a dozen steps will take us where we wish to go. With its rush and roar echoing yet in our ears, we have turned the corner from prosperity to poverty. We stand upon the domain of the tenement. . . .

Jewtown

The tenements grow taller, and the gaps in their ranks close up rapidly as we cross the Bowery and, leaving Chinatown and the Italians behind, invade the Hebrew quarter. . . .

Bayard Street, with its synagogues and its crowds, gave us a foretaste of it. No need of asking here where we are. The jargon of the street, the signs of the sidewalk, the manner and dress of the people, their unmistakable physiognomy, betray their race at every step. Men with queer skull-caps, venerable beard, and the outlandish long-skirted kaftan of the Russian Jew, elbow the ugliest and the handsomest women in the land. The contrast is startling. The old women are hags; the young, houris *. . . . There is no mistaking it; we are in Jewtown.

It is said that nowhere in the world are so many people crowded together on a square mile as here. The average five-story tenement adds a story or two to its stature in Ludlow Street and an extra building on the rear lot, and yet the sign "To Let" is the rarest of all there. Here is one seven stories high. The sanitary policeman whose beat this is will tell you that it contains thirty-six families, but the term has a widely different meaning here and on the avenues. In this house, where a case of small-pox was reported, there were fifty-eight babies and thirty-eight children that were over five years of age. In Essex Street two small rooms in a six-story tenement were made to hold a "family" of father and mother, twelve children, and six boarders. The boarder plays as important a part in the domestic economy of Jewtown as the lodger in the Mulberry Street Bend. These are samples of the packing of the population that has run up the record here to the rate of three hundred and thirty thousand per acre. . . . At Rivington Street let us get off and continue our trip on foot. It is Sunday evening west of the Bowery. Here, under the rule of Mosaic law, the week

* Nymph in Mohammedan folklore.—Ed.

of work is under full headway, its first day far spent. . . . Let us . . . see how Sunday passes in a Ludlow Street tenement.

Up two flights of dark stairs, three, four, with new smells of cabbage, of onions, of frying fish, on every landing, whirring sewing machines behind closed doors betraying what goes on within, to the door that opens to admit the bundle and the man. A sweater,* this, in a small way. Five men and a woman, two young girls, not fifteen, and a boy who says unasked that he is fifteen, and lies in saying it, are at the machines sewing knicker- bockers, "knee-pants" in the Ludlow Street dialect. The floor is littered ankle-deep with half-sewn garments. In the alcove, on a couch of many dozens of "pants" ready for the finisher, a bare-legged baby with pinched face is asleep. A fence of piled-up clothing keeps him from rolling off on the floor. The faces, hands, and arms to the elbows of everyone in the room are black with the color of the cloth on which they are working. The boy and the woman alone look up at our entrance. The girls shoot sidelong glances, but at a warning look from the man with the bundle they tread their machines more energetically than ever. The men do not appear to be aware even of the presence of a stranger.

They are "learners," all of them, says the woman, who proves to be the wife of the boss, and have "come over" only a few weeks ago. She is disinclined to talk at first, but a few words in her own tongue from our guide set her fears, whatever they are, at rest, and she grows almost talka- tive. . . . There are ten machines in the room; six are hired at two dollars a month. For the two shabby, smoke-begrimed rooms, one somewhat larger than ordinary, they pay twenty dollars a month. She does not complain, though "times are not what they were, and it costs a good deal to live." Eight dollars a week for the family of six and two boarders. How do they do it? She laughs, as she goes over the bill of fare, at the silly question: Bread, fifteen cents a day, of milk, two quarts a day at four cents a quart, one pound of meat for dinner at twelve cents, butter, one pound a week at "eight cents a quarter of a pound." Coffee, potatoes, and pickles complete the list. At the last calculation, probably, this sweater's family hoards up thirty dollars a month, and in a few years will own a tenement somewhere and profit by the example set by their landlord in rent-collecting. It is the way the savings of Jewtown are universally invested, and with the natural talent of its people for commercial speculation the investment is enormously profitable.

On the next floor, in a dimly lighted room with a big red-hot stove to keep the pressing irons ready for use, is a family of man, wife, three children, and a boarder. . . . The boarder pays sixty-five cents a week. He is really only a lodger, getting his meals outside. The rent is two dollars and twenty- five cents a week, cost of living five dollars. Every floor has at least two, sometimes four, such shops. Here is one with a young family for which life is bright with promise. Husband and wife work together; just now

* Slang for sweatshop operator.—Ed.

the latter, a comely young woman, is eating her dinner of dry bread and green pickles. Pickles are favorite food in Jewtown. They are filling, and keep the children from crying with hunger. Those who have stomachs like ostriches thrive in spite of them and grow strong—plain proof that they are good to eat. The rest? "Well, they die," says our guide, dryly. No thought of untimely death comes to disturb this family with life all before it. In a few years the man will be a prosperous sweater. Already he employs an old man as ironer at three dollars a week, and a sweet-faced little Italian girl as finisher at a dollar and a half. She is twelve, she says, and can neither read nor write; will probably never learn. How should she? The family clears from ten to eleven dollars a week in brisk times, more than half of which goes into the bank. . . .

The majority of the children seek the public schools, where they are received sometimes with some misgivings on the part of the teachers, who find it necessary to inculcate lessons of cleanliness in the worst cases by practical demonstration with wash-bowl and soap. "He took hold of the soap as if it were some animal," said one of these teachers to me after such an experiment upon a new pupil, "and wiped three fingers across his face. He called that washing." In the Allen Street public school the experienced principal has embodied among the elementary lessons, to keep constantly before the children the duty that clearly lies next to their hands, a characteristic exercise. The question is asked daily from the teacher's desk: "What must I do to be healthy?" and the whole school responds:

"I must keep my skin clean,
Wear clean clothes,
Breathe pure air,
And live in the sunlight."

It seems little less than biting sarcasm to hear them say it, for to not a few of them all these things are known only by name. In their everyday life there is nothing even to suggest any of them. Only the demand of religious custom has power to make their parents clean up at stated intervals, and the young naturally are no better. As scholars, the children of the most ignorant Polish Jew keep fairly abreast of their more favored playmates, until it comes to mental arithmetic, when they leave them behind with a bound. It is surprising to see how strong the instinct of dollars and cents is in them. They can count, and correctly, almost before they can talk.

REFORMING THE TENEMENTS

No one who is at all familiar personally with tenement house life in New York, no one who without personal familiarity reads the description

Robert W. De Forest and Lawrence Veiller, *The Tenement House Problem* (New York, 1903), pp. 3–9.

of tenement house life from the point of view of the tenant and inspector contained in the special paper on this subject which forms part of this report, can fail to realize that the chief evil to be remedied is the tenement house itself.

Adequate light and air, perfect sanitation, even passable home environment, cannot be provided by the best tenement house which is commercially possible on Manhattan Island—that is, by the best tenement house which can be built with sufficient prospect of income to warrant its erection. Such a tenement house, even if only five stories high, occupying only 65 percent of the lot and accommodating only three families on a floor, situated, as it either is at the outset or soon will be, among other buildings of the same or greater height, must necessarily lack, especially in its lower apartments, some of these desirable conditions. Ideal conditions in these particulars can only be attained when each family occupies its own separate house. The fewer families in each house and the larger air space around it, the nearer approach to this ideal.

Inquiry naturally directs itself, therefore, first to the question whether the inherent evils of the tenement house system can be remedied, and whether we can look forward at any near future to housing the working classes of New York in separate or smaller houses as the laboring men of many other cities are accommodated. The near realization of rapid transit and closer and quicker connection with the Boroughs of Brooklyn and Queens by bridge and tunnel would seem to make such a development possible [but] . . . it is evident that the bulk of the laboring classes will still continue to live in tenement houses.

A family which now pays from $12 to $18 a month for its apartment in a tenement house must be able to pay at least $20 a month for a separate house in the suburbs, a reason sufficient in itself to keep it in the tenement. Other influences—familiarity with tenement life, which, however distasteful to previous generations, has now perforce grown into a habit, the natural inclination of our large foreign population to group itself in neighborhoods on national lines, and other causes equally potent—all tend in the same direction.

Concluding, therefore, that the tenement house system must continue in New York, the question presents itself, What evils not inherent in the system admit of remedy? These are the practical questions before the Commission. The most serious evils may be grouped as follows:—

(1) Insufficiency of light and air due to narrow courts or air shafts, undue height, and to the occupation by the building or by adjacent buildings of too great a proportion of lot area.

(2) Danger from fire.

(3) Lack of separate water-closet and washing facilities.

(4) Overcrowding.

(5) Foul cellars and courts, and other like evils, which may be classed as bad housekeeping.

Of the three first-named groups of evils, all are evils of construction

These four photographs trace changes between 1900 and 1914 in the design of so-called air shafts in New York City tenements. These brick houses were four to five stories tall and sometimes held more than thirty families. The air shaft provided the only light and air in the interior rooms, since these houses were built attached to each other on both sides. (Other cities, however, had different types of cheap housing, each with its inadequacies.) In New York the first such tenements in the late 1880s were built with scarcely any city rules to limit the builder. One result was the first air shaft shown, 12 inches wide by 6 feet long and four to five stories deep. Due to protest, law, and other changes, there followed the 2-foot-6-inch shaft, shown from the inside in the second picture; the famous "reform" or dumbbell shaft with "bridge" fire escapes (another novelty); and finally the "new law court" type of inner space of 12 by 25 feet, which was used throughout the city even for middle-income tenants after 1913. Earlier buildings continued to be used, however, since they were not condemned.   *National Archives*

which admit of remedy both in buildings hereafter constructed and those which already exist, if that remedy can wisely be applied. . . .

Tenement house reform would not be practical which went so far as to put a stop to building new tenement houses. Now would it be practical if it compelled such extensive changes in old tenements that owners would turn them to other uses.

The result in both cases would be to decrease the supply of tenement accommodation, and to either force more people into this diminished space, which would mean more overcrowding, or to force some people out, in which case competition would raise rents.

Reform of such a kind would harm most the very persons it sought to aid. . . .

The Typical New York Tenement

Some knowledge of the prevailing kind of New York tenement house must necessarily precede any consideration of its evils and their remedies. It is known as the "double-decker," "dumb-bell" tenement, a type which New York has the unenviable distinction of having invented. It is a type unknown to any other city in America or Europe.

Although the housing problem is one of the leading political questions of the day in England, the conditions which exist there are ideal compared to the conditions in New York. The tall tenement house, accommodating as many as 100 to 150 persons in one building, extending up six or seven stories into the air, with dark, unventilated rooms, is unknown in London or in any other city of Great Britain. It was first constructed in New York about the year 1879, and with slight modifications has been practically the sole type of building erected since, and is the type of the present day. It is a building usually five or six or even seven stories high, about 25 feet wide, and built upon a lot of land of the same width and about 100 feet deep. The building as a rule extends back 90 feet, leaving the small space of ten feet unoccupied at the rear, so that the back rooms may obtain some light and air. This space has continued to be left open only because the law has compelled it. Upon the entrance floor there are generally two stores, one on each side of the building, and these sometimes have two or three living rooms back of them. In the center is the entrance hallway, a long corridor less than 3 feet wide and extending back 60 feet in length. This hallway is nearly always totally dark, receiving no light except that from the street door and a faint light that comes from the small windows opening upon the stairs, which are placed at one side of the hallway. Each floor above is generally divided into four sets of apartments, there being seven rooms on each side of the hall, extending back from the street to the rear of the building. The front apartments generally consist of four rooms each and the rear apartments of three rooms, making altogether fourteen upon each floor, or in a seven-story house eighty-four rooms exclusive of the stores and rooms back of them. Of these fourteen rooms on each floor, only four receive direct light and air from the street or from the small yard at the back of the building. Generally, along each side of the building is what is termed an "air shaft," being an indentation of the wall to a depth of about 28 inches, and extending in length for a space of from 50 to 60 feet. This shaft is entirely enclosed on four sides, and is, of course, the full height of the building, often from 60 to 72 feet high. The ostensible purpose of the shaft is to provide light and air to the five rooms on each side of the house which get no direct light and air from the street or yard; but as the shafts are narrow and high, being enclosed on all four sides, and without any intake of air at the bottom, these rooms obtain, instead of fresh air and sunshine, foul air and semi-darkness. Indeed it is questionable whether the rooms would not be more habitable and more sanitary with no shaft at all, depending for their light and air solely upon the front and back rooms into which they open; for each family, besides having the foul air from its own rooms to breathe, is compelled to breathe the emanations from the rooms of some eleven other families; nor is this all, these shafts act as conveyors of noise, odors, and disease, and when fire breaks out serve as inflammable flues, often rendering it impossible to save the buildings from destruction.

A family living in such a building pays for four rooms of this kind a rent of from $12 to $18 a month. Of these four rooms only two are large enough to be deserving of the name of rooms. The front one is generally about 10 feet 6 inches wide by 11 feet 3 inches long; this the family use as a parlor, and often at night, when the small bedrooms opening upon the air shaft are so close and ill-ventilated that sleep is impossible, mattresses are dragged upon the floor of the parlor, and there the family sleep, all together in one room. In summer the small bedrooms are so hot and stifling that a large part of the tenement house population sleep on the roofs, the sidewalks, and the fire-escapes. The other room, the kitchen, is generally the same size as the parlor upon which it opens, and receives all its light and air from the "air shaft," or such a supply as may come to it from the front room. Behind these two rooms are the bedrooms, so called, which are hardly more than closets, being each about 7 feet wide and 8 feet 6 inches long, hardly large enough to contain a bed. These rooms get no light and air whatsoever, except that which comes from the "air shaft," and except on the highest stories are generally almost totally dark. Upon the opposite side of the public hall is an apartment containing four exactly similar rooms, and at the rear of the building there are, instead of four rooms on each side of the hallway, but three, one of the bedrooms being dispensed with. For these three rooms in the rear the rent is generally throughout the city from $10 to $15 a month. In the public hallway, opposite the stairs, there are provided two water-closets, each water-closet being used in common by two families and being lighted and ventilated by the "air shaft," which also lights and ventilates all the bedrooms. In the newer buildings there is frequently provided, in the hallway between the two closets, a dumb-waiter for the use of the tenants.

U.S. SENATE REPORT ON WOMAN AND CHILD LABOR

We find by far the largest proportion of mothers working outside their homes in two distinctively American communities, in the southern places, in the northern towns.

Of course, in drawing conclusions, we must always remember that we have a special selection of families to deal with, namely, the families where one or more of the children were just leaving school to go to work. . . . Table 26 shows the complete membership of the families.

TABLE 26.—MEMBERSHIP OF FAMILY.

	Paw-tucket, R. I.	Woon-socket, R. I.	Colum-bus, Ga.	Geor-gia and Ala-bama coun-ties.	Colum-bia, S. C.	Ply-mouth, Pa.	Hazle-ton, Pa.	Total.
Total families......................	99	167	63	52	53	82	58	574
MALE WAGE-EARNERS.								
16 and over, including father..........	168	303	70	77	69	114	82	883
Under 16.........................	53	72	51	42	48	53	33	352
Total......................	221	375	121	119	117	167	115	1,235
FEMALE WAGE-EARNERS.								
16 and over, including mother........	75	184	39	46	49	31	49	473
Under 16.........................	42	84	30	26	32	38	17	269
Total......................	117	268	69	72	81	69	66	742
CHILDREN AT SCHOOL.								
Families having children at school...	70	127	38	29	28	63	45	400
Average number of children at school per family......................	1.9	2.3	2.2	1.7	1.5	2.0	1.9	2.0
CHILDREN AT HOME.								
Families having children at home....	34	64	32	27	20	47	24	248
Average number of children at home per family......................	1.6	1.9	1.4	1.6	1.6	1.9	1.6	1.7
NATURAL FAMILY AT HOME.								
Lowest number per family..........	2	2	2	2	3	2	2	2
Highest number per family..........	12	13	9	11	11	10	11	13
Average number per family..........	6.3	7.4	6.1	6.3	6.0	6.5	6.4	6.6

U.S. Senate, *Report on Condition of Woman and Child Wage-Earners in the United States* (Washington, 1911–12) 19 Volumes. Vol. VIII, pp. 75, 83, 98–101; Vol. XIII, pp. 150–54; Vol. XVI, pp. 36–38, 40–41, 196–97.

Looking first at the wage-earners, it appears that there are 2.15 male to 1.29 female wage-earners per family. . . .

Table 34 shows the earnings of the heads of families by locality. It will be noticed that not only were there very few families having female heads but that very few of these female heads were working for wages and that their earnings, when they were so working, were generally small, both absolutely and in proportion to the family income. . . .

TABLE 34.—EARNINGS OF HEADS OF FAMILIES DURING PAST YEAR.

	Paw-tucket, R. I.	Woon-socket, R. I.	Colum-bus, Ga.	Geor-gia and Ala-bama coun-ties.	Colum-bia, S. C.	Plym-outh, Pa.	Hazle-ton, Pa.	Total.
Total number of families............	99	167	63	52	53	82	58	574
MALE HEADS OF FAMILY.								
Total number.......................	82	151	44	44	40	72	48	481
Number earning wages..............	81	143	41	43	38	70	47	463
Lowest earnings per head...........	$60	$115	$130	$74	$102	$254	$215	$60
Highest earnings per head..........	$1,898	$2,565	$2,600	$1,500	$1,480	$2,000	$1,200	$2,600
Average earnings per head..........	$621	$572	$826	$445	$523	$617	$561	$593
Average earnings per family having male head......................	$1,277	$1,375	$1,225	$1,048	$1,057	$940	$1,004	$1,186
FEMALE HEADS OF FAMILY.								
Total number.......................	17	16	19	8	13	10	10	93
Number earning wages..............	3	4	8	4	6	3	4	32
Lowest earnings per head...........	$149	$77	$26	$263	$52	$52	$24	$26
Highest earnings per head..........	$344	$628	$728	$517	$468	$81	$156	$728
Average earnings per head..........	$278	$408	$295	$376	$163	$65	$123	$250
Average earnings per family having female head.....................	$1,055	$1,025	$679	$744	$772	$640	$798	$834

Turning from the heads of families to other members, we find a curious variation in the earnings, as shown in Table 35. In general, male workers 16 or over earned more than the same class of female workers. . . .

TABLE 35.—AVERAGE EARNINGS PER PERSON OF SPECIFIED CLASSES OF MEMBERS OF FAMILIES, AVERAGE AMOUNT PAID TO FAMILY, AND PER CENT OF FAMILY INCOME RECEIVED FROM SUCH MEMBERS DURING THE YEAR, BY LOCALITY.

[The averages and percentages shown in this table apply, in each case, only to the number of families reporting the specified classes of members.]

Classes of members.	Pawtucket, R. I. (99 families).			Woonsocket, R. I. (167 families).			Columbus, Ga. (63 families).			Georgia and Alabama counties (52 families).		
	Average earnings.	Average amt. paid to family.	Percentage of family income.	Average earnings.	Average amt. paid to family.	Percentage of family income.	Average earnings.	Average amt. paid to family.	Percentage of family income.	Average earnings.	Average amt. paid to family.	Percentage of family income.
Male heads	$621	$621	55.3	$572	$572	41.6	$826	$826	66.1	$445	$445	51.8
Female heads	278	278	5.9	408	408	18.0	295	295	20.5	376	376	35.7
Other males 16 and over (not boarders and lodgers)	339	305	33.9	385	368	39.0	375	343	34.4	318	268	30.0
Other females 16 and over (not boarders and lodgers)	326	312	38.7	312	307	34.8	250	233	30.1	254	246	37.4
Boarders and lodgers (members of families)	535	171	20.3	398	132	18.6	447	87	14.0	375	74	26.6
Boys under 16	142	129	12.0	143	138	10.8	160	148	17.5	120	115	14.5
Girls under 16	115	109	10.9	127	124	9.9	115	112	17.1	119	115	17.8
Children 14 and 15	130	120	11.5	134	130	10.7	177	163	17.0	150	143	18.7
Children under 14				6	6	.6	105	102	13.6	87	85	12.0

Classes of members.	Columbia, S. C. (53 families).			Plymouth, Pa. (82 families).			Hazleton, Pa. (58 families).		
	Average earnings.	Average amt. paid to family.	Percentage of family income.	Average earnings.	Average amt. paid to family.	Percentage of family income.	Average earnings.	Average amt. paid to family.	Percentage of family income.
Male heads	$523	$523	53.5	$617	$617	65.1	$561	$561	59.8
Female heads	163	163	11.6	65	65	3.6	123	123	6.7
Other males 16 and over (not boarders and lodgers)	286	269	28.6	371	322	44.1	337	281	33.6
Other females 16 and over (not boarders and lodgers)	296	288	38.7	115	110	13.9	208	185	27.2
Boarders and lodgers (members of families)	372	60	11.8	476	108	9.5	448	114	15.3
Boys under 16	148	142	19.8	145	139	17.2	153	145	17.1
Girls under 16	148	146	20.6	97	94	12.8	97	95	13.3
Children 14 and 15	186	182	22.0	133	128	15.7	137	130	16.3
Children under 14	108	104	18.9	103	98	11.2	142	142	15.6

Attitude of Parents in Regard to Sending Children to School Longer

The two following tables show what parents said of their ability and willingness to send the children to school longer, and also illustrate their discrimination between ability and willingness. Taking all the places together, of the 612 children reported on, the parents of 242, or 39.5 percent, were able and willing, 23, or 3.8 percent, were able but unwilling, 250, or 40.8 percent, were unable but willing, and 97, or 15.9 percent, were unable and unwilling to send their children to school longer.

The willingness or unwillingness of parents to continue their children in school, correlated with their professed ability or inability to do so, is shown in Table 50.

TABLE 50.—CHILDREN CLASSIFIED BY ABILITY AND WILLINGNESS OF PARENTS TO SEND THEM TO SCHOOL LONGER.

Ability of parents to send children to school longer.	Children whose parents were willing or unwilling to send them to school longer.					
	Willing.		Unwilling.		Total.	
	Number.	Per cent.	Number.	Per cent.	Number.	Per cent.
PAWTUCKET, R. I.						
Able	42	97.7	1	2.3	43	100.0
Unable	36	60.0	24	40.0	60	100.0
Total	78	75.7	25	24.3	103	100.0
WOONSOCKET, R. I.						
Able	46	86.8	7	13.2	53	100.0
Unable	63	54.3	53	45.7	116	100.0
Total	109	64.5	60	35.5	169	100.0
COLUMBUS, GA.						
Able	31	96.9	1	3.1	32	100.0
Unable	40	88.9	5	11.1	45	100.0
Total	71	92.2	6	7.8	77	100.0
GEORGIA AND ALABAMA COUNTIES.						
Able	16	69.6	7	30.4	23	100.0
Unable	34	94.4	2	5.6	36	100.0
Total	50	84.7	9	15.3	59	100.0
COLUMBIA, S. C.						
Able	33	94.3	2	5.7	35	100.0
Unable	24	100.0	....	....	24	100.0
Total	57	96.6	2	3.4	59	100.0
PLYMOUTH, PA.						
Able	41	95.3	2	4.7	43	100.0
Unable	34	82.9	7	17.1	41	100.0
Total	75	89.3	9	10.7	84	100.0
HAZLETON, PA.						
Able	33	91.7	3	8.3	36	100.0
Unable	19	76.0	6	24.0	25	100.0
Total	52	85.2	9	14.8	61	100.0
ALL LOCALITIES.						
Able	242	91.3	23	8.7	265	100.0
Unable	250	72.0	97	28.0	347	100.0
Total	492	80.4	120	19.6	612	100.0

The following table shows the number and percentage of children whose parents said they were both able and willing to send them to school longer:

NUMBER AND PER CENT OF CHILDREN WHOSE PARENTS SAID THEY WERE ABLE AND WILLING TO SEND THEM TO SCHOOL LONGER.

Locality.	Total reporting.	Children whose parents said they were able and willing to send children to school longer.	
		Number.	Per cent.
Columbia, S. C.	59	33	55.9
Hazleton, Pa.	61	33	54.1
Plymouth, Pa.	84	41	48.8
Pawtucket, R. I.	103	42	40.8
Columbus, Ga.	77	31	40.3
Woonsocket, R. I.	169	46	27.2
Georgia and Alabama counties.	59	16	27.1
Total	612	242	39.5

This shows about two-fifths of the children leaving school of their own choice. In view of the frequent assumption that children, particularly young children, found at work are there because they wish to be, it seems worth while to notice the age of those thus leaving. In Pawtucket and Woonsocket the question does not arise; whatever the child's sentiments the law requires attendance until he is 14, and so far as this investigation discloses the law seems generally enforced. . . . The 154 children from other places who apparently left school of their own choice form about two-fifths— 41.8 percent—of all the children from these places.

Looking first at the ages of this group of 154 children, we find they range as shown in Table 51.

TABLE 51.—NUMBER AND PER CENT OF CHILDREN LEAVING SCHOOL OF THEIR OWN CHOICE, BY AGE.

Age.	Number.	Per cent.
Under 12 years.	22	14.3
12 years.	19	12.3
13 years.	38	24.7
14 and 15 years.	75	48.7
Total	154	100.0

The preponderance of the older children shows very strikingly in this table, very nearly three-fourths being from 13 to 15 years old. Apparently the desire to leave school among the children whose parents are both able and willing to send them longer coincides very closely with the restless age.

This seems still more markedly the case if we analyze the causes leading the younger children to leave school. The entire group of children studied contained 54 children under 12 who had left school to work, of whom the 22 under consideration form practically two-fifths. . . .

It will be noticed that where young workers were most numerous and began work at the earliest ages, comparatively few of those working under 12 had any choice in the matter, and only two left on account of a real dislike for school. The weariness of the school routine, the lack of interest and the restlessness which caused so much of the dissatisfaction with school seem to develop, or at least to become effective, in the adolescent period.

A question naturally arises as to the ground of unwillingness in the case of those parents who said they were able but unwilling to send children to school longer. Table 52 gives the data relating to these cases:

TABLE 52.—REASONS FOR UNWILLINGNESS OF PARENTS WHO WERE ABLE BUT UNWILLING TO SEND THEIR CHILDREN TO SCHOOL LONGER.

PAWTUCKET, R. I.

Sex.	Age.	Grade last attended.	Kind of school.	Race of father.	Father's occupation.	Per capita weekly income.[a]	Reasons for parents' unwillingness.
M.	16	8	Parochial.	Irish...	Hostler, bottling works.	[b] $3.15	Child cared too much for play while in school.

WOONSOCKET, R. I.

Sex.	Age.	Grade last attended.	Kind of school.	Race of father.	Father's occupation.	Per capita weekly income.[a]	Reasons for parents' unwillingness.
M.	14	3	Public ..	Fr. Can.	Laborer, cotton-mill.	$3.08	"Old enough to work." (Boy wanted to go to school very much.)
M.	15	6	...do.....	...do....	Carpenter.....	3.29	"Old enough to work." If he wants more education he can get it at night school.
M.	15	3	...do.....	...do....	Butcher.......	5.06	"At 14 a boy ought to work. He is too old for school."
M.	14	3	...do.....	...do....	Peddler.......	4.21	Thought studying cause of child's headaches. Too hard for him.
F.	14	6	...do.....	...do....	Tobacco dealer	6.36	Needed in father's store. Father did not see use of too much schooling.
F.	16	7	Convent	Irish...	Letter carrier [b]	[b] 2.10	Child wanted to help, and custodian has no objection "if she gets something to do that won't kill her."
F.	14	(c)	Public ..	Fr. Can.	Carpenter.....	3.98	Want child to help swell the savings before they go back to Canada.

COLUMBUS, GA.

Sex.	Age.	Grade last attended.	Kind of school.	Race of father.	Father's occupation.	Per capita weekly income.[a]	Reasons for parents' unwillingness.
M.	14	5	Parochial.	Amer ..	Drayman.....	$4.27	Mother thought 14 time for a boy to begin work.

GEORGIA AND ALABAMA COUNTIES.

Sex.	Age.	Grade last attended.	Kind of school.	Race of father.	Father's occupation.	Per capita weekly income.[a]	Reasons for parents' unwillingness.
M.	8	2	County .	Amer ..	Grocer and barber.	$1.88	Poor school; learned bad manners; etc.; was suspended; can not afford to send him to city school.
M.	15	7	Public ..	...do....	Overseer, cotton-mill.	2.60	These boys (brothers) were restless in school and parents thought work good for them for a while. Will probably return later.
M.	14	5	...do.....	...do....	...do	2.60	
M.	13	2	County .	...do....	Watchman, cotton-mill.	1.10	Poor school; incompetent teachers; can not afford to live in city.
F.	14	5	Public ..	...do....	Clerk, dry goods.	2.06	Poor school; incompetent teachers; no discipline in schoolroom.
F.	14	1	County .	...do....	Carder, cotton-mill.[d]	.48	"Teacher whipped child so." Could only have sent her 4 months longer.
F.	13	4	Public ..	...do....	Order man, cotton mill.	1.98	Child has weak eyes, is nervous. Mother thought mill work less strain.

COLUMBIA, S. C.

Sex.	Age.	Grade last attended.	Kind of school.	Race of father.	Father's occupation.	Per capita weekly income.[a]	Reasons for parents' unwillingness.
M.	10	1	Public ..	Amer ..	Laborer, cotton-mill.	$2.82	Poor school. Child learned nothing. Refused to have child vaccinated.
M.	12	3	...do.....	...do....	Carpenter.....	(c)	Father a drunkard. Would not buy books. Indifferent regarding education of boy.

PLYMOUTH, PA.

Sex.	Age.	Grade last attended.	Kind of school.	Race of father.	Father's occupation.	Per capita weekly income.[a]	Reasons for parents' unwillingness.
M.	14	8	Public ..	Amer ..	Miner.........	$3.25	Had opportunity to learn plumbing. (His own and his parents' ambition.)
M.	14	5	...do.....	...do....	Carpenter.....	1.92	Had opportunity to work in store. (His own and parents' ambition.) Had been sick.

a After deducting rent and expenses for sickness and death and income from all children of same age as child specified and from younger children.
b Custodian; own father deserted child.
c Not reported.
d Stepfather; own father dead.

Conclusion

The prevailing standard of living among the majority of the cotton-mill workers of the South is not high. From the facts presented in the foregoing pages, it is plain that low wages are the chief factor in determining the prevailing standards of living. Even in those cases where the incomes are fairly high the fact that they fluctuate from week to week is not conducive to the adoption of a standard as high as might be indicated by the total income.

The opportunities offered the people to improve their condition are limited. They rarely have a choice as to the kind of house they must live in. Overcrowding is as likely, or even more likely, to occur in a family with a large income than in one with a small income, for large incomes usually mean a large family, always a large number of workers.

Certain other factors, less tangible, perhaps, have a bearing upon the prevailing standard of living. These may be referred to as limitation of ideals. Often where the income is large the home is most unattractive, with bare floors and a few necessary articles of furniture. Nothing appears comfortable, nothing beautiful. The casual observer would say that the family was living in poverty, yet they might have plenty of good food, plenty of fire, and the children might be well dressed. The explanation for this state of affairs is simple. It is not that these mill girls and boys are vain, extravagant creatures, thinking only of personal adornment. Most of them have never seen a well-furnished house. Their friends live as they do. There is no shame in inviting them to a house that is bare. They see, however, in the shop windows and on the people they pass in the street a display of clothing that sets for them a higher standard as regards clothing than they have in other respects.

One other important feature enters into the lives of most of these people. Relatively few of them live in large cities. In a city, there are a great many things that enrich the poor man's life that he does not have to pay for directly out of his income. There are parks and playgrounds, baths, libraries, art galleries, public lectures, etc. But the cotton-mill family has none of these. Its members must depend on their own financial resources and upon the limited opportunities of the mill village for all their pleasure and for any stimulating influences which may enter into their lives.

Family Budgets in Detail

FAMILY NO. 1

This [Southern] family represents the aristocratic element among cotton-mill people, if such it can be called. One of the daughters married the son of the superintendent of the mill and this gives to the family some prestige in the community. It is probably safe to assume that the family represents as high a standard as has been attained by Southern cotton-mill workers.

The sex, age, occupation, earnings, and contributions of the different members of the family are shown in the following table:

MEMBERSHIP AND INCOME OF FAMILY NO. 1, 1908.

Relationship.	Sex.	Age.	Occupation.	Industry.	Earnings during year.	Amount paid to family during year.
Husband [1]						
Wife	F.	44	Housekeeper			
First child	F.	21	Spinner	Cotton..	$486.85	$486.85
Second child	M.	16	Doffer	...do....	268.75	268.75
Third child	F.	10	At school			
Boarders and lodgers:						
Son-in-law No. 1	M.					
Married daughter No. 1..	F.					[2] 140.00
Baby	F.					
Son-in-law No. 2	M.					[3] 156.00
Married daughter No. 2..	F.					[4] 48.00
Son-in-law No. 3	M.					[3] 156.00
Married daughter No. 3..	F.					[5] 36.00
Total						1,291.60

[1] Deceased.
[2] Board and lodging for 5 months.
[3] Board and lodging for 1 year.
[4] Board and lodging for 4 months.
[5] Board and lodging for 3 months.

The house in which the family lives is not owned by the mill company but is one of the better houses rented from private individuals. The rent is $10 per month. There are five rooms, with a hall and porch. Three rooms are bedrooms, each containing beds. The parlor, which contains a couch bed, is used as a bedroom. The couch, a piano bought on the installment plan, lace curtains, a large rug, rocking chairs, pictures, and a center table give the room a cheerful appearance not usually seen in cotton-mill houses. The kitchen and dining room are one. There is a large range and plenty of kitchen utensils. The hall furnishings, consisting of a hatrack and matting for the floor, were bought on the installment plan and are not fully paid for.

All members of the family are in good health, and during the past year have not had any severe illness.

The amusements of the family are more varied than those of many others of the community. During the winter the unmarried daughter goes to the theater nearly every week. In the summer the members of the family frequently go to the amusement parks. During the past summer the mother was sent to the country for a vacation. This cost $20.

The food is good and plentiful. The menu shows that the family had meat for breakfast and supper. For dinner they had vegetables, but no meat other than the bacon with which the vegetables were cooked.

The following table shows the annual expenditures of the family during the year:

EXPENDITURES OF FAMILY No. 1, 1908.

Item.	Amount.	Item.	Amount.
Food..........................	$534.00	Newspapers........................	$6.74
Rent..........................	120.00	School books........................	2.75
Clothing..........................	205.63	Church contributions..................	2.00
Fuel (wood $43, coal $18)................	61.00	Amusements........................	98.00
Light..........................	9.88	Laundry........................	50.00
Tobacco..........................	18.20	Sundries........................	20.80
Drinks..........................	5.20	Furniture........................	12.00
Medicine..........................	6.00		
Doctor's bills..........................	6.00	Total........................	¹1,207.60
Insurance..........................	49.40		

¹ Not including a debt of $5 for furniture.

MENU OF FAMILY NO. 1, WEEK ENDING JANUARY 3, 1909.

Monday

BREAKFAST: Ham, sausage, biscuit, coffee, sugar, butter, sirup.

DINNER: Baked sweet potatoes, stewed Irish potatoes, collards with bacon, corn bread, biscuit, coffee.

SUPPER: Ham, Irish potatoes, biscuit, coffee, butter, sirup.

Tuesday

BREAKFAST: Fried pork (fresh), biscuit, butter, sirup, coffee, sugar.

DINNER: Peas and bacon, butter beans, sweet potatoes, Irish potatoes, buttermilk, corn bread, biscuit, coffee.

SUPPER: Beefsteak, Irish potatoes, biscuit, butter, coffee, sugar, sirup.

Wednesday

BREAKFAST: Fried pork, ham, butter, cheese, biscuit, coffee, sugar.

DINNER: Cabbage with bacon, Irish potatoes, sweet potatoes, corn bread, biscuit, coffee, sugar.

SUPPER: Steak, rice, biscuit, butter, sirup, coffee, sugar.

Thursday

BREAKFAST: Pork, sausage, biscuit, butter, sirup, coffee, sugar.

DINNER: Collards and bacon, Irish potatoes, sweet potatoes, corn bread, biscuit, butter, buttermilk.

SUPPER: Beefsteak, rice, biscuit, coffee, sirup, sugar.

Friday

BREAKFAST: Pork, rice, biscuit, butter, coffee, sugar.

DINNER: Peas, bacon, butter beans, sweet potatoes, fried pork, onions, pickles, corn bread, biscuit, coffee, sugar.

SUPPER: Ham, cheese, biscuit, butter, coffee, sirup, sugar.

Saturday

BREAKFAST: Pork and rice, biscuit, butter, sirup, coffee, sugar.

DINNER: Collards, bacon, Irish potatoes, sweet potatoes, corn bread, biscuit, coffee, sugar.

SUPPER: Oyster stew, fried pork, biscuit, butter, sirup, coffee, sugar.

Sunday

BREAKFAST: Pork, oyster stew, biscuit, butter, coffee, sugar.

DINNER: Beans, Irish potatoes, sweet potatoes, pork, biscuit, corn bread, coffee, sugar.

SUPPER: Ham, biscuit, butter, sirup, coffee, sugar.

This is an English family [in Massachusetts] consisting of the father, mother, and 7 children. The father has been in this country 20 years. The membership and the age, occupation, and earnings of the members are shown in the following table:

MEMBERSHIP AND INCOME OF FAMILY NO. 97, 1908-9.

Relationship.	Sex.	Age.	Occupation.	Industry.	Earnings.	Amount paid to family.
Husband...........	M.	42	Weaver...........	Cotton..	[1] $309. 40	[1] $309. 40
Wife..............	F.	42	Housekeeper......	....	....	....
First child........	F.	16	Weaver...........	Cotton..	[2] 276. 71	[2] 276. 71
Second child.......	F.	15	.....do..........	...do.....	[1] 253. 40	[1] 253. 40
Third child........	M.	13	At school........	....	....	....
Fourth child.......	M.	11	.....do..........	....	....	....
Fifth child........	M.	6	At home..........	....	....	....
Sixth child........	F.	4	.....do..........	....	....	....
Seventh child......	F.	1	.....do..........	....	....	....
Total.........	......	.....	....	....	....	839. 51

[1] Earnings for 41 weeks.   [2] Earnings for 43 weeks.

The above earnings represent the earnings of the father and the second child for 41 weeks and of the first child for 43 weeks. Prior to this their earnings could not be obtained, for they were at work in other mills.

The family occupies four rooms in a tenement in which six families live. Three of the rooms are used for sleeping; the fourth is the kitchen and general living room. Gas is used for lighting and also for cooking to some extent.

The average value of food consumed per week per man unit for the year covered was $1.56. Following is the menu of family No. 97 for two days:

First day

BREAKFAST: Coffee, bread, butter, eggs.
DINNER: Corned beef and cabbage, potatoes, apple pie, tea, bread, butter.
SUPPER: Ham, bananas, tea, bread, butter.

Second day

BREAKFAST: Coffee, bread, butter, eggs.
DINNER: Boiled beef, potatoes, tea, bread, butter, apple pie.
SUPPER: Ham, eggs, tea, bread, butter.

The house is very plainly furnished. The floor of the kitchen is covered with oilcloth. There are a sewing machine and a few chairs. The windows are not curtained.

The members have all been in good health except the mother. She has had an abscess on her breast, said to have been caused by nursing her baby.

The annual expenditures of the family are as follows:

EXPENDITURES OF FAMILY NO. 97, 1908-9.

Item.	Amount.	Item.	Amount.
Food	$486. 20	Newspapers	$8. 84
Rent	104. 00	Church contributions	46. 80
Cloth¡	210. 11	Amusements	1. 00
Fuel	32. 00	Washing	13. 00
Light	18. 00	Sundries	14. 50
Tobacco	7. 80	Barbering	6. 70
Medicine	5. 00	Poll tax	2. 00
Doctor's bills	12. 00		
Insurance	59. 80	Total	1,032. 95
Lodge dues	5. 20		

The family saved nothing during the year, but have about $150 in the bank, which they had been able to save in former years. They pay cash for all of their groceries, so that no store account could be obtained. . . .

Infant Mortality and Employment of Mothers

An examination of the details concerning some of the cases [in Fall River, Massachusetts, 1908] where the mother returned to work may help to explain the causes of death. Of the mothers who returned to work outside the home, 11 returned during the first month after childbirth and 18 during the second month. . . . It will be especially worth while to examine the details in regard to the lives of these 11 children, for during the first month the maximum percentage of breast feeding will be found, and any improper feeding there found will be representative of similar conditions affecting an increasing proportion of the children in later months.

CHILDREN WHOSE MOTHERS RETURNED TO WORK UNDER ONE MONTH

Mother returned to work as dressmaker outside the home at nine days; child died at one month and eight days of gastroenteritis (and malnutrition); child not nursed at all, milk absent; fed on cow's milk (not bottled) * scalded; child sick all its life; mother had tuberculosis of the hip; cared for by friend in mother's absence. Mother, French Canadian.

Mother returned to housework and sewing outside the home at 10 days; child died at six months of pneumonia; from the beginning was breast fed once at night, at other times fed with cup and spoon on undiluted cow's milk (not bottled) from grocery; child cared for by its aunt in mother's absence. Mother, Portuguese.

Mother returned to work in mill at two weeks; child died at six months of bronchitis; breast fed exclusively two weeks, then at night, but during day given condensed milk "when baby cried;" bottle "cleaned once or twice

* Milk was poured into a container supplied by customer.—Ed.

A photograph by Lewis W. Hine, one of the foremost photographer-chroniclers of the life of the new urban tenement world. This view is from a large series of interiors by him of the tenement dwellers at their work. Perhaps meant ironically because of the presence of the children, this picture is called "Tenement Homework." The family, as in earlier generations, works as a unit at home with materials supplied by a businessman or his agent, usually on piecework pay rather than an hourly wage. This family is making one of the new cheap fancy products of the machine, artificial flowers. Both the flower fabrics and their basic forms were produced by machines and then distributed to the families to be finished. Pictures like this do not often show a man present, suggesting that the work was to supplement a father's labor elsewhere, or that the work was considered fit largely for women and children.   *Library of Congress*

every day;" child strong at birth, but weakened by lack of fresh air and improper food; cared for by neighbor. Mother, Syrian.

Mother returned to work in mill at two weeks; child died at four and one-half months of gastroenteritis; not nursed at all, although mother had milk; fed on condensed milk and cow's milk (not bottled); long-tube bottle used, "washed when needed;" "table food" at four months; grandmother cared for child in mother's absence; Coderre's Infant's Sirup. Mother, Portuguese.

Mother returned to work in mill at two weeks; child died at seven months of pneumonia; child not nursed at all, although mother had milk; fed on condensed milk and cow's milk (not bottled) from grocery, also bread and crackers; child dressed too warmly and kept in hot rooms and seldom taken out of doors; cared for by neighbor in mother's absence. Mother, Portuguese.

Mother returned to work in mill at two weeks; child died at four months of bronchitis; fed exclusively on cow's milk (not bottled) from grocery; mother's milk deficient; child strong at birth and gained steadily at first, but kept in close quarters without fresh air, which debilitated it; cared for by its grand-mother in mother's absence. Mother, Portuguese.

Mother returned to work in mill at three weeks; child died at eight months of bronchitis; child nursed exclusively for three weeks, then given condensed milk, and at four months crackers and milk; mother's milk deficient; fed every hour; "always hungry;" not taken out-of-doors, "too cold;" child cared for by its sister in mother's absence. Mother, French Canadian.

Mother returned to work in mill at three weeks; child died at five months of gastroenteritis; child nursed exclusively two weeks; mother's milk then deficient and child was nursed at night and given Eskay's Food, barley water, and white of egg for four and one-half months; began to fail when mixed feeding was given; sick two months; cared for by neighbor in mother's absence. Mother, English.

Mother returned to work in mill at three weeks; child died at one month and five days of suffocation, mother lying on child; child not nursed at all, given cow's milk with crackers soaked in hot water or milk; in mother's absence cared for by woman with whom she boarded; illegitimate child. Mother, Portuguese.

Mother returned to housework in boarding house at three weeks; child died at 25 days of infantile debility; not nursed at all, although mother had milk; was boarded out and fed exclusively on condensed milk; sick from birth; illegitimate child; mother only 16 or 17 years old. Mother, Irish.

Mother returned to work in mill at four weeks; child died at three months of pneumonia; nursed exclusively two weeks, then given condensed milk; Gover's Soothing Sirup given; child not taken out of doors often; cared for by a friend of mother in mother's absence. Mother, French Canadian.

It would ordinarily be assumed, in the absence of the detailed information given above, that the primary cause of death in the case of each of these 11 children was the employment of the mother outside the home and her consequent inability to care for the child in its early infancy. An examination of the details given above shows that except in the two cases where breast feeding continued up to the time of the mother's return to work, and possibly in one other case—that is, in 8 out of the 11 cases—improper feeding began while the mother was at home and before her return to work necessitated the withdrawal of her care. . . .

It would thus appear that the beginning of improper feeding and unintelligent care in almost all of these cases preceded the mother's return to work, and that even in those cases where feeding other than nursing did not begin until the withdrawal of the mother's care it was still apparent that she must have been responsible for the character of the feeding.

In 5 cases the lack of sufficient fresh air is noted. While in some of these cases it is clear that this was due to the belief that exposure to cold air was injurious, in some of the cases at least it is probable that it was due directly to the mother's absence and inability to take the child out of doors. The debility certain to result from improper feeding and the lack of fresh air would naturally tend to render the children easy victims of bronchitis or pneumonia, the recorded cause of death in 6 of the 11 cases.

Character of Feeding Before and After Mother Went to Work of Children Whose Mothers Went to Work in the Second Month

An examination of the histories of the 18 children whose mothers returned to work in the second month does not disclose quite so bad a record of improper feeding and care. Twelve went to work at one month, 2 at five weeks, 2 at six weeks, 1 between six and seven weeks, and 1 at seven weeks. Fourteen were reported well and strong at birth, 3 not well, and the condition of 1 was not reported. . . .

It would . . . appear that here, as with the children whose mothers returned to work under 1 month, the beginning of improper feeding and unintelligent care in the majority of the cases preceded the mother's return to work.

SOCIAL INSURANCE FOR OLD AGE

What is the modern problem of old age? It is the problem of poverty caused by inability to find employment because the productive power has waned—and waned not temporarily, but forever. Evidently, in this form, the problem could not exist until the majority of mankind became dependent upon a wage-contract for their means of existence. It may be said that the problem has always existed, because there always were old men and women. In a primitive agricultural community, however, where the patriarchal family prevails, there can be no acute old-age problem. The authority of the patriarch is paramount and lasts longer than his productive powers. When no longer able to lead a plow, he is still looked up to for advice. The family is one large consumption unit, its members all prosper or starve together. . . .

Most aged persons are not actually starving to death in the United States, even when not in receipt of organized public or private charitable relief. Neither were they presumably starving in Great Britain, France, or any country which was forced to institute old-age pension systems. After all, some of them hold on with grim desperation to an opportunity to earn a wage. Not many succeed, to be sure. To return to the United States statistics. There were in 1900 some 1,065,000 men sixty-five years or over engaged in gainful occupations, out of a total of 1,555,000 of that age. But of 1,065,000 men nearly one half were farmers; and professional men, bankers, brokers, manufacturers, corporation officers, and merchants constituted another 15%, leaving only about one-third for wage-earners. The question is: how many of the 500,000 men over sixty-five years of age and not employed were being supported by charity or private aid; how

I. M. Rubinow, *Social Insurance* (New York, 1913), pp. 302–17.

many of the 1,400,000 women over sixty-five years of age had the comforts of their own homes, and how many were burdens to a workingman's family? And how many of the 500,000 or 600,000 wage-workers, sixty-five years or older, were earning enough for any approach to a physiological standard? Perhaps nothing short of an old-age pension system will bring forth exact answers to these questions.

This, then, is briefly, the situation and the problem. What are the remedies? In absence of any systematic social method of dealing with the problem, three ways are open to the aged workman who is unable to find employment, or, when employed, unable to earn the amount needed even for a modest living:

(1) Savings; (2) dependence upon children or relatives; and (3) finally, public charity. . . .

That in thousands of cases children or relatives are forced to give help is a fact too well known to be disputed. But it is a condition which usually exists, and is this sort of relief always possible, and if possible, desirable?

The strongest emphasis on this remedy for old-age destitution was recently made by the Massachusetts Commission on Old-Age Pensions. The secretary of the Commission, Professor F. Spencer Baldwin, has repeatedly emphasized the same argument in articles and lectures. It was used as one of the main reasons against the desirability of an old-age pension system in the state of Massachusetts. In the report of the Commission it is stated in the following energetic language:

> *The disintegrating effect on the family.* A non-contributory system would take away, in part, the filial obligation for the support of aged parents which is a main bond of family solidarity. It would strike at one of the forces that have created the self-supporting, self-respecting American family. The impairment of family solidarity is one of the most serious consequences to be apprehended.

There is a good, old-fashioned, atavistic nobility of sentiment about this argument which will greatly please all good men and women except those who have to be supported by their children, and those who have to support their parents and also their own families on a wage-earner's budget. Scientifically the argument is certainly original, because it assumes the basis of the family to be the support of the older generation by the younger, while it has always been fairly well agreed upon by all students of society that the shoe was on the other foot, and that the care of the children by the parents was the proper function of family. It further seems to assume that we love our burdens, and that when parents cease being burdens the children cease loving them.

It assumes that the standing of a superannuated parent in a family is in an inverse proportion to the amount he is able to contribute to the family budget. It is an appeal to an ideal of a patriarchal family which has been dead for a century in every industrial country, and which really never had any strong hold upon American life. Of course, its inapplicability to the aged single man or the aged spinster aunt will be evident. For it certainly cannot be claimed that the support of all spinster aunts is also a fundamental principle of American family solidarity. Then, again, even married people may not have any children, or may have lost them. One must remember that New England was practising race suicide long before the term ever became popular. As a matter of fact, the very data gathered by the Commission show that of the inmates of almshouses and benevolent homes over 25% were single, and of those receiving outdoor relief 15%.

Furthermore, these data also show how these almshouses and homes do break down the solidarity of the American family. Of their inmates, 42% had adult children living at time of entrance, of the several thousand pensioners receiving outdoor relief 60% had adult children at the time of investigation, and 59% other near relatives. It is really surprising that the Commission did not recommend discontinuance of aid, both institutional and outdoor, because of the demoralizing effect upon said children and relatives.

However, the same table which conveys the information just quoted shows that while there were children in some 60%, only in 22% were they able to render aid; that this proportion was only some 10% in case of the inmates of homes, and about 50% in case of persons receiving outdoor relief. Moreover, it appears from another table that some 40% were receiving aid from children or relatives, as outdoor relief is seldom bountiful.

The long and short of this dependence upon family solidarity is just this:

1. That in a number of cases the aged poor are single individuals.
2. Or if married or widowed, have no children.
3. And if there are adult children or other relatives they are unable to render any aid, or, at any rate, sufficient aid.
4. Or if they are able, may not be willing to do so.

But, nevertheless, there must be thousands of families where children are either unable or unwilling to render aid to the superannuated workers, but do it, nevertheless, because of deep attachment to the parents, or family pride revolting against application to charity, and that the filial obligation is thus enforced by a neglectful society with the effect of frequently depressing a standard of life already too low, or forcing the old father or mother to eat the daily bread unwillingly yielded, in pain and humiliation, or—preventing the formation of a new family by the dutiful son or daughter, because of the existing obligation towards the ruins of the old family. And these are the results of trying to apply an eighteenth-century ideal to twentieth-century conditions.

In view of the failure of individual methods, such as private savings, and semi-social methods, such as family solidarity, to meet the problem in a satisfactory way, the burden, or a very large share of it, is thrown upon the primitive social method of poor-relief, whether public, semi-public, or private, by individual alms-giving. That charity—private charity, church charity, and public poor-relief—has done a good deal since time immemorial almost no one will deny. But it is just as evident that this cannot be considered as a final settlement of the problem of destitution. Even if poor-relief were capable of assuming the care of all those who need it, it would be far from satisfactory. In Great Britain, where the aged pauper population is proportionately the greatest in the world, the number of people receiving poor-relief served more to accentuate the need for some systematic and satisfactory way, than to evidence that the problem had been solved. For it is admitted by modern society that alms-giving and alms-receiving are degrading and demoralizing, and that alms-giving should be restricted as far as possible. Modern philanthrophy defends its right of existence on the plea that it works for the rehabilitation of the individual and family; and the situation of the superannuated worker is not such as to permit of rehabilitation.

Poor-relief, in all countries, carries with it a social stigma, and in most a definite loss of the prerogatives of free citizenship. Outdoor poor-relief meets the constant danger of malingery and exploitation, and institutional poor-relief is gruesome to every one except the senile, the invalid, or physically or mentally defective. The majority of people, even of the poorest class, have a wholesome antipathy to poor-relief, and institutional relief is considered the last hope. But even aside from these moral aspects of poor-relief, materially it has never been sufficient, either quantitatively, or qualitatively, to solve the problem of old age.

Moreover, poor-relief, as the only solution of the problem, is highly unsatisfactory, not only from humanitarian considerations, but also for "sound business reasons." By its objectionable character to the wage-worker, it fails to furnish any incentive for voluntary retirement. The problem of old age has a direct bearing upon efficiency in production, and, therefore, upon the employer's profit. The reasons forcing the older men out of the field of production have already been mentioned. In practice, the elimination of the aging worker does not proceed as easily and smoothly as all that. Some employers are humane. And where the humane employer's place has been taken by a corporation "without a body to be kicked, without a soul to be damned," the actual hiring and firing may be done by foremen, privates of yesterday. It may be easy to establish rules of admission, but not so simple to enforce rules about wholesale discharge. Age may be lied about, and the decline in efficiency may only be noticeable to the nearest workman. Besides, there is the union to be reckoned with, and no establishment can preserve any degree of efficiency if it is in constant turmoil of labor conflicts. Thus, the need of some systematic provision for retirement adds additional weight to the importance of the old-age problem.

Growing Up in San Francisco, 1900–1915

One major problem with oral histories of family experiences is separating nostalgic and special elements from general and objective
views. Although historians must guard against such distortions
in assessing answers to the query "What was family life like, back there,
then?," they must also recognize that, however distorted, the memories
form a standard by which older Americans—and those they may influence—
feel, act, and even legislate on family policy.

To what degree do these memories (recorded circa 1975) of San Francis-
cans who were about as old as the century seem distorted by nostalgia?
Do the memories excessively flatter or represent the so-called "nice home"
contrasted with the families across the tracks? What darker images of old
San Francisco (about the time of the great earthquake of 1906) are available
to Americans to compare with the more arcadian visions of childhood
and family life invoked in these interviews? What are some differences
and distinctions even within these recollections? What might seem distinctive or distorted if these recordings were analyzed under headings like
parental authority, religious and moral ideals, and so on? What might
we learn about the "good old days" by comparing these with similar records
of still earlier generations of childhoods in San Francisco? Or by using
recordings from other locales of the same period? In reconstructing something of the family structure, relations, and values behind these memories,
what, seemingly, are the missing elements and emphases? To whom, really,
beyond the interviewer, are these memoirs addressed? For whom, generally,
do American families speak when asked or when spontaneously giving
forth about bygone good or bad days?

OLD SAN FRANCISCANS REMEMBER

A Man, Age 80

Q: Comparing then and now, what would be the greatest difference in
living in San Francisco when you were growing up and now?

Frederick M. Wirt, director, "Growing Up in the City Project" (photocopy of typed transcript, 1977). Donated Oral Histories Collection, The Bancroft Library, University of California, Berkeley. Courtesy The Bancroft Library.

A: Well, I think what I would point out is that life, all of life, was much more simple. By that I mean we got along with what we had, and oftentimes that wasn't much. There were very few people—we were just talking about it a few days ago—there very few people having means of transportation, which makes your supermarkets today. We had so many institutions that were simple things, like the corner grocery store, which part of it was devoted to meat. Very seldom you ever had a thing like a baker shop. The mothers, most of our mothers, cooked—baked—pies and cakes. That's why we used to buy flour by the bulk. Twenty-five pounds of flour. The store is the same way. The grocery store, you ordered a pound of coffee and they ground it right there. Had a barrel of pickles which the man himself made; sauerkraut, he had a barrel of that and he made that. You went down—when I'd go to the store, I was nine, ten years of age—and pick up the groceries. Most of those places also delivered, and you had charge accounts. The grocerymen, there was a lot more respect in their honesty and their respect and their word. Today, you have to establish credit. The grocerymen knew all your family problems. Sometimes they'd talk about family difficulties, and when you finished, he'd give you a slice of bologna or salami, a stick of candy. When you think of it, not many people had a horse and buggy, no automobiles. I remember when the first automobile came out, 1915. It wasn't until 1920 that my folks bought a Model T. But to get places, you'd go in a trolley car.

Q: So you think the big difference is the simplicity of life.

A: Yes. We stayed home. Once in a while, you'd visit friends, but it'd be on a special occasion, you know. Drop by on Christmas for a little while. At home you played cards, sometimes the family'd play checkers. I used to play checkers with my father. But just three of us, we used to play casino, you know. Keep score. . . .

Q: Was San Francisco in your early days kind of a collection of little villages with green space in between them?

A: Yes, your neighborhood; you identified yourself more with neighborhoods than you do today. You see, the Mission in my time was probably eighty-five percent Irish. Today it's about eighty-five percent Mexican. But where do you live? "In the Mission District," "In the Sunset," "North Beach," "I'm a South-of-Market boy." That kind of thing prevailed. "Well, surely you're from Richmond, that's just the new part of town. I'm from the Mission, that's the real San Franciscan, real native." That kind of stuff. That established a kind of a pride and identity.

A Woman, Age 72

A: My father was very religious. He had been brought up in a very religious home. We went to Sunday school right from the start. I sang. At the age of three, I was solo singer in the church and sang Swedish songs. Mother would accompany me on the piano, and we were all confirmed in, it was a Swedish Covenant church, which is one of the Protestant churches. I would definitely say that the background is religious. It resulted in my two brothers not going to church at all when they got through. They'd had enough of it.

Q: What were your reactions, when very young, to this religious training?

A: I knew no other way of life. My father was so strict, from the old school— he probably didn't mean to be—that one night, I came to the dinner table, and I was so full of high spirits I just started to sing. I had to leave the table and go finish my dinner in the kitchen all alone.

Q: This was on Sunday?

A: No, this was just during the week. Oh, you didn't sing at the table.

Q: How often did you have to go to church? Just Sunday?

A: Sunday. Well, I would say as far as I'm concerned, Sunday was Sunday school. Then I had to sit through this Swedish service, which was so boring because I didn't understand it. It was just a nightmare. This was cruel for the young people, but that's what we had to do. Then when I grew older, we had Christian Endeavor about seven o'clock, and we had evening services about eight o'clock. Then later on, we sang in the choir. Then we had an after-meeting, a sort of revival meeting. So Sunday was practically spent in church all day long. It was horrible.

Q: Did you have any Wednesday-night or weekday services to attend?

A: Oh, we didn't have to do that. They had a Wednesday-night prayer meeting, but as young people we didn't attend that.

Q: Sunday school, what would that consist of?

A: Well, unfortunately, again you see, this was the—we really didn't try to learn Swedish. We should have, and when I look back—this is ridiculous—but we were more or less ashamed of it. We just ignored it, which is ridiculous because in Sunday school we were taught in Swedish. That was boring. Then the service, of course, was boring also. Instead of picking up the language and understanding what it was all about, we didn't. We all regretted it when we grew up.

Q: What did church mean to you if it was all in a language you couldn't understand?

A: Well, it was a way of life. Mother played in the string band and sang in the choir, and Dad was a deacon. Mother practically ran the church. All the people, our friends, were part of the church. They all sang in the choir and they all were musical. It was, just definitely, religion in the house which like today television might be in the home. It was just a way of life.

Q: Tell me how religion as a part of daily life worked. Give me some illustrations if you can.

A: Well, we certainly had our conscience, we were keenly aware of our conscience, and we lived our religion. It was just part of us. We knew right from wrong so well that hardly anyone would have ever thought of going astray. Not only from punishment from the family, but our own conscience. It was just sort of like having God live right in your home, really. That's the way we were brought up. It was fine. I'm sure it didn't do us any harm, but where we failed, we should have learned the language, and then we would have been in more accord with the whole thing.

Q: Your brothers rejected it?

A: My brothers rejected it. They had all they could take and they never went back.

Q: How much of that stayed with you?

A: Oh, well, in all fairness, when I left home and married the first time, I thought this was the way life should be lived. Not taking your whole Sunday up. I just loved the freedom of it. But then later, when all sorts of things began to happen, I came back to the church. Now, my church is my whole life. I do volunteer work there as a receptionist. It's my whole life now, again. So you see, it's at the beginning and the end.

Q: Your father and mother were thus very close in reinforcing this religion.

A: Oh, yes.

Two Sisters, Ages 70 and 74

Q: Looking back on these things, what do you think were some of the good effects of that early training?

A-1: I think it was a wonderful guideline, in doing the right thing and always trying to do a good job and always doing the right job, never doing anything dishonest, never treating another person in a way that you would not want to be treated yourself. We received a great moral code from the religious training, but we got most of it from our father and his sister. A very strong moral code. We are still very close, my sister and my other sister.

A-2: The values are there and that's what I see missing today, the values are given to you, and that's great. So much of the way this was done was wrong, the rigidity and the terrible guilt, more than children can take, but it's too bad they couldn't separate from that. The method of doing it, I would say, needs—

Q: What would you say, then, were some of the not-so-good effects of that religious training?

A-2: It closes a person's mind to the point that they do not think for themselves. If they want to think for themselves, they feel, "I'm not supposed to." Someone else has done the thinking for you. The young people today are thinking for themselves.

A-1: Interesting trade-off, that if you close off thinking you increase the value of, the effect of, the value training. If you permit more openness in looking at this, the value training is less emphatic.

A Woman, Age 72

Q: We learn somewhere along the line how to be a mother or wife. What comes to mind first when you think about your earliest training about being a girl?

A: Well, I have a very vivid memory of coming home with my friend. Mother was always there. That's one thing, to divert just a moment, I think is wrong with conditions today, that Momma's not home, waiting for the children when they come home from school. That's the thing. She was there, always with a starched, clean apron and a clean gingham dress, with cookies and milk. Supervised our activities. I'm just sure that this is one of the big failings, and there are a lot of people that belong to this school, but I remember so well, I started to act up and became very rambunctious. Mother reproached me, and she said—no, I said, "Who do you think I am? A rooster?" This was in front of my schoolmates. My mother said, "I'd like to think that you are a little lady." Do you know, I'm seventy-two years old, and I still cringe when I think of that. It was so effective. Imagine. I was probably seven when that happened. That was the goal, to be a little lady.

Q: Do you remember doing anything that the boys used to do?

A: No, I was with dolls. I always played with dolls.

Q: You didn't play baseball or basketball?

A: No.

Q: Did you have any early training about what a good mother should be like? Did your mother, for example, talk about what your role would be as a mother?

A: Yeah, I would say that she was just great. She set such a beautiful example. She worked so hard, and then in the afternoon she always got cleaned up, and some of us don't bother today. We go all day long in the same garb that we work in the house. But Mother always dressed in starched clothes, starched aprons. Then in those days, no transportation of any kind. They had what they called their days at home. Mother's day at home would probably be every third Thursday. Another lady would be every third Wednesday. Then, if you could, you knew that lady would be home, and it was like open house, and you could go over and visit. Then they always would have sandwiches and cake and cookies and coffee, of course. Coffee to Swedish people is what beer is to the Germans and the wine to the French. So then they'd clean up their house even more so, and all this good food would be ready. You would never know who would drop in, but everybody had on their calendars: so-and-so's day at home.

Q: Did you participate in any of those days?

A: Oh, I went with her everywhere. Sure, I went everywhere. Then, at home, we'd know when there was activity.

Q: Was that fun to go with your mother to these things? These adult visits.

A: Not really, but I didn't know any better. Sometimes, somebody else would bring someone to play with. Mother would say, I can hear her say, "Oh, she's such a good child to take out. She never says boo." I used to wonder, Why would anyone say boo?

Q: Did your mother give you any formal training in cooking or housecleaning?

A: She tried. She tried, but I just wasn't gaited that way. I was made for office work and writing letters, and I never have been domesticated. She tried so hard, but you have to learn. Once I got married, I learned.

Q: What kind of training did you have to be a wife?

A: Well, I guess probably by example.

Q: What was a good wife supposed to be like then?

A: Well, you certainly kept a clean house and you kept yourself clean, and you certainly should be a fairly good cook, and be active in church, go about raising the children and taking care of their friends and their schooling. As a matter of fact, in our family, Mother was, as I say, she was the dominant factor. Dad was a good man, but he just worked and went to church Sunday morning and read the Bible, and that was about it.

Q: Did he ever take you out for fun?

A: Oh, yes.

Q: Just the two of you.

A: Oh, every Sunday, almost every Sunday, we would go to church—it's still there. . . .

Q: Did your father ever take you out on a date, as we now call it? Just you two: a movie, for example?

A: Oh, movies were—oooooooh. And they were five cents; we called them nickelodeons. Ice-cream sodas were five cents. But movies, when we lived in Turlock—and by now, I'm just ready to come back to the city, so we'll say I'm seventeen or eighteen—a friend and I went to a movie with our two boyfriends, and her mother and my father were waiting for us when we got outside. We were told that we were headed straight for hell. Just for going to a movie on Sunday night. That's how strict we were brought up.

Middle-Class Marriage, 1920s

S cholarly examination of American family life in the twentieth century added yet another genre to the earlier advice manuals and moral musings about the family. Two of the best and most enduring of these portraits appeared in 1929 and 1933. Along with the chapters on family matters in the U.S. government's *Recent Social Trends* (1933), those in the Lynds' sociology classic *Middletown* present valuable summary views of family life about one third of the way through the century. *Middletown* and its follow-up a decade later, *Middletown in Transition*, were studies of the purportedly typical small American city; in fact, Muncie, Indiana.

The technique of finding one community and of examining it in depth as a microcosm of national life is regarded as one of the most productive methods of empirical social science in the United States. The first question thus raised by this selection from the chapter on marriage and making a home is one that is still perplexing. What are the distinguishing elements that entitle studies to be called accurate depictions of the *typical* American town or family? What seems to make Middletown typical of America? How would we define or establish typicality or Americanness? What about "modern" or "occidental" or "WASP" or other rival or complimentary descriptions? Can any author's bias be discerned in this supposedly impartial account of how Middletowners make and conduct their families? What words suggest the authors' affection and approval? Which of their phrases imply censure or skepticism? Do statistics seem to be used often and well enough to document generalizations? In what degree do the assumptions of these families conflict or coincide with their aims—that is, their ideals and ideal images of themselves? How, for example, do social ideals of power and prestige that may derive largely from the worlds of politics and business affect the "private" family virtues of love, fidelity, and companionship?

MARRIAGE IN MIDDLETOWN

It would appear that more people are marrying young in Middletown today. Explanation of this apparent drift toward more and earlier marriages

Robert S. and Helen Merrell Lynd, *Middletown* (New York, 1929), pp. 111–19. Copyright 1929 by Harcourt Brace Jovanovich; copyright 1957 by Robert S. and Helen M. Lynd. Reprinted by permission of the publisher.

may lie in part in such changes, noted elsewhere, as the cessation of apprenticeship, which gives a boy of eighteen a man's wages at a machine, the increased opportunities for wives to supplement the family income by working, the relatively greater ease and respectability of dissolving a marriage today, the diffusion of knowledge of means of contraception, and the growing tendency to engage in leisure-time pursuits by couples rather than in crowds, the unattached man or woman being more "out of it" in the highly organized paired social life of today than a generation ago when informal "dropping in" was the rule.

Marriage consists in a brief ceremonial exchange of verbal pledges by a man and woman before a duly sanctioned representative of the group. This ceremony, very largely religious in the nineties, is becoming increasingly secularized. In 1890, 85 percent of the local marriages were performed by a religious representative and 13 percent by a secular agent, while in 1923 those performed by the religious leaders had fallen to 63 percent, and the secular group had risen to 34 percent of the total. A prominent local minister accounted for the prevalence of divorces in Middletown in 1924 by the fact that "there are too many marriages in secular offices away from the sanctity of the churches." The marriage ceremony relaxes the prohibition upon the mutual approaches of the two persons to each other's persons and as regards the sexual approach makes "the wrongest thing in the world the rightest thing in the world." The pair usually leave the homes of their parents at once and begin to make a home of their own; the woman drops the name of her father for the name of her husband.

A heavy taboo, supported by law and by both religious and popular sanctions, rests upon sexual relationships between persons who are not married. There appears to be some tentative relaxing of this taboo among the younger generation, but in general it is as strong today as in the county-seat of forty years ago. There is some evidence that in the smaller community of the eighties in which everybody knew everybody else, the group prohibition was outwardly more scrupulously observed than today. A man who was a young buck about town in the eighties says, "The fellows nowadays don't seem to mind being seen on the street with a fast woman, but you bet we did then!". . .

The choice of a mate in marriage is nominally hedged about by certain restrictions—legal, religious, and customary. . . . Further informal demands, made by the fluid sentiments of the group, have apparently altered little since the nineties, although they have been given somewhat greater legal recognition. Foremost among these is the demand for romantic love as the only valid basis for marriage. Theoretically, it is the mysterious attraction of two young people for each other and that alone that brings about a marriage, and actually most of Middletown stumbles upon its partners in marriage guided chiefly by "romance." Middletown adults appear to regard romance in marriage as something which, like their religion, must be believed in to hold society together. Children are assured by their elders that "love" is an unanalyzable mystery that "just happens"—"You'll know when the right one comes along," they are told with a knowing smile. . . .

And yet, although theoretically this "thrill" is all-sufficient to insure permanent happiness, actually talks with mothers revealed constantly that, particularly among the business group, they were concerned with certain other factors; the exclusive emphasis upon romantic love makes way as adolescence recedes for a pragmatic calculus. Mothers of the business group give much consideration to encouraging in their children friendships with the "right" people of the other sex, membership in the "right" clubs, deftly warding off the attentions of boys whom they regard as undesirable for their daughters to "see too much of," and in other ways interfering with and directing the course of true love. . . .

Middletown wives appear in part to accept the impression of them that many of their husbands have. "Men are God's trees; women are his flowers," and "True womanliness is the greatest charm of woman," the recent mottoes of two of the local federated women's clubs, suggest little change from the prevailing attitude reflected in a commencement essay in 1891, "Woman Is Most Perfect When Most Womanly." . . .

In general, a high degree of companionship is not regarded as essential for marriage. There appears to be between Middletown husbands and wives of all classes when gathered together in informal leisure-time groups relatively little spontaneous community of interest. The men and women frequently either gravitate apart into separate groups to talk men's talk and women's talk, or the men do most of the talking and the women largely listen. . . . One of the commonest joint pursuits of husbands and wives is playing cards with friends. A few read aloud together, but this is relatively rare, as literature and art have tended to disappear today as male interests. . . . The automobile appears to be an important agency in bringing husbands and wives together in their leisure, counteracting in part the centrifugal tendency in the family observable in certain other aspects of Middletown's life.

Among the working class, leisure activities and other relations between married couples seem to swing about a somewhat shorter tether than do those of business folk. Not infrequently husband and wife meet each other at the end of a day's work too tired or inert to play or go anywhere together; many of them have few if any close friends. . . . This frequent lack of community of interests, together with the ideas each sex entertains regarding the other, appears in many families in a lack of frankness between husband and wife, far-reaching in its emotional outcome. "One thing I always tell my young men when they marry," said the only one of the six leading ministers who gives any instruction to people he marries, "is that they must get over any habit of thinking that they must be frank and tell everything they know to their wives.". . .

Traditionally this institution of marriage is indissoluble. "What God hath joined together let no man put asunder," commands the religious marriage ritual. But the trend toward secularization noted in the performance of the marriage ceremony appears even more clearly in the increased lifting of the taboo upon the dissolution of marriage. With an increase, between 1890 and 1920, of 87 percent in the population of the county in which Middletown is located, the number of recorded divorces for the four years 1921–24 has increased 622 percent over the number of divorces in the county in the four years 1889–92. There were nine divorces for each 100 marriage licenses issued in 1889 and eighteen in 1895. . . . After fluctuating about the latter figure for fifteen years, the total in 1909 first passed twenty-five divorces for each 100 marriage licenses, and six years later thirty. In 1918 it was fifty-four for each 100 marriage licenses; 1919, thirty-nine; 1920, thirty-three; 1921, fifty-five; 1922, forty; 1923, thirty-seven; 1924, forty-two.

The frequency of divorces and the speed with which they are rushed through have become commonplaces in Middletown. "Anybody with $25 can get a divorce" is a commonly heard remark. Or as one recently divorced man phrased it, "Anyone with $10 can get a divorce in ten minutes if it isn't contested. All you got to do is to show non-support or cruelty and it's a cinch.". . .

Traditionally, voluntary control of parenthood is strongly tabooed in this culture, as is all discussion of sexual adjustment involved in mating, but this prohibition is beginning to be somewhat lifted, a fact perhaps not unrelated to the increasing secularization of marriage noted above. The widely divergent habits of different persons in regard to control of parenthood reveal strikingly the gap found in so many cases to exist between the habits of different groups of people living together in the same community. All of the twenty-seven women on the business class who gave information on this point used or believed in the use of some method of birth control and took it for granted. Only one woman spoke of being uncertain as to whether she had been wise in limiting her family as she had. Of the seventy-seven wives of workers from whom information was secured on this subject, only thirty-four said that they used any means of birth control. . . .

The behavior of the community in this matter of the voluntary limitation of parenthood—in this period of rapidly changing standards of living, irregular employment, the increasing isolation and mobility of the individual family, growing emphasis upon child-training and upon education and other long-term family plans such as insurance and enforced home ownership on a time payment basis—presents the appearance of a pyramid. At the top, among most of the business group, the use of relatively efficacious contraceptive methods appears practically universal, while sloping down from this peak is a mixed array of knowledge and ignorance, until the base of ignorance is reached. Here fear and worry over pregnancy frequently walk hand in hand with discouragement as to the future of the husband's job and the dreaded lay-off. . . .

With the spread of the habit of married women's working, women are less willing to continue an unsatisfactory marital arrangement. Said the

lawyer quoted above, "If a woman has ever worked at all she is much
more likely to seek a divorce. It's the timid ones that have never worked
who grin and bear marriage. Unemployment always increases the number
of women seeking a divorce." In one sturdy, self-respecting family the
daughter of twenty-three and the son of twenty-one have both been married
and divorced and are living at home again:

> "My daughter's husband," said the mother, "is at the house six days a
> week and they have an awfully good time together, but they just couldn't
> get on about money matters. Now she has her own money and he has his
> and there's no trouble. That was the trouble with my son and his wife, too.
> They split up over money."

. . . The way in which these antecedents of divorce are imbedded in
the whole complex of Middletown's culture touching the adjustments between a man and his wife is suggested by comparing what Middletown
regards as minimum essentials of marriage with conditions actually existing
in many Middletown homes, particularly those of the working class, among
whom, according to lawyers handling divorce cases, divorce is more frequent. The husband must "support" his family, but, as pointed out above,
recurrent "hard times" make support of their families periodically impossible for many workers; the wife must make a home for her husband and
care for her children, but she is increasingly spending her days in gainful
employment outside the home; husband and wife must cleave to each other
in the sex relation, but fear of pregnancy frequently makes this relation
a dread for one or both of them; affection between the two is regarded
as the basis of marriage, but sometimes in the day-after-day struggle this
seems to be a memory rather than a present help. Not one of the sixty-
eight working-class wives mentioned her husband in answering the question
as to the things that give her "courage to go on when thoroughly discouraged." More than one wife seems to think of her husband less as an individual than as a focus of problems and fears—anxiety about loss of job,
disappointment over failure in promotion, fear of conception—the center
of a whole complex of things to be avoided. To many husbands their
wives have become associated with weariness, too many children, and other
people's washings. . . .

There are some homes in Middletown among both working- and busi-
ness-class families which one cannot enter without being aware of a constant
undercurrent of sheer delight, of fresh, spontaneous interest between husband and wife. But such homes stand out by reason of their relative rarity.
In others where this quality is less apparent, marriage is doubtless the
deepest reality in the lives of the pair. For many couples, however, for
whom thought of the divorce court may never figure even as a remote
possibility, marriage seems to amble along at a friendly jog-trot marked
by sober accommodation of each partner to his share in the joint undertaking of children, paying off the mortgage, and generally "getting on."

Depression Families

The "Great Depression" that began in 1929 and the Civil War are the only severe social traumata the United States has known. For families the depression years of the 1930s brought a nationwide pummeling. Only Southerners on the paths of the armies in the 1860s experienced desolation directly. After 1929, loss of businesses and jobs, loss of savings, loss of life insurance, loss of status through seeking work below one's qualifications and self-image, loss of higher education for older children and the need, instead, for children to find work that would pay— all these and more were familiar blows to families everywhere in the United States.

As a general social crisis, the Depression inspired an extraordinary record of reports, investigations, fiction, plays, musicals and memoirs. For family life a major question remains whether the disasters weakened or strengthened ties. Did the loss of jobs, money, and schooling put family members more at each other's throats or force more members onto the labor market to help cut expenses or to find work in distant places?

Three different family experiences during the Depression decade are recorded in these selections. From the reports of the Works Progress Administration (WPA) comes the sketch of the Donner family of Dubuque, Iowa. What specific losses and psychological changes did this family experience? With what likely effects on their feelings for each other? Were there any gains from Depression experiences? Contrast the categories of expenses given in the budget of a middle-class management couple in 1939 (comfortable throughout the Depression and just then purchasing a house) with categories or outlays that the Donners may have had to forego or never knew. Which of the budget categories would not have appeared commonly or at all in family budgets earlier in the century or when the Depression had passed? Is there any evidence in the budget that this couple knew hard times at all? Might they have profited from Depression prices, cheap help, low interest rates? (The husband was in the lumber business.)

One of the most dramatic Depression disasters was the notable increase in families losing their farms or farm work because of low prices, poor management, and dust storms. In desperation, they took to the roads to find cash elsewhere. There was already migration before 1929, however, largely from shrinking markets and the expansion of agribusiness at the expense of the smaller independent family farmer or the local farm laborer. The jump in number of migrants after 1930 and the leap in *rate* of their dispossession, coupled with the country's greater sensitivity to dislocation and disasters, put the Okies (Oklahomans) and Arkies (Arkansans) into the newspapers and newsreels and onto the agendas of state and federal legislators and bureaucrats. By the mid-1930s, at least a million Americans were "on the road" but in a nation ill-equipped to handle their presence even when there was goodwill.

The last selection records the origins, marriage patterns, and family style of several California clans of migrants, some of whom gave up city life and jobs for the "fruit tramp" life. Included are a family tree and a chart and map of travel. Many of our usual categories for thinking about American families seem to presume their staying in place, but what did family movement such as that shown on the map mean for family activities like schooling, medical and dental care, writing letters and receiving mail, courting, friendships, and knowing the whereabouts of relatives? How much of the distress of the migrants seems traceable to being poor and underemployed rather than being on the move? How does migration affect family relations with community and government services for families that presume long-term local residence? Do migrants represent special cases of "Americans on the move" (a startling phenomenon of American family and social history) rather than a largely unprecedented or exceptional type of family? Is it (or was it), in other words, the American norm for most families to remain settled or, cyclically, to move, set down, scatter, then move again with or without resources?

THE DONNERS

Interviewing completed
March 15, 1938

Mr. Donner	53
Mrs. Donner	48
Louise	14
Dick	06

In good years, while Mr. Donner had his own printing business in Chicago, it "was nothing" for him to take the children downtown on Saturday afternoons and spend $2 or $3 on trivialities for each of them, and Dick and Louise "never thought of going into a drugstore" without having sun-

J. N. Webb with J. A. Bloodworth and E. J. Greenwood, *The Personal Side* (Washington, D.C., WPA Division of Research, 1939), pp. 283–90.

daes or sodas. When, in the early thirties, the business started downhill, both Mr. and Mrs. Donner were even more concerned about the children than about the business. Though they tried not to let Louise and Dick know how worried they themselves were, they did explain that now there was less money to spend because "business was bad." As it happened, the children surprised their parents by their casual acceptance of deprivations. They used to tell their father not to buy the things they especially wanted unless "business was good." They did, though, expect Christmas toys in 1933, for they still believed in Santa Claus.

Mr. Donner has had no private employment since the spring of 1934, when he finally gave up the printing business which he had owned and operated for 15 years. Then he and Mrs. Donner and the two children came to Dubuque to Mrs. Donner's parents. Since the fall of 1934 he has been employed most of the time on emergency work projects. He is now a WPA timekeeper.

He looks the part of the business man that he has been. He is broad and well-built, well-dressed, and well-groomed. Both Mr. and Mrs. Donner are cordial and gracious and talk rather freely about their depression experiences.

When Mr. Donner was 13 years old his family moved from Dubuque to Chicago. After completing a 2-year business college course in 1907, he began work in the office of a Chicago insurance firm. He was soon promoted to salesman; he continued at this job until 1918, when he took over a Chicago printing establishment. His mother had inherited the business from her uncle, and Mr. Donner purchased it from his mother. He continued to make payments to his mother until 1931; the business was paid for only "just before it was lost." Through the twenties the business had prospered. Mr. Donner employed from 12 to 30 men; "at a conservative estimate" the business was worth $15,000 in 1929, and Mr. Donner's income averaged about $300 a month.

Awareness of the depression came early to the Donners, who had savings in one of the first banks to fail after the 1929 stock market crash. The Chicago bank that went under early in November, 1929 paid only 30 percent of the total deposits. Through 1930 and 1931 Mr. Donner's business was fairly good; he considered himself rather fortunate, for many of his friends had already begun to suffer heavy losses.

Mr. Donner continued to hope to meet "prosperity just around the corner" as long as he dared, but the time came when he could no longer wait for prosperity. He thinks now that he held on too long, but he had no way of knowing that the depression would last so long, and that in the end he would save nothing from his business. He hated to discharge his employees, so kept as many as possible as long as possible. He also hated to see his huge presses standing idle. All of the family's assets were converted into cash to be put into the business, and besides, Mr. Donner borrowed from relatives money which he has only recently succeeded in repaying. The Donners gave up the large home which they had been renting but had hoped to buy as soon as the business was paid for, put their furniture in storage, and moved into furnished rooms. The furniture has now been reclaimed, but it "just missed" being sold for storage.

Finally, Mr. Donner had fired all of his employees, sold some of his presses, and rented a part of the floor space. But he still couldn't give up altogether. He was gathering up what orders were to be had even when he did the printing, the delivering, and the bookkeeping all alone. He was worrying so continually and so excessively that he lost 35 pounds in a few months and couldn't sleep at night.

Mrs. Donner had lived in Dubuque until her marriage. Her parents still have their Dubuque home, a huge but somewhat ramshackle place in a good residential neighborhood. Mrs. Donner and her parents had been urging Mr. Donner to give up his business and move to Dubuque over a period of some 6 to 7 months before he finally consented to do so. He had been thinking that if he couldn't support his family in Chicago, what chance would he have in Dubuque? But there were at last only two alternatives; either the Donners would go on relief in Chicago or they would come to Dubuque to Mrs. Donner's parents. Neither possibility was a very happy one, but above all things Mr. Donner was anxious to remain off relief rolls; so he came to Dubuque in the spring of 1934.

Mrs. Donner's family had the second floor of their home made into an apartment for the Donners, who have their own entrance. The apartment is roomy and airy and attractively furnished. For about 5 months after coming to Dubuque, Mr. Donner was unemployed, though he managed to keep busy—he was so anxious to have "something to do"—by painting the doors and window frames and sashes of the family's home. He had kept in touch with the employment office, as well as with "every factory in Dubuque." His first job came when he was assigned as a common laborer, on a nonrelief basis, to the Dubuque lock and dam project. His work consisted largely of gathering up lumber and carrying it to, or away from the scene of operations.

Although Mrs. Donner was glad enough for her husband to be working at anything, it hurt her to see him put on overalls for the first time in his life. "He had never had a pair of overalls, not even when he was a little boy." Mrs. Donner managed not to say anything until he was out of the house, but as soon as he had gone she ran into the bedroom and began to cry; she thought she "just couldn't stand it." When her brother insisted on knowing what was the matter, and she told him, he laughed at her for worrying about Mr. Donner; his putting on the overalls and going out on a job like that just "showed the stuff he had in him." Mrs. Donner thinks that only the "strong-minded" have lived through the depression without becoming either too bitter or too resigned.

Mr. Donner continued to work on the locks until he got a brief-lived job with a tanning company, then hiring many extra persons to handle Government orders for leather mittens and jackets to be distributed among the relief clients. Mr. Donner understands that most of the employees were assigned on a relief basis, but the company had the privilege of hiring a certain proportion of nonrelief employees. For his work as packer and, later, as cutter Mr. Donner was paid 40¢ an hour. This work, too, was quite different from anything he had ever done in the past; he had scarcely even seen factory machines in operation. The first day he operated a ripping machine, he pushed one hide a little too near the needle, which ripped off a finger nail. After having worked for several months for the tanning company, Mr. Donner was laid off, along with many other workers, when the special orders were filled.

His next job was as timekeeper on a WPA project; he was assigned on a nonrelief basis through the employment office. Mr. Donner attributes his assignment to one of the better jobs to his "good education" and to his experience as bookkeeper when he had his own business. For the past 2 years he has been working as timekeeper on WPA projects.

Mr. Donner feels that the depression really hit hardest the families like his, who had been used to a relatively "high standard of living." For 25 years Mr. Donner's earnings had averaged not less than $300 a month. Since he now earns only about $90 a month, he thinks that his income has been reduced, proportionately, more than that of the average WPA worker. He is nevertheless sympathetic with relief clients and especially with the WPA workers who earn "a few dollars a month" less than he.

These past several years, the Donners have heard a great deal about the unemployed men who don't want to work and won't look for jobs and about the "shovel-leaners" on WPA jobs. "Of course," Mr. Donner says, "there are a few loafers on WPA projects; but there are also a few loafers on jobs in private industry." But on the whole, as Mr. Donner knows from having seen hundreds of WPA workers come and go, they are most eager to have employment and to do what is expected of them, or even "more than is expected." "Besides," Mr. Donner explains, "several factors should be taken into account before any of the WPA workers can be criticized for not doing a first-rate job: many of the men working as common laborers haven't been accustomed to hard physical labor; a good proportion of them have large families to support on their earnings of $12 a week and are always undernourished. And the men really shouldn't be expected to do $25 worth of work for $12." . . .

Mr. Donner does not see any immediate prospect of his leaving the WPA rolls. Business today is little better than when Mr. Donner returned to Dubuque more than 3 years ago, and "numbers of WPA rolls in the county are increasing." From his correspondence with friends in Chicago and other cities Mr. Donner gathers that conditions elsewhere are much the same as in Dubuque. . . . For many years, Mr. Donner has been interested in social legislation; he approves of the Social Security Act in general, though he is dubious about the need for so large a reserve for the old-age benefits fund. As one having some knowledge of insurance, he believes that such a reserve is greater than necessary to meet all demands that would be made on the fund over any given period of time, and would "take too much money out of circulation."

What Mr. Donner would really like is to return to Chicago and go into the printing business again. If business is again "as good as it was last summer when most of the Dubuque factories were working 24 hours a day," there may be some possibility of his returning to Chicago; in the meantime, there is none. He has done everything he can to find a job other than on WPA projects: he has taken four civil service examinations, and has kept applications on file with the State employment office and with all of the local factories. There is nothing more to be done. He is not particularly hopeful of finding work; neither is he particularly discouraged. There is no bitterness or resentment evident in his expression of attitudes and opinion.

FAMILY BUDGET, 1939

Account of Household Expenditures for the month of *JUNE* 19 39

Savings Account Bonds	Payment on Property	House Furnishings	Total Daily Expense	Day of Month	Item	Amount		Carfare Express	Laundry and Supplies	Stationary Postage Daily Papers	House Supplies Renovating
		1.03			Rent	56.00	1	6.50		.75	
					~~Water~~		2			.05	
					~~Ice~~		3			.05	
					~~Electricity~~		4				
					~~Illuminating Gas~~		5			.05	
					Telephone	4.45	6			.05	
					~~Garbage~~		7		1.06	.05	
	400				FUEL—~~Coal~~		8			.47	
		.26			Wood		9			.05	
					~~Gas~~		10			.05	
					~~Electric~~		11				
					~~Oil~~		12			1.35	
					Life Insurance		13			.05	
		.35					14			.05	
		.26			Health Ins. Lodges		15	.15		.05	
							16		.65	.05	
					Unemployment and Old Age Tax	5.52	17				
					Accident Ins.		18				
					Fire Ins.		19		.22	.10	
		.23			Taxes		20			.05	
					Union Dues		21		.53	.05	
					Wages—hired help		22				
							23			.05	
					call chg paid	1.00	24			.05	
							25				
							26		.79	.35	
							27			.15	
							28			.05	
							29			.05	
							30			.75	
							31				
	400	2.13				66.97		6.65	3.25	3.77	
		402.13									80.64

Family budget, 1939, from anonymous family records opened to the editors.

(Cont'd)

| | HEALTH | | | FOOD | | | | | |
| | BUDGET ALLOW. $___ | | | BUDGET ALLOWANCE $___ | | | | | |
	Physician Nurse Medicine	Dentist Tooth Preparations	Barber Toilet Articles	Staples	Butter Eggs Milk	Fruits and Vegetables	Meats Fish Shellfish	~~Bakery Goods~~ Meals out	Ice Cream Candies Etc.
1		.40	5.00					.21	
2				.10		.30	.40		6.40
3				.52	.27		.25	1.70	1.02
4									
5								.26	
6				.10	1.76			2.55	
7									
8						.68	.19		
9			.80	.29	.27				
10									1.25
11									
12				.68	.26		.75		
13									1.25
14				.12		.69		.26	.05
15								1.64	
16				.25		.79	1.50		
17								3.75	
18									.14
19					.32	.92	.34	.31	3.32
20			.80	.72		.75			
21				.32	.12	.75	.10	.31	.05
22									
23								.85	2.78
24				.39	.32	.19	1.25		
25									.30
26				.25		.67	.20	.31	.62
27								1.12	1.25
28				.14	.11			1.46	
29								.47	1.39
30	1.03			.37		.73		.31	
31									
	1.03	40	6.60	5.25	3.43	6.47	4.98	15.51	19.82
			8.03						55.66

FAMILY BUDGET, 1939 (Cont'd)

	CLOTHING				ADVANCEMENT			RECREATION			EXTRAS
	BUDGET ALLOWANCE $___				BUDGET ALLOW. $___			BUDGET ALLOW. $___			
	Under- clothing Lingerie Stockings	Outer Clothing Dresses Hats Etc.	Cleaning Dyeing Pressing	Shoes Repairs Rubbers	Books Maga- zines	Church Charity Gifts	Lectures Education Clubs	Excur- sions Vacations	Theatre Social or Athletic Functions	Train, Boat or Carfare Auto Expense	
1		1.24					7.75			10.03	
2		8.19			.05						
3			3.16						1.10	1.00	
4											
5									4.40		
6											
7							.50				
8					.20						
9					.10						
10	3.04									.55	
11										.80	
12											1.03
13											
14											1.44
15					.05					.50	
16						2.00					
17		3.92		7.00						1.10	
18										1.00	
19											
20											1.09
21		5.15									
22					.05				1.75		
23										.15	
24											
25					.46					.40	
26											.97
27								1.00			
28		1.85									
29			1.00								
30				.05							
31											
		23.39	4.15	7.00	.96	2.00	8.25	1.00	7.25	15.53	4.53
				34.54			11.21			23.78	4.53

A photograph of a California fruit tramp and his family taken in 1935 by the now-famous American photographer Dorothea Lange. It is part of her large series of pictures of American faces under the stress of the Great Depression. Lange's views generally suggested an underlying dignity and humanity in the dispossessed, although at times she seems beholden to the modern myth of the superior virtue of the oppressed. Whatever her "moral message," the photography *qua* photography made her one of America's masters.   *Library of Congress*

MIGRANT FAMILY LIFE

In the packing houses fruit is carried to the workers on an endless chain. The fruit changes, but the chain continues, unceasingly, endlessly, constantly driving the worker to keep up with its speed. The life of the fruit tramp is like the fruit on the endless chain. The trek continues year after year; individuals return to the same places at approximately the same time. They perform the same work in the same fields or packing houses, but the situation remains unchanged.

This group referred to by themselves, their employers, and the public as "fruit tramps" may be divided roughly into four classifications: pickers, packers, boxmakers, and loaders. Usually the entree of the inexperienced person is through the medium of picking. Fruit tramps range from the lone individual through families and even into clans. The personages of whom this history is written represent such a clan.

Harassed by debts, their credit exhausted, and impressed by enthusiastic reports of good money earned in the fruit fields, Gene Hillis and his wife, Lucy, decided to "try their luck." They disposed of their few surplus belongings, and packing their two old cars with newly purchased camp equipment, left San Francisco in August, 1923, to begin their trek as fruit tramps. In addition to Gene and his wife, the group included his four daughters: Valerie, Thelma, Minnie, and Olive.

Almost thirteen years have elapsed since that first migration. As the daughters married the group was augmented by their husbands, and later by their progeny. Lucy's brothers, their wives, and children have periodically joined the group. Even Lucy's aged parents have become familiar with the laborious life in the field, and relatives and in-laws, with their wives and children, have still further swelled the clan. In the comparatively good years from 1928 through 1931 when this clan worked at full strength, there were thirty-five members, directly or indirectly related, employed in the fields and packing houses on the West Coast, primarily California.

The two major groups with which this history is concerned are the Hillis and Peterson families. Valerie Hillis was the first of the children to assume family status; Bob Peterson was the first outsider to contribute to the growth of the clan. This occurred in the early fall of 1923. Valerie was fifteen years old; Bob reached his eighteenth birthday a few days after they declared that they "were married." Both the Peterson and Hillis families are representative of middle-class American stock. . . .

Individual family groups who planned to relinquish the [migratory] life found it increasingly difficult to do so.* As time passed, however, they realized that their migratory life offered no opportunity for stability and

* See accompanying chart and family tree.—Ed.

State Relief Association of California, *Migratory Labor in California* (San Francisco, 1939), passim.

FRUIT TRAMP FAMILY, 1910–1936
RESIDENCE, OCCUPATION, LIVING QUARTERS

DATES		LOCATION		LENGTH OF STAY	OCCUPATION OR CROPS HARVESTED	TYPE OF LIVING QUARTE
ARRIVAL	DEPARTURE	COUNTY	STATE			
Oct. 1910	Jan. 1911	Summit	UT*	3 mos.	Barbering	2-room flat
Jan. 1911	Oct. 1920	Beaver	UT	10 yrs.	Barbering, trapping	House of relative
Oct. 1920	Feb. 1926	Daggett	UT	5½ yrs.	Barbering, trapping	3 dif. house 1-3R, 2-4
Feb. 1926	Oct. 1926	Gem	ID*	8 mos.	Barbering	House
Oct. 1926	May 1929	Canyon	ID	3½ yrs.	Barbering	40-acre farm with hous
June 1929	July 1929	Cowlitz	WA*	1 mo.	Apples	Tents
July 1929	Sept. 1929	Benton	WA	1½ mos.	Apples	Tents
Sept. 1929	Sept. 1929	Yakima	WA	2 wks.	Hops	Tents
Sept. 1929	Sept. 1929	Benton	WA	1 wk.	Hops	Tents
Sept. 1929	July 1930	Walla Walla	WA	9 mos.	Hops	Tents
July 1930	Aug. 1930	Kittitas	WA	3 wks.	Sheep herding	Tents
Aug. 1930	Aug. 1930	Ada	ID	3 wks.	Hay	Abandoned church bl
Aug. 1930	Sept. 1930	Pierce	WA	1 wk.	Hops	Tents
Sept. 1930	Sept. 1930	Benton	WA	1 wk.	Hops	Tents
Oct. 1930	July 1931	Clarke	WA	8 mos.	Trapping	Old store
July 1931	Oct. 1931	Cowlitz	WA	3½ mos.	Apples, pears	Tents
Oct. 1931	Nov. 1931	Shasta	CA*	1 wk.	No work	Tents
Nov. 1931	May 1932	Madera	CA	7½ mos.	Cotton, figs	Tents, 2 cabins
May 1932	Oct. 1932	Monterey	CA	5 mos.	Lettuce	Tents
Oct. 1932	Nov. 1932	San Luis Obispo	CA	1 mo.	Peas	Tents
Nov. 1932	Feb. 1933	Tulare	CA	3 mos.	Oranges, olives	Tents
Feb. 1933	Apr. 1933	Monterey	CA	2 mos.	Peas	Tents
Apr. 1933	May 1933	San Luis Obispo	CA	1 mo.	Peas	Tents
May 1933	July 1933	San Mateo	CA	2 mos.	Peas	Tents
July 1933	Aug. 1933	Santa Clara	CA	1 mo.	Hops, pears	Tents
Aug. 1933	Sept. 1933	Sonoma	CA	1 mo.	Hops, pears	Tents
Sept. 1933	Sept. 1933	Napa	CA	1 wk.	Hops	Tents
Sept. 1933	Feb. 1934	Tulare	CA	5 mos.	Peas, oranges, grapes	Tents
Feb. 1934	Mar. 1934	Monterey	CA	1 mo.	Peas	Tents
Mar. 1934	Apr. 1934	San Luis Obispo	CA	1 mo.	Peas	Tents
Apr. 1934	July 1934	San Luis Obispo	CA	3 mos.	Peas	Tents
July 1934	Aug. 1934	San Benito	CA	1½ mos.	Apricots	Tents
Aug. 1934	Aug. 1934	Sutter	CA	1 mo.	Hops, peaches	Tents
Aug. 1934	Oct. 1934	Benton	WA	2 mos.	Apples, hops	Tents
Oct. 1934	Dec. 1934	Tulare	CA	2 mos.	Oranges	Tents
Dec. 1934	Apr. 1935	San Bernardino	CA	4 mos.	Oranges	Tents
Apr. 1935	June 1935	Tulare	CA	2 mos.	Lettuce, young berries	Tents
June 1935	July 1935	Contra Costa	CA	1½ mos.	Apricots	Tents
July 1935	July 1935	San Benito	CA	6 dys.	No work	Tents
July 1935	Aug. 1935	Sutter	CA	1 mo.	Peaches	Tents
Aug. 1935	Sept. 1935	Benton	WA	3 wks.	Hops, apples	Tents
Sept. 1935	Oct. 1935	Benton	WA	1 mo.	Hops, apples	Tents
Oct. 1935	Dec. 1935	Tulare	CA	2 mos.	Oranges	Abandoned house
Dec. 1935	Mar. 1936	San Bernardino	CA	3 mos.	Oranges	Tents

* UT—Utah; ID—Idaho; WA—Washington; CA—California.

FRUIT TRAMP FAMILY, 1910–1936
FAMILY MEMBERSHIP AND TRAVEL

SIZE OF FAMILY					TRAVELS		
TOTAL	ADULTS OVER 18	PRE-SCHOOL CHILDREN	CHILDREN OF SCHOOL AGE	CHILDREN IN SCHOOL	DIRECTION	APPROX. MILEAGE	MODE OF TRAVEL
2	2	–	–	–	–	–	–
3–7	2	1–3	1–3	1–3	S.	54	Wagon
7–9	2	1–4	3–6	3–6	N.	70	Hired truck
11	2	3	6	6	N.	450	Train
12	2	3	7	7	W.	26	Train
9	3	–	6	–	W.	400	'23 Ford truck
9	3	–	6	–	S.	90	'23 Ford truck
9	3	–	6	–	S.	130	'23 Ford truck
9	3	–	6	–	S.	40	'23 Ford truck
9	3	–	6	7	W.	20	'23 Ford truck
9	3	–	6	–	E.	100	'25 Chev. tour.
9	3	–	6	–	E.	100	'26 Chev. truck
9	3	–	6	–	W.	200	'26 Chev. truck
9	3	–	6	5	S.	40	'26 Chev. truck
9	3	–	6	5	W.	20	'26 Chev. truck
9	3	–	6	–	N.	20	'26 Chev. truck
9	3	–	6	–	S.	450	'26 Chev. truck
9	4	–	5	4	S.	250	'26 Chev. truck
9	4	–	5	4	W.	90	'26 Chev. truck
9	4	–	5	4	S.	35	'26 Chev. truck
9	5	–	4	4	E.	160	'26 Chev. truck
9	5	–	4	4	W.	160	'26 Chev. truck
9	5	–	4	4	N.	150	'26 Chev. truck
9	5	–	4	–	N.	80	'26 Chev. truck
9	5	–	4	–	S.	50	Nash sedan
9	5	–	4	–	N.	150	Chev. truck
9	5	–	4	–	S.	50	Chev. truck
9	5	–	4	–	S.	250	Chev. truck
9	5	–	4	4	W.	160	'28 Pontiac
9	5	–	4	4	S.	10	'25 Chev. tour.
9	5	–	4	4	N.	160	'25 Chev./trailer
9	5	–	4	–	N.	40	'25 Chev./trailer
9	5	–	4	–	N.	180	'25 Chev./trailer
9	5	–	4	4	N.	500	'25 Chev./trailer
9	5	–	4	4	S.	280	'25 Chev./trailer
9	5	–	4	4	S.	280	'25 Chev./trailer
9	5	–	4	4	N.	150	'25 Chev./trailer
9	5	–	4	–	N.	100	'29 Chry./trailer
9	5	–	4	–	S.	140	'29 Chry./trailer
9	5	–	4	–	N.	220	'29 Chry./trailer
9	5	–	4	3	N.	650	'29 Chry./trailer
9	5	–	4	3	N.	20	'29 Chry./trailer
9	5	–	4	3	S.	900	'29 Chry./trailer
9	5	–	4	3	S.	280	'29 Chry./trailer

held forth no hope of economic security for themselves or their offspring. Employment at lathing usually became scarce in the late spring. With the coming of May and the ripening of fruit, the consciousness of available jobs and immediate cash remuneration would come to the fore, and always culminated in a return to the fields and packing houses. . . .

While the families retained their own identity, there was a strong tendency toward interdependence socially and economically among the families comprising the clan. When in the same community they lived together, or in close proximity. If one family had money and another was in financial straits it was understood that assistance would be extended. Money would be given and the transfer was not considered as a loan. No effort was made to repay such advances, nor was a refund expected.

While occasionally there were quarrels within the group, considering the number of individuals involved, the variety of personalities and temperaments, there was comparative harmony. Their clannishness tended to develop a "closed shop." The outsiders with whom the girls had social relationships would be drawn into the group rather than members of the clan projecting themselves into other groups. Thelma was the only daughter who deserted the life of the fruit tramp. . . .

Social life of the clique was as different from the conventional social amenities as the rest of their existence. Lack of community restraint allowed for conduct that would have been severely frowned upon under normal living conditions. As a result they worked hard during the day and played equally as hard at night. Cards, dancing, drinking parties, moonlight rides terminating in reckless sexual abandonment were the rule rather than the exception. They found fruit tramps to be a tolerant class; that is, tolerant of promiscuity but intolerant of prostitution.

When the family first entered the fields, Gene and Lucy were not aware of current attitudes regarding personal conduct. As time passed and the freedom of the life induced a careless attitude on the part of the girls toward sexual irregularities they realized the real seriousness of the situation and the dangers facing their adolescent daughters. They frowned upon the prevailing sexual promiscuity and attempted to prevent the inevitable. The children developed caution and not only concealed their conduct from their parents, but protected one another.

As children were born into the clan another problem presented itself. According to the dictates of the life, both parents worked, necessitating taking the children into the field or making arrangements for their care. . . . When extremely young they were carried into the fields in a basket or box, which was placed in a shady spot close enough to the mother for her to observe the child as she worked. They grew up in this environment of endless migration. At six or seven they reached out their immature, childish hands to pick the fruit. They knew no other life and accepted this as other children accept normal surroundings. . . .

Attitudes toward children and their care among the members of the clan varied considerably. With one couple cleanliness was a mania and

THE ENDLESS TREK

Fruit Tramp Families, 1850-1934

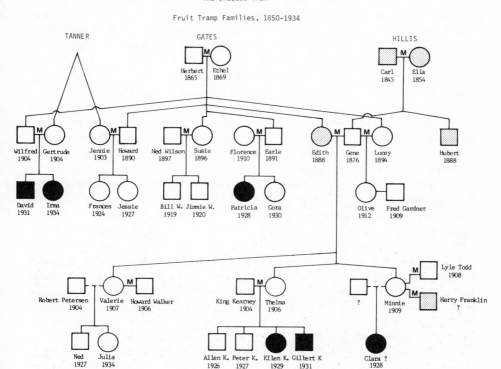

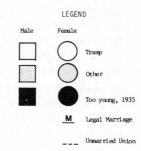

LEGEND

Male	Female	
□	○	Tramp
▨	◍	Other
■	●	Too young, 1935
M		Legal Marriage
_ _ _		Unmarried Union

their children their major interest. When this mother returned from work
at night she ignored her exhaustion and concentrated on her children.
She bathed them, washed their clothing, and frequently sewed their torn
dresses and shirts or made new clothes to replace those that had worn
out. Both she and her husband were patient with the children. Either they
fed them before they ate or allowed the children to eat with them, first
scrutinizing them carefully to be sure they came to the table clean. They
made a conscientious effort not to express their irritability through impa-
tience or unfair treatment of the children. Frequently they played games
with the youngsters and assisted them in the preparation of their lessons.

The opposite extreme was represented by another couple whose three
children were relatively neglected. They accompanied the parents to the
fields and were required to work. Careless of her own person, the mother
was equally so with the children. She paid little attention to their personal
appearance. Clothing for them was purchased several sizes too large on
the theory that children should grow into clothes. Lack of surplus clothing,
and the rough life, caused the clothing to be worn out long before the
youngsters could do so; consequently they always appeared badly dressed.
The parents not only ate first but frequently showed little interest in what
was left over for the children. The mother was not bothered about cleanliness or state of repair; as a result the personal appearance of the family
was one of neglect and carelessness, and too frequently irritability on the
part of the parents resulted in physical discomfort for the children.

Regular attendance at school was impossible. In some instances the children were required to work in the fields to help meet the family budget.
Even when parents were willing to have the children attend school, the
frequent changes resulted in irregularity of class placement. Transfer cards
were usually forgotten. They changed from location to location in haste,
and time consumed visiting the schools was often considered as wasted.
Frequently the departure occurred over a week end, or in the evenings
when access to records was impossible. This caused delay in proper placement in the next school. The only consistent education of the children
of this clan has been secured during the winter months when they settled
in one of the larger cities. On these occasions the children attended school
regularly, the mothers kept house, and the fathers worked at their
trade. . . .

Lack of regular school attendance on the part of the children resulted
in their usually missing periodic physical examinations. The lack of available
clinics together with a carelessness toward health conditions resulted in
latent illnesses of the children being undiscovered until the illness reached
an advanced state. Bright's disease, tuberculosis, and infected tonsils were
discovered among the children of the clan after the family had been on
relief in one of the large cities for several months. If caught in early stages,
the resultant sanitorium care might have been unnecessary, thereby preventing expense to the community and suffering to the children. . . .

Since the depression the situation has become much worse for members of the group. Wages have been reduced, and they have learned that local individuals who heretofore would have scorned working either in the fields or packing houses have turned to such labor to meet their budgets. The tramps resent this as they feel their knowledge was gained through years of hard work, and is deserving of first consideration.

MIGRATION OF FRUIT TRAMP FAMILY JANUARY 1935 TO MARCH 1936

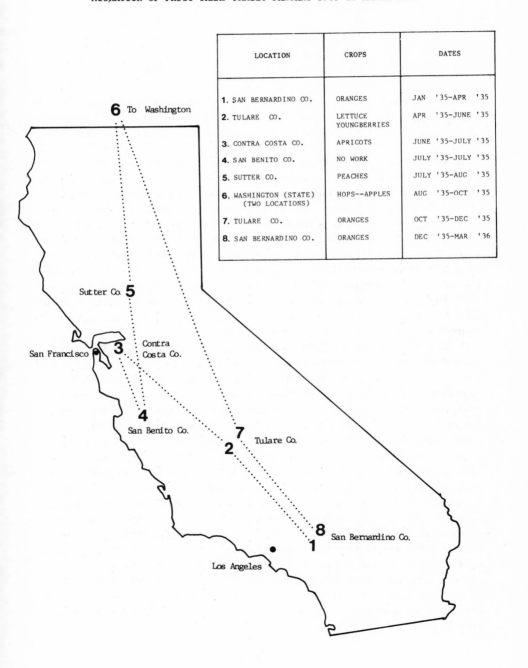

LOCATION	CROPS	DATES
1. SAN BERNARDINO CO.	ORANGES	JAN '35–APR '35
2. TULARE CO.	LETTUCE YOUNGBERRIES	APR '35–JUNE '35
3. CONTRA COSTA CO.	APRICOTS	JUNE '35–JULY '35
4. SAN BENITO CO.	NO WORK	JULY '35–JULY '35
5. SUTTER CO.	PEACHES	JULY '35–AUG '35
6. WASHINGTON (STATE) (TWO LOCATIONS)	HOPS--APPLES	AUG '35–OCT '35
7. TULARE CO.	ORANGES	OCT '35–DEC '35
8. SAN BERNARDINO CO.	ORANGES	DEC '35–MAR '36

6 To Washington

Sutter Co. 5

San Francisco

3 Contra Costa Co.

4

San Benito Co.

7 Tulare Co.

2

8 San Bernardino Co.

1

Los Angeles

FAMILY AS WILL AND IDEA

The Not-So-Nice "Nice Home"

Accompanying the turn-of-century concern with the family life of the "other half" of poor and immigrant Americans, was a long-growing fear of the inadequacies of "our better homes." By 1903, when *The Home* by Charlotte Perkins Gilman appeared, the demand for "domestic reform" had already been apparent for several generations. The campaign had started about 1830 among popular moralists who were clearly circumspect, fearing charges of invading the privacy and sanctity of the home and of the rights of parents. By the late nineteenth century, however, ideamongering Americans had developed a hearty appetite for advice about the home and family. Would-be reformers gained confidence, armed now with the authority of science, with advanced educations, and with income as professional writers. Under their surveillance the "crisis of the family" seems to have become routinized and ritualized. Every generation after 1830 had been told the family faced new challenges: sin, heredity, materialism. The dual task was preserving the American home while paradoxically changing it to prepare for the perilous future.

Against this background of a tradition of crisis and critique, Mrs. Gilman published her notable indictment of the commonly idealized American family life. Who might be the audience for such works? By 1905 the national population was nearing 100 million. How many of these Americans were adequately described by Mrs. Gilman's call to reform? To what extent did the "boldness" of this criticism assume, again paradoxically, more liberation within the family—more education, more leisure, more enlightenment, more comfort among the very women whose ignorance or sloth Mrs. Gilman deprecated? Have such books thus helped to create the discontents about the American home that they pretend to discover? How does it happen, for so it seems, that the more "enlightened" our American families have become in the twentieth century, the more preoccupied they seem to become with their own limitations and thereby the less satisfactory reform becomes in bringing family peace and harmony? What purpose other than reform might be served by the ritualized consuming of family-advice literature? How could the nice family, at least as Mrs. Gilman views it, be in a crisis, be criticized, and simultaneously be invoked by other writers as a standard for families of the "other half"? Was there, perhaps, an unstated malaise common to both "halves"?

MAKING NICE HOMES BETTER

What is here sought is simply to give a general impression of the continual flux and growth of the home as an institution, as one under the same laws as those which govern other institutions, and also of the check to that growth resultant from our human characteristic of remembering, recording, and venerating the past. The home, more than any other human phenomenon, is under that heavy check. The home is an incarnate past to us. It is our very oldest thing, and holds the heart more deeply than all others. The conscious thought of the world is always far behind the march of events; it is most so in those departments where we have made definite efforts to keep it at an earlier level, and nowhere, not even in religion, has there been a more distinct, persistent, and universal attempt to maintain the most remote possible status.

"The tendency to vary," that inadequate name for the great centrifugal force which keeps the universe swinging, is manifested most in the male. He is the natural variant, where the female is the natural conservative. By forcibly combining the woman with the home in his mind, and forcibly compelling her to stay there in body, then, conversely, by taking himself out and away as completely as possible, we have turned the expanding lines of social progress away from the home and left the ultra-feminised woman to ultra-conservatism therein. Where this condition is most extreme, as in the Orient, there is least progress; where it is least extreme, as with us, there is the most progress; but even with us, the least evolved of all our institutions is the home. Move it must, somewhat, as part of human life, but the movement has come from without, through the progressive man, and has been sadly retarded in its slow effect on the stationary woman. . . .

The home has changed much in physical structure, in spite of itself. It has changed somewhat in its functions, also in spite of itself. But it has changed very little—painfully little—dangerously little, in its governing concepts. Naturally ideas change with facts, but if ideas are held to be sacred and immovable, the facts slide out from under and go on growing because they must, while the ideas lag further and further behind. . . .

What progress has been made in our domestic concepts? The oldest—the pre-human. But shelter, safety, comfort, quiet, and mother love, are still with us, still crude and limited. Then follow gradually later sentiments of sanctity, privacy, and sex-seclusion; and still later, some elements of personal convenience and personal expression. How do these stand as compared with the facts? Our safety is really insured by social law and order, not by any system of home defence. Against the real dangers of modern life the home is no safeguard. It is as open to criminal attack as any public building, yes, more. A public building is more easily and effectively watched and guarded than our private homes. Sewer gas invades

Charlotte Perkins Gilman, *The Home, Its Work and Influence* (New York, 1903), pp. 28–35, 315–22.

the home; microbes, destructive insects, all diseases invade it also; so far as civilised life is open to danger, the home is defenceless. So far as the home is protected it is through social progress—through public sanitation enforced by law and the public guardians of the peace. If we would but shake off the primitive limitations of these old concepts, cease to imagine the home to be a safe place, and apply our ideas of shelter, safety, comfort, and quiet to the City and State, we should then be able to ensure their fulfilment in our private homes far more fully.

The mother-love concept suffers even more from its limitations. As a matter of fact our children are far more fully guarded, provided for, and educated, by social efforts than by domestic; compare the children of a nation with a system of public education with children having only domestic education; or children safeguarded by public law and order with children having only domestic protection. The home-love and care of the Armenians for their children is no doubt as genuine and strong as ours, but the public care is not strong and well organised, hence the little Armenians are open to massacre as little Americans are not. Our children are largely benefited by the public, and would be much more so if the domestic concept did not act too strongly in limiting mother love to so narrow a field of action.

The later sentiments of sanctity and the others have moved a little, but not much. *Why* it is more sacred to make a coat at home than to buy it of a tailor, to kill a cow at home than to buy it of a butcher, to cook a pie at home than to buy it of a baker, or to teach a child at home than to have it taught by a teacher, is not made clear to us, but the lingering weight of those ages of ancestor-worship, of real sacrifice and libation at a real altar, is still heavy in our minds. We still by race-habit regard the home as sacred, and cheerfully profane our halls of justice and marts of trade, as if social service were not at least as high a thing as domestic service. This sense of sanctity is a good thing, but it should grow, it should evolve along natural lines till it includes all human functions, not be forever confined to its cradle, the home.

The concept of sex-seclusion is, with us, rapidly passing away. Our millions of wage-earning women are leading us, by the irresistible force of accomplished fact, to recognise the feminine as part of the world around us, not as a purely domestic element. The foot-binding process in China is but an extreme expression of this old domestic concept, the veiling process another. We are steadily leaving them all behind, and an American man feels no jar to his sexuo-domestic sentiments in meeting a woman walking freely in the street or working in the shops.

The latest of our home-ideas, personal convenience and expression, are themselves resultant from larger development of personality, and lead out necessarily. The accumulating power of individuality developed in large social processes by the male, is inherited by the female; she, still confined to the home, begins to fill and overfill it with the effort at individual expression, and must sooner or later come out to find the only normal field for highly specialised human power—the world.

Thus we may be encouraged in our study of domestic evolution. The forces and sentiments originating in the home have long since worked out to large social processes. We have gone far on our way toward making the world our home. What most impedes our further progress is the persistent retention of certain lines of industry within domestic limits, and the still more persistent retention of certain lines of home feelings and ideas. Even here, in the deepest, oldest, darkest, slowest place in all man's mind, the light of science, the stir of progress, is penetrating. The world does move—and so does the home. . . .

The change we require does not involve the loss of one essential good and lovely thing. It does not injure womanhood, but improves it. It does not injure childhood, but improves it. It does not injure manhood, but improves that too.

What is the proposed change? It is the recognition of a new order of duties, a new scale of virtues; or rather it is the practical adoption of that order long since established by the facts of business, the science of government, and by all great religions. Our own religion in especial, the most progressive, the most social, gives no sanction whatever to our own archaic cult of home-worship. . . . This antiquated method of serving the family *does not serve them to the best advantage.* In what way does a man best benefit his family? By staying at home and doing what he can with his own two hands—whereby no family on earth would ever have more than the labour one affectionate amateur could provide; or by going out from the home and serving other people in a specialised trade—whereby his family and all families are gradually supplied with peace and plenty, supported and protected by the allied forces of civilisation?

In what way does a woman best benefit her family? By staying at home and doing what she can with her own two hands—whereby no family ever has more than the labour one affectionate amateur can provide—or by enlarging her motherhood as man has enlarged his fatherhood, and giving to her family the same immense advantages that he has given it? We have always assumed that the woman could do most by staying at home. Is this so? Can we prove it? Why is that which is so palpably false of a man held to be true of a woman? "Because men and women are different!" will be stoutly replied. Of course they are different—in sex, *but not in humanity.* In every human quality and power they are alike; and the right service of the home, the right care and training of the child, call for human qualities and powers, not merely for sex-distinctions.

The home, in its arbitrary position of arrested development, does not properly fulfil its own essential functions—much less promote the social ones. Among the splendid activities of our age it lingers on, inert and blind, like a clam in a horse-race.

It hinders, by keeping woman a social idiot, by keeping the modern child under the tutelage of the primeval mother, by keeping the social conscience of the man crippled and stultified in the clinging grip of the domestic conscience of the woman. It hinders by its enormous expense;

making the physical details of daily life a heavy burden to mankind; whereas, in our stage of civilisation, they should have been long since reduced to a minor incident.

Consider what the mere protection and defence of life used to cost, when every man had to be a fighter most of his life. . . . Organisation among men has reduced this wasteful and crippling habit of being every-man-his-own-soldier. We do not have to carry a rifle and peer around every street-corner for a hidden foe. As a result, the released energy of the ninety percent of men, a tenth being large allowance for all the fighting necessary, is now poured into the channels that lead to wealth, peace, education, general progress.

Yet we are still willing that the personal care of life, the service of daily physical needs, shall monopolise as many women as that old custom of universal warfare monopolised men! Ninety percent of the feminine energy of the world is still spent in ministering laboriously to the last details of bodily maintenance; and the other tenth is supposed to do nothing but supervise the same tasks, and flutter about in fruitless social amusement. This crude waste of half the world's force keeps back human progress just as heavily as the waste of the other half did.

By as much as the world has grown toward peace and power and unity since men left off spending their lives in universal warfare, will it grow further toward that much-desired plane when women leave off spending their lives in universal house-service. The mere release of that vast fund of energy will in itself increase all the facilities of living; but there is a much more important consequence.

The omnipresent domestic ideal is a deadly hinderance to the social ideal. When half our population honestly believe that they have no duties outside the home, the other half will not become phenomenal statesmen. This cook-and-housemaid level of popular thought is the great check. The social perspective is entirely lost; and a million short-sighted homes, each seeing only its own interests, cannot singly or together grasp the common good which would benefit them all.

That the home has improved as much as it has is due to the freedom of man outside it. That it is still so clumsy, so inadequate, so wickedly wasteful of time, of money, of human life, is due to the confinement of woman inside it.

What sort of citizens do we need for the best city—the best state—the best country—the best world? We need men and women who are sufficiently large-minded to see and feel a common need, to work for a common good, to rejoice in the advance of all, and to know as the merest platitude that their private advantage is to be assured *only* by the common weal. That kind of mind is not bred in the kitchen. . . .

This little ganglion of aborted economic processes, the home, tends to a sort of social paralysis. In its innumerable little centres of egoism and familism are sunk and lost the larger vibrations of social energy which should stimulate the entire mass. . . .

The home, in its ceaseless and inexorable demands, stops this great process of specialisation in women, and checks it cruelly in men. A man's best service to society lies in his conscientious performance of the work he is best fitted for. But the service of the home demands that he do the work he is best paid for. Man after man, under this benumbing, strangling pressure, is diverted from his true path in social service, and condemned to "imprisonment with hard labour for life."

The young man, for a time, is comparatively free; and looks forward eagerly to such and such a line of growth and large usefulness. But let him marry and start a home, and he must do, not what he would—what is best for him and best for all of us; but what he must—what he can be sure of pay for. We have always supposed this to be a good thing, as it forced men to be industrious. As if it was any benefit to society to have men industrious in wrong ways—or useless ways, or even slow, stupid, old-fashioned ways! . . . Having a family to support, in the most wasteful possible way, multiplies a man's desire for money; but in no way multiplies his ability, his social value.

Therefore the world is full of struggling men, putting in for one and trying to take out for ten; and in this struggle seeking continually for new ways to cater to the tastes of the multitude, and especially to those of the rich; that they may obtain the wherewithal to support the ten, or six, or simply the one; who though she be but one and not a worker, is quite ready to consume more than any ten together! . . .

The position is this: the home, as now existing, costs three times what is necessary to meet the same needs. It involves the further waste of nearly half the world's labour. It does not fulfil its functions to the best advantage, thus robbing us again. It maintains a low grade of womanhood, overworked or lazy; it checks the social development of men as well as women, and, most of all, of children. The man, in order to meet this unnecessary expense, must cater to the existing market; and the existing market is mainly this same home, with its crude tastes and limitless appetites. Thus the man, to maintain his own woman in idleness, or low-grade labour, must work three times as hard as is needful, to meet the demands of similar women; the home-bound woman clogging the whole world.

Change this order. Set the woman on her own feet, as a free, intelligent, able human being, quite capable of putting into the world more than she takes out, of being a producer as well as a consumer. Put these poor anti-quated "domestic industries" into the archives of past history; and let efficient modern industries take their place, doing far more work, far better work, far cheaper work in their stead.

With an enlightened system of feeding the world we shall have better health—and wiser appetites. The more intelligent and broad-minded woman will assuredly promote a more reasonable, healthful, beautiful, and economical system of clothing, for her own body and that of the child. The wiser and more progressive mother will at last recognise child-culture as an art and science quite beyond the range of instinct, and provide for the child such surroundings, such training, as shall allow of a rapid and enormous advance in human character.

The man, relieved of two-thirds of his expenses; provided with double supplies; properly fed and more comfortable at home than he ever dreamed of being, and associated with a strong, free, stimulating companion all through life, will be able to work to far better purpose in the social service, and with far greater power, pride, and enjoyment.

The man and woman together, both relieved of most of their personal cares, will be better able to appreciate large social needs and to meet them. Each generation of children, better born, better reared, growing to their full capacity in all lines, will pour into the world a rising flood of happiness and power. Then we shall see social progress.

The New Woman *v.* the Modern Home

As woman in the early twentieth century increasingly frequented clubs, businesses, reform movements, social work, and voting booths, all her new roles were sensed as threats to the home, to husband, and to child-rearing. But many of the "new women" were also embarked on contradictory tasks. In 1914 Walter Lippmann, one of the more philosophic progressives, asked how reformers could square their enthusiasm for careers for women with their even stronger conviction that modern American capitalism and business life could not command the respect of thinking men and women let alone the loyalty of the millions of poorer people who had little choice but to work or die.

A more developed view of the "modern family" divided against itself came from a highly esteemed book of the same period, *The Century of the Child.* The author was Ellen Key, a Swedish sociologist, and the book was translated into several languages, becoming a minor classic in the American sociology of the family during the first quarter of this century. Generally concerned, as its title suggests, with enhanced possibilities in the new century for raising happier and better children, Key's book dealt with a wide variety of family and cultural topics bearing on her title theme. The question raised in this selection is like Lippmann's, whether modern woman at work and modern woman as scientific parent can reconcile her roles. To what extent, however, does Key misconstrue the biological basis of modern parenthood and the demands of modern work? Does more and better technology for home tasks also change the dimension of the problems perceived here? Are there other conflicts within the "new" world of the twentieth century that affect the family to the extent that a new, good, freer womanhood must struggle not only against old oppressions but also against other new and approved "goals" in marriage and parenthood? Who in the family is to sacrifice what and for whose good and by what right in pursuit of perfection and happiness?

THE CENTURY OF THE CHILD

In our programme of civilisation, we must start out with the conviction that motherhood is something essential to the nature of woman and the

Ellen Key, *The Century of the Child* (New York, 1913), chapter 2.

Congress and the President

Legalize and Immortalize

Mothers' Day

Second Sunday in May

A PROCLAMATION

"Whereas, by a joint resolution, approved May 8, 1914, designating the second Sunday in May as Mothers' Day, and for other purposes, the President is authorized and requested to issue a proclamation calling upon the government officials to display the United States flag on all government buildings, and the people of the United States to display the flag at their homes, or other suitable places on the second Sunday in May, as a public expression of our love and reverence for the mothers of our country;

"And, Whereas, by the said joint resolution it is made the duty of the President to request the observance of the second Sunday in May as provided for in the said joint resolution;

"Now, therefore, I, Woodrow Wilson, President of the United States of America, by virtue of the authority vested in me by the said joint resolution, do hereby direct the government officials to display the United States flag on all government buildings, and do invite the people of the United States to display the flag at their homes, or other suitable places, on the second Sunday of May, as a public expression of our love and reverence for the mothers of our country. In witness whereof I have set my hand and caused the seal of the United States to be hereunto affixed.

"Done at the city of Washington this 9th day of May, in the year of our Lord, one thousand nine hundred and fourteen and of the Independence of the United States one hundred and thirty-eight.

"WOODROW WILSON.

"By the President.

"WILLIAM JENNINGS BRYAN,

"Secretary of State."

A long campaign for official national recognition of America's debts to its mothers came to fruition in 1914 when Congress and President Wilson joined to "immortalize" Mother's Day. It has been celebrated on the same Sunday in May ever since. It is ironic that this homage came at a time when the traditional roles for which the mother was honored were changing rapidly, with the old-fashioned mother being attacked as a drudge and out of step with the era of science, efficiency, and involvement in community affairs.

way in which she carries out this profession is of value for society. On this basis we must alter the conditions which more and more are robbing woman of the happiness of motherhood and are robbing children of the care of a mother. Or, we must begin with the assumption that motherhood is not essential: then everything must continue to go on as it is going on now, and work directed towards external spheres with its satisfaction in the joy of creation, of ambition, of gain, of enjoyment, of independence, will be more and more the end towards which women will arrange their plan of life. For this end they will modify their fundamental habits and remould their feelings. . . . By a new ideal innumerable women are now driven from a life directed inwards to a life directed outwards. . . .

I would not put the slightest hindrance, however, in the way of a single isolated woman pursuing her own path freely, if it leads her even to the most unusual forms of labour and attempts to make a living. But for the sake of women themselves, for the sake of children, for the sake of society, I wish men as well as women to think earnestly over the present position of things. They will see that in the near future, one of two things must be chosen. Either there must be such a transformation of the way in which modern society thinks and works that the majority of women will be restored to motherhood, or the disintegration of the home and the substitution of general institutions will inevitably result. There is no alternative.

Undoubtedly it required the whole egoistic self-assertion of woman, all her efforts towards individuality, her temporary separation from home and from family, her independent efforts to make a living to convince man and society of the following truths: that woman is not solely a sexual being, not solely dependent on man, the home and the family, no matter in what form these may exist. Only in this way could woman fulfil her destiny as wife and mother with really free choice. Only in this way could she secure the right of being regarded as man's intellectual equal in the field of the home and the family, the recognition that in her way she was just as complete a being as he. . . .

Those who believe they can fulfil their duties as mothers and at the same time can accomplish other valuable work have never made the experiment of education. The long continued habit of alternately caressing and striking one's children is not education. It needs tremendous power to do one's duty to a single child. This by no means signifies giving up to the child every hour of one's time, but it does mean that our soul is to be filled by the child, just as the man of science is possessed by his investigations and the artist by his work. The child should be in one's thoughts when one is sitting at home or walking along the road, when one is lying down or when one is standing up. This devotion, much more than the hours immediately given to one's children, is the absorbing thing; the occupation which makes an earnest mother always go to any external activity with divided soul and dissipated energy. Therefore the mother, if she gives her children the share they need, can devote to social activities only her occasional attention. And for the same reason she should be entirely free from working to earn her living during the most critical years of the children's training. . . .

From the point of view of women's rights, it is said, in reply to these opinions of mine, that motherhood can be made infinitely easier by a natural method of life, that work can be very well combined with it. It is said that children soon grow out of needing the protection of their mother, that the mothers can then devote themselves entirely to their work. They contend, besides, that motherhood is no unconditional obligation; that people are fully justified in making different individual arrangements; one woman wishes to become a mother, another not. The one gets married with the hope of becoming a mother; the other with the resolution of avoiding maternity. The third does not marry at all. Attempts to generalise on this matter in which individual freedom has every right to be recognised, they consider reactionary. Full freedom for the woman, married or unmarried, to choose her work and to continue it; full freedom to choose motherhood or to do without it, this they say is the way to free woman, this is the line of progress. Here woman is subject to that economic law which has made it necessary for her to work for her own living. Just as woman's household work has been superseded by factory work, so too, they say, will the maternal obligations of woman be fulfilled collectively, and the difficulties on which the so-called reactionary members of the women's rights movement base their arguments, will in the future only arise in exceptional cases. As regards these arguments, I have already shown that I recognise fully the right of the feminine individual to go her own way, to choose her own fortune or misfortune. I have always spoken of women collectively and of society collectively.

From this general, not from the individual standpoint, I am trying to convince women that vengeance is being exacted on the individual, on the race, when woman gradually destroys the deepest vital source of her physical and psychical being, the power of motherhood.

But present-day woman is not adapted to motherhood; she will only be fitted for it when she has trained herself for motherhood and man is trained for fatherhood. Then man and woman can begin together to bring up the new generation out of which some day society will be formed. In it, the completed man—the Superman—will be bathed in that sunshine whose distant rays but colour the horizon of to-day.*

---

* The writer was influenced by the German philosopher Friedrich Nietzsche, and by the eugenics movement before World War I.—Ed.

The Contraception Revolution

Previous documents implied the great length of the public struggle to legitimize the use of birth control. By the end of the nineteenth century in America and Western Europe, almost four generations of proselytizing had yielded mounting fires of public concern for and against legalized contraception. At the same time, birth statistics and other evidence after about 1870 strongly suggest the quiet private spread of birth control among married couples. By 1910 it is probably safe to assume that many better-off and better educated American families had somehow obtained the information and means to prevent conception. One says "somehow" since, in addition to the predominance of opposition within religion and custom, laws across the United States made it criminal for anyone, including nurses and doctors, to provide birth-control advice or devices. The contrast between the growing, if illegal, practice and the public stance of opposition made hypocrisy yet another feature of the contraception debate. The contradiction also implied clearly that class lines generally described the border between those who did and those who did not know how to practice contraception; the well-to-do often could obtain what was almost impossible for the poor.

After another half century of strife beyond 1900, marked by gradual legalization and growing contrast between public profession and private practice, in 1965 the United States Supreme Court held in the Griswold case that contraception was a matter of private and personal choice and, as such, not subject to the intrusion of law. Although this decision left unaddressed such complexities as the position of minor children seeking birth-control means and the obligations of public clinics to provide birth-control help if demanded by patients, the Griswold case ended centuries of public enforcement of the birth-control aspects of sexual morality inside or outside marriage. The court answered none of the great moral and social issues raised in a century of war for and against contraception. But as opponents contended, the decision—to forbid legislation on such private sexual choices—in effect, did establish and further a social morality of greater marital freedom.

The selections that follow present various aspects of the contraception revolution in American family life. Margaret Sanger was probably the most famous American proponent of birth control. For her, and typical of her generation of progressive Americans on the issue, the use of contraceptive devices at will was a moral right of women and men and an ethical goal for America and humanity in general. The famous chapter from her autobiography is a graphic (although, some allege, distorted) personal experience but an accurate general depiction of what the early twentieth-century world without birth-control information meant to millions of individuals and families. The next selection, a program from an international conference about a decade later, poses questions of why and how birth control became rapidly a worldwide crusade and why it was able to reach so far beyond the pragmatic matter of individual choice or convenience to basic questions of the future of humanity. The final selections present several Roman Catholic arguments in connection with contraception. Although the highest authority in the Catholic Church had repeatedly condemned mechanical means of birth control, the Papacy had also come to sanction "conjugal love," thus complicating the choices of Catholics. Despite the greater publicity given to the Pope's opposition to contraception, there was strong opposition also among Orthodox Jews, various Protestants, and even some black groups fearing inundation by whites. Two different views of Catholic couples show even further divisions among Catholics on the Church's recommended "rhythm method" of avoiding conception.

Whatever the particulars in any general view, everyone involved in the birth-control debate believed it involved a momentous change both in the history of human biology and evolution as well as in the culture of mankind.

To begin to appreciate the scope of the revolution in family and social life that took place, we need pose merely one general question: What difference does it make in family life whether or not one has available reliable birth-control methods? This question at once divides into innumerable considerations of male and female "psychologies" and cultural roles, of class distinctions, of religious and moral outlooks and choices. Just to mention such reverberations suggests that the debate over contraception probably provides the most important focus for analyzing changes in family life in this century.

MARGARET SANGER'S FIGHT FOR BIRTH CONTROL

Awakening and Revolt

Early in the year 1912 I came to a sudden realization that my work as a nurse and my activities in social service were entirely palliative and consequently futile and useless to relieve the misery I saw all about me. . . .

Margaret Sanger, *My Fight for Birth Control* (New York, 1931), pp. 46–61 passim. Reprinted by permission of Dr. Grant Sanger.

When I look back upon that period it seems only a short time ago; yet in the brief interval conditions have changed enormously. At that time it was not the usual thing for a poor woman to go to a hospital to give birth to her baby. She preferred to stay at home. She was afraid of hospitals when any serious ailment was involved. That is not the case today. Women of all classes are more likely to have their babies in lying-in hospitals or in private sanatoriums than at home; but in those days a woman's own bedroom, no matter how inconveniently arranged, was the usual place for confinement. That was the day of home nursing, and it gave a trained nurse splendid opportunities to learn social conditions through actual contact with them.

Were it possible for me to depict the revolting conditions existing in the homes of some of the women I attended in that one year, one would find it hard to believe. There was at that time, and doubtless is still today, a sub-stratum of men and women whose lives are absolutely untouched by social agencies. . . .

In this atmosphere abortions and birth become the main theme of conversation. On Saturday nights I have seen groups of fifty to one hundred women going into questionable offices well known in the community for cheap abortions. I asked several women what took place there, and they all gave the same reply: a quick examination, a probe inserted into the uterus and turned a few times to disturb the fertilized ovum, and then the woman was sent home. Usually the flow began the next day and often continued four or five weeks. Sometimes an ambulance carried the victim to the hospital for a curettage, and if she returned home at all she was looked upon as a lucky woman.

This state of things became a nightmare with me. There seemed no sense to it all, no reason for such waste of mother life, no right to exhaust women's vitality and to throw them on the scrap-heap before the age of thirty-five. . . .

I heard over and over again of their desperate efforts at bringing themselves "around"—drinking various herb-teas, taking drops of turpentine on sugar, steaming over a chamber of boiling coffee or of turpentine water, rolling downstairs, and finally inserting slippery-elm sticks, or knitting needles, or shoe hooks into the uterus. I used to shudder with horror, as I heard the details and, worse yet, learned of the conditions *behind the reason* for such desperate actions. Day after day these stories were poured into my ears. I knew hundreds of these women personally, and knew much of their hopeless, barren, dreary lives. . . .

Finally the thing began to shape itself, to become accumulative during the three weeks I spent in the home of a desperately sick woman living on Grand Street, a lower section of New York's East Side.

Mrs. Sacks was only twenty-eight years old; her husband, an unskilled worker, thirty-two. Three children, aged five, three and one, were none too strong nor sturdy, and it took all the earnings of the father and the ingenuity of the mother to keep them clean, provide them with air and proper food, and give them a chance to grow into decent manhood and womanhood.

Both parents were devoted to these children and to each other. The woman had become pregnant and had taken various drugs and purgatives, as advised by her neighbors. Then, in desperation, she had used some instrument lent to her by a friend. She was found prostrate on the floor amidst the crying children when her husband returned from work. Neighbors advised against the ambulance, and a friendly doctor was called. The husband would not hear of her going to a hospital, and as a little money had been saved in the bank a nurse was called and the battle for that precious life began.

It was in the middle of July. The three-room apartment was turned into a hospital for the dying patient. Never had I worked so fast, never so concentratedly as I did to keep alive that little mother. Neighbor women came and went during the day doing the odds and ends necessary for our comfort. The children were sent to friends and relatives and the doctor and I settled ourselves to outdo the force and power of an outraged nature.

Never had I known such conditions could exist. July's sultry days and nights were melted into a torpid inferno. Day after day, night after night, I slept only in brief snatches, ever too anxious about the condition of that feeble heart bravely carrying on, to stay long from the bedside of the patient. With but one toilet for the building and that on the floor below, everything had to be carried down for disposal, while ice, food and other necessities had to be carried three flights up. It was one of those old airshaft buildings of which there were several thousands then standing in New York City.

At the end of two weeks recovery was in sight, and at the end of three weeks I was preparing to leave the fragile patient to take up the ordinary duties of her life, including those of wifehood and motherhood. Everyone was congratulating her on her recovery. All the kindness of sympathetic and understanding neighbors poured in upon her in the shape of convalescent dishes, soups, custards, and drinks. Still she appeared to be despondent and worried. She seemed to sit apart in her thoughts as if she had no part in these congratulatory messages and endearing welcomes. I thought at first that she still retained some of her unconscious memories and dwelt upon them in her silences.

But as the hour for my departure came nearer, her anxiety increased, and finally with trembling voice she said: "Another baby will finish me, I suppose."

"It's too early to talk about that," I said, and resolved that I would turn the question over to the doctor for his advice. When he came I said: "Mrs. Sacks is worried about having another baby."

"She well might be," replied the doctor, and then he stood before her and said: "Any more such capers, young woman, and there will be no need to call me."

"Yes, yes—I know, Doctor," said the patient with trembling voice, "but," and she hesitated as if it took all of her courage to say it, "*what* can I do to prevent getting that way again?"

"Oh ho!" laughed the doctor good naturedly, "You want your cake while you eat it too, do you? Well, it can't be done." Then, familiarly slapping her on the back and picking up his hat and bag to depart, he said: "I'll tell you the only sure thing to do. Tell Jake to sleep on the roof!"

With those words he closed the door and went down the stairs, leaving us both petrified and stunned.

Tears sprang to my eyes, and a lump came in my throat as I looked at that face before me. It was stamped with sheer horror. I thought for a moment she might have gone insane, but she conquered her feelings, whatever they may have been, and turning to me in desperation said: "He can't understand, can he?—he's a man after all—but you do, don't you? You're a woman and you'll tell me the secret and I'll never tell it to a soul."

She clasped her hands as if in prayer, she leaned over and looked straight into my eyes and beseechingly implored me to tell her something—something *I really did not know*. It was like being on a rack and tortured for a crime one had not committed. To plead guilty would stop the agony; otherwise the rack kept turning.

I had to turn away from that imploring face. I could not answer her then. I quieted her as best I could. She saw that I was moved by the tears in my eyes. I promised that I would come back in a few days and tell her what she wanted to know. The few simple means of limiting the family like *coitus interruptus* or the condom were laughed at by the neighboring women when told these were the means used by men in the well-to-do families. That was not believed, and I knew such an answer would be swept aside as useless were I to tell her this at such a time.

A little later when she slept I left the house, and made up my mind that I'd keep away from those cases in the future. I felt hopeless to do anything at all. I seemed chained hand and foot, and longed for an earthquake or a volcano to shake the world out of its lethargy into facing these monstrous atrocities.

The intelligent reasoning of the young mother—how to *prevent* getting that way again—how sensible, how just she had been—yes, I promised myself I'd go back and have a long talk with her and tell her more, and perhaps she would not laugh but would believe that those methods were all that were really known.

But time flew past, and weeks rolled into months. That wistful, appealing face haunted me day and night. I could not banish from my mind memories of that trembling voice begging so humbly for knowledge she had a right to have. I was about to retire one night three months later when the telephone rang and an agitated man's voice begged me to come at once to help his wife who was sick again. It was the husband of Mrs. Sacks, and I intuitively knew before I left the telephone that it was almost useless to go.

I dreaded to face that woman. I was tempted to send someone else in my place. I longed for an accident on the subway, or on the street—anything to prevent my going into that home. But on I went just the same. I arrived a few minutes after the doctor, the same one who had given her such noble advice. The woman was dying. She was unconscious. She died within ten minutes after my arrival. It was the same result, the same story told a thousand times before—death from abortion. She had become pregnant, had used drugs, had then consulted a five-dollar professional abortionist, and death followed.

The doctor shook his head as he rose from listening for the heart beat. I knew she had already passed on; without a groan, a sigh or recognition of our belated presence she had gone into the Great Beyond as thousands of mothers go every year. I looked at that drawn face now stilled in death. I placed her thin hands across her breast and recalled how hard they had pleaded with me on that last memorable occasion of parting. The gentle woman, the devoted mother, the loving wife had passed on leaving behind her a frantic husband, helpless in his loneliness, bewildered in his helplessness as he paced up and down the room, hands clenching his head, moaning, "My God! My God! My God!"

One after another these pictures unreeled themselves before me. For hours I stood, motionless and tense, expecting something to happen. I watched the lights go out, I saw the darkness gradually give way to the first shimmer of dawn, and then a colorful sky heralded the rise of the sun. I knew a new day had come for me and a new world as well.

It was like an illumination. I could now see clearly the various social strata of our life; all its mass problems seemed to be centered around uncontrolled breeding. There was only one thing to be done: call out, start the alarm, set the heather on fire! Awaken the womanhood of America to free the motherhood of the world! I released from my almost paralyzed hand the nursing bag which unconsciously I had clutched, threw it across the room, tore the uniform from my body, flung it into a corner, and renounced all palliative work forever.

I would never go back again to nurse women's ailing bodies while their miseries were as vast as the stars. I was now finished with superficial cures, with doctors and nurses and social workers who were brought face to face with this overwhelming truth of women's needs and yet turned to pass on the other side. They must be made to see these facts. I resolved that women should have knowledge of contraception. They have every right to know about their own bodies. I would strike out—I would scream from the housetops. I would tell the world what was going on in the lives of these poor women: I *would* be heard. No matter what it should cost. *I would be heard.* . . .

I asked doctors what one could do and was told I'd better keep off that subject or Anthony Comstock* would get me. I was told that there were laws against that sort of thing. This was the reply from every medical man and woman I approached.

Then I consulted the "up and doing" progressive women who then called themselves Feminists. Most of them were shocked at the mention of abortion, while others were scarcely able to keep from laughing at the idea of my making a public campaign around the idea of too many children. "It can't be done," they said. "You are too sympathetic. You can't do a thing about it until we get the vote. Go home to your children and let things alone.". . .

The following spring found me still seeking and more determined than ever to find out something about contraception and its mysteries. Why was it so difficult to obtain information on this subject? Where was it hidden? Why would no one discuss it? It was like the missing link in the evolution of medical science. It was like the lost trail in the journey toward freedom.

At the end of six months I was convinced that there was no practical medical information on contraception available in America. I had visited the Library of Congress in Washington, I had pored over books in the library of the New York Academy of Medicine and in the Boston Public Library, to find only the information no more reliable than that already obtainable from "back fence gossip" in any small town. . . .

Wherever I turned, from every one I approached I met the same answer: "Wait!" "Wait until women get the vote." "Wait until the Socialists are in power." "Wait for the Social Revolution." "Wait for the Industrial Revolution." Thus I lost my faith in the social schemes and organizations of that day.

Only the boys of the I.W.W.† seemed to grasp the economic significance of this great social question. At once they visualized its importance, and instead of saying "Wait" they gave me names of organizers in the silk, woolen and copper industries, and I offered their assistance to get any facts on family limitation I secured direct to the workingmen and their wives.

Again "Big Bill" Haywood came to my aid with that cheering encouragement of which I was so sorely in need. He never wasted words in advising me to "wait." I owe him a debt of gratitude which I am proud to acknowledge. It was he who suggested that I go to France and see for myself the conditions resulting from generations of family limitation. This idea,

---

* A famous and controversial proponent of laws to enforce private morality.—Ed.

† International Workers of the World was a radical labor organization principally active in the far northwestern states and then headed by W. D. "Big Bill" Haywood.—Ed.

together with my interest in the social experiment then going on in Glasgow, convinced me that I was to find new ways to solve old problems in Europe. I decided to go and see.

Sixth International

Neo-Malthusian and Birth Control Conference

THURSDAY, MARCH 26th

9:30–12:00   FECUNDITY AND CIVILIZATION

> *Chairman,* PROF. E. M. EAST
> "Americanism and Birth Control," *Prof. W. P. Montague*
> "General Idea of Optimum Population," *Prof. Henry P. Fairchild*
> "The Family Allowance System in the Light of Population Problems," *Prof. Paul H. Douglas*
> "The Excesses of Birth Control," *Dr. Louis I. Dublin*
> "The Racial Responsibilities of the Physician," *Prof. Samuel J. Holmes*

12:00–1:00   DISCUSSION

2:00–5:00   DIFFERENTIAL BIRTH RATE

> *Chairman,* PROF. RAYMOND PEARL
> "Is the Voluntary Control of Human Population an Idle Dream?" *Prof. F. B. Sumner*
> "Decreasing Birth Rate in the United States," *Prof. Walter Willcox*
> "The Effect of Overpopulation on Chinese Character," *Prof. Ellsworth Huntington*
> "Some Neglected Aspects of the Population Problem," *Prof. Malcolm A. Bissell*
> "Race Suicide Fallacy," (paper), *J. O. P. Bland*
> "Small Families and Willing Work," (paper), *Dr. Binnie Dunlop*

5:00–6:00   DISCUSSION AND RESOLUTIONS

7:30 P.M.   PIONEERS' DINNER

> *Chairman,* HEYWOOD BROUN
> Paper by ALICE DRYSDALE VICKERY, to be read by *Dr. C. V. Drysdale*

Sixth International Neo-Malthusian and Birth Control Conference Program (New York, 1925), in *Sanger Papers,* Library of Congress.

Dr. Aletta Jacobs   *Holland*
Mr. G. Hardy   *France*
Margaret Sanger   *America*
Kitty Marion   *America*
Dr. Norman Haire   *England*
Dr. Johann Ferch   *Austria*
Fru Thit Jensen   *Denmark*

FRIDAY, MARCH 27th

9:30–12:00   Health of the Community

Chairman, Dr. Benjamin T. Tilton
"The Birth Control Necessity in Our Crowded East Side, from a Physician's Point of View,"   *Dr. Benjamin T. Tilton*
"Factors in Maternal Mortality,"   *Dr. Norman Haire*
"Eugenics, Euthenics and Birth Control and Their Relation to Some of the Problems of the Present Day,"   *Dr. S. Adolphus Knopf*
"Medicine's Responsibility in the Birth Control Movement,"   *Dr. Wm. Allen Pusey*
"Realities and Ideals,"   *Dr. Rachelle S. Yarros*
"Contraceptive Advice and the Medical Profession,"   *Dr. Morris H. Kahn*
"The Educational Phase of Social Hygiene," (paper),   *Elisabeth McManus*

12:00–1:00   Discussion

2:00–5:00   Economics—Poverty and Child Labor

Chairman, Rev. John Haynes Holmes
"Poverty and Birth Control,"   *Dr. Alice Hamilton*
"Juvenile Delinquency and the Family,"   *Dr. Miriam Van Waters*
"Does Russia Want Birth Control?"   *Dr. Peter Tutyshkin*
"The Labor Problems in India,"   *Prof. Taraknath Das*
"The Labor Problem of Mexico,"   *Roberto Haberman*
"Mothers Clinics in Austria," (with lantern slides),   *Dr. Johann Ferch*
"Poverty and Plague in China,"   *Dr. Wu Lien-teh*
"Birth Control in Relation to Child Employment,"   *Owen Lovejoy*
"Housing Problem in England,"   *Dr. C. V. Drysdale*

8:00–10:00   Evening Session—War and Population

Chairman, Dr. C. V. Drysdale
"Overpopulation as a Prime Factor in the Cause of War,"   *Prof. John C. Dura*
"Birth Control or War,"   *Rosika Schwimmer*
"Has France a Population Problem?"   *Mr. G. Hardy*

"Germany and Peace,"   *Dr. Helene Stocker*
"League of Low Birth-rate Nations,"   *Harold Cox*
"War and Overpopulation,"   *Dr. Ferdinand Goldstein*

DISCUSSION

SATURDAY, MARCH 28th

9:30–12:00   EUGENICS AND WELFARE

Chairman, PROF. P. W. WHITING
"Selection, the Only Way of Eugenics,"   *Prof. P. W. Whiting*
"Unnatural Selection and Its Resulting Obligations,"   *Dr. C. C. Little*
"A Eugenic Birth-rate for France,"   *Dr. G. de Lapouge*
"What Are the Criteria for Racial Control?"   *Dr. Ira S. Wiley*
"On Birth Control,"   *Prof. Corrado Gina*
"The Distribution of Birth Control Practices,"   *Prof. Roswell Johnson*
"Should the State Demand a Health Certificate for Marriage,"   *Prof. Dr. Lad. Haskovec*
"Survival of the Unfit," (with lantern slides),   *Dr. Max G. Schlapp*
"The State and Birth Control,"   *E. S. P. Haynes*

12:00–1:00   DISCUSSION

2:00–5:00   BIOLOGICAL AND ALLIED PROBLEMS

Chairman, DR. C. C. LITTLE
"The Evolutionary Meaning of Birth Control," (paper),   *Havelock Ellis*
"A Study of the Inheritance of Internal Glandular Disturbances,"   *Dr. Walter Timmer*
"Mechanism of Sex-determination,"   *Dr. Calvin Bridges*
"Relation of Certain Endocrine Troubles to Birth Control,"   *Dr. Wm. N. Berkeley*
"The Problems of Hedonistic Sex Relations,"   *Dr. Adolf Meyer*

SUNDAY, MARCH 29th

2:30–5:00   CONTRACEPTION

(For Physicians Only—and by Invitation)

Chairman, DR. JAMES F. COOPER
"Birth Control Methods, Satisfactory and Unsatisfactory,"   *Dr. Norman Haire*
"The Clinical Research Department of the American Birth Control League,"   *Dr. Hannah M. Stone*
Papers by Gammeltoft   *(Denmark)*
              Davidson   *(England)*

Gottschalk   *(France)*
Duehrssen   *(Germany)*

DISCUSSION

MONDAY, MARCH 30th

9:30–12:00   SEX AND REPRODUCTION

Chairman, DR. G. V. HAMILTON
"Sex and Reproduction,"   *Dr. A. A. Brill*
"Psychic Release of Sex, Apart from Reproduction,"   *Dr. Helene Stocker*
"Marriage and Birth Control,"   *Prof. Wm. F. Ogburn*
"Relationship of the Neuroses and Divorce to Ignorance of Contraceptive Information,"   *Dr. W. F. Robie*
"Is Sexuality Love?"   *Grace Potter*
"False Social Barriers to Woman's Psychic Release,"   *Doris Stevens*

12:00–1:00   DISCUSSION

2:00–5:00   RELIGIOUS AND MORAL FACTORS

Chairman, REV. DR. WM. H. GARTH
"The Present Status of the Church on Birth Control,"   *Rev. Dr. Wm. H. Garth*
"Birth Control and Biblical Interpretation,"   *Rev. Dr. Frank S. C. Wicks*
"Assured Romance,"   *Rev. Nelson Junius Springer*
"Fear and Morality,"   *Rev. Dr. A. Ray Petty*
"Conduct as a Science,"   *Prof. Harry Elmer Barnes*
"Mice, Men and Morals,"   *Dr. C. C. Little*
"Why the Church Should Champion Birth Control,"   *Rev. Dr. Charles Francis Potter*
Concluding Remarks,   *Rabbi Stephen S. Wise*

DISCUSSION

8:30–10:00   PUBLIC MEETING Scottish Rite Hall, 315 West 34th Street

THE MEDICAL STATUS OF BIRTH CONTROL

Chairman, NORMAN THOMAS
"Some Popular Objections to Birth Control Considered,"   *Norman Thomas*
"The Physician and Public Health,"   *Dr. Norman Haire*
"World-wide Problem of Peace,"   *Dr. C. V. Drysdale*
"Civilization and the 'End of the World,' "   *Fru Thit Jensen*
"The Medical Status of Birth Control,"   *Dr. James F. Cooper*
"The Children's Era,"   *Margaret Sanger*
"The Feminist Movement and Birth Control,"   *Ruth Hale*

THE POPE ON HUMAN LIFE

II. Doctrinal Principles

The problem of birth, like every other problem regarding human life, is to be considered, beyond partial perspectives—whether of the biological or psychological, demographic or sociological orders—in the light of an integral vision of man and of his vocation, not only his natural and earthly, but also his supernatural and eternal vocation. And since, in the attempt to justify artificial methods of birth control, many have appealed to the demands both of conjugal love and of "responsible parenthood," it is good to state very precisely the true concept of these two great realities of married life. . . .

Conjugal love reveals its true nature and nobility when it is considered in its supreme origin, God, who is love, "the Father, from whom every family in heaven and on earth is named.". . .

Hence conjugal love requires in husband and wife an awareness of their mission of "responsible parenthood," which today is rightly much insisted upon, and which also must be exactly understood. Consequently it is to be considered under different aspects which are legitimate and connected with one another.

In relation to the biological processes, responsible parenthood means the knowledge and respect of their functions; human intellect discovers in the power of giving life biological laws which are part of the human person.

In relation to the tendencies of instinct or passion, responsible parenthood means that necessary dominion which reason and will must exercise over them.

In relation to physical, economic, psychological and social conditions, responsible parenthood is exercised, either by the deliberate and generous decision to raise a numerous family, or by the decision, made for grave motives and with due respect for the moral law, to avoid for the time being, or even for an indeterminate period, a new birth.

Responsible parenthood also and above all implies a more profound relationship to the objective moral order established by God, of which a right conscience is the faithful interpreter. The responsible exercise of parenthood implies, therefore, that husband and wife recognize fully their own duties towards God, towards themselves, towards the family and towards society, in a correct hierarchy of values.

In the task of transmitting life, therefore, they are not free to proceed completely at will, as if they could determine in a wholly autonomous way the honest path to follow; but they must conform their activity to the creative intention of God, expressed in the very nature of marriage and of its acts, and manifested by the constant teaching of the Church.

Humanae Vitae, U.S. Catholic Conference (Washington, D.C., 1968), pp. 4–8.

These acts, by which husband and wife are united in chaste intimacy, and by means of which human life is transmitted, are . . . noble and worthy, and they do not cease to be lawful if, for causes independent of the will of husband and wife, they are foreseen to be infecund, since they always remain ordained towards expressing and consolidating their union. In fact, as experience bears witness, not every conjugal act is followed by a new life. God has wisely disposed natural laws and rhythms of fecundity which, of themselves, cause a separation in the succession of births. Nonetheless the Church, calling men back to the observance of the norms of the natural law, as interpreted by their constant doctrine, teaches that each and every marriage act . . . must remain open to the transmission of life.

That teaching, often set forth by the magisterium, is founded upon the inseparable connection, willed by God and unable to be broken by man on his own initiative, between the two meanings of the conjugal act: the unitive meaning and the procreative meaning. Indeed, by its intimate structure, the conjugal act, while most closely uniting husband and wife, capacitates them for the generation of new lives, according to laws inscribed in the very being of man and of woman. By safeguarding both these essential aspects, the unitive and the procreative, the conjugal act preserves in its fullness the sense of true mutual love and its ordination towards man's most high calling to parenthood. We believe that the men of our day are particularly capable of seizing the deeply reasonable and human character of this fundamental principle.

It is in fact justly observed that a conjugal act imposed upon one's partner without regard for his or her condition and lawful desires is not a true act of love, and therefore denies an exigency of right moral order in the relationships between husband and wife. Likewise, if they consider the matter, they must admit that an act of mutual love, which is detrimental to the faculty of propagating life, which God the Creator of all, has implanted in it according to special laws, is in contradiction to both the divine plan, according to whose norm matrimony has been instituted, and the will of the Author of human life. To use this divine gift destroying, even if only partially, its meaning and its purpose is to contradict the nature both of man and of woman and of their most intimate relationship, and therefore it is to contradict also the plan of God and His will. On the other hand, to make use of the gift of conjugal love while respecting the laws of the generative process means to acknowledge oneself not to be the arbiter of the sources of human life, but rather the minister of the design established by the Creator. In fact, just as man does not have unlimited dominion over his body in general, so also, with particular reason, he has no such dominion over his generative faculties as such, because of their intrinsic ordination towards raising up life, of which God is the principle. . . .

In conformity with these landmarks in the human and Christian vision of marriage, we must once again declare that the direct interruption of the generative process already begun, and, above all, directly willed and procured abortion, even if for therapeutic reasons, are to be absolutely excluded as licit means of regulating birth.

CHRISTIAN TRADITION AND CONTRACEPTION

The act of coitus is sacred, is invested with a nonhuman immunity. It is sacramental for Christians and non-Christians alike. Why is it thus? Because by means of it God permits two human beings to join in the creative task of producing human life. The unique power of this act is such that every instance of its exercise must be treated reverently, as one would treat a sacrament. The criticisms based on the function of the biological system, the analogies drawn from animal behavior, even the arguments showing that to absolutize this value destroys other marital values—all these miss the point. This act is absolute, interference with its natural function is immoral, because it is the act from which life begins.

It would be possible to read the teaching of the theologians and canonists, popes and bishops, for over seventeen hundred years, as embodying this position. To do so would require isolating a single strand of the teaching from other reasons and treating it, abstracted from all contexts, as dispositive of the morality of any act which, in the exercise of coitus, "intentionally deprives it of its natural power and strength.". . . To predict that this position would not be the option adopted by the Church would be to presume beyond the purview of history. . . .

The recorded statements of Christian doctrine on contraception did not have to be read in a way requiring an absolute prohibition. The doctrine had been molded by the teaching of the Gospels on the sanctity of marriage; the Pauline condemnation of unnatural sexual behavior; the Old Testament emphasis on fertility; the desire to justify marriage while extolling virginity; the need to assign rational purpose and limit to sexual behavior. The doctrine was formed in a society where slavery, slave concubinage, and the inferiority of women were important elements of the environment affecting sexual relations. The education of children was neither universal nor expensive. Underpopulation was a main governmental concern. The doctrine condemning contraception was formulated against the Gnostics, reasserted against the Manichees, and established in canon law at the climax of the campaign against the Cathars. Reaction to these movements hostile to all procreation was not the sole reason for the doctrine, but the emphases, sweep, and place of the doctrine issued from these mortal combats.

The environmental changes requiring a reconsideration of the role accumulated only after 1850. These changes brought about a profound development of doctrine on marriage and marital intercourse: love became established as a meaning and end of the coital act . . . women were emancipated and marriages in the West came to be based on personal decision. . . . Suppose the test of orthodoxy were, Would Augustine or Thomas be surprised if he were to return and see what Catholic theologians are teaching today? By this criterion, the entire development on the purposes of marital intercourse would have been unorthodox. But it is a perennial mistake to confuse repetition of old formulas with the living law of the Church. The Church, on its pilgrim's path, has grown in grace and wisdom.

That intercourse must be only for a procreative purpose, that intercourse in menstruation is mortal sin, that intercourse in pregnancy is forbidden, that intercourse has a natural position—all these were once common opinions of the theologians and are so no more. Was the commitment to an absolute prohibition of contraception more conscious, more universal, more complete, than to these now obsolete rules? These opinions, now superseded, could be regarded as attempts to preserve basic values in the light of the biological data then available and in the context of the challenges then made to the Christian view of man.

At the core of the existing commitment might be found values other than the absolute, sacral value of coitus. Through a variety of formulas, five propositions had been asserted by the Church. Procreation is good. Procreation of offspring reaches its completion only in their education. Innocent life is sacred. The personal dignity of a spouse is to be respected. Marital love is holy. In these propositions the values of procreation, education, life, personality, and love were set forth. About these values a wall had been built; the wall could be removed when it became a prison rather than a bulwark.

CATHOLIC MARRIAGES

[*Couple No. 1*]

At any rate the children came and we worried about being able to afford them—financially, physically, psychologically. Maybe we would have done better with them if they had been better spaced. Maybe one or more of them suffer from some grievous flaw that could have been avoided if we had had fewer of them. . . .

The consensus seems to be that they are pretty good kids, healthy, smart, and doing well in school. Pretty good schools too. Well fed, well clothed, well housed. We would be heartbroken if we had to part with any one of them. All our worries *seem* to have been unfounded. God did provide. Until the last few years we were in debt a good deal, so maybe in all

Michael Novak, ed., *The Experience of Marriage* (New York, 1964), pp. 24–27, 56–57. Reprinted by permission of the author.

honesty it should be said that our creditors provided too, and maybe this was unfair. But mostly they were the phone company and the oil company waiting an extra month or two, and I can't really feel too bad about that.

I think it is accurate to say that our worries were mostly unfounded, that every baby *is* born with a loaf of bread under its arm, that God *does* provide.

Even so, we did use the rhythm [method] and sometimes it worked. And we did not have as many children as we might have, and probably that was a good thing. So I am not going to say that nobody should fret about birth control. I think it is beyond dispute that some people are having more children that they can begin to take care of and raise as decent human beings.

The most I can bring myself to say is this: From our own experience, it seems that most people worry more than they should about having too many children and that it is better to lean in the direction of having what you think is too many rather than too few. With us this worked out marvelously well. I thank God with all my heart for how marvelously well it worked out.

So I will worry about whether my wife has the physical and psychological strength to have more children. It is no longer necessary to worry about the finanical resources, but I would worry less about that anyway. . . .

Before I start to worry about limiting my own family for . . . global, demographic reasons I think it will be necessary for somebody like the Pope or an ecumenical council to tell me so. It is just too sensational a departure from everything they have been telling me up to date.

Now for the other thing. . . . My wife said that she found it was possible "to abstain altogether for a time without any serious danger of aberrations." For her this is certainly true. And for me it is also true, but there is a difference between possibility and probability. In other words, even where there is no abstinence there is always the serious danger of sin, if only from adulterous thoughts. And the longer the *enforced* abstinence—that is, enforced by fear of conception—then the greater becomes the danger of sin, whether in the direction of adultery or in the direction of treading too close to the line of onanism or false orgasm.

So I fret about birth control for several reasons. I would like to know when we are going to conceive so that every conception might indeed be a free act of will, a free and meaningful act of cooperation with God's creation, and not an accident. Secondly, I fret about it because I would like to be able to make love to my wife more frequently—complete and perfect love, that is—not simply because this would make it more easy to be chaste in my relations with her and with other women, but also because it would contribute to making our life together more beautiful, more nearly perfect.

For these reasons, and because so many people in the world are so clearly in the position where they cannot afford to have more children, I am conscious of a certain amount of resentment that the Church is not doing more to promote a safer, better, and more easily accessible method of using the rhythm. . . . It almost reminds one of the bit in the epistle of St. James: "Here is a brother, here is a sister, going naked, left without the means to secure their daily food; if one says to them, Go in peace, warm yourselves and take your fill, without providing for their bodily needs, of what use is it?" . . . I cannot help but believe that if the Church were really to put the full force of its weight behind it, enough money and enough interest could quickly be raised to promote research that would soon come up with a cheap, simple way of determining when a woman is fertile and when she is sterile, so that the rhythm method would be far more often a safe and sure way and not, as some wag put it, a kind of Vatican roulette.

I cannot bring myself to question the Church's teaching on birth control. Almost instinctively, almost intuitively, I feel that the Church is right. It is almost as if my very flesh shrinks from the idea of employing any kind of mechanical device or pill to frustrate conception, to interfere with the natural performance of the act of love. Actually, there are two things here, two separate shrinkings. One is a shrinking from meddling with the internal, natural biology of the female, say, by the use of a pill to change the natural fertility of the woman to sterility. The other shrinking, which also has an aesthetic quality, is the shrinking from using some kind of device to prevent the sperm from meeting the ovum. It seems to me to violate the fitness of things, and with me personally this is enough to say, without expanding on more involved statements of natural law.

[Couple No. 2]

Conscientious parents, it seems to us, simply cannot have as many children today as the previous generation did. They must be responsible for their children and their children's education for more years than their parents were. Living space becomes increasingly more expensive, and this is only one of the many ways in which more money, effort, and time are needed to raise each child today than were needed fifty years ago. The more we learn about the child's medical, psychological, nutritional, educative, emotional, and physiological needs, the greater becomes the parents' obligation toward the child to meet those needs. The fact that our grandparents raised ten children does not mean that today's parents of small families are slackers. What was considered adequate care of a child fifty years ago would not be adequate today. To have more children than one can give conscientious care to is an injustice to them; one must give them more than love.

Since the number of fertile years of marriage is growing and the number of children a couple can have is getting smaller, it seems inevitable at this point that rhythm is increasingly going to be *the* Catholic way of marriage. If this is true, God help the Catholic family—because we have found rhythm unnatural, unhealthy, and spiritually destructive. A parallel might be drawn. For those couples who have little good to say to each other and for whom talking is only an outlet for the ego, talking by the calendar would have little serious effect and perhaps would even be beneficial. But for the husband and wife who are truly building a marriage, intercourse is as unselfish as their conversation. The importance of the pleasure involved in intercourse is trivial compared with the importance of further building their whole relationship.

It is time Catholics stopped talking about marital love in terms of rights, indulgence, and the allaying of concupiscence. Quite clearly, a major part of the problem is that those who have been doing most of the talking (and legislating) have never tried to build a marriage. It is time we talked about making love to one's spouse as one of the essential dynamics of the married relationship, entailing as much obligation, difficulty and effort, and possessing as great an importance, as earning a living, keeping house, or raising the children. It is time we stopped thinking of sexual desire as primarily a way of seeing to it that children get conceived. Intercourse between husband and wife is an important goal in itself, and at the same time a means toward building a good, sacramental marriage in which to raise children and seek salvation.

We would like to have children in a just, charitable, and responsible fashion and to maintain a normal, whole, married relationship. And that seems almost impossible to us now.

Out of Corners and Closets

S exuality in bewildering diversity has been a characteristic of marital and family relations throughout history, but there have been ages when social codes have tried strenuously either to deny this diversity or restrict it. Restriction in the past, understandably, has dealt better with behavior than with feelings. Before the nineteenth century, American society seems to have been less restrictive about sexuality than in so-called Victorian times, when opinion and law strongly supported premarital chastity, expressed opposition to autoeroticism, adultery, and divorce, tolerated marital intercourse for child begetting, and upheld an ideal of sexual passivity for proper ladies in marriage. Public censure of "libertines" and prostitutes, and persecution of groups like the polygamous Mormons, were different ways to emphasize the exclusive desirability of lifelong, monogamous, heterosexual, and sexually low-keyed marriage. Since it was assumed correctly that sexuality is essentially a matter of feelings rather than behavior, guilt and anxiety were expected to dampen emotions in marriage that might have led to robust sexual feeling and the freer activity that later came to be called "polymorphous perversity" (no limits on sexual enjoyment of the entire body).

The so-called sexual revolution in twentieth-century America seems less novel than a cyclical re-emergence of a more full-blown sexual freedom. Recently, American law and attitude have increasingly sanctioned the open expression of sexual stances in ever-proliferating variety. To "come out of the closet" has not been merely a new ideal for homosexuals. The continuing so-called "revolt against Victorianism" has also tried to encourage less guilty feelings about the range and intensity of all sexual curiosity and appetite. That American culture needed less chastity had been a persistent theme of some of its critics for a long time. But had the massive defeats for chastity as an ideal and practice in this century implied concomitant defeats for delicacy of erotic feeling and for the sexual dignity or integrity of others?

The selections that follow try to recreate some of the high points in recent changes in the family setting of sexuality. The documents on birth control elsewhere in the volume have first bearing on the so-called sexual revolution, for, as the question was repeatedly put, if contraception is used during intercourse how can one pretend any longer that the sole or principal purpose of intercourse is to create children? What did the sanctioning of contraception for Americans thus imply about the legitimacy of their sexual feelings and expression?

Within the family, one important answer to this question has been implicit in the "scientific" marriage manual that replaced its more circumspect (and often suspect) predecessors of the nineteenth century. One of the all-time best-sellers of its type, Dr. Marie Stopes's *Married Love* (1918) became available inexpensively in the 1920s. It was hawked increasingly and frankly in respectable newspapers and magazines, although, at first, with the ad's pledge that it would arrive in a "plain brown wrapper." Millions of copies were sold, but one can only speculate to what diversity of interest and purpose. The book concentrated, some sympathizers thought excessively, on the right and need for women to achieve intense orgasm simultaneously with the male. Specific advice on "mechanics" was thin. Does this paramount theme of the book, together with the mammoth sales, suggest anything reliable about the anxiety, guilt, inadequacy, and other negative as well as positive feelings of Americans about their married love? What can it mean that the title is not "sex in marriage" or "marital sex" but "married *love?*" What had there been in "good marriages" if not Dr. Stopes's notion of love?

If most American marriages were "good," as convention held, why did the divorce rate steadily rise? The national diversity and stringency of divorce laws at the start of the century, as well as the high public censure of divorce, seemed to many critics a disservice to marriage and the family. Divorce available only for adultery or for abuse or long desertion seemed to condemn many to continuing dreadful mistakes in choosing mates. It also increasingly invited hypocrisy about a marriage when partners secretly sought outside satisfaction and brought the need for sex and the ideal of fidelity within marriage into unwarranted conflict. The idea of "experiment" in American marriages slowly emerged from old shadows, purportedly first as an alternative to impossible or shameful divorce and then as an alternative to traditional marriage itself. Meanwhile, the divorce rate climbed steadily after 1900. After 1965, especially, the rate moved up to its recent peak of slightly beyond 40 percent of all marriages. Therapists and sociologists, however, estimate that there probably were psychological and other grounds for divorce in 70 percent of marriages, thus giving America a presumed "good marriage" rate of no more than 30 percent.

Statistics about the incidence of infidelity apart from that in divorce suits are unreliable, but, as the publication of *The Companionate Marriage* (1927) implies, in the 1920s one type of "infidelity" was becoming an open style or habit. Respectable publishers sold the book, and respectable people bought and discussed it. The principal author was Ben Lindsey, a well-known Colorado judge with honorable credentials from his reform efforts for juvenile crime and punishment, for more liberal divorce laws, and for the problems of youths' and women's rights. His account of the increasing varieties of marital experience raised one basic question about growing freedom for sexual behavior: Does it lead to greater happiness?

Early in the century an accepted equation among divorce and sex reformers was that easier divorces or freer sexual expression would lead to a happier marriage. What was the reasoning behind such notions? By 1980 the earlier confidence and clarity about better marriages had yielded to another ideal: being free from law and opinion to please oneself about marriage and "sexual orientation." Generally, by 1980, starting and ending legalized marriage had become relatively easy and inexpensive. In many localities "live-in" and "consort" arrangements (however small in numbers) were open and tolerated or, even more, beyond the concern of most people. Although a very large percent of Americans still lived within households with legally constituted marriages, increasingly, the husband or wife had been married previously. In California, perhaps the national laboratory for experiments on forms of family life, the revised Family Law of 1970 dropped the historic word "divorce." Instead, the law provided for "no-fault dissolution of marriage" and almost sex-blind provisions for child custody, alimony, and disposition of property. In several states by 1980, old ideals were further challenged as in the case given below, by "gays" who asked (unsuccessfully) that legal marriage be provided for homosexual couples, including equal rights with heterosexual marrieds in seeking to adopt children or to keep custody of children from previous conventional marriages.

Clearly, this century has produced more open diversity and ease in marriage and sexual choice generally. But was marriage like other aspects of family life somehow victimized by a "revolution of rising expectations"? Had marriage, because of the new freedom and an ideal of a realizable perfection, become less happy, more challengeable, more fragile? If it was easier to start and more legitimate to end a marriage, was there greater intolerance about its demands? How do we reconcile the very high proportion of Americans living in and thus seeming to seek conventional legal marriages with the divorce rate of two out of five for every recorded marriage, accompanied by a very high remarriage rate? Beyond ideals of love, respect, and honor, what made a marriage or kept it going? In consulting the Census Bureau table on marriage and divorce since 1910, what happens overall to the marriage rate during the years compared with the divorce rates for the period? In what ways do these indexes supplement or contradict each other? The figures on the chart are, of course, extracted from millions of decisions to break legal marriages. What other categories of information, statistics, and records of experiences would we need for an accurate portrait of what marriage and family have come to mean to Americans, sexually and in other respects?

MARRIED LOVE

So many people are now born and bred in artificial and false surroundings, that even the elementary fact that the acts of love should be *joyous*
is unknown to them. When I first wrote this book that was true of the
great majority of English-speaking people. To-day, so rapidly has the new
outlook spread, it may seem unbelievable, yet the then Secretary of the
Royal Society of Medicine told me on its publication that my theme was
revolutionary and offered unimaginable joy to married men, saying "It is
a veritable new gospel to be told we can have a mutual joy in the sex act
in married life." A distinguished American doctor made this characteristic
statement: "I do not believe mutual pleasure in the sexual act has any
particular bearing on the happiness of life." ("Amer. Med. Assoc. Rep.,"
1900.) This is, perhaps, an extreme case, yet so many distinguished medical
men, gynaecologists and physiologists, were either in ignorance or error
regarding some of the profoundest facts of human sex-life, that it is not
surprising that ordinary young couples, however hopeful, should break
and destroy the joy that might have been their lifelong crown. . . .

It seems strange that those who search for natural law in every province
of our universe should have neglected the most vital subject, the one which
concerns us all infinitely more than the naming of planets or the collecting
of insects. Woman is *not* essentially capricious; some of the laws of her
being might have been discovered long ago had the existence of law been
suspected. But it has suited the general structure of society much better
for men to shrug their shoulders and smile at women as irrational and
capricious creatures, to be courted when it suited them, not to be studied.

Vaguely, perhaps, men have realised that much of the charm of life
lies in the sex-*differences* between men and women; so they have snatched
at the easy theory that women differ from themselves by being capricious.
Moreover, by attributing to mere caprice the coldness which at times comes
over the most ardent woman, man was unconsciously justifying himself
for at any time coercing her to suit himself.

Circumstances have so contrived that hitherto the explorers and scientific
investigators, the historians and statisticians, the poets and artists have
been mostly men. Consequently woman's side of the joint life has found
little or no expression. Woman, so long coerced by economic dependence,
and the need for protection while she bore her children, has had to be
content to mould herself to the shape desired by man wherever possible,
and she has stifled her natural feelings and her own deep thoughts as
they welled up.

Most women have never realised intellectually, but many have been dimly
half-conscious, that woman's nature is set to rhythms over which man has
no more control than he has over the tides of the sea. While the ocean
can subdue and dominate man and laugh at his attempted restrictions,

Dr. Marie Stopes, *Married Love* (New York, 1918), pp. 30–39.

woman has bowed to man's desire over her body, and, regardless of its pulses, he approaches her or not as is his will. Some of her rhythms defy him—the moon-month tide of menstruation, the cycle of ten moon-months of bearing the growing child and its birth at the end of the tenth wave— these are essentials too strong to be mastered by man. But the subtler ebb and flow of woman's sex has escaped man's observations or his care.

If a swimmer comes to a sandy beach when the tide is out and the waves have receded, leaving sand where he had expected deep blue water— does he, baulked of his bathe, angrily call the sea "capricious"?

But the tenderest bridegroom finds only caprice in his bride's coldness when she yields her sacrificial body while her sex-tide is at the ebb.

There is another side to this problem, one perhaps even less considered by society. There is the tragic figure of the loving woman whose love-tide is at the highest, and whose husband does not recognise the delicate signs of her ardour. In our anæmic artificial days it often happens that the man's desire is a surface need, quickly satisfied, colourless, and lacking beauty, and that he has no knowledge of the rich complexities of love-making which an initiate of love's mysteries enjoys. To such a man his wife may indeed seem petulant, capricious, or resentful without reason.

Welling up in her are the wonderful tides, scented and enriched by the myriad experiences of the human race from its ancient days of leisure and flower-wreathed love-making, urging her to transports and to self-expressions, were the man but ready to take the first step in the initiative or to recognise and welcome it in her. Seldom dare any woman, still more seldom dare a wife, risk the blow at her heart which would be given were she to offer charming love-play to which the man did not respond. To the initiate she will be able to reveal that the tide is up by a hundred subtle signs, upon which he will seize with delight. But if her husband is blind to them there is for her nothing but silence, self-suppression, and their inevitable sequence of self-scorn, followed by resentment towards the man who places her in such a position of humiliation while talking of his "love."

So unaware of the elements of the physiological reactions of women are many modern men that the case of Mrs. G. is not exceptional. Her husband was accustomed to pet her and have relations with her frequently, but yet he never took any trouble to rouse in her the necessary preliminary feeling for mutual union. She had married as a very ignorant girl, but often vaguely felt a sense of something lacking in her husband's love. Her husband had never kissed her except on the lips and cheek, but once at the crest of the wave of her sex-tide (all unconscious that it was so) she felt a yearning to feel his head, his lips, pressed against her bosom. The sensitive interrelation between a woman's breasts and the rest of her sex-life is not only a bodily thrill, but there is a world of poetic beauty in the longing of a loving woman for the unconceived child which melts in mists of tenderness toward her lover, the soft touch of whose lips can thus rouse her mingled joy. Because she shyly asked him, Mrs. G.'s husband gave her one swift unrepeated kiss upon her bosom. He was so ignorant that he did not know that her husband's lips upon her breast melt a wife to tenderness and are one of a husband's first and surest ways to make her physically ready for complete union. In this way he inhibited her natural desire, and as he never did anything to stir it, she never had any physical pleasure in their relation. Such prudish or careless husbands, content with their own satisfaction, little know the pent-up aching, or even resentment, which may eat into a wife's heart, and ultimately may affect her whole health.

COMPANIONATE MARRIAGE

Preface

Companionate Marriage is legal marriage, with legalized Birth Control, and with the right to divorce by mutual consent for childless couples, usually without payment of alimony.

Companionate Marriage is already an established social fact in this country. It is conventionally respectable. Sophisticated people are, without incurring social reproach, everywhere practicing Birth Control and are also obtaining collusive divorce, outside the law, whenever they want it. They will continue the practice, and no amount of prohibitive legislation can stop them. . . .

Technically *the Companionate and Trial Marriage have certain features in common but* one *is not the* other. *Both would normally avail themselves of Birth Control and divorce by mutual consent. Both would place a minimum of obstruction in the way of childless couples wishing a divorce. And both recognize the fact that when men and women marry they can never be perfectly certain that their marriage will turn out to be a permanent success. But there the similarity ends.*

For the emphasis—*the psychological emphasis—is altogether different. All men and women who are sensible and honest know when they marry that there is at least a possibility of failure ahead. But they assume that the chance is remote. They have confidence in their ability to weather all storms and make port. It is their intention to do that, and to make such adjustments as may be necessary to that end. That is* marriage. *That is the spirit of marriage. It involves the same recognition of risk that goes into trial marriage, but it stoutly proposes to overcome and nullify that risk. It emphatically does not propose to seek divorce the moment the flame of romantic passion begins to cool.*

Now the trouble with this attitude in ordinary marriage is that not enough account is taken of the risk. If the Trial Marriage psychology puts too much emphasis on the risk, the psychology of traditional marriage bull-headedly ignores it altogether. The result is that couples who make a mistake in their choice of each other find that in getting into marriage they have walked into a trap. . . . The Companionate would not invite many such persons. Nor, since it would offer small hope of alimony, would it attract ladies of the "gold-digger" type. It would give marriage a chance to breathe and live; it would give it room in which to grow; it would give it soil in which to put forth roots; and it would establish it on a better basis than it has yet known. . . .

The couples who mutually agree that adultery is all right are a strange and interesting phenomenon in American life to-day. And what I have so far observed leads me to believe that such agreements are far more common than even students of these matters have any idea of. There is no means of telling to what extent the thing is happening, of course, because such agreements, when they exist, are sedulously secret. In many cases I have no doubt there is no candid agreement, but simply a tacit ignoring of the facts. In other cases, where the couple no longer care for each other, there may be some such agreement, with no further sex relations in their own marriage. But when couples that love each other enter on such an apparently anomalous course, that is surely indicative that something extraordinary is happening to one of the most firmly established of our customs.

One of the most remarkable and clear-cut cases of this sort that has ever come to my attention through the statements of the parties themselves was that of a couple whom I will call Mr. and Mrs. Frederick Blank. They have wealth, education, and enough leisure to think about things, and, if you will, get into mischief. Their social position is first rate. They don't run with a fast set; they go to social functions only occasionally; and they apparently stick pretty closely to their home.

Mrs. Blank is a very attractive woman, and men are attentive wherever she appears. She divorced her first husband on grounds of incompatibility. Apparently there is no prospect that she will ever separate from her second husband for a similar cause—for most persons, I think, would consider them compatible to a fault. . . . Mrs. Blank began to tell me some things about herself. Her husband, she said, had recently had an affair with a girl—not this girl; and she on her part had been through similar experiences, after her present marriage, with men she liked.

"Does your husband know it?" I asked.

"Of course," she said placidly. "We agree on these things. We love each other, but we enjoy these outside experiences; so why not take them? I think we care more for each other on account of them."

It isn't often that I get paralysis of the tongue, but I got it then. I simply sat and looked at her. I had suspected this kind of thing was going on, but here was the evidence. Here was a new one. Sex scrapes were old stuff; collusion for the obtaining of a divorce was as old as divorce laws; statutory rape was an item of my daily routine; and unbelievable coincidences in human lives were the kind of thing I expected as a matter of course. But here was collusion in adultery on the part of people who were as far from gross vulgarity as any you would be likely to find in a day's run.

Perceiving my astonishment, Mrs. Blank smiled.

"This is a new one on me," I said at last. "I have suspected it might be going on. I have known of such cases where neither party admitted it to the other. I have known cases where they admitted it because they had ceased to care for each other. I have known women who tolerated unfaithfulness on the part of their husbands; and a few husbands who tolerated it on the part of their wives. But this—in a marriage you say is a love-match—" I could proceed no farther.

"Oh, Judge," she exclaimed. "What's the harm—aside from the fact that we have always been told it was wrong? If he has an affair with a girl he takes a fancy to, it really means nothing more to him or to me than if he took her to dinner or the theater. It is all casual and harmless unless one *thinks* harm into it. Society says there is harm in it, and that it strikes at the roots of the Home. But as a matter of simple, biological fact does it do any harm whatever in our particular case; and as a matter of sociological fact, does it strike at the roots of our Home? I maintain that it makes us both happier, and that our Home is a lot better off than the virtuous homes where husbands and wives chafe and fret in bondage. We are free, and our married life is ideal,—in spite of the whole world saying, 'It can't be done!'

"This thing, " she went on, "is what thinking makes it—not what society's thinking makes it, but what his thinking makes it, and the girl's thinking, and my thinking, and the thinking of the men who win my friendship to that ultimate degree. And if the thing is what *thinking* makes it rather than what *custom* makes it, then custom has no authority in this matter unless we are obligated to agree with custom and obey it. I deny that it has any such authority. We propose to disagree with custom in our thoughts as much as we see fit, and in our acts up to any point where we don't infringe on other people's rights."

"But that's just the point, isn't it?" I suggested. "Other people's rights—and society's rights."

"We have not violated any such rights," she answered. "What we have done is our own business and that of the friends with whom we have shared our intimacies. It concerns nobody else."—Then she added with a laugh, "The minister of my church will stand up and tell you that such and such an Old Testament worthy had concubines and several wives; and if you ask him he'll tell you further that this was perfectly moral *then*—right in the sight of God, but one of the seven deadly sins *now*. To which I answer: Even the customs of God seem to change. Why not those of men?—Custom is always pronouncing something right in one age or country, and wrong in another. What is pure in one region is impure in another. Which is which? And when even the Bible changes face on the matter, who is to decide? The individual, of course. That's the way I look at it, Judge. I think there is no such intrinsic thing as Purity and Impurity. They are abstractions; and they have been one and the same thing repeatedly in human history."

"I should like to know," I said, "how you came around to this way of thinking. You were strictly brought up. I take it that you did not break away from all that early training without a struggle and some misery. How did it come about?"

"I found out that he was having an intrigue with a girl," she answered. "He looked it. He went around like a whipped dog, and he would never look me in the eye. When I accused him he went white, and tried to deny it; but I told him what I knew, and then, when there was no way out, he owned up. . . . He could talk all right as soon as he found I was ready to listen. It was an agonizing business, but the upshot, after many hours, during which the taxi called and was dismissed, was that I agreed to condone what he had done. Only he was never to do it again—never—never.

"That quarrel lasted us for six months. Outwardly everything was calm, but the air in our house was tense. I wondered what Frederick was thinking about; but if I asked him,—well, of course, you can't find out that way.

" 'Frederick,' I said to him one day, 'you're under a strain. There's something on your mind. I think I can guess it. Have you been out with any one?'

"He jumped up furiously. 'I told you I was through,' he snarled, 'and I'm keeping my word. So forget it.'

" 'Are you keeping it in your thoughts?' I asked. And then, without giving him a chance to answer, I added, 'I've been thinking things over, Frederick. This present arrangement won't do. Telling people they mustn't do things makes them want to do them. I've made that mistake with you. Suppose we arrange it this way—that I'm to give you full liberty—and that you are to give me the same.'

"Judge, I wish you could have seen his face. It was a study. The utter conflict of emotions! On the one hand a yearning for the freedom he craved for himself; and on the other the old notion about female chastity—the double standard. He *owned* me; for *me* to go adventuring was quite different. I'd be polluted and unclean.

" 'I don't want it,' he said shortly. 'I wish you'd drop it and forget it.'

" 'Oh,' I said. 'You don't want it. Are you sure? Or is it that you want it for yourself but not for me—exactly like a man!' And I felt myself going into a rage.

" 'Well,' he asked, 'would you like me to say that I'd be willing to share you with some one else? You know you wouldn't! You'd feel insulted.'

"With that I realized that that was just the way I would have felt. I didn't know whether to laugh or cry, I was so mixed up.

" 'Wouldn't you?' he reiterated.

" 'Yes,' I owned, 'I would. But that's one way of looking at it, and an irrational way at that. We can't go on the way we have been; and I'm not going to let you get away with any double standard. We couldn't live together on that basis either. If you want to drop your masculine notions about purity and property and meet me on the level, we'll try out the thing *you* started.'. . .

"So, Judge, that's the way it came about. Nobody could be more surprised than I am at the outcome. After the first shock was over the tension in our home disappeared. We had no reservations. We were able to speak our minds on all this. Little mishaps ceased to irritate us. Everything was different. We felt like free souls in voluntary service to each other.—As for these outside affairs, there have not been many.

"The world would say we are wrong. It would call *me* unclean, and my husband merely unconventional. It would receive him socially and make me an outcast for the very same conduct. And yet it has not affected me any differently from what it has him—though we have a social superstition which says it has.". . .

[I responded] "I am sure, that whatever you may feel about the rightness of what you are doing, you will agree with me that so violent a tampering with an established social custom, and with one's own habits of thought and feeling, is dangerous in a high degree—dangerous to the happiness of those who attempt it, and possibly dangerous to the stability of society."

"It all depends on whether one knows how to handle dynamite," she answered. "Some persons should not touch it. What makes our course safe is that we understand each other, and that we don't impose our opinions, and, if you like, our bad example, on the outside world. We are very careful not to get found out. I don't mean that in any cynical spirit, but I mean it."

"Perhaps, " I ventured, "you will permit me to say that your story sounds more like promiscuity than what you call many marriages."

She flushed. "I'm not afraid of the word," she said with spirit. "That's all it is—a word. If you mean by promiscuity that I am to be had for the asking, you are mistaken. But I know you don't think that. I know you understand the thought in my mind better than that. These are genuine attachments, deep friendships, intimate companionships. The sex part is an incident, and a rather rare one so far as I am concerned. I am very particular, though I may not sound like it. I suppose most persons would not believe me when I say that sex, as such, plays a very minor rôle in these affairs, and often no rôle at all. But that is because most persons are so repressed that they can't think of intimate friendship between a man and a woman in anything but the sex sense. I was that way. But I've genuinely gotten beyond it, simply by letting go.

"What I mean is that I do what I want to do, and that I find it increasingly easy to do it without my fears and my old habits of thought tearing me to pieces inside. Save for the restraints contingent on other people's rights, there isn't a repression in my body. I think that is the way one should be in order to be healthy and happy.". . . Mrs. Blank laughed, a trifle bitterly, I thought. "Oh, Judge, lies are such terrible things. Why can't we all speak the truth? Tell *me* the truth, Judge. What do you think of me?"

"I think you're rich but honest," I said. "You would like to have me tell you that I think you are doing right. In like manner most conventional persons would reproach me bitterly for not telling you that you are an impure woman and a highly immoral person. But I could not do the work I am engaged in if I permitted my mind to form fixed judgments on human behavior. You must excuse me therefore from taking sides. It is part of my job not to take sides. I simply note the facts; and I find them interesting because they are among the indications that some sort of a social change is on the way."

CALIFORNIA FAMILY LAW, 1970

Title 3. Dissolution of Marriage

CHAPTER 1. GENERAL PROVISIONS

4500. Marriage is dissolved only by (1) the death of one of the parties or (2) the judgment of a court of competent jurisdiction decreeing a dissolution of the marriage.

4501. The effect of a judgment decreeing a dissolution of the marriage is to restore the parties to the state of unmarried persons. . . .

4506. A court may decree a dissolution of the marriage or legal separation on either of the following grounds, which shall be pleaded generally:

(1) Irreconcilable differences, which have caused the irremediable breakdown of the marriage.

(2) Incurable insanity.

4507. Irreconcilable differences are those grounds which are determined by the court to be substantial reasons for not continuing the marriage and which make it appear that the marriage should be dissolved.

4508. (a) If from the evidence at the hearing and contained in the confidential questionnaire, the court finds that there are irreconcilable differences, which have caused the irremediable breakdown of the marriage, it shall order the dissolution of the marriage or a legal separation. If it appears that there is a reasonable possibility of reconciliation, the court shall continue the proceeding for a period not to exceed 30 days. During the period of the continuance, the court may make any order for the support and maintenance of the parties, the custody, support, maintenance, and education of the minor children of the marriage, attorney fees, and for the preservation of the property of the parties. At any time after the termination of such 30-day period, either party may move for the dissolution of the marriage or a legal separation, and the court may enter its judgment decreeing such dissolution or separation.

(b) The court may not render a judgment decreeing the legal separation of the parties without the consent of both parties unless one party has

Statutes and Amendments of California, Sacramento, 1970 (1969 Regular Session), pp. 3323–48.

not made a general appearance and the petition is one for legal separation. A judgment decreeing the legal separation of the parties shall not bar a subsequent judgment decreeing the dissolution of the marriage rendered pursuant to a petition for dissolution filed by either party.

4509.   In any pleadings or proceedings for legal separation or dissolution of marriage under this part, including depositions and discovery proceedings, evidence of specific acts of misconduct shall be improper and inadmissible, except where child custody is in issue and such evidence is relevant to establish that parental custody would be detrimental to the child, or at the hearing where it is determined by the court to be necessary to establish the existence of irreconcilable differences.

4510.   A marriage may be dissolved on the grounds of incurable insanity only upon proof, including competent medical or psychiatric testimony, that the insane spouse was at the time the petition was filed, and remains, incurably insane. . . .

4514.   When an interlocutory judgment has been entered . . . and six months have expired from the date of service of a copy of summons and complaint, or the date of appearance of the respondent, the court on motion of either party, or upon its own motion, may enter the final judgment dissolving the marriage, and such final judgment shall restore them to the status of single persons, and permit either to marry after the entry thereof. . . .

4516.   During the pendency of any proceeding under Title 3 (commencing with Section 4500) or Title 4 (commencing with Section 4600) of this part, the superior court may order the husband or wife, or father or mother, as the case may be, to pay any amount that is necessary for the support and maintenance of the wife or husband and for the support, maintenance, and education of the children, as the case may be. . . .

Title 4. Custody of Children

4600.   In any proceeding where there is at issue the custody of a minor child, the court may, during the pendency of the proceeding, or at any time thereafter, make such order for the custody of such child during his minority as may seem necessary or proper. If a child is of sufficient age and capacity to reason so as to form an intelligent preference as to custody, the court shall consider and give due weight to his wishes in making an award of custody or modification thereof. Custody should be awarded in the following order of preference:

(a) To either parent according to the best interests of the child, but, other things being equal, custody shall be given to the mother if the child is of tender years.

(b) To the person or persons in whose home the child has been living in a wholesome and stable environment.

(c) To any other person or persons deemed by the court to be suitable and able to provide adequate and proper care and guidance for the child.

Before the court makes any order awarding custody to a person or persons other than a parent, without the consent of the parents, it must make a finding that an award of custody to a parent would be detrimental to the child, and the award to a nonparent is required to serve the best interests of the child. Allegations that parental custody would be detrimental to the child, other than a statement of that ultimate fact, shall not appear in the pleadings. The court may, in its discretion, exclude the public from the hearing on this issue. . . .

Title 6. Property Rights of the Parties

4801. (a) In any judgment decreeing the dissolution of a marriage or a legal separation of the parties, the court may order a party to pay for the support of the other party any amount, and for such period of time, as the court may deem just and reasonable having regard for the circumstances of the respective parties, including the duration of the marriage, and the ability of the supported spouse to engage in gainful employment without interfering with the interests of the children of the parties in the custody of such spouse. . . .

Title 8. Husband and Wife

5100. Husband and wife contract toward each other obligations of mutual respect, fidelity, and support.

5101. The husband is the head of the family. He may choose any reasonable place or mode of living, and the wife must conform thereto.

5102. Neither husband nor wife has any interest in the property of the other, but neither can be excluded from the . . . other's dwelling except as provided.

5103. Either husband or wife may enter into any engagement or transaction with the other, or with any other person, respecting property, which either might if unmarried; subject, in transactions between themselves, to the general rules which control the actions of persons occupying confidential relations with each other. . . .

5107. All property of the wife, owned by her before marriage, and that acquired afterwards by gift, bequest, devise, or descent, with the rents, issues, and profits thereof, is her separate property. The wife may, without the consent of her husband, convey her separate property.

5108. All property owned by the husband before marriage, and that acquired afterwards by gift, bequest, devise, or descent, with the rents, issues, and profits thereof, is his separate property. The husband may, without the consent of his wife, convey his separate property. . . .

5110. All other real property situated in this state and all other personal property wherever situated acquired during the marriage by a married person while domiciled in this state is community property. . . .

5125. . . . The husband has the management and control of the community personal property, with like absolute power of disposition, other than testamentary, as he has of his separate estate; provided, however, that he cannot make a gift of such community personal property, or dispose of the same without a valuable consideration, or sell, convey, or encumber the furniture, furnishings, or fittings of the home, or the clothing or wearing apparel of the wife or minor children that is community, without the written consent of the wife. . . .

5127.   Except as provided in Section 5128, the husband has the managament and control of the community real property, but the wife, either personally or by duly authorized agent, must join with him in executing any instrument by which such community real property or any interest therein is leased for a longer period than one year, or is sold, conveyed, or encumbered; provided, however, that nothing herein contained shall be construed to apply to a lease, mortgage, conveyance, or transfer of real property or of any interest in real property between husband and wife. . . .

1761.   Prior to the filing of any proceeding for dissolution of marriage, legal separation, or judgment of nullity of a voidable marriage, either spouse, or both spouses, may file in the conciliation court a petition invoking the jurisdiction of the court for the purpose of preserving the marriage by effecting a reconciliation between the parties, or for amicable settlement of the controversy between the spouses, so as to avoid further litigation over the issue involved. . . .

1770.   . . . If, however, after the expiration of such period, the controversy between the spouses has not been terminated, either spouse may institute proceedings for dissolution of marriage, legal separation, or judgment of a nullity of a voidable marriage. The pendency of a proceeding for dissolution of marriage, legal separation, or declaration of nullity shall not operate as a bar to the instituting of proceedings for conciliation under this chapter.

HOMOSEXUAL MARRIAGE AND THE LAW

RICHARD JOHN BAKER ET AL., APPELLANTS,

v.

GERALD NELSON, CLERK OF HENNEPIN COUNTY
DISTRICT COURT, RESPONDENT.

Supreme Court of Minnesota.

Oct. 15, 1971.

Mandamus proceeding by applicants for marriage license. The District Court . . . ruled that clerk of county district court was not required to issue marriage license to applicants who were of the same sex and specifically directed that license not be issued to them, and appeal was taken. The Supreme Court . . . held that statute governing marriage does not authorize marriage between persons of the same sex, and such marriages

"Baker *v.* Nelson," *191 Northwestern Reporter* (2nd Series, 1972), pp. 185–87.

are accordingly prohibited, and that such statute does not offend the First, Eighth, Ninth or Fourteenth Amendments to the United States Constitution.

Affirmed. . . .

OPINION

PETERSON, Justice.

The questions for decision are whether a marriage of two persons of the same sex is authorized by state statutes and, if not, whether state authorization is constitutionally compelled.

Petitioners, Richard John Baker and James Michael McConnell, both adult male persons, made application to respondent, Gerald R. Nelson, clerk of Hennepin County District Court, for a marriage license, pursuant to Minn.St. c. 517.08. Respondent declined to issue the license on the sole ground that petitioners were of the same sex, it being undisputed that there were otherwise no statutory impediments to a heterosexual marriage by either petitioner.

The trial court . . . ruled that respondent was not required to issue a marriage license to petitioners and specifically directed that a marriage license not be issued to them. This appeal is from those orders. We affirm.

[1] 1. Petitioners contend, first, that the absence of an express statutory prohibition against same-sex marriages evinces a legislative intent to authorize such marriages. We think, however, that a sensible reading of the statute discloses a contrary intent.

Minn.St. c. 517, which governs "marriage," employs that term as one of common usage, meaning the state of union between persons of the opposite sex. It is unrealistic to think that the original draftsmen of our marriage statutes, which date from territorial days, would have used the term in any different sense. The term is of contemporary significance as well, for the present statute is replete with words of heterosexual import such as "husband and wife" and "bride and groom."

We hold, therefore, that Minn.St. c. 517 does not authorize marriage between persons of the same sex and that such marriages are accordingly prohibited.

[2] 2. Petitioners contend, second, that Minn.St. c. 517, so interpreted, is unconstitutional. There is a dual aspect to this contention: The prohibition of a same-sex marriage denies petitioners a fundamental right guaranteed by the Ninth Amendment to the United States Constitution, arguably made applicable to the states by the Fourteenth Amendment, and petitioners are deprived of liberty and property without due process and are denied the equal protection of the laws, both guaranteed by the Fourteenth Amendment.[1]

---

[1] We dismiss without discussion petitioners' additional contentions that the statute contravenes the First Amendment and Eighth Amendment of the United States Constitution.

These constitutional challenges have in common the assertion that the right to marry without regard to the sex of the parties is a fundamental right of all persons and that restricting marriage to only couples of the opposite sex is irrational and invidiously discriminatory. We are not independently persuaded by these contentions and do not find support for them in any decisions of the United States Supreme Court.

The institution of marriage as a union of man and woman, uniquely involving the procreation and rearing of children within a family, is as old as the book of Genesis. . . . This historic institution manifestly is more deeply founded than the asserted contemporary concept of marriage and societal interests for which petitioners contend. The due process clause of the Fourteenth Amendment is not a charter for restructuring it by judicial legislation.

Griswold v. Connecticut, 381 U.S. 479, 85 S.Ct. 1678, 14 L.Ed.2d 510 (1965), upon which petitioners rely, does not support a contrary conclusion. A Connecticut criminal statute prohibiting the use of contraceptives by married couples was held invalid, as violating the due process clause of the Fourteenth Amendment. The basic premise of that decision, however, was that the state, having authorized marriage, was without power to intrude upon the right of privacy inherent in the marital relationship. . . .

The equal protection clause of the Fourteenth Amendment, like the due process clause, is not offended by the state's classification of persons authorized to marry. There is no irrational or invidious discrimination. Petitioners note that the state does not impose upon heterosexual married couples a condition that they have a proved capacity or declared willingness to procreate, posing a rhetorical demand that this court must read such condition into the statute if same-sex marriages are to be prohibited. Even assuming that such a condition would be neither unrealistic nor offensive under the Griswold rationale, the classification is no more than theoretically imperfect. . . .

Loving v. Virginia, 388 U.S. 1, 87 S.Ct. 1817, 18 L.Ed.2d 1010 (1967), upon which petitioners additionally rely, does not militate against this conclusion. Virginia's antimiscegenation statute, prohibiting interracial marriages, was invalidated solely on the grounds of its patent racial discrimination. As Mr. Chief Justice Warren wrote, "Marriage is one of the 'basic civil rights of man,' fundamental to our very existence and survival. . . . To deny this fundamental freedom on so unsupportable a basis as the racial classifications embodied in these statutes, classifications so directly subversive of the principle of equality at the heart of the Fourteenth Amendment, is surely to deprive all the State's citizens of liberty without due process of law. The Fourteenth Amendment requires that the freedom of choice to marry not be restricted by invidious racial discriminations."

Loving does indicate that not all state restrictions upon the right to marry are beyond reach of the Fourteenth Amendment. But in commonsense and in a constitutional sense, there is a clear distinction between a marital restriction based merely upon race and one based upon the fundamental difference in sex.

We hold, therefore, that Minn.St. c. 517 does not offend the First, Eighth, Ninth, or Fourteenth Amendments to the United States Constitution.

No. 80. Live Births, Deaths, Marriages, and Divorces: 1910 to 1978

[Prior to 1960, excludes Alaska and Hawaii. Figures for deaths and death rates for 1910–1930 are for death-registration States only. Beginning 1970, excludes births to, and deaths of, nonresidents of the U.S. See Appendix III. See also *Historical Statistics, Colonial Times to 1970*, series B 1–5, B 142, B 167, B 214, and B 216]

YEAR	NUMBER (1,000)					RATE PER 1,000 POPULATION					
	Births [1]	Deaths Total	Deaths Infant [2]	Marriages [3]	Divorces [4]	Births [1]	Deaths Total	Deaths Infant [2]	Marriages [3]	Divorces [4]
1910	2,777	697	(NA)	948	83	30.1	14.7	(NA)	10.3	.9
1915	2,965	816	78	1,008	104	29.5	13.2	99.9	10.0	1.0
1920	2,950	1,118	130	1,274	171	27.7	13.0	85.8	12.0	1.6
1925	2,909	1,192	135	1,188	175	25.1	11.7	71.7	10.3	1.5
1930	2,618	1,327	142	1,127	196	21.3	11.3	64.6	9.2	1.6
1935	2,377	1,393	120	1,327	218	18.7	10.9	55.7	10.4	1.7
1940	2,559	1,417	111	1,596	264	19.4	10.8	47.0	12.1	2.0
1945	2,858	1,402	105	1,613	485	20.4	10.6	38.3	12.2	3.5
1950	3,632	1,452	104	1,667	385	24.1	9.6	29.2	11.1	2.6
1955	4,097	1,529	107	1,531	377	25.0	9.3	26.4	9.3	2.3
1960	4,258	1,712	111	1,523	393	23.7	9.5	26.0	8.5	2.2
1962	4,167	1,757	105	1,577	413	22.4	9.5	25.3	8.5	2.2
1963	4,098	1,814	103	1,654	428	21.7	9.6	25.2	8.8	2.3
1964	4,027	1,798	100	1,725	450	21.0	9.4	24.8	9.0	2.4
1965	3,760	1,828	93	1,800	479	19.4	9.4	24.7	9.3	2.5
1966	3,606	1,863	86	1,857	499	18.4	9.5	23.7	9.5	2.5
1967	3,521	1,851	79	1,927	523	17.8	9.4	22.4	9.7	2.6
1968	3,502	1,930	76	2,069	584	17.5	9.7	21.8	10.4	2.9
1969	3,600	1,922	75	2,145	639	17.8	9.5	20.7	10.6	3.2
1970	3,731	1,921	75	2,159	708	18.4	9.5	20.0	10.6	3.5
1971	3,556	1,928	68	2,190	773	17.2	9.3	19.1	10.6	3.7
1972	3,258	1,964	60	2,282	845	15.6	9.4	18.5	11.0	4.1
1973	3,137	1,973	56	2,284	915	14.9	9.4	17.7	10.9	4.4
1974	3,160	1,934	53	2,230	977	14.9	9.2	16.7	10.5	4.6
1975	3,144	1,893	51	2,153	1,036	14.8	8.8	16.1	10.1	4.9
1976	3,168	1,909	48	2,155	1,083	14.8	8.9	15.2	10.0	5.0
1977	3,327	1,900	47	2,178	1,091	15.4	8.8	14.1	10.1	5.0
1978, prel.	3,329	1,924	45	2,243	1,122	15.3	8.8	13.6	10.3	5.1

NA Not available.   [1] Through 1955, adjusted for underregistration.   [2] Infants under 1 year, excluding fetal deaths; rates per 1,000 registered live births.   [3] Includes estimates for some States through 1969 and also for 1976, and marriage licenses for some States for all years except 1973 and 1975.   [4] Includes reported annulments

U.S. Department of Commerce, Bureau of the Census, *Statistical Abstract* (Washington, 1978), Chart 80.

Abortion—Unfinished Debate

The legalization of abortion in America continued arguments already familiar from the campaign to legitimize contraception. Abortion seems to many only another method to interfere against conception. By the 1960s, however, when legalization of abortion became a heated national issue, the country was also waging new battles about women's rights and opportunities, generally called "women's liberation." Although a woman's right to control her own body was a theme occasionally heard in the earlier birth-control debate, it became a loud constant during the abortion controversies. The U.S. Supreme Court had already held that birth control was basically a matter of personal choice and private morality into which government should not intrude. Some now added for abortion, "Whether a woman is married or not." And some also said, "Whether her husband agrees or not."

Despite the many implications of abortion for limiting family size, the issue went beyond contraception, most dramatically when the fire of the opponents centered on the "murder" of the fetus. Although Roman Catholics were divided on the issue of abortion and many non-Catholics also opposed legalization, Catholics provided much of the energy of the opposition, especially against using public money for clinics for elective abortion where the "murders" would be performed. The opposition cry for the "right to life" seemed a projection into the prenatal period of the so-called rights of children. But how could the two moral causes, the rights of women and of unborn children, be reconciled? If there was a "higher law" that morally limited what a woman could do with her own body or what a doctor could do with a fetus, who would define and apply it as public policy and against whose contrary notion of "conscience"? And why, as some anti-abortionists did propose, exempt the lives of assumedly defective fetuses or of those whose mothers were victims of rape or incest? What also did the "higher law" demand, and what would be done practically, about abandoned or abused infants who had a right to decent nurture but had been born to neglect because they came against the mothers' wishes?

How did the attempt to define "life" within the womb bear on the issue? What, for example, was the specific time at which a fetus gained humanity and thus a "right" not to be aborted? Even if one took a materialistic view of "life," not a transcendent moral stance, when did "vitality" enter the fetus? Why not at conception? If not "human" then, when and why and how human?

Aside from these troubling and debated issues, how did abortion affect family relations? Only another method of family limitation, was one prosaic emphasis, a backup, perhaps, for faulty contraception during coitus. What of abortion being available—and anonymously—to minor daughters of families as their right, regardless of parental wishes? Would the availability of abortion largely or solely on a wife's initiative and against the husband's wishes throw any substantial shadow over family relations? If unwanted babies helped poison family lives, was the "good of the family" and of those already living preferable to giving life to the unwanted child? What of one seemingly wanted and gestating baby but whose health and well-being would be predictably severely at risk in known "bad family" settings? Were particular cases so varied and complex that forceful moral standards or laws would create as much grief as relief? But for another turn, and as in the earlier case of legalized contraception, was not the libertarian standard of "personal choice," once given legal protection, sanctioning what many citizens believed was immoral murder or God-forbidden evil? How could conservatives, deprecating further intrusion of state and public into family life, justify adding another law telling families what they could or could not do? What was happening in American public feeling about "family-related issues" that could account for both the rapidity of the "abortion revolution" and the storm of controversy it engendered?

The selections on abortion try to recapitulate the amazing history of the swift victory for its legalization and to present some conflicting religious views about legalization. Among the latter, Calvin J. Eichhorst is a Lutheran, Mary Daly is a Catholic professor of theology, and John T. Noonan an eminent scholar of Catholic doctrine who had not opposed Catholics using contraception.

THE ABORTION REVOLUTION

The changes which took place in Britain and the Commonwealth during the 1960s and early 70s, while rapid compared with previous experience, were tortoise-like beside events soon to follow in the USA. The movement for liberal abortion started more slowly there, but in the space of six years went from modest reform, in some states, to total repeal in others and ended with a revolutionary judgement by the Federal Supreme Court. The Supreme Court strongly asserted the rights of the pregnant woman and carefully limited the role of the State with respect to the woman and her

Malcolm Potts, Peter Diggery, John Peel, "The American Revolution," in *Abortion* (Cambridge, England, 1977), Chapter 10, passim. Copyright 1977 by Cambridge University Press. Reprinted by permission of Cambridge University Press.

fetus, producing a profoundly new abortion situation in the USA—and the world. . . .

JANE ROE AND MARY DOE

By 1971, 17 cases relating to abortion had been referred to the Supreme Court. . . . The Supreme Court reviewed the laws with respect to the Fourteenth and Ninth Amendments. They concluded "that the right of personal privacy includes the abortion decision, but that this right is not unqualified and must be considered against important state interest in regulation."

The Supreme Court had to consider the appellant's contention that the fetus is a person "within the language and meaning of the Fourteenth Amendment." The Court pointed out that the Constitution only uses the word "person" in situations where it is unequivocally referring to an individual already born and concludes, considering the historical background of the situation already referred to above, that "the word 'person,' as used in the Fourteenth Amendment, does not include the unborn." They tempered this conclusion with the observation that "It is reasonable and appropriate for a state to decide that at some point in time another interest, that of the health of the mother or her potential human life, becomes significantly involved. The woman's privacy is no longer sole and any right of privacy she protests must be measured accordingly." With wisdom the Court decided, "We need not resolve the difficult question of when life begins. When those trained in the respective disciplines of medicine, philosophy and theology are unable to arrive at any consensus, the judiciary, at this point in the development of man's knowledge, is not in a position to speculate as to the answer." . . . The Court . . . summarised much of its thinking in the following paragraph:

> We do not agree that, by adopting one theory of life, Texas may override the rights of the pregnant woman that are at stake. We repeat, however, that the state does have an important and legitimate interest in preserving and protecting the health of the pregnant woman, whether she be a resident of the state or a non-resident, who seeks medical consultation and treatment there, and that there is still *another* important and legitimate interest in protecting the potentiality of human life. These interests are separate and distinct. Each grows in substantiality as the woman approaches term and, at a point in pregnancy, each becomes "compelling."

The Court considered that these interests become "compelling" at the end of the first trimester. At this point the state may set up regulations concerning the qualifications of the person to perform abortion and facilities where it is performed. Prior to that time the attending physician, "in consultation with his patient, is free to determine, without regulation by the State, that in his medical judgment the patient's pregnancy should be terminated. If that decision is reached, the judgment may be effectuated by an abortion free of interference by the state." . . .

The two dissenting Judges found

nothing in the language or history of the Constitution to support the Court's judgment. The Court simply fashions and announces a new Constitutional right for pregnant mothers and, with scarcely any reason or authority for its action, invests that right with sufficient substance to override most existing State abortion statutes. The upshot is that the people and legislators of the 50 States are Constitutionally disentitled to weigh the relative importance of the continued existence and development of the fetus on the one hand against the spectrum of possible impact on the mother on the other hand. . . .

RESULTS

The widespread availability of abortion on request led to a reduction in illegal abortion and in maternal and infant deaths and to a fall in the number of unwanted children. There was a very low mortality rate for the operation itself. . . . A number of homes for unmarried mothers closed and homes that once had a waiting list turned to placing advertisements on radio stations. Yet others, in the phrase of the *Wall Street Journal,* undertook some degree of "diversification"—for example, taking in emotionally disturbed teenagers. Guttmacher told of a medically qualified abortionist with 25 years' experience of illegal practice who complained after the passage of repeal legislation that he had not "seen a single patient for the past two weeks."

Repeal brought equality as between different ethnic groups. In one series of 200 women receiving therapeutic abortions in 1968–70, 92 percent were white. After repeal, the highest legal abortion rates were among black women. Kramer summarises the statistics (over 1970–71) and their implications:

Prior to liberalization of New York's abortion law, the total fertility rate of blacks was 2.85, as compared to 2.15 for whites. . . . In the course of just 18 months, the . . . rate of blacks fell to 2.11, the replacement level, while white fertility declined much more modestly to 1.84. . . . The evidence is compelling that . . . by enabling blacks to avert . . . births, and thereby to reproduce at a rate more compatible with the well-being of the family unit, abortion legalization may rank as one of the great social equalizers of our time.

In 1973 at least 745,400 legal abortions were performed in the USA. The Supreme Court ruling was associated both with a rise in the total number of legal abortions and with a redistribution of services. States that had previously had a restrictive attitude witnessed a two- to three-fold jump in legal abortion numbers. States that had a middle-of-the-road attitude, and often limited abortion to local residents, experienced a 70 percent increase. While states such as New York and Washington, which had previously served many out-of-state women, did approximately a quarter fewer abortions. . . .

Public Opinion and Medical Attitudes

FEMINIST GROUPS

Feminist organisations adopted the cause of abortion law reform or repeal as a rallying point. In the social history of the movement, abortion may have been as significant as a unifying goal to the movement as the movement was to changing abortion attitudes. . . .

ROMAN CATHOLIC ATTITUDES

Many Catholics attempted to distinguish their own deep convictions from the right of the community to freedom of action. The Bill repealing the abortion law in Hawaii was sponsored by Senator Vincent Yano, a Roman Catholic with ten children, and allowed to pass by a Roman Catholic Governor. In October 1970 the *Catholic Medical Quarterly* discussed the possibility that refusal to abort a woman might be interpreted as denial of that woman's rights under the law. In Pennsylvania a local group was formed called Roman Catholics for the Right to Choose. It claimed 500 members in 1971, and a spokesman said, "our Church should not attempt to use civil law to impose its moral philosophy upon our non-Catholic neighbors." In June 1972, a Gallup poll found 56 percent of Catholics believed that "the decision to have an abortion should be made solely by the woman and her physician." Dr Mary Daly, Professor of Theology in Boston College, was willing to testify on behalf of abortion law repeal before the Social Welfare Committee of the Massachusetts legislature in 1971. Several Catholic legislators in New York State voted for the repeal Bill, and that extraordinary piece of legislation would not have passed without their support. A colourful individual incident was well publicised in 1974 when a Massachusetts priest refused to baptise a baby of Catholic parents who supported the right of American women to abortion. A New York Jesuit and director of Catholics for a Free Choice later performed the baptism on the steps of the Church of the Immaculate Conception. He was dismissed from the Order, although other Jesuits continued to campaign. . . .

PUBLIC OPINION

Most systems of legislation favour the status quo. In the USA, as in several other countries, individual opinion has been more strongly in favour of liberal abortion than public institutions and group attitudes would suggest. In 1968 a Gallup survey showed that 15 percent of the public approved of liberalised abortion laws; in November 1969 a similar survey found 40 percent approved. In June 1972, 64 percent of a 1574 sample of Americans over 18 years of age and drawn from 300 localities believed that the decision to have an abortion should be made solely by the woman and her doctor. Six months earlier it had only been 57 percent, while ten years earlier, in 1962, 74 percent of Americans in a Gallup sample had *disapproved* of abortion for economic reasons. . . .

Counter Movements

By mid-1971, once the actions of the Supreme Court had been set in motion and when most communities were able to seek abortions in the liberal states, the pressure for reform weakened and the explosion of change died down.

At the same time, the passage of liberal abortion legislation in some states of America generated an organised opposition. Often largely supported by Catholics (although, as stated previously, not expressing the feelings of all Catholics), it also included some right-wing groups and individuals from Fundamentalist sects. When draft legislation attempting to widen the Californian statutes was discussed at a hearing in the State Capital in Sacramento in 1970 it was attended by such groups as United of Life, Right to Life League, Friends of the Fetus, Voice of the Unborn, League Against Neo-Fascism, and the Blue Army Against Satan. By mid-1972 the National Committee for the Right to Life had 250 affiliates. All traded on the rare case of late termination when the fetus has shown signs of life and inflated the anxieties of young nurses. . . .

Not all reaction, however, was extreme. In New York, official Roman Catholic diocesan guidelines forbade a doctor or nurse to enter into "direct participation" in an abortion operation, but specifically permitted Catholic personnel to care for a woman before and after an operation, to lay out instruments in the operating theatre, to explain the operation to the patient, and to witness consent forms. Neither was it all negative. In the spring of 1971 Archbishop Terence Cardinal Cooke of New York launched a programme called *Birthright* to aid women with unwanted pregnancies to find help or seek abortion. . . .

State and Federal Legislation

. . . Following the Supreme Court ruling in January 1973, there was a burst of abortion legislation all over the USA. Some of it came out of the ruling itself, which invited legislative attention to "protecting the health of the pregnant woman" and the "potentiability of human life," especially as the woman approaches term. Other legislation attempted to set back the Supreme Court ruling, and bills known to be unconstitutional were nevertheless passed. This method of counteraction slowed progress at the state level on the principle that it can take a long time, and cost a lot of money, to remove obstacles, even when demonstrably unconstitutional. . . .

CONSTITUTIONAL AMENDMENTS

Within eight days of the Supreme Court ruling, Congressman Hogan of Maryland moved an amendment stating, "Neither the United States, nor any State, shall deprive any human being, from the moment of conception, of life without due process of law; nor deny to any human being, from the moment of conception, within its jurisdiction, the equal protection of its laws." . . . In practice such amendments, while preventing governmental abortion services, might have no effect on private services ("if a legislative body permitted, but did not *cause* the death of any fetus, it would not, under well-established legal principles, be depriving any fetus of life without due process of law"). It would be an impossible task to enforce any "right-to-life" amendments without a wholesale invasion of the woman's right to privacy—theoretically every miscarriage would require investigation, to rule out deliberate abortion.

Amendments to the Constitution require a two-thirds majority of both houses of Congress, and subsequently need to be ratified by three-quarters of all states within seven years. By the end of 1974 no "right-to-life" amendment had accumulated more than 40 sponsors, although a minimum of 218 is needed to raise the issue in the House. . . .

The "right-to-life" amendments would disallow truly therapeutic abortions, run counter to the thought and practice of the majority of Americans, and leave the critical question of defining a "human being" unsolved. As the Supreme Court showed, it is a question which is insoluble in purely legal terms.

DEATH PEDDLER ABORTIONISTS

The substance is a report on the "Symposium for the Implementation of Therapeutic Abortion," held at the International Hotel, Los Angeles, California, January 22–24, 1971. The cast of speakers reads like a Who's Who among abortion proponents. Questions about human life in the womb or the search for grounds to justify an abortion had no place at this conference. The case was already decided. Abortion is an unquestionable good— a right of every woman. The task is to create the optimal conditions for realizing the good and exercising the right. . . .

In the world of abortion there is no need to justify the technological process of killing; rather, "compulsory pregnancy" must be justified. Most mind-boggling of all is talk of the "fetal right not to be born." What kind of sense does this make, especially since that to which the right is attributed must never be called human? What analogies would help us understand this rhetorical device or retort? A society that would expend much time and energy arguing for the right of the most helpless stage of human life to be killed—which after all is what it is—would be sick indeed. . . . In Los Angeles the woman's right to use her body as she pleases is an absolute in a relativistic value system.

I wonder how many liberals—including avant-garde Catholics of this

Calvin J. Eichhorst, a review of Paul Marx, O.S.B., *The Death Peddlers: War on the Unborn* in *America* (March 4, 1972), pp. 242–43.

cast—have vigorously opposed killing kids with napalm or bombing them from 20,000 feet but have no qualms about salting them out of the womb or sucking them up with vacuum aspirators.

A straight shot of the abortion reality such as the author provides in this report might show those who dillydally on the issue that those who are numbered among pro-life groups are not alarmists at all. We see abortion for what it is—war on the unborn.

ABORTION AND SEXUAL CASTE

Patriarchal religion—in its various forms with their varying degrees of intensity—functions to legitimate sexual caste, affirming that it is in harmony with "nature" and "God's plan." It does this in a number of interrelated ways, and I am proposing that rigidity on the abortion issue should be seen as part of the syndrome. It is less than realistic to ignore the evidence suggesting that within Roman Catholicism the "official" opposition to the repeal of anti-abortion laws is profoundly interconnected—on the level of motivations, basic assumptions, and style of argumentation—with positions on other issues. Such interconnected issues include birth control, divorce, the subordination of women in marriage and in religious life, and the exclusion of women from the ranks of the clergy. . . .

Since the condition of sexual caste has been camouflaged so successfully by sex role segregation, it has been difficult to perceive anti-abortion laws and anti-abortion ethical arguments within this context. Yet it is only by perceiving them within this total environment of patriarchal bias that it is possible to assess realistically how they function in society. If, for example, one-sided arguments using such loaded terminology as "the *murder* of the unborn *child*" are viewed as independent units of thought unrelated to the kind of society in which they were formulated, then they may well appear plausible and cogent. However, once the fact of sexual caste and its implications have been unveiled, such arguments and the laws they attempt to justify can be recognized as consistent with the rationalizations of a system that oppresses women but incongruous with the experience and needs of women. . . .

Women did not arbitrarily choose abortion as part of their platform. It has arisen out of the realities of their situation. On its deepest level, I think the issue is not as different from the issue of birth control as many, particularly liberal Catholics, would make it appear. There are deep questions involved which touch the very meaning of human existence. Are we going to let "nature" take its course or take the decision into our own hands? In the latter case, who will decide? What the women's movement is saying is that decisions will be made affecting the processes of "nature," and that women as individuals will make the decisions in matters

Mary Daly, "Abortion and Sexual Caste," *Commonweal*, 95 (Feb. 4, 1972), pp. 415–19.

most intimately concerning themselves. I think that this, on the deepest level, is what authoritarian religion fears. Surely its greatest fear is not the destruction of life, as its record on other issues reveals.

ABORTION AND PRIVACY

The Abortion Cases and their sequelae took from the American family much of its status in the law. *The Abortion Cases* themselves had created a liberty in which the most fundamental strand in the structure was deprived of support in the law—a mother was relieved of the duty to care for her offspring, if they were unborn, and was given the liberty to destroy them. With this strand removed, much of the remaining legal structure was dismantled by the cases that followed. . . . Rights that had been thought older and more fundamental than the state became delegations of power from the state. Even the right to procreate became a state-delegated power when it was exercised by a male. As the state had no power to stop abortion, it had no power to protect its delegation of procreation to a man. Parents' interest in their grandchildren was denied. Parents' interest in an [abortion] operation affecting the body, emotions, and conscience of their daughter became a matter of litigation where the state must furnish the daughter with counsel. The abortion decision became a matter of litigation between minor child and the state, which the parents need never know about. The liberty of abortion became larger than any liberty located in the family structure.

Such a view of the childbearing woman was now imputed to the Constitution that she became a solo entity unrelated to husband or boy friend, father or mother, deciding for herself what to do with her child. She was conceived atomistically, cut off from family structure. The *Boston Herald* ran a picture of young girls seeking an abortion in the same months that Justice Blackmun wrote *Planned Parenthood* v. *Danforth.* The girls wore bags over their heads. Without a family identity, these carriers of children were anonymous and parentless. As they prepared to destroy their own children, they put on masks and became faceless.

John T. Noonan, *A Private Choice: Abortion in America in the Seventies* (New York, 1979), p. 95.

Family Liberation

Some observers view recent campaigns for "women's liberation" as a delayed but logical expression of the equal rights pledged to humanity in 1776. Until relatively recently, however, the limits of work power and of technology had helped reinforce fear and prejudice to keep women in the home. Labor-market opportunities came after World War II for women to move beyond the family to other interests and roles or, if they chose as men had, to move toward other goals while also having a mate, a marriage, and a home with children. Weakened sanctions against women outside the family setting and the refinement of technology, labor, and the work force found millions of women ready to move on from being mere fill-ins, as "Rosie-the-Riveter" was for men during the war. Then as now, however, most moved into low-level clerical and sales jobs. More schooling and educational opportunity, pressures to earn more money, and greater confidence from media images and from such battles as those won for the ballot, for birth control, for higher education—all contributed to the renewed push in the 1960s to complete the American agenda for family freedom and equality, and not merely for women. Rising expectations, not despair or complete frustration under male tyranny, provided women with inspiration and energy. Soon, there was resentment, as millions of women, now permanently in the work force and with proven qualifications, found widespread evidence of unequal pay for equal work.

"What will happen to the family?" was an immediate wail over women's new demands, just as it had been ever since women began to claim their rights in the 1840s. One impact on traditional family arrangements was in the division of labor and the distribution of time and tasks in the home. If women increasingly were out of the home during business hours, or if husbands returned from work before their wives, who would have dinner waiting, children bathed and fed, and drinks mixed (in families that took "drinks")?

The "new feminism," however, went far beyond another cycle of problems of families with women in full-time careers. From the most diverse biases and ideologies there came an all-out assault on "sexism" in American life. "Male chauvinist" became as loud an epithet as "fascist" had been— with little distinction between the two and limited awareness of the tyrannies of sex and culture that drove and possessed men also. In the all-out push for full equal rights for women, every traditional female role became open to question. Not only men but the family itself were indicted for their age-old fostering of frustrating sexual-cultural identities.

The selections that follow raise a few of the issues about how families help prepare women for their various sex-linked roles. On another salient of the family front, housework is also subject to a strong moral and practical attack that at least reveals some of its concealed inanities even with machines at home and bakeries and laundromats nearby. In reading such pieces, try to distinguish questions of historical and sociological fact from assertions about family power and organization that are largely polemical. How clearly settled is it, for example, that there is little in male or female biology that dictates inviolable roles; that, on the contrary, all there is to male or female is an accident of time and circumstance? Aside from the "merely biological" (sic) techniques of mating and begetting, does all else in family life have only "culture"—and changeable culture—as its explanation? If this broad proposition is accepted, what are its implications for the future founding and furbishing of family and family life? Even if somehow "contrived," is the "culture" of the family *necessarily* suspect or limitlessly alterable for the better?

With families now open game and indictable for every aspect of their oldest work in creating sex roles, the modern spluttering American war on the father or mother "figure" becomes steadier and more bitter. Three different poems about family are presented from three well-known American women poets of the last generation. What voices of our time speak through these poems or invite such themes? In what ways, for what reasons, are fathers loved and hated in these works? What specific and practical changes in fathers and mothers could have given these children and their fathers what they seem to have missed? Had "happiness," "liberation," "fulfillment" etc. become so absolute and compelling for men and women that no family (or culture) could avoid disappointing them?

THE POLITICS OF HOUSEWORK

Though women do not complain of the power of husbands, each complains of her own husband, or of the husbands of her friends. It is the same in all cases of servitude; at least in the commencement of the emancipatory movement. The serfs did not at first complain of the power of the lords, but only of their tyranny.

—*John Stuart Mill,* On the Subjection of Women

Liberated women—very different from women's liberation! The first signals all kinds of goodies, to warm the hearts (not to mention other parts)

Pat Mainardi, "The Politics of Housework" (New York, 1970). Reprinted by permission of the author.

of the most radical men. The other signals—*housework*. The first brings sex without marriage, sex before marriage, cozy housekeeping arrangements ("You see, I'm living with this chick") and the self-content of knowing that you're not the kind of man who wants a doormat instead of a woman. That will come later. After all, who wants that old commodity anymore, the Standard American Housewife, all husband, home, and kids. The New Commodity, the Liberated Woman, has sex a lot and has a Career, preferably something that can be fitted in with the household chores—like dancing, pottery, or painting.

On the other hand is women's liberation—and housework. What? You say this is all trivial? Wonderful! That's what I thought. It seemed perfectly reasonable. We both had careers, both had to work a couple of days a week to earn enough to live on, so why shouldn't we share the housework? So I suggested it to my mate and he agreed—most men are too hip to turn you down flat. "You're right," he said, "It's only fair."

Then an interesting thing happened. I can only explain it by stating that we women have been brainwashed more than even we can imagine. Probably too many years of seeing television women in ecstasy over their shiny waxed floors or breaking down over their dirty shirt collars. Men have no such conditioning. They recognize the essential fact of housework right from the very beginning. Which is that it stinks. Here's my list of dirty chores: buying groceries, carting them home and putting them away, cooking meals and washing dishes and pots, doing the laundry, digging out the place when things get out of control, washing floors. The list could go on, but the sheer necessities are bad enough. All of us have to do these things, or get some one else to do them for us. The longer my husband contemplated these chores, the more repulsed he became, and so proceeded the change from the normally sweet considerate Dr. Jekyll into the crafty Mr. Hyde who would stop at nothing to avoid the horrors of—*housework*. As he felt himself backed into a corner laden with dirty dishes, brooms, mops, and reeking garbage, his front teeth grew longer and pointier, his fingernails haggled, and his eyes grew wild. Housework trivial? Not on your life! Just try to share the burden.

So ensued a dialogue that's been going on for several years. Here are some of the high points:

"I don't mind sharing the housework, but I don't do it very well. We should each do the things we're best at."
Meaning: Unfortunately I'm no good at things like washing dishes or cooking. What I do best is a little light carpentry, changing light bulbs, moving furniture (*how often do you move furniture?*).
Also Meaning: Historically the lower classes (black men and us) have had hundreds of years' experience doing menial jobs. It would be a waste of manpower to train someone else to do them now.
Also Meaning: I don't like the dull stupid boring jobs, so you should do them.

"I don't mind sharing the work, but you'll have to show me how to do it."

Meaning: I ask a lot of questions and you'll have to show me everything everytime I do it because I don't remember so good. Also don't try to sit down and read while I'm doing my jobs because I'm going to annoy hell out of you until it's easier to do them yourself.

"We used to be so happy!" (Said whenever it was his turn to do something.)
Meaning: I used to be so happy.
Meaning: Life without housework is bliss. *(No quarrel here. Perfect agreement.)*

"We have different standards, and why should I have to work to your standards? That's unfair."

Meaning: If I begin to get bugged by the dirt and crap I will say "This place sure is a sty" or "How can anyone live like this?" and wait for your reaction. I know that all women have a sore called "Guilt over a messy house" or "Household work is ultimately my responsibility." I know that men have caused that sore—if anyone visits and the place *is* a sty, they're not going to to leave and say, "He sure is a lousy housekeeper." You'll take the rap in any case. I can outwait you.

Also Meaning: I can provoke innumerable scenes over the housework issue. Eventually doing all the housework yourself will be less painful to you than trying to get me to do half. Or I'll suggest we get a maid. She will do my share of the work. You will do yours. It's women's work.

"I've got nothing against sharing the housework, but you can't make me do it on your schedule."

Meaning: Passive resistance. I'll do it when I damned well please, if at all. If my job is doing dishes, it's easier to do them once a week. If taking out laundry, once a month. If washing the floors, once a year. If you don't like it, do it yourself oftener, and then I won't do it at all.

"I *hate* it more than you. You don't mind it so much."

Meaning: Housework is garbage work. It's the worst crap I've ever done. It's degrading and humiliating for someone of *my* intelligence to do it. But for someone of *your* intelligence . . .

"Housework is too trivial to even talk about."

Meaning: It's even more trivial to do. Housework is beneath my status. My purpose in life is to deal with matters of significance. Yours is to deal with matters of insignificance. You should do the housework.

"This problem of housework is not a man-woman problem! In any relationship between two people one is going to have a stronger personality and dominate."

Meaning: That stronger personality had better be *me*.

"In animal societies, wolves, for example, the top animal is usually a male even where he is not chosen for brute strength but on the basis of cunning and intelligence. Isn't that interesting?"

Meaning: I have historical, psychological, anthropological, and biological justification for keeping you down. How can you ask the top wolf to be equal?

"Women's liberation isn't really a political movement."
Meaning: The Revolution is coming too close to home.
Also Meaning: I am only interested in how *I* am oppressed, not how I oppress others. Therefore the war, the draft, and the university are political. Women's liberation is not.

"Man's accomplishments have always depended on getting help from other people, mostly women. What great man would have accomplished what he did if he had to do his own housework?"
Meaning: Oppression is built into the System and I, as the white American male receive the benefits of this System. I don't want to give them up.

Postscript

Participatory democracy begins at home. If you are planning to implement your politics, there are certain things to remember.

1. He *is* feeling it more than you. He's losing some leisure and you're gaining it. The measure of your oppression is his resistance.

2. A great many American men are not accustomed to doing monotonous repetitive work which never ushers in any lasting let alone important achievement. This is why they would rather repair a cabinet than wash dishes. If human endeavors are like a pyramid with man's highest achievements at the top, then keeping oneself alive is at the bottom. Men have always had servants (us) to take care of this bottom strata of life while they have confined their efforts to the rarefied upper regions. It is thus ironic when they ask of women—where are your great painters, statesmen, etc? Mme. Matisse ran a millinery shop so he could paint. Mrs. Martin Luther King kept his house and raised his babies.

3. It is a traumatizing experience for someone who has always thought of himself as being against any oppression or exploitation of one human being by another to realize that in his daily life he has been accepting and implementing (and benefiting from) this exploitation, that his rationalization is little different from that of the racist who says "Black people don't feel pain" (women don't mind doing his shitwork), and that the oldest form of oppression in history has been the oppression of 50 percent of the population by the other 50 percent.

4. Arm yourself with some knowledge of the psychology of oppressed peoples everywhere, and a few facts about the animal kingdom. I admit playing top wolf or who runs the gorillas is silly, but as a last resort men bring it up all the time. Talk about bees. If you feel really hostile, bring up the sex life of spiders. They have sex. She bites off his head.

The psychology of oppressed people is not silly. Jews, immigrants, black men, and all women have employed the same psychological mechanisms to survive: admiring the oppressor, glorifying the oppressor, wanting to be like the oppressor, wanting the oppressor to like them, mostly because the oppressor held all the power.

5.   In a sense, all men everywhere are slightly schizoid—divorced from the reality of maintaining life. This makes it easier for them to play games with it. It is almost a cliché that women feel greater grief at sending a son off to war or losing him to that war because they bore him, suckled him, and raised him. The men who foment those wars did none of those things and have a more superficial estimate of the worth of human life. One hour a day is a low estimate of the amount of time one has to spend "keeping" oneself. By foisting this off on others, man gains seven hours a week—one working day more to play with his mind and not his human needs. Over the course of generations it is easy to see whence evolved the horrifying abstractions of modern life.

6.   With the death of each form of oppression, life changes and new forms evolve. English aristocrats at the turn of the century were horrified at the idea of enfranchising working men—were sure that it signaled the death of civilization and a return to barbarism. Some working men were even deceived by this line. Similarly with the minimum wage, abolition of slavery, and female suffrage. Life changes but it goes on. Don't fall for any line about the death of everything if men take a turn at the dishes. They will imply that you are holding back the Revolution (their Revolution). But you are advancing it (your Revolution).

7.   Keep checking up. Periodically consider who's actually *doing* the jobs. These things have a way of backsliding so that a year later once again the woman is doing everything. After a year make a list of jobs the man has rarely if ever done. You will find cleaning pots, toilets, refrigerators, and ovens high on the list. Use time sheets if necessary. He will accuse you of being petty. He is above that sort of thing—(housework). Bear in mind what the worst jobs are, namely the ones that have to be done every day or several times a day. Also the ones that are dirty—it's more pleasant to pick up books, newspapers, etc., than to wash dishes. Alternate the bad jobs. It's the daily grind that gets you down. Also make sure that you don't have the responsibility for the housework with occasional help from him. "I'll cook dinner for you tonight" implies it's really your job and isn't he a nice guy to do some of it for you.

8.   Most men had a rich and rewarding bachelor life during which they did not starve or become encrusted with crud or buried under the litter. There is a taboo that says that women mustn't strain themselves in the presence of men: we haul around 50 pounds of groceries if we have to but aren't allowed to open a jar if there is someone around to do it for us. The reverse side of the coin is that men aren't supposed to be able to take care of themselves without a woman. Both are excuses for making women do the housework.

9.   Beware of the double whammy. He won't do the little things he always did because you're now a "Liberated Woman," right? Of course he won't do anything else either. . . .

I was just finishing this when my husband came in and asked what I was doing. Writing a paper on housework. Housework? he said, *Housework?* Oh my god, how trivial can you get. A paper on housework.

Little Politics of Housework Quiz

The lowest job in the army, used as punishment is: (a) working 9–5; (b) kitchen duty (K.P.).

When a man lives with his family, his: (a) father (b) mother does his housework.

When he lives with a woman (a) he (b) she does the housework.

(a) his son (b) his daughter learns preschool how much fun it is to iron Daddy's handkerchief.

From the *New York Times*, 9/21/69: "Former Greek Official George Mylonas pays the penalty for differing with the ruling junta in Athens by performing household chores on the island of Amorgos where he lives in forced exile" (with hilarious photo of a miserable Mylonas carrying his own water). What the *Times* means is that he ought to have (a) indoor plumbing (b) a maid.

Dr. Spock said (*Redbook* 3/69): "Biologically and temperamentally, I believe, women were made to be concerned first and foremost with child care, husband care, and home care." Think about: (a) *who* made us (b) why? (c) what is the effect on their lives (d) what is the effect on our lives?

From *Time* 1/5/70: "Like their American counterparts, many housing project housewives are said to suffer from neurosis. And for the first time in Japanese history, many young husbands today complain of being henpecked. Their wives are beginning to demand detailed explanations when they don't come home straight from work, and some Japanese males nowadays are even compelled to do housework." According to *Time*, women become neurotic: (a) when they are forced to do the maintenance work for the male caste all day every day of their lives or (b) when they no longer want to do the maintenance work for the male caste all day every day of their lives.

TRAINING FOR WOMAN'S PLACE

The Presumed Incompatibility of Family and Career

If we were to ask the average American woman why she is not pursuing a full-time career, she would probably not say that discrimination had discouraged her; nor would she be likely to recognize the pervasive effects

S. L. Bem and D. J. Bem, "Case Study of a Non-Conscious Ideology: Training the Woman to Know Her Place," in *Beliefs, Attitudes and Human Affairs* by D. J. Bem (Monterey, Calif.: Brooks/Cole Publishing Company, 1970). Reprinted by permission of the publisher.

of her own sex-role conditioning. What she probably would say is that a career, no matter how desirable, is simply incompatible with the role of wife and mother.

As recently as the turn of the century, and in less technological societies today, this incompatibility between career and family was, in fact, decisive. Women died in their forties and they were pregnant or nursing during most of their adult lives. Moreover, the work that a less technological society requires places a premium on mobility and physical strength, neither of which a pregnant woman has a great deal of. Thus, the historical division of labor between the sexes—the man away at work and the woman at home with the children—was a biological necessity. Today, it is not.

Today, the work that our technological society requires is primarily mental in nature; women have virtually complete control over their reproductive lives; and most important of all, the average American woman now lives to age 74 and has her last child before age 30. This means that by the time a woman is 35 or so, her children all have more important things to do with their daytime hours than to spend them entertaining some adult woman who has nothing fulfilling to do during the entire second half of her life span. . . .

Accordingly, the traditional conception of the husband-wife relationship is now being challenged, not so much because of widespread discontent among older, married women, but because it violates two of the most basic values of today's college generation. These values concern personal growth, on the one hand, and interpersonal relationships on the other. The first of these emphasizes the individuality and self-fulfillment; the second stresses openness, honesty, and equality in all human relationships.

Because they see the traditional male-female relationship as incompatible with these basic values, today's young people are experimenting with alternatives to the traditional marriage pattern. Although a few are testing out ideas like communal living, most seem to be searching for satisfactory modifications of the husband-wife relationship, either in or out of the context of marriage. An increasing number of young people claim to be seeking full equalitarian relationships. . . .

More and more young couples really are entering marriages of full equality, marriages in which both partners pursue careers or outside commitments which carry equal weight when all important decisions are to be made, marriages in which both husband and wife accept some compromise in the growth of their respective careers for their mutual partnership. Certainly such marriages have more tactical difficulties than more traditional ones: It is simply more difficult to coordinate two independent lives rather than one-and-a-half. The point is that it is not possible to predict ahead of time on the basis of sex, who will be doing the compromising at any given point of decision.

It should be clear that the man or woman who places career above all else ought not to enter an equalitarian marriage. The man would do better to marry a traditional wife, a wife who will make whatever sacrifices his career necessitates. The woman who places career above all else would do better—in our present society—to remain single. For an equalitarian marriage is not designed for extra efficiency, but for double fulfillment.

The Woman as Mother

In all marriages, whether traditional pseudo-equalitarian or fully equalitarian, the real question surrounding a mother's career will probably continue to be the well-being of the children. All parents want to be certain that they are doing the very best for their children and that they are not depriving them in any important way, either materially or psychologically. What this has meant recently in most families that could afford it was that mother would devote herself to the children on a full-time basis. Women have been convinced—by their mothers and by the so-called experts—that there is something wrong with them if they even want to do otherwise. . . . If you don't feel that your two-year-old is a stimulating, full-time, companion, then you are probably neurotic.

In fact, research does not support the view that children suffer in any way when mother works. Although it came as a surprise to most researchers in the area, maternal employment in and of itself does not seem to have any negative effects on the children; and part-time work actually seems to benefit the children. Children of working mothers are no more likely than children of non-working mothers to be delinquent or nervous or withdrawn or anti-social; they are no more likely to show neurotic symptoms; they are no more likely to perform poorly in school; and they are no more likely to feel deprived of their mothers' love. . . .

The major conclusion from all the research is really this: What matters is the quality of a mother's relationship with her children, not the time of day it happens to be administered. This conclusion should come as no surprise; successful fathers have been demonstrating it for years. Some fathers are great, some fathers stink, and they're all at work at least eight hours a day.

Similarly, it is true that the quality of substitute care that children receive while their parents are at work also matters. Young children do need security, and research has shown that it is not good to have a constant turnover of parent-substitutes, a rapid succession of changing baby-sitters or housekeepers. . . . Clearly, this is why the establishment of child care centers is vitally important at the moment. This is why virtually every women's group in the country, no matter how conservative or how radical, is in agreement on this one issue: that child care centers ought to be available to those who need them. . . .

At the moment, the majority of . . . working women must simply "make do" with whatever child care arrangements they can manage. Only 6% of their children under 6 years of age currently receive group care in child-care centers. This is why child-care centers are a central issue of the new feminist movement. This is why they are not just an additional luxury for the middle-class family with a woman who wants to pursue a professional career.

But even the woman who is educationally and economically in a position to pursue a career must feel free to utilize these alternative arrangements for child care. For once again, America's sex-role ideology intrudes. Many people still assume that if a woman wants a full-time career, then children must be unimportant to her. But of course, no one makes this assumption about her husband. No one assumes that a father's interest in his career necessarily precludes a deep and abiding affection for his children or a vital interest in their development. Once again, America applies a double standard of judgment. Suppose that a father of small children suddenly lost his wife. No matter how much he loved his children, no one would expect him to sacrifice his career in order to stay home with them on a full-time basis—even if he had an independent source of income. No one would charge him with selfishness or lack of parental feeling if he sought professional care for his children during the day.

It is here that full equality between husband and wife assumes its ultimate importance. The fully equalitarian marriage abolishes this double standard and extends the same freedom to the mother. The equalitarian marriage provides the framework for both husband and wife to pursue careers which are challenging and fulfilling and, at the same time, to participate equally in the pleasures and responsibilities of child-rearing. Indeed, it is the equalitarian marriage which has the potential for giving children the love and concern of two parents rather than one. And it is the equalitarian marriage which has the most potential for giving parents the challenge and fulfillment of two worlds—family and career—rather than one.

PARENTS IN POEMS

Daddy

SYLVIA PLATH

You do not do, you do not do
Any more, black shoe
In which I have lived like a foot
For thirty years, poor and white,
Barely daring to breathe or Achoo.

Daddy, I have had to kill you.
You died before I had time—
Marble-heavy, a bag full of God,

Ghastly statue with one grey toe
Big as a Frisco seal

And a head in the freakish Atlantic
Where it pours bean green over blue
In the waters off beautiful Nauset.
I used to pray to recover you.
Ach, du.

In the German tongue, in the Polish town
Scraped flat by the roller
Of wars, wars, wars.
But the name of the town is common.
My Polack friend

Says there are a dozen or two.
So I never could tell where you
Put your foot, your root,
I never could talk to you.
The tongue stuck in my jaw.

It stuck in a barb wire snare.
Ich, ich, ich, ich,
I could hardly speak.
I thought every German was you.
And the language obscene,

An engine, an engine
Chuffing me off like a Jew.
A Jew to Dachau, Auschwitz, Belsen.
I began to talk like a Jew.
I think I may well be a Jew.

The snows of the Tyrol, the clear beer of Vienna
Are not very pure or true.
With my gypsy ancestress and my weird luck
And my Taroc pack and my Taroc pack
I may be a bit of a Jew.

I have always been scared of *you,*
With your Luftwaffe, your gobbledygoo.
And your neat moustache
And your Aryan eye, bright blue.
Panzer-man, panzer-man, O You—

Not God but a swastika
So black no sky could squeak through.
Every woman adores a Fascist,
The boot in the face, the brute
Brute heart of a brute like you.

You stand at the blackboard, daddy,
In the picture I have of you,
A cleft in your chin instead of your foot
But no less a devil for that, no not
Any less the black man who

Bit my pretty red heart in two.
I was ten when they buried you.
At twenty I tried to die
And get back, back, back to you.
I thought even the bones would do.

But they pulled me out of the sack,
And they stuck me together with glue.
And then I knew what to do.
I made a model of you,
A man in black with a Meinkampf look

And a love of the rack and the screw.
And I said I do, I do.
So daddy, I'm finally through.
The black telephone's off at the root,
The voices just can't worm through.

If I've killed one man, I've killed two—
The vampire who said he was you
And drank my blood for a year,
Seven years, if you want to know.
Daddy, you can lie back now.

There's a stake in your fat black heart
And the villagers never liked you.
They are dancing and stamping on you.
They always *knew* it was you.
Daddy, daddy, you bastard, I'm through.

Girl's-Eye View of Relatives

PHYLLIS MCGINLEY

First Lesson

The thing to remember about fathers is, they're men.
A girl has to keep it in mind.
They are dragon-seekers, bent on improbable rescues.
Scratch any father, you find

Phyllis McGinley, "Girl's-Eye View of Relatives," in *Times Three* (New York, 1961). Copyright © 1959 by Phyllis McGinley. Originally appeared in *The New Yorker*. Reprinted by permission of Viking Penguin Inc.

Someone chock-full of qualms and romantic terrors,
Believing change is a threat—
Like your first shoes with heels on, like your first bicycle
It took such months to get.

Walk in strange woods, they warn you about the snakes there.
Climb, and they fear you'll fall.
Books, angular boys, or swimming in deep water—
Fathers mistrust them all.
Men are the worriers. It is difficult for them
To learn what they must learn:
How you have a journey to take and very likely,
For a while, will not return.

To the Dead of Family Wars

ELIZABETH SWADOS

To boys and girls whose mothers' and fathers'
Minds took long walks down late-night halls.
To boys and girls who in baby dreams,
Saw mothers and fathers scraping the strength off selves,
Like bark off trees.
To boys and girls whose mothers and fathers put them to sleep,
Not with goodnight eyes,
But goodbye.
To boys and girls who saw their mothers' and fathers' lives spread out,
Like caged bird wings.
To boys and girls whose mothers and fathers would
One minute give a chance,
And the next close it up like
Fat cardboard books.
To boys and girls who grew slim and adolescent
While mothers and fathers swelled with
Middle-aged wool.
When mothers and fathers stared blankly,
When mothers and fathers started screaming lines from old movies.
To boys and girls whose mothers and fathers drunkenly wished
For an incredible lie
Worth keeping.
To boys and girls who now weep,
Because you wished you'd met
Your mother's or father's shadow
On a dark talk porch,

In dream rockers.
I say,
Make laws against regret,
Otherwise, you'd have to start with Adam and Eve.
The line is long and waiting.
They were unsavable by you.
They were unseen by their own parents themselves.
It is so long this song and so yearning.
To boys and girls too young to know,
When eyes are cold and scared.
To boys and girls who in baby memories
Remember a squeeze to stop crying
So violent that it could not
Have meant
Anything but violence.
To boys and girls who in their adolescence sneak
Downstairs disturbingly found
A mother and father coiled in a chair,
Locked in consequence.
I say,
There is so much mother pull,
There is so much father pull,
And so little human decency.
To boys and girls who read half-done mother and father war letters,
And watch the gardens overgrow
With weeds.
To boys and girls half secret with womanhood and manhood,
Who have to pry open too soon,
Because mothers and fathers die or kill themselves
According to the laws of angry, random
Grownup Gods.
To boys and girls weeping, now half man, half woman
Because you wished you'd got your parents' signature,
On a definite night on a talk porch,
In dream chairs holding family hands,
Talking love words,
I say,
Make laws against regret.
Otherwise, you'd have to start with Adam and Eve,
And the line waits endlessly,
And the song is so long and so yearning.

Three Classics on Child-Rearing

Of all the varieties of advice books and manuals about family matters that poured forth in the nineteenth century, those on child care probably predominated. By 1900, seventy-five years of literature for parents on bringing up babies had brought a change from an early hortatory tone and moral concern about the inborn "essence" of the child to an evolutionary emphasis on observed facts and scientific interpretation of its development. The child existed; any "essence" was created. The flood of nurture literature has only grown in the twentieth century. Those books that became "classics," and from which these selections are taken, reached sales in tens of millions. Such concern for children may suggest that worry about their nurture surpasses any other approved purpose of marriage and family life. In the family calculus of Americans, for husband and wife to fail each other or their God or their society seems increasingly less serious than to fail their children.

Try to discover and account for both the continuities and differences in emphasis and tone, i.e., detached or "involved," of these three selections. For whom do such books seem to have been written? What sense of parental responsibility is being inculcated? How much trust is being granted to adult spontaneity and how much to disciplined intelligence, at least as conceived by these authors? Is there an implication that a perfectly happy and healthy child is within grasp and that failure to produce one represents some ultimate fault of character, will, and mind? To what degree is the American family depicted as primarily a child-rearing and child-perfecting institution, the setting and source of the child-centered culture that foreigners have repeatedly discerned in the United States?

INFANT CARE

DEPARTMENT OF LABOR,
CHILDREN'S BUREAU,
July 22, 1914.

SIR: I transmit herewith the second monograph in the Care of Children series.

This issue discusses the care of the baby to the close of the second year.

Mrs. Max West, *Infant Care,* U.S. Department of Labor, Children's Bureau (Washington, 1914), pp. 7, 30–31, 59–63.

It is written by Mrs. Max West, who wrote the first number of this series, entitled "Prenatal Care," and the same method has been used in its preparation—namely, exhaustive study of the standard literature on the hygiene of infancy as well as consultations with physicians, nurses, and other specialists in this field.

Like the preceding one of the series, it is addressed to the average mother of this country. There is no purpose to invade the field of the medical or nursing professions, but rather to furnish such statements regarding hygiene and normal living as every mother has a right to possess in the interest of herself and her children. It endeavors to present the accepted views of the best authorities at the present time. . . .

Feeding

PROCESS OF DIGESTION

In order to comprehend the principles which underlie the proper feeding of infants, it is well to understand what is involved in the process of digestion and what food elements are needed for the growth, maintenance, and repair of the body. . . . All these are found in milk, and in no other food which the infant is capable of digesting. Therefore milk is the one proper infant food.

BREAST FEEDING

The milk necessary for the normal healthy growth of every infant mammal, including the human species, is created for it in the breast of its mother. . . . No other argument than this simple physiological one should be needed to induce a thoughtful mother to nurse her baby at the beginning of his life, but if further demonstration is needed the evidence on every hand of the comparative failure of artificial feeding, at least as far as young babies are concerned, should be convincing.

Statistics gathered from this country and many others show that breast-fed babies have a much greater chance for life than those who are bottle fed, and also that the infant illnesses, not only those of the digestive tract but many other varieties, afflict bottle-fed infants much oftener and much more seriously than those who have breast milk. But not only does breast milk protect the nursing baby from illness and increase materially his chance for life, but it practically insures that his development shall proceed in a normal, orderly fashion. . . . Undoubtedly in many cases grown people would have escaped many of the defects and deficiencies with which they have to contend if they had passed the period of infancy in perfect health.

These are the impelling reasons why mothers should nurse their babies. Other less important reasons are that if the mother takes care of the baby herself it is much easier to nurse than to feed by a bottle, that breast milk is practically free from disease germs, and that it is fed to the baby at a uniform temperature from beginning to end of the nursing. . . .

Habits, Training, and Discipline

Habits are the result of repeated actions. A properly trained baby is not allowed to learn bad habits which must be unlearned later at great cost of time and patience to both mother and babe. The wise mother strives to start the baby right.

SYSTEMATIC CARE

In order to establish good habits in the baby, the mother must first be aware what they are, and then how to induce them. Perhaps the first and most essential good habit is that of regularity. This begins at birth, and applies to all the physical functions of the baby—eating, sleeping, and bowel movements. The care of a baby is readily reduced to a system unless he is sick. Such a system is not only one of the greatest factors in keeping the baby well and in training him in a way which will be of value to him all through life, but reduces the work of the mother to the minimum and provides for her certain assured periods of rest and recreation.

As a sample of what is meant by a system in baby care the following plan is suggested, which may be variously modified to suit particular cases:

6 A.M., baby's first nursing.
Family breakfast; children off to school.
9 A.M., baby's bath, followed by second nursing.
Baby sleeps until noon.
12 to 12.30, baby's noon meal.
Out-of-door airing and nap.
3 to 3.30 P.M., afternoon nursing.
Period of waking.
6 to 7 P.M., baby's supper and bed.

It is quite feasible to have the baby's night meal at 11.30 or 12 o'clock, in order to give the mother a chance to spend an occasional evening in pleasant recreation. . . .

BAD HABITS

Some of the bad habits which a baby learns are these:

Crying.—Crying ought not to be classed as a bad habit without some modification, for although a well-trained baby does not cry very much he has no other means of expressing his needs in the early months of life, and his cry ought to be heeded. But when a baby cries simply because he has learned from experience that this brings him what he wants, it is one of the worst habits he can learn, and one which takes all the strength of the mother to break. Crying should cease when the cause has been removed. If the baby cries persistently for no apparent cause, the mother may suspect illness, pain, hunger, or thirst. The first two of these causes will manifest other symptoms, and the actual need for food may be discovered by frequent weighing. But if finally, after careful scrutiny of all these conditions, no cause for the crying can be found, the baby probably wants to be taken up, walked with, played with, rocked, or to have a light, or to have some one sit by him—all the result of his having learned that crying will get him what he wants, and sufficient to make a spoiled, fussy baby, and a household tyrant whose continual demands make a slave of the mother. It is difficult to break up this habit after it has once been formed, but it can be done. After the baby's needs have been fully satisfied he should be put down alone and allowed to cry until he goes to sleep. This may sound cruel, and it is very hard for a young mother to do, but it will usually take only a few nights of this discipline to accomplish the result. In some cases persistent crying may be due to causes not readily discernible by the mother; in this event, the opinion of a good doctor as to the cause of the crying should be sought. . . .

Bed wetting.—It requires great patience and persistence on the mother's part to teach the baby to control the bladder. Some babies may be taught to do this during the day by the end of the first year, but it is ordinarily not until some time during the second year that this is accomplished. It is necessary to put the baby on the chamber at frequent intervals during the day. Bed wetting may be due to some physical weakness if it persists in children 3 years old and over. A doctor should be consulted. In ordinary cases, it may suffice if no liquid food is given in the late afternoon and if the baby is taken up the last thing before the mother retires.

EARLY TRAINING

The training in the use of individual judgment can be begun even in infancy: a child should early be taught to choose certain paths of action for himself; and if he is continually and absolutely forbidden to do this or that he is sometimes seriously handicapped later, because he does not know how to use his own reasoning faculties in making these choices. On the other hand, obedience is one of the most necessary lessons for children to learn. A wise mother will not abuse her privilege in this respect by a too-exacting practice. For the most part she can exert her control otherwise than by commands, and if she does so her authority when exercised will have greater force and instant obedience will be more readily given.

Most of the naughtiness of infancy can be traced to physical causes. Babies who are fussy, restless, and fretful are usually either uncomfortable in some way because they have not been properly fed and taken care of, are sick or ailing, or have been indulged too much. On the other hand, babies who are properly fed, who are kept clean, and have plenty of sleep and fresh air, and who have been trained in regular habits of life, have no cause for being "bad" and are therefore "good."

It must not be forgotten that the period of infancy is a period of education often of greater consequence than any other two years of life. Not only are all the organs and functions given their primary education, but the faculties of the mind as well receive those initial impulses that determine very largely their direction and efficiency through life. The first nervous impulse which passes through the baby's eyes, ears, fingers, or mouth to the tender brain makes a pathway for itself; the next time another impulse travels over the same path it deepens the impression of the first. It is because the brain is so sensitive to these impressions in childhood that we remember throughout life things that have happened in our early years while nearer events are entirely forgotten. If, therefore, these early stimuli are sent in orderly fashion, the habits thus established and also the tendency to form such habits will persist throughout life.

CONDITIONED BEHAVIOR, 1925

The home we have with us—inevitably and inexorably with us. Even though it is proven unsuccessful, we shall always have it. The behaviorist has to accept the home and make the best of it. His task is to try to get the mother to take a new view of what constitutes the care of an infant— of her responsibility for her experiment in child bearing.

Since the behaviorists find little that corresponds to instincts in children, since children are made not born, failure to bring up a happy child, a well adjusted child—assuming bodily health—falls upon the parents' shoulders. The acceptance of this view makes child-rearing the most important of all social obligations.

The behaviorists believe that there is nothing from within to develop. If you start with a healthy body, the right number of fingers and toes, eyes, and the few elementary movements that are present at birth, you do not need anything else in the way of raw material to make a man, be that man a genius, a cultured gentleman, a rowdy or a thug.

So much for general behavior, the behavior that you can directly observe in your children. But how about the things you cannot observe? How about *capacity, talent, temperament, personality,* "mental" constitution and "mental" characteristics, and the whole inward emotional life? . . . How about its loves—its affectionate behavior? Isn't that "natural"? Do you mean to say the child doesn't *"instinctively"* love its mother? Only one thing will bring out a love response in the child—stroking and touching its skin, lips, sex organs and the like. It doesn't matter at first who strokes it. It will "love" the stroker. This is the clay out of which all love—maternal, paternal, wifely or husbandly—is made. Hard to believe? But true. A certain amount of affectionate response is socially necessary, but few parents realize how easily they can overtrain the child in this direction. It may tear the heart strings a bit, this thought of stopping the tender outward demonstration of your love for your children or of their love for you. But if you are convinced that this is best for the child, aren't you willing to stifle a few pangs? Mothers just don't know, when they kiss their children and pick them up and rock them, caress them and jiggle them upon their knee, that they are slowly building up a human being totally unable to cope with the world it must later live in. . . . You can see invalidism in the making in the majority of American homes. . . .

Should the Mother Never Kiss the Baby?

There is a sensible way of treating children. Treat them as though they were young adults. Dress them, bathe them with care and circumspection. Let your behavior always be objective and kindly firm. Never hug and kiss them, never let them sit in your lap. If you must, kiss them once on the forehead when they say good night. Shake hands with them in the morning. Give them a pat on the head if they have made an extraordinarily good job of a difficult task. Try it out. In a week's time you will find how easy it is to be perfectly objective with your child and at the same time kindly. You will be utterly ashamed of the mawkish, sentimental way you have been handling it. . . .

If you haven't a nurse and cannot leave the child, put it out in the backyard a large part of the day. Build a fence around the yard so that you are sure no harm can come to it. Do this from the time it is born. When the child can crawl, give it a sandpile and be sure to dig some small holes in the yard so it has to crawl in and out of them. Let it learn to overcome difficulties almost from the moment of birth. The child should learn to conquer difficulties away from your watchful eye. No child should get commendation and notice and petting every time it does something it ought to be doing anyway. . . . In conclusion, won't you then remember when you are tempted to pet your child that mother love is a dangerous instrument? An instrument which may inflict a never healing wound, a wound which may make infancy unhappy, adolescence a nightmare, an instrument which may wreck your adult son or daughter's vocational future and their chances for marital happiness.

Night and Day Time Care

THUMB SUCKING

. . . The effect of thumb sucking upon the child's personality is the most serious aspect of all. It is an infantile type of reaction which when carried over beyond the age of infancy ends in a pernicious habit almost impossible to break. Indeed if carried through adolescence in the modified form of nail biting, finger biting, cuticle picking or finger picking, it becomes practically impossible to break. It is then classed as a neurotic trait.

The act brings with it a kind of soothing or quieting effect like a drug. As long as the individual is allowed to engage in it he is perfectly docile in all of his reactions. Scold him about it, try to check it and he becomes irritable and uneasy. Apparently when the child has his fingers in his mouth *he is,* speaking broadly, *blocked to all other stimuli.* Hence the persistent thumb sucker cannot be as easily made to respond to toys and other objects upon which we normally train children. The outside world doesn't get a good chance at him. He doesn't conquer his world. He becomes an "exclusive," an auto-erotic. With his fingers safely in his mouth the child may sometimes not even react to dangerous stimuli. Our own experiments at Johns Hopkins show that even when stimuli which are known to produce fright are shown to the thumb sucking child they lose their power to arouse him.

How can we correct thumb sucking? The answer is, *cure it during the first few days of infancy.* Watch the baby carefully the first few days. Keep the hands away from the mouth as often as you are near the baby in its waking moments. And always when you put it into its crib for sleep, see that the hands are tucked inside the covers—and if you examine the sleeping infant from time to time see when you leave it that the hands are under the covers (when the child gets older—over one year of age—you will want to see that the hands are left *outside* the covers when put to bed. . . .

If the habit develops in spite of this early scrutiny, consult your physician about the infant's diet. Tell him about the thumb sucking. If after changes in the diet thumb sucking persists, then take more drastic steps to break the habit. Sew loose white, canton flannel mitts with no finger or thumb divisions to the sleeves of the night gown and on all the *day dresses, and leave them on for two weeks or more—day and night.* So many mothers leave them on only at night. Unless the child is watched every moment the hand will at one time or another get back to the mouth. You must be careful to see that the dress or night gown is fastened securely but not tightly at the throat—else if the infant is persistent he will learn to disrobe himself to get at his hands. If the habit still persists make the material of the mitts of rougher and rougher material.

I have tried many methods that will not work. Those clumsy aluminum mitts are ineffective. The child bangs himself over the head and eyes and nine times out of ten gets out of them in one way or another. Pasteboard tubes over the elbow joint are used in some good hospitals but they are cruel. The child cannot rub an irritation or scare away a fly or mosquito. Coating the fingers with bitter aloes has never worked out for me. Occasionally the infant goes right ahead without baulking at the aloes, or if he does make a wry face or two he soon goes on serenely. I've never had any success with taping the finger. Either he picks the tape off after a time (if one year of age or over) or else sucks the finger, tape and all.

I have tried punishment—sharply rapping the finger with a pencil. This is beautifully effective while the experimenter is around but at night the habit reasserts itself. Scolding and corporal punishment likewise have proved wholly ineffective.

DR. SPOCK, 1976

A Letter to the Reader of This New Edition

There are hundreds of small changes in this third edition, twenty-two years after the book first appeared and eleven since the publication of the second edition. Many of them were made necessary by scientific advances, such as the Sabin oral polio vaccine, measles vaccine, cold-mist humidifiers for croup and colds. . . .

The principal change that has occurred in my own outlook on child rearing has been the realization that what is making the parent's job most difficult is today's child-centered viewpoint. I don't merely refer to the few parents who kowtow to their tyrannical children or the larger number who have been intimidated by all the advice they've received from us pediatricians, psychologists, psychiatrists and pedagogues, and are hesitant to give their children the firm leadership they need, for fear they might do the wrong thing. I mean the tendency of many conscientious parents to keep their eyes exclusively focused on their child, thinking about what he needs from them and from the community, instead of thinking about what the world, the neighborhood, the family will be needing from the child and then making sure that he will grow up to meet such obligations. Even to hear this latter point of view expressed is a little startling to many Americans.

I think we've brought up our children not only less ready to do their part in solving the world's urgent problems but actually less happy in the sense of less fulfilled. For human beings, by and large, can only be really happy when they feel they are part of something bigger than themselves and when a lot is expected of them and when they are living up to these expectations.

But the reason why, as parents and professionals, we haven't taught our children their place in the world and their obligation to it is that most of us have not been at all clear about our own place in the universe or about the meaning of human existence, the way people were in earlier centuries. . . .

The main reason for this 3rd revision (4th edition) of *Baby and Child Care* is to eliminate the sexist biases of the sort that help to create and perpetuate discrimination against girls and women. Earlier editions referred to the child of indeterminate sex as he. Though this in one sense is only a literary tradition, it, like many other traditions, implies that the masculine sex has some kind of priority.

In discussing the clothes and playthings parents buy their children and the chores they assign them, I took it for granted that there should be a

deliberate distinction between boys and girls. But this early-childhood differentiation begins in a small way the discriminatory sex stereotyping that
ends up in women so often getting the humdrum, subordinate, poorly
paid jobs in most industries and professions, and being treated as the
second-class sex.

I always assumed that the parent taking the greater share of the care
of young children (and of the home) would be the mother, whether or
not she wanted an outside career. Yet it's this almost universal assumption
that leads to women feeling a much greater compulsion than men to sacrifice
a part of their careers in order that the children will be well cared for.
Now I recognize that the father's responsibility is as great as the mother's.

Enjoy Your Baby

Don't be afraid of him. You'd think from what some people say about
babies demanding attention that they come into the world determined to
get their parents under their thumb by hook or by crook. This isn't true.
Your baby is born to be a reasonable, friendly human being.

Don't be afraid to feed him when you think he's really hungry. If you
are mistaken, he'll merely refuse to take much.

Don't be afraid to love him and enjoy him. Every baby needs to be
smiled at, talked to, played with, fondled—gently and lovingly—just as
much as he needs vitamins and calories. That's what will make him a person
who loves people and enjoys life. The baby who doesn't get any loving
will grow up cold and unresponsive. . . .

Love and enjoy your child for what he is, for what he looks like, for
what he does, and forget about the qualities that he doesn't have. I don't
give you this advice just for sentimental reasons. There's a very important
practical point here. The child who is appreciated for what he is, even if
he is homely, or clumsy, or slow, will grow up with confidence in himself,
happy. He will have a spirit that will make the best of all the capacities
that he has, and of all the opportunities that come his way. He will make
light of any handicaps. But the child who has never been quite accepted
by his parents, who has always felt that he was not quite right, will grow
up lacking confidence. He'll never be able to make full use of what brains,
what skills, what physical attractiveness he has. If he starts life with a handicap, physical or mental, it will be multiplied tenfold by the time he is
grown up. . . .

We've been through a big transition. It's hard to get any perspective
on this topic without taking a historical view. Styles in strictness vary from
one period to another. The Victorian Age was quite strict, for instance,
about manners and modesty. In the twentieth century, especially after
World War I, a reaction set in. Several factors pushed it along. The great
American pioneers in educational research, like John Dewey and William
Kilpatrick, showed that a child learns better and faster with a method of
teaching that makes allowance for his particular readiness to progress and
that recognizes his eagerness to learn if the subject matter is suitable.

Freud and his followers showed that harsh toilet training or frightening a child about sex can distort his personality and lead to neurosis. Studies of delinquents and criminals revealed that most of them had suffered more from lack of love in childhood than from lack of punishment. These discoveries, among others, encouraged a general relaxation in child discipline and a greater effort to give children what they seemed to need as individuals. . . .

But it's not possible for a civilization like ours to go through such a change of philosophy—it really amounts to a revolution—without raising doubts in many parents' minds and without getting some parents thoroughly mixed up. It's basic human nature to tend to bring up your children about as you were brought up. It's easy enough to pick up new ideas about vitamins and inoculations. But if your upbringing was fairly strict in regard to obedience, manners, sex, truthfulness, it's natural, it's almost inevitable, that you will feel strongly underneath about such matters when raising your own children. You may have changed your theories because of something you've studied or read or heard, but when your child does something that would have been considered bad in your own childhood, you'll probably find yourself becoming more tense, or anxious, or angry than you imagined possible. This is nothing to be ashamed of. This is the way Nature expects human beings to learn child care—from their own childhood. This is how different civilizations have managed to remain stable and carry on their ideals from generation to generation.

Parents who become confused with new theories are often of two kinds. There are, first of all, those who have been brought up with too little confidence in their own judgment. If you don't dare trust yourself, you have to follow what someone else says, willy-nilly. A second group are those parents who feel that they were brought up too severely. They remember the resentment they felt toward their parents at times, and they don't want their children to feel that way about them. But this is a very difficult approach. If you want to raise your children the way you were raised, you have a definite pattern to follow. You know just how obedient, how helpful, how polite, you want them to be. You don't have to stop and think. But if you want to treat them quite differently than the way you were treated—more indulgently, for instance, or more as equals—you don't have any pattern of how far to carry it. If things begin to get out of hand—if, for example, your child begins to take advantage of your permissiveness—it's harder to find your way back onto the right track. The child makes you mad, all right, but the madder you get the guiltier you feel for fear you'll step into the very pattern you were determined to avoid. . . .

Stick to your convictions. I think that good parents who naturally lean toward strictness should stick to their guns and raise their children that way. Moderate strictness—in the sense of requiring good manners, prompt obedience, orderliness—is not harmful to children so long as the parents are basically kind and so long as the children are growing up happy and friendly. But strictness is harmful when the parents are overbearing, harsh, chronically disapproving, and make no allowances for a child's age and individuality. This kind of severity produces children who are either meek and colorless or mean to others.

Parents who incline to an easygoing kind of management, who are satisfied with casual manners as long as the child's attitude is friendly, or who happen not to be particularly strict—for instance, about promptness or neatness—can also raise children who are considerate and cooperative, as long as the parents are not afraid to be firm about those matters that do seem important to them.

When parents get unhappy results from too much permissiveness, it is not so much because they demand too little, though this is part of it. It is more because they are timid or guilty about what they ask or because they are unconsciously encouraging the child to rule the roost.

What Are Your Aims in Raising a Child?

The rearing of children is more and more puzzling for parents in the twentieth century because we've lost a lot of our old-fashioned convictions about what kind of morals and ambitions and characters we want them to have. We've even lost our convictions about the purpose of human existence. Instead we have come to depend on psychological concepts. They've been helpful in solving many of the smaller problems but they are of little use in answering the major questions.

Flaming Youth

Concern for the future and for the "world the young will inherit" has been constant in family history since colonial days. It is less clear when young people became identified as distinctive generations, as in the phrase "the current generation," or when youth became both a cause and symbol of degeneracy and cultural despair. There are clear signs of such identifications from at least the 1850s, with concurrent traditional wails about the failure of the family and God's judgment on family life for producing threats to the republic and offenses to heaven. Later cries in the 1920s were probably more pervasive and more shrill, but they cannot be gauged adequately as mere incidents in American "postwar disillusion" or as part of a general revolt at the time against village mores and puritanism.

The proclaimed excesses of youth in the 1920s were a compound of sex, alcohol, tobacco, dancing, dress, automobiles, vocabulary. What extremes there were, were rooted in earlier, deep changes in the familial and social roles of young people. A new youth seems almost inevitable by 1920, given what had happened to family tasks, work, and the work force, in education and means of recreation. One usable formula posits that for a century before 1920 the age of adulthood and responsibility was progressively postponed as more young Americans went to school but, at the same time, the age of admission to adult pleasure, tastes, and styles was progressively lowered. By 1920 the variety of pleasures—movies, cars, sports—and their easier accessibility for all seem to have invited the "wild carryings-on" among those eighteen to twenty-two or so who seemed so shocking. One says "seems," because for such phenomena statistical evidence is impossible and/or unavailable. Some facts and common sense suggest that most youth did not yet have the leisure, money, or freedom that "flaming" or even a "flivver" required. For most, perhaps the flame of a cigarette or that between lovers on the local movie screen marked the limits of "rebellion." Still, complaints about youth's attitudes and mores came from even remote communities, and the battles fought about the charges suggest a national sense of apocalypse and Armageddon. Even those commentators who realistically resisted the wilder tales seem agreed that families had less to say to and less control over their children and that the general culture, especially school and "peer group" influences, was making large gains at the expense of the home. Whatever the case, a distinctive youth culture outside the family seems to have become an American staple by 1930.

This selection from a barrage of comment raises long-range issues about familial purposes and models and controls for children. To what extent had play, in a broad sense of the word, become a general American possibility? Families in America's rich industrial society enjoyed or anticipated shorter hours, strong purchasing power, high productivity, and a torrent of goods. What problems thus follow for families used to thinking of diligent preparation of children for hard work and moral seriousness, not frivolity? Young people had better education, falling economic value, entered the labor market later (in deference to "respect for childhood"), and in countless ways had their needs and status protected by American law and ideas of equality and freedom. Weren't these conditions, however abused, part of the general promise of a pursuit of happiness? Since 1900 what had the young seen happen to classic family chores that had made life less frivolous, tasks like baking bread, doing the laundry, and "putting up" fruits and vegetables? What were they to do with more leisure, suddenly finding at their doors easy, cheap and "auto" transportation? Like adults, they too were customers for movie houses, theaters, and dance halls. For the best reasons of soft pedagogics they were learning less about jobs in school and being asked to master less for all their longer schooling. They too found churches more "social" and religion more secular, and also found the mere hand labor they had to sell outdated by machinery. From all this, does what has happened to youth in aspirations and attitudes as well as behavior reveal what is happening to America as an advanced industrial society?

THE CASE AGAINST THE YOUNGER GENERATION

Sensational criticism of our young people has been reaching us from time to time from the churches, the colleges, and numerous scandalized members of the younger generation itself. If the newspapers are less outspoken than a year ago, when THE DIGEST investigated these matters by questionnaire, the change appears to be not so much a result of improvement in our young people as of indifference toward conditions that have lost their "news punch." To many an observer this indifference is alarming, as it seems to indicate that we are acquiescing in what such observers call a moral and spiritual revolution whose consequences can hardly be other than subversive of the principles upon which manners and morals are based. Indeed, "revolution" is not the harshest word we hear. One critic prefers to term it "devolution." Another calls it "devilution.". . .

"The Case Against the Younger Generation," *Literary Digest*, June 17, 1922.

From the Stanford "Chaparral."

A COLLEGE VIEW

This picture, with an accompanying bit of verse, represents a typical, if humorous, conception of the frivolous young girl of to-day. It appeared first in a Stanford University college paper, and was copied by *The Collegiate World*, which circulates in the various colleges. The accompanying verses run:

Who was this wild and winsome coot
That made poor Adam pull the boot
And taste of that forbidden fruit?
A Flapper.

This Cleopatra maiden fair
For whom great Cæsar tore his hair,
Who was this vamp so debonair?
A Flapper.

Who was this biddy called Salome
That robbed John Baptist of his dome,
The one that made mere man leave home?
A Flapper.

Who is it now that flashes by
With scanty clothes and dropping eye,
For whom some sap would gladly die?
A Flapper.

Who strokes the profs upon their nobs,
And on their shoulders gently sobs
While some swell mark from them she robs?
A Flapper.

Who it is spends their hard-earned kale
Who makes this plant a woeful tale
Who is more deadly than the male?
A Flapper.

"The Flapper"

Perhaps the crux of the question may be stated in this way: Is society, especially the younger part of it, undergoing a revolution in morals, in manners, or in both?

In so broad and diverse a land as America, conditions, of course, are not everywhere the same, and the replies fall naturally into two classes, those revealing conditions that are deplorable, and those which show that the young folks are returning to normalcy. . . .

"There is such a thing as Bolshevism in the moral and spiritual spheres," declares George W. Sandt, D.D., editor of the *Lutheran;* and, in his opinion:

We are suffering from its effects at the present time. A spirit of libertinism is abroad among our youth. There is little or no respect for parents and superiors in many of our homes and schools and churches. There is an ominous absence of reverence for things sacred, of noble ambition and earnest moral purpose, and a bold and brazen defiance of decency and modesty in dress and speech and conduct. Women paint and powder and drink and smoke, and become an easy prey to a certain class of well-groomed and well-fed highlivers, whose chief business is 'to pluck the blush of innocency from off the cheek of maidenhood and put a blister there.' Pleasure—madness and love of luxury have become epidemic.

In view of . . . this complaint, one asks, not unnaturally, "What are we going to do about it?" The questionnaire has brought in a curiously uniform array of answers. While many of them emphasize the need for a revival of old-fashioned religious instruction and many more demand a reform of the movies and of current fiction, an overwhelming majority declare that improvement can come only from influences brought to bear in the home. If girls dress indecently, dance shockingly, go traveling around the country at night in chaperonless automobiles, encourage the "snuggle puppy" in his "petting," smoke cigarets, drink whatever they can find to drink, swear like pirates, and talk freely of things they ought to leave unmentioned, our correspondents ask, "Where are their mothers?" If boys are as wild, where are their fathers? All through the mass of replies from horrified onlookers runs this censure of the American home. The great need, we are told, is a reassertion of parental authority. Indeed, it is probable that this view would be indorsed even by the correspondent who asserts that in his own community the youngsters have been helped along the road to righteousness by the attentions they are receiving from the Ku Klux Klan. . . .

In the meantime, members of the Parents League of Brooklyn have decided not only that conditions are capable of improvement but also that a certain set of edicts may help in the process. League members, reports the *New York Times,* will see that several blue laws for the young are enforced in their own families, and will try to extend the movement to other Brooklyn homes. The rules which are to be applied to flappers run as follows:

1. Hours for evening parties are limited from 8:30 to 12. It's curfew after midnight.
2. Parties are to be held only on Friday and Saturday nights.
3. Simple, refined clothes are to be worn at all times.
4. Chaperones must be present at all parties.
5. Chaperones will accompany the girls home.
6. Censorship over the plays and movies to be attended.
7. Improper dancing forbidden.
8. No refreshments served after dances.
9. Not more than one party to be attended on the same evening.

Here are the rules which the smaller boys and girls, those of primary school age, must observe:

1. Entertain in small groups.
2. Serve very simple refreshments at parties.
3. All games must be supervised.
4. Use simple favors and no prizes.
5. Parties must end at 8:30 P.M.

6. Simple afternoon dress is to be worn on all occasions.

7. No movies or theaters, except those recommended by the school or investigated and approved by parents.

"We can do nothing with the older boys and girls, whose customs have become more or less established," said Mrs. Otto Affeld, . . . president of the league. Girls over 18 years of age are left to whatever rules their parents prescribe.

INTERVENING

A Rationale for Intervention

Besides the growing sense of crisis about the family after 1900 and the piecemeal but rapid increase in the agencies and proposals to help the family, a philosophy or, at least, reasoned grounds for "intervention" from outside the family seemed essential. Jane Addams and other early social workers had variously described what Addams called the subjective and objective necessities for settlement-house work among the urban poor, one of the most effective of the early interventions. The subjective grounds were the sentiments of young, well-educated American women that they were called to do more than accept the easily entered, but too often "empty," life of middle-class marriages and homemaking. The objective basis was the growing size and seeming irreduceability of distress among millions of families—the problems would not go away— and the inability of many families to fend adequately for themselves against the new giants of the city, the corporations, the bureaucracies, and hostile other Americans. Very often answers seemed to lie in public intervention.

Florence Kelley of New York City was a leader in that effort. Her book on laws that were needed was not an exercise in abstractions, for it helped bring new agencies and new laws in both New York and Washington to deal with problems that families could not or would not handle for themselves. One early victory for Miss Kelley was the establishment of the federal government's Children's Bureau in 1914, and another was a series of New York laws trying to control and eliminate child labor within the state. Kelley also fought hard for compulsory, longer, improved schooling.

If child labor could be more decent and realistic than it was in 1905, would more general schooling for adolescents remain quite as compelling an ideal as it seemed then? In the subsequent light of what universal schooling has meant for children, has mandating it until they reach the later teens made children more discerning, better citizens and voters, more moral, more happy, wiser family members, healthier mates, safer drivers, or less susceptible to the corruptions of money, power, drugs, nicotine, or alcohol? Were attempts like Kelley's to shrink parents' control over the labor of their children, and to substitute more schooling for jobs, as good for the family or the children as "intervention" unequivocally pretended? Did the heated battle for an "ethical gain" obscure the forces within much-vaunted "education" that could alienate children from parents, disturb family life, and also sunder children from work ideals and skills that most adolescents, at least, should never have lost?

Most of the issues connected generally with intervention in this century are implicit in the early Kelley assumptions about the "ethical gain" of restricting child labor and lengthening education. But did the good of the child, of the family, of the state, and of society conflict much more with each other than enthusiasts for this or that ethical gain through intervention understood? What ironies came in the wake of the success of this famous plea? The article, several generations later, from 1978 (see p. 666), should suggest some.

LEGISLATING FOR BETTER FAMILIES

The Right to Childhood

The noblest duty of the Republic is that of self-preservation by so cherishing all its children that they, in turn, may become enlightened self-governing citizens. The children of to-day are potentially the Republic of 1930. As they are cherished and trained, so will it live or languish a generation hence. The care and nurture of childhood is thus a vital concern of the nation. For if children perish in infancy they are obviously lost to the Republic as citizens. If, surviving infancy, children are permitted to deteriorate into criminals, they are bad citizens; if they are left illiterate, if they are overworked and devitalized in body and mind, the Republic suffers the penalty of every offense against childhood.

An unfailing test of the ethical standards of a community is the question, "What citizens are being trained here?"

Where young children die by thousands, the ethical standards of the community are, so far, bad. For science has long shown how to minimize infant mortality. The failure of a community to follow the teachings of science in this direction is a moral dereliction of the gravest character. The death from preventable disease of thousands of young children in the tenement houses of the city of New York, occurring year after year, from generation to generation, stamps the ethical standards of the metropolis as bad beyond belief. For the exposure of infants on the highways of China is not more obvious to the people of China, than the preventable mortality of infants in New York City has for years been obvious to the people of the United States. It is, moreover, one of the incredible things of our civilization that this excessive infant mortality, from generation to generation, is left to local boards of health and to local philanthropies, whose inability to cope with it its persistence has long conspicuously proved.

The legislation of the last few years, intended to secure improved housing

Florence Kelley, *Some Ethical Gains Through Legislation* (New York, 1905), pp. 3–99, passim.

for the people of New York City, although it is still wholly inadequate, constitutes one of the fundamental ethical gains of our generation. For it marks the beginning of that social protection of infant life without which the right to childhood is illusory; and for want of which thousands of potential citizens in the great cities have, within the last half century, been lost to the Republic.

It would seem at first glance to be a universally acknowledged right of the human being to receive during the first months of life food, clothing, shelter and nurture without even passive coöperation on its own part beyond swallowing food, wearing clothing and sleeping in a quiet, warm, clean place. Yet within one generation it has been necessary to enforce with fines and imprisonment, statutes and ordinances for the purpose of stopping large numbers of infants less than one year old from being used to contribute to the income of their owners by being exposed in the arms of begging women upon the streets of the great cities. The colder the night and the later the hour, the more overwhelming the appeal to the pity of the passer-by and the greater the pecuniary value to its owner (not by any means always its mother), of such an instrument for securing income.

Before the enactment of the statute which put an end in New York City to this misuse of infants, a belief was current that, if the public should cease to contribute to their support, starvation might be the alternative for both woman and child. But women and infants do not starve in New York. The suppression of this exploitation of infants is a clear gain for the moral sense of the community, not only because the lives and health of the babies are protected, but because a perverted and unwholesome outlet for unreasoning pity is cut off, and a higher form of reasonable care for childhood is substituted therefor.

Following babyhood, the years from the first to the seventh birthday are so far held sacred to sleep, play and rapid growth that most states exempt children during this period from compulsory attendance at school. The belief is generally held, that the strain of school life is excessive for the health and welfare of so many children at this age as to make compulsion of doubtful public benefit.

YOUNG CHILDREN WORKING IN TENEMENT HOUSES

Yet, in the spring of 1903, a kindergartner in New York City, on missing from her class an Italian brother and sister aged four and five years, and visiting them in their homes, was told by their mother that they could not be spared from their work to go to the kindergarten. They were engaged in wrapping colored paper around pieces of wire, to form the stems of artificial flowers which the family manufactured in their tenement home, the older sisters making the leaves and petals, and the other members of the group forming whole flowers and sprays.

The children were pointed out to the attendance agent who explained that, even under the statute of 1903, the compulsory attendance law exempted the younger child for three years and the older for two, assuming that each would then enter school on reaching the seventh birthday. The factory inspector, when the facts were brought to his attention, observed that the case did not appear to constitute a violation of the factory law, since the children were not receiving wages, and the group at work did not exceed the number authorized under the license to manufacture artificial flowers in their tenement home.

The question then arose whether such employment constituted cruelty under the statutes of New York. The danger attending taking the children and their parents into court upon a charge of cruelty was, that it might be found that this parental exploitation of young children within the home did not technically constitute cruelty in the judicial sense; and such a decision might then be construed by the colony of artificial flower makers as approval of similar employment of small children upon a scale even larger than at present. Or, such employment might be held to constitute cruelty, the children might be removed from the custody of their parents and sent, perhaps at the cost of the city, to one of the subsidized sectarian institutions, and a whole new series of hardships thus caused, not less grave than those already suffered by the children.

Such exploitation of very young children within the family circle is practised whenever manufacture in tenements is tolerated. These children are types of employees in New York, Chicago, Philadelphia, and all other cities in which tenement dwellings are turned into workshops. This form of domestic overwork of little children can be eliminated by the effective prohibition of manufacture in the tenements (a measure sure to be enacted within a few years in the interest of the public health) and in no other way. Until this prohibition is enacted and enforced, there will be, wherever the needle-trades and other industries are carried on in homes, virtually no lowest limit above the age of three years for the employment of children in families. For children can pull out basting threads, sew on buttons, paste boxes and labels, strip tobacco and perform a multitude of simple manipulations as readily as they can learn the kindergarten occupations. . . .

YOUNG CHILDREN IN DOMESTIC WORK

Far more difficult to reach by statute is the oppression of little girls under the burden of household drudgery at cost of school attendance. The Little Mothers' Association registers one of the bitter ironies of child life in New York City. The girls whose dreary lives it cheers are under the legal age for working for wages. Many of them attend school just enough to save their parents from the penalties attaching to keeping a truant in the family, but so irregularly that progress with the class is impossible and school life is one long discouragement. For these children, whose exploitation is largely due to sheer parental shiftlessness and selfishness, that new provision must in the long run prove a godsend which now requires a child before beginning to work for wages, to show that it has completed the curriculum of the first five years of the public schools and has, within

Groups of messenger boys like these were common sights around the many telegraph offices
that dotted large American cities around 1905
when this picture was taken. The boys received
little or no wages from the telegraph companies
but raced off to deliver the "wires" for whatever
tips they could get. Since making money was
their principal objective, and since they knew
streets, houses, and neighborhoods well, they
were also available for other types of both licit
and illicit communications. Such trade made
them into one of the symbols of the wickedness
of child labor and of the dangers of "the streets"
for children. The warning sign of the time attests
to these concerns. Lewis W. Hine, the photographer, produced many similar pictures of messenger boys and newsboys for the National Child
Labor Committee. This view comes from a series
entitled "Street Trades."   *Library of Congress*

the last preceding school year, attended school one hundred and thirty days. This measure places a premium, in the shape of wage-earning capacity at the fourteenth birthday, upon steady progress in school and, therefore, upon regular attendance. When this fact penetrates the minds of the parents, the "little mothers" will doubtless find less opposition at home to their efforts to escape from the baby, the washtub, and the scrubbing brush, and to take refuge in the schoolroom.

The statute thus reënforces parental duty and stays the pressure of drudgery upon defenseless children within the family. Unfortunately, it is too slight and indirect. The "little mothers" need direct help and protection almost as much as the tiny makers of artificial flowers in the tenements. The next step might well be the adoption of an objective standard applied to the child herself. If it were required that a girl must weigh eighty pounds and measure sixty inches in height, the test to be made with scales and measuring rod in the school, besides being able to read fluently and write legibly in the English language, before leaving school, the danger of oppression of little girls within the family circle would be greatly reduced.

No modern community recognizes the old *patria potestas,* the Roman right of the father to put his child to death. But in the intimate circle of family life there lingers deeply rooted the belief in the right of either parent to exploit childhood for money, or for personal relief from work by the substitution of the child in the performance of domestic tasks. And the public conscience is slower to recognize the need of intervention in this than in any other form of cruelty.

With the statutory prolongation of childhood in the form of child labor laws, there emerges the need of assuring to the children the practical benefit due them with their legal immunity from work. In the Republic, childhood must be sacred to preparation for citizenship. Hence the public schools offer instruction in the interest of the community. But for the children here under discussion, mere offering is not enough. There must be compulsion incarnate in the attendance agent. Through this official the community enters the home, as it enters the workshop, the store and the factory, to enforce upon the adult the child's claim to this high privilege. There is no longer discussion with the parent as to the advantage to himself accruing from the education of his child. The child's right has been recognized and made a part of the life of the community. . . .

MESSENGER BOYS

All the circumstances attending the work of telegraph and messenger service render it especially unfit for young, growing boys. The irregular hours, and the still more irregular meals, picked up in the intervals of message serving and consisting commonly of bread or cake with the vilest coffee, contribute to sapped vitality and broken health. Such meals foster the craving which seems universal among workers upon the streets, for cigarettes and liquor. The incessant temptation to overcharge is in turn enhanced by the longing for these stimulants. The temptation to purloin money and to overcharge makes thieves of hundreds of children. The ease with which overcharges may be collected and the relative safety from detection sap the habit of honesty in nearly all messenger boys. The writer has had wide experience of working boys and has never known a messenger who did not, sooner or later, succumb to the temptation to overcharge. . . .

Let us assume that, in spite of all its disadvantages, some rare boy survived a long term of employment in the telegraph and messenger service and emerged with digestion unhurt by irregular meals and coffee drinking; nerves sound in spite of lost sleep and cigarette-smoking; character untainted by evil companionship and the overwhelming temptation to dishonesty. What has such a boy to show for the years he has spent in delivering messages? He has no trade, no craft, no skill of any kind, no discipline of mind or body to fit him for rising in any direction. The irregularity of his work has unfitted him for any sustained effort when he has passed the age for accepting children's wages. One of the problems of the settlements is to find work for boys who have outgrown the messenger's uniform. The lads have learned nothing which is of any value to them. There is no versatility in them which might make them desirable employees in the hobble-de-hoy age. Their eagerness to make a record of speed and promptness has all oozed away. They are no longer dazzled at the prospect of earning $4.00 a week. They know most exactly the purchasing power of the wages they are likely to receive, and balancing the fatigue and exertion against the pay, they simply sit still and wait for something to turn up, rather better pleased if nothing can be found for them to do. Not every boy is morally ruined by this work; but the earlier he enters upon it, and the longer he remains in it, the greater the probability of his ruin. . . .

Child, State, and Nation

In the century since the movement for child labor laws began with Sir Robert Peel's act, in 1802, effort has been devoted chiefly to placing about the labor of children restrictions based upon age or school attendance; and these have been found unsatisfactory by reason of the willingness of parents to perjure themselves. It is the tendency of the present to consider the fitness of the child itself for the prospective occupation. Under the present statute of New York, for instance, a child must be "of normal development and in sound health" before receiving the certificate of the local board of health without which it cannot legally begin to work.

Effective legislation involves the child, the parent, the employer, the officials charged with the duty of enforcing the statutes, and the community which enacts the laws, provides the schools for the children when these are prohibited from working, supports and authorizes the officers who enforce the laws, prescribes penalties for their violation and assists dependent families in which children are below the legal age for work. In the long run, the effectiveness of the laws depends upon the conscience of the community as a whole far more than upon the parents and the employer taken together. . . .

An effective child labor law rests upon certain prohibitions, among which are the following:

LABOR IS PROHIBITED

(1) for all children under the age of fourteen years,
(2) for all children under sixteen years of age who do not measure sixty inches and weigh eighty pounds,
(3) for all children under sixteen years of age who cannot read fluently and write legibly simple sentences in the English language,
(4) for all children under the age of sixteen years, between the hours of 7 P.M. and 7 A.M., or longer than eight hours in any twenty-four hours, or longer than forty-eight hours in any week,
(5) for all children under the age of sixteen years in occupations dangerous to life, limb, health or morals.

THE CHILD

Effective legislation requires that before going to work the child satisfy a competent officer appointed for the purpose, that it
(1) is fourteen years of age, and
(2) is in good health, and
(3) measures at least sixty inches and weighs eighty pounds, and
(4) is able to read fluently and write legibly simple sentences in the English language, and
(5) has attended school a full school year during the twelve months next preceding going to work.

THE PARENT

Effective child-labor legislation requires that the parent
(1) keep the child in school to the age of fourteen years and longer if the child has not completed its required school work, and
(2) take oath as to the exact age of the child before letting it begin to work, and
(3) substantiate the oath by producing a transcript of the official record of the birth of the child, or the record of its baptism, or some other religious record of the time of the birth of the child, and must
(4) produce the record of the child's school attendance, signed by the principal of the school which the child last attended. . . .

THE SCHOOL

The best child-labor law is a compulsory education law covering forty weeks of the year and requiring the consecutive attendance of all the children to the age of fourteen years. It is never certain that children are not at work, if they are out of school. In order to keep the children, however, it is not enough to compel attendance,—the schools must be modified and adapted to the needs of the recent immigrants in the North and of the poor whites in the South, affording instruction which appeals to the parents as worth having, in lieu of the wages which the children are forbidden to earn, and appeals to the children as interesting and attractive. These requirements are so insufficiently met in the great manufacturing centers of the North, that truancy is in several of them, at present, an insoluble problem. No system of child-labor legislation can be regarded as effective which does not face and deal with these facts.

The evolution of the vacation school and camp and play centers promises strong reënforcement of the child-labor laws, which are now seriously weakened by the fact that the long vacation leaves idle upon the streets children whom employers covet by reason of the low price of their labor, while parents, greedy for the children's earnings and anxious lest the children suffer from the life of the streets, eagerly seek work for them. Nothing could be worse for the physique of the school child than being compelled to work during the summer; and the development of the vacation school and vacation camp alone seems to promise a satisfactory solution of the problem of the vacation of the city child of the working class. . . .

More important, however, than the enactment of the foregoing provisions is the maintenance in the community of a persistent, lively interest in the enforcement of the child-labor statutes. Without such interest, judges do not enforce penalties against offending parents and employers; inspectors become discouraged and demoralized; or faithful officers are removed because they have no organized backing while some group of powerful industries clamors that the law is injuring its interest. Well-meaning employers grow careless, infractions become the rule, and workingmen form the habit of thinking that laws inimical to their interest are enforced, while those framed in their interest are broken with impunity.

Upon parents there presses incessant poverty, urging them to seek opportunities for wage-earning even for the youngest children; and upon the employers presses incessant competition, urging them to reduce the payroll by all means fair and foul. No law enforces itself; and no officials can enforce a law which depends upon them alone. It is only when they are consciously the agents of the will of the people that they can make the law really protect the children effectively.

A UNITED STATES COMMISSION FOR CHILDREN

If the right to childhood is recognized, it follows that the welfare of the children is a legitimate interest of the nation, for the right rests upon the future citizenship of the children. The interest of the nation, as such, has not hitherto found articulate expression, and it is desirable that it should do so. It is therefore suggested that there be constituted a Commission for Children, whose functions should be to correlate, make available, and interpret the facts concerning the physical, mental and moral condition and prospects of the children of the United States, native and immigrant.

Crusades for Home and Family

T These extracts from the archives of well-known American organizations date from the first decades of this century. They are only
samples of the record of an extraordinary offensive and growing
network to save the American family and home. What threats to home,
daughters, and motherhood called these people to arms? What specific
ideals did they wish to rescue or preserve? How did these women reconcile
their new worldly activism—they were attacked sarcastically as the "woman-
club type"—with the traditional confinement of women to the home,
kitchen, nursery, and garden? Are there class or other social distinctions
discernible within these documents—that is, between some types of homes
and others? With what different implications for organizing public policy
and social agencies? Do these organizations seem liberal, conservative,
progressive, or something else? If their words suggest confidence and control, rigidity and discipline, sin and redemption, solidarity and uniformity
in family styles and objectives, are these descriptions of an America and
a family life with which Americans are still comfortable? Or can we sense
some deep change of "tone" in ways of thinking about the family as the
twentieth century moved on?

NATIONAL CONGRESS OF MOTHERS

Tenth Annual Report

In May, 1907, at Los Angeles, California, the National Congress of Mothers will celebrate the tenth anniversary of its existence.

The organization came into being in the spring of 1897, holding its
first meeting in Washington, D.C. From the Atlantic to Pacific is a stride
that well typifies the growth of the work.

The first call sent out was born of the needs of parents for a fuller
comprehension of their duties toward their own children. The call today

Phoebe Apperson Hearst Correspondence and Papers, The Bancroft Library, University
of California, Berkeley.

The National Congress of Mothers

Earnestly invites you to participate in the

First International Congress

to be held in

Washington, D. C.
March 10=17, 1908

Subject of Consideration

The Welfare of the Child

President Roosevelt opens International Congress by welcoming delegates at White House and giving address

President Roosevelt says:

"I take the heartiest interest in your First International Congress to deal with the welfare of the children.

"I am delighted that you have planned to bring the representatives of the nations together to confer upon such a subject.

"What I can personally do to help you will, of course, be done.

"I shall hope to welcome your delegates at the White House, and there to greet them, and to express to them my deep realization of the importance of their work and my profound sympathy with it."

Governors of Every State in the Union are Appointing Delegates to this Congress

The
National Congress of Mothers of the United States

has been studying the needs of childhood for the past ten years, and through its local circles and annual conferences has endeavored to unify the best thought of the nation on the wisest measures to be adopted to secure the highest physical, mental and moral development of the coming race.

With the purpose of stimulating world-wide interest in these subjects, this International Congress has been called.

Suggested Topics

Helps to Parents | Child Study; Physical, Mental, Spiritual.

Moral Training | In the Home; the Sunday School; the Day School.

Education |
Compulsory Education.
Stimulation of Parental Responsibility; Parent-Teacher Associations.
The School Curriculum; Physical Exercises.
Manual Training; Household Economies.
Industrial Schools.
Coeducation.

Provision for the Helpless and Defective |
The Deaf; the Blind.
The Epileptic and Insane.
The Mentally Deficient and Dependent.

Preventive and Protective Agencies |
Playgrounds; Public Baths.
Day Nurseries.
Libraries; Boys' and Girls' Clubs.

Treatment of Erring Children |
Causes of Delinquency, Truancy, Vagrancy, Theft, Immorality.
Placing out in Homes.
Juvenile Courts; Probation.
Reformatories.

Legislation |
Special Schools; Regulation of Child Labor.
Protection of the Home and the Child.
Marriage and Divorce.
Tenement Laws.
Pure Food Laws.
Juvenile Courts.
Establishing Parks and Playgrounds.

What is your city, state or nation doing to raise the standards of care and guardianship of children?

has widened until it embraces in its scope not only the needs of parenthood but the needs of childhood everywhere.

The Congress has correspondents in every State of the Union. Letters of inquiry as to methods of work and requests for help have been received from nearly every country in the world.

From the beginning the Congress has stood for the development of a wiser, better trained parenthood. To this end it has enlisted the coöperation and aid of specialists, educators, physicians, lawyers and others, and has accumulated valuable material which is available for and has been used by thousands, who have never been able to come into close personal touch with the Congress in the way of attending conferences. Much of this part of the work is done by correspondence in the home.

The Congress publishes many leaflets, which have proved extremely useful. The reports of its meetings, containing papers and discussions, are printed from time to time in the Congress magazine which is issued monthly with the exception of July and August. The Congress also has a full list of loan papers. The papers are largely by specialists. They are clearly typewritten, well mounted and encased in a heavy manila envelope. They can be borrowed for three weeks, for 10 cents each.

Departments of Work

Trained Parenthood
Books and Book Lists
Child Labor
Household Economics
Education
Juvenile Court and Probation Work
Legislation
Civic Betterment
Parent-Teacher Association
The Press

Influence of the Congress

The work of the Congress extends from the homes of the wealthiest and most cultured to the homes of the poorest and the lowliest, and the help it gives is eagerly sought by thousands of mothers. It is applying the best thought of earnest, intelligent men and women to the problems of child-care throughout the land. It is bringing to the solution of these problems the results of the psychological and biological investigations of our learned men and women, and is influencing organizations and individuals to coöperate in this movement for more intelligent parenthood, truer insight into child nature, and better understanding of all that tends to its fullest and highest development.

This is an age of specialization, and on what more important object can the mothers of the nation focus their thought and work than on the children?

The wisdom of experienced and intelligent motherhood, applied to all that pertains to childhood, whether in home, school, institution, reformatory or factory, can do more to raise the social and civic conditions of our country than any other one thing. The children of the world need the loving protection and consideration of enlightened womanhood, and organized motherhood stands for the same wise, loving thought and care for the children of the world that a wise, loving mother gives to her own little ones.

CALIFORNIA CONGRESS OF MOTHERS

Activities of the New Century Club of Oakland, 1917

Neighborhood work begun on private lines in that section of West Oakland known as "The Point" in 1898 resulted in the formation of the Oakland New Century Club two years later. In 1902 the Club became a part of the State Federation and also of that larger body, the General Federation of Women's Clubs.

> To establish and maintain schools of domestic science, including cooking and sewing schools; to promote the establishment and maintenance of boys clubs and girls' clubs; to establish and maintain free libraries and reading rooms; to promote the establishment and maintenance of kindergarten schools, vacation schools, public playgrounds, and public parks; to promote in any and all ways the proper care, education, and training of the young, to the end that they may become self-sustaining and intelligent, useful members of society,

have been the aims of the Club from the very first. Some of these things have been achieved; some we are still working for. We have seen cooking, sewing, and manual training installed in the public schools of Oakland since the days when we were pioneers in the field, and now the kindergarten, which we maintained for so many years, is part of the public school system, profiting by all that is latest and best in kindergarten methods, while holding its own under the fostering care of the New Century Club. We have worked in the past—and we shall leave no effort untried in our attempts to obtain a playground for the throngs of children who live "South of the tracks." These children are too far removed from De Fremery Park, and the overcrowded condition of the Prescott school playground leaves no room for the very little ones.

Through the various committee chairmen and our resident worker, a finger is kept on the pulse of the activities that tend toward the social and industrial welfare of the community. The neighbors take their problems to the house mother, who is generally able to point the avenue of relief. Sometimes the Health Department of the city is appealed to, sometimes the Probation Officer is needed, or a policeman, or it may be a question for the Associated Charities or visiting nurse, or only a trifling matter that can be adjusted by a note to a schoolteacher. But however simple or complex the problem, the clubhouse is the center, and the Club stands (through its representatives) ever ready to inform, guide, or advise.

A garment class for young girls is held every Saturday, where the girls are taught not only to make up garments from *new* material but are instructed in the art of renovating—which includes ripping, pressing, and turning mother's old dress into a new frock for Liza Lou!

A club of young women—all laundry workers—meets every Tuesday evening for an hour and a half of crocheting, embroidery, or plain sewing, followed by a half hour of music. Except for sickness, there are never any absentees Tuesday evenings.

A class of twenty mothers of the neighborhood meets twice a month for demonstration cooking at the capable hands of Mrs. E. Booge. Mrs. Booge, who gives her services, teaches not only how to concoct appetising, economical dishes; she raises housework to an art beautiful, and inspires in her hearers a love for the hitherto despised duties.

Besides these clubs of the altogether utilitarian sort, there are social, gymnastic, and basketball clubs. Five clubs of girls ranging from seven to sixteen years of age meet afternoons after school hours; three small boys' clubs also meet after school and Saturdays, and three older boys' clubs have the use of the gymnasium four evenings of each week. There are occasional community dances on the free evenings.

The great unsolved problem of this and every other club in the State is the Americanization of the alien. Since August 1914, hundreds of young men—mostly Greeks and Austrians—have come to our city. They are so numerous and so herded together that they do not yet see the need of learning our language. How to make them *see* the need, how to make them avail themselves of our night schools, is the question that confronts every one of us.

The New Century Club numbers but 50 members. The dues are small, but the members are prodigious workers, and with the aid of card parties, dances, and an annual Christmas bazaar, the necessary money is raised to defray the running expenses of the house, provide a Christmas present for every kindergarten child, and perform other acts of philanthropy that come within our ken.

CAMP FIRE GIRLS

Constitution and By-Laws, 1912

ARTICLE I   Name.

Section 1.   The name of this corporation shall be: THE CAMP FIRE GIRLS, INC.

ARTICLE II   Purpose.

Section 1.   The Purpose of this corporation shall be to perpetuate the spiritual ideals of the home under the new conditions of a Social community, through the organization of girls and women into units divided by age, into Camp Fires and a Junior Organization.

Section 2. The organization shall endeavor to aid in the formation of the habits making for health and vigor, the out-of-door habit and the out-of-door spirit.

Section 3. The organization shall endeavor to show that the common things of daily life are the chief means of beauty, romance and adventure.

Section 4. The organization shall endeavor to devise and put into use ways of measuring and creating standards of woman's work.

Section 5. The organization shall endeavor to give to girls and women incentive ideals and objects for doing "team work," for "keeping step."

Section 6. The organization shall endeavor to foster intimate relations between mothers and daughters by giving status and social recognition to the work of the Mother.

Section 7. The organization shall endeavor to develop among girls and women a sympathetic understanding of the newer economic relationships into which women are coming.

Section 8. The organization shall definitely undertake to improve the social life in the community of each of its constituent groups through the promotion of such community social activities as pageants, celebrations, social centers, organized vacations, and tramping, amateur drama, and music.

ARTICLE III   Local Membership.

Section 1. Any girl of good moral character, at least twelve years of age, is eligible to election as a member of any "Camp Fire" of the organization.

Section 2. Any girl of good moral character under twelve years of age is eligible to election as a member of the junior order of this organization by whatever name it may be called.

Section 3. The members of the local "Camp Fires" shall be divided into three classes, designated as follows, and such other classes as may be created:

> a.   "Wood Gatherers."
> b.   "Fire Makers."
> c.   "Torch Bearers."

Section 4. The qualification for admission to membership in the foregoing classes shall be as set forth in the Camp Fire Girls Manual, to be hereafter adopted by the Executive Committee of the Board of Directors of the Camp Fire Girls.

ARTICLE IV.   Camp Fires and the Junior Order.

Section 1. The unit of organization shall be called a "Camp Fire." The membership of any local Camp Fire shall consist of not less than six nor more than twenty girls. Each Camp Fire shall be presided over by a woman of suitable age, character and attainment, who shall be called the "Guardian of the Fire."

Section 2. The Board of Directors shall have power to make rules and regulations for the conduct and control of a junior order of Camp Fire Girls, consisting of those under twelve years of age. . . .

Minutes of National Board Meeting, 1912

There seems to be no question but that we have found the way to the hearts and lives of girls. In spite of our not having given out any publicity material for six months, without public propaganda of any kind, without having any copies of the manual for six months, the work has spread by word of mouth and from girl to girl till on February first there were 48,000 Camp Fire girls—that is only nine months after the work was given to the public.

Mothers say that the girls have a new attitude toward the home—common interests between mother and daughter have been deepened; and the fact that beauty and romance are to be found in everyday things has been made evident.

Teachers, settlement, and church workers say that it increases the effectiveness of their work as nothing else has ever done.

The question is no longer what it was a year ago:—does this movement possess a universal appeal to girls? Now it is this:—Can we secure that strong conservative guidance which will so lead, control, and use this enthusiasm that it shall result in a true and deep spiritual movement? This work seems so imperative that at the request of our Board of Managers the President has resigned from the Sage Foundation to give his entire time to the Camp Fire Girls.

As to our needs:—A sufficient fund to carry on the work as it now stands is our most urgent need. . . .

Our deepest, unfilled need is to establish regular means of communication with the Guardians—for in their hands the success of the entire work lies. They need to be kept in contact with the best work done everywhere and, of not less importance, to be constantly exposed to contagious enthusiasm. There were on February first 1,578 Guardians. The cheapest and most effective available mode of communication is to print a four-page circular letter or bulletin every month. This can be done for $100 per month.

We need to get college girls interested and intelligent on this work that they may act as Guardians when they return from college to their own communities. A capable woman should be devoted to this work both by visitation and by correspondence. An equally able woman should spend her time in contact with Guardians now in the field—strengthening and inspiring their work. Two field Guardians for these services with their expenses would not cost per month less than $700.

Making Families Healthier

M ost of the literature about American families in the twentieth century stresses moral concerns: happiness, freedom, liberation, growth. And much of this literature is directed to (not necessarily consumed by) serious people schooled well beyond literacy. A preoccupation with ideals, however, may blind us to the power of the nonideological elements that have recently so deeply affected the making and conduct of families. Changes in demography, work, public sanitation affect *all* Americans (however differently) and especially the vast majority beyond or beneath "ideas" flowing from the media and schools.

This selection from Morris Fishbein, M.D., one of the "household names" among home health guides, recapitulates the stunning changes in the conditions of family physical health since 1900. In the century after 1800 the American life expectancy at birth had increased about one third, but between 1900 and 1980 that same index had jumped another 50 percent, with an average life expectancy at birth well beyond 70 years, and with prospects lengthening the longer one lived.

What are the types of change in health conditions, in Dr. Fishbein's account, that seem most important since 1900? Try to compare the American changes with similar categories and statistics for Western European nations, and Latin American, Asian, or African lands.

However admired and desired, longer lives have not necessarily meant healthier ones. Other physical ailments endure or replace conquered enemies like cholera or yellow fever, and psychological disorders increasingly seem to add to the burdens of longer lives. How, then, do greater awareness of life and the enlarged rituals of good health, like brushing teeth, affect family expectations generally and, specifically, the allocation of income for health and attitudes toward and provisions for bad health. Does "ailing"—a chronic condition of earlier centuries—seem to become unnatural and morally discomforting to hear about or see? What demands can the sick, especially children and the aged, make on the well? How do rising expectations for good health affect the family sense of life purpose? Are statistical possibilities for good health at least as tantalizing and frustrating for the family as they are encouraging and energizing?

MODERN FAMILY HEALTH

Changing Life Expectancy

In 1959 . . . the life cycle of man is about 70 years, contrasted to only 24 hours for some insects, around 10 years for a dog, 20 years for a horse, 100 years for some elephants and 300 for others, 1000 years for a whale. The life cycle is the years one is constituted to live barring infectious disease or accident. The seventy years of the life cycle of man may be divided into infancy, childhood, adolescence, adulthood, old age, and senility. Infancy would include the years from birth to six years of age; childhood up to 13 years, at which age puberty occurs and adolescence begins. Adulthood begins from 18 to 21 years of age, old age from 55 to 60, and senility somewhere after 70. Middle age is usually the years from 40 to 55.

Most of the increase in life expectancy has come as a result of new discoveries in medicine which have overcome the tremendous rates for infant mortality which used to prevail in the past. Before 1900 as many as one-fourth of all the babies born died before they were one year old. Today the rate is around one-tenth of what it used to be. Improvements in prenatal care, obstetrical care, and the elimination of most of the severe infectious diseases of childhood are responsible. Such diseases as diphtheria, scarlet fever, whooping cough, measles, infantile paralysis, dysentery, tuberculosis and pneumonia are no longer constant threats to health and life. . . . Through the discovery and use of the antibiotic drugs practically all infections are being controlled if diagnosed promptly. Among the most significant has been the control of the venereal diseases.

The great epidemics of the past which devastated great nations have been abolished by the adoption of sanitary measures, by inoculation against those for which preventive vaccines and serums are available and by the continued practice to some extent of isolation and quarantine. Thus poliomyelitis, which at various times has affected from 25,000 to 50,000 Americans in a single year, involved in 1957 around 8000 people. This result was brought about by the discovery of the Salk vaccine and attempts at immunization of everyone under forty years of age.

Smallpox, which for centuries was one of the great scourges of mankind, is now practically nonexistent in the United States due to the use of smallpox vaccination. . . . Diphtheria used to be a serious and highly fatal disease. The death rate dropped from 40 per million population in 1900 to the disappearing point in 1950. This disease is controlled by inoculation with a toxoid. . . .

Among the most fatal of diseases during the early parts of the century were the infections of the intestinal tract such as typhoid fever and various forms of dysentery and attacks by intestinal parasites. Typhoid fever is so rare today that many physicians have never seen a case. This advance has been brought about by good sanitation which provides pure food and water, disposal of sewage, and also by inoculation with typhoid and paratyphoid vaccines. . . .

Venereal diseases used to produce vast amounts of disability and destruction of the tissues of human beings. . . . Then came specific chemotherapy for syphilis with the use of Ehrlich's salvarsan or arsphenamine; and finally, the monumental discovery that penicillin could control these diseases resulted in curing gonorrhea in 24–48 hours and syphilis in a week. . . .

Dental caries which used to destroy the teeth of growing children are beginning to yield to the fluoridation of water supplies and to widespread practice of dental hygiene.

The functions of seeing and hearing are being conserved similarly by knowledge of the causation of blindness and deafness and by direct attacks through modern methods of prevention and cure. . . .

The facts that have been stated are an indication of the tremendous change that has taken place in our knowledge of the incidence of illness and the causes of death in the last fifty years. This rapid change is continuing and has resulted in the creation of a new problem—namely, the care of the aged. Around 1900 about 2 percent of the population were over 65 years of age. In 1950, 8 percent of a much larger population are over 65 years of age. In 1960 the United States will have about 15 million people over 65 years of age, of which 2 million will be over 80 years of age. Out of this has come a new specialty called geriatrics, which is care of the aged, as contrasted with pediatrics, the care of the child.

The older people suffer with chronic diseases and disabilities which give great concern. Practically no one dies of old age as such. They succumb rather to conditions that involve single organs, such as the lungs, the liver, the kidneys, the heart, the stomach, or the brain. . . .

One of the greatest areas of discovery in the twentieth century has been the field of so-called dietary deficiency diseases. With the determination that such conditions as scurvy are due to a deficiency of vitamin C, rickets to a deficiency of vitamin D, xerophthalmia to a deficiency of vitamin A, polyneuritis a result of deficiency of thiamin, increasing attention has been given to studies of the vitamins and most of these conditions brought under control. . . .

Significant also in modern health control is the great advance of surgery as a method not so much for the removal of mutilated and defective portions of the body, as for reconstruction and rehabilitation with restoration of normal physiology. . . .

You and Your Doctors

Medicine was practiced formerly almost wholly in the doctor's office and in the patient's home. Today the hospital is the center of medical care. In the United States about ten thousand hospitals are available, varying in size from ten beds to more than three thousand beds. The hospitals also are frequently specialized, including children's hospitals, orthopedic hospitals, eye hospitals, mental hospitals, tuberculosis sanitariums, and even hospitals devoted entirely to cancer and skin diseases.

In 1900 hospitals catered largely to surgical operations and severe infections. In 1960 the chief work of the hospitals concerns obstetrics and accidents. . . .

THE GENERAL PRACTITIONER

The old-time doctor depended largely on listening, feeling, thumping, and observing, utilizing his five senses, but modern science has invented devices which extend and amplify every one of these senses. For instance, the old-time doctor would look at his patient, observing particularly the color of the white of the eye, the tongue, the palm of the hand, and the rest of the skin, and would make a quick guess as to whether or not anemia was a factor in the patient's illness. The modern physician simply requests the laboratory technician to get some of the patient's blood, which is then studied by a variety of techniques which determine exactly the amount of hemoglobin, or red coloring matter, and the numbers and varieties of red blood cells, white blood cells, and other cells; thus the physician has an exact index of the quality of the blood. . . .

COMMUNITY RESOURCES

In our larger cities the available medical resources are so complex and numerous that many physicians are themselves unaware of all the community has to offer. For the exceedingly poor, the public hospitals provide emergency services, clinics, dispensaries, beds for general medicine, surgery, and obstetrics, pediatrics departments, psychiatric departments, and even such highly specialized services in some instances as respiratory centers. Many communities provide, in addition, diagnostic clinics which are available particularly for tuberculosis and venereal diseases. The Veterans Administration has hospitals scattered throughout the United States for general medical services, and some hospitals particularly for cancer. In addition, the United States Public Health Service has its great health center in Bethesda, Maryland, together with numerous institutes of research, and also hospitals in seaports which carry on the marine services established more than a hundred years ago. The hospitals in towns and villages are most frequently community hospitals. As the towns grow, various organizations, particularly those of the churches, Presbyterian, Methodist, Baptist, Catholic, and Jewish, have often developed their own hospitals. In larger cities there are municipal hospitals, county hospitals, and often state hospitals. . . . In any large city the welfare agencies have available lists of medical institutions and medical services which may be utilized by those in the city. The structure of medical services is thus definitely complicated, but it is now so vast that no one need go without medical service provided he can determine where to call upon it.

One Career in Public Health, 1915–1965

This selection should suggest within the lifetime and activities of one professional man the extraordinary growth of public organizations to "intervene" in family health since the early years of this century. What are the implications of each and all of these activities for traditions of family autonomy and semi-isolation from society, for the role and claims of experts, for the scope of government, for free choice and legal obligation in building a family life? Which of these seem directed specifically at the poor, which to society at large, and with what general lines of differentiation?

DR. R. A. BOLT

Essentials in a maternal and child health program as developed during fifty years in which R.A.B. has taken an active part:

Importance of complete and accurate birth registration:
Birth registration area organized in 1915.
Birth registration area completed in 1933.
Prenatal care on part of competent physician from as early in pregnancy as possible.
Supervision and training of midwives.
Instruction of expectant mothers and fathers.
Prevention of ophthalmia neonatorium [and] state laws for prophylaxis.
Breast feeding.
Improvement in milk supplies and pasteurization of milk.
Improvement in hospitalization for obstetric cases.
Study of maternal mortality.
Cost of obstetric services.

Richard Arthur Bolt was a prominent physician in the San Francisco area who spent much of his professional life in organizing child and family health activities. This selection is from his *Reminiscences Concerning His Career in Public Health,* reproduced from original documents owned by The Bancroft Library, University of California, Berkeley. Courtesy, The Bancroft Library.

TENEMENT HOUSE DEPARTMENT OF THE CITY OF NEW YORK
Borough of MANHATTAN

DIPHTHERIA

The following is a 1903 tenement inspection report form, partly printed and partly handwritten, from the Tenement House Department of the City of New York, Borough of Manhattan. The inspector's findings and recommendations include:

I found the facts to be as follows:

Accumulation garbage, rubbish, dirt, papers, etc. in yard, front areaway, N. & S. shafts, interior court.

Painted walls & whitewashed ceilings. 3 W.C. compts. halls... stories dirty.

Plaster on walls of above W.C. compts. broken & defective.

Seats of middle W.C. compts. 3 story broken & defective.

Two ash cans, not adequate for 33 families.

Inspector 116 Dist.
Chief Inspector

Report Reviewed

Street Ave. C. No. 117 Dist. 116 Borough of Manhattan

To the Tenement House Commissioner, Sir:—
I recommend that the following orders be issued in this case:

- Remove the accumulations of rubbish from the yard, front areaway, N. & S. shafts, interior court, etc.
- Thoroughly cleanse the walls and ceilings of the three w.c. compartments in the halls on the 1,2,3,4,5,6,7 stories, etc.
- Remove from the walls all broken, loose and defective plaster in the said w.c., etc.
- Repair the seat of the middle w. c. in the hall on the 3rd story.
- Provide proper and separate receptacles for ashes.

A tenement inspection report of 1903 from New York City. The words speak for themselves and show part of the world Dr. Bolt inherited. The investigator noted the presence of diphtheria, one of the great summer killer epidemics, especially threatening to children. Reading the report carefully will chronicle what tenement dwellers and reformers had to contend with. Note particularly the last line of the inspector's written findings and the recommendation of his chief. Note also the bureaucracy already required just for tenement inspection. For the year 1903, more than 50,000 such violations were reported. The number of effective corrections initiated by such reports is difficult to determine.

National Archives

Education of mothers in infant and child care.

Development of infant welfare centers as part of health centers.

Health Center of Alameda County, California.

Periodic check-up of infants and preschool children by physician.

Follow-up of instructions to mothers in the homes by public health nurses.

Development of standards for examination of children in schools.

Medical inspection of school children with provisions for correction of defects.

Instruction of medical students, nurses and dentists in preventive pediatrics.

Hygiene Department and School of Public Health, University of California.

Development of state bureaus of maternal and child health.

Development of U.S. Children's Bureau.

Nutrition programs—educational and service.

Health programs for day nurseries, nursery schools, emergency day care centers.

Development of juvenile courts and probation system.

The Vote and Family Life

A persistent characteristic of American calls for reform of family life has been the tendency to foretell deliverance from all evils in each reform proposal (contraception, simplified divorce, abortion, education of parents, etc.). Similarly, severe opponents have predicted universal degeneration. In retrospect, most family reforms either changed far less than deifiers or damners had foreseen or the changes had largely unforeseen consequences. Both these effects became strikingly apparent after the success of seventy years of struggle for the ballot for women. From the beginnings in the 1840s, the suffrage campaigners leaped from their basic moral proposition that women were as entitled as men to express their political choice, to the most elaborate mystique of what woman as mate, wife, mother, lover of peace and harmony, binder of wounds, keeper of hearth fires, and more would do for the world if she was enfranchised. Generally, even without the hosannas, the ballot for women was welcomed for strengthening other progressive or liberal social ideals. Those who favored women's suffrage and either refused to confuse the issue with social prophecy or were skeptical that women at the polls would—or had to—change the world, received far less attention than paradisiacal partisans or apocalyptic enemies.

In the extraordinary range of arguments about women's suffrage, there were constant references to its implications for woman's family roles and for family life in general. From this huge record of debate, the selection from Jane Addams stresses the need for the vote as a pragmatically logical extension of the womanly role as homemaker and protector of the domestic virtues. Her plea appeared in 1910 in a series of guest columns on votes for women in the leading American woman's magazine, the *Ladies' Home Journal.* Among others who expressed contrary views were ex-President Grover Cleveland and the eminent divine Lyman Abbott. The other pieces in the series are worth reading as a convenient compendium of major ideas of the day not long before the constitutional guarantee was finally obtained in time for American women to vote (heavily for Warren Harding) in the national election of 1920.

The question raised by Jane Addams was clever: Given the threats of the new century to the family, how could the traditional home or the improved home be protected adequately without giving the principal home-maker the necessary political power to do her job better? Distinguishing the conservative and novel views of the family from each other in the Addams piece will expose some of the deeper dilemmas about women's roles within family life in the new century. Beyond this, what views of women's virtues, psychology, and roles had led many suffrage enthusiasts to endow the ballot with such portentous meaning? Why did women seem by nature and/or "acculturation" conservative (for better or worse), daring or experimental (for better or worse), vengeful, or compassionate; why so seldom, simply, variously "human"? In any case, did the right to vote logically depend at all on an assessment of women's "nature" or past cultural roles in the family setting? And if it did, was the right for males any less dependent on similar assessments about the nature of "masculin-ity" and with equal degrees of conjecture and risk?

In fact, the fight for the ballot perennially invoked, pro and con, notions of woman's nature as a family creature. To what degree did disappointments with the results of receiving the ballot represent errors about her "nature" or her history? Do there seem to be any lessons from the campaign for the suffrage to condition expectations of what other demands for women may bring? How insightful is it to view all moves for women's rights (vote, careers, birth control, abortion) in twentieth-century America as essentially built around an unchanging core of arguments? What are these ideas? How reliable are they as guides to campaigners and observers?

The piece from *Are Women People?*, from a collection by the poet and wit Alice Duer Miller, may suggest the broad variety of suffragette propa-ganda. It is also a terse listing of some of the commonest "cheap shot" arguments against woman's ballot. Which of these, however, or their ob-verse, is basically germane to the suffrage issue?

WHY WOMEN SHOULD VOTE

For many generations it has been believed that woman's place is within the walls of her own home, and it is indeed impossible to imagine the home when her duty there shall be ended or to forecast any social change which shall release her from that paramount obligation.

This paper is an attempt to show that many women today are failing to discharge their duties to their own households properly simply because they do not perceive that as society grows more complicated it is necessary that woman shall extend her sense of responsibility to many things outside of her own home if she would continue to preserve the home in its entirety. One could illustrate in many ways. A woman's simplest duty, one would say, is to keep her house clean and wholesome and to feed her children

Jane Addams, "Why Women Should Vote," *Ladies' Home Journal*, XXVII (January, 1910), pp. 21–22.

properly. Yet if she lives in a tenement house, as so many of my neighbors do, she cannot fulfill these simple obligations by her own efforts because she is utterly dependent upon the city administration for the conditions which render decent living possible. Her basement will not be dry, her stairways will not be fireproof, her house will not be provided with sufficient windows to give light and air, nor will it be equipped with sanitary plumbing, unless the Public Works Department sends inspectors who constantly insist that these elementary decencies be provided. Women who live in the country sweep their own dooryards and may either feed the refuse of the table to a flock of chickens or allow it innocently to decay in the open air and sunshine. In a crowded city quarter, however, if the street is not cleaned by the city authorities, no amount of private sweeping will keep the tenement free from grime; if the garbage is not properly collected and destroyed, a tenement-house mother may see her children sicken and die of diseases from which she alone is powerless to shield them, although her tenderness and devotion are unbounded. She cannot even secure untainted meat for her household, she cannot provide fresh fruit, unless the meat has been inspected by city officials, and the decayed fruit, which is so often placed upon sale in the tenement districts, has been destroyed in the interests of public health. In short, if woman would keep on with her old business of caring for her house and rearing her children she will have to have some conscience in regard to public affairs lying quite outside of her immediate household. The individual conscience and devotion are no longer effective.

Chicago one spring had a spreading contagion of scarlet fever just at the time that the school nurses had been discontinued because businessmen had pronounced them too expensive. If the women who sent their children to the schools had been sufficiently public-spirited and had been provided with an implement through which to express that public spirit, they would have insisted that the schools be supplied with nurses in order that their own children might be protected from contagion. In other words, if women would effectively continue their old avocations, they must take part in the slow upbuilding of that code of legislation which is alone sufficient to protect the home from the dangers incident to modern life. One might instance the many deaths of children from contagious diseases the germs of which had been carried in tailored clothing. Country doctors testify as to the outbreak of scarlet fever in remote neighborhoods each autumn, after the children have begun to wear the winter overcoats and cloaks which have been sent from infected city sweatshops. That their mothers mend their stockings and guard them from "taking cold" is not a sufficient protection when the tailoring of the family is done in a distant city under conditions which the mother cannot possibly control. The sanitary regulation of sweatshops by city officials is all that can be depended upon to prevent such needless destruction. Who shall say that women are not concerned in the enactment and enforcement of such legislation if they would preserve their homes?

Even women who take no part in public affairs, in order that they may give themselves entirely to their own families, sometimes going so far as to despise those other women who are endeavoring to secure protective legislation, may illustrate this point. The Hull-House neighborhood was at one time suffering from a typhoid epidemic. A careful investigation was made, by which we were able to establish a very close connection between the typhoid and a mode of plumbing which made it most probable that the infection had been carried by flies. Among the people who had been exposed to the infection was a widow who had lived in the ward for a number of years, in a comfortable little house which she owned. Although the Italian immigrants were closing in all around her, she was not willing to sell her property and to move away until she had finished the education of her children. In the meantime she held herself quite aloof from her Italian neighbors and could never be drawn into any of the public efforts to protect them by securing a better code of tenement-house sanitation. Her two daughters were sent to an Eastern college; one June, when one of them had graduated and the other still had two years before she took her degree, they came to the spotless little house and to their self-sacrificing mother for the summer's holiday. They both fell ill, not because their own home was not clean, not because their mother was not devoted, but because next door to them and also in the rear were wretched tenements, and because the mother's utmost efforts could not keep the infection out of her own home. One daughter died and one recovered but was an invalid for two years following. This is, perhaps, a fair illustration of the futility of the individual conscience when woman insists upon isolating her family from the rest of the community and its interests. The result is sure to be a pitiful failure.

One of the interesting experiences in the Chicago campaign for inducing the members of the Charter Convention to recommend municipal franchise for women in the provisions of the new charter was the unexpected enthusiasm and help which came from large groups of foreign-born women. The Scandinavian women represented in many Lutheran Church societies said quite simply that in the old country they had had the municipal franchise upon the same basis as men since the seventeenth century; all the women formerly living under the British Government, in England, Australia, or Canada, pointed out that Chicago women were asking now for what the British women had long had. But the most unexpected response came from the foreign colonies in which women had never heard such problems discussed and took the prospect of the municipal ballot as a simple device— which it is—to aid them in their daily struggle with adverse city conditions. The Italian women said that the men engaged in railroad construction were away all summer and did not know anything about their household difficulties. Some of them came to Hull-House one day to talk over the possibility of a public wash-house. They do not like to wash in their own tenements; they have never seen a washing-tub until they came to America, and find it very difficult to use it in the restricted space of their little kitchens and to hang the clothes within the house to dry. They say that in the Italian villages the women all go to the streams together; in the town they go to the public wash-house; and washing, instead of being lonely and disagreeable, is made pleasant by cheerful conversation. It is asking a great deal of these women to change suddenly all their habits of living, and their contention that the tenement-house kitchen is too small for laundry-work is well taken. If women in Chicago knew the needs of the Italian colony they would realize that any change bringing cleanliness and fresh clothing into the Italian household would be a very sensible and hygienic measure. It is, perhaps, asking a great deal that the members of the city council should understand this, but surely a comprehension of the needs of these women and efforts toward ameliorating their lot might be regarded as matters of municipal obligation on the part of voting women.

The same thing is true of the Jewish women in their desire for covered markets which have always been a municipal provision in Russia and Poland. The vegetables piled high upon the wagons standing in the open markets of Chicago become covered with dust and soot. It seems to these women a violation of the most rudimentary decencies and they sometimes say quite simply, "If women had anything to say about it they would change all that."

If women follow only the lines of their traditional activities, there are certain primary duties which belong to even the most conservative women, and which no one woman or group of women can adequately discharge unless they join the more general movements looking toward social amelioration through legal enactment.

The first of these, of which this article has already treated, is woman's responsibility for the members of her own household that they may be properly fed and clothed and surrounded by hygienic conditions. The second is a responsibility for the education of children: (a) that they may be provided with good schools; (b) that they may be kept free from vicious influences on the street; (c) that when working they may be protected by adequate child-labor legislation.

(a) The duty of a woman toward the schools which her children attend is so obvious that it is not necessary to dwell upon it. But even this simple obligation cannot be effectively carried out without some form of social organization, as the mothers' school clubs and mothers' congresses testify, and to which the most conservative women belong because they feel the need of wider reading and discussion concerning the many problems of childhood. It is, therefore, perhaps natural that the public should have been more willing to accord a vote to women in school matters than in any other, and yet women have never been members of a Board of Education in sufficient numbers to influence largely actual school curricula. If they had been, kindergartens, domestic science courses, and school playgrounds would be far more numerous than they are. More than one woman has been convinced of the need of the ballot by the futility of her efforts in persuading a business man that young children need nurture in something besides the three R's. Perhaps, too, only women realize the influence which the school might exert upon the home if a proper adaptation to actual needs were considered. An Italian girl who has had lessons in cooking at the public school will help her mother to connect the entire family with American food and household habits. That the mother has never baked bread in Italy—only mixed it in her own house and then taken it out to the village oven—makes it all the more necessary that her daughter should understand the complications of a cooking-stove. The same thing is true of the girl who learns to sew in the public school, and more than anything else, perhaps, of the girl who receives the first simple instruction in the care of little children, that skillful care which every tenement-house baby requires if he is to be pulled through his second summer. The only time, to my knowledge, that lessons in the care of children were given in the public schools of Chicago was one summer when the vacation schools were being managed by a volunteer body of women. The instruction was eagerly received by the Italian girls, who had been "little mothers" to younger children ever since they could remember.

As a result of this teaching I recall a young girl who carefully explained to her Italian mother that the reason the babies in Italy were so healthy and the babies in Chicago were so sickly was not, as her mother had always firmly insisted, because her babies in Italy had goat's milk and her babies in America had cow's milk, but because the milk in Italy was clean and the milk in Chicago was dirty. She said that when you milked your own goat before the door you know that the milk was clean, but when you bought milk from the grocery store after it had been carried for many miles in the country "you couldn't tell whether or not it was fit for the baby to drink until the man from City Hall, who has watched it all the way, said that it was all right." She also informed her mother that the "City Hall wanted to fix up the milk so that it couldn't make the baby sick, but that they hadn't quite enough votes for it yet." The Italian mother believed what her child had been taught in the big school; it seemed to her quite as natural that the city should be concerned in providing pure milk for her younger children as that it should provide big schools and teachers for her older children. She reached this naïve conclusion because she had never heard those arguments which make it seem reasonable that a woman should be given the school franchise, but no other.

(b) But women are also beginning to realize that children need attention outside of school hours; that much of the petty vice in cities is merely the love of pleasure gone wrong, the over-restrained boy or girl seeking improper recreation and excitement. It is obvious that a little study of the needs of children, a sympathetic understanding of the conditions under which they go astray, might save hundreds of them. Women traditionally have had an opportunity to observe the play of children and the needs of youth, and yet in Chicago, at least, they had done singularly little in this vexed problem of juvenile delinquency until they helped to inaugurate the Juvenile Court movement a dozen years ago. The Juvenile Court Committee, made up largely of women, paid the salaries of the probation officers connected with the court for the first six years of its existence, and after the salaries were cared for by the county the same organization turned itself into a Juvenile Protective League, and through a score of paid officers are doing valiant service in minimizing some of the dangers of city life which boys and girls encounter.

This Protective League, however, was not formed until the women had had a civic training through their semi-official connection with the Juvenile Court. This is, perhaps, an illustration of our inability to see the duty "next to hand" until we have become alert through our knowledge of conditions in connection with the larger duties. We would all agree that social amelioration must come about through the efforts of many people who are moved thereto by the compunction and stirring of the individual conscience, but we are only beginning to understand that the individual conscience will respond to the special challenge largely in proportion as the individual is able to see the social conditions because he has felt responsible for their improvement. Because this body of women assumed a public responsibility, they have seen to it that every series of pictures displayed in the five-cent theater is subjected to a careful censorship before it is produced, and those series suggesting obscenity and criminality have been practically eliminated. The police department has performed this and many other duties to which it was oblivious before, simply because these women have made it realize that it is necessary to protect and purify those places of amusement which are crowded with young people every night. This is but the negative side of the policy pursued by the public authorities in the fifteen small parks of Chicago, each of which is provided with halls in which young people may meet nightly for social gatherings and dances. The more extensively the modern city endeavors on the one hand to control and on the other hand to provide recreational facilities for its young people, the more necessary it is that women should assist in their direction and extension. After all, a care for wholesome and innocent amusement is what women have for many years assumed. When the reaction comes on the part of taxpayers, women's votes may be necessary to keep the city to its beneficent obligations toward its own young people.

(c) As the education of her children has been more and more transferred to the school, so that even children four years old go to the kindergarten, the woman has been left in a household of constantly narrowing interests, not only because the children are away, but also because one industry after another is slipping from the household into the factory. Ever since steam power has been applied to the processes of weaving and spinning, woman's traditional work has been carried on largely outside of the home. The clothing and household linen are not only spun and woven, but also usually sewed, by machinery; the preparation of many foods has also passed into the factory, and necessarily a certain number of women have been obliged to follow their work there, although it is doubtful, in spite of the

large number of factory girls, whether women now are doing as large a
proportion of the world's work as they used to do. Because many thousands
of those working in factories and shops are girls between the ages of fourteen and twenty-two, there is a necessity that older women should be interested in the conditions of industry. The very fact that these girls are not
going to remain in industry permanently makes it more important that
someone should see to it that they shall not be incapacitated for their
future family life because they work for exhausting hours and under unsani-
tary conditions.

If woman's sense of obligation had enlarged as the industrial conditions
changed, she might naturally and almost imperceptibly have inaugurated
the movements for social amelioration in the line of the factory legislation
and shop sanitation. That she has not done so is doubtless due to the
fact that her conscience was slow to recognize any obligation outside of
her own family circle, and because she was so absorbed in her own household that she failed to see what the conditions outside actually were. It
would be interesting to know how far the consciousness that she had no
vote and could not change matters operated in this direction. After all,
we see only those things to which our attention has been drawn, we feel
responsibility for those things which are brought to us as matters of responsibility. If conscientious women were convinced that it was a civic duty
to be informed in regard to these grave industrial affairs, and then to
express the conclusions which they had reached by depositing a piece of
paper in a ballot box, one cannot imagine that they would shirk simply
because the action ran counter to old traditions.

To those of my readers who would admit that although woman has no
right to shirk her old obligations, that all of these measures could be secured
more easily through her influence upon the men of her family than through
the direct use of the ballot, I should like to tell a little story. I have a
friend in Chicago who is the mother of four sons and the grandmother
of twelve grandsons who are voters. She is a woman of wealth, of secured
social position, of sterling character and clear intelligence, and may, therefore, quite fairly be cited as a "woman of influence." Upon one of her
recent birthdays, when she was asked how she had kept so young, she
promptly replied: "Because I have always advocated at least one unpopular
cause." It may have been in pursuance of this policy that for many years
she has been an ardent advocate of free silver, although her manufacturing
family are all Republicans! I happened to call at her house on the day
that Mr. McKinley was elected President against Mr. Bryan for the first
time. I found my friend much disturbed. She said somewhat bitterly that
she had at last discovered what the much-vaunted influence of woman
was worth; that she had implored each one of her sons and grandsons,
had entered into endless arguments and moral appeals to induce one of
them to represent her convictions by voting for Bryan! That, although
sincerely devoted to her, each one had assured her that his convictions
forced him to vote the Republican ticket. She said that all she had been

able to secure was the promise from one of the grandsons, for whom she had an especial tenderness because he bore her husband's name, that he would not vote at all. He could not vote for Bryan, but out of respect for her feelings he would refrain from voting for McKinley. My friend said that for many years she had suspected that women could influence men only in regard to those things in which men were not deeply concerned, but when it came to persuading a man to a woman's view in affairs of politics or business it was absolutely useless. I contended that a woman had no right to persuade a man to vote against his own convictions; that I respected the men of her family for following their own judgment regardless of the appeal which the honored head of the house had made to their chivalric devotion. To this she replied that she would agree with that point of view when a woman had the same opportunity as a man to register her convictions by vote. I believed then, as I do now, that nothing is gained when independence of judgment is assailed by "influence," sentimental or otherwise, and that we test advancing civilization somewhat by our power to respect differences and by our tolerance of another's honest conviction.

This is, perhaps, the attitude of many busy women who would be glad to use the ballot to further public measures in which they are interested and for which they have been working for years. It offends the taste of such a woman to be obliged to use indirect "influence" when she is accustomed to well-bred, open action in other affairs, and she very much resents the time spent in persuading a voter to take her point of view, and possibly to give up his own, quite as honest and valuable as hers, although different because resulting from a totally different experience. Public-spirited women who wish to use the ballot, as I know them, do not wish to do the work of men nor to take over men's affairs. They simply want an opportunity to do their own work and to take care of those affairs which naturally and historically belong to women, but which are constantly being overlooked and slighted in our political institutions.

In a complex community like the modern city, all points of view need to be represented; the result of diverse experiences need to be pooled if the community would make for sane and balanced progress. If it would meet fairly each problem as it arises, whether it be connected with a freight tunnel having to do largely with businessmen, or with the increasing death rate among children under five years of age, a problem in which women are vitally concerned, or with the question of more adequate street-car transfers, in which both men and women might be said to be equally interested, it must not ignore the judgments of its entire adult population.

To turn the administration of our civic affairs wholly over to men may mean that the American city will continue to push forward in its commercial and industrial development and continue to lag behind in those things which make a city healthful and beautiful. After all, woman's traditional function has been to make her dwelling-place both clean and fair. Is that dreariness in city life, that lack of domesticity, which the humblest farm dwelling presents, due to a withdrawal of one of the naturally coöperating forces? If women have in any sense been responsible for the gentler side of life which softens and blurs some of its harsher conditions, may they not have a duty to perform in our American cities?

In closing, may I recapitulate that if woman would fulfill her traditional responsibility to her own children; if she would educate and protect from danger factory children who must find their recreation on the street; if she would bring the cultural forces to bear upon our materialistic civilization; and if she would do it all with the dignity and directness fitting one who carries on her immemorial duties, then she must bring herself to the use of the ballot—that latest implement for self-government. May we not fairly say that American women need this implement in order to preserve the home?

RHYMES FOR SUFFRAGE TIMES

Our Own Twelve Anti-Suffragist Reasons

1. Because no woman will leave her domestic duties to vote.
2. Because no woman who may vote will attend to her domestic duties.
3. Because it will make dissension between husband and wife.
4. Because every woman will vote as her husband tells her to.
5. Because bad women will corrupt politics.
6. Because bad politics will corrupt women.
7. Because women have no power of organization.
8. Because women will form a solid party and outvote men.
9. Because men and women are so different that they must stick to different duties.
10. Because men and women are so much alike that men, with one vote each, can represent their own views and ours too.
11. Because women cannot use force.
12. Because the militants did use force.

Why We Oppose Women Travelling on Railway Trains

1. Because travelling in trains is not a natural right.
2. Because our great-grandmothers never asked to travel in trains.
3. Because woman's place is the home, not the train.
4. Because it is unnecessary; there is no point reached by a train that cannot be reached on foot.
5. Because it will double the work of conductors, engineers, and brakemen who are already overburdened.
6. Because men smoke and play cards in trains. Is there any reason to believe that women will behave better?

Alice Duer Miller, *Are Women People?: A Book of Rhymes for Suffrage Times* (New York, 1915).

The World of Therapy

Families have always had ideal views of themselves beyond their mere moods and ideas of the moment. The ideal image of the American family used to be found in the Bible and in church or village codes of behavior, but in the twentieth century American family ideals have drawn decreasingly on religion, custom, and local word-of-mouth. Along with the preacher or local moralist, a vast array of "authorities," from school-teachers and scientists to distant sociologists and advertising agencies, have given the family new ideas for measuring itself. Few of these recent ideas seem more pervasive than the notions of family life drawn from psychotherapy—"therapy" for short. Medical records show that by 1980 tens of millions of members of American families have experienced therapy directly, either in clinics or in sessions in private offices. Most doctors also use psychiatric advice and medication for emotional problems accompanying physical treatment. The lingo of therapy for describing routine daily difficulties is even more widespread, with words like uptight, neurotic, and depressed becoming commonplace usage.

The document that follows is an invitation to consider only one of the many ways therapists have for understanding an individual family in contemporary America. Dozens of such "schools" of therapy proliferated in the United States after World War II.

"Counseling" can be directed to short-term treatment and relief from a specific problem, like a young man's inability to hold a job. Longer and deeper treatment can involve a thorough attack on the sources of personality and aim at a basic reorientation of instinctual life. The treatment of immediate symptoms or "problems" is usually what is meant by "therapy"; the second type of treatment may require full-scale psychoanalysis over many years. All psychoanalysis is therapy but some shorter-term, symptom-relief therapy can be psychoanalytically based if it uses theories and techniques deriving from Sigmund Freud (1856–1939), the founder of modern psychiatry.

In America, widespread disagreement with Freud has involved both his description of individual development (the "dynamics" of growth) and his long and slow, psychoanalytic, method of therapy. Freud stressed the dominance in man of powerful sexual instincts, their determining effect on character and life in the first six years of life, and the intractable sources of behavior in the "unconscious" part of the mind. Dissent from these notions began soon after the earliest publication of Freud's claims and has been strong enough to hold Freudian analysis in America to a minority of physicians. Most patients today are treated by less expensive and extensive "revisionists." These are therapists, most not M.D.s, who have revised, or "Post-Freudians" who have thoroughly rejected, Freud's views of dynamics and treatment.

"Family therapy," to which this interview is loosely allied, accepts as do most therapists the great importance of family in affecting the character and behavior of any individual. Since problems of personality always involve "interactive behavior" and the feelings of others, the *family* therapist does not treat the single patient but draws family members into the treatment and moves from one to the other in clarifying difficulties. The family may be sick, not merely one member. The family setting also provides an opportunity to observe faces, body movements, and other indicators of "response" of the members, not merely to hear single replies to the therapist's repeated question, "What do *you* think about that?"

In reading this extract from an actual family interview—the names alone are fictional—try to list the *social* aspects of this family's trouble, perhaps the experience of the Great Depression, the ethnic background, or changes in the father's career. What, however, does the evidence of their *personal* relations suggest about the kind of people they are, in attitudes toward themselves and toward others? Who "wears the pants"? How does the father feel about his wife and she about him? Does the boy (and father?) seem to have been taught to feel guilt or excessive passivity about expressing his own wishes or dreams? When, how far back, did the son learn his life lessons? Does he seem "doomed" and is his "character" fate? Is he a "born loser"?

Such questions cannot be answered from this short document, but stressing lifelong social influences (family, class, status, school, "peers") on all the characters involved and the need to change current conditions—or, discounting much of this, emphasizing the early, intimate and dominating effects of parents on small children—will edge you, broadly, toward either Freudian or revisionist therapy.

A FAMILY INTERVIEW

TOM (SON): I think everyone should go to college, even though I—I don't really intend to. . . .

DR. P: Why did you decide not to?

A Chance to Grow (Boston, WGBH Educational Foundation, 1967), pp. 73–100 passim. Reprinted by permission of Norman Paul, M.D. and the WGBH Educational Foundation, Boston.

TOM: Well, I look at it, I suppose, the way most teenagers look at it in the respect that well, gee, I've gone to school for twelve years—why should I go any more? But I think I've got an advantage over, shall I say, a normal high school student, where I go, go to a vocational high school. I know . . . I don't think I really need the further education that a normal high school student would need.

DR. P: So you feel the college education is better for someone else, not for you?

TOM: Well, that seems kind of a hard way to put it, really. I mean, I can go to school; I can go to a number of schools, Franklin, for one, and continue my education in the automotive field, and for that matter become an engineer. But, uh, I don't know if I really want to get that involved in the automotive field. I mean, I like it—I love it, as a matter of fact—but I really don't think I—I really want to get that involved . . . that I really need it, unless I was planning on going to work for some place like General Motors. And when I say going to work for General Motors, I mean going right to the top and working for General Motors or Chrysler Products, Ford, or one of the big companies. I just plan to, with a little bit of luck, open my own garage.

JOE (FATHER): Well, of course, we always wanted one of the boys, or one of the children, to have, you know, have college educations but our children are more or less—well, of course, myself, when I was—in my time, college was almost impossible for us to, you know, to obtain. In the first place we couldn't have afforded it and I was a good deal like my first three boys. . . . The minute that high school came you want to go to work with your hands. You want to take whatever knowledge that you've got and go to work, you know, to make money. . . . As far as I'm concerned, I've done all right, but I don't know today, the education is a little different. There was many a time when I really knew that if I had more education, I could make money a little easier, you know, I could figure things out better. The other way, I had to really work for it, you know. That's what I, what I'm trying to get. I wish that he would go, continue his education.

DR. P: Well, he says he's planning to, but not in any formal college way.

JOE: Well, that's more or less, that's his, that's for himself to make up his mind. We'll always find a way to support the situation if he wanted to make it.

DR. P: He told you this before, or is this—

JOE: No, I'm—well, I've—we have always told the boys that if any of them wanted to go to college that we'd always find the money to, you know, to let them go to college.

DR. P: Maybe they sort of copied your style.

JOE: Well, it's possible.

TOM: They would have liked to see me go to college, well, like any parent would, naturally you know, to have—they'd like to see their son or daughter go further in education and be smarter, this, that and the other one, and where was I, but . . . just to be able to say they had at least one out of ten go to college which they haven't got yet, although.

DR. P: Do you feel you disappointed them?

TOM: Yes, I do, as a matter of fact. I do kind of wish I had gone to college for that one reason though. But the way I looked at it I figured—I figured if I had gone to college that would've been the only reason I would've gone to college, see, would be, should I say, make them happy, that one of the ten went to college.

JOE: Well, he's got more or less the same idea that I've—that I've been thinking about more or less talking to him about. That I would love to be able to have something for Tom and his brother, Jim as, you know, as a shop, as his brother, Jim, of course, is—he's like myself. He works. He likes body work. So, we'll say that he started—they started a shop with an ignition shop, tune-ups, he would do the tuning up and the brother would do the body work. I think they could make, you know, a good living at it. In fact I know they could, because I've been in it for years and years, and I know that there's a good living, you know, there's a good living in it. I was ready, you know, to buy a garage down here in Brookline Street, and I could have put him to work; I could have put the three or four brothers to work. And—but I had to mortgage my house. My house was all paid for. And the bank wanted to give me $15,000 to mortgage the house. And I could have paid that back. I got a lawyer, cost me $500 to look over the whole situation, and I had been in that location for years and years, and I knew what the station was, and all the businesses down there wanted me to take it. Well, I kept on coaxing and coaxing, and no, no, no, so I says, well, I'll get this lawyer to call you up. Had him for years and years. And he says, gee—you know, I knew him personally for years—and he says, You know I don't steer you wrong. I says, That's right. He says, If you buy this place, you'll be made in four or five years. He showed me the figures of how much gas they used to put out, and I could have put my body business there. And I could have put my mechanics there. I would have been—I wouldn't have had to work myself; I would have really just run the place. Well finally, she *(laugh)*—the house is under her name and my name, and we couldn't—

DR. P: Oh, your wife wouldn't sign it?

JOE: She wouldn't sign. So I had—that's when I came here. I had to give up the whole thing.

DR. P: How long ago was this?

JOE: This was four years ago. I was gonna throw—they wanted $45,000 for the property and everything. Just down here on Brookline Street, for gas station and garage. There was $500 there in rent coming in. And, you know, they used to rent spaces. It was a big piece of property.

DR. P: Yeah.

JOE: No, she wouldn't go along with me, so I says, well *(laugh)*, let's forget it. I—I—

DR. P: You're shaking your head, Tom. Do you remember that?

TOM: Oh, do I remember that!

JOE: I could have put the whole family to work there.

DR. P: Yeah.

JOE: The whole family. I would have been all set.

TOM: I was right behind you all the way. . . . I guess you could come close to saying it broke my heart when he sold his garage, because I really wanted to go into it. If not, when Mother wouldn't sign, you know, when—when he wanted to buy that station. I was quite perturbed about the whole matter. . . .

ANNOUNCER: Six months after graduation our students were visited again. First we will hear Tom interviewed with his parents. . . .

TOM: I'm going into the service.

DR. P: When?

TOM: In January. *(Pause)* Gonna join the Air Force, or I have joined.

DR. P: You already signed?

TOM: Last night. *(Pause)*

DR. P: And when do you have to leave?

TOM: In January. They didn't give any definite date, just January. *(Pause)* I can't wait. *(Laughter)*

DR. P: You can't wait?

TOM: No.

DR. P: Why did you decide to join?

TOM: Well, I—um *(pause)* a number of things really. Er—*(pause)* for one thing one of my friends was going in *(laugh)* er, no I figured they'd get me sooner or later. They'd draft me. Because I got a physical notice, and usually right after you take your physical, providing you pass your physical, you—er, you're called—er, in about sixty to ninety days, for the Army, and I don't want to go into the Army.

DR. P: What have you been doing since we last met?

TOM: Well, I quit my job at the garage, for one thing.

DR. P: When?

TOM: One, they weren't paying. *(Pause)*

DR. P: They weren't paying you at all?

TOM: Two—no, they—you know, I mean, don't get me wrong, they were paying but they weren't paying me enough. But then again the reason they weren't paying me enough was because there was no work. Half the time I sat around twiddling my thumbs. Another reason also is when I wasn't working on cars they tried to make me do stock work when I was hired as a mechanic, which I didn't like at all. . . . And—oh, they had me doing a number of things as a matter of fact, besides mechanics. I didn't like that because I was hired as a mechanic, not a stock boy, or anything else they had me do, so I didn't like that, so after I quit I figured—

DR. P: When did you quit? When you'd—

TOM: Oh, gee, I don't—

DR. P: We're now in the end of November, approximately.

TOM: Hmmm. Gee, I think it was in August—yeah, I think it was in August I quit. So I was having—I didn't think I'd have a tough time finding a job, but as it turned out I was having a very tough time finding a job so—

DR. P: As a mechanic?

TOM: As a mechanic. Oh, well, more or less, I mean I was being kind of fussy.

DR. P: Oh, you were fussy?

TOM: I mean I wasn't really, just—I mean, there was plenty of jobs come up like gas stations and that, but . . . I want to stay away from gas stations, I don't like gas stations. So, I *(pause)* there just got to a point that I— you know, bills were piling up and I was running an automobile, so a friend of mine happened to be working in this place and he says that they needed someone so I went over—I'm working there ever since.

DR. P: That was when? In September? October?

TOM: I don't know. I guess August or September—thereabouts. But I like it, you know, wouldn't want to stay there but *(laugh)* like it.

DR. P: I gathered that you had counted on your father starting a garage after you had graduated from high school?

TOM: I'm almost positive I definitely would have furthered my education in the automotive field had my father had a garage when I got out of high school—definitely.

DR. P: Well, how do you feel hearing him say that because there's no garage he's electing to go into the service?

JOE: Well, it makes me—it doesn't make me feel good, naturally, because I wish I would have had the financial backing without Ma *(laughs)* to really start a shop—you know, we could have gone together and—ah, it's not hard to make a living in that type of business, I mean, if you know it, all I would have had him continue his studies from his school, you know, in actual work and then when his brother, James, would have been out of the service he coulda joined in and by that time we woulda had a pretty good little business picked up.

DR. P: How do you feel hearing Tom make a strong point about if there was a garage he wouldn't be going in the service?

MOTHER: Well, I haven't given it much thought, but right now I—if Dad did have the garage and Tom was going to stay with him—that, that would suit me much more than him going in the service, but my other boys went in the service with—Dad had the garage. They worked with him in the garage and they became dissatisfied after a while and decided to go in the service and put in their time and then when they came out, they stayed, they've all stayed in the automotive field.

TOM: I think all high school seniors before they graduate from high school all figure, well, I'll go out and get a good job and I'll be all set, but *(laughs)* that isn't the way it happens. I know it myself. I had—I'd have no trouble at all finding a job, a good job, making good money, right off the bat. But I have found out different, and it's a lot different from what I thought it was going to be. I mean—I mean like when we first met at—at the high school. I never thought that—in January—I'd be going in the service. That was the farthest thing from my mind. I figured I'd have a good job— by January, I figured I was going to be a millionaire. *(Laughter)* I guess that's—that's the best way to put it. I really never thought I'd be going in the service. I figured I'd be set. But as it is I'm not. *(Laughter)* I get kind of disgusted with myself because I think in the last two years—no, not even two years; last year, I think—I've had about, you know, seven or eight jobs, and I get kinda disgusted with myself seeing that I can't— figuring that I can't hold a job, and a lot of people say that, you know, it takes time to get adjusted and this, that, and the other thing, but when I look around . . . you know, and they say, Well, gee, we got out of high school . . . they all sound like they're going to stay there for quite a while and that, and then I look at myself and I've got a job now but I won't be staying there long and I had a job and I wasn't there too long, and I had a job before that and I wasn't there too long—it kind of, you know, gets me nervous.

DR. P: Nervous in what sense?

TOM: Well, I don't know. I'm—this is one reason that—why I want to go into service, I figure they'll—if anybody will teach me *(pause)* they'll teach me.

DR. P: Teach you what?

TOM: This is what I'm getting at—I'm not too sure *(laughter . . .)* I don't know whether I want to be taught how to work *(slight laugh)* or how to get along with people. I'm really not sure why I can't hold a job, whether it's that I don't work hard enough. I don't look at it that way; I think I work hard enough and I seem to get along with people well, but there's something. . . .

DR. P: Well, has anybody told you?

TOM: No, no one has ever told me why, you know, what—what—what it is. I don't know. They just keep on sayin', Well, you know it takes time to get adjusted and this and that, but *(small pause)* I don't know, the way I look at it I've had a lot of time to adjust and I'm not adjusting *(small laugh)*. . . .

DR. P: Are you disappointed in yourself?

TOM: More or less, yes, because of the idea, I don't know—like I say, I'm just afraid that there's something wrong *(sigh)*.

DR. P: When I first met you, you seemed to suggest that the world was going to be your oyster.

TOM: Yes, well *(laughs)* this—no, I—well, like I said, see, I figured by January instead of going into service I'd be a millionaire. I didn't figure I'd be having any kind of a hard time finding a job, or having any trouble at all moving along in this world, but I found out a lot different. I'm having a very hard time understanding this crazy world of ours. I mean, here—here I've got three brothers that graduated, two brothers that graduated from a vocational high school and they're doing completely opposite—not completely opposite, but I mean completely different things from what they took up in high school. I don't understand why they went to this school. I went to school to learn, I mean cars. This is why I can't understand my—my mother wants me to go to work in Polaroid Corporation. It's a waste of four years of high school. I used to eat like a horse, now I eat absolutely nothing. I eat because—I used to love food. I used to eat because I enjoyed eating, now I eat because I have to eat.

DR. P: Since when? Around graduation?

TOM: Since around graduation *(small laugh)*. I mean, you know, I just don't care to eat anymore. My mother makes me two sandwiches for lunch; I'll be lucky if I can finish one of 'em. I don't know *(laughs)*. . . .

MANY NATIONS, MANY RACES

Making Families American

Only recently have Americans used the word "ethnic" to describe the many nationalities and races in the United States. And only recently have we recognized how basic to our history race and nationality questions have been. "Ethnicity" runs strongly through American history from our beginnings with, for example, the first blacks as slaves (1619) and the Dutch in New York (1623) coming to this country at the same time as the English. The common phrases "old American stock" or "old American family," apart from any social cachet, refer to ancestors who settled in America usually at least before the Civil War. Most black families are thus old Americans. But such phrases are also used to imply "blueblood" ancestors who were white and from the British Isles, even preferably from England. To claim "old American" in this sense, as a social distinction for a family, is really to stamp them not "pure" American but Anglo-American. Strictly speaking, the only old and "pure" Americans are the native Americans we have, the so-called Indians.

Probably no institution of American life has been more beset by the dilemmas of ethnicity than the family. By the year 1850, centuries of intermittent ethnic conflict had still not prepared Anglo-American families for the next three massive assaults on their sense of primacy in the land. About one million poor Irish-Catholic immigrants after 1846 deeply upset Northern Protestant society. Americans in all sections were even more challenged after 1865 when four million black slaves were suddenly freed from slavery to begin a century of travail with whites. Almost simultaneously, the nation also had to undergo the wrenching changes that came with rapid and massive industrialization and urbanization. These dual revolutions were made more painful, however, by expansion of ethnic antagonism into a revolution in its own right, basically a challenge to live without the single communal identity of the past: from 1880 to 1914 came the major shock of twenty million immigrants, largely from Eastern and Southern Europe, who poured into America with little or no restriction. Like earlier arrivals, the one social institution they brought with them, or quickly sought to re-establish, was family. As families or as individuals, those who debarked after 1880 were viewed by most Americans already here as disturbingly "new," somehow basically different from the earlier "old" immigrants. The daily con-

Family photos from America's old Chinatowns seem rare. This group of a well-to-do grandfather with his grandchildren in holiday dress was taken by Arnold Genthe, the well-known photographer and early chronicler of San Francisco's Chinese.

Library of Congress

flicts among these immigrants were very often along family lines, with Italians against Greeks and Jews against Christians and so forth. By 1910 the race and ethnic struggles had become huge and diverse and were further complicated by the effects of class and status considerations. The documents here can raise only a few basic questions about families and ethnicity since 1900. They feature Jewish and Chinese families as "case studies."

Jewish families from Western Europe have been in America since colonial times. Their numbers have always been small. Contrary to prejudice and myth, most remained among the petty bourgeoisie and wage laborers. There are indications, however, that the proportion of Jews moving from modest origins into the ranks of wealth and the professions is above the average for other immigrants. One special factor in understanding Jewish-American family history is that, like Catholics, Jews have different national origins and their own conflicts about social and religious rank. America received Jews from Mediterranean lands (the Sephardim), from Western Europe (largely Germany), and from Eastern Europe and Russia (the Ashkenazim). Most American Jews spring from the last group, which heavily dominated the almost two million Jewish arrivals in America from 1880 to 1914. Some of what subsequently was thought of as Jewish in America, other than in religion, is a Jewish gloss on East European cultures of the late nineteenth century. West European and Sephardic Jews tended to look down on the more humble or "vulgar" Jews from eastern lands. Jewish Americans, as did Polish, Irish, and Italian Catholics, thus fought among themselves as well as with "Yankees" for status and produced their own elites. Still, despite these special stresses, the history of all Jewish families in America resembles the general immigrant tale of what happened to them and what happened to America as result of their struggle.

There have been three major attempts to explain what happened to immigrant minorities in American history. The first policy to be used, the harshest as method and the least accurate as description, is called "Americanization." Immigrants would be welcomed and given equal opportunities (they rarely were) if they foreswore the "old country" and became "American"—that is, Anglo-American—in language, custom, and even belief. (Ultimately, many Americanizers hoped both Jews and Catholics would become Protestant Christians.) The second policy and idea came as a response against the first, early in the twentieth century. According to this theory, the "melting pot," immigrants continually "contribute" distinctive gifts (but not distinctive vices) to an ever-changing amalgam of Americanism. The Anglo-Saxon or white Anglo-Saxon Protestant (WASP) is only one element in the amalgam. It has great weight but no special moral prestige. At any moment "American" is a blend or a hybrid. The third description is probably the most realistic historically and the most demanding as an attitude or basis for policy. It dates from about 1915 and is called cultural pluralism or, simply, pluralism. Immigrants neither capitulate to Americanization nor melt in a generation or two into an amalgam.

They persevere and resist America. "Americanism" thus becomes increasingly complex and diverse, with many strong, coexisting and conflicting strains of race and nationality. Much that is distinctive among arriving immigrants in language, religion, and custom battles successfully for survival. These old cultures are in certain respects also touched or tinted by the rest of American diversity. Jewish families, for example, transform a traditional Jewish patriotic holiday of Chanukah into an analog of Christmas (itself made in an American version), but these families may also celebrate Christmas—devoid, however, of religious elements.

In all three policies and descriptions, it should be apparent that family is the frontier of the encounter between American and ethnic "identities." Unlike the two other descriptions, pluralism in action does not imply clarity or stability for the family but ever-shifting tension and anxiety-ridden conflicts. There is usually public peace on the surface of daily life, but underneath, in almost every aspect of the family and of the general culture, there is constant contest and division, with hatred as well as "tolerance," and only occasionally the official "love" and "understanding." By 1980, however, there is mounting evidence that the pluralism as fact may be giving way to some kind of amalgam after all.

After 1880, the largest settlement of East European Jews in the United States was in New York City in a district of "teeming tenements" called the Lower East Side. (See the selection from Jacob Riis.) The people from this area produced an extraordinary Jewish-American culture, much of it in Yiddish, the Jewish language deriving from medieval German. Among several Yiddish newspapers the *Jewish Daily Forward,* under a redoubtable editor, Abraham Cahan, is the most famous. This paper served as daily channel between the evolving Jewish-American culture and the complex American-Christian world beyond. The most famous feature of the paper was the advice column started by Cahan himself in 1906, which commented on letters to the editor about an astonishing variety of problems of daily life. "Bundle of Letters" is the translation of "Bintel Brief," the Yiddish title of the column. Those reprinted here come from different periods of the history of the *Forward.* The most fruitful questions in reading them are also usefully applied to other ethnic-American sources: What seems distinctively ethnic—that is, Jewish—in this selection? What is the "American" custom or ideal with which there is conflict? What are the dilemmas that follow? What seem to be the solutions and their costs? What are the particular strengths of the "American way" in this case? What are the advantages of the old custom? What are the disadvantages of both?

Jews were especially set off from other Americans by their non-Christian and historically reviled religion. Chinese—like other Asians—were also set apart, by the physical appearances of race. Thousands of Chinese, largely without their families, were imported in the middle of the nineteenth century as "coolie labor" on the West Coast, particularly for the building of railroads. The major port city of San Francisco quickly became and remained the major enclave of Chinese in the United States, although by

1914 many Japanese and some Filipinos and other Asians had also arrived in the area. This Asian immigration was the first to be regulated on the basis of race, in the 1880s. Eventually, the "tide of Orientals" became a trickle, and in 1924, on racial grounds, almost all East Asians were barred, an exclusion that lasted for several generations.

Although every nationality among immigrants seemed to outsiders bizarre and somehow menacing—Italians being gangsters, Frenchmen sexual adventurers, and so on—the Chinese seem to have aroused unusual suspicions. In part this was owing to a long tradition in the Occident of viewing China as exotic, mysterious, and "distant." But within the United States the Chinese religion, the use of opium and incense and household idols, the seeming impenetrability of a language without a Western "alphabet," their quarreling self-government associations called tongs, and their alleged penchants for "white slave" girls and cruelty to women and enemies—all these became part of an elaborate special mythology about the Chinese as a potent example of the "yellow peril." Among the Chinese themselves, of course, the views of life were quite different. For example, like many non-oriental traditionalist societies, pride in family, ancestral customs, and paternal authority were deep concerns. However, historic pride in being Chinese translated within America as "clannish" and exclusive and secretive. Coming as many Chinese did from the crowded cities of China, their immigrants tended to stay in their own enclaves in "Chinatowns" in San Francisco, New York, and other places, and this concentration of their "exotic" culture advertised by "oriental faces," dress, and "pig tail" hair style seems to have increased the dread of their secret powers and murderous threats. The hostility against Chinese bred by such fantasies tended to keep them to "their own kind," so a circular process of separation was set in motion similar to that for other immigrant groups. And on the highly charged American ethnic frontiers, the Chinese also gave otherwise squabbling nationalities in places like California a highly visible common foe and assumedly racial inferior.

The historical records of Chinese Americans have recently been enriched, as have those for other ethnic groups, by oral histories. These are intended primarily to record the memories of still-living immigrants. They also allow a properly trained interviewer to encourage recollection of specific events or compare individual memories with forgotten facts that the skilled interviewer tactfully resuscitates. The first interview in this section comes from an oral history project with Asian-Americans living in the San Francisco area about the year 1970. This one deals especially with Chinese-American family conflicts but, it is well to note, about a generation after the most traumatic and publicized period of Chinese immigrant experience, the years before about 1920. The interview is with a San Francisco woman, thirty-six years old in 1965, who was born in China and came to the United States with her parents. By the 1930s and 1940s, when this woman was young, it seems that her parents' Chinese culture was still dominant. The second selection, from another oral history project, does go back to the earlier time of the fantasized "yellow peril." A seventy-two-year-old American woman (born in 1903) of Swedish parentage and also from the San Francisco area, records her impressions of the Chinese and other minorities of her childhood. One "ethnic" thus reflects on other nationalities and races. There is enough here at least to suggest elements of the "ethnic identities" of both the Swedes and Chinese, but are these elements distinctively Chinese or Swedish rather than, generally, "ethnic" or "American"? For example, do the Swedish American's views of the Chinese seem peculiar to her own or a few other ethnic groups, or are these "American" views taken over by Swedes and others? Or are these views of Chinese associatable primarily with a wider group, whites living in Western societies? Of such complexity generally are all questions about what "Americans" and "ethnics" think of each other.

Does the interview with the Chinese American suggest that the Chinese family has amalgamated Chinese and American ideas and practices or that some Chinese and American ideas were not radically different? Does the harshness to the Chinese child stem from her being a female among Chinese as well as crippled? Are immigrants generally coarser about "handicaps" than "softie" Americans? Are the problems with her intermarriage reminiscent of attitudes of other ethnics and minorities? Are those problems also found, in other guises, among white Americans much more distant from immigrant days? Why, generally, has the making of marriages been so sensitive an issue for American families? Can marriage be said to be a touchstone of ethnic family contention with America? How much do the Chinese views represent a positive assertion of family identity and how much a "defense," and against what?

Many questions posed about Jewish immigrants are also relevant for the Chinese. Should we expect the Chinese to be any more intense about their old identity than the Jews? Do they seem less or more permeable to the "American" culture? How did "Chinatown," an offense to outsiders and a defense to insiders, differ from what Jacob Riis called "Jewtown" or from enclaves of "Little Italy" and many other similar ethnic fortresses? What special problems did physical characteristics of race pose for Asians wishing to "pass" into the American world—or to be left alone? Although there were strong temptations among immigrants (particularly from their children, who served as scouts on the ethnic frontiers) to make their families more "American," what features of Jewish or Chinese life could serve as standards for criticizing—and changing—the "American" family? How did immigrant families construe the classic "open American invitation" to immigrants to "become one of us"? What price did the immigrant family pay for "belonging" to America and following its ideals and practices? How much of either pluralistic diversity or take-it-or-leave-it Americanism can distinctive ethnic family styles endure?

The tensions bred by pluralism are further illustrated by the final selection on the problems of Roman Catholic family identity. Those families following the official Roman Church teachings on marriage are also deeply affected by the attitudes and practices of non-Catholics. They share with them, however, aspirations for wealth, power, and success that conflict with official Catholic hostility to materialism. Which ideals have been winning since 1900?

Like the Jews, that other great non-Protestant religious minority, Roman Catholics in America have always been diverse. Their faith, however, has been distinguished by, among other things, the seeming authority and visibility of their church. Yet, from Rome to the American parishes, at least recently, churchmen have differed on major family matters like divorce, mixed marriage, contraception, abortion, secular schooling, and dietary observances. How then take the piece by a Catholic scholar which asks, "How can we continue to have identifiable Roman Catholic families in modern America?" What costs must be paid to maintain or compromise with that identity?

JEWS AND AMERICA

Worthy Editor,

I consider myself a progressive woman who thinks there should be no difference between Jews and Christians. Years ago when I was a girl and sometimes heard that parents would not allow their children to marry a Christian, I maintained that they should not interfere. I believed that a fine Christian was as good as a fine Jew.

Now, however, when my daughter has fallen in love with a Gentile, I have become one of those mothers who interferes because I am against this match. I am not one of those fanatic parents who warn their children that they will disown them because of it, but I'm trying with goodness to influence my daughter to break up with the boy.

My daughter argues with me: "Why? You always used to say that all people are equal." She is educated, she knows how to talk to me, and often I have no answers to her arguments. But I feel this is no match for my daughter. Her friend comes here often, and as a person he appeals to me, but not as a husband for her.

I don't know how to explain it. He is intelligent, quiet and gentle, but somehow his nature and his way of thinking are different from that of a Jew. His parents are American Yankees, never miss a Sunday at church and speak with reverence of President Coolidge. When I think that they might become my in-laws and their son my daughter's husband, I tremble. I feel—a mother's heart feels—that my daughter could never get used to these people.

Isaac Metzker, *The Bintel Brief* (New York, 1972), pp. 147–48, 156–57, 166–68. Translation and introduction copyright © 1971 by Isaac Metzker. Reprinted by permission of Doubleday & Company, Inc.

When one is young and in love, one is in the clouds and sees no flaws. But when love cools down, she will see it's no good. I see it in advance. True, it could happen that she could marry a Jewish man and after the wedding not be able to stand him. But with a Jew it's still different.

I would very much like to hear your opinion about this.

Respectfully,
A Mother

ANSWER:

You yourself answered everything in your letter, and our opinion is the same as yours. Your daughter should also understand that the match is not a good one. But she is infatuated with the young man. And when one is in love, then all the sensible arguments are worthless.

* * *

Worthy Editor,

I am sure that the problem I'm writing about affects many Jewish homes. It deals with immigrant parents and their American-born children.

My parents, who have been readers of your paper for years, came from Europe. They have been here in this country over thirty years and were married twenty-eight years ago. They have five sons, and I am one of them. The oldest of us is twenty-seven and the youngest twenty-one.

We are all making a decent living. One of us works for the State Department. A second is a manager in a large store, two are in business, and the youngest is studying law. Our parents do not need our help because my father has a good job.

We, the five brothers, always speak English to each other. Our parents know English too, but they speak only Yiddish, not just among themselves but to us too, and even to our American friends who come to visit us. We beg them not to speak Yiddish in the presence of our friends, since they can speak English, but they don't want to. It's a sort of stubbornness on their part, and a great deal of quarreling goes on between our parents and ourselves because of it.

Their answer is: "Children, we ask you not to try to teach us how to talk to people. We are older than you."

Imagine, even when we go with our father to buy something in a store on Fifth Avenue, New York, he insists on speaking Yiddish. We are not ashamed of our parents, God forbid, but they ought to know where it's proper and where it's not. If they talk Yiddish among themselves at home, or to us, it's bad enough, but among strangers and Christians? Is that nice? It looks as if they're doing it to spite us. Petty spats grow out of it. They want to keep only to their old ways and don't want to take up our new ways.

We beg you, friend Editor, to express your opinion on this question, and if possible send us your answer in English, because we can't read Yiddish.

Accept our thanks for your answer, which we expect soon,

Respectfully,

I. and the Four Brothers

ANSWER:

We see absolutely no crime in the parents' speaking Yiddish to their sons. The Yiddish language is dear to them and they want to speak in that language to their children and all who understand it. It may also be that they are ashamed to speak their imperfect English among strangers so they prefer to use their mother tongue.

From the letter, we get the impression that the parents are not fanatics, and with their speaking Yiddish they are not out to spite the children. But it would certainly not be wrong if the parents were to speak English too, to the children. People should and must learn the language of their country.

* * *

Dear Editor,

My husband and I came from Galicia to America thirty-three years ago right after we were married. At home I had received a secular education, and my husband had been ordained as a rabbi. However, he did not want to be a rabbi here, and since we had brought along a little money from home, we bought a small business and made a good living. My husband is religious but not a fanatic. I am more liberal, but I go to *shul* with him on *Rosh Hashanah* and *Yom Kippur*.

We have five children—two boys and three girls. The boys went to a *Talmud Torah,* and the girls, too, received a Jewish education. We always kept a Jewish home and a *kosher* kitchen.

Our eldest son is now a college teacher, tutors students privately, and earns a good deal of money. He is married, has two children, four and seven years old. They live in a fine neighborhood, and we visit them often.

It happened that on Christmas Eve we were invited to have dinner with friends who live near our son and daughter-in-law, so we decided to drop in to see them after the meal. I called up, my daughter-in-law answered the telephone and warmly invited us to come over.

When we opened the door and went into the living room we saw a large Christmas tree which my son was busy trimming with the help of his two children. When my husband saw this he turned white. The two grandchildren greeted us with a "Merry Christmas" and were delighted to see us. I wanted to take off my coat, but my husband gave me a signal that we were leaving immediately.

Well, I had to leave at once. Our son's and daughter-in-law's pleading and talking didn't help, because my husband didn't want to stay there another minute. He is so angry at our son over the Christmas tree that he doesn't want to cross the threshold of their home again. My son justifies himself by saying he takes the tree in for the sake of his children, so they won't feel any different than their non-Jewish friends in the neighborhood. He assures us that it has nothing to do with religion. He doesn't consider it wrong, and he feels his father has no right to be angry over it.

My husband is a *kohen** and, besides having a temper, he is stubborn, too. But I don't want him to be angry at our son. Therefore I would like to hear your opinion on this matter.

With great respect,
A Reader from the Bronx

ANSWER:

The national American holidays are celebrated here with love and joy, by Jews and Gentiles alike. But Christmas is the most religious Christian holiday and Jews have nothing to do with it. Jews, religious or not, should respect the Christmas holiday, but to celebrate it would be like dancing at a stranger's wedding. It is natural that a Jew who observes all the Jewish traditions should be opposed to seeing his son and grandchildren trimming a Christmas tree.

But he must not quarrel with his son. It is actually your husband's fault because he probably did not instill the Jewish traditions in his son. Instead of being angry with him, he should talk to his son and explain the meaning of Christmas to him.

CHINESE AND AMERICA

Q: When your parents learned you were going to marry a white person, were they surprised?

A: Yes they do. They really get mad at me. They planning to—ah, find the Chinese guy in Taiwan or Hong Kong or . . . like that, like the handicapped person. . . . Yeah, so far I been married twice in my life and those people white. And every time I ask my folks' advice and they say don't ask me you over twenty-one, I don't care to who you marry to, and—you know, so forth, so on. Really hard for me to tell my mother what kind of trouble I'm am or they have their own too. But they misunderstand . . . the kids . . . like me, special. I mean physical I need lots of help. But they self[ish]. They never thought I will be learning or they—

Q: Never give you the chance to learn skills.

---

* A Jew especially enjoined to uphold the law of Moses.—Ed.

Combined Asian American Resources Project, Asian American Oral History Composite (photocopy of typed transcript, 1977), Donated Oral Histories Collection, The Bancroft Library, University of California, Berkeley. Courtesy, The Bancroft Library.

A: Yeah, right.

Q: The American people have many handicap centers to learn skills. The Chinese people think we Chinese can take care of our own people, they don't go outside to ask agencies to help us.

A: Right, that way I miss my education.

Q: They didn't bother to send you to handicap schools?

A: No, no, no. They was a' busy their own business and we got a lots of kids and I don't get a chance to go to school [except] the Chinese, and when Chinese writing I learn until fourth grade almost fifth grade, and then I have to stop, and, ah—

Q: They didn't want you to continue?

A: No, that time I was not important, you know. Well, upset or something bother me, I kept it inside, I didn't tell to nobody and then special when the person don't understand. I just ignore them, I just don't want to talk about my problem until when I grow up. That a wrong thing. I have to talk to someone get advice, like that. My mother, my mother understand me very well. My father is a little different. He's funny, when something not right or something wrong, whoever at home he always pick on that person. But I proud of him, he never pick on my mother but he pick on daughter or son, whoever at home, and he just jump on you, and I never say bad behind my father whatever he do or right or wrong, we never say anything to him. . . .

Q: What are your opinions about how Chinese treat handicapped people?

A: Well, they terrible thing. I remember when I was young in China, very very seldom see handicapped. If they do have one, they lock them in a room or kill them when they born or they can do anything. Because they afraid to lose face, and that's why they—special if you're a girl. And the handicapped they hate the idea. Waste the food. Other words, waste the money on everything, the handicapped. But my parents different because they the modern mind. They believe God—yeah, Jesus Christ—and that's why they still kept me alive. See, well, of course, we have so many brother sister, pretty soon the love is changed. The pressure, all those difficulties at my parents and mother.

Q: How come you don't see very many cripple people in Chinatown?

A: Well to my opinion the people they don't want to mention about their handicapped. If—ah, they do, the people look them down. That's—ah, my opinion, you know, and that's why lots of people they hide the truth, like, ah—"Guess what I have? A handicapped in my house." They never mention that, always kept in a corner inside . . . just selfish.

Q: Do you think the Chinese people will change their old ideas about handicapped people in America? Because in America you can see there are many programs to help handicapped people. Many programs in schools. Handicapped people can go to all schools now. You know, to—Where I go to school, at San Francisco State, they have special programs, elevators to help handicapped people, so they can use elevators. All through the state they try to help—ah, cripple people. Any way they can. Like in restrooms they have special facilities, to make—special things to make it easy to use restrooms. And special parking lots. Parking spaces for the handicapped people.

A: I know.

Q: They understand handicapped people may be useful in society. That they shouldn't be ignored. Do you think the Chinese people—the old . . . the old ideas will be lost—that the selfish ideas will be gone in America? That the Chinese people are changing their minds for the better to help handicapped people? Do you think the Chinese people in America now will change their ideas to help handicapped people, their own handicapped?

A: That's—ah, depend the person idea. And, of course, lots of the handicap's parents that don't understand the kid. The children feeling that that's they are, no chance because—ah, they are stupid or whatever they want to think. But I hope so too. We living in America, we not living in China. We should change and learn the right way to understand the handicap people. Of course, difficult for the handicap person to go out, oh, like in the wheelchair or go somewhere. At least you know you're safe, special this year. I know that. But they change the world a lot and make it easier for handicap just like you say. Go to school, learn some special skill like that. I'm very happy that's why the opportunity. I'm waiting because I'm the one want to learn and I don't know how. And the normal body, that's the person not handicap, should try to understand the unable body. See, that way grow up everything still . . . fine in the future.

Q: So before, your parents did not appreciate your marriage, that you marry a white person—they didn't like it. The point is that you're over twenty-one, you can do what you want. They didn't care what you want?

A: Right.

Q: And also you told me that your sister also marry interracial?

A: Oh, yeah, right. She marry the Japanese guy, and also my brother marry the tow gee,* born here. She's Chinese and she's born here.

Q: Did your parents like that?

A: Well, we three are brother and sister. We marry different nationality, and of course you can hear the complaint and this and that. You *never* please them, though. That's sure.

_____
* Chinese expression for "our own."—Ed.

Q: So your parents didn't like it when your sister married a Japanese person?

A: Nope.

Q: Do your parents live far from your brother and sister now?

A: Oh, they still live in San Francisco. Not that far. But I don't know. They say we are changed. They didn't realize they are changed too. No other word after they get something settled down . . . getting better. Our love is different, because my brother getting marry and sister and so did I. Different problems. But when we needed advice or trouble coming up we go to see the parents. But they not 'preciation, they always mention about past ten years or twenty years before and they don't talking about right now. They talk about the past. And we usual don't go to see them or don't want to call them up. It very, very difficult to please my folk, you know they mean?

Q: To please your family right?

A: Yeah.

Q: How did the Japanese parents—did they think it was okay for their son to marry a Chinese person?

A: No, the mother against that too.

Q: The Japanese mother?

A: Yeah, she wants us—she have only one son, see. The whole family only one son and she wanted marry to the Japanese woman, not the Chinese. When my sister marry she was very, very young. She was eighteen, over eighteen, and she leaving, although first is because the family problem tore her apart. Well we want to get out soon as possible. I left home first, that's why my parents say even I'm cripple, I learn the bad thing. I hurt them . . . a lot. But I was thinking my future. I have to do something, because I figure I stay home I always like the slave, you know—do this, do that, take care of the brother and sister, you know.

Q: Your parents' old-fashioned ideas hurt you because they did not want to help handicapped people. But, do you say that—do you still have these old-fashioned ideas or are you Americanized?

A: They old-fashion. They live in the United States many many years, but they idea still the Chinese customs, you know. We remember—my brother, sister, the three of us—oldest say that you guy come to the United States four-five years, suddenly the idea everything changed. Why? You know. But you have to change, to change—because you're living your friendships, or working, or . . . you know.

SWEDISH-AMERICANS AND "ETHNICS"

Q: You were raised in a neighborhood which was rather diverse, different ethnic and religious backgrounds?

A: Definitely. We had everything except colored. This is interesting. We had two colored girls in the first grade at school. Their names were Antoinette and Oreol and they were my best friends. I would bring them home; Mother would give us milk and cookies. Nobody knew the difference. I often wondered why it was, there was no reason for my picking them out as my chums, but they were the only two colored ones. I've often wondered about that. My mother must have wondered why, but of course she never questioned it.

Q: Did you have any pictures of what an ethnic group was like as a group? For example, what were your reactions to the Irish?

A: Well, we had them all in our classes. It was just—we had lots of them. It seemed like—I would say, in looking back, we probably didn't play with any whose ancestors had been here a long time. This probably was true because it was San Francisco, where everybody came West, you see. Really the last place that they could go, San Francisco is.

Q: Do you remember, at that time, having some notion that the Irish were different from the Italians, who were different from the Latins, who were different from the Chinese?

A: We really, if we were to look down on anyone, it was the Chinese. They were at the bottom of the ladder, as far as I can recall.

Q: Did you have contact with them?

A: Um. They used to walk around Chinatown with chairs on their heads. They repaired chairs, see, that was their trade and stock—they repaired chairs. So you always saw pictures of them with a band over their head and one chair over each shoulder. As a child, that's always as we imagined them.

Q: Did you meet any of their children?

A: There were no children in the class, as I recall. No oriental. This is interesting. We had been brought up, of course, on white slavery, and the horrors of white slavery. As a child, my father would take me through Chinatown, and there really were opium dens at that time, and they were playing cards. We could smell it as we walked by, and, of course, all these horrible tales about white slavery. I just would hang on to my father's hand.

Frederick M. Wirt, director, "Growing Up in the City Project," Donated Oral Histories Collection, The Bancroft Library, University of California, Berkeley. Courtesy, The Bancroft Library.

Q: The Chinese were somehow connected with white slavery?

A: Oh, yes. We grew up on that, that they had a regular market. It was true, I'm sure, a lot of it, that they would kidnap white girls and sell them into slavery. It couldn't have been all word of mouth. I hated to go through Chinatown. I just dreaded it. Dad would take me occasionally, and I was just petrified for fear they'd come up and snatch me in the doorway, because all the places were down underground, you see. You walked down to their homes and gambling place.

Q: So you would have Chinese down at the bottom of this ladder?

A: Yes. Never socially at all.

Q: How about blacks?

A: The only two I recall are the ones that I played with in school. The rest were predominantly Irish and German and Italian.

Q: How about the Italians? How would they rate on the ladder?

A: Well, we all played together as children. That's the one thing. I don't recall. You see, the Swedish church would obviously only have Swedish people. People were lonely and they just gravitated to the church where they spoke Swedish. To the day my father—he came over when he was fourteen, and he was fifty-nine when he died—and to the day he died, he would say "enyoy" instead of "enjoy." The "j" is "y" is Swedish. The reason we moved to Turlock* was that it was every Swedish man's dream to have a little farm of their own and be independent. And we bought ten acres in Turlock; we moved down. He never did farm because he had his business in Turlock as a tailor. We had to have a regular income. But there we were, five thousand people in Turlock, and I would assume almost all of them were Swedish. Twenty-eight churches and one theater. If you went to the theater again, you were a social outcast. If you were a Mason or an Elk, there was no way. You had to go to one of the churches. Being together then, you see, they never gave themselves a chance to learn our language anymore than I gave myself a wonderful opportunity to learn Swedish language.

Q: In San Francisco, do you recall if the boys had gangs?

A: Oh, yes. Oh, yes.

Q: Were they ethnic gangs?

A: No, not really. Again, I would say they were all Irish. I recall one day—

Q: The gangs you knew were all Irish?

A: No, not necessarily. No, I would say that they were of every nationality. One day I was walking home, and a gang had taken and tied my brother,

* Turlock, California, about 200 miles from San Francisco.—Ed.

who was six years older than myself, to a telephone pole, and they had rope all the way. I don't know what they intended to do, but of course I ran home screaming. Mother came down the steps, and when the boys saw her, you can imagine they took off. But I would say that this was a gang, just boys, who probably did it just for the devilment of it. No personal thing at all. . . .

THE AMERICAN CATHOLIC FAMILY

A religious minority can retain its specifically religious identity either by isolating itself from the alien influences of the dominant culture, as some groups such as the Mennonites are striving to do, or by selective integration. American Catholics have always opted for the latter solution, but until relatively recently, as we have indicated, the major portion of them remained fairly isolated, owing to their ethnic and regional urban concentration, immigrant and culturally alien origins, and consequently lower socioeconomic status. This incidental form of isolation is rapidly ceasing to exist, with the result that they are planning to experience the full impact of their increasingly secularized social environment. . . .

The rejection of belief in the sacramental character of the marriage bond in societies with a Protestant majority eventually led to the gradual establishment of a legal system providing for relatively facile dissolution of the bond by the civil courts, with the result that popular expectancies and patterns of conduct relating to entrance into marriage, the solution of marital conflicts, and openness to extra-marital relationships came to be based on the assumption that divorce was always possible. . . .

Whenever such a change is accepted by the majority, it is gradually "geared into" the entire social system; that is, it becomes "institutionalized" in the sense that related social structures, attitudes and practices tend to be modified in terms of it. . . .

American couples who reject contraceptive family limitation, yet accept contemporary cultural goals and behavioral patterns in all other respects, are bound to experience serious strain and frustration, for they cannot make use of the [contraceptives] which enable their contemporaries to maintain some measure of social equilibrium or balance. Unless such couples are fully aware of the normally anticipated consequences of their decision relating to the use of conjugal relations and family size, and develop patterns of conduct, marital goals and life expectations that take these consequences fully into account, they will soon find themselves caught in an unending series of contradictory expectancies, needs, and requirements. . . .

Members of a minority must participate in a social system not only geared

John L. Thomas, S.J., *The American Catholic Family: A Sociological Perspective*, U.S. Catholic Conference (Washington, D.C., 1974), pp. 11–14.

to goals and values they often cannot accept, but which has achieved some type of working balance or equilibrium by introducing practices they must consider morally pathological. Like all families they must work out some *modus vivendi* in their changing environment, but the adjustments and adaptations they make must be developed within . . . moral norms consistent with their distinctive religious beliefs.

If the foregoing facts and observations are substantially correct, we may safely conclude that the American Catholic community will encounter special difficulties in providing the understanding, motivation, and support that are required for the effective maintenance and transmission of its marriage and family values. In particular, the faithful must acquire a clear understanding of the religious foundations of these values, that is, of the superordinate system or complex of distinctively Catholic beliefs which gives these values their normative significance and makes them matters of ultimate concern. Today, perhaps as never before, these values are being challenged in both theory and practice. Under such conditions, they can continue to "make sense," to attract lasting commitment, and to provide the essential moral guidelines for making discerning choices when adjusting to change, only if the faithful are trained to view them within their comprehensive, integral credal context as a matter of course. Moreover, owing to increased education and social mobility, as well as to the "normative ambiguity" and "credibility gap" resulting from recent developments and controversies within the Church, the upcoming generation of American Catholics are no longer likely to accept their family values solely on the basis of authority or tradition.

At the same time, the powerful supernatural, juridical, social, and psychological sanctions that formerly operated to encourage conformity and inhibit deviance have been seriously eroded. Whether we consider the balanced Christian "sense of sin" normally acquired in early home and school training, or the more general respect for authority structures and authority itself, we can easily document a notable attrition particularly among adolescents and young adults but also as a pervasive component of the total "climate of opinion" affecting all members of society. This anomic or normless orientation of contemporary American thoughtways is bound to result in a considerable "withdrawal of affect" from Catholic family values, together with a marked diminution of needed mutual encouragement and support even on the part of minority group members.

Although these secularizing trends undoubtedly vary in strength from diocese to diocese and have a different impact on different social classes within each diocese, no perceptive observer of the contemporary scene can deny that they have serious implications for practical programs of action relating to marriage and the family. Stated in summary fashion this means that in designing a feasible pastoral approach to the challenging new issues we face in regard to sex, love, marriage, and the family, we can no longer assume that the faithful fully understand the total Christian context of relevant beliefs within which acceptable solutions must be formulated. In the practical order, this implies that we take as our starting point what might be called the essential religious vocation of Christians that they receive at baptism and which calls them to union with Christ in his mission of building up the Kingdom through operative charity, that is, through progressive love of God and neighbor. The marriage vocation, like all other Christian vocations, involves a further or more specific determination of this essential religious vocation. In other words, it defines the essential relevant relationships through which and within which conjugal partners are to manifest their love of God and neighbor. Although these essential relationships are ultimately founded on the bisexual character of the human species as God created it, and they consequently involve some basic "givens," their specific determinations will depend on the sociocultural situations within which the family operates as well as on the religious context of beliefs within which they are interpreted.

This means that as a voluntary total sharing of the whole of life, marriage is both "covenant" or "contract" and "community." As a mysterious two-in-one-flesh potentially procreative unity involving a unique sacramental givenness it is community, and this constitutes its unchangeable aspect. As a union of love and life involving what is culturally conditioned and freely chosen it is covenant or contract, and this is its voluntary, dynamic aspect. Among different family systems, as well as among individual marriages, primary concern may be placed on either covenant or community, on what each partner chooses to give or what is "given" in the nature of things; but both are involved in every marriage.

Black Families: Dilemma and Debate

Trauma and frustration are themes dominating both white and black accounts of black family life. It thus seems against the grain when historians find that, amid the viciousness of slavery, some American blacks did manage to have family lives that were viable and supportive. Many whites who feel the weight of America's racist past are recurrently astonished at contemporary evidence of the social conservatism of black families on issues like school curriculum or discipline or on their seemingly indefatigable eagerness for their children to cash in on American capitalism. How many are there of the classic "broken, hopeless lives" and "alienated" radicalism of the dispossessed?

Despite the dismaying defeats that marked black lives in America after Reconstruction and that became by 1910 a dance of death in lynchings and Jim Crow culture, black Americans and their families were not downed. Along with the numbing real-life pains of living through its "downs" as well as "ups," the twentieth century overall shows general improvement in the place of blacks in American life. Rates of change, relative shares of life, steadiness of growth for blacks lag behind those for whites. But, overall, rising expectations, not despair, have fed both progress in the prosaics of life for the majority of blacks (income, health, housing) as well as the militancy of black minorities who ignore or dismiss such changes.

If there was any large complacency about blacks among white Americans in 1965, after about a decade of civil rights turmoil and black militancy, it seemed shattered by the publication in that year of the so-called Moynihan report, which depicted "The Negro Family" as caught in a national "tangle of pathology." A small mountain of studies of black families, mostly pessimistic, had accumulated by the 1960s with, increasingly, blacks themselves as investigators and authors. None of these seem to have had the impact of the Moynihan report. After ten years of wrenching but successful civil rights movements, of black social advances, with national energy newly enlisted in a "war against poverty" and in a strong Voting Rights Act of 1965, a nationally prestigious white politician-sociologist uttered an American unutterable: Money and will were not working their expected American miracles; time and tide were running against the hope for the mass of

blacks to equal whites in American life; much that had seemed hopeful
for blacks, such as the successful desegregation of the armed forces, also
bred frustration and despair about more desired civilian opportunities.

The uproar about the report seemed to confuse its statements of fact
about black family sociology (which, in important respects, *were* questionable) with a racist contention that blacks seemed *constitutionally* susceptible
to a "pathological" family life and unable to use opportunities given them.
Careful reading of the entire document, which space prohibits printing
here, easily shows the genuineness of Daniel Patrick Moynihan's liberal,
progressive, reformist, man-of-good-will, antiracist credentials, as well as
the tough-mindedness that had occasionally annoyed other liberals on other
issues. He was, after all, passionately and long-committed to breaking the
chains of pathology by a massive federal Negro family policy.

If there is any general criticism to be made of the report, might it not
center on how black families in America had lived oblivious to, or even
beyond, their "pathology," however traumatic their lives may have seemed
to white and black observers? Themes of disease, debauchery, and dread
had so dominated the writing on and by blacks that it seemed odd suddenly
to indict Moynihan's "pathology" thesis or other pessimistic generalizations
about the black family. If the experiences of blacks had been crushing to
despair, where and how had any of the many escapes from the nightmare
occurred? What was the source of encouragement for any to escape from
the pathology? Either the system *was* too closed for hope or, after all,
not that closed, for past and future accomplishments.

The critics of Moynihan's work filled newspapers and periodicals with
comment ranging from some cool appraisals to largely indignant demur
or denunciation. Perhaps the most effective reply was by Moynihan's fellow
sociologist, Herbert J. Gans,* a highly regarded student of contemporary
American mores. Gans denied that Moynihan was either a racist or a defeat-
ist. He emphasized Moynihan's intention to help more blacks to an equality
of *results* with whites, not of abstract "opportunities" in American society.
Gans regretted that the lack of specific proposals in the report made it
seem basically contradictory—that is, Negroes were to be helped toward
equality, but *presently* their family life and roles seemed to make them incapable of achieving it. Taken quickly, Gans agreed, these contentions could
invite black and reformer resignation or strengthen white prejudice against
racially "hopeless" blacks, taken as being inherently unequal and incapable
of rising to the proposed opportunities of adequate jobs, higher income,
and cohesive family lives.

Gans's warnings about Moynihan's sociological findings were even more
telling because they posed not Gans's own moral questions but, simply,
how true the report's traumatic accounts were. Calling on other findings,
neglected by or underplayed by Moynihan, Gans contended:

---

* See Herbert J. Gans, "The Negro Family, Reflections on the Moynihan Report," *Commonweal*, October 15, 1965.

1. "Broken families" did not induce failure at school, delinquency, drug usage, or mental illness *as much as* did poverty and low social status.
2. Families break up for many reasons, and removing one member— e.g., an angry, unemployed black father—may be a healthy and realistic move.
3. Matriarchal families, as among blacks, have not been proven to be intrinsically pathological, even for their boys, and, together with the large "kinship system" of black females, are "surprisingly stable" on the female side. They thereby compensate for the lack of males.
4. Boys from such families often do well in life and make stable marriages. If there seems to be "pathology" present in their childhood it may be the *personal* and objective problem of a mother's emotional weakness or peculiar range of cultural skills rather than the *structural* problem of missing fathers. Thus a family with a single mother may be "healthier"—less prone to pathology—than one with a merely marginal father. The lower-class black family may survive *best*, may find the most viable and realistic solution *available*, by rejecting its men.
5. Since illegitimacy is not as condemned or censured among the poor as it is among comfortable classes, the price in pathological feeling from being treated as a bastard or a promiscuous woman is less than middle-class white observers may understand. Having any child, regardless of its illegitimacy, for black girls often means becoming an adult and playing the important role of mother over the family. In a world with low odds on happiness, having babies can mean feeling prowess and usefulness. "Illegitimacy" may not seem much of a price to pay.

The illegitimacy issue raised by Gans implies a wide range of other moral and political questions summarizable in this way: Which of the implicitly normal white middle-class family goals of "health," "security," "happiness," and "progress" can confidently be posited as better goals for blacks than those they currently pursue? If analysis of these standards among *whites* could be incorporated into public policy, might the country need two or more national family policies, not one? Was there, in other words, any evidence of a trans-racial *American* family pathology that urged caution both about the uniqueness of black family "sickness" and any rush to have blacks jump from their own small frying pan into a national fire?*

BLACK FAMILIES AND AMERICAN LIFE

The United States is approaching a new crisis in race relations. . . . The most difficult fact for white Americans to understand is that . . . the

---

* See also the selection "Family: An Endangered Species," page 670.

Daniel P. Moynihan and Paul Barton, *The Negro Family: The Case for National Action*, U.S. Department of Labor, Office of Planning and Research (Washington D.C., 1965).

circumstances of the Negro American community in recent years has probably been getting *worse, not better.*

Indices of dollars of income, standards of living, and years of education deceive. The gap between the Negro and most other groups in American society is widening.

The fundamental problem, in which this is most clearly the case, is that of family structure. The evidence—not final, but powerfully persuasive—is that the Negro family in the urban ghettos is crumbling. A middle-class group has managed to save itself, but for vast numbers of the unskilled, poorly educated city working class the fabric of conventional social relationships has all but disintegrated. There are indications that the situation may have been arrested in the past few years, but the general post-war trend is unmistakable. So long as this situation persists, the cycle of poverty and disadvantage will continue to repeat itself. . . .

The Negro American Family

At the heart of the deterioration of the fabric of Negro society is the deterioration of the Negro family.

It is the fundamental source of the weakness of the Negro community at the present time. . . . It is more difficult, however, for whites to perceive the effect that three centuries of exploitation have had on the fabric of Negro society itself. Here the consequences of the historic injustices done to Negro Americans are silent and hidden from view. But here is where the true injury has occurred: unless this damage is repaired, all the effort to end discrimination and poverty and injustice will come to little.

The role of the family in shaping character and ability is so pervasive as to be easily overlooked. The family is the basic social unit of American life; it is the basic socializing unit. By and large, adult conduct in society is learned as a child. . . .

But there is one truly great discontinuity in family structure in the United States at the present time: that between the white world in general and that of the Negro American.

The white family has achieved a high degree of stability and is maintaining that stability.

By contrast, the family structure of lower-class Negroes is highly unstable, and in many urban centers is approaching complete breakdown. . . .

In every index of family pathology—divorce, separation, and desertion, female family head, children in broken homes, and illegitimacy—the contrast between the urban and rural environment for Negro families is unmistakable. . . .

UNEMPLOYMENT AND POVERTY

The impact of unemployment on the Negro family, and particularly on the Negro male, is the least understood of all the developments that have contributed to the present crisis. There is little analysis because there has been almost no inquiry. Unemployment, for whites and nonwhites alike, has on the whole been treated as an economic phenomenon, with almost no attention paid for at least a quarter-century to social and personal consequences. . . .

The fundamental, overwhelming fact is that *Negro unemployment,* with the exception of a few years during World War II and the Korean War, *has continued at disaster levels for 35 years.* . . .

Because in general terms Negro families have the largest number of children and the lowest incomes, many Negro fathers literally cannot support their families. Because the father is either not present, is unemployed, or makes such a low wage, the Negro woman goes to work. Fifty-six percent of Negro women, age 25 to 64, are in the work force, against 42 percent of white women. This dependence on the mother's income undermines the position of the father and deprives the children of the kind of attention, particularly in school matters, which is now a standard feature of middle-class upbringing. . . .

Negro women not only have more children, but have them earlier. Thus in 1960, there were 1,247 children ever-born per thousand ever-married nonwhite women 15 to 19 years of age, as against only 725 among white women, a ratio of 1.7:1. The Negro fertility rate overall is now 1.4 times the white, but what might be called the generation rate is 1.7 times the white. . . .

This population growth must inevitably lead to an unconcealable crisis in Negro unemployment. The most conspicuous failure of the American social system in the past 10 years has been its inadequacy in providing jobs for Negro youth. Thus, in January 1965 the unemployment rate for Negro teenagers stood at 29 percent. This problem will now become steadily more serious. . . .

A cycle is at work; too many children too early make it most difficult for the parents to finish school. . . .

Low education levels in turn produce low income levels, which deprive children of many opportunities, and so the cycle repeats itself. . . .

THE TANGLE OF PATHOLOGY

In a word, most Negro youth are in *danger* of being caught up in the tangle of pathology that affects their world, and probably a majority are so entrapped. Many of those who escape do so for one generation only: as things now are, their children may have to run the gauntlet all over again. That is not the least vicious aspect of the world that white America has made for the Negro.

Obviously, not every instance of social pathology afflicting the Negro community can be traced to the weakness of family structure.

If, for example, organized crime in the Negro community were not largely controlled by whites, there would be more capital accumulation among Negroes, and therefore probably more Negro business enterprises. If it were not for the hostility and fear many whites exhibit towards Negroes, they in turn would be less afflicted by hostility and fear and so on. There is no one Negro community. There is no one Negro problem. There is no one solution. Nonetheless, at the center of the tangle of pathology is the weakness of the family structure. Once or twice removed, it will be found to be the principal source of most of the aberrant, inadequate, or antisocial behavior that did not establish, but now serves to perpetuate, the cycle of poverty and deprivation.

It was by destroying the Negro family under slavery that white America broke the will of the Negro people. Although that will has reasserted itself in our time, it is a resurgence doomed to frustration unless the viability of the Negro family is restored.

MATRIARCHY

A fundamental fact of Negro American family life is the often reversed roles of husband and wife.

Robert O. Blood, Jr., and Donald M. Wolfe, in a study of Detroit families, note that "Negro husbands have unusually low power," and while this is characteristic of all low-income families, the pattern pervades the Negro social structure: "the cumulative result of discrimination in jobs . . . , the segregated housing, and the poor schooling of Negro men." In 44 percent of the Negro families studied, the wife was dominant, as against 20 percent of white wives. "Whereas the majority of white families are equalitarian, the largest percentage of Negro families are dominated by the wife."

The matriarchal pattern of so many Negro families reinforces itself over the generations. This process begins with education. Although the gap appears to be closing at the moment, for a long while, Negro females were better educated than Negro males, and this remains true today for the Negro population as a whole. . . .

THE FAILURE OF YOUTH

[The] account of Negro youth growing up with little knowledge of their fathers, less of their fathers' occupations, still less of family occupational traditions, is in sharp contrast to the experience of the white child. . . . White children without fathers at least perceive all about them the pattern of men working.

Negro children without fathers flounder—and fail.

Not always, to be sure. The Negro community produces its share, very possibly more than its share, of young people who have the something extra that carries them over the worst obstacles. But such persons are always a minority. The common run of young people in a group facing serious obstacles to success do not succeed. . . .

The effect of broken families on the performance of Negro youth has not been extensively measured, but studies that have been made show an unmistakable influence. . . .

This difference in ability to perform has its counterpart in statistics on actual school performance. Nonwhite boys from families with both parents present are more likely to be going to school than boys with only one parent present, and enrollment rates are even lower when neither parent is present.

When the boys from broken homes are in school, they do not do as well as the boys from whole families. Grade retardation is higher when only one parent is present, and highest when neither parent is present. . . .

A study of Negro apprenticeship by the New York State Commission Against Discrimination in 1960 concluded:

> Within the minority community, skilled Negro "models" after whom the Negro youth might pattern himself are rare, while substitute sources which could provide the direction, encouragement, resources, and information needed to achieve skilled craft standing are nonexistent.

Recent psychological research demonstrates the personality effects of being reared in a disorganized home without a father. One study showed that children from fatherless homes seek immediate gratification of their desires far more than children with fathers present. Others revealed that children who hunger for immediate gratification are more prone to delinquency, along with other less social behavior. . . .

THE ARMED FORCES

. . . Service in the United States Armed Forces is the *only* experience open to the Negro American in which he is truly treated as an equal: not as a Negro equal to a white, but as one man equal to any other man in a world where the category "Negro" and "white" do not exist. If this is a statement of the ideal rather than reality, it is an ideal that is close to realization. In food, dress, housing, pay, work—the Negro in the Armed Forces *is* equal and is treated that way.

There is another special quality about military service for Negro men: it is an utterly masculine world. Given the strains of the disorganized and matrifocal family life in which so many Negro youth come of age, the Armed Forces are a dramatic and desperately needed change: a world away from women, a world run by strong men of unquestioned authority, where discipline, if harsh, is nonetheless orderly and predictable, and where rewards, if limited, are granted on the basis of performance.

The theme of a current Army recruiting message states it as clearly as can be: "In the U.S. Army you get to know what it means to feel like a man."

At the recent Civil Rights Commission hearings in Mississippi a witness testified that his Army service was in fact "the only time I ever felt like a man.". . .

ALIENATION

The term alienation may by now have been used in too many ways to retain a clear meaning, but it will serve to sum up the equally numerous ways in which large numbers of Negro youth appear to be withdrawing from American society. . . .

There is a larger fact about the alienation of Negro youth than the tangle of pathology described by . . . statistics. It is a fact particularly difficult to grasp by white persons who have in recent years shown increasing awareness of Negro problems.

The present generation of Negro youth growing up in the urban ghettos has probably less personal contact with the white world than any generation in the history of the Negro American.

Until World War II it could be said that in general the Negro and white worlds lived, if not together, at least side by side. Certainly they did, and do, in the South.

Since World War II, however, the two worlds have drawn physically apart. . . .

In the North, despite strenuous official efforts, neighborhoods and therefore schools are becoming more and more of one class and one color. . . .

The Case for National Action

The object of this study has been to define a problem, rather than propose solutions to it. . . . We have shown a clear relation between male employment, for example, and the number of welfare dependent children. Employment in turn reflects educational achievement, which depends in large part on family stability, which reflects employment. Where we should break into this cycle, and how, are the most difficult domestic questions facing the United States. We must first reach agreement on what the problem is, then we will know what questions must be answered. . . .

What then is that problem? We feel the answer is clear enough. Three centuries of injustice have brought about deep-seated structural distortions in the life of the Negro American. At this point, the present tangle of pathology is capable of perpetuating itself without assistance from the white world. The cycle can be broken only if these distortions are set right.

In a word, a national effort towards the problems of Negro Americans must be directed towards the question of family structure. The object should be to strengthen the Negro family so as to enable it to raise and support its members as do other families. After that, how this group of Americans chooses to run its affairs, take advantage of its opportunities, or fail to do so, is none of the nation's business. . . .

Such a national effort could be stated thus:

The policy of the United States is to bring the Negro American to full and equal sharing in the responsibilities and rewards of citizenship. To this end, the programs of the Federal government bearing on this objective shall be designed to have the effect, directly or indirectly, of enhancing the stability and resources of the Negro American family.

FAMILIES AS FICTION AND FANTASY

Families in the Media

Family life was one of the commonest themes in newspapers and magazines of the nineteenth century, a time of rapid growth in mass literacy. The media* expanded into silent motion pictures by 1910, in the 1920s into radio and talking "movies" and, after 1945, into television. This technology brought simultaneously to millions of Americans the sight and voices of families other than their own. "With what effect?" remains a continuing puzzle. Some writers depict the mass audience as helpless victims of continuous manipulation to "conform." Others find Americans more selective amid or calloused by the barrage of words and pictures of worlds beyond their own. Although pictures and spoken words in the media probably affect most Americans of today more deeply than print ever did, it is difficult to generalize about intentions or effects. We know that media audiences are huge and diverse. We know that fans develop strong loyalties to favorites but also antipathies or indifference to characters or stories that win other millions. We know what images millions *seem* to see and what story writers and directors *say* they portray about families, but of what audiences *really* see, how they take it, and what it leads to we can still say little. Nevertheless, the family image remains one of the most potent for affecting American expectations and styles of life. Advertising agencies and "idea men," writers, actors, directors, and others have, collectively, a multi-billion-dollar stake in "getting their messages across" or in "how to get people excited."

Descriptions and examples of a few of the more famous "media" families convey some idea of what images modern American audiences have been exposed to and what writers or producers guessed their audiences wanted as "family fare."

The samples from the media include themes from one of the most popular "love magazines" of the 1930s, *True Story*. This monthly had sales of hundreds of thousands of copies and readers in the millions. *True Story* also was the basis for one of the most popular radio shows of the decade, *The Court of Human Relations*, a weekly series of enactments of "real-life" situations that had appeared in the magazine. The radio audience was

* Jargon derived from "medium of expression."

613

asked to submit opinions on the difficulties of these radio families. The selection here is from summaries of the most provocative sixty histories that had a calibrated range of effects on the reporting audience. Included are the advertising agency's ratings of impact and its analysis for prospective sponsors of the kinds of family themes that "get people excited." Would we agree with the rating of what the stories seem to say? What can such "true stories" tell us about actual American families or of their perceptions of what is "real"? Should we resist the basic contention that the stories are "true," not to imply that they are made-up but that they adequately convey the behavior and feelings of family members in the ostensible real life situation?

Another selection is four daily strips from the immensely popular *Blondie* comics, still a favorite in 1980, more than forty years after its inception as a King Features enterprise. Again, how did readers understand Blondie and her husband, Dagwood? Was she a lovable and lovely, although "daffy," wife and mother, or was she domineering and manipulative, really "ruling the roost" despite her "dizziness"? Can we claim any importance for the comic strip's being named "Blondie," not "The Bumsteads" or "Dagwood"? How much can one comic strip, no matter how popular or seemingly revealing, tell us about general styles of American families?

It is just as difficult to build a sense of America's views of itself from the hundreds of movies that have dealt with family themes. That audiences (as shown in the poll below) classified *Gone With the Wind* primarily as a family film suggest how tricky labels are. In the 1930s, the heyday of the talking movies, "family films" had an extraordinary range. Among the most popular—most admissions paid—were the Andy Hardy series starring the young Mickey Rooney. All these turned on the adventures of the sixteen-or-so-year-old Andy trying to solve his problems with girls, money, and his small-town "typically American" family headed by his correct but kindly father, Judge Hardy. The very successful sixteen Hardy films (1936–58) were appealing for their "real life" portraits of the good old American family and for their reassuring nostalgia. The series thus epitomized and probably set the aims of many other family movies. However settings and plot varied and however threatened it was, the film family like the Hardys overcame money worries, illness, and sexual temptation to restore peace, order, and propriety. In the once-common Hollywood happy ending husbands and wives settled with and for each other, parents and children were reconciled. Interlopers are expelled and those who break the family code too severely are punished, even killed. In the forty years after *The Jazz Singer* (1927) Hollywood produced few films that were irreverent about the family, and immigrant, black, and "ethnic" families scarcely existed on the screen. *The Jazz Singer* did depict an undisguised religiously orthodox Jewish family but its characters were such stereotypes and the son's struggle to become an "American" success in show business was so sympathetically shown that audiences could be reassured that no main-line American family ideal was being threatened. Similarly, in *The Grapes of Wrath* (1940), the classic "social conscience" film of the Great Depression, the poorest and most oppressed of the "common people" vindicated traditional ideals of honesty, hard work, and sexual propriety.

After about 1960 when public taste and the Hollywood code became less finicky, there was greater diversity and less piety in family films. Ethnic families and destructive family relationships were depicted. *The Godfather* (1972) and *The Godfather Part II* (1974) summed up many of these changes: the Corleone family of Italo-American mobsters was unmistakably and enduringly "ethnic"; the family business was, openly, crime; betrayal and hostility coexisted with internal loyalty to the family. All of America still seemed a society made for family but family had now gone corrupt. At the end of the saga, however, came familiar, reassuring retribution. The American son of the Godfather has become master of the rackets. He finds the American dream of immense power and wealth but his private life is in a shambles. His family has been destroyed en route to success.

From radio and television we have synopses and samples from two of the most popular daytime and evening family dramas. From radio in the 1930s we have the evening show *One Man's Family,* and from daytime TV the "soap opera" *Days of Our Lives.*

Beyond the problems of intentions, unintended meanings, and audience perceptions these classics from the media raise other questions. What do the *titles* of the shows suggest the audience is supposed to see and hear? Does there seem to be any reason for one type of show to have run largely in the evening and the other to have appeared only in the morning or afternoon? Is one more a "family show" while the other is a woman's, homemaker's, wife's, or mother's show? What makes one or the other more a *family* show? That daytime audiences for soap operas include millions of men and unmarried women is another fact that adds to the chronic complexity in assessing the roles of media families in recent American life.

The media since 1900 have also included means to increase hearing, playing, and singing popular songs. The sheet music of the twentieth century was printed in ever larger quantities thanks to modern presses. Phonograph records increased rapidly in variety, quality, and availability, and recorded music over radio and on movie sound tracks filled the American air with "hits" and "old-time favorites." Overwhelmingly, since 1900, love has been the main theme of the American popular song, but with endless variations on that theme. Only a small minority of love songs, however, indicate marriage as the aim or setting of love. Still, some of the greatest hits have had lyrics about love in marriage, and a sampling of those from the first half of the twentieth century will be found below.

Serious historical questions about popular songs are a peculiarly difficult task, since to begin with they involve hearing, primarily, not seeing, and they stir so-called "musical emotions" as well as our store of images and associated feelings and ideas. In reading these lyrics, without their music, in what ways do any "pictures" of marriage change from 1905 to about

1930, and then from 1930 to 1950? What seems permissible or desirable to say in 1905, and what seems to be sayable two generations later? What do these changes tempt us to believe is happening to the place of and expectations associated with marriage during a half century? In that period and today, American society remains strongly a marriage culture, in practice and profession. What then are we to think if most of its popular songs are about either love without mention of marriage (no proof, however, that marriage is not *meant*) or, increasingly, about marriage bringing or creating love problems? Are these songs one way to reflect increasing dissatisfactions with marriage, infidelity, and the commoner use of divorce?

FAMILIES IN MAGAZINES

With True Story apparently succeeding in stirring up more excitement among the people who are its readers than has any other magazine ever published (as evidenced by the greatest voluntary reader demand in the history of the magazine business), increasing numbers of advertising men have been examining the magazine as a laboratory of human emotions. . . .

One of the True Story departments most examined has been the Home Problems Forum, probably because it has offered the most conveniently measurable index of what gets people excited. Each month a controversial problem involving certain basic human emotions and viewpoints is presented. Everyone of these problems stems from actual experience since they are written from real life by True Story's own readers. This is consistent with True Story's editorial policy. For the best solution from a reader, a series of prizes is offered. These prizes are kept modest ($15, $10, $5) deliberately so that response may be credited to the problem rather than to the cash!

Some problems bring letters by the thousands—others by the thin hundreds.

The following pages contain summaries of . . . psychological situations which have been presented in the True Story Home Problems Forum during the past five years—together with the relative ranking of their ability to get people excited. . . .

Should Wife Be Compelled to Work?

Sophie has worked during the 10 years of her marriage to Jack. She dislikes her work but her husband wants her to keep at it, his excuse being they must save for the future. In addition, Sophie does all her own housework. She is not allowed to handle her own money, which goes into a joint account. Sophie wants to quit work since there is no real need for her to do it. Jack sees nothing wrong in her working. *What do you think about this?* [Excellent]

Editors, True Story, *How to Get People Excited* (New York, 1937), passim.

What Should We Tell Our Children?

Elsie and Stan are the parents of an unusually bright boy of 8. They do not agree on his upbringing. Stan thinks he should be conversant with the details of marital and sex life. Elsie objects. She thinks his attitude can only make the boy sex-conscious at an age when he cannot understand its meaning. She believes this will result in a perverted mental attitude toward life. *How do you feel about this problem?* [Excellent]

Son Objects to Mother's Work

Margaret finds it difficult to get work after her husband's death. She tries living with each of her married children but cannot get along, and is especially unhappy in her son Frederick's home. Her children cannot afford to give her an income. She wants to have a newsstand so that she can support herself. Frederick says this would embarrass him and keep him from getting a better position. He wants her to come and live with his family again. But she was so unhappy there she does not want to. *What would you do?* [Very good]

Should Mother Marry Again?

Susan was left a widow with four small children at the youthful age of 27. All through the years she has cared for them, and now Susan is 54 and her children are all married. She wants to marry Peter, age 60, a wealthy widower who is in love with her. Her children do not want her to marry. *How do you feel about Susan's problem?* [Very good]

Shall Wife Forgive Errant Husband?

Helen goes home to her parents, who live in a town where there is a good hospital, to have her baby. Later she discovers that her husband George has had an affair with another woman while she was away. Unable to stand her husband, she takes baby away to her sister's home, where the child dies. She is too dazed to resist George when he comes to take her home, but feels there can be no happiness for them now. George says he loves her and wants another chance. *What do you think?* [Good]

Wife Deserts Family for Singing Career

Six years ago Stella left her husband, Frank, and their 6-year-old child in order to further her singing career. Frank, though bitter because of her desertion, follows her career and, when he finds she has been a failure, offers to take her back, not because he loves her but because the child needs a mother. Stella, though still in love with Frank and the child, feels she cannot go back. Fears her husband will think she came back for a home and not because she still loves him. *What would you do?* [Good]

Should He Adopt Wife's Child?

Harvey was shocked to learn that his wife Sue had had an illegitimate child prior to their marriage. They have two children of their own. Sue wants to adopt the boy. Harvey wants him sent to an orphanage. Fears he may be a bad influence on his own children—furthermore, he says he could not stand the sight of him. *What's your opinion?* [Fair]

Wife Incompatible

Sarah, mid-Victorian in her ideas, has brought her three children up to be self-righteous little prigs with none of the instincts of normal boys and girls. Her husband, Luke, has been forced to give up his friends due to her narrow-mindedness and nagging. Sarah is anxious to separate. Luke, though unhappy, is willing to do a great deal to keep his children—if Sarah will give in a little. *What is your suggestion?* [Fair]

Should Wife Grant Divorce?

After 11 years of seemingly happy marriage, Fred suddenly wants a divorce. He loves another woman and wants to marry her. Henrietta, his wife, is willing to live with him as a comparative stranger, so that the children might not be deprived of his love. To Fred this is intolerable. He thinks being held in this way would cause him soon to hate her. *What would you advise?* [Poor]

Separate Bedrooms

Mary and Howard, engaged to be married, have bought a house. Because she was one of many children and has never had any privacy, Mary insists that they have separate rooms. She says she has dreamed all her life of a room of her own. Howard cannot understand her refusal to share his room at night. He can only feel that it is because of something lacking in their relationship. *How would you settle this problem? Do you sympathize with Howard, or do you think Mary's attitude is right?* [Poor]

Wife Lets Maid Care for Child

Marie likes to help her husband, Dean, in his office. She has recently hired a new maid to take care of her young son. While waiting for a street car the boy is instantly killed and the maid injured for life. Dean blames Marie. Says she should not have left the boy in care of an incompetent maid. Feels he can no longer live with her and wants a divorce. Marie says the same thing might have happened if she were with the boy. *What do you think?* [Very Poor]

Doesn't Approve of Mother-in-Law

Vilma's mother, a nightclub hostess, wants to come to live with her daughter. Vilma's husband, John, objects to his mother-in-law, whom he has been led to believe was on the stage, and whom he sees for the first time in his eight years of marriage. During the Depression years the mother helped considerably in a financial way. Vilma wants her mother to come to live with her and the grandchildren, who are very fond of her. John wants the children to have nothing to do with her and will pay back the money when he can. *With whom do you agree?* [Very Poor]

FAMILIES IN ADVERTISING

The Saturday Evening Post, 1915

Advertisements using family imagery appeared in the nineteenth century. Usually a small idealized sketch of a baby or wife-mother was used to suggest purity or reliability. As advertising expanded after 1900, ads became more elaborate and extravagant. These five ads for well-known household soaps appeared in the most important family and women's magazines of the decades 1910–50. They show changes in the family image to which advertisers appealed, and important shifts in language and mood.

ACTUAL
VISITS
TO P & G
HOMES
No. 1

14 little blouses blowing on the line

WHEN we saw those blouses, and counted them, and surveyed the rest of the beautiful, fresh-looking clothes snapping in the crisp breeze, we simply had to stop in for a talk with their owner.

Mrs. Marshall* proved to be one of those cordial, friendly people you just can't help liking. Her house was friendly, too — with bright chintzes, glistening white woodwork, and welcoming, comfortable chairs.

"How do you do it?" we asked her when we found she'd done that whole wash herself. "There are *fourteen* blouses on that line!"

"There aren't always so many," she laughed. "Somehow Dick and Bobby each needed a clean blouse every day last week. But even fourteen blouses aren't so much work as they once were, since I've used P and G Naphtha Soap. I suppose that pleases you!" she added.

Hints from Mrs. Marshall

"*Before putting the clothes to soak, I always have lukewarm water in the tub. I never put the clothes in first and then run in hot and cold water. Hot water, striking the clothes, sets the dirt. Also, the first few drops are often rusty and make stubborn stains. With P and G I soak my clothes only during breakfast, not over night. This loosens even the most ground-in dirt without rubbing.*"

"Indeed it does," we replied. "How do you notice the difference?"

"By comparison. Like most women, I've tried a good many soaps, but P and G simply outdoes them all. It gets the clothes clean so quickly, without ever fading their colors. I never have to rub hard any more, or boil every week. And I not only use it in the laundry but everywhere else in the house from kitchen to bathroom."

Of course, Mrs. Marshall is only one of the millions of women who think this way about P and G, and that is why P and G is the largest-selling laundry soap in America. You see, it does everything better! And it makes no difference whether the water is hard or soft, cold or hot, P and G always gives beautiful, quick, safe results. Don't you think it ought to be doing *your* work, too?

*Of course, this isn't her real name.

PROCTER & GAMBLE

THE LARGEST-SELLING LAUNDRY SOAP IN AMERICA

THERE *is no mystery about the supremacy of P and G — it is simply a better soap.*

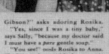
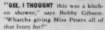
The Saturday Evening Post, 1935

"almost like a Fels-Naptha wash !"

"Sunny wash days are wonderful! 'Specially now, when I can't always get Fels-Naptha.

"Wash day weather never bothered me when Fels-Naptha Soap was plentiful. On rainy days I'd do a whole wash with Fels-Naptha, hang it in the basement and my things would be as white and sweet as though they'd dried in the sun.

"Oh, well . . . as long as the Fels people are making soap for my Jim and the other boys in the service, I can't complain. And I guess we'll have our Fels-Naptha Soap back before long . . ."

We like to think the average American wife or mother says something like this as she carries on without many ordinary necessities—like Fels-Naptha Soap.

We wish she could have Fels-Naptha Soap for *every* wash day. But while we're making soap that helps keep Jim the cleanest fighting man in the world, sometimes she'll have to do without.

And the lady in the picture is right . . . she'll have her Fels-Naptha Soap back, before long.

Fels-Naptha Soap
BANISHES "TATTLE-TALE" GRAY

53

Wonderful Ivory Snow...

safest possible soap for diapers and everything that touches baby's tender skin

Leaves baby things far softer than strong soaps or detergents!

Softer, safer for your baby's tender skin, that's how diapers, baby things come out washed with Ivory Snow! It leaves them far softer than strong soaps or detergents, and free of irritating deposits that could chafe your baby's skin.

All nice hand or machine washables stay nice longer with Ivory Snow care. It guards gay colors, leaves woolens soft and fluffy. It's granulated for efficiency in your washing machine, too!

IVORY SNOW

GIANT ECONOMY SIZE

99 44/100% PURE ®

COMMENDED PARENTS MAGAZINE

The only soap both Ivory-safe and granulated for efficiency!

Ladies' Home Journal, 1955

FAMILIES IN COMICS

Just Between Boys!

Vacuum Cleaner Has a Bagful.

Chic Young, *Blondie: 100 Selected Top Laughs of America's Best Loved Comic* (Philadelphia, 1944).
© 1944 King Features Syndicate, Inc. Reprinted by permission.

One Is Enough!

"I'll Take Vanilla!"

FAMILIES IN MOVIES

The Jazz Singer (1927, Warner Bros.). This was the first movie to incorporate sound in some scenes. Al Jolson played the restless son of a pious Jewish cantor and rejects a similar career for himself to find success as a Broadway singer. The enraged father is eventually reconciled with his son before dying. The son dedicates his hit song, "Mammy," to his adoring mother on the big opening night. May McAvoy played the mother.

The Museum of Modern Art/Film Stills Archive

Andy Hardy Meets Debutante (1939, MGM). The Hardy films often turned around the troubles of the son played by Mickey Rooney. Girls, money, cars, and boyish projects deeply try the patience of the forebearing, consoling mother (Fay Holden) and eventually require steadying by the stern father Judge Hardy (Lewis Stone). Andy's girlfriends included familiar types like the sweet and steady girl-next-door, the daring sex-pot, and the alluring, big-city girl in town on a visit.   *The Museum of Modern Art/Film Stills Archive*

The Grapes of Wrath (1940, 20th Century-Fox). The Joads, a large migrant family, forced from its farm in Oklahoma, travel to California for a new chance. The "common people" included Henry Fonda, Jane Darwell, and John Carradine.

The Museum of Modern Art/Film Stills Archive

The Magnificent Ambersons (1942, RKO). An unusually realistic movie for the time made by the young, irreverent Orson Welles. A patrician family of the 1880s loses its money and its power. Joseph Cotten, Dolores Costello, and Agnes Moorehead played the major roles. *The Museum of Modern Art/Film Stills Archive*

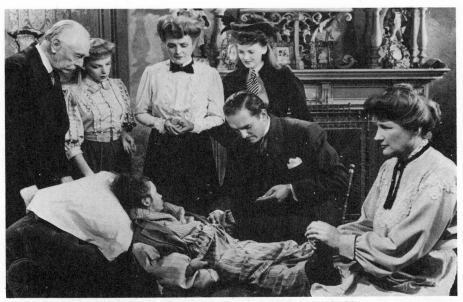

Meet Me in St. Louis (1944, MGM). As the great St. Louis Fair of 1904 prepares to open, a comfortable family faces a series of mild stresses but all turns out well in time for them to ride the new electric trolley to the wondrous fair. The family included Judy Garland, Margaret O'Brien, Mary Astor, and Leon Ames.

The Museum of Modern Art/Film Stills Archive

The Best Years of Our Lives (1946, Goldwyn). Another all-star cast, including Myrna Loy, Fredric March, and Teresa Wright, showed how three veterans coming back from World War II to three different families in the same town dealt with the problems of "readjustment."   *The Museum of Modern Art/Film Stills Archive*

Shane (1953, Paramount). A western in which a peaceful small family of homesteaders is befriended by a mysterious gunslinger who helps save the farm from the "bad guys" and strengthens the family's ties before he has to move on. Alan Ladd, Jean Arthur, Van Heflin, and Brandon de Wilde were the principals.

The Museum of Modern Art/Film Stills Archive

Giant (1956, Warner Bros.). This was a saga of two generations of a Texas ranch family on its climb to immense Texan-scale success in the era of oil and gas. The all-star cast featured Rock Hudson, Elizabeth Taylor, and James Dean.

The Museum of Modern Art/Film Stills Archive

Cat on a Hot Tin Roof (1958, MGM). Elizabeth Taylor, Paul Newman, and Burl Ives were the principals in this melodrama of the modern South by Tennessee Williams. The rich "Big Daddy" of the plantation is dying but deeply worried about the inadequacies of both of his sons as his successors. Paul Newman rallies to the challenge.

The Museum of Modern Art/Film Stills Archive

The Godfather Part II (1974, Paramount-Coppola). **This followed the similarly immensely successful** *The Godfather*. **It showed the struggle for mastery of the mob by the youngest son and chosen heir of the founder of the Corleone clan. The film included splendid flashbacks to the Sicily and New York City ghetto of the youth of the Godfather. Robert De Niro and Al Pacino were the stars.** *The Museum of Modern Art/Film Stills Archive*

THE TEN BEST

FORTY YEARS: THE TEN
BEST FAMILY FILMS

The Sound of Music
Gone With the Wind
Meet Me in St. Louis
Cheaper by the Dozen
Mrs. Miniver
Little Women
Life with Father
I Remember Mama
You Can't Take It with You
How Green Was My Valley

Christian Science Monitor poll, 1972.

THE TEN MOST POPULAR
DAYTIME RADIO SHOWS

When a Girl Marries
Stella Dallas
Romance of Helen Trent
Arthur Godfrey
Our Gal Sunday
Young Dr. Malone
Young Widder Brown
Ma Perkins
Big Sister
Pepper Young's Family

Rating in *New York Times*, 1949.

FAMILIES ON RADIO

One Man's Family was created by Carlton E. Morse in 1932 and "dedicated to the mothers and fathers of the younger generation and to their bewildering offspring." It went on the air for the first time [on NBC] in 1932. The final broadcast, pre-recorded, went on the air . . . twenty-seven years later in 1959. *One Man's Family* was a serial drama, appearing as a weekly half-hour program through June 1950, and thereafter as a daily quarter-hour program, for a total of 3,256 separate episodes. . . .

One Man's Family presented a continuing saga of the generations in a single, happy, American family. . . . The evidence available in the listing of programs and ratings compiled . . . tells us that it was generally the most popular radio network program available to audiences when it was on the air. . . .

Content

The principal theme of the series was: The American family and home life are vital to the continuance of the nation's ideals and freedoms, and they are in danger of deterioration or destruction. The *Family* was dedicated to this theme, and it permeated nearly every one of Morse's scripts. Specific statements of it were given mainly to the older and more authoritative characters or to the announcer. Here is a semi-humorous treatment of the idea of deterioration:

HENRY (father): From fifteen to eighteen a boy or girl never listens to the words you say to them. They only listen to your tone of voice. From that they decide a parent's either preaching, or angry, or else doesn't know what's going on.

HAZEL (daughter—*amused*): Oh, that's a little bit exaggerated, Father.

HENRY: I have it out of the mouth of one of those young people himself.

TEDDY (adopted granddaughter—*amused*): How do you mean, Father Barbour?

HENRY: I was walking by the high school the other noon, and I overheard a not-yet-dry-behind-the-ears Young Swain say to his hardly-out-of-adolescence Lady Love, "What makes with the ancestors, infant mortality? I called three times last night and got the vinegar treatment every time."

HAZEL: *(laughs)*

HENRY: To which the Beautiful Young Thing replied, "Johnny, Momma just doesn't like you. I don't know what I'm going to do with her." Our Hero shrugged. "Well, that's parents for you. They're either in the pulpit, in a pet, or innocent."

Walter F. Sheppard, "Some Notes on *One Man's Family*," *Journal of Broadcasting*, vol. 14, no. 2 (Spring, 1970), pp. 183–95.

HAZEL *(amused):* I've caught similar bits of dialogue.

HENRY: And that's the young people's idea of their parents—either preaching, angry, or else too dumb to know what's going on. What a commentary on modern family life.

Secondary themes included: Personal freedom is permissible within the boundaries of family life; Motherhood is to be honored and is a woman's natural destiny; Our society is changing and social improvements will probably result; and Nature is a source of joy and pleasure, and closeness to nature is important to the health of the individual and society. There are numerous examples of these themes in the scripts:

PAUL (son): . . . You think of us—the Barbour children—as *your* family. I'm afraid we think of ourselves as separate entities.

HENRY: Paul, you never tire of belittling the importance of family ties, do you?

PAUL: You are mistaken, Dad. I merely think you overrate those ties and insist so vehemently on their strict observance that you make them a little galling at times.

* * *

HENRY: I remember . . . how she [Fanny—wife] accepted motherhood as the greatest blessing that could be bestowed on her. The cynicism and resentment of some of these modern girls today is beyond my understanding after these years with Fanny. . . .

PAUL: The people of this country are at last awake. They are thinking, having opinions, expressing themselves. They may be thinking along wrong lines, their opinions may be silly, and they may express themselves badly; but this is only the beginning. Out of all this ferment will come ideas, good ideas, progressive ideas. And only one thing can come of it—advancement, growth, development.

* * *

HENRY: My boy, I can get down on my knees and work in that soil for a couple of hours and I'm a new man. Renewed in spirit and strength. The soil's a great thing, Jack. It wasn't named Mother Earth for nothing. We're part of her. We need her constantly.

Subsidiary to the themes are observations, discussions, comments, statements of advice, and lecturettes on almost every topic imaginable. The subjects naturally include such family matters as relations between the generations, child-rearing, and marriage. They also range widely over other aspects of life and behavior—the importance of a sense of humor, how to react to death, sexual relations, tolerance to others. Their content goes from glib superficiality through plain common sense to observations and discussions that are outspoken and unexpected for a highly popular family program.

FAMILIES ON TELEVISION

DR. TOM HORTON and his wife, Alice, head a large, old-fashioned family in Salem, U.S.A., where Tom is Chief of Internal Medicine at University Hospital. The problem-plagued Horton brood originally consisted of five children: Addie (recently deceased) and Tommy (twins, in their mid-forties), Mickey (late thirties), Bill (mid-thirties), and Marie (late twenties). Addie, who married singer DOUG WILLIAMS before her death, is the mother of Julie (mid-twenties) and Steve (late teens), who was raised in Europe and now lives in Paris. Mickey is a successful attorney wed to psychiatrist LAURA HORTON, and they have a son, Michael, Jr. (mid-teens). Bill is still the bachelor. Tommy, now a widower, lives in the Horton household with his daughter, Sandy. Marie is a nun. Julie, Addie's daughter with the late BEN OLSON, has recently made Tom and Alice great-grandparents with the birth of her son, David. . . .

Sixteen years ago the Hortons were a happy family, all still living together—with the exception of the oldest son, TOMMY HORTON, who was missing in action in Korea. Then ADDIE HORTON OLSON, married to wealthy banker BEN OLSON, moved to Europe with him. DR. TOM HORTON and his wife, ALICE HORTON, felt little joy at their daughter's sudden departure. But they did have a consolation in that Addie and Ben left their daughter, JULIE OLSON, to be raised by her grandparents. Young Julie, however, never forgave her mother for deserting her.

Julie became the tortured and motherless young girl searching for love and friendship wherever she could find them. Unfortunately she tended to find both in all the wrong places.

Her one-time best chum from high-school days, SUSAN MARTIN, eventually became her bitter rival and the cause of many of her heartaches. The friendship was first severely strained when Julie found out that Susan was carrying the child of DAVID MARTIN, to whom Julie was then secretly engaged. Julie, however, stepped aside and let the two marry, even stoically agreeing to become Susan's maid of honor, but bitterness raged between the two women when Susan, after the birth of her child, refused to divorce David so that Julie could marry him.

While the two rivals steamed, DR. BILL HORTON, a brilliant young surgeon attempting to follow in his father Tom's footsteps at University Hospital, met and fell in love with a fellow intern, DR. LAURA SPENCER, who was specializing in psychiatry. They became engaged, but when Bill discovered that he could no longer operate because of an infirmity in his hands, he suddenly left Salem.

As if fate were punishing Susan and David for their sins, tragedy engulfed them. Shortly after their son, RICHARD MARTIN, was born, his father, David, was playing with him on a swing and the child was killed accidentally. Susan went out of her mind and shot David Martin!

Susan was put on trial for his murder. Since she was a patient of Laura Spencer's and was being defended by MICKEY HORTON, Bill's brother, Laura and Mickey had to spend a great deal of time together. Laura, distraught over Bill's continued absence from Salem, began to return Mickey's affections. The outcome of Mickey's defense was Susan's acquittal on the charge of murder on the basis of temporary insanity—established during the trial by Laura's expert psychiatric testimony. Laura married Mickey, and Bill returned to Salem—heartbroken to find that his brother and fiancée had wed.

Shattered though he was, Bill had to turn his attentions to a young doctor whom he had brought home with him. Burned and tortured during the Korean war, the young doctor had undergone extensive plastic surgery, which completely changed his appearance, and was still suffering from the amnesia inflicted by shell shock. MARIE HORTON, the Horton's youngest daughter, was instantly attracted to the handsome doctor and fell in love with him. Later, when the young man was revealed to be her missing brother, Tommy Horton, Marie was able to retain her sanity only by becoming a nun. KITTY HORTON, to whom Tommy was married before leaving for Korea, had returned to Salem with their daughter, SANDY HORTON, and she immediately began causing trouble for everyone.

Meanwhile, Bill couldn't forget Laura. The thought of the woman he loved being married to his own brother haunted him day and night. Having to work with her every day at the hospital made it even worse for him. One night at the hospital the pressure became too much for him, and he raped her. Soon after, she became pregnant and knew that it had to be Bill's child. By then Tom Horton knew that Mickey was sterile and could never father his own child, and so confronted Laura with this knowledge. She was forced to admit that Bill had raped her. Tom was beside himself but dared not say anything for fear someone would tell Mickey the truth about himself.

After Bill's son, MICHAEL HORTON, was born, the interfering Kitty Horton got hold of a tape recording of a conversation between Laura and Tom Horton that proved Michael's true parentage. She threatened Bill with revealing the truth to the whole world. A struggle between the two of them took place, and Kitty, who already had a heart condition, died on the spot. During Bill's trial for supposedly killing her, he repeatedly refused to say what caused the struggle in order to protect Mickey from the truth, and was finally sentenced to six months in prison for manslaughter.

MARRIAGE IN SONGS

In My Merry Oldsmobile (1905)
Vincent Bryan and Gus Edwards

Come away with me, Lucille,
In my merry Oldsmobile.
Down the road of life we'll fly,
Automo-bubbling, you and I.
To the church we'll swiftly steal,
Then our wedding bells will peal.
You can go as far as you like with me
In my merry Oldsmobile.

For Me and My Gal (1917)
Edgar Leslie and E. Ray Goetz–George W. Meyer

The bells are ringing, for me and my gal.
The birds are singing, for me and my gal.
Everybody's been knowing,
To a wedding they're going.
And for weeks they've been sewing,
Every Susie and Sal.
They're congregating for me and my gal.
The parson's waiting for me and my gal.
And sometime I'm gonna build a little home
For two, for three, or four or more,
In love-land, for me and my gal.

Till We Meet Again (1918)
Raymond B. Egan and Richard A. Whiting

Smile the while you kiss me sad adieu,
When the clouds roll by I'll come to you.
Then the skies will seem more blue
Down in lovers' lane, my dearie.
Wedding bells will ring so merrily,
Every tear will be a memory,
So wait and pray each night for me,
Till we meet again.

Ma (He's Making Eyes at Me) (1921)
Sidney Clare and Con Conrad

Ma, he's making eyes at me.
Ma, he's awful nice to me.
Ma, he's almost breaking my heart,

I'm beside him, mercy, let his conscience guide him.
Ma, he wants to marry me,
Be my honey bee.
Every minute he gets bolder,
Now he's leaning on my shoulder,
Ma, he's kissing me.

Ain't We Got Fun (1921)

Gus Kahn & Raymond B. Egan–Richard A. Whiting

Bill collectors gather 'round and rather haunt the cottage next door,
Men the grocer and butcher sent, men who call for the rent.
But within, a happy chappy and his bride of only a year
Seem to be so cheerful, here's an earful of the chatter you hear.

Just to make their trouble nearly double, something happened last night.
To their chimney a gray bird came, mister Stork is his name.
And I'll bet two pins, a pair of twins just happened in with the bird.
Still they're very gay and merry, just at dawning I heard:

CHORUS 1:

Every morning, every evening, ain't we got fun.
Not much money, oh, but honey, ain't we got fun.
The rent's unpaid, dear, we haven't a bus,
But smiles were made, dear, for people like us.
In the winter, in the summer, don't we have fun.
Times are bum and getting bummer, still we have fun.
There's nothing surer—the rich get rich and the poor get children.
In the meantime, in-between time, ain't we got fun.

CHORUS 2:

Every morning, every evening, don't we have fun.
Twins and cares, dear, come in pairs, dear, don't we have fun.
We are only started as mommer and pop.
Are we down-hearted? I'll say we're not.
Landlord's mad and getting madder, still we have fun.
There's nothing surer—the rich get rich and the poor get laid off.
In the meantime, in-between time, ain't we got fun.

CHORUS 3:

Night or daytime, it's all playtime, ain't we got fun.
Hot or cold days, any old days, ain't we got fun.
If wifie wishes to go to a play,
Don't wash the dishes, just throw them away.
Streetcar seats are awful narrow, ain't we got fun.
They won't smash up our Pierce Arrow, we ain't got none.

They've cut my wages—but my income tax will be so much smaller.
When I'm paid off, I'll be laid off, Ain't we got fun.

Tea for Two (1924)

Irving Caesar and Vincent Youmans

I'm discontented with homes that are rented, so I have invented my own.
Darling, this place is a lover's oasis where life's weary chase is unknown.
Far from the cry of the city where flowers pretty caress the streams,
Cosy to hide in, to live side by side in, don't let it abide in my dream.

Picture you upon my knee, just tea for two and two for tea,
Just me for you and you for me alone.
Nobody near us to see us or hear us, no friends or relations on weekend
    vacations,
We won't have it known, dear, that we own a telephone, dear.
Day will break and you'll awake and start to bake a sugar cake
For me to take for all the boys to see.
We will raise a family, a boy for you, a girl for me—
Oh, can't you see how happy we would be.

Blue Room (1926)

Richard Rodgers and Lorenz Hart

HE: All my future plans, dear, will suit your plans,
   Read the little blue prints.
   Here's your mother's room, here's your brother's room,
   On the wall are two prints.
   Here's the kiddies' room, here's the biddy's room,
   Here's a pantry lined with shelves, dear.
   Here I've planned for us something grand for us
   Where we two can be ourselves, dear.

SHE: From all visitors and inquisitors
   We'll keep our apartment.
   I won't change your plans. You arrange your plans
   Just the way your heart meant.
   Here we'll be ourselves and we'll see ourselves
   Doing all the things we're scheming.
   Here's a certain place, cretonne-curtain place
   Where no one can see us dreaming.

We'll have a blue room, a new room, for two room
Where every day's a holiday because you're married to me.
Not like a ball room, a small room, a hall room
Where you can smoke your pipe away
With your head upon my knee.
We will thrive on, keep alive on
Just nothing but kisses, with mister and misses
On little blue chairs.
I'll wear my trousseau, and Robinson Crusoe
Is not so far from worldly cares
As our blue room far away upstairs.

My Blue Heaven (1927)

George Whiting and Walter Donaldson

When whip-poor-wills call
And evening is nigh,
I hurry to my blue heaven.
A turn to the right,
A little white light
Will lead you to my blue heaven.
You'll see a smiling face, a fireplace, a cozy room,
A little nest that's nestled where the roses bloom.
Just Mollie and me
And baby makes three,
We're happy in my blue heaven.

Soon (1930)

George Gershwin and Ira Gershwin

VERSE 1:

I'm making up for all the years
That I waited;
I'm compensated
At last.
My heart is through with shirking;
Thanks to you it's working
Fast.
The many lonely nights and days
When this duffer
Just had to suffer
Are past.

Life will be a dream song,
Love will be the theme song.

REFRAIN:

Soon—the lonely nights will be ended;
Soon—two hearts as one will be blended.
I've found the happiness I've waited for:
The only girl that I was fated for.
Oh! Soon—a little cottage will find us
Safe, with all our cares far behind us.
The day you're mine this world will be in tune.
Let's make that day come soon.

REFRAIN 2:

Soon—my dear, you'll never be lonely;
Soon—you'll find I live for you only.
When I'm with you who cares what time it is,
Or what the place or what the climate is?
Oh, Soon—our little ship will come sailing
Home, through every storm, never failing.
The day you're mine this world will be in tune.
Let's make that day come soon.

It's De-Lovely (1936)

Cole Porter

VERSE 1:

He: I feel a sudden urge to sing
    The kind of ditty that invokes the spring,
    So control your desire to curse
    While I crucify the verse.
She: This verse you've started seems to me
    The Tin-Pantithesis of melody,
    So spare me, please, the pain,
    Just skip the damn thing and sing the refrain.
He: Mi, mi, mi, mi,
    Re, re, re, re,
    Do, sol, mi, do, la, si,
She: Take it away.

REFRAIN 1:

The night is young, the skies are clear,
So if you want to go walking, dear,
It's delightful, it's delicious, it's de-lovely.
I understand the reason why
You're sentimental, 'cause so am I,
It's delightful, it's delicious, it's de-lovely.
You can tell at a glance
What a swell night this is for romance,
You can hear dear Mother Nature murmuring low:
"Let yourself go."
So please be sweet, my chickadee,
And when I kiss you, just say to me,
"It's delightful, it's delicious,
"It's delectable, it's delirious,
"It's dilemma, it's delimit, it's deluxe, it's de-lovely."

VERSE 2

She: Oh, charming sir, the way you sing
　　　Would break the heart of Missus Crosby's Bing,
　　　For the tone of your tra la la
　　　Has that certain je ne sais quoi.
He: Oh, thank thee kindly, winsome wench,
　　　But 'stead of falling into Berlitz French
　　　Just warble to me, please,
　　　This beautiful strain in plain Brooklynese.
She: Mi, mi, mi, mi,
　　　Re, re, re, re,
　　　Do, sol, mi, do, la, si,
He: Take it away.

REFRAIN 2:

Time marches on and soon it's plain
You've won my heart and I've lost my brain,
It's delightful, it's delicious, it's de-lovely.
Life seems so sweet that we decide
It's in the bag to get unified,
It's delightful, it's delicious, it's de-lovely.
See the crowd in that church,
See the proud parson plopped on his perch,
Get the sweet beat of that organ, sealing our doom,
"Here goes the groom, boom!"
How they cheer and how they smile
As we go galloping down that aisle.

"It's divine, dear, it's diveen, dear,
"It's de wunderbar, it's de victory,
"It's de vallop, it's de vinner, it's de voiks, it's de-lovely."

REFRAIN 3:

The knot is tied and so we take
A few hours off to eat wedding cake,
It's delightful, it's delicious, it's de-lovely.
It feels so fine to be a bride,
And how's the groom? Why, he's slightly fried,
It's delightful, it's delicious, it's de-lovely.
To the pop of champagne,
Off we hop in our plush little plane
Till a bright light through the darkness cozily calls,
"Niag'ra Falls."
All's well, my love, our day's complete,
And what a beautiful bridal suite,
"It's de-reamy, it's de-rowsy,
"It's de-reverie, it's de-rhapsody,
"It's de-regal, it's de-royal, it's de-Ritz, it's de-lovely."

REFRAIN 4:

We settle down as man and wife
To solve the riddle called "married life,"
It's delightful, it's delicious, it's de-lovely.
We're on the crest, we have no cares,
We're just a couple of honey bears,
It's delightful, it's delicious, it's de-lovely.
All's as right as can be
Till, one night, at my window I see
An absurd bird with a bundle hung on his nose—
"Get baby clo'es."
Those eyes of yours are filled with joy
When Nurse appears and cries, "It's a boy,"
"He's appalling, he's appealing,
"He's a polywog, he's a paragon,
"He's a Pop-eye, he's a panic, he's a pip, he's de-lovely."

REFRAIN 5:

Our boy grows up, he's six feet three,
He's so good looking, he looks like me,
It's delightful, it's delicious, it's de-lovely.
He's such a hit, this son of ours,
That all the dowagers send him flowers,
It's delightful, it's delicious, it's de-lovely.
So sublime is his press

That in time, L. B. Mayer, no less,
Makes a night flight to New York and tells him he should
Go Hollywood.
Good God!, today, he gets such pay
That Elaine Barrie's his fiancée,
"It's delightful, it's delicious,
"It's delectable, it's delirious,
"It's dilemma, it's delimit, it's deluxe, it's de-lovely."

Where Is the Life That Late I Led? (1949)
Cole Porter

VERSE:

Since I reached the charming age of puberty
And began to finger feminine curls,
Like a show that's typically Shuberty
I have always had a multitude of girls.
But now that a married man, at last, am I,
How aware of my dear, departed past am I.

REFRAIN 1:

Where is the life that late I led?
Where is it now? Totally dead.
Where is the fun I used to find?
Where has it gone? Gone with the wind.
A married life may all be well,
But raising an heir
Could never compare
With raising a bit of hell.
So I repeat what first I said,
Where is the life that late I led?

PATTER 1:

In dear Milano, where are you, Momo,
Still selling those pictures of the scriptures in the duomo?
And Carolina, where are you, Lina,
Still peddling your pizza in the streets o' Taormina?
And in Firenze, where are you, Alice,
Still there is your pretty, itty-bitty Pitti palace?
And sweet Lucretia, so young and gay-ee?
What scandalous doin's in the ruins of Pompeii!

REFRAIN 2:

Where is the life that late I led?
Where is it now? Totally dead.
Where is the fun I used to find?
Where has it gone? Gone with the wind.
The marriage game is quite all right,
Yes, during the day
It's easy to play
But oh what a bore at night.
So I repeat what first I said,
Where is the life that late I led?

PATTER 2:

Where is Rebecca, my Becki-weckio,
Again is she cruising that amusing Ponte Vecchio?
Where is Fedora, the wild virago?
It's lucky I missed her gangster sister from Chicago.
Where is Venetia, who loved to chat so,
Could still she be drinkin, in her stinkin' pink palazzo?
And lovely Lisa, I thank you, Lisa,
You gave a new meaning to the leaning tow'r of Pisa.

REFRAIN 3:

Where is the life that late I led?
Where is it now? Totally dead.
Where is the fun I used to find?
Where has it gone? Gone with the wind.
I've oft been told of nuptial bliss
But what do you do,
A quarter to two,
With only a shrew to kiss?
So I repeat what first I said,
Where is the life that late I led?

HOW FAMILIES LIVE NOW

Variations on the Theme "Family"

Despite extraordinary, open and tolerated diversification, the American family in the late twentieth century largely means a legalized marriage of a man/husband and woman/wife, probably with children and living together in one household. By 1980 the great majority of Americans lived with such arrangements. Divorce and remarriage had made big inroads on this convention, and large numbers of legal spouses had been married previously. There was something strikingly odd in the strength and persistence of the traditional family setting, since so much of the sociology, law, court trials, social surveys, and psychiatry that made the headlines had repeatedly announced the death and passing of the family. Beyond sensationalism, however, serious study irrefutably revealed how many old family functions had disappeared or been lost to outsiders by 1950. With the extraordinary easing of sexual mores, even "having sex" (as a new expression oddly put it) scarcely depended on marriage or that old alternative, prostitution. Had the family then finally become largely what some historians had emphatically posited it had become several centuries earlier, a group tied primarily by affection? Or, but for children, would there be much marriage even if there was affection? In pursuit of a perfect affection or to salvage some affections from wrecked marriages, perhaps 15 percent of Americans in the last generation have practiced or preached or known family life in new modes or live without family. From the wide range of recent experiments, several documents are presented.

From the variegated revived enthusiasm for communes, one manifesto sets out a "radical solution" for families feeling in deep conflict with American culture. After 1950, hundreds, possibly more than a thousand of such familial experiments were made, from California to Maine, based on broadly similar sentiments of a new love and cooperation. Most of their records are probably lost to historians, but a strong consensus holds that most of these experiments failed rather quickly, whatever symbolic or partial victories they may have attained in their own view. The would-be communard had known the average American standard of living and expectations. "Programmed" or "conditioned" as they were, how much independence of telephones, clothes washers, hospitals, and medical care (however ideologically suspect) can communards in practice forego? Put otherwise, can the old family be fought without using or depending on some of its tools, like money or electricity or antibiotics? More deeply, can a community founded on a familial ideal of love and cooperation avoid raising the coercive power of guilt and shame when it foreswears law and open force? What "liberation" is that?

At the extreme, the ideal of a new and free family life brought one great national shock and horror, the commune of Jonestown in Guyana in South America. In the summer of 1978, a life of love and redemption that had started among the dispossessed of the San Francisco area turned into a nightmare of totalitarianism. It had a charismatic and apocalyptic leader with the out-of-a-novel name of Reverend Jim Jones. There was the religious con man's financial bilking and swindling, ugly sexual abuse and emotional exploitation, and a final orgy-at-gunpoint of a drug-induced death/suicide for most of the almost 1,000 members. Guns, loudspeakers, and other "technologies" in the hands of elite guards deliberately using fear were elements of a real-life version of twentieth-century love gone madly perverse. Most communes, of course, were light years away from this apocalypse, but extremes, like Jonestown or the "Moonies," suggest unsuspected contradictory tendencies within self-willed new and moral love societies. What, for example, does the hostile account in the final selection about a psychoanalytic familial "commune" in New York City imply about the authoritarian potential of any family in which one "figure" really dominates? Does the contemporary abstraction "good of the family," in this case translated as "therapeutically essential for health," obscure supposedly foresworn "neurotic drives" to power, acted-out immoral fantasy, and sexual abuse? Does a family ideal of complete love and cooperation by its very absolutism and blinding abstract quality invite such results? Is one major problem of any "ideal family" not purity of love as professed but the moral worth of the will that can make or break the traditional family of affection as well as any of its modern substitutes?

Apart from recent ideological communal experiments with the family ideal, Americans also sought or coped with private "alternative families." Two of these, the single parent and the growing number of stepparents, present their problems and claims in documents below; the selection on homosexual marriage (page 500) may also be relevant here. They prompt the question asked by some psychiatrists: Can a family without a female mother and mother figure or a male father and father figure adequately cope with the needs of young children? But are marriages with a mother or a father who fails to do the job (and what *are* those jobs?) preferable to the "single parent" household or to living with one parent and a stepparent? Some teachings of psychiatry also suggest that all families must and do "fail"; no human will or family control can be without large flaws. Husbands, wives, and children inevitably inflict deep wounds on each other, bringing frustration and alienation. In this view also, love can suffocate; conflict and anger are often legitimate and healthy. If such warnings are valid, albeit generalized, how much investment can be made in altered *structures* of families? If psyches were good *enough*, how much would "structure" matter? But how much do structures tax and taint psyches, perhaps already frail enough, in most cases? These few selections raise such questions about all recent searches for alternatives to the traditional family.

FAMILY LIVING: A RADICAL SOLUTION

The radical left movement has long protested the existing economy, and has assumed the responsibility of continually seeking a better solution to contemporary conditions. A basic change in life-style is the most obvious method of attacking the bond to the established quagmire. Communal living has proved to be a successful alternative to the single family unit, and has provided valuable resources to the movement.

Living in single family units, the establishment has us right where they want us. We are urged to be economically independent from each other, encouraged to be possessive of our material assets in every way, encouraged to believe that we cannot trust our brothers to care about us and that we should therefore not care about them. The media leads us to believe that only consuming more products will relieve us of the constant pressures we feel in this oppressive society by showing us that happy, fulfilled people use their product. If we are frustrated and unhappy, the blame must lie within ourselves and we must not reveal ourselves too closely to others. We must mistrust others' interests in our personal lives as a direct threat to our self-reliance. We are, therefore, forced to compete with each other almost constantly—for the most beautiful body, the nicest home, the best stereo tape recorder, the latest gadgets on the market, even for the most "well-adjusted" children. . . .

Because communal living costs less, each individual is set free from the economic necessity of working at a dull, frustrating job because he can't afford to take one that pays less. He is also free to work part time if he wants more time for other activities, or is free not to work at all if there is the need. Housecleaning, yard-work, and general maintenance are much less time consuming and burdensome when the responsibilities are shared. The aspect of substantially increased free time is doubly important to the movement because of all the things that need to be done, but are now being done by just a few people. Communal living would give those already deeply involved some time to themselves and would give others time to become more involved. Related to this is the aspect of group living as an educational tool. One is exposed to a much more diverse store of knowledge than in a nuclear family situation. This is mentally stimulating and enjoyable, and especially helpful to the movement when ideas of radical change are shared.

In a communal setup there is a great emphasis on human relationships.

"Family Living: A Radical Solution," *The Green Revolution,* June, 1969.

This pushes the value of consumer products even lower than it already is in many of our minds. Human relationships can also become much more satisfying when those in the group are honest about their feelings towards themselves and towards each other. There is new perspective put on relationships when members of a group share their observations and feelings about those relationships. The deeper and more important human relationships become to an individual, the less he cares or even thinks about being a consumer and loyally supporting the market. This puts us exactly where the establishment does not want us. And a very important place for us to be.

PARENTS WITHOUT PARTNERS

Who Are We?

We are an international organization of custodial and non-custodial single parents—widowed, divorced, separated, or never married—who, since the first Chapter was organized in 1957, have joined together for mutual help so that our single-parent homes can provide a happy family environment in which to bring up our children.

Our purposes are basically educational: with professional help, we conduct a program in which lectures, discussions, publications, and recreational activities aid the single parent in coping with the many problems that must be faced in a single-parent home. . . .

What Do We Do?

. . . Publish "The Single Parent" magazine, the only publication dealing solely with the problems of single-parenthood. Featured are articles on child-rearing, income taxes, remarriage, psychological problems and adjustments, education, and a host of others.

Prepare and distribute educational materials and program aids. . . .

Authorize and conduct research into the many unexplored areas of single-parent living.

Conduct annual international conference, and supervise the many zone and regional conferences that take place during the year.

Maintain close relationships with, and seek the help of, professional people concerned with our special areas of interest, and work with educational institutions to improve our programs and activities.

Through a dynamic informational program, bring single-parent problems to the attention of the public and of government agencies.

Individual chapters organize and conduct programs to fit the needs of their members. They do this through—

Parents Without Partners (Washington, D.C., 1967).

- Monthly educational programs, with professional speakers and panelists, on such subjects as "How to Live as a Single Parent"; "Parent-Child Relationships in a One-Parent Home"; "Sex Education for Children"; etc.
- Discussion groups, at which members "talk out" their problems and share experiences with each other. Some discussion groups may be planned only for the widowed, or the divorced or separated, but others can deal with specific topics such as "Remarriage"; "Dating and Relating"; "How to Deal with Loneliness"; etc.
- Chapter newsletters, containing a calendar of events plus information useful to the single parent.
- Recreational and social activities for both adults and children, providing a comfortable environment for interaction free of the "fifth wheel" feeling.

What Can We Do for You?

Our society is generally based on the traditional two-parent home and does not really understand the special problems faced by the millions who must bring up their children alone. Parents Without Partners, Inc., is uniquely fitted to help you, because our members themselves have gone through and experienced the challenges accompanying the loss of a mate, and the struggle to establish a new kind of life.

PWP can help you. You will find sympathetic and understanding people with whom you can share your experiences, problems, and hopes. You can gain a new perspective as you discover that you are not alone, and that others have triumphed over the same kind of difficulties you are facing. You can learn to accept what you must, while you strive toward a more successful way of life.

Your children need not be "victims" of a one-parent situation. From the new insights you can gain, you can be a better parent, and your children will benefit—not only from the activities planned for them, but from the new strength and self-reliance you can derive from the educational program and from your association with friendly people "in the same boat."

THE HALF-PARENT

The belief that they deviate from the normal is a burden carried by stepfamilies. It is an unnecessary burden, for the unbroken home is a myth and always has been. There is nothing new about all this changing of spouses (sequential polygamy, the anthropologists call it) and all these stepchildren. The stepfamily, a mended broken home, is a normal and traditional family pattern.

Why then has Western society never come to terms with the stepparent? Why have no customs been evolved to ease relations between stepparents and stepchildren? . . .

Brenda Maddox, *The Half-Parent* (New York, 1975), chapter 12. Copyright © 1975 by Brenda Maddox. Reprinted by permission of the publisher, M. Evans and Company, Inc.

A society determined to have divorce on demand has not done its homework. Where is the conventional wisdom for getting along with a stepchild? Where are the instructive pamphlets from the Department of Health, Education, and Welfare, "So You're Going to be a Stepfather!"? Where are the mimeographed notices from the Parent-Teachers Association saying that stepfathers are welcome to attend meetings? Where is the social-welfare counseling for the man whose wife is pressing him to adopt her child?

The answer is obvious. The guidance is not there because society cannot face the fact that it has exchanged one unworkable ideal for another. It has given up indissoluble marriage because, like premarital chastity, it was unrealistic. But it has not given up the belief that an unbroken happy home is essential for a child's sound emotional development. To examine the darker feelings inherent in the step-relationship stirs anxieties that are too strong for the P.T.A. and Parents Without Partners. They may be too strong for social agencies as well. "We have nothing to offer a stepparent," said an experienced social worker, head of a large organization dedicated to helping unmarried mothers. "There are no norms, no standards for stepparenthood," she said. "And if we did meet the man who was going to marry an unwed mother, which is unlikely—she won't bring him to us—if we tried to explore with him some of the possible tensions with the child, we might scare him off."

There may not be norms for successful stepparenthood. But there are expectations. From what stepparents say about themselves, from gossip, from the press, from stories, from what other relatives say, I have extracted four.

1. A stepparent must be seen not to be cruel.

2. A stepparent must not try to usurp the place of the natural parent.

3. A stepparent must supply whatever elements of parenting a stepchild lacks or the spouse demands.

4. A stepparent must love the stepchild.

It should be obvious that these expectations conflict. They set a trap into which hundreds of thousands of unsuspecting adults walk every year. Stepparenthood is a relationship that pits the myth of the Cruel Stepparent against the Instant Parent, *The Sound of Music* against *Snow White,* Julie Andrews against the Wicked Queen. The Instant Parent myth is more ubiquitous than people realize. . . .

Research has shown that a surprisingly large percentage of children consider their homes happy or very happy before divorce. So what is to be done about irreconcilables? Children do not like divorce or substitute parents. Adults demand the freedom to live with whom they love. . . . There is no formula for eliminating the strains between stepparent and stepchild, but more honesty and less pretending can only help. Both adult and child should be kept free from the expectation that they love each other, that they act as parent and child. If love grows, well and good. If not, fine, too. All that should be demanded on both sides is politeness. The special tensions of the family then need to be recognized. . . .

What are the differences in operating as a stepfamily, not as a biological family? What face should they put to the world? How do they want to be introduced? What should they all call each other? . . .

Comparisons with other families being inevitable, stepfamilies should learn where the true comparisons lie. Not with mothers and fathers, but with new babies and with parents-in-law. Intruders, rivals, one generation with interests in conflict with another. If there is anything "natural" in the step-relationship, it is the element of rivalry. We have come to live with the fact that not only children but even *fathers* are jealous of new babies. That stepparents and stepchildren resent each other is not so ugly a thought that it needs to be left hidden.

I think attempts to abolish the *step-* terms are ridiculous. They stem from the faith in positive thinking that has produced such absurdities as "mental health" and "chairperson." If the connotation is unpleasant, the reason should be faced, not glossed over with a change of label. . . .

If the *step-* terms were used more openly, the step-relationship could come out from under cover. Stepparents would be visible in their millions. It may be impracticable for censuses to count stepfathers, but there are informal ways that the status might be recognized and a social role defined. Schools could help a lot. Schools should routinely expect four parents per child on social occasions, and principals and teachers should acknowledge the remarried. "We are happy to welcome so many parents and stepparents here today."

It seems to me that there may be a solution short of full conversion to matriarchy. Fatherhood, vague as it is, has always had two aspects—biological and sociological. A stepfather could be allowed to assume some of the sociological functions of a male parent around the house without infringing on the legitimate father's rights. Stepfathers could be encouraged to teach their stepchildren skills, and they could be pressed into service in helping the children make the transition into the adult world. If they were allowed to have sex-linked duties toward the child, as stepmothers have, they would feel less like third wheels and perhaps press less fiercely for parental rights. . . .

At the same time, fair's fair. A society that wants nearly a million divorces a year cannot afford to be embarrassed when the children in a household don't have the same surname as their father and mother. Like millions of other children, they have their father's name and their mother has remarried. What is difficult about that?

A remarrying society needs to get rid of a lot of archaic ideas. One is . . . that divorce totally severs a marriage. Some enlightened people (enlightened usually by expensive lawyers) arrange arbitration procedures when they divorce in order to resolve, without reopening old wounds, the inevitable decisions and conflicts of opinion that arise over the children of the marriage as time goes by. . . .

I think I can answer my stepson's question now. Why did we have all those arguments? Because we pretended. We masqueraded as a nuclear family and we were not. And we let ourselves imagine that unbroken homes are happier than they are. . . . The stepfamily is open and tough. It is not a bad place to live for those who can accept the uncomfortable fact that many of the tensions between stepparents and stepchildren will be inevitable as long as spouses are replaceable and parents are not.

A TOTALITARIAN THERAPEUTIC FAMILY

"The whole aim of Sullivanian therapy," said a man who had, for a short while, broken through the magic circle and dated a Sullivanian, "is to encourage and facilitate independence and autonomy. But from what she [his date] said about the therapists, they seem to be very directive. They try to make patients fit into some mold. There was a definite party line. I don't know if it helped them—it often helps people to become religious.". . .

Estimates of the group's size vary from 350 to 600 members. There are approximately 40 therapists (who are also patients of one another); and, since each therapist can theoretically handle up to twenty patients, the community may very well number as many as 800—although not all of them are part of the inner circle, members who live with and socialize exclusively with each other. [They] follow the teachings of the eminent American psychiatrist Harry Stack Sullivan, but are now involved with this ingrown group. (Sullivan himself died on January 14, 1949, and was not connected to the Sullivanians in any way. In fact, some analysts claim that the group has perverted Sullivan's thought, and its name is misleading.)

The members of the group's inner circle started sharing apartments in the early 1960s as much for economic reasons as for ideological ones. Now, in many of the apartments, members live in barracks. When they have sleep-over dates, they sign up for the apartment's date room, "a sex room," as one former member described it.

During the summer, the Sullivanians migrate to a commune; when they travel abroad, they travel in packs. . . .

As is the case when making generalizations about any community, the likes and dislikes are not absolutely true of all Sullivanians; nevertheless, the group is fundamentally authoritarian, and most members follow the current fashions. And the fashions are set not only by the leading therapists, but also by certain members who, because of their professional success, have status within the community. . . .

Start asking questions about the group and you run up against a barrier of silence. . . . A utopian experiment—which the Sullivanian community in many ways seems to be—needs to limit its contact with the outside world in order to maintain the illusions that sustain it.

The problem is that to maintain and enforce limited external contact a

David Black, "Totalitarian Therapy on the Upper West Side," *New York Magazine*, December 15, 1975, pp. 54–66. Copyright © David Black, 1975. Reprinted by permission of the author.

group must become totalitarian, exacting a severe price from anyone in the group who does not follow party policy, and using leverage (like threatening to expose intimate and confidential records of a former patient's therapy sessions) to keep dropouts from spreading group secrets. They hold psyches hostage.

"Sullivan's notion—similar to Erik Erikson's later on—was that there were various necessary stages of development in the maturation of a person," explained another therapist who had been tied to the Sullivanian group, "and that certain types of required experience have to happen at these various stages of development. If they don't happen, there are going to be faulty integrations of experience at that level, which in turn will have an effect on the next stage, and so on. The effects are cumulative, very much as in embryonic development.". . .

Because this theory of development is so central to Sullivanian thought, Sullivanian therapists feel strongly that one should try to identify what area has been neglected in the patient's psychological evolution and then try to repeat the experience that was missing at that particular period of development. . . .

"We live in a dangerous world," the first sentence of [Sullivan's] *The Conditions of Human Growth* proclaims, so it's important to have someone keeping track of you. The buddy system is transposed from swimming at camp to all of a person's experience. If you start to sink, someone will be there to shout for help. Not a bad idea, although in practice it tends to encourage dependency rather than strengthen one's self-reliance and self-trust. . . .

Even more important than recapitulating infant cuddling, breast-feeding, and adolescent palships is duplicating the experience of living within a family. Not the old destructive family—it is Sullivanian dogma that all families (all non-Sullivanian families) are destructive; all parents, especially all mothers, are monsters—but a new, healthy, supportive family of Sullivanian therapists and patients.

To make this new family experience work, one must free oneself from blood relatives, a painful process not only for the Sullivanian patient, but also for the patient's kin who are being abandoned.

"Three years ago, when our daughter was living in New Haven, she got involved in the feminist movement and became a lesbian," said the father of a girl who is currently living among the Sullivanians. "When she moved to New York, she found this group of Sullivanians and joined them. We haven't had any connection with her for the past two years."

As he spoke, he kept pausing, not so much to search for words as to gasp for breath, as though sorrow and resentment had thinned his air; he lived in the rarefied atmosphere of grief. It was obvious that he had loved his daughter and had been no worse, perhaps better, than most fathers. . . .

In committing yourself to your new family of Sullivanians, however, you must bend to the authority of the therapists, the parent figures, just as you had to submit to your blood parents when you were a child. In trying to escape the restrictions of the blood family, the Sullivanians re-create those restrictions anew.

"When I lived . . . among the Sullivanians," said a Sullivanian dropout, "I'd had thirteen years of co-op-summer-house experience. But this was the first time it was not coed. I lived with nine women. I found the whole life-style insane. It was too regimented for me. There were things that were going on, and if you didn't participate, it was your problem."

As at a summer camp, the Sullivanians were expected to fill their time attending classes given by other patients: dance classes, art classes, acting classes, writing classes, etc. When you worked, you were supposed to work with another patient. If you wanted to work alone, play alone, be alone, you were accused of being antisocial. . . .

Being alone is dangerous. Being alone may allow one to find strength that is not dependent upon the group. . . .

"There's a joke," said a former Sullivanian. "You can always tell two Sullivanians on Broadway because they both have their date books out. The trick is not to spend a lot of time with any one person. Because then it becomes exclusive and you're *focusing*. There were jokes about 'hocus-focus.' So you have to make lots of dates for different things with different people. And you need this date book to keep it all straight.". . .

Because of such close contact among members of the group, Sullivanians live with the illusion of intimacy—that is, until they drop out of the community. Abruptly, all their intimate friends and lovers start avoiding them. Because the group has cut off all contact with non-Sullivanians, members are dependent on the group for everything—friendships, affairs, housing, in some cases even a job. So, when members are told not to consort with a dropout, they have no choice but to obey or to have their lives shattered by being cast out of the community themselves. . . .

Although it is easy to get thrown out of the group, it is difficult to make the decision to leave. Every patient I spoke to who had quit told the same story. In their last sessions, they were accused of being psychotic or paranoid schizophrenics (favorite Sullivanian insults), desperate, on the brink of disaster. "You can only survive the world if you are in therapy," one former Sullivanian said, explaining Sullivanian dogma, "and the only true therapy is Sullivanian therapy." Another former Sullivanian was able to break from the group only after his Sullivanian roommates had him committed, against his will, to Sheppard-Pratt in Baltimore.

One of the reasons the group is so paranoid about dropouts who may spread tales about the community is that a number of its therapists lack traditional formal training.

"I've heard that they are even training therapists who are only in their late teens," said an analyst who has a number of patients who have been members of the Sullivanian community. . . .

"The unconscious dynamic that keeps that place going is a rage against the mother who didn't satisfy all the child's needs," said another therapist who has followed the group's progress from the outside over a period of many years. "And, of course, a mother never can, never does satisfy all a child's needs. The Sullivanian community as an institution is set up to continue that rage. Although they seem to be promoting an antimonogamous position—which sounds reasonable in many respects—what they are actually promoting is the notion that there should have been one perfect person in the patient's life—the mother. And since the mother failed to be a perfect partner in a one-to-one relationship, you have to keep away from any other one person. But you can't go around hating all your life. Or idealizing. The freedom they talk about is really totalitarian. If you don't hold to the party line, then that's it. That kind of institution makes people's choices for them, and a condition of belonging is to accept the choices that are made.". . .

"If you're young," said a recent dropout, "if you don't have a home, [if you have] no husband or wife, no children, no friends, the group provides people to live with, a social life, a world where you're accepted. Just watch out if you join and be very, very careful."

"If you're going to mortgage your psyche," another former believer said, "read the fine print first."

FAMILY HORIZONS, 1980

Structure and Stresses

S ome of the most impressive and reliable evidence about the structure of American family life has come recently from the U.S. Bureau of the Census. Over the years it has recruited outstanding statisticians and demographers to deal with the highly complex range of facts about how Americans live now. Among its achievements the Census Bureau often releases short and literate "recent findings." From those published in the 1970s come two selections which have already been referred to in connection with other documents on twentieth-century families. Given the increasingly combative arguments about what America's families are, what they are good for, and where they are going, these two essays in their own right provide a solid base to check against mere speculation, cultural grievance, and biases of various sorts. In all fairness, however, they too should be read for evidence of bias: for example, in favor of the traditional family, or for excessive "sanity," or insensitivity to forces that may disrupt the merely probable statistically projected future. It should be profitable to compare these reports with the views of the family in the 1979 news reports on recent tensions and crises and with a current view of women in the labor force.

THE FUTURE OF THE AMERICAN FAMILY

Slowdown in Population Change

A reasonable expectation is that further changes in American family life will significantly lessen during the next two decades. . . . Even the *high* projected rates of change in population growth, enrollment, and the labor force during the 20 years between 1970 and 1990 are consistently smaller than the corresponding rates of change that had already taken place during the 20 years between 1950 and 1970.

The prospect of such a slowdown in social change could turn out to be seriously in error; particularly if some unforeseen change of great conse-

Paul C. Glick, "The Future of the American Family," *Current Population Reports,* U.S. Bureau of the Census, Series P-23, No. 78 (Washington, 1978).

quence should develop in the meantime. But several aspects of the present situation are at least consistent with an outlook of less change ahead.

In the first place, the decline in the birth rate during the last two decades has provided much momentum to a wide variety of other changes. . . . The relevant fact here is that this decline has gone about as far as it can go, and most demographers do not expect it to rise very significantly in the next decade or two.

In the second place, the great amount of increase in school and college enrollment during the last two decades has influenced other changes but is most unlikely to be repeated again in the next couple of decades. The proportion of young people who graduate from high school has been on a plateau of about 85 percent during the 1970s. The proportion of men in their late twenties who have completed a year or more of college after graduating from high school has reached 60 percent, and the comparable proportion of women has approached 50 percent; these levels are 10 or more percentage points higher than a decade ago and seem unlikely to rise by a similar amount during the next decade.

In the third place, the recent rate of increase in the proportion of women in the labor force has been dramatic, going up from 38 percent in 1960 to 48 percent in 1977. Without a continuing decline in the birth rate and with less increase in the educational level of the young adult population, along with other changes not mentioned, the odds seem to favor a slackening of the rate of increase in the labor force participation of women over the next decade or two. The worker rate for men has been declining for several years; this trend may diminish or be slightly reversed in future years by the lifting of the mandatory retirement age and by the easing of entry into the labor force by young men (and women) a decade or two from now because of the relatively small size of the cohorts that will be seeking to be absorbed into the labor market at that time.

These slackening changes in the birth rate, the enrollment rate, and the labor force participation rate seem likely to have a dampening impact on patterns of future change in family life.

Changes in the Family Life Cycle

Longtime trends in demographic variables that are used to study the family life cycle have been primarily affected by downward trends in the birth and death rates. This conclusion was reached . . . on the basis of an analysis of changes over the 80-year period from the early 1900s through the 1970s.

Aside from the baby boom after World War II, the birth rate has followed a generally downward direction until the present time. The average family that was formed in the early years of the twentieth century included four children, whereas the average family formed in the 1930s included three children. Families formed during the familistic era of the 1950s had one additional child, but those forming at the present time expect to have only two children, on the average.

Today's young family of two children stands in sharp contrast with their great-grandparents' family of four children. Other things being equal (though they may not be), one would expect that the father and mother of today can spend more time with each of their children and with each other apart from their children. The period of child-rearing has been shortened by about 3 years; and the period after the children leave home has been increased by 11 years (from 2 years to 13 years), largely as a consequence of the improvement in survival rates among adults.

Accordingly, young couples today can expect to live as a "child-free" twosome for about 14 more years than their elders, with most of the increase coming in middle age and later. These 14 years represent nearly one-third of the entire 44 years of married life for the shrinking proportion of couples with continuous first marriages. The degree of satisfaction those later years bring depends on many tangible and intangible factors concerning how well the two relate to each other and to their grown children. (All but a few—between 5 and 10 percent—will have some children.) That satisfaction has a good chance of being affected by the rising status of women and the concomitant increase in singlehood and divorce. The extent to which young adults are postponing marriage and to which adults of all ages are dissolving their marriages in divorce will be treated in the next two sections of this statement.

Will the Postponement of Marriage Continue?

. . . Evidence of much more postponement of marriage now than formerly is provided by the increase of one-half between 1960 and 1977 in the proportion of women 20 to 24 years of age who had never married (from 28 percent in 1960 to 45 percent in 1977). During this period the same rate of increase was recorded in the postponement of marriage among women in their late twenties (from 10.5 percent to 16.1 percent). . . .

The longer the pattern of increasing postponement of marriage persists, the more likely the prospect becomes that the extent of lifetime singlehood among young adults of today will increase. . . .

The Marriage and Divorce Rates Have Stabilized; Will They Remain Stable?

. . . The future propensity of young adults to marry cannot be forecast with a great degree of confidence. Nevertheless, there are reasons to expect the proportion of young adults who marry to level off or to rise moderately for a few years and then to rise still more after that time. . . .

If the focus is on the more remote period of one or two decades from now, the prospects for an increasing proportion of young adults to marry should be better because of the greater ease with which the labor market should be able to absorb the relatively small cohort of young adults at that time. Of course, changes in the sizes of age groups during successive stages of the life cycle and simultaneous changes in employment conditions are not the only critical variables affecting the level of the marriage rate, but they are surely two of the most important variables.

The future course of the divorce rate is also difficult to forecast. But to the extent that the level of divorce is related to the level of marriage, the prospect for divorce to decline somewhat in the next few years seems reasonable. . . .

What Is the Outlook for Change Among One-Parent Families?

Despite substantial increases in divorce and informal living arrangements during the last couple of decades, the preponderant majority of people still live in households maintained by a nuclear family. Specifically, 7 of every 8 of the 213 million persons in the noninstitutional population of the United States in 1977 were residents of nuclear family households:

 77 percent were in husband-wife households; and
 10 percent were in one-parent households; thus,
 87 percent were in nuclear family households.
  7 percent were living alone as one-person households;
  1 percent were in households of unmarried couples; and
  5 percent were in various other living arrangements.
100 percent. (In 1970, 1 percent of all persons were in institutions.)

That is the big picture. One feature of it that may be particularly surprising is the smallness of the proportion of *persons* living in the households of one-parent families. An obvious reason is that such families include only one parent instead of two. Another is that only 54 percent of all families have any "own" children under 18 years of age in the household.

But some of the 79 percent of children under 18 in 1977 living with two parents were living with a stepparent or were born to their current parents after one or both had remarried. . . .

On balance, there are still close to 4 of every 5 young children living with two parents and most of the rest living with one parent. Even so, this situation is significantly different from that in 1960 when 7 of every 8 lived with two parents—more often their own natural parents then than now.

The Family (in Modified Form) Will Go On

This paper has documented some of the substantial changes that have been occurring in regard to marriage, family size, and living arrangements and has offered some opinions about likely future changes in these aspects of family life. In spite of the demonstrable delay in marriage, the decline in family size, the upturn in divorce, and the increasing diversity of living arrangements, the overwhelming majority of American people still live in nuclear families. . . . This assertion is not meant to minimize the extent of recent changes but to imply that the American people have been showing a great degree of resilience in coping with pressures that affect their family life and are likely to continue to do so. . . .

The judgment presented here is that most of the changes in family life over the next two decades will be small as compared with those during the last two decades. Of course, the future changes in some respects, such as the living arrangements of unmarried young adults, may continue to change considerably in view of the recency of the sharp increase in the experimentation in this area.

Underlying many of the Nation's family problems during the 1960s and 1970s has been the difficulty of coping with the tremendous task of absorbing into the social system the massive number of young adults who were born during the period of high birth rates after World War II. High unemployment rates and inflated prices for consumer products and services must have also contributed to the increasing delay in marriage, the reduction in births, the evident difficulty of keeping marriages intact, and associated changes in the composition of households.

The delay in marriage should have the favorable side effect of expanding the range of social relations before marriage, thereby increasing the chances that a rational choice of a marriage partner will be made at a more mature age than formerly. Through a cumulative process, delayed marriage also generally means still further delayed childbearing. . . .

The advantages of having a large family in an agrarian economy no longer apply to the current American scene. In earlier times the mother of many children usually found her time fully occupied with household duties, but now half of the mothers (usually with only one, two, or possibly three young children) are using their high school or college education to gain employment outside the home. Once these mothers have overcome the obstacles to such employment, few of them are likely to forego the advantages, particularly those women with no children below school age. . . .

Delaying marriage has been associated with an increase in the work experience of women who have never married. This experience makes women more employable as they enter marriage, and increasingly makes it possible for them to work on a continuous basis with a few months off for childbearing. The more employable they become and the fewer children they have as a partial consequence thereof, the more economically independent young mothers become and the more likely they are to seek a divorce if their marriage comes under serious stress.

Thus, the new options that have emerged during the last generation or two for women to become well-educated, to obtain employment outside the home, to limit the size of their family, and to end an unsatisfactory marriage in divorce, have created a setting in which an increase in divorce should not be very surprising. The new options have therefore come at a price. . . . But the price is not too high insofar as it has made divorce a real alternative to a marriage that becomes a threat to the mental health and general well-being of persons who are directly involved. . . .

During the last two decades social pressure has been diminishing for young adults to marry, to have children, and to stay married. During the next decade or two social pressure may also be expected to diminish for both a working mother and her husband to be employed on a full-time basis. Relaxation of pressures in these ways would be expected to increase the quality of the marriages that are initiated and of those that remain intact.

PERSPECTIVES ON HUSBANDS AND WIVES

In the past few years, Census Bureau reports on the current composition of the American household and family have tended to emphasize such changes as increases in the number of persons living alone, gains in the number of unmarried couples, and the growing proportion of mothers maintaining one-parent families. As striking as the growth of these groups has been, only a minority of the total population is likely to experience any of these types of living arrangements for more than a short-term interval. Often that interval is a transitional period between marriages or a period that precedes or follows the far more universal living experience of marriage.

Past history indicates that almost everyone will be either a husband or a wife at some point in their life. Typically, a person who has entered a marital union will stay in that union for the remainder of their life, although a growing proportion will not. Similarly, most of these married persons will eventually have children, or take a job, or both, although some husbands and wives will forego one or both of these options.

Traditionally, most married women, and particularly those who were mothers, have accepted the demands and rewards of work inside the home. Only the husband was encouraged to continue his education, or enter the labor force, and thereby provide most, if not all, of the family's income. As long as this situation continued, it was perhaps not surprising that many persons considered it sufficient to describe the social and economic status of the family by referring only to the characteristics of the husband—his education, his occupation, his income, etc.

Today's wives, however, are increasingly likely to have completed high school and perhaps some years of college, to participate in the labor force, and to contribute to the family income. Thus, the demarcation between many of the roles of husbands and wives has become less distinct. The sole breadwinner has given way in many instances to dual breadwinners. Similarly, many working wives and mothers are coming to expect more involvement and assistance from their husbands in carrying out the child-rearing and housekeeping responsibilities of the family.

In light of these developments, total reliance on the characteristics of the man when describing married couples is likely to result in misleading conclusions which do not always correspond to reality. A recent report to a United Nations conference on the revision of concepts related to

Stephen Rawlings, "Perspectives on American Husbands and Wives," *Current Population Reports*, U.S. Bureau of the Census, Series P-23, No. 77 (Washington, 1978).

family and household data pointed out that it is still sufficient to describe single-parent families in terms of the age, sex, employment status, occupation, etc., of one person. This approach, however, is no longer appropriate with married couples, for the life patterns and conditions of married couples (with or without children) are the product of various combinations of the husband's and wife's social and economic characteristics. . . .

Age at Marriage

Marriage is something that virtually all Americans experience at some time in their lives. Some may postpone marriage, while others enjoy it, endure it, or terminate it; but very few people can, or wish to, escape it completely. One-half of the men currently make their initial entry into marriage by the age of 24.0 years. One-half of the women marry for the first time by the age of 21.6 years.

The age at which people marry is determined by many forces, including economics, warfare, and the pool of available potential mates. In the years since the mid-1950s, these factors have interacted in such a way so as to bring about nearly a 1½-year increase in the median age at which men and women first marry. As one consequence, the median age at first marriage today is about the same as it was in 1940. Throughout this century, the median age at first marriage has fluctuated between about 22 and 26 years for men, and between about 20 and 22 years for women, but these fluctuations have been much less dramatic than the recent changes in the proportion of persons who have been delaying marriage.

Very few people marry in their teens. The relative rarity of teenage marriage accounts for the fact that in 1977, 98 percent of the men 14 to 19 years of age and 91 percent of their female counterparts had never been married. The pace of matrimony after young adults reach their twenties, however, is sufficient to bring about a rapid decline in the proportion of persons who have never married. Among those 25 to 34 years old in 1977, only 20 percent of the men and 12 percent of the women were still single; among those 45 to 54, the corresponding figures were 6 percent and 4 percent. In future years, the proportion of men and women who never marry at any time during their lives may be expected to rise a few percentage points above these low levels, according to present estimates. . . .

Education, Family Size, and Presence of Children

The average size of married-couple families [surveyed] was 3.42 persons. Married couples with exactly 4 years of high school had the largest families, on the average (3.49 persons). . . .

Education, Labor Force Participation, and Income

. . . It was much less common for both the husband and the wife to be in the labor force among couples who completed less than 4 years of high school (27 percent), than among college-graduate couples (62 percent). Conversely, neither spouse was in the labor force in 30 percent of the couples with less than 4 years of high school, but this was true for only 6 percent of the college-graduate couples. . . .

The fact that husbands and wives were often both workers in college-graduate couples doubtless contributes to the fact that these couples also had higher family incomes than couples who had completed fewer years of school. For example, the median family income of college-graduate couples ($26,645) was more than twice the corresponding income ($10,434) among couples who had completed less than 4 years of high school.

Social Characteristics of Younger and Older Couples

As couples move from young adulthood toward their more mature years, they experience a series of changes. In their early years, the couple's family is generally larger and somewhat more stationary. At full maturity, the characteristics of the couple are again likely to change. The discussion [below] deals with married couples in relation to the age of the husband and wife.

Age, Family Size, and Presence of Children

Among couples in which the spouses were both either 14 to 24 years old or 25 to 34 years old, the average family size was 3.40 persons. Approximately one-half of these families were composed of two persons (the husband and wife) or the couple plus one additional family member. Almost always, this third person was their own child, but in a very few instances it was some other relative, such as a brother or sister, of one of the persons maintaining the family. The average number of children under 18 years of age in these families was 1.36.

By the time both the husband and wife approached their middle years (age 35 to 44), family size had grown to an average of 4.66 persons . . . and the average number of children under 18 in these "early midlife" families was 2.24 persons.

As the husband and wife continued to grow older, their children, if any, had begun to reach young adulthood and leave their parental home to form households of their own. Once the couple reached retirement age (65 years and over), average family size had declined to 2.22 persons. About 87 percent of these families consisted of just the husband and wife, and rarely was the additional relative a child under 18. . . .

Employment Characteristics of Married Couples

Until a decade or two ago, it was possible to obtain a reasonably clear picture of the economic characteristics of married-couple families simply by examining the employment status and income of the husband. The importance of such information diminishes, however, as more wives enter the labor force and contribute significantly to the family's income. . . .

Participation in the Labor Force

Although husbands are less likely now than formerly to be the sole bread-winner for the family, the proportion who were in the labor force in March 1977 was still relatively high (81 percent). In that year, close to one-half (47 percent) of all married women were in the labor force; that level of participation is substantially higher than in the past. . . .

Working Wives and Mothers

Married women who had one or more children under 18 years of age were just as likely to be members of the labor force (48 percent) as married women who did not have such a child (45 percent). There are substantial differences when consideration is given to the age of the wife as well as the presence of children. . . .

The age of the child is often a critical factor in determining whether the mother enters or remains in the labor force. The participation rate for wives whose only children at home were age 14 to 17 was about 57 percent, whereas the rate for those whose children were all under age 6 was only 40 percent.

Working Wives by Education and Income Level

Regardless of whether a wife has children or not, the more years of school she has completed, the more likely she is to be a member of the labor force. Among wives who were not high school graduates, only a third were working or job hunting, whereas two-thirds of those who had completed more than 4 years of college were in the labor force. If the wife had 4 or more years of college, was under age 45, and had no children under 18, her participation rate soared to about 90 percent.

Wives do not necessarily enter the work force in proportion to their degree of economic need. For example, married women in 1977 were most likely to be in the work force if their husbands had incomes of $10,000 to $14,999; they had a higher participation rate (54 percent) than the comparable group of women whose husbands had incomes of less than $3,000 (43 percent).

If one looks at married-couple families from the standpoint of their joint labor-force participation, one finds that married couples with both spouses working or seeking work had a median family income of $19,327. If only the husband was in the labor force, the median family income was about $3,000 lower, or $16,267. If the situation was reversed, and only the wife was a member of the labor force, the median income was $12,450.

Work Experience of Married Couples

. . . The 1977 data show that the husband was the family's *sole* earner in only 26 percent of the married-couple families. More common were couples in which there were 2 earners, the husband and wife (36 percent).

The proportion of couples in which the wife was the only earner was quite low (4 percent). . . .

Income of Married Couples

The median family income for all married-couple families in 1976 was about $16,271. As one would expect, the presence of more than one earner in the family was associated with a relatively high median family income. Also as expected, the lowest median income ($6,761) was that for families with no earners at all. The median income for families with the husband as the only earner was $14,543, as compared with medians of $17,570 for those with two earners (the husband and wife), and $20,203 for those with the husband and some other relative as the earners. In families with at least three earners (one of which was the husband), the median income was $23,474.

For white married-couple families the median income was $16,554; in comparison, black couples had a median income of $13,280, and Spanish-origin couples, $11,969.

About 20 percent of all married-couple families had incomes of $25,000 or more in 1976. An additional 36 percent had incomes of at least $15,000 but less than $25,000, and, similarly, 38 percent had incomes of at least $5,000 but less than $15,000. Finally, 6 percent had incomes of less than $5,000. (The 1976 poverty threshold for a nonfarm family of four, according to Federal government guidelines, was $5,815.)

SAVING THE FAMILY FROM INTERVENTION

The U.S. is the only Western nation that does not have a formal family policy—the same thing, many say, as having an anti-family policy. But the impact of government and other outside agencies on the family is already so pervasive that it has provoked a grass-roots parents' revolt. The National Parents' Rights Coalition . . . in Chicago, promises that "anyone who has an impact on the family, from politicians and bureaucrats to educators and the media, will hear from us and face our power." In Washington, the Coalition of Family Organizations lobbies for tax breaks and other family support. Meanwhile, the American Family Society is promoting a slick new magazine, "Family Time," devoted to self-help projects, and also puts out a checklist for locating possible sources of family instability.

Why is the family in trouble? One major reason is that traditions no longer dictate life patterns for most adult Americans. Now people have more options—to get married or not, to have children or not, to stay married or not, to work or not. . . . A second reason is that the sheer

"Saving the Family," *Newsweek*, May 15, 1978, pp. 63–90, passim. Reprinted by permission of *Newsweek*.

cost of raising a child is enough to make any potential parent pause—and current parents shudder. At 1977 prices, a family of four, earning between $16,500 and $20,000 a year, can expect to spend $54,297 to support a child to the age of 18, excluding the expense of higher education.

Finally, parents feel increasingly powerless in the face of institutional interference. The growth of social services, health care and public education has robbed them of their traditional roles as job trainers, teachers, nurses and nurturers. And their control over their children's lives is threatened by the pervasive—and increasingly authoritative—influences of television, schools and peer groups. . . .

The Vanishing "Ideal"

By the middle of the nineteenth century Americans established the first and eventually the most powerful institutional counterpoise to the autonomous nuclear family: the compulsory, free public school. From that point on, schools were expected to do what educators assumed that families, especially those of immigrants, could not accomplish on their own—teach skills, develop work habits and instill approved social values. In the course of the following century, almost every other traditional function of the family passed out of the home and into the hands of institutions and professional providers, from care of the sick to support of the poor, from the preparation of food to instruction in leisure activities. . . .

Government: Hitting Home

"Everything the Federal government does affects the family," a Congressional researcher observed last week. "When it passes defense appropriations it can affect job opportunities. A new highway may affect where a child goes to school. It's hard to imagine how the government doesn't impact the family." State and local governments also impinge on family life, yet only recently has anyone begun to measure these effects. Now, researchers are discovering that government actions may reverberate through a whole range of consequential family decisions, from where the family lives to what it eats to whether it remains a family at all.

One group working from the new perspective is the Family Impact Seminar, established at George Washington University in 1976. Seminar members have identified 331 domestic-assistance programs, accounting for $247.4 billion in 1976 funds, that directly or indirectly impact on families. But researchers are already learning how difficult it is to identify government actions as clearly pro- or anti-family. School breakfast and lunch programs, for example, seem a boon to working mothers; but on the other hand, they may encourage mothers to leave home, and they put an important slice of children's nutrition in the hands of school officials. . . .

These are some of the problems family specialists are focusing on:

CAN TWO PAY TAXES AS CHEAPLY AS ONE?

Over the years, both single and married taxpayers have argued that the income-tax laws discriminated against them. The rule permitting married couples to file a joint return resulted in a lower tax than would be paid by spouses filing separately. A 1969 reform attempted to balance things, but produced another anomaly: under present law, those most heavily penalized are a husband and wife earning equal wages. A sample computation by the Brookings Institution shows that a couple earning $10,000 each would pay $200 more on a joint return than if they could file as singles. No one has yet figured out how to pass a tax system that would remain progressive—with higher rates for higher incomes—but still avoid discriminating against working couples.

SHOULD MOM GO TO WORK?

Equal-opportunity laws, legalized abortion, school breakfast and lunch programs, the pressures of inflation and the general *Zeitgeist* seem to say yes. But day-care funds remain restricted, part-time jobs are scarce and there is little vocational training available for older women re-entering the work force. Meanwhile, although the social-security bite keeps growing, many women never get the benefit of their own contributions. Under the existing system, the family's chief wage-earner—usually the husband—gets a monthly retirement pension roughly proportional to his total earnings. His spouse, whether she worked or not, can receive a dependent's benefit of half that amount, thus giving nonworking wives a "free ride." And many working wives find that their own benefits are smaller than those they can receive as an adjunct of their husbands.

IS THE BIG, HAPPY FAMILY OUT OF DATE?

The $750 tax deduction for children and elderly dependents once clearly favored larger families. But it has shrunk to a pittance alongside the inflation-swollen costs of nurturing children. At the same time, higher social-security benefits are encouraging grandparents to live apart from the nuclear family.

ARE COURTS PROMOTING THE BREAKUP OF THE FAMILY?

Courts are clearly having an impact, especially at the state level. State courts set alimony levels and award custody of children; they have also eased the requirements for divorce. In April 1977, the District of Columbia passed a no-fault divorce law designed to cut red tape and legal fees in the dissolution of marriages. While some attorneys say the law has made no difference, divorce cases jumped to 2,392 in the six months from May through October 1977, compared with 1,664 in the previous six months. Naturally, a general relaxation of divorce statutes has touched off comparable rises.

WHAT HAPPENS TO THE CHILDREN?

State courts also put children in foster homes, often resulting in bitter disputes between foster parents and biological parents. The children themselves seldom have any choice. The Carnegie Council on Children reports that in 1976, about 100,000 minors were removed from their homes under "neglect" laws—usually based on parents' inability to provide them with necessities. In the 1930s and '40s, such court action was more routine than it is now. . . .

IS WELFARE AN ANTI-FAMILY PROGRAM?

Welfare has been—and seems bound to remain—the most nettlesome family policy issue. Under the present system, millions of American households share around $200 billion of Federal support annually through such programs as Aid to Families with Dependent Children, food stamps, Medicaid and rent subsidies. AFDC has long been a target of liberals who charge it promotes family breakups by denying benefits when an unemployed father lives in the home. Yet the rule is still operative in more than half the states, and, if nothing else, it may discourage divorced welfare mothers from remarrying.

The Administration has promised to get rid of man-in-the-house restrictions and provide firmer income support for families. But by calculating benefits on the basis of "household units" instead of individual need, the President's proposed welfare reform would still penalize related persons living under one roof. An unwed mother, for instance, would lose $66 of her maximum $250 a month if she and her child moved in with an uncle who was ineligible for aid. She would retain her full benefits if she lived with a boyfriend, but would lose part of them if she married him.

WHERE WILL THE FAMILY LIVE?

Obviously, the decision is influenced by practical considerations, including family finances and accessibility to schools and jobs. But critics feel the government has played an important role in population shifts to the suburbs with such policies as building highways at the expense of mass transit, easier requirements for suburban builders and tax advantages for homeowners. The $9.9 billion in 1977 deductions for real-estate taxes and mortgage-interest payments probably had a greater impact on family housing opportunities than all Federal programs offering subsidized public housing.

A highway built through a residential neighborhood can have a direct and devastating impact on family organization. A Duke Center study has pinpointed one such community, Crest Street, bordering the Duke campus. Crest Street is a remarkably close-knit community of long-term black homeowners, the majority of whom work within walking distance of their homes. Most residents are also related to one another and help one another with shopping, child care and other neighborly chores. But Crest Street is slated to be wiped out unless the Durham (N.C.) city council vetoes a proposed expressway interchange later this month. And fears are that, under the present Environmental Policy Act, all the State Highway Department must do to win approval is to affirm that it has given consideration to the expressway's impact on "community cohesion."

No one contends that such government policies actually dictate the way a family lives, but they clearly affect the broad process of family choices. Thus, the Carter Administration has set itself a formidable task by coming out four-square for a "pro-family" policy. First of all, officials will have to sort out what is pro or anti, and policy planners will have to find a way of reconciling those who advocate vigorous action and those who are wary of any further government intrusion. Ultimately, the most unassailable argument may be that the intrusion is already a fact.

FAMILY: AN ENDANGERED SPECIES

The American family was pictured as an endangered species by hundreds of citizens voicing concern about issues ranging from inflation to the rising influence of cults.

The long litany of complaints and fears poured out during [a] hearing held to obtain information for three White House Conferences on Families to be held next summer [1980] in Baltimore, Minneapolis and Los Angeles.

To the Reverend Robert L. Pruitt, joblessness is the most serious problem facing millions of Americans and their families, particularly blacks. "The crisis in America," he said, "is not Iran or oil but jobs."

To Lee Bullitt, teen-age pregnancies and lack of sex education is a threat to family stability. Last year in the District of Columbia, she said, 92 percent of all births to teen-agers were out of wedlock.

Other witnesses, testifying in various Senate and House committee rooms, touched on such issues as child abuse and neglect, abortion, gambling abuse, support of elderly parents, lack of child care facilities for working mothers, battered wives, domestic violence, poverty and impact of pornography on the family.

Others said family stability was threatened by violence within the home, lack of adequate housing, rising costs of essential services and by the disruptive influence of various cults on young people and their parents.

While acknowledging that the challenge to family life is both real and serious, Patricia Roberts Harris, secretary of the Department of Health, Education and Welfare, said in a speech opening the hearing that she was sure the family would survive. "I suspect concern over the possible disintegration of the family has been present in every society throughout the history of civilization," she said.

"Threats to Families Outlined at Hearing," New York Times News Service, Washington, D.C., November 30, 1979.

WOMEN WORKERS, 1980

As more women surged into the work force in the 1970s than during any other decade in this century our economy went through a giant revolution. Among the questions the revolution raised:

What is now "normal" for the employment-unemployment ratio? What is the "normal" proportion of after-tax income that should go for savings? What is a "typical" family today as compared to families a couple of decades ago?

More than half of all women 16 years old and over—about 43 million—are now part of the work force. As a result, the once "typical" family with a working husband, a wife who is a full-time homemaker and two children has become a statistical rarity. This family now accounts for only 7 percent of married-couple families. Instead, today's "typical" family has two or more wage-earners.

What's more, there are now roughly 8.5 million women who have no husbands and who are supporting families alone.

On top of these fundamental changes is the great, enduring shift of our economy from a goods-producing to a service-oriented one.

These forces have raised our living standards, stabilized employment and, in times of inflation, encouraged two-paycheck couples to spend more and save less instead of cutting back as was the "normal" reaction in the past.

Does all this mean that economic predictions based on historical precedent are automatically thrown off-target? . . . "Congressional committees or groups of skilled economists about economic and employment issues [are] still looking at them in historical terms," Janet Norwood, commissioner of labor statistics, [says]. "But there have been such radical changes in the labor force that I think history is not going to repeat itself."

Norwood and other experts are skeptical about . . . pessimistic forecast[s] because . . . the big upswing of baby-boom teen-agers and women entering the labor force may already have passed through the economy, so a slowdown in the creation of new jobs may not push up the unemployment rate as quickly or to the heights predicted.

The growth in the number of two wage-earner families may continue to encourage these couples both to spend and borrow more. For even if one wage-earner is laid off, the combination of unemployment insurance and another worker's earning may reduce families' tendencies to cut back on spending.

Yet, despite these obvious socio-economic changes and the complex impact they are having on our economy, other basic characteristics of the job market remain unchanged.

Most women, for example, still hold jobs as secretaries, file clerks or

Sylvia Porter, "Women Workers: Change vs. Economic Patterns," Field Enterprises, February 5, 1980.

other clerical staff—and while these are relatively recession-proof jobs, they are low-wage jobs, and the contributions of the women who hold them to their families' total income is comparatively meager.

Despite some outstanding exceptions of women who have climbed to or near the top, only a tiny percentage of women have made major inroads into occupations that were all-male just a decade or two ago.

The predominance of women in lower-paying fields is a prime reason that today's average full-time woman worker still brings home less than half the paycheck of her male counterpart.

But the explanations are far more complicated than the simple "lower-paying fields" would seem to imply. Discrimination on the basis of sex (as well as race, age, color and religion) remains rampant in our so-called advanced society. A woman does earn less than a man doing the identical work in a vast number of instances. The male-female "earning gap" is widening, not narrowing. Female elementary and high school teachers, for example, make only about 85 percent of what male teachers in the same posts earn—and the prime explanation has to be discrimination.

SELECTED BIBLIOGRAPHY
FOR PART THREE

Banner, Lois W. *Women in Modern America: A Brief History.* New York: Harcourt Brace Jovanovich, 1974.

Chafe, William H. *The American Woman: Her Changing Social, Economic, and Political Roles, 1920–1970.* New York: Oxford University Press, 1974.

Elder, Glen H., Jr. *Children of the Great Depression: Social Change in Life Experience.* Chicago: University of Chicago Press, 1974.

Fass, Paula S. *The Damned and the Beautiful: American Youth in the 1920s.* New York: Oxford University Press, 1977.

Filene, Peter G. *Him-Her Self: Sex Roles in Modern America.* New York: Mentor, 1976.

Handlin, Oscar. *The Uprooted.* New York: Grosset and Dunlap, 1957.

Hareven, Tamara K., and Randolph Langenbach. *Amoskeag: Life and Work in an American Factory-City.* New York: Pantheon, 1978.

Jacobson, Paul H. *American Marriage and Divorce.* New York: Rinehart, 1959.

Kennedy, David M. *Birth Control in America: The Career of Margaret Sanger.* New Haven: Yale University Press, 1970.

Keniston, Kenneth. *All Our Children: The American Family Under Pressure.* New York: Harcourt Brace Jovanovich, 1977.

Lasch, Christopher. *Haven in a Heartless World: The Family Besieged.* New York: Basic Books, 1977.

O'Neill, William L. *Everyone Was Brave: A History of Feminism in America.* New York: Times Books, 1972.

Stack, Carol B. *All Our Kin: Strategies for Survival in a Black Community.* New York: Harper & Row, 1974.

Staples, Robert, ed. *The Black Family: Essays and Studies.* Belmont, Calif.: Wadsworth Publishing Co., 1970.

Yans-McLaughlin, Virginia. *Family and Community: Italian Immigrants in Buffalo, 1880–1930.* Ithaca, N.Y.: Cornell University Press, 1977.

GENERAL BIBLIOGRAPHY

BIBLIOGRAPHIES

Berkin, Carol, and Mary Beth Norton. *Women of America: A History*. Boston: Houghton Mifflin Company, 1979.

Bremner, Robert. *Children and Youth in America: A Documentary History*. 3 vols. Cambridge, Mass.: Harvard University Press, 1971–74.

Gordon, Michael. *The American Family in Social-Historical Perspective*. 2nd ed. New York: St. Martin's Press, 1978.

Jacobs, Sue E. *Women in Perspective: A Guide for Cross-Cultural Studies*. Urbana: University of Illinois Press, 1974.

Sicherman, Barbara, et al. *Recent United States Scholarship on the History of Women*. Washington: American Historical Association, 1980.

American Quarterly, annual bibliographical issue.

The Journal of American History, bibliographies in each issue.

JOURNALS

American Quarterly
Journal of Family History
Journal of Interdisciplinary History
Journal of Social History

DOCUMENTS

Axtell, James, general ed. *The American People*. 10 vols. West Haven, Conn.: Pendulum Press, 1973.

Baxardall, Rosalyn, et al., eds. *America's Working Women: A Documentary History, 1600 to the Present*. New York: Random House, 1976.

Blassingame, John W., ed. *Slave Testimony: Two Centuries of Letters, Speeches, Interviews, and Autobiographies*. Baton Rouge: Louisiana State University Press, 1977.

Brownlee, W. Elliot and Mary M. *Women in the American Economy: A Documentary History, 1675–1927*. New Haven: Yale University Press, 1976.

Cott, Nancy. *The Root of Bitterness: Documents of the Social History of American Women*. New York: E. P. Dutton and Co., 1972.

Greven, Philip J., Jr., ed. *Child-Rearing Concepts, 1628–1861*. Itasca, Ill.: F. E. Peacock Publishers, Inc., 1973.

Lerner, Gerda, ed. *Black Women in White America: A Documentary History.* New York: Random House, 1973.

BOOKS

Abbott, Edith. *Women in Industry.* 2 vols. New York: D. Appleton and Company, 1910.

Anderson, Michael. *Family Structure in Nineteenth Century Lancashire.* Cambridge, Eng.: Cambridge University Press, 1971.

Ariès, Philippe. *Centuries of Childhood: A Social History of Family Life.* New York: Vintage Books, 1960.

Calhoun, Arthur W. *A Social History of the American Family.* 3 vols. Cleveland: Clark, 1917.

Cott, Nancy F., and Elizabeth Pleck, eds. *A Heritage of Her Own: Recent Essays in Work, Family, and Feminism.* New York: Simon and Schuster, 1979.

Degler, Carl N. *At Odds: Women and the Family from the Revolution to the Present.* New York: Oxford University Press, 1980.

de Mause, Lloyd, ed. *The History of Childhood.* New York: Harper & Row, 1975.

Demos, John, and Sarane Spence Boocock, eds. *Turning Points: Historical and Sociological Essays on the Family.* Chicago: University of Chicago Press, 1978.

Ditzion, Sidney. *Marriage, Morals, and Sex in America: A History of Ideas.* New York: Octagon Books, 1970.

Frazier, E. Franklin. *The Negro Family in the United States.* Chicago: University of Chicago Press, 1939.

Gutman, Herbert G. *The Black Family in Slavery and Freedom, 1750–1925.* New York: Pantheon, 1976.

Handlin, Oscar and Mary F. *Facing Life: Youth and the Family in American History.* Boston: Little, Brown, 1971.

Hareven, Tamara K., ed. *Family and Kin in Urban Communities, 1700–1930.* New York: New Viewpoints, 1977.

————. *Transitions: The Family and the Life Course in Historical Perspectives.* New York: Academic Press, 1978.

Hartman, Mary S., and Lois W. Banner, eds. *Clio's Consciousness Raised: New Perspectives on the History of Women.* New York: Harper & Row, 1974.

Himes, Norman E. *Medical History of Contraception.* New York: Gamut, 1963.

Howard, George. *A History of Matrimonial Institutions.* 3 vols. Chicago: University of Chicago Press, 1904.

Kett, Joseph F. *Rites of Passage: Adolescence in America, 1790 to the Present.* New York: Basic Books, 1977.

Rabb, Theodore K., and Robert I. Rotberg, eds. *The Family in History: Interdisciplinary Essays.* New York: Harper & Row, 1973.

Reed, James. *From Private Vice to Public Virtue: The Birth Control Movement in American Society Since 1830*. New York: Basic Books, 1977.

Rosenberg, Charles E., ed. *The Family in History*. Philadelphia: University of Pennsylvania Press, 1975.

Ryan, Mary P. *Womanhood in America: From Colonial Times to the Present*. New York: New Viewpoints, 1975.

Tilly, Louise A., and Joan W. Scott, *Women, Work, and Family*. New York: Holt, Rinehart and Winston, 1978.

Thematic Index

NOTE: This index covers only documents printed in this volume. Page numbers refer to the *first page* of the document containing the theme.

Abortion
 debate on, 506, 511, 512, 513
 legalization of, 506
 as murder, 511
 as private decision, 513
 statistics on, 506
Acculturation, 29, 383, 402, 406, 553, 557, 596, 600, 602
 See also "Americanization"
Adoption, 295, 381, 650
 See also Children, custody of; Guardians
Adultery, 22, 98, 363, 367, 492
 as grounds for divorce, 18, 363
 penalties for, 78, 98
 proscriptions against, 79, 82, 85
Advertising, familial themes in, 616
Alternative families, 337, 339, 340, 342, 648, 649, 650
 See also Communal families; Utopian families
"Americanization," 383, 402, 406, 553, 557, 593, 596, 600, 602
Apprentices, 160, 385
 See also Orphans

Bachelor, 18, 230, 232
 suitability as guardian, 295
Bastardy, 18, 22, 65, 82, 320, 363, 607, 670
 See also Fornication; Sexuality, illicit
Birth control, *see* Contraception
Birth rate, 657
Black (Negro) families, *see* Family, black; Family, slave
Boarders, 402, 406, 412

Catholic-Americans, 483, 506, 602
 See also Acculturation; "Americanization"

Ceremonies, 76, 79, 125, 222, 223
 See also Marriage, ceremonies; Rituals
Charity, 426, 552
 See also Intervention in families by
Childbirth, 128, 129, 130
 death in, 129, 130
Child labor, 160, 216, 218, 219, 385, 402, 412, 423, 545, 547
 and education, 412, 545
 in factories, 218, 219, 412
 laws, 412, 545
 in tenements, 402, 412, 423, 545
Child nurture, *see* Child-rearing
Child-rearing, 141, 143, 145, 149, 152, 153, 276, 297, 300, 304, 306, 465, 528, 532, 535, 620
 changes in, 657
 Indian, 149
 manuals, 132, 141, 143, 287, 304, 306, 528, 532, 535
 methods, 141, 306, 528, 532, 535
 See also Fathers; Mothers
Children
 abuse of, 160, 352, 357
 character of, 141, 143, 145, 297, 300, 305, 308, 465, 523, 532, 535
 custody of, 158, 160, 295, 381, 497, 650
 death of, 13, 205, 233, 285, 288, 325, 356, 357
 departure from home of, 10, 205, 281, 285
 education of, 18, 306, 412
 health of, 412, 566
 idealization of, 205, 233, 285, 287, 288, 325
 obedience and punishment of, 18, 132, 133, 141, 143, 149, 152, 297, 300, 304, 306, 528, 532, 535

Children *(cont.)*
responsibilities of, for aged-parents, 133, 162, 285
sentimentalization of death of, 205, 233, 288, 325
slum, 383, 402, 423, 545, 547
Chinese-Americans, 596
Comics, families in, 625
Communal families, 337, 339, 340, 648, 653
See also Alternative families; Utopian families
Contraception, 253, 436, 470, 476, 483
abortion linked to, 470
campaign for, 253, 470, 476
legality of, 470
methods, 253, 262, 263, 476, 483
practice of, 258, 262, 263, 436, 483
religion and, 258, 450, 483, 513, 602
Court decisions on
divorce, 363
guardianship, 168, 295
homosexual marriage, 500
parents' rights *v.* the state, 380
slave families, 314, 316
Court records, 91, 98, 160, 164, 295, 314, 316, 375, 380, 500
Courtship, 27, 29, 37, 40, 41, 46, 53, 57, 61, 122, 237, 239, 243, 637
etiquette, 237, 243
Indian, 27
inter-racial, 29
slave, 122
satires of, 61
songs of, 637
Cultural conflict, *see* Acculturation; "Americanization"

Daughters, 22, 46, 57, 64, 72, 98, 149, 160, 166, 183, 205, 208, 216, 219, 233, 285, 287, 356, 375, 523
See also Children
Death
age at, 13
of child, 13, 205, 233, 285, 325, 352, 356, 357
in childbirth, 129, 130
of spouse, 13, 108
See also Orphans; Widows
Demography, 10, 11, 13, 657
See also Statistics
Desertion, 91
Discipline of children, *see* Child-rearing; Children, obedience and punishment of
Disease, 292, 562
See also Children, health of; Death

Disownment, 51, 205, 281
Divorce
court decisions on, 363
effect of, on families, 607, 649, 650
frequency of, 436, 503, 657
grounds for, 18, 363, 497
and guardianship, 650
rate, 657
See also Stepchildren; Stepfamilies; Stepparents
"Double standard," 492
Dowry, 18, 46, 53, 72
Drunkenness, *see* Intemperance

Education, 18, 160, 216, 657, 662
Equality
and family, 192, 210, 648
of sexes, 118, 208, 210, 243, 459, 492, 512, 570, 578
Extended families, 10, 13, 70, 222, 223, 227, 318, 320, 323, 337, 342, 607

Factories, 216, 218, 219, 402, 406, 412
Family
black, 122, 314, 316, 318, 320, 321, 323, 333, 607
Catholic, 483, 506, 602
changes in, 515, 520, 657, 670, 671
Chinese, 596
devotions, 18, 141, 222, 430
farm, 184, 186, 214, 332, 447
economy, 214, 216, 218, 412
entertainment, 222, 627, 633, 635
as foundation of social order, 18, 22, 133, 149, 199, 375, 666
future of, 515, 520, 657, 666, 670
health, 255, 293, 402, 412, 562
ideal, 85, 132, 133, 249, 300, 337, 339, 340, 648
impact of poverty and unemployment on, 98, 214, 216, 332, 383, 402, 412, 449, 607, 670
income, 412, 446, 662
Indian, 27, 149, 192, 193
Italian, 402, 406
Jewish, 402, 406, 593
law, 18, 33, 76, 158, 164, 295, 314, 316, 363, 381, 497, 545, 668
matriarchal, 607
migrant, 451
politics concerning, 570
and public policy, 18, 295, 314, 316, 380, 382, 412, 545
separation of, 10, 183, 189, 201, 216, 219, 281, 285, 314, 316, 318, 323, 325

Family *(cont.)*
  size of, 11, 13, 166, 168, 183, 222, 412, 504, 657, 670
  slave, 122, 314, 316, 318, 323, 325
  stability and structure of, 657, 670
  therapy, 580
  ties, 139, 149, 169, 201, 216, 222, 223, 229, 267, 272, 273, 280, 285, 318, 323, 426, 648, 650, 653
  violence within, 91, 98, 352, 356, 360, 363, 373, 375
Fathers, authority and role of, 46, 57, 72, 133, 141, 143, 152, 186, 199, 201, 205, 208, 216, 295, 297, 300, 320, 523, 607
  See also Child-rearing; Parents
Fornication, 18, 33, 65, 320, 363, 607, 670
  See also Bastardy; Sexuality, illicit
Foster homes, 160, 295, 385, 650, 666
Freudianism, 580
Frontier impact on families, 183, 184, 189, 195, 196

"Generation gap," 540, 593, 596
Ghetto, 402, 406, 593, 596, 607
Grandfather, 228
Grandmother, 222, 229
Great Depression, 442, 447, 451
Guardians, 158, 162, 295, 381, 649, 650
  See also Adoption; Court decisions on; Orphans

Health
  child and family, 255, 292, 402, 412, 562, 566
  maternal, 128, 129, 130, 249, 412, 470, 566
  See also Death; Disease
Home
  idealization of, 249, 265, 272, 273, 276, 278, 280, 282, 283, 285, 300, 306, 620, 627, 633
  as refuge, 249, 265, 280, 282, 285, 570
  threats to, 255, 258, 325, 352, 356, 360, 465, 570
Homesteading, 189, 195, 196
Homosexual marriage, 500
Household, size of, 11, 657
Housework, 189, 195, 196, 249, 430, 515
  See also Wives, duties of
Housing, 111, 112, 196, 331, 332, 374, 395, 402, 406, 408, 409, 412, 567
Husbands
  authority and role of, 85, 91, 98, 105, 118, 184, 186, 262, 263, 295, 436, 607, 617

  and wives, 85, 91, 98, 103, 105, 111, 122, 125, 255, 258, 316, 323, 342, 344, 430, 436, 515, 520, 580, 607, 617, 627, 633, 635

Illegitimacy, *see* Bastardy; Fornication
Immigrants, 10, 11, 383, 402, 406, 483, 593, 596, 600
  attitudes toward schools, 402, 406
  See also Acculturation; "Americanization"; Catholic-Americans; Chinese-Americans; Irish-Americans; Italian-Americans; Jewish-Americans; Swedish-Americans
Impotence as grounds for annulment, 96
Indians (Native Americans), 192, 193
  child-rearing, 149
  courtship, 27
  marriage, 27
Inequality of sexes, *see* Women, inequality of
Infanticide, 22
Infant mortality, 13, 127, 412, 502
  See also Children, death of
Inheritance, 46, 70, 72, 160, 166, 169
  See also Disownment; Wills
Intemperance, impact on families of, 352, 356, 360, 373
Intermarriage, 29, 35, 593, 596, 600
  See also Inter-racial relationships
Inter-racial relationships, 29, 35, 122, 320, 363
Intervention in families
  by charitable agencies, 360, 383, 385, 553, 558, 570, 668
  by courts, 91, 98, 164, 295, 314, 316, 380, 545, 666
  by public agencies, 380, 382, 385, 402, 406, 470, 553, 558, 566, 580, 666
Irish-Americans, 600
Italian-Americans, 404, 406

Jewish-Americans, 402, 406, 593

Labor, *see* Child labor, in factories; Women, work of; Working-class families
Legislation concerning families, 18, 33, 76, 158, 360, 402, 406, 497, 545, 666
  See also Intervention in families by courts
Liberty, family as source of, 152, 199, 276, 339, 633, 648
Life expectancy, 562
Love songs, 61, 254, 280, 637

Marriage
  age at, 201, 237, 662
  annulment of, 497

Marriage *(cont.)*
  ceremonies, 27, 76, 77, 323, 436
  choice, 37, 40, 41, 46, 53, 57, 64, 79, 122,
    205, 237, 239, 436
  contracts, 70, 72, 73
  dissolution of, 497
  education and, 662
  employment and, 662
  forms, 27, 76, 79, 82, 316, 323, 492,
    500
  homosexual, 500
  ideals of, 27, 85, 103, 239, 249, 254, 492,
    617, 627, 633, 635, 637
  illegal, 94, 316, 500
  Indian, 27
  inter-racial, 29, 35, 122, 320, 363
  laws, 18, 76, 497
  manuals, 85, 249, 490
  parental power over, 18, 46, 53, 57, 64,
    72, 201, 205
  postponement of, 53, 201, 205, 237,
    657
  prohibitions against, 33, 51, 79, 160,
    205
  property and, 27, 41, 46, 53, 57, 64, 70,
    72, 73, 166, 168, 201, 205, 230, 239, 316,
    436, 497, 662, 671
  reasons for, 37, 41, 53, 64, 122, 205, 237,
    342, 436, 482, 483, 616, 627, 633, 635,
    637
  reform of, 490, 492, 497, 515, 662
  satire of, 63, 71, 230, 232, 253, 255, 617,
    627, 637
  slave, 316, 320, 321, 323
Marriages of specific persons, 91, 98, 103,
    105, 108, 110, 111, 122, 125, 262, 263,
    269, 316, 321, 323, 363, 367, 442
Married life, *see* Husbands, and wives; Mar-
    riages of specific persons
Masters, servants and, 33
    and slaves, 33, 122, 314, 318, 321, 323,
    330, 363
Maternal health, *see* Health, maternal
Migrant families, 451
Migration, 10, 11, 91, 183, 184, 186, 451
Mormonism, 342, 344
Mothers (motherhood), 128, 129, 139, 201,
    205, 233, 272, 273, 274, 276, 278, 280,
    282, 283, 284, 300, 325, 402, 412, 436,
    459, 465, 525, 532, 535, 554, 555, 616,
    633, 635
    See also Child-rearing; Wives, duties of
Movies, families in, 627
Moynihan thesis, 607

Negro, *see* Family, black

Old age, 133, 164, 169, 272, 426, 562
Orphans, 158, 160, 295, 381, 385
    See also Guardians

Parents
    authority of, 18, 27, 51, 72, 132, 133, 141,
      149, 152, 199, 201, 205, 208, 216, 276,
      300, 304, 305, 306
    foster, 158, 233, 385
    organizations of, 353, 557, 649
    responsibility of children for, 133, 166, 285
    single, 160, 219, 607, 649, 657
    step, 70, 166, 168, 233, 381, 653
    See also Child-rearing; Fathers; Mothers
Piety, *see* Religion
Plantations, 330, 331, 332
Poems, 103, 128, 129, 139, 222, 227, 255,
    280, 308, 523, 525, 526
Polygamy, 342, 344
Poverty, 98, 160, 214, 216, 332, 383, 402,
    412, 442, 497
    in old age, 164, 426
    relief of, 426
Pregnancy
    fear of, 129, 130
    prevention of, 258, 262, 263, 470, 476,
      480, 482, 483
    teenage, 607, 670
    See also Childbirth; Contraception
Property, *see* Marriage, property and
Prostitution, 600
Psychiatry, 580, 653
Public agencies, *see* Intervention in families
Public health, 562, 566
Public policy, families and, 295, 380, 382,
    385, 402, 406, 545, 657, 666

Race relations, 33, 122, 318, 320, 321, 323,
    363, 600, 607
Radio, families on, 633
Reform of family, 22, 85, 249, 278, 300, 337,
    339, 340, 360, 459, 465, 490, 515, 645,
    653, 657, 666
Reform schools, 380, 382, 385
Religion
    conversion, 285
    family order and, 27, 85, 141, 149, 210,
      297, 337, 342, 375, 430, 603
    nurture of, 18, 141, 149, 276, 282, 436
    piety in children, 85, 141, 145, 149
Remarriage (second marriage), 40, 41, 46, 72,
    166, 168, 295, 650, 657
Retirement, 426

Rituals
    courtship, 27, 61, 65, 79, 237, 243, 637
    familial, 222, 223
    funeral, 374
    marriage, 18, 27, 70, 72, 73, 76, 79, 323, 436
    See also Ceremonies

Schools
    attitudes toward, 402, 406, 412
    reform, 380, 382, 385
Settlement house, 570
Servants, indentured, 10, 33, 98, 160
Sex discrimination, 118, 208, 210, 671
Sex roles
    female, 85, 111, 139, 149, 249, 276, 278, 304, 333, 459, 465, 515, 520
    male, 85, 141, 143, 186, 249, 300, 436
    See also Fathers; Husbands; Mothers; Wives
Sexual liberation, 490, 500
Sexuality, 27, 55, 122, 255, 320, 490
    control of, 27, 37, 53, 65, 255, 258, 262, 263, 320, 480
    diversity in, 27, 320, 500
    illicit, 22, 33, 55, 65, 82, 98, 122, 363, 367
    inter-racial, 33, 122, 320, 321, 323, 363
    marital, 27, 37, 53, 85, 96, 98, 105, 122, 255, 262, 263, 320, 323, 363, 480, 482, 490
    regulation of, 18, 35, 160, 337, 480, 482
    See also Fornication
Single men, *see* Bachelor
Single-parent family, 160, 219, 607, 649, 657
Single women, *see* Widows; Women, unmarried
Slaves
    breakup of families of, 122, 314, 316, 318, 323
    courtship among, 122, 320
    family ties of, 33, 314, 316
    laws regulating, 33, 314, 316
    See also Family, black
Slums, 313, 402, 406, 593
    See also Ghetto
Social work and the family, 470, 553, 557, 558, 666
Songs, 61, 184, 232, 254, 280, 637
Sons, 72, 139, 149, 152, 160, 168, 169, 201, 208, 216, 276, 281, 285, 373, 430, 540, 580, 607, 627
    See also Children; Parents
Spinster, *see* Single women

Statistics, marriage-remarriage, 503
Stepchildren, 70, 166, 168, 233, 381, 653
Stepfamilies, 653
Stepparents, 70, 166, 168, 233, 381, 653
Swedish-Americans, 429, 600

Television, families on, 635
Tenements, 402, 406, 570
"Teen-agers," 540, 558
    See also Youth and youth culture
Therapy
    family, 580
    groups, 653
Threats to the family, 91, 98, 122, 160, 184, 186, 189, 216, 249, 316, 318, 323, 325, 344, 352, 356, 373, 375, 570, 607, 648, 653, 666, 670
    from death, 129, 160
    from intemperance, 352, 356, 360
    from poverty, 98, 164, 216, 333, 383, 402, 406, 412, 426, 449, 670
    from sale of slaves, 316, 318, 323, 325
    from violence, 91, 98, 122, 352, 356, 373, 375, 523, 526

Utopian families, 337, 339, 340, 342, 648, 649, 650
    See also Alternative families; Communal families

Violence, *see* Family, violence within; Threats to the family
Voluntary organizations, 360, 383, 553, 555, 558
    See also Intervention in families

Welfare, 426, 442, 666
Westward movement, *see* Frontier impact on families; Migration
Widows, 41, 70, 98, 160, 219
Wills, 160, 166, 168
    See also Dowry; Inheritance
Wives
    abuse of, 91, 98, 344, 352, 356, 363, 373
    duties of, 85, 111, 139, 149, 249, 263, 265, 267, 276, 278, 300, 304, 436, 459, 465, 515, 520, 528, 532, 535, 648, 657
    farm, 184, 189, 196, 214, 333, 449
    and husbands, *see* Husbands, and wives
    political action of, 360, 570
    satire of, 230, 617
    working, 111, 218, 402, 459, 515, 535, 662, 670, 671

Wives *(cont.)*

See also Child-rearing; Husbands, and wives;
Marriage; Mothers; Parents

Women

character of, 85, 110, 222, 276, 325, 375,
465, 490, 520, 553, 557, 570, 633

inequality of, 118, 208, 210, 243, 469, 492,
515, 570, 578, 671

issues concerning, 278, 360, 570

liberation of, 492, 497, 515

role of, 85, 249, 278, 300, 333, 436, 469,
515, 520, 662, 671

unmarried, 216, 219, 227, 412

vote of, 570

work of, 111, 189, 218, 333, 402, 412, 423,
459, 657, 662, 666, 671

See also Daughters; Mothers; Widows;
Wives

Working-class families, 216, 218, 383, 402,
406, 412, 426, 430, 442, 451, 470, 593,
607

budgets of, 418

diet of, 418

housing of, 402, 406, 423

Youth and youth culture, 540